MOBILE CONFEDERATES
FROM SHILOH TO SPANISH FORT
❖ ❖ ❖ ❖ ❖ ❖ ❖
THE STORY OF THE 21ST ALABAMA INFANTRY VOLUNTEERS

Private Malachi L. Stabler, Co. G

21st Alabama Infantry Volunteers CSA
Abstracted Compiled Service Records

Arthur E. Green

HERITAGE BOOKS
2012

Dedicated to my Grandfather
John C. Green, Pvt. Co. B 38th Alabama Infantry
and sincere thanks to Charlie for his loyalty

HERITAGE BOOKS
AN IMPRINT OF HERITAGE BOOKS, INC.

Books, CDs, and more—Worldwide

For our listing of thousands of titles see our website
at
www.HeritageBooks.com

Published 2012 by
HERITAGE BOOKS, INC.
Publishing Division
100 Railroad Ave. #104
Westminster, Maryland 21157

Copyright © 2012 Arthur E. Green

Other Heritage Books by the author:
Southern Boots and Saddles: The Fifteenth Confederate Cavalry C.S.A., First Regiment Alabama and Florida Cavalry, 1863–1865
Too Little Too Late: Compiled Military Service Records of the 63rd Alabama Infantry CSA with Rosters of Some Companies of the 89th, 94th and 95th Alabama Militia CSA

All rights reserved. No part of this book may be reproduced or transmitted in any form or by any means, electronic or mechanical, including photocopying, recording or by any information storage and retrieval system without written permission from the author, except for the inclusion of brief quotations in a review.

International Standard Book Numbers
Paperbound: 978-0-7884-5376-2
Clothbound: 978-0-7884-3440-2

Contents

History 5

Introduction to Compiled Service Records 17

Roster 19

Appendix 376

Bibliography 387

MOBILE CONFEDERATES

History

The secession of the State of Alabama from the United States of America was accomplished by election at State Convention in Montgomery on January 11, 1861. On February 18, 1861, Jefferson Davis took the Oath of Office on the portico of the Alabama Capitol, and Montgomery became the seat of the new government. During December and January, Alabama Governor A. B. Moore had taken possession of US fortifications at Fort Morgan, Fort Gaines and the Arsenal at Mount Vernon.[1]

Alabama was the fourth state to secede, and the delegates of the seceded states met at Montgomery, Alabama, and organized The Confederate States of America on February 4, 1861.

The 21st regiment of Alabama Volunteers, 3rd Brigade, District of Gulf, organized and mustered into state service in the months of April, May, June, July, August and September 1861 and mustered into Confederate service on October 13, 1861, for 12 months. Some early enlistments were in the 2nd Alabama Infantry serving under Colonel Harry Maury at Fort Morgan where they learned artillery warfare. There is some indication that the 21st existed as a State Regiment before October of 1861 as 1st Regiment 1st Alabama Volunteers. Enlistments show enrollments at Baldwin County, Mobile and Halls Mill on October 13, 1861. A few members show enlisting as early as October 7, 1861. Others recruits were enlisted in the Confederate Army and reorganization was done from the remnants of the disbanded State 2nd Alabama Regiment and 1st Regiment 1st Alabama Volunteers.

The regiment formed officially on October 13, 1861, at Halls Mill, Alabama, about ten miles west of Mobile near the intersection of Three Notch Road and the Old Spanish Trail or Pascagoula Road. They occupied Camp Governor Moore or Camp Moore and nearby Camp Memminger. There were reported to be at least nine Alabama Infantry commands in that area.

The records show that later recruits were enlisted from Marengo, Clarke, Wilcox, Baldwin and Sumter Counties in Alabama with a sprinkling from other areas. The remainder of the Confederate men was made up from the disbanded Alabama State 2nd Alabama Regiment and the 1st Regiment of Alabama Volunteers.

James Crawford was chosen as colonel on July 22, 1861, and Colonel Crawford resigned in April of 1862 to be replaced with Charles D. Anderson who was elected as colonel on May 8, 1862, at the reorganization of the 21st Alabama. Anderson remained in command of the regiment until his surrender of Fort Gaines on August 8, 1864. Charles Anderson was from Galveston, Texas, and attended West Point and served in the 4th US Artillery before the War.

The 21st regiment of Alabama Volunteers, 3rd Brigade, District of Gulf organized in the months of April, May, June, July, August and September 1861 and mustered into Confederate service on October 13, 1861, for 12 months. See Whiting, Nathan 1st Lt.

It was unusual that the regiment divided itself into two battalions. Battalion No. 1 consisted of Companies A, B, C and F while 2nd Battalion consisted of Companies D, E, I and K. Then James Crawford is shown as having enlisted in April in Battalion No. 3. We must guess that Companies G and H made up Battalion No. 3. Sossaman's

---

[1] Confederate Military, History V111 – Lt. General Joseph Wheeler

detachment appears later as a third (or fourth division) and some of its men were assigned to man Battery Huger in upper Mobile Bay. Many of the 21st men had received training and instruction as artillerists as stated at Fort Morgan and were used as such at Forts Gaines, Morgan, Powell and the Bay Batteries as well as Oven Bluff on the Tombigbee River and Choctaw Bluff on the Alabama River about 60 miles north of Mobile. Choctaw Bluff is on the west bank of the Alabama River south of Jackson, Alabama, and a Brook Cannon still is in position there. Oven Bluff is on the Tombigbee River near the Salt Works.

Companies were formed and identified as Company A - Washington Light Infantry, No. 2, Mobile; Company B - The Montgomery Guards; Company C - Marengo Rifles or Witherspoon Guards; Company D - Battle Guards; Company E - Chamberlain Rifles - Woodruff Rifles or Mobile Rifles No. 2; Company F - Baldwin Rifles No. 2; 1st Co. G - Spanish Guards; 2nd Company G - Swanson Guards No. 1; Company H - Swanson Guards No. 2; Company H - French Guards; Company I – United Rangers or Independent Rifles and Company K - The Mobile Cadets.

The 21st was ordered by General G. P. T. Beauregard to leave Camp Memminger near Hall's Mill on March 3, 1862, for Fort Pillow, Tennessee. General Forrest had captured the Federal Outpost on the Mississippi River on April 12, 1863. They arrived at Memphis, Tennessee, on March 7, 1862, and were conveyed by steamer *Scotchman* to Fort Pillow on March 8, but were removed to Corinth, Mississippi, on March 18. The regiment picked up a few new recruits at Fort Pillow in their short stay. You will find in the service records 21st men who were captured at Fort Donaldson north of the area on the Cumberland River in Tennessee on February 16, 1862. Obviously from the men's records some of the 21st Alabama force was at the upper river forts early on before the regiment made the move north. Later a few men were captured at Port Gibson, Mississippi, on May 1, 1863. It is unknown what roll they played as the 21st was not officially in the vicinity.

April 1863 the regiment found itself ordered and encamped near Corinth, Mississippi, in anticipation of an action near Pittsburg Landing. The action was to be called the Battle of Shiloh. They marched north from Corinth, Mississippi, to near Shiloh in April 1863 and slept on the field in the rain.

April 6 and 7, 1862, Battle of Shiloh, Tennessee, the 21st served in the Army of Mississippi, that was commanded by Albert S. Johnston, 2nd Corps; Major General Braxton Bragg, 2nd Division; Brigadier General Jones M. Withers, 1st Brigade and Brigadier General A. H. Gladden. Gladden's Brigade consisted of 21st, 22nd, 23rd, 26th Alabama Regiments; 1st Louisiana; Robertson's Battery and Gages' Battery. General Gladden was mortally wounded by cannon fire about 8 a.m. on April 6, and his command was passed to Colonel W. D. Adams, who continued the attack until he fell wounded in the head at 12:30 p.m. The command passed to Colonel Z. C. Deas of the 22nd Alabama who also fell to multiple wounds

At the Battle of Pittsburg Landing or Shiloh, Lt. S. W. Cayce reports that near Monterey on April 6 and 7, the 21st Alabama Infantry lost 198 men killed, wounded and missing, including five color bearers.[2] He, as lieutenant, was placed in command of the 21st by General Gladden on April 5.

---

[2] OR. Vol X/1 S#10

The unit was engaged at Farmington, Mississippi, on May 9 and 10.

A report for June 1862, camped near Tupelo, Mississippi, shows many wounded and ill were sent away to internal hospitals at the evacuation of Corinth on or near June 1.

Men captured at Shiloh were sent to prison at Camp Douglas, Illinois, or Camp Morton, Indiana, and were exchanged. Some of those injured who were wounded or captured at the hospital were treated at Hickory Street USA, General Hospital in St. Louis and paroled at Mrs. R. W. Seris' home. Most of these men reached Atkins Landing near Vicksburg for exchange aboard the steamer *John H. Done* in September and November 1862 and made their way back to the regiment.

On April 16, 1862, the Confederate Congress enacted the Enrollment Act, which extended the one-year volunteers' enlistments for two additional years and made liable for the draft all white men between the ages of 18 and 35 unless they volunteered or were legally exempt

On May 6, 1862, Braxton Bragg of Mobile, Alabama, a veteran of the Mexican War, was appointed commander of the Army of Mississippi. He immediately ordered all 12-month volunteer units to hold reorganization elections as allowed by the Enrollment Act.

June 1862, camped near Tupelo, Mississippi, many wounded and ill were sent away to internal hospitals at the evacuation of Corinth on or near June 1.

July 4, 1862, Company H, French Guards were transferred to the 1st Louisiana Regulars.

September 24, 1862, all companies of the 21st Alabama Infantry were mustered at Fort Morgan, Alabama, for bounty and each member paid $50 bounty. Some men refused to accept the bounty.

On October 6, 1862, Special Order No. 236 assigned 1st Battalion Companies A, B, C and F, with Colonel Anderson in command, to Choctaw and Oven Bluff; 2nd Battalion Companies D, E, I and K remained at Fort Morgan.[3]

This data from captions and records of events US Archives Microfilm File M-311 Roll 284 gives company assignments with dates.

Company A

September 24, 1862 — Fort Morgan for bounty
December 31, 1862, to April 30, 1863 — Mobile, Alabama.
April 26, 1863, Detached from the Battalion and ordered to report at Mobile. - May 5, 1863, ordered to report at Selma. - May 26, 1863, ordered from Selma to report to Gen. Slaughter at Mobile.
May and June, 1863 — Fort Stonewall, Ala.
April 26, 1863, ordered from Choctaw Bluff to Mobile. – May 5, 1863, ordered from Mobile to Selma. – May 20, 1863, ordered from Selma to Mobile. – June 8, 1863, ordered from Mobile to Choctaw Bluff. – June 24, 1863, moved into camp three miles from Fort Stonewall Choctaw Bluff.
September and October 1863 — Fort Morgan, Ala.

---

[3] From That Terrible Field - James M. Williams edited by John Kent Folmar

Ordered from Point Clear, Ala. to Spring Hill, Ala. October 24, 1863. - Arrived at Spring Hill October 26, 1863. - Ordered to Fort Morgan October 28, 1863. – Arrived at Fort Morgan October 29, 1863.

Company B

September 24, 1862	Fort Morgan, Ala.
March and April 1863	Oven Bluff
May and June 1863	Camp near Fort Stonewall Jackson

– Removed from Fort Sidney Johnston (Oven Bluff) to Rosie Hill near Fort Stonewall Jackson (Choctaw Bluff) on the 25th day of June 1863.

September and October 1863   Fort Morgan

Company C

September 24, 1862	Fort Morgan for bounty
December 31, 1862 to April 30, 1863	Mobile, Ala.

– April 26, 1863, detached from the Battalion and ordered to report at Mobile - May 5, 1863, Ordered to report at Selma. - May 20, 1863, Ordered to report to General Slaughter at Mobile.

May and June 1863   Fort Stonewall – Ordered to report to General C. D. Anderson at Choctaw Bluff on the 8th of June 1863, - Moved from Choctaw Bluff to Rosie Hill on the 24th of June 1863.

September and October 1863   Fort Morgan, Ala.

Company D

September 24, 1862	Fort Morgan for bounty
November and December 1862	Fort Morgan
July and August 1863	Fort Grant

– Ordered from Fort Morgan to Fort Grant by Colonel Smith commanding the 3rd Brigade August 21, 1863.

September and October 1863	Fort Grant
November and December 1863	Fort Powell
September and October 1864	Battery Huger

Company E

September 24, 1862	Fort Morgan for bounty
November and December	Fort Morgan
July and August 1863	Fort Morgan
September and October 1863	Fort Morgan

Company F

September 24, 1862	Fort Morgan for bounty
March 1 to June 30, 1863	Fort Stonewall
September and October 1863	Fort Morgan

– Ordered form Point Clear to Spring Hill near Mobile October 22, 1863. – Reached Spring Hill. October 23, 1863. – Ordered from Spring Hill to Fort Morgan on October 27, 1863. - Reached Fort Morgan on October 28, 1863.

Company I

September 24, 1862	Fort Morgan for bounty
July and August 1863	Fort Morgan
September and October 1863	Fort Morgan

Company K

November and December 1862	Fort Morgan
July and August 1863	Fort Morgan
September and October 1863	Fort Morgan
September and October 1864	Brown Warehouse – Mobile, Ala.

April 30, 1863, two men were killed at Fort Morgan when a cannon exploded. One was the gunner and the other Lieutenant Colonel Charles S. Stewart. Colonel Stewart is buried in Magnolia Cemetery at Mobile, Square 7, Lot 48. Lieutenant Colonel James M. Williams was his successor. The gunner was not identified and may not have been a member of the 21st Alabama.

From OR. August 1863, Organization of Department of the Gulf with General Dabney Maury in command shows reports 1st Battalion of the 21st Alabama under command of Brigadier General James Cantey Forts Morgan and Gaines 2nd Battalion under the command of Colonel W. L. Powell.

November 1863, 21st is in General F. A. Shoup Brigade

December 1863, 21st is in Brigadier General Edward Higgins Brigade

January 1864, 21st is in Higgins Brigade.

On April 3, 1864, Captain Melville C Butt, Co. C requisitioned the following for his company D; 42 jackets, 28 caps, 30 shirts, 41 pair drawers and 13 pair shoes as the men lost their clothing in the evacuation of Fort Powell.

For the month of May 1864, 1st Lt. J. Brainard, Co. K filed a requisition from Fort Powell that indicated forces assigned were; 1 officer, 2 subalterns, 54 non-com officers and privates.

August 5, 1864, Battle of Mobile Bay

Major General D. H. Maury reports from Mobile on August 5, 1864. Seventeen of the enemy's vessels (14 ships and 3 iron-clads) passed Fort Morgan this morning. The Tecumseh, a monitor, was sunk by Fort Morgan. The Tennessee surrendered after a desperate engagement with the enemy's fleet. Admiral Buchanan lost a leg and is a prisoner. The Selma was captured. The Gaines was beached near the hospital. The Morgan is safe and will try and run up tonight. The enemy fleet has approached the city. A monitor has been engaging Fort Powell all day. D. H. Maury, Major General [4] Maury, was in command of Department of Alabama, Mississippi and East Louisiana.

August 7, 1864, destruction of Fort Powell

Fort Powell was a substantial earth fortification that lay beside Grant's Pass north of Dauphin Island and south of Alabama Port. It guarded the protected passage for vessels taking the inside route of Dauphin Island. On August 5, 1864, it was reported that a Federal Monitor ran close up and cannonaded it for several hours while five gun

---

[4] O. R. Series 1 – Vol XXXIX/1 [S#77]

boats in Mississippi Sound bombarded it at long range. No man or officer was wounded and only a ten-inch gun carriage was disabled. August 8, 1864, Major General Dabney Maury reported that Lt. Colonel Williams, commanding Fort Powell, evacuated and blew up the fort. General Maury writes that Powell had, under his bomb proof, 30-days water and two months provisions and was armed with hand grenades, revolvers, muskets and howitzers. He had eight heavy guns to use against vessels. Fort Powell was connected by telegraph to Fort Gaines and Mobile. Maury reports that on the morning of August 5 there were 70 Negroes with trenching tools in the fort. The guns on the east face were mounted and in fighting order but not yet covered by the parapet. One of the salvaged cannon from Fort Powell is now relocated in the median of Government Street in Mobile just west of Water Street.

August 8, 1864, surrender of Fort Gaines. General Maury reports that Colonel Charles D. Anderson of the 21st Alabama Regiment "shamefully" surrendered Fort Gaines with its garrison of 600 men and six months provisions at 9:30 a.m. General Page had observed Anderson's communication by signal flag of truce and was directed by signal guns and telegraph, "Hold on to your fort." When General Page arrived at Fort Gaines, he found Anderson aboard the Yankee fleet arranging the terms of capitulation. Fort Gaines, according to General Maury, was garrisoned by 6 companies of the 21st Alabama, 2 companies of the 1st Alabama Battalion, 40 Pelham Cadets, 120 reserves and about 40 marines. It is unclear exactly which six companies were present at Fort Gaines and which were at Fort Morgan, Fort Powell and other locations. The three ten-inch guns were dismounted during the bombardment. Twenty guns were reported to be in good order.

We are very fortunate that a first person eyewitness account survives of the surrender of Fort Gaines and is shared by Mobile family descendants. While not directly related to the 21st Alabama, it is worth including as the officer was present during the surrender of Fort Gaines. In a letter to his brother on September 5, 1864, from US military prison, a native of Mobile, who was a member of the Confederate Marine Corps, gives his impression of the actions and surrender at Fort Gaines, Dauphin Island. His name was 2nd Lt. John Lawrence Rapier, and he served as Adjutant to Major W. R. Brown. He was, after the war, to become the sole owner of the Mobile Register. The spelling, grammar and opinions are his. He writes in part:

Military Prison, Union Press
New Orleans, Sept. 5th. 1864.

Dear Tom ….We reached the Fort at Sunrise on the 4th ult. At one P. M. a double turreted Monitor moved up & threw a dozen shell at the Fort, doing no damage; having 3 ten-inch Columbiads to bear upon them we gave her a few shots, at every discharge two of them would be dismounted, showing gross negligence in our officers, as the guns were in no condition to fight. The Monitor having remained as long as she saw fit, went away. About 1 A. M. our Battn. Took the "piquet line" 1,100 yards from the fort; daylight showed us the enemy's infantry about 600 yards, in our front, soon we began a lively skirmish; the enemy had foolishly allowed us to advance to the edge of a pine forest, thus we (I mean our side, not our Battan.) voluntarily took the weakest position on the bare sand hills & beach & in the Palmetto, yielding to the enemy the cover of the wood & a strong abattis, which served them – not us. In half and hour we had 3 men killed & 8 wounded. Major Brown determined to advance & take possession of cover in the woods. At this moment, we rec'd the astounding order from Col. Anderson to fall back into the fort, it had to be obeyed, but its stupidity was evident. The enemy would of course advance his sharpshooters & no one would have been able to show his head above the work, with out at least being shot at. Luckily the order was countermanded, when we had fallen back about 400 yards, we then advanced to within 20 yds. of our old line. Whilst we were making these moves, like the "King of France, " a most terrible bombardment had opened on Fort Morgan; and our gallant fleet, it was <u>till</u> <u>then</u> the grandest sight I had ever witnessed – Farragut's entire fleet 22 or 24 vessels in line of battle slowly advancing, firing broadside after broadside. Fort Morgan was hidden from our site, the noise was "something like Daddies' gun only a tarnation louder." Soon the fleet moved by a flank right down on the fort. I could see them as they as they moved up & as they passed on, but I could not see them when they were immediately opposite the fort. The ships looked dressed for some great gala day – ensigns flying from every mast & and never ceasing their fire one moment as they came onward. They now began to pay us some little attention, but not enough to distract us from the scene which I though surpassed the first part of the fight. Soon a cheer arose, it was taken up at Fort Gaines – we knew something had happened. Shortly, a courier from "Gaines" came to tell us that a Monitor, one of the 4 in the Yankee fleet, had gone down with all on board, Hurrah: All this time, our fire with the enemy's infantry had been pretty brisk, they had also opened a land battery on tow places – Parrots, from the land side. The fleet had passed & all the great noise had quieted, save firing at some distance towards Bon Secour Bay. We afterwards learned that, the gallant, old Pat Murphy, after fighting 3 vessels with his little "Selma" had been forced to surrender. We could now mind our own business for awhile. The enemy showed no desire to advance. Major B. sent to the fort to beg a few shots from our 32 prds. to silence the Parrot Battery & keep the enemy's skirmishers quiet; whilst the courier was gone, I looked about at the "situation" – 3 Monitors & 14 wooden ships of war, in easy range of Fort Gaines, 2½ miles to my right in the Bay, some 4 or 5 vessels & as many mortar schooners in the Gulf, 5 miles off; Granger with his forces across the Island in the fort's rear, then <u>our</u> front. Well we were surrounded, but with a cool & bull-dog commander, though the fort was shamefully good for nothing, there was room for glory & and a good fight. I wondered what had become of the Tennessee, with the Strs. Morgan and Gaines. I learned soon, that Gaines was beached under the guns of Fort Morgan; Bennett, her brave commander grappled the foe like a lion, they were too many for him – he disengaged his sinking ship & reaching the beach, she sunk, with 18 shot holes in her hull, machinery ruined, & vessel <u>dead</u>. The Morgan – kept up a long taw fight doing considerable damage to the enemy, her boats boarded, & burnt a vessel which was disabled by a shot from Fort Morgan. The great Tennessee was not long in showing herself, she fought the enemy's fleet one after the other, as they passed her & and now they were all in a heap off Fort Gaines. Here comes the Tennessee; yes, here she comes – right for the enemy's fleet; they scatter before her, yes, 3 ironclads & 14 wooden vessels mounting 200 guns would run from one, with 6 guns, did not shame & and the scarcity of water prevent them. The skirmishing on land ceases by tacit agreement. Now comes a sight that throws all others in the shade… Well, they scatter before her – she makes for the flagship – she nearly reaches her, but Farragut glides from in front of her prow; the T. bores several holes in her antagonist, then puts about; the

MOBILE CONFEDERATES

whole fleet gathers around her – starboard, port, beam, bow, quarter – on every point – What a noise! The Tenn. fires with great rapidity, chiefly the broadside guns, which are in charge of Lt. Raney of our corps. The Bay for a mile around, is boiling with the ricochet of the shot and shell. The Brooklyn moves past – delivers her broadside, then the Hartford, followed by the Richmond – but that is nothing; they make no impression. That brave old Admiral Buchanan in contempt of danger, stands on the shield, when the Brooklyn at 30 yards, delivers her broadside; the concussion knocks him over but he is not hurt, & some fellow from the tops of the B. in his rage, dashes his opera glasses at him. Soon the Tennessee disappears & a black cloud of smoke takes her place; her smoke stack is shot away – the fight goes on however, gushes of white smoke through the black, show whenever gives a blow. Four of the enemy's vessels, one after the other, run down upon her at full speed, but to get their prows knocked off or stove in; the T's motions become slower & slower, she emerges from the fleet & crawls toward Fort Morgan, she goes but four or five hundred yards., almost stand still, 2 monitors run near her, (one, the Manhattan has a 15 inch gun) they come up, touching her, then let her have it again – She does not answer – she has surrendered. Fort Gaines has plucked up courage to open on the woods with her 32's - & and though overshooting very far, makes the enemy's battery keep respectful silence. One of the Monitors gives the fort four shots, & and in turn we are silenced. Why? Respondit Anderson. The enemy can enfilade my parapets: however, these were the last cannon shot, but two from our fort. The piquet lines continue their firing during that day & about nightfall our skirmishers on the left, lost their position through mismanagement, or something worse, of the officer command of that part of the line. I will not name him. Before morning however, we regained our lost line. On the morning of the 5th, the enemy's fire was not quite so brisk, but more accurate; though they killed on one, & wounded few, still the shots aimed at individuals came more uncomfortably near, than on the day before. Tow sharpshooters in trees in the woods threw 30 shots, from 6 inches, to ten feet, from Major B. & myself, distance of 500 yds. Our Battn. had been relieved at daylight & Major B. & myself were relieved at 10 A. M. (6th). We gave up our line intact. We had scarcely been in the Fort 20 minutes, when our piquets were seen falling back in hot haste, nor could we tell why; the Yankees did not advance, & scarcely fired a shot. Major Johnson, the veri[d]est coward I ever knew, commanded on that day. Col. A. sent his word to stop retreating, & advance his line; he advanced about one hundred yds. & sent word that he could go no further as the enemy pressed him; (his line was then 500 yds. From the fort, he having lost 600 yds.) This was false, for the enemy had not advanced 10 feet. During the previous night, Col. A had imitated the example of Herman Cortez – you remember that this chieftain burnt his ships when he landed on the Mexican beach – Well, Col. A had eleven boats, I thnk capable of carrying 250 to 300 men each trip – well, 9 of these, he had hauled up & and cut to pieces, placing a guard on the other two. In the course of the morning, finding that Fort Powell, at Grant's Pass, had been evacuated and blown up, he telegraphed the fact to Gen. Page, & added: "I will follow the example of our gallant Admiral." All this indicated fight, we all expected it. But Alas: What a sequel we had to all this bluster. At 2 or 3 P. M. our double turreted friend moved up, & gliding along about ¾ of a mile from the fort (in the Bay began throwing up a few "shells of ocean, "their firing was pretty close. But a "miss is good as a mile", & this could have been applied to every shell, with the exception of two; one struck the top of a 32, rifled & and injured it some – the other fell in the fort yard, knocked down two iron pillars & exploding, killed two men who were sleeping in one of the casements, & wounding one other; these were the only two that struck the fort. Then came two shots from our two 10 inch guns, & this was our last kick on our side. The monitor stopped firing in about an hour, having thrown about 20 shell. Then slight, very slight, firing at the piquets for the rest of the evening. I went to sleep inside the glacis at 9 P. M., having to rise early next morning to go on duty. At 4 A. M. Capt. Sherman (late of your office) woke me up & told me that the fort was about to surrender. You can probably imagine my astonishment. Upon asking him, he told me that a council of war had been held, & that Col. A. had determined for the sake of humanity to surrender.to the fleet. I have quit using oaths, but I plead guilty of having thought, & still thinking – Col. A. and humanity be d__d. Just at daylight two white flags left the fort, one for the enemy's land forces to pray that they stop shooting at us, as we were under truce with the fleet, and the other to the fleet, - to get terms of capitulation. The army, kindly forbore hurting us & Farragut sent word that we should surrender to the "Combined Naval & Army Forces, & that he would send "terms" at an early hour. All now was quiet, & whilst waiting for the return of Farragut's flag, let me tell you about this council of war, which threw disgrace upon the Arms of the Confederacy. Fort G. was garrisoned by seven companies of the 21st Ala. Regt. commanded by Col. A. & Major Johnson; the Regt. had fought at Shiloh, & since then, has been in & around Mobile; it has rec'd many recruits, those, who when the conscript laws finally seized (ceased) looking at their despairing families & meditating the dangers of a battle-field rushed into the 21st., as safer even than the Marine Corps; We reinforced this garrison; our Battn. had fourteen officers – of these fourteen, but three were at the "Council" Major Brown, one of them, arriving during the proceedings, opposed the surrender with all his power but to no avail. He was overruled. (I do not pretend to say that none of our officers would have consented to the shameful affair, on the contrary, I know that some would have.) After this council, some of the officers got up a paper to excuse the Col., in which it was set fourth that, the fort was a slaughter house, that the men would not fight etc., etc. This, nearly all the officers signed, some I must say, without reading in. It will be published. You will not see Lt. Fendall's (C. S. M. C.) or my name there. Though I admit that the fort was worthless, still it was so, through the fault of the officers sent there by our government, & we are now, all of us, parts of one large body – our country, & and if the rascals sent there to take the fort tenable did not do their duty, it does not take away from the disgrace attached, to the surrender of 818 officers and men, 19 cannon, 1000 small arms, lots of exploding stuff & provisions for 3 to 6 months. We could have held the fort out one or two weeks more, lost 150 men, killed as many Yankees – but the flag would have gone down with honor. As for the men not fighting – I deny this; I can say that I saw (in my own crowd, I know nothing of the others) no signs of giving up, they would have fought. I don't think, that in our army, because a man is a private, that "We Officers' should pretend that he has no patriotism. "Tis absurd; I was as honorable a personage when a private in the Chasseurs, as I am now, or ever will be. I repeat – that the men would have fought, had not the "white flag" been see to issue from Hd. Qtrs … Then, I did hear some speak of surrender. Farragut did not answer till night. In the meantime, Fort Morgan tried with all her might to find what we were up to; she signaled, fired signal guns, but all to no purpose – Fort Gaines did not answer. During the day I heard a good deal of talk about fighting – Oh: so bloodily – if Farragut did not come to terms. I knew this was all bosh – they had been offered the Fort, even before they thought of asking for it. Of course they would offer but one – "<u>unconditional</u>" & now, we had shown our weakness, & there was no fight in the Fort. At nightfall F's Boat came, Col. Anderson went off in the fleet to sign the papers of capitulation. During his absence Genl. Page came over; he was surprised and vexed, & I heard it said, that he made some tough remarks; he ordered that the Fort should be held. Shortly after his departure for Fort M., Col. A. returned from the fleet, & the deed was done – terms – "Unconditional." The fort to be delivered the next morning at 8 o'clock. You know how surrenders are made, I will not describe the ceremony, I hate to think it over. At 2 P. M. I was on a "tinclad" on my way to the ocean steamer, now gunboat Bienville, & we reached her about 3…………….[2nd Lt. John Lawrence Rapier was imprisoned at Union Press, one of the lower cotton steam presses at New Orleans and escaped. He was assigned to the gunboat Morgan and surrendered at Nanna Hubba Bluff, Alabama in 1965]

Major General Dabney Maury reports on August 8, 1864, that the outer line of defense for Mobile Gaines, Morgan and Powell was supplied with 300 rounds per gun while those near the city only are provisioned with no more that 200 rounds per gun. Total number of men in the whole District is about 6,000 about 1,000 whom have been under fire and a large number of citizens. The city probably has more women and children in it that any time since the war began. [5]

The men captured at Fort Gaines on August 9, were sent initially to New Orleans, Louisiana, and many were imprisoned at Steam Levee Press No. 4, on Tchoupitoulas Street in the Modern-day Warehouse District. The able bodied were transferred to Ship Island, on October 25, 1864, to be paroled and exchanged at Ship Island on January 4, 1865. Many made their way, as they should have, back to the regiment. Those men captured at Fort Morgan on August 23, 1864, were sent to New Orleans and transferred back to Ship Island then on to New York to be imprisoned at the notorious Elmira Prison. Several 21st Alabama Infantry men died and are buried there.

August 23, 1864, surrender of Fort Morgan. The enemy fleet had attacked Fort Morgan on Friday, August 5, at 6:30 a.m. and US land forces had landed east and at Navy Cove then progressed toward the fort. Three monitors and the captured ex CSN Tennessee launched a naval bombardment on August 13. Land forces bombarded and kept up a steady fire on the fort beginning August 15. All but two cannon were disabled after the extreme fire from ship and land batteries on August 21. Some of walls had been breached and the citadel had burned due to heavy cannon fire. Finally on August 23, CS Brigadier Richard L. General Page ordered his guns spiked, his powder destroyed and Fort Morgan surrendered.

January 4, 1865, those men who were captured at Fort Gaines in August and imprisoned at Ship Island, Mississippi, were exchanged and made their way back to the regiment to fight at Spanish Fort or Blakeley.

April 9, 1865, surrender of Spanish Fort and Blakeley. Only members of Companies C and D were assigned at Blakeley. Men who were captured at Spanish Fort and Blakeley were taken directly to Ship Island, Mississippi, arriving on April 13, for imprisonment. They were paroled at Ship Island and transferred for exchange to

---

[5] OR Series 1 Vol. XXXIX [S#77]

Vicksburg, Mississippi, on May 1, 1865. It is of interest that some of the men captured at Fort Gaines and sent to Ship Island, Mississippi, were paroled January 4, in time to reach the regiment and were captured again at Spanish Fort or Blakeley in April and sent back again to Ship Island. They would not be released this time until May or June 1865.

[*From Mobile Register and Advertiser Sunday April 2, 1865*] *Privates* **Elam** *and* **Winn** *of the 21st Alabama Regiment were shot to death with musketry at Blakeley at 6 o'clock P. M. on Friday – These men deserted to the enemy some time since but were subsequently apprehended, tried, condemned, and suffered the extreme penalty of the law, as above stated.*]

Co. H. 21st Alabama, Infantry surrendered with **Holtzclaw's Brigade** CSA commanded by Captain A. B. Carrinton surrendered at Citronelle.

A Federal newspaper, *The Mobile Daily News Vol No. 1,* published on April 13, 1865, reports that when the federal forces disembarked below the city (of Mobile) acting Adjutant Inspector General Laughrin of Major General Granger's Staff and Captain Franklin of the U. S. Navy, proceeded on shore and accompanied General Veach and Benton to the city limits where they were met by Mayor R. H. Slough and a delegation of the city authorities. The Mayor was presented a document stating that the city is menaced by a large land and naval force and demanded immediate and unconditional surrender. The document was signed by Major General Gordon Granger and Acting Rear Admiral H. K. Thacher. The Mayor responded with a reciprocal document acknowledging the receipt of the federal paper and stated the city had been evacuated by military authorities, and the city was under his control, and he conceded to their demands. When General Banks arrived, Colonel Laughton had a carriage in waiting at the wharf where General Banks and Brigadier General Andrews, Provost Marshal, were transported to the Mayor's office to carry out further details for taking formal possession of the city.

Major General Granger and staff moved into the Battle House, and the band belonging to General Slack's command played in front of the hotel that evening. This newspaper No. 1 was on 8 ½ by 11 sheet and only a single page.

U. S. Major General E. R. S. Canby and Confederate Lt. General Richard Taylor, with their staff, met at the Jacob Magee Farm house near Kushla, Alabama, a few miles northwest of Mobile along the Mobile and Ohio Railroad west of Eight Mile to discuss terms of surrender and a cease fire on April 29, 1865.

May 4, 1865 - Surrender by Lt. General Richard Taylor CSA to Major General E. R. S. Camby USA at Citronelle, Alabama, along the Mobile and Ohio Railroad beneath an oak tree.

May 13, 1865, the bulk of the men of the 21st Alabama Infantry were paroled at Meridian, Mississippi.

Introduction to Compiled Service Records

These abstracted muster rolls are from US National Archives microfilm file M – 311, Rolls 284-290. They were made available for copying by the Mobile Public Library, Special Collections, History and Genealogical Branch. Our gratitude to the library is significant in that the loan allowed this endeavor to come to competition.

Every reasonable effort was made to garner useful information for inclusion with the Roster. Some microfilm is unreadable due to poor photography or printing and cannot be transcribed. The fact that many men could not read or write and poor clerical skills produced a variety of spellings of names. Researchers are advised to check all conceivable spellings of names when using this roster. Some files contain original paper work and have been noted with an *. If considerable paper work is in the man's file a double ** will follow the entry. In general, spelling is as shown in the original records especially as to medical terms. Where exact locale such as a state is inferred I have added that information. The material contained herein is from the National Archives microfilm for the most part; however, where additional data is available from news accounts or other sources that has been appended as well. [Brackets or italics signify material from other sources than the service record film.] These records are not intended to be all-inclusive, and you are urged to consult the Compiled Service Records of US National Archives.

There are a number of cards among the records that are designated "a consolidated Report of Deserters from the Reserve Corp Army of Mississippi, Brigadier Gen. Withers commanding." In most cases it appears that the soldier was shown as wounded at Shiloh and was not a deserter. It is supposed that they simply used a standard card for reporting.

Dates are often confusing in these records but have been reported as found in the compiled military service records. Where glaring conflicts appear it is pointed out.

These soldiers were paid for clothing on commutation. They furnished their own clothing and the Confederate Government re-reimbursed them or sometimes paid them for clothing not received. In other instances they drew Government Issue clothing as you can see from the officer's requisitions. Many records denote the payment for clothing not drawn in kind; other records show the Confederate Government issued clothing. Apologies are offered in advance for errors or emissions. There is no intent to slight the members of the 21st Alabama Infantry that joined from other Alabama Counties such as Clarke, Sumter, Wilcox, Baldwin or Marengo Counties in the title *Mobile Confederates*
AEG

MOBILE CONFEDERATES

Roster 21st Alabama Infantry

A

Aaron, J., Corp. Co. I
His name appears for payment on a descriptive list for May 31, to August 31, 1862. Paid $39 on April 17, 1863, by C. S. Wallach.

Abrahms, Joseph, Pvt. Co. A
Enlisted on October 13, 1861, at Mobile, Alabama, by Major Hessee. Company muster roll for September 24, 1862, for payment of bounty shows him present. He refused to take the bounty. He appears present on a muster roll for September 24, 1862.

Ackerman, Joseph, C., Pvt. Co. A
Discharged at Corinth, Mississippi, on May 3, 1862, for disability.

Acton, J. G., Pvt. Co. F
Enlisted on September 10, 1862, at Shelby County by I. M. Davis for three years. Muster roll for March to June 30, 1862, reports him present, sick in hospital. Muster roll for September/October 1863, reports him absent sick since July 25, 1863. There is a reference card in his file dated September 28, 1863, stating "Deserter."

Acton, J. V., Pvt. Co. F
Enlisted on September 10, 1862, at Shelby County by I. M. Davis for three years or the war. Muster rolls for March to June 30, 1862, report him present. Muster roll for September/October 1862 reports him present. He drew clothing on March 31, and June 1, 1864. POW captured at Fort Gaines, Alabama, on August 8, 1864, received at Ship Island, Mississippi, from New Orleans on October 25, 1864. Exchanged at Ship Island on January 4, 1865. POW captured at Spanish Fort, Alabama, on April 8, 1865. Received at Ship Island on April 10, 1865. Transferred from Ship Island to Vicksburg, Mississippi, on May 1, 1865. There is a reference card in his file dated Sept. 28, 1863, stating "Deserter."

Adams, Homer, Pvt. Co. A
His name appears on a regimental return for June 1862. He was discharged at Tupelo, Mississippi, on June 16, 1862, for disability. Paid for service on June 17, 1862.

Adams, John, Pvt. Co. A
Enlisted on October 13, 1861, at Mobile, Alabama, by Major Hessee for the war. Company muster roll for September 24, 1862, for payment of bounty shows him present. Company muster roll for December 31, 1862, to April 30, 1863, reports him present. Muster rolls for May/ June 1863 also September/October 1962 report him present. His name appears on a consolidated report dated June 28, 1862, near Tupelo, Mississippi., sent to Corinth Hospital and from there to interior hospital on May 26, 1862, by order of

Surgeon Heustis. Drew clothing at Camp Anderson on June 14, 1864. POW captured at Fort Morgan on August 23, 1864, at New Orleans sent to New York on Sept. 27, 1864. Received at Elmira, New York, on October 8, 1864. He died November 21, 1864, at Elmira of pneumonia. Effects were one jacket, one pair pants and one pair shoes.

Adams, M., Pvt. Co. C

Enlisted on October ? 1863, by Lt. Wragg for three years or the war. Company muster rolls for September/October 1863 report him present. He drew clothing on March 31, and June 1, 1864. POW captured at Fort Gaines, Alabama, on August 8, 1864. Received at Ship Island, Mississippi, from New Orleans on October 25, 1864. He was exchanged on January 4, 1865. POW captured at Blakeley, Alabama, on April 9, 1865. Received at Ship Island on April 15, 1865. Transferred to Vicksburg, Mississippi, on May 1, 1865. Exchanged on parole at Camp Townsend May 6, 1875.

Adams, Timoleon, Pvt. Co. A

Enlisted at Point Clear, Alabama, on October 19, 1863, by Captain Cothran for three years or the war. Company muster roll for September/October 1863 shows him present.

Aderhold, Issac, Pvt. Co. B

POW captured at Champion Hill, Mississippi, on May 17, 1863, and sent to Memphis, Tennessee, May 25, 1863.

Agee, J. D., Pvt. Co. C

Enlisted on February 17, 1862, at Marengo County, Alabama, by Lt. Northrup for three years or the war. Company muster rolls for December 31, 1862, to April 1863, and May/ June 1863 report him present. September/October 1863 muster roll reports him present and having lost one H (haversack) sack worth $1. Admitted to Post Hospital at Fort Morgan on November 23, 1863, with pneumonia. He died on December 2, 1863.

Agee, K., Pvt./Sgt. Co. C see **Agee, Kennon** or **Agee, C. H. K**

Agee, Kennon, Agee, C. H. K.

Enlisted at Fort Gaines, Alabama, on November 22, 1861, by Capt. Rembert for three years or the war. Regimental return for June 1862, reports that he was wounded at Shiloh and furloughed. Company register for Battle of Shiloh April 6, 1862, reports he was wounded in the left shoulder on April 6, 1862, at 4 P. M. crossing Old Field while advancing. Company muster roll for September 24, 1862, for payment of bounty shows him present. Company muster rolls for December 31, 1862, to April 1863 and May/June 1863 report him present. Promoted to 3rd Corporal from the ranks on June 6, 1863. Muster roll for September/October 1863 roll reports him present. POW surrendered at Citronelle, Alabama, on May 4, 1865, and paroled at Meridian, Mississippi, on May 13, 1864. Residence shown as Marengo County, Alabama. Here is he is shown as 4th Sergeant.

Agee, Robert L., Pvt. Co. E

Drew clothing on June 1, 1864. POW captured at Fort Gaines, Alabama, on August 9, 1864, sent to Ship Island, Mississippi, and exchanged on January 4, 1865. Received at Ship Island from New Orleans on October 25, 1864. He is shown as a POW confined at Steam Levee Press No. 4 at New Orleans on September 29, 1864, sent to hospital. He was admitted to St. Louis USA Hospital General Hospital at New Orleans, Louisiana, on September 24, 1864, with diarrhoea. Returned to confinement on October 15, 1864. Surrendered at Citronelle, Alabama, on May 4, 1865. Paroled at Meridian, Mississippi, on May 13, 1864. Residence shown as Shiloh, Marengo County, Alabama.

Agee, W. R., Pvt. Co. K

Enlisted on September 17, 1862, at Fort Morgan, Alabama, by Captain Dorgan for the war. Drew clothing on December 19, 1863, and June 20, 1864. Drew pay at Mobile on August 16, 1864, at $11 per month. Company muster roll for September/October 1864, reports him absent sick at Claiborne since October 20. "Furnished certificate from Medical Board". POW received at Ship Island, Mississippi, on April 10, 1865, captured again at Spanish Fort, Alabama. Transferred from Ship Island to Vicksburg, Mississippi, on May 1, 1865. He signed for clothing as **W. R. Agee Jr.**

Agnes, V., Pvt. Co. G

Discharged on February 28, 1862.

Ahern, John, Pvt. Co. D

Killed at Battle of Shiloh on April 6, 1862. Wounds in the head and left breast in the A.M. at First Camp. Payment of $13.20 made to Catherine Ahern his widow. Born in Ireland, five foot seven inches, dark complexion, black eyes, and sandy hair. **

Aiken, E. T. Pvt. Co. E see **Akin, A. J.**

Akin, A. J. Pvt. Co. E

Drew clothing on March 31, and June 1, 1864. POW captured at Fort Gaines, Alabama, on August 8, 1864. Received at Ship Island, Mississippi, from New Orleans, on October 25, 1864. Exchanged on January 4, 1865. Paroled at Montgomery, Alabama on May 30, 1865. His parole is in his file. He is described as six feet one inch, dark hair, hazel eyes, and dark complexion.

Albert, J., Pvt. Co. K

Enlisted at Fort Morgan, Alabama, on July 4, 1863, by Captain Dorgan for the war. His name appears on a descriptive list and account for bounty. He drew clothing on July 10, and December 19, 1863.

Alberti, Ant, (**Albside**) Pvt. Co. H

Killed at Farmington on picket on May 13, 1862.

Aldridge, James L., Pvt./Sergeant Co. C

Enlisted at Mobile, Alabama, on January 15, 1862, by Captain McVoy for three years or the war. Company muster roll for bounty at Fort Gaines, Alabama, September 24, 1862, reports him present. Company muster roll for December 31, 1862, to April 1863, at Fort Gaines reports him present. Company muster roll for September/October 1863, reports him present and having lost one haversack at $1 and one canteen at $2. Reported absent on surgeon's certificate. for June 1862. Drew clothing on March 21, 1864. POW captured at Fort Gaines on August 8, 1864. Received at Ship Island from New Orleans on October 25, 1864. Exchanged at Ship Island on January 5, 1865. POW captured at Spanish Fort on April 9, 1865. Received at Ship Island on April 15, 1865. Transferred from Ship Island to Vicksburg, Mississippi, on May 1, 1865. There is paper work in his file of poor quality.*

Aldridge, James K., Pvt. Co. G

Paid $9.90 on August 20, 1863, at Montgomery, Alabama, for commutation of rations while on furlough from August 26, to September 23, 1863. Drew clothing on May 3, March 21 and June 1, 1864. Admitted to Ross Hospital at Mobile, Alabama, on January 6, 1865, with debilitas and scurvy. Furloughed on January 17, 1865, for 60 days.*

Aldridge, James S. see **Aldridge James,** Pvt./Sgt. Co. C

Alexander, James J., Pvt. Co. E

His name appears on a roll of POW's in the Engineer Department of the Confederate States commanded by Colonel Minor Meriwether, that were surrendered at Citronelle, Alabama, on May 4, 1865, by Lt. General Richard Taylor. He was paroled at Meridian, Mississippi, on May 10, 1865. Residence shown as Mobile, Alabama.

Allan, Z. D., Pvt. Co. C/G

Enlisted on April 6, 1863, at Choctaw Bluff, Alabama, by Captain Smith for three years or the war. Drew clothing March 31, May 5, and June 1, 1864. Company muster roll for December 31, 1862, to April 30, 1863, reports him present. Company muster roll for May/June 1864, reports him present sick in quarters. September/October muster roll reports him absent sick in hospital at Mobile since October 25, 1863. His name appears on a roll for commutation of rations, $9.90, while on furlough from November 20, to December 19, 1863. POW captured at Fort Gaines, Alabama, on August 8, 1864. Received at Ship Island, Mississippi, from New Orleans on October 25, 1864. He died at Ship Island on November 22, 1864, of diarrhoea, and was buried in Grave No. 26.

Allen, A. J. see **Allen Elijah J.** Pvt. Co. I

Allen, Edwin, Pvt./Corp. Co. A

Enlisted on October 13, 1861, at Mobile, Alabama, by Major Hessee. He appears present on company muster rolls from September 24, 1862, through October 1863. Drew clothing on March 31, May 20, and June 14, (at Camp Anderson). Signed by his mark. POW captured at Fort Morgan, Alabama, on August 23, 1864. Sent to New York on

September 27, 1864. Received at Elmira, New York, on October 8, 1864, from New Orleans. He was released on June 14, 1865. Signed Oath of Allegiance to the USA at Elmira, New York, on June 14, 1865. Residence Windsor County (?), fair complexion, auburn hair, blue eyes, six foot.

Allen, Elijah J., Pvt. Co. I

Enlisted on October 13, 1861, at Halls Mill, Alabama, by Major Hessee. Regimental return for June 1862 shows him sent to interior hospital on June 28, 1862. Muster roll for bounty dated September 24, 1862, reports him absent detached by order of General Jackson on August 1, 1862, A. Q. M. Company muster roll for June/July 1863, reports him present but absent without leave on August 9, to 12. Company muster roll for September/October 1863, reports him present but absent without leave for 2 days. Drew clothing on March 31, 1864. POW captured at Fort Gaines, Alabama, on August 8, 1862, confined at Steam Levee Press No. 4 at New Orleans on September 29, 1864. Sent to hospital on September 29, 1864, and admitted to St. Louis USA General Hospital with acute diarrhoea on Oct. 2, 1864, returned to confinement on October 3, 1864. He was admitted to the same hospital on October 11, 1864, with pneumonia. He died October 11, 1864, and was buried on October 12, 1864. Age 21, wife N. M. Allen, Mobile, Alabama, Grave 391 Monument Cemetery. There are good copies of his death certificate in his file.*

Allen, Jefferson, Pvt. Co. I filed with **Allen, John E.** Pvt. Co. I

Admitted to St. Louis USA General Hospital at New Orleans on August 15, 1864, with fever intermitten qout. Returned to confinement on August 22, 1864. Age 21, he was on Ward K. (See also **Allen, J. S.**)

Allen, J. M., Pvt. Co. D

Enlisted on July 22, 1863, at Montgomery, Alabama. Company muster rolls from July 1863 until December 1863 report him present. Drew clothing on June 20, 1864. Drew pay at Mobile on August 15, 1864, for service November 1, 1863, until June 30, 1864, at $11 per month. Signed by his mark. A company muster roll for September/October 1864, reports him absent sick in hospital in Montgomery since September 17, 1864. His name appears on a hospital muster roll at Ladies' Hospital at Montgomery, Alabama, November 15, 1864, as a patient. POW surrendered by Lt. General Richard Taylor at Citronelle, Alabama, on May 4, 1865. Paroled at Meridian, Mississippi, on May 13, 1865.

Allen, John, E., Pvt. Co. I

Enlisted on October 13, 1861, at Halls Mill, Alabama, by Major Hessee. Regimental return for June reports he was sent to hospital on May 28, 1862. His name appears on a consolidated list June 28, 1862, near Tupelo, Mississippi, sent to interior hospital from Corinth. He is reported present for bounty on September 24, 1862. Company muster rolls for July through October 1863 report him present. Drew clothing on June 1, 1864. Admitted to Ross Hospital at Mobile, Alabama, on June 23, 1864, with febris interimit. Returned to duty on July 19, 1864. POW captured at Fort Morgan, Alabama, on August 23, 1864. Admitted to St. Louis USA General Hospital at New

Orleans on August 26, 1864, with diarrhoea, age 32. Returned to confinement on August 30, 1864. Sent to New York from New Orleans on September 27, 1864. Received at Elmira, New York, on October 8, 1864. Paroled at Elmira on February 9, 1864, and sent to James River for exchange. Transferred for exchange on February 13, 1865. Appears on a roll of POW's at Point Lookout, Maryland, among 3038 paroled prisoners received at Boulwares and Cox's Wharf, James River, February 20 and 21, 1865. He appears on a register at General Hospital Howard's Grove at Richmond, Virginia, on February 21, 1864.

Allen, J. S., Pvt. Co. I filed with **Allen John E.**, Pvt. Co. I
Confined at Steam Levee Press No. 4 at New Orleans on August 15, 1864. Sent to hospital on August 15, 1864.

Allen, M. Pvt. Co. D
Appears on a regimental return for June 1862, as being on detached service as a carpenter. Drew $22 on September 4, 1862, for service July 1, to September 4, 1862.

Allen, N. W. Pvt. Co. C see **Allan, Z. D.**

Allen, Perry W., Pvt. Co. I
Enlisted October 13, 1861, at Halls Mill, by Major Hessee. Sent to interior hospital on May 28, 1862. His name appears on a consolidated list on June 28, 1862, near Tupelo, Mississippi, sent to interior hospital from Corinth. Admitted to Post Hospital at Fort Morgan, Alabama, on March 20, 1863, with rubeola, returned to duty on April 1, 1863. He appears present on company muster rolls for July through October 1863. Drew clothing on March 31, 1864. Admitted to Post Hospital at Fort Morgan on July 29, 1864, with int. fev. quot., retuned to duty on August 6, 1864. POW captured at Fort Morgan on August 23, 1864. Sent to Elmira, New York, from New Orleans. Received at Elmira on October 8, 1864. His name appears on a list of prisoners at Elmira on April 15, 1865, that wish to take the Oath of Allegiance to the USA and remain North during the war. Released on May 14, 1865. Resident of Mobile, Alabama, dark complexion, dark hair, blue eyes, five foot ten inches.

Allen, S., Pvt. Co. K
A resident of Mobile County, Alabama. POW surrendered by Lt. General Richard Taylor at Citronelle, Alabama, on May 4, 1865. He was paroled at Meridian, Mississippi, on May 10, 1865.

Allen, Samuel, Pvt. Co. A
Discharged on April 11, 1862, by reason of defective eyesight. Age 19, born in Alabama, five foot nine and one half inches, dark complexion, black eyes, a clerk by profession. Appears on extra duty in Captain Maury's Corps for the months of June and July 1864, as assistant clerk. His discharge is in his file.*

Allen, William, Pvt. Co. I

POW captured at Fort Gaines, Alabama, on August 8, 1864. Received at Ship Island, Mississippi, from New Orleans on October 25, 1864. Exchanged on January 4, 1865.

Allen, William A., Pvt. Co. D

Enlisted on October 13, 1861, at Mobile, Alabama, by Captain Butts for the war. His name appears on a consolidated list on June 28, 1862, near Tupelo, Mississippi, sent to interior hospital from Corinth and on to hospital in Mobile. Company muster roll for bounty on September 24, 1862, reports him present. Transferred to Co. H, 1st Battalion Alabama Artillery on December 8, 1862.

Allen, William B., Pvt. Co. A

Enlisted on January 13, 1862, at Fort Gaines, Alabama. Company muster roll for bounty on September 24, 1862, reports him absent in Gainesville (Fort Gaines?) hospital. Company muster roll for December 31, 1862, until April 30, 1863, reports him present but with forfeiture of pay to the CSA from September 13, 1862, to January 16, 1863, by order of G. C. M. (General Court Marshal). Company muster rolls report him present for May, June, September and October 1863. Drew clothing on March 31, 1864. POW captured at Fort Morgan on August 23, 1864. Received at Elmira, New York, on October 8, 1864, from New Orleans. Released on June 14, 1865. A resident of Demopolis, Alabama, fair complexion, auburn hair, blue eyes, five foot eight inches. Note descriptive list for five soldiers is in **Keane, Edward,** Drummer's file May 21, 1862.
Allen, William B., Pvt., age 23, gray eyes, dark hair, fair complexion, five foot ten inches, born Marengo County a teacher, enlisted January 13, 1862, at Fort Gaines, $50 bounty received.

Allen, W. T., Pvt. Co. C

His name appears on a roll of POW's of Co. C, 21st Alabama Infantry under the command of Captain F. N. Smith that were surrendered by Lt. General Richard Taylor at Citronelle, Alabama, on May 4, 1865. He was paroled at Meridian, Mississippi, on May 13, 1865. Residence shown as Marengo County, Alabama.

Allen, Z. J. filed with **Allan, Z. D.**

Allen, Z. M. filed with **Allan, Z. D.**

Allman, Benjamin Frank, Sgt./2nd Lt. Co. E

Enlisted October 13, 1861, at Mobile, Alabama, by Captain Chamberlain for the war. Company muster roll for bounty on September 24, 1862, reports him present as does roll for November and December 1862. Drew clothing on March 16, 1863. Admitted to Post Hospital at Fort Morgan, Alabama, on July 4, 1863, with syphilis, returned to duty on July 10. Company muster roll for July/August 1863, reports him absent sick with surgeon's certificate. Company muster roll for September/October 1863, reports him absent on leave from October 27, until November 11. Elected to 2nd Lt. on May 11, 1864, and promoted on May 16. POW captured at Fort Gaines, Alabama, on August 8, 1864. Admitted to St. Louis USA General Hospital in New Orleans, on August 20, 1864, with fever remitten. Returned to confinement on August 24, 1864. Age 23. His name appears on a roll of POW's that escaped confinement at 21 Rampart Street in New Orleans on September 20, 1864. Drew $80 per month as Lt. See personal papers of **M. C. Burke**. There are several pay vouchers, his Parole of Honor and a letter are in his file.**

> Headquarters M. D. W. W.
> Office of Com. Of Prisons
> September 7, 1864.
> Sirs,
>> You will send to the St. Louis Hospital under <u>guard</u> Lieut. Allman 21st Alabama, whose uncle is reported as dying.
>> He will be allowed to remain there for a short time and then will be returned to the prison.
>> The Guard will remain with him & return him.
>>> Signed

Allman, Frank, Sgt./2nd Lt. filed with **Allman, Benjamin F.**

Allnet, J., Pvt. Co. C filed with **Albrest, J.**

Albrest, J., Pvt. Co. C
POW captured at Blakeley, Alabama, on April 9, 1865. Received at Ship Island, Mississippi, on April 15, 1865, transferred to Vicksburg, Mississippi, on May 1, 1865.

Amerson, A. Y., Pvt. Co. D
His name appears on a Medical Director's Office register at Howard's Grove Hospital in Richmond, Virginia, on October 8, 1864. Remarks: Canton, Mississippi.

Anderson, C. D., Colonel
Served for a time as Major in the 20th Alabama Infantry. Rank from March 16, 1861. Elected Colonel on reorganization of the 21st Regiment on May 8, 1862. Shown present at Tupelo, Mississippi, for the Month of May 1862. Transferred to Choctaw Bluff, Alabama, on October 6, 1862. Signed receipt of 25,000 buck and ball cartridges in 25 packing boxes at Choctaw Bluff in November 1862. Drew forage for two private horses at Point Clear, Alabama, on August 31, 1863. Paid $195 per month plus $9 for five years service as Colonel on June 30, 1864. POW captured at Fort Gaines, Alabama, on August 8, 1864. Received at Ship Island, Mississippi, from New Orleans on November 25, 1864. Exchanged at Ship Island on January 4, 1864. Surrendered by Lt. General Richard Taylor and signed a Parole of Honor at Meridian, Mississippi, on May 17, 1865. His parole, requisitions, pay vouchers and other materials are in his file. **
Born in South Carolina. Admitted to the Academy on September 1, 1846. On July 26, 1856, he was a 2nd Lt. USA 4th Artillery, at age 25 and resided in Galveston, Texas. Iney A. Anderson is shown as his widow. Died November 21, 1902, at Galveston, Texas. There is no record of him being a Brigadier General.

Anderson, Hopeley E., Pvt./Corp. Co. E

Enlisted on October 13, 1861, at Mobile, Alabama, by Captain Chamberlain for the war. Wounded at Shiloh on April 6, 1862. Wounded in the thigh slightly at 7 A. M. while advancing on 1st Battery. He appears present on company muster rolls from September 24, 1862, for bounty, until October 1863. Drew clothing on March 1, and June 1, 1864. POW captured on August 8, 1864, at Fort Gaines, Alabama. Received at Ship Island, Mississippi, from New Orleans on October 26, 1864. Exchanged at Ship Island on January 5, 1865. Surrendered by Lt. General Richard Taylor at Citronelle, Alabama, on May 4, 1865. Paroled at Meridian, Mississippi, on May 13, 1865. He is shown as 3rd Corporal of Co. E.

Anderson, M. C., Pvt. Co. G

His name appears on a register of POW's paroled at Montgomery, Alabama, on June 3, 1865. His parole shows Wm. C. Anderson. florid complexion, dark hair, blue eyes, five foot eight inches. His parole is in his file.*

Anderson, Wm. C., see **Anderson, M. C.**

Anderson, William H., Surgeon

Mustered into Confederate service on October 13, 1861. Transferred on December 1, 1861. Succeeded by **R. H. Redwood**. Company muster roll for November 1, 1861, at Fort Gaines shows him absent on detached service in Mobile as Medical Purveyor.

Anderson, Wade, L., Pvt. Co. E

Enlisted on September 8, 1862, at Shelby County, Alabama, by W. J. Davis for the war. Company muster rolls for November/December 1862, July/August 1863 and September/ October 1862, all report him present. He drew clothing on March 31, and June 1, 1864, and signed by his mark. POW captured at Fort Gaines, Alabama, on August 8, 1864. Received at Ship Island, Mississippi, from New Orleans on October 25, 1864. Exchanged at Ship Island on January 4, 1865.

Andrews, W. H., 2nd Lt. Co. G

Appointed 2nd Lt. on March 24, 1864. Drew $80 for service January 1, to March 23, 1864. He drew clothing on March 1, and March 31, 1864. Granted 10 days leave by General Maury on June 25, 1864. POW captured at Fort Gaines, Alabama, on August 8, 1864. Confined at 21 North Rampart Street, New Orleans, Louisiana. Admitted to St. Louis USA General Hospital at New Orleans, on September 16, with fev. intermit and variolois. Transferred to General Hospital Barracks on September 19, age 24. Escaped from barracks September 29, 1864. There is paperwork in his file.*

Antonio, Pvt. Co. G

Admitted to Ross Hospital at Mobile, Alabama, on August 8, 1864, with diarrhoea, acuta, and rheumatism. Sent to general hospital on August 9, 1864.

Armistead, B. B., Pvt. Co. C

Admitted to Post Hospital at Fort Morgan, Alabama, on November 11, 1863, with catarrh, retuned to duty on November 18, 1863. Drew clothing on June 1, 1864. POW captured at Fort Gaines, Alabama, on August 8, 1864. Received at Ship Island, Mississippi, from New Orleans on October 25, 1864. Exchanged at Ship Island on January 4, 1865. POW captured at Blakeley, Alabama, on April 9, 1865. Received at Ship Island on April 15, 1865. Transferred from Ship Island to Vicksburg, Mississippi, on May 1, 1865.

Armistead, J. W., Pvt. Co. C

Enlisted on February 10, 1863, at Choctaw Bluff, Alabama, by Captain Smith for the war. Company muster rolls for December 3, 1862, to April 30, 1863, report him present. Muster rolls for May/June, and September/October 1863, report him present. Drew clothing on March 31, and June 1, 1864. POW captured at Fort Gaines, Alabama, on August 8, 1864. Admitted to St. Louis USA General Hospital at New Orleans on September 13, 1864, with diarrhoea, returned to prison September 26, 1864, age 36. Received at Ship Island, Mississippi, from New Orleans on October 25, 1864. Exchanged at Ship Island on January 4, 1865.

Armor, William, Pvt./Sgt. Co. E see **Armour, William**

Armour, William, Pvt./ 2nd Lt. Co. E/F

Enlisted on October 13, 1861, at Mobile, Alabama, by Captain Chamberlain for three years or the war. Sent to interior hospital on May 27, 1862. Drew clothing on March 14, 1863. Transferred from Co. E, 2nd Battalion to Co. F, 1st Battalion as 1st Sergeant, on September 17, 1863. Drew clothing on March 31, and June 1, 1864. POW captured at Fort Gaines, Alabama, on August 8, 1864. Admitted to St. Louis USA General Hospital at New Orleans on August 22, 1864, with diarrhoea, returned to prison on August 29, 1864, age 23. Received at Ship Island, Mississippi, from New Orleans on October 25, 1864. Exchanged at Ship Island on January 4, 1865. Surrendered by Lt. General Richard Taylor at Citronelle, Alabama, on May 4, 1865. Paroled at Meridian, Mississippi, on May 12, 1865. His parole is in his file.*

Armstead, B. B., Pvt. Co. C see **Armistead, B. B.**

Armstead, J. W., Pvt. Co. C see **Armistead, J. W.**

Armstrong, James S., Pvt. Co. B

POW captured May 17, 1863, at Champion Hill, Mississippi, by the Army of the Tennessee, sent to Memphis, Tennessee, on May 25, 1863.

Armsted, J. W., Pvt. Co. C see **Armistead, J. W.**

Armstrong, P. P., Pvt. Co. D

Enlisted on July 22, 1863, at Montgomery, Alabama, by Enrolling Officer for the war. Company muster roll for July/August 1863, reports him present. Admitted to Post

Hospital at Fort Morgan, Alabama, on August 4, 1863, with feb remit. Returned to duty on August 20. Company muster roll for September/October 1863, reports him present under arrest. Company muster roll for November/December 1863, reports him under sentence of General Court Marshal. Drew clothing June 20, and in August 1864. Company muster roll September/October 1864, reports him absent in General Hospital at Mobile, since October 7, 1864.

Arnett, John, Pvt. Co. I

Enlisted on October 13, 1861, at Halls Mill, Alabama, by Major Hessee for the war. Regimental return for June 1862, reports that he was sent to interior hospital on May 28, 1862. His name appears on a list of men who returned without arms or with captured arms, Wither's Division, 1st Brigade. Transferred to Captain Hutchinson's Company of Engineers on August 20, 1862. His name appears on a consolidated roll June 28, 1862, sent to an interior hospital from Corinth by Dr. Heustis. Appears on detached service with Engineering Department by General Forney on December 6, 1862. Bounty paid on January 30, 1863. There are signed pay vouchers in his file.* He was paid $11 per month.

Arnett, W., Pvt. Co. I

Enlisted on October 13, 1861, at Halls Mill, Alabama. Regimental return for June 1862, reports that he was sent to interior hospital on May 28, 1862. His name appears on roll June 28, 1862, sent to an interior hospital from Corinth by Dr. Heustis. Born North Carolina, age 18 years, five foot six inches, hazel eyes, light hair, dark complexion, by profession a spirits maker. Discharged on October 23, 1862, due to disability. His discharge and a pay voucher are in his file.* He signed by his mark.

Aranmelilch, Michael, Pvt. Co. H see **Asonosilich, M.**

Ashby, Samuel, Pvt. Co. D

Enlisted on October 13, 1864, at Mobile by Captain Butt for one year. Drew clothing on June 20, 1862. A regimental return for June 1862, reports that he was sent to an interior hospital at the evacuation (of Corinth). A consolidated report near Tupelo on June 28, 1862, shows that he was sent to hospital in Mobile from hospital at Corinth by surgeon. He appears present on a company muster roll for bounty on September 24, 1862. Company muster roll for November/December 1862, reports that he has deserted since November 8, 1862.

Ashley, W. B., Pvt. Co. H

His name appears on a register of claims of deceased soldiers from Alabama, which were filed for settlement. Filed by Hon. John R. Rolls on February 7, 1863. Paid $30.26.

Asonosilich, Michale, Pvt. Co. H

Regimental return for June 1862, reports that he was sent to the rear on May 28. His name appears on a consolidated report near Tupelo, Mississippi, on June 28, 1862, as having been sent to the interior from Corinth at the time of the evacuation. Paid $113 on

MOBILE CONFEDERATES

November 12, 1863, for service from March 1, 1862, until October 31, 1862. He signed by his mark. His pay voucher is in his file*.

Auburt, F. H., Pvt. Co. K
Enlisted on October 13, 1861, at Mobile, Alabama, by Captain Stewart for the war. A report near Tupelo, Mississippi, on June 21, 1862, reports him on furlough since May 29. Appears present on company muster roll for September 24, 1862, sent to general hospital on May 28, 1862. Company muster roll for November/December 1862, reports him present and detailed as Acting Postal Clerk Q. M. by order of Captain Stewart. Company muster rolls; July/August, 1863, September/October 1863, and September/October 1864, report him present. Drew clothing on July 10, 1863, December 19, 1863, and June 30, 1864. Paid $11 on August 15, 1864. POW captured at Spanish Fort, Alabama, on April 8, 1865. Received at Ship Island, Mississippi, on April 10, 1865. Transferred from Ship Island to Vicksburg, Mississippi, on May 1, 1865.

Augustini, Biggie, Pvt. Co. G
His name appears on a register of claims for soldiers from Alabama, filed by J. R. Eastham, Attorney on June 24, 1862. Born Genoa, Italy. Paid $49.56 on July 14, 1862, to Francis Augustini, Mother? Widow? Age 21, five foot four inches, white complexion, dark eyes, dark hair, by profession a restaurant keeper. Residence Mobile, Alabama. Paid to December 19, 1861. (Date of Death?) There is paperwork in his file.**

Augustini, Pierre, 2nd Lt. Co. H
He enlisted on October 13, 1861. He was elected 2nd Lt. on October 15, 1861. A register dated November 1, 1861, reports him present at Fort Gaines, Alabama. Wounded seriously in the left arm on April 6, 1862, 7 A. M while advancing on attack of 1st Battery at Shiloh, Tennessee. He was honorably discharged by General Bragg. Paid $282.66, on November 22, 1862, for service. There is paperwork in his file**.

Austin, John, A., Pvt. Co. B
POW captured at Champion Hill, Mississippi, on May 17, 1863. Captured by the Army if the Tennessee (USA) and sent to Memphis, Tennessee, on May 23, 1863.

Austin, T. J., Pvt. Co. C/A
Enlisted at Choctaw Bluff, Alabama, on January 3, 1863, by Colonel Anderson for three years or the war. Transferred to Co. A on March 31, 1863. Company muster roll to April 30, 1863, reports him present at Choctaw Bluff as does rolls for May/June 1863, and September/October 1863. Paid $22 on September 12, 1863. Drew clothing on March 31, and June 16, 1864, (Camp Anderson). POW captured at Fort Morgan, Alabama, on August 23, 1864. Sent to New York on September 27. Received at Elmira, New York, on October 8, 1864, from New Orleans. Died at Elmira on July 7, 1865, of chron. diarrohea. He was buried in grave No. 2978. Signed by his mark. Note Descriptive list for five soldiers is in **Keane, Edward,** Drummer's file, May 21, 1862.
Austin, J. T., Pvt., age 26, gray eyes, black hair, dark complexion, five foot eight and one half inches, a farmer, enlisted at Clarke County, Alabama, by Colonel Anderson for the war, $50 bounty received.

Austin, W. A., Pvt. Co. C/A, also shown as **Oston**

Enlisted at Choctaw Bluff, Alabama, on February 1, 1863, by Colonel Anderson for three years or the war. Transferred to Co. A on March 31, 1863. Company muster roll to April 30, 1863, at Choctaw Bluff reports him present. May/June 1863, roll reports him absent sent to General Hospital at Selma, Alabama, on May 8, 1863. Company muster roll at Choctaw Bluff for September/October, reports him present but absent without leave from July 4, to September 26, 1863. Admitted to Post Hospital at Fort Morgan, Alabama, on November 1, 1863, with contusio. Returned to duty on November 16, 1863. Drew clothing on March 31, and June 14, 1864, (Camp Anderson).

Averett, Amason M., Pvt. Co. G

Drew clothing on March 3, and June 1, 1864. Admitted to Ross Hospital at Mobile, Alabama, on January 6, 1865, with diarrhoea and debililtia. He died on January 22, 1865. Left $15 in effects with surgeon in charge. There is paperwork in his file.*

Averheart, Thomas D., Pvt. Co. D

Enlisted at Fort Powell, Alabama, on January 8, 1864, by Captain Butt for the war. Drew clothing in August 1864. Company muster roll for September/October 1864, reports him absent on furlough of sixty days, granted by Medical Board on October 7, 1864.

Averheart, T. M., Pvt. Co. D

Enlisted on March 12, 1861, at Prattville, Alabama, by Lt. Whiting for three years. Company muster roll for July/August 1863, reports him present, indebted to the Government for one saber bayonet. September/October 1863, muster roll reports him present and is due (from) him eight dollars for bayonet. On November/December 1863, roll he is reported present and he is paid $134.13 less $20.50 drawn. Drew clothing on June 20, 1864, and paid $11 on August 15, 1864. POW captured at Blakeley, Alabama, on April 9, 1865. Received at Ship, Island, Mississippi, on April 15, 1865. Transferred from Ship Island to Vicksburg, Mississippi, on May 1, 1865. [*He was a member of the Robinson Springs UCV Camp 396. He died in Jefferson County, Alabama.*]

Avery, D. D., Pvt. Co. D.

Enlisted on October 13, 1861, at Mobile, Alabama, by Captain Butt for one year. Present for bounty on September 24, 1862. Muster rolls for November/December 1862, July/August 1863, September/October 1863, and November/December 1863, report him present. Admitted to Post Hospital at Fort Morgan, Alabama, on June 4, 1864, with vulnus (wound) returned to duty on June 8, 1864. Drew clothing June 20, and in August 1864. He was paid $17 on August 15, 1864. Signed by his mark. September/October 1864, roll reports him absent in guardhouse at Mobile since October 13, 1864.

Avery, William A., Pvt. Co. D

Enlisted on October 13, 1861, at Mobile, Alabama, by Captain Butt for one year. Present for bounty on September 24, 1862. Muster rolls for November/December 1862, July/August 1863, September/October 1863, and November/ December 1863, all report him present. Paid commutation of clothing $65.18 on October 31, 1863. Admitted to

MOBILE CONFEDERATES

Ross Hospital at Mobile on March 30, 1864, with diarrhoea acuta. Returned to duty on April 2. Muster roll for September/October 1864, reports him absent sick in hospital in Mobile since September 26, 1864. Drew clothing, April 15, June 20, and in August 1864. He was paid $11 for service on August 15, 1864.

B

Babbitt, J. H., Pvt. Co. C
 His name appears on a list of prisoners that died at Camp Butler, Chicago, Illinois, on June 8, 1864.

Baber, Anonymous, Pvt. Co. A
 He enlisted on February 1, 1863, at Choctaw Bluff, Alabama, by Captain Cothran for the war. Muster roll for May/June 1863 reports him present. Muster roll for September/October 1863, reports him absent, detached July 25, 1863, A. Q. M. Department by order of Colonel Anderson. Last paid on August 31, 1863, by Captain McVoy. Note Descriptive list for five soldiers is in **Keane, Edward,** Drummer's file, May 21, 1862.
Baber, A., Pvt., age 36, blue eyes, light hair, fair complexion, five foot nine inches, born N.C.? Rutherford, a farmer, enlisted Clarke Co. Alabama, by Colonel Anderson for the war, $50 bounty received.

Badger, William, S., 2nd Lt./1st Lt. Co. A/H
 His name appears on a company muster roll for bounty on September 24, 1862. Elected 2nd Lt. Co. A on May 8, 1862. Promoted to 2nd Lt. Co. A on August 30, 1862. Transferred from Fort Morgan, Alabama, to Choctaw Bluff, Alabama, on October 6, 1862. Promoted to 1st Lt. Co. H on March 24, 1864. Company muster roll for December 31, 1862, to April 30, 1863, reports him present. He requisitioned 60 pair of shoes for Co. A on May 25, 1863, at Mobile, Alabama. Company Muster rolls for May/June, September/October 1863, report him present. POW captured at Fort Gaines, Alabama, on August 8, 1864. Received at Ship Island, Mississippi, on November 25, 1864, from New Orleans. Exchanged at Ship Island on January 5, 1865. See personal papers of **M. C. Burke.** Lt. Badger was paid $80 per month as a 1st Lt. He was surrendered by Lt. General Richard Taylor at Citronelle, Alabama, and signed a Parole of Honor at Meridian, Mississippi, on May 11, 1865. His parole and other paper work is in his file.**

Bahan, Patrick, Pvt. Co. A
 Enlisted on August 15, 1862, at Fort Morgan, Alabama, by Captain Williams. Company muster roll for bounty on September 24, 1862, reports him present. Discharged on February 20, 1863. Paid $40.33 for service on February 28, 1863. Signed by his mark. Born Ireland, age 31, 5 foot 5 inches, fair complexion, hazel eyes, black hair, a laborer by occupation.

Bailey, George T., Pvt. Co. A/F
 Enlisted on February 10, 1863, at Choctaw Bluff, Alabama, by Captain Cothran for the war. Company muster roll for December 31, 1862, to April 30, 1863, reports him

32

present. Muster rolls for May/June 1863 and September/October 1863, report him present. Drew clothing on March 31, and June 14, 1864. POW captured at Fort Morgan, Alabama, on August 23, 1864. Received at Elmira, New York, on October 8, 1864, from New Orleans. Transferred for exchange on February 13, 1865, forwarded via Point Lookout, Maryland. Received at Boulwares and Cox's Wharf, James River on February 20 and 21, 1865, among 3038 paroled prisoners of war. Surrendered by Lt. General Richard Taylor and paroled at Demopolis, Alabama, on May 11, 1865.

Bailey, John, Pvt. Co. B/D

Enlisted on October 13, 1861, at Mobile, Alabama, by Major Hessee for the war. Wounded at Shiloh on April 6, 1862, 7 A. M. slightly in the right thigh on attack 1st Battery while advancing. POW captured at the hospital on April 7, at Pittsburg Landing, Tennessee, on April 7, 1862. Received at Camp Chase, Ohio, on June 3, 1862, exchanged on August 25, 1862. He arrived at Vicksburg, Mississippi, September 11, 1862, on board the steamer *Jno. H. Done* among 1020 prisoners for exchange. Eyes gray, hair dark, complexion light, five foot seven inches, age 26. Company muster roll for December 31, 1862, to April 30, 1863, reports him present. Muster rolls for March/April 1863, May/June 1863 and September/October 1863, report him present. Admitted to Post Hospital at Fort Morgan, Alabama, on November 28, 1863, with interr. Fever, returned to duty on December 5. POW captured at Spanish Fort, Alabama, on April 8, 1865. He was received at Ship Island, Mississippi, on April 10, 1865, and transferred from Ship Island to Vicksburg on May 1, 1865. There is a signed pay voucher in his file.*

Bailey, William N., Pvt. Co. A

Enlisted on October 13, 1861, at Mobile, Alabama, by Major Hessee. Company muster roll for bounty on September 24, 1862, reports him present and that he refused to take the bounty. He appears on a report near Tupelo, Mississippi, on June 28, 1862, sent to Corinth Hospital and from there to the interior by order of Surgeon Heustis. He is shown on a receipt roll for pay at Choctaw Bluff, Alabama, as a laborer from December 1, 1862, to February 10, 1863. Paid 25 cents per day. Muster roll for December 31, 1862 to April 30, 1863; report that he died March 24, 1863, at Choctaw Bluff, Alabama

Baily, A. M., Pvt. Co. F

Enlisted on August 22, 1862, at Jefferson County, Alabama, by W. G. Pool for the war. Company muster roll for March 1, to June 30, 1863, reports him present and on extra duty as butcher in Commissary Department since June 2, 1862, by order of Colonel Anderson. On extra duty at Choctaw Bluff January 1863, as a butcher. He died July 2, 1863, at Fort Stonewall, Clarke County, Alabama. Age 27, 5 foot 11 inches, fair complexion, light hair, light eyes, a farmer, born in Shelby County, Alabama. Martha Baily, widow was paid $58.98 for his service. There is paperwork in his file.*

Baily, John, Pvt. Co. B see **Bailey, John**

Baily, U. J., Pvt. Co. F

Enlisted August 26, 1862, at Shelby County, Alabama, by W. J. Davis for three years or the war. Drew clothing March 31, and June 1, 1864. POW captured at Fort

Gaines, Alabama, August 8, 1864. He was a patient at the hospital at New Orleans on September 10, 1864, with gastritis and returned to prison September 16, 1864, age 26. Received at Ship Island, Mississippi, from New Orleans on October 25, 1864. Exchanged at Ship Island on January 4, 1865. Age 23, hair red, eyes gray, complexion fair, and five foot nine inches, born in Shelby County, Alabama. "Deserted."

Baily, William N., Pvt. Co. A see **Bailey, William N.**

Bainer, A, Sgt./Pvt. Co. F/D

Enlisted on October 13, 1861, at Baldwin County, Alabama, by Captain McCoy for one year. He appears present as 4th Sgt. on a company muster roll for bounty on September 24, 1862. Muster roll for March 1, to June 30, 1862, reports him as 5th Sgt, sick in hospital, lost one haversack at 20 cents. Regimental return for June 1862, reports him on detached service in Pioneer Corps. September/October 1863, muster roll reports him absent detached to fish by General Maury on August 23, 1863. September/October 1864, muster roll reports that he was assigned as a Pvt. to Co. D by order and detached to Battery Huger by order of Colonel Fuller, due $62.13 for clothing not drawn. POW surrendered by Lt. General Richard Taylor at Citronelle, Alabama, on May 4, 1865, and paroled at Meridian, Mississippi, on May 13, 1864. Admitted to Yandell Hospital, Meridian, on April 1, 1865.

Baines, A., Sgt./Pvt. Co. F see Bainer, A

Baker, A., Pvt. Co. B

Drew clothing April 16, May 20 and June 1, 1864. On extra duty as a teamster for three weeks in September 1863, paid 25 cents per day. POW captured at Fort Gaines, Alabama, on August 8, 1864. Received at Ship Island, Mississippi, on October 25, 1864, from New Orleans. Died of dysentery on Ship Island on December 11, 1864. He was buried in grave No. 77.

Baker, D. A., Pvt. Co. C

Enlisted September 22, 1862, at Talladega, Alabama, by G. A. Cary for three years or the war. Company muster roll for December 31, 1862, to April 30, 1863, reports him present. May/June 1863, roll reports him absent on sick leave for 15 days from June 29. This rolls shows he lost a cartridge box at $2.50, a cap pouch at $1, a waist belt at 75 cents, a bayonet scabbard and plate at $1 and ten caps and ten cartridges at $1. He drew clothing on May 31 and June 1, 1864. September/October 1863, roll reports him present and having lost one canteen at $2. POW captured at Fort Gaines, Alabama, on August 8, 1864. Received at Ship Island, Mississippi, on October 25, 1864, from New Orleans. Exchanged at Ship Island on January 5, 1865. POW surrendered by Lt. General Richard Taylor at Citronelle, Alabama, on May 4, 1865. He was paroled at Meridian, Mississippi, on May 13, 1865. A resident of Dallas County, Alabama.

Baker, John, Corporal Co. F

Enlisted on October 13, 1863, in Baldwin County, Alabama, by Captain McCoy for one year. Wounded at Shiloh April 6, 1862, at 3 P. M. slightly in the foot while advancing on the center. He appears present on a company muster roll for bounty on September 24, 1862. Company muster roll March to June 1863, reports him present and having lost one canteen at 25 cents. September/October 1863, roll reports him absent, detached on duty at Choctaw Bluff by Colonel Anderson. He drew clothing on June 1, 1864, and signed by his mark. POW captured at Fort Gaines, Alabama, on August 8, 1864. Received at Ship Island, Mississippi, on October 25, 1864, from New Orleans. Applied at this time to take the Oath (of Allegiance to the USA). He was exchanged at Ship Island on January 4, 1865.

Baker, R. E., 1st Lt. & Ordnance Officer

POW captured at Fort Gaines, Alabama, on August 8, 1864. Received at Ship Island, Mississippi, on November 2, or 5, 1864, from New Orleans. Exchanged at Ship Island on January 5, 1865.

Baker, Thomas, J., Pvt. Co. I

His name appears on a Regimental return for the month of June 1863. June 17. Grand Junction, died hospital.

Baker, W. F., Pvt./2nd Lt. Co. C

Enlisted at Selma, Alabama, on February 6, 1863, by Major Gee for three years or the war. Drew $50 signing bounty on February 13, 1863. Company muster roll for May/June 1863; reports him present, sick in quarters, lost cartridge box at $2.50, lost cap pouch at $1, bayonet scabbard at $1, and plate with belt at 75 cents. Muster roll for September/October 1863 shows him present. Admitted to Post Hospital at Fort Morgan, Alabama, on November 18, 1863, with pneumonia. Returned to duty on December 2. Admitted again to Post Hospital at Fort Morgan on January 12, 1864, with pneumonia. Returned to duty on January 23. Drew clothing March 31 and June 1, 1864. POW captured at Fort Gaines, Alabama, on August 8, 1864. Here he is shown as a Lieutenant. Received at Ship Island, Mississippi, on October 25, 1864, from New Orleans. Exchanged at Ship Island on January 4, 1864. He was surrendered by Lt. General Richard Taylor at Citronelle, Alabama, and paroled at Meridian, Mississippi, on May 10, 1865. His Parole of Honor is in his file.

Baker, W. G., Pvt. Co. A

Paid $88 on November 1, 1862, for service and $50 bounty for a total of $138.

Baker, William, Pvt. Co. C see **Baker, W. F.**

Baldwin, R. P., Corp./2nd Lt. Co. E see **Baldwyn, Ralph P.**

Baldwyn, Ralph P., Corporal/2nd Lt. Co. E

Enlisted on October 13, 1864, at Mobile, Alabama, by Capt. Chamberlain for the war. Regimental return on June 1862, reports him having been sent to interior hospital on May 27. Company muster roll for September 24, 1862, for bounty reports him present. November/December 1862, July/August 1863 and September/October 1863, muster rolls all report him present. He drew clothing on March 16, 1863, and March 31, 1864.

Elected 2nd Lt. on May 16, 1864. POW captured at Fort Gaines, Alabama, on August 8, 1864. Received at Ship Island, Mississippi, from New Orleans on November 5, 1864, and exchanged at Ship Island, on January 4, 1865. He signed a Parole of Honor at Meridian, Mississippi, on May 10, 1865. He was surrendered by Lt. General Richard Taylor at Citronelle, Alabama, and paroled at Meridian, Mississippi, on May 10, 1865. His parole and other paper work is in his file.*

Ball, William M., Pvt. Co. E
Enlisted on October 13, 1864, at Mobile, Alabama, by Capt. Chamberlain for the war. Company muster roll for November/December 1862, reports him absent without leave, omitted on last pay roll. Regimental return for December 1862, reports him absent without leave since December 30. July/August and September/October 1863, muster roll reports him detached with the Signal Corps on June 5, 1863, by orders of Colonel Powell. He is paid several times as a signal operator until August 31, 1864. There is paperwork in his file.*

Ballard, I. J., Pvt. Co. F
His name appears on a roll of POW's that were stragglers, paroled at Selma, Alabama, in June 1865. Residence shown as Wilcox County, Alabama.

Ballonge, C., Co. A
His name appears on a regimental return for June 1862.

Banley, S., Pvt. Co. I see **Barley, Stephen**

Barrow, John C., Pvt. Co. C
His name appears on a list of payments to discharged soldiers. Discharged on September 25, 1862.

Barber, G., Pvt. Co. G
His name appears on a regimental return for June 1862, as having been sent to hospital May 28. His name also appears on a consolidated report of deserters near Tupelo, Mississippi, on June 28, 1862, as having been sent to interior from Corinth at the time of evacuation.

Barelli, Battisto, Corp. Co. G
Paid $52 for service from March 1, to June 30, 1862, plus $52 for traveling, subsistence and clothing at Mobile, Alabama, on July 21, 1862, by Geo. W. Holt. His signed pay voucher is in his file.*

Barger, J., Pvt. Co. I
His name appears on a register of payments on descriptive lists for service May 1, to June 30, 1863. Paid $22 on August 1, 1863.

Barley, J. A., Pvt. Co. I filed with **Barley, James.**

Barley, James, Pvt. Co. I

Enlisted at Fort Morgan, Alabama, on March 24, 1863, by Captain Vass for the war. Admitted to Fort Morgan Post Hospital on May 25, 1863, with chills and fever, returned to duty on May 30. Company muster roll for July/August 1863, reports him present, absent without leave from 3, to 5 July. September/October 1863, muster roll reports him present. POW captured at Fort Gaines, Alabama, on August 8, 1864. He was admitted to St. Louis USA General Hospital at New Orleans on September 1, 1864, with diarrhoea and remit. fever. Returned to prison September 12, age 24. He was readmitted with chronic diarrhoea on September 18 and returned to prison on November 2, 1864. Received at Ship Island, Mississippi, from New Orleans on October 29, 1864. Died of dysentery at Ship Island on November 24, 1864, and buried in grave No. 41.

Barley, Stephen, Pvt. Co. I

Enlisted on March 1, 1862, at Halls Mill, Alabama, by Lt. Cayce for the war. He is shown present on muster roll for bounty on September 24, 1862. Muster rolls for July/August 1862, and September/October 1862, report him present. Admitted to Fort Morgan Post Hospital with diarrhoea, on September 23, 1863, and returned to duty on September 26. Drew clothing March 31, 1864. POW captured at Fort Gaines, Alabama, on August 8, 1864. He was received at Ship Island, Mississippi, from New Orleans on October 25, 1864. Exchanged at Ship Island January 4, 1865. POW surrendered by Lt. General Richard Taylor, on May 4, 1865, at Citronelle, Alabama, and paroled at Meridian, Mississippi, on May 13, 1865. Residence is shown as Marengo County, Alabama.

Barnes, Asa D., Pvt. Co. C

Enlisted on March 7, 1863, at Choctaw Bluff, Alabama, by Lt. Northrup for three years or the war. Died in hospital at Choctaw Bluff, of disease on May 6, 1863. Death claim filed in Jasper County, Mississippi, by attorney for David W. Barnes father of Asa D. Barnes. Born in Marengo County, Alabama, 19 years of age, dark eyes, dark hair, dark complexion, six foot, a planter by occupation. Paid $99.20 for service. There is paperwork in his file.*

Barnes, J. R., Pvt. Co. C

His name appears on a regimental return for June 1862, as absent on surgeon's certificate. His name appears on a consolidated report near Tupelo, Mississippi, on June 28, 1862, as having been sent to interior hospital from Corinth by surgeon at the time of evacuation.

Barnes, Louis B., Pvt. Co. D

Enlisted at Demopolis, Alabama, on November 13, 1863, for the war. He drew clothing on June 20, 1864. Admitted to Ross Hospital at Mobile, Alabama, on January 22, 1864, with hepatitis, returned to duty on Feb. 17. Admitted to Ross Hospital at Mobile with ascites on August 8, 1864, and returned to duty on August 9. Admitted to 1st Mississippi CSA Hospital at Jackson, Mississippi, on August 13, 1864, with ascites, and returned to duty on August 24. POW surrendered by Lt. General Richard Taylor on May 4, 1865, at Citronelle, Alabama, and paroled at Meridian, Mississippi, on May 13, 1865.

MOBILE CONFEDERATES

Barnes, T. J., Musician, Co. C

Enlisted in Linden, Alabama, on July 29, 1863, by L. McLeod for three years or the war. A resident of Choctaw County, Alabama. He appears on a descriptive list at Point Clear, Alabama, October 12, 1863, age 36, gray eyes, dark hair, fair complexion, six foot one inch, a farmer born in Sumter, District South Carolina, paid $50. He was admitted to Post Hospital at Fort Morgan, Alabama, on October 31, 1863, with int. fev. and returned to duty on November 21, 1863. Company muster roll for September/October 1863, reports him present. A resident of Choctaw County, Alabama. He drew clothing on March 31 and June 1, 1864. POW captured at Fort Gaines, Alabama, on August 8, 1864. Received at Ship Island, Mississippi, from New Orleans on October 25, 1864. Exchanged at Ship Island on January 5, 1865. POW Surrendered by Lt. General Richard Taylor at Citronelle, Alabama, on May 4, 1865, and paroled at Meridian, Mississippi, on May 13, 1865.

Barr, G. D., Pvt. Co. C see also **Jamie Barr**

Enlisted at Marengo County, Alabama, on February 11, 1863, by Lt. Northrup for three years or the war. Company muster rolls for December 31, 1862, to April 30, 1863, May/June 1863, September/October 18673, all report him present. On the latter roll he is shown as having lost one canteen at $2. There is a discharge in his file for general debility dated May 5, 1863. He is shown as being 24 years old, born in Rockingham, North Carolina, six foot, light complexion, blue eyes, sandy hair and a planter by profession. He was paid for service from December 9, 1961, to May 5, 1863. He drew clothing on March 31 and June 1, 1864. POW captured at Fort Gaines, Alabama, on August 8, 1864. He was received at Ship Island, Mississippi, from New Orleans, on October 25, 1864 and exchanged at Ship Island on January 5, 1865. Surrendered by Lt. General Richard Taylor at Citronelle, Alabama, on May 4, 1865. Paroled at Meridian, Mississippi, on May 13, 1865. His discharge is in his file.* There may be two individuals in this set of records.

Barr, James, Pvt. Co. C

Enlisted in Company C, 21st Regiment of Alabama Volunteers on October 13, 1861, at Clio, Alabama, by Captain James A. Rembert to serve 12 months. Born Rockingham, North Carolina, age 33, six foot one inch, light complexion, blue eyes, sandy hair, and a merchant when enlisted. James M. Barr was discharged by surgeon at Corinth, Mississippi, on April 25, 1862, because of a hernia. He is also shown as enlisting at Marengo County, Alabama, on February 11, 1863, by Lt. Northrup for three years or the war. Company muster roll for December 31, 1862, to April 30, 1863, reports him present and never paid. May/June 1863, muster roll reports him sick in Selma. July 17, to August 31, 1863, hospital muster roll at General Hospital Point Clear, Baldwin County Alabama, reports him present and having enlisted at Choctaw Bluff on February 13, 1863, by Lt. Northrup. September/October company muster roll reports him absent detached as a nurse at hospital at Point Clear, Alabama, by order of Colonel Anderson on October 11, 1863. Admitted to Post Hospital at Fort Morgan, Alabama, on December 6, 1863, with icterus (jaundice). Returned to duty on January 4, 1864. POW captured at Fort Gaines, Alabama, on August 8, 1864. Confined and sent to hospital in the Steam Levee Press, No. 4 at New Orleans on October 4, 1864. St. Louis USA General Hospital,

New Orleans reports he was admitted on October 4, 1864, with acute diarrhoea, and returned to prison on October 20, age 37. Received at Ship Island, Mississippi, from New Orleans on October 25, 1864. Exchanged at Ship Island on January 4, 1865. His discharge is in his file.*

Barr, James M., Pvt. Co. C see **Barr James**

Barrett, G. H., Pvt. Co. A see **Bassett, George H.**

Barrett, J. W., Pvt. Co. H see **Banet, John W.**

Barrett, John W., Pvt. Co. H
POW captured at Fort Gaines, Alabama, on August 8, 1864. POW admitted to St. Louis General Hospital at New Orleans on September 17, 1864, with fev. intermit. And returned to prison on September 28, 1864, age 36. His name appears on a morning report as POW confined at Steam Levee Press No. 4 New Orleans on September 29, 1864. Received at Ship Island, Mississippi, from New Orleans on October 25, 1864. He was exchanged at Ship Island on January 5, 1864. POW surrendered by Lt. General Richard Taylor at Citronelle, Alabama, on May 4, 1865. Paroled at Gainesville, Alabama, on May 13, 1865.

Barrier, Charles, Pvt. Co. B
Enlisted on October 13, 1861, at Mobile, Alabama, by Major Hessee for three years or the war. He is reported present on a company muster roll for bounty on September 24, 1862. Muster rolls for March/April 1863, May/June 1863, and September/October 1863, all report him present. He was appointed 3rd Corporal by Colonel Anderson on September 1, 1863. He drew clothing on March 31 and June 1, 1864. Admitted to Ross Hospital at Mobile, Alabama, on June 27, 1864, with ophthalmia (pain in the eye). Returned to duty on July 12. POW captured at Fort Gaines, Alabama, on August 8, 1864. Received at Ship Island, Mississippi, from New Orleans on October 25, 1864. Exchanged at Ship Island on January 5, 1864. POW surrendered by Lt. General Richard Taylor at Citronelle, Alabama, on May 4, 1865 and paroled at Gainesville, Alabama, on May 13, 1865.

Barrilae, Charles, Pvt. Co. B see **Barrier, Charles**

Barriere, Charles, Pvt. Co. see **Barrier, Charles**

Barrun, (Barron) William, Pvt. Co. C
Enlisted by Captain J. M. Rembert at Marengo County, Alabama. He was discharged at Choctaw Bluff, Alabama, by reason of being over 35 years of age on October 13, 1862. Born in Marengo County, Alabama, age 52, 5 foot 8 inches, dark complexion, dark eyes, dark hair, and a planter by profession. Paid $15.76 for his service from September 1, 1862. His discharge is in his file.*

Bassett, George H., Pvt. Co. A

Enlisted at Mobile, Alabama, on October 13, 1861, by Major Hessee for three years or the war. He is reported present on a company muster roll for bounty on September 24, 1862. Company muster rolls for March/April 1863, May/June 1863, and September/October 1863, all report him absent on detached service as clerk for General Withers since December 26, 1861. He appears on a statement of clerks serving as extra duty men in the various Staff Departments of Withers' Division, Polk's Army of Tennessee, issued at Shelbyville, Tennessee, in March 1863. Detached as a clerk in the AAG Department as orderly for General Withers by General Withers in October 1862. His name appears on a list of clerks employed in the various offices and bureaus at the Military Post of Mobile, Alabama, by authority of Major General Maury, in July 1864, employed as a druggist, detailed at the request of the Surgeon General. POW with Medical Purveyors Department CSA employed by Surgeon R. Miller, surrendered by Lt. General Richard Taylor at Citronelle, Alabama, on May 4, 1865. Paroled at Columbus, Mississippi, on May 16, 1865. There is considerable paperwork and pay vouchers in his file.**

Basso, F. (Frank), Pvt. (Co. G)

He appears present on a muster roll of Captain Sossaman's Detachment of the 21st Regiment Alabama Infantry for September and October 1864. Enlisted at Mobile, Alabama, on November 1, 1862, by Lt. Sewell for the war. On March 23, 1864, he was ordered back to his regiment from detailed service with Ordnance Department at Fort Morgan. He drew clothing on June 1, 1864, signed by his mark.*

Bastie, L. M., Pvt. Co. E

Enlisted on September 10, 1861, at Eutah (Eutaw), Alabama, by Captain Watkins for the war. His name appears on a hospital muster roll at Madison House Hospital, Montgomery for November 15, 1864. He was shown as a patient from November 8, 1864.

Baswell, J. A., Pvt. _

His name appears on a roll of POW's at Camp Butler, Springfield, Illinois, captured at Fort Donaldson on February 16, 1862. He died March 28, 1862.

Bates, H., Sgt. Co. C

He appears on a consolidated report near Tupelo, Mississippi, June 28, 1862, furloughed on surgeons certificate for 30 days to June 29. He also appears on a list of men who returned without arms or with captured arms in Winters' Division, 1st Brigade. A regimental return for June 1862, reports him absent on sick furlough.

Baxter, William, Pvt. Co. I

Drew clothing on March 31, 1864, and signed by his mark. Enlisted at Cedar Point, Alabama, on June 30, 1864, by Colonel Miller for the war. Company muster roll for September/October 1864, reports him present. He was assigned extra duty as a teamster. Admitted to City Hospital at Mobile, Alabama, wounded. POW captured April

12, 1865, in hospital at Mobile surrendered by Lt. General Richard Taylor and paroled at Mobile on May 11, 1865. Residence shown as Mobile.

Bayless, A. J., Pvt. Co. A see **Bayles, Andrew**

Bayles, Andrew, Pvt. Co. A.
Enlisted in Jefferson, County, Alabama, on April 28, 1862, by I. W. Bass for three years or the war. He appears present on company muster rolls December 31, 1862, to April 30, 1863 and May/June 1863. Drew clothing March 31 and June 14, 1864. Muster roll for September/October 1863, report him absent, sent to hospital on October 25, 1863. Admitted to Post Hospital at Fort Morgan on December 17, 1863, with int. fever. Returned to duty on December 25, 1863. POW captured at Fort Morgan, Alabama, on August 23, 1864. Sent to New York, on September 27, 1864. Entered Elmira, New York, on October 8, 1864. Died at Elmira of pneumonia on October 21. Left 2 jackets, 1 pair pants, 2 pair drawers, 1 shirt. He was buried in grave No. 707.

Bazer, Nathan, Pvt. Co. K
Enlisted on August 29, 1864, at Mobile, Alabama, by Major Stone for the war. He was transferred to the Conscript Camp at Notasulga, Alabama, by order of Major Stone, Enlistment Officer on October 18, 1864. POW surrendered by Lt. General Richard Taylor at Citronelle, Alabama, on May 4, 1865, and paroled at Meridian, Mississippi, on May 15, 1865. Residence shown as Wayne County, Mississippi.

Brazor, Nathan, Pvt. Co. K see **Brazer, Nathan**

Beach, H., Pvt. Co. I see **Buck, Henry**

Beam, J. M., Corp./Pvt. Co. F
Enlisted on November 27, 1863, at Point Clear, Alabama, by Captain Dale for the war. He appears present on company muster roll for September/October 1864. Promoted from ranks on September 1, 1864. POW surrendered by Lt. General Richard Taylor at Citronelle, Alabama, on May 4, 1865, and paroled at Meridian, Mississippi, on May 13, 1865. Residence shown as Mobile, Alabama.

Bears, R. W., Pvt. Co. E see **Beers, R. W.**

Beasley, Edward, Pvt./Corp. Co. E
Enlisted June 2, 1863, at Fort Morgan, Alabama, by Captain Sossaman for the war. Company muster roll for July/August 1863, reports him present and he appears present on company muster roll for September/October 1864. Promoted from ranks on September 1, 1864. He drew clothing on March 31, 1864. Admitted to Ross Hospital at Mobile, Alabama, on July 25, 1864, with paralysis. Returned to duty on August 6.

Beasly, Edward, Pvt./Corp. Co. E see **Beasley, Edward**

Beasly, J. W., Corporal Co. G

Drew clothing March 3, March 31 and June 2, 1864. POW captured at Fort Gaines, Alabama, on August 8, 1864. Received at Ship Island, Mississippi, on October 25, 1864, from New Orleans and exchanged at Ship Island on January 5, 1865. His name appears on the proceedings of the Hospital Examining Board at Mobile, Alabama, on March 9, 1865, as having been furloughed from Maury's command for 60 days due to general debility following having small pox and scurvy contracted at Ship Island.

Beaumont, William D., Pvt. Co. D

He was discharged at Fort Gaines, Alabama, on December 21, 1861, due to infirmity. Born Tuscumbia, Alabama, age 42, five foot seven and one half inches, dark complexion, dark eyes, and dark hair. Paid $49.93 for his service on July 19, 1862. His certificate of disability and pay voucher is in his file.*

Beers, Robert W., Pvt. Co. E

Enlisted on October 13, 1862, at Mobile, Alabama, by Captain Chamberlain for the war. Wounded in left thigh (flesh) at Shiloh on April 6, 1862, while charging 1st Battery advancing. POW captured at Shiloh in hospital on April 6, 1862. He was admitted to USA No. 2 General Hospital (Marine) at Evansville, Indiana, on April 15, 18(62?) with vulnus sclopeticum (gunshot wound), sent to Indianapolis April 29. He appears on a roll of POW's at Camp Morton, Indiana, not dated and a roll of POW's at POW Headquarters Hoffman Battalion, Depot Prisoners of War near Sandusky, Ohio, (Johnson's Island) arrived from Camp Morton on August 26, 1862, sent to Vicksburg, Mississippi, (for exchange) September 1. "Rec'd the forgoing list of Prisoners of War – eleven hundred and four in number – On board steamer *Jno. H. Done* near Vicksburg, Miss. Sept. 20. 1862. - N. G. Watts, Major C. S. A. & Agent for exchange of prisoners." "Declared exchange at Atkins Landing Nov. 10, 1862." He appears absent on September 24, 1862, muster roll for bounty and is shown as an exchanged prisoner now in Mobile. Company muster roll for November/December 1862, reports him absent on detached duty at General Forney's Headquarters by order. November and December 1862, regimental returns report him detached as clerk in General Forney's office at Mobile on October 22, 1862, by order of General Forney. Drew clothing on March 15, 1863. May 12, 1863, Special Order No. 78/1 transferred Pvt Beers to Captain Williams Co. Lt. Artillery in East Tennessee. Paid $50 bounty on December 17, 1863. He appears on a hospital muster roll of General Hospital Miller (also know as Convalescent Hospital) at Spring Hill, Alabama, for November/December & January/February 1864, detailed as a ward master and present. There is considerable paper work in his file.***

Beers, William, H., 1st Sgt./2nd Lt. Co. A

Enlisted at Mobile, Alabama on October 13, 1861, by Major Hessee for the war. Company muster roll for bounty on September 24, 1862, reports him present. December to April 30, 1863, May/June 1863, September/October 1863, company muster rolls reports him present. He was admitted to Post Hospital at Fort Morgan on November 1, 1863, with int. fev. and returned to duty on November 3. Drew clothing on March 31, 1864. Elected 2nd Lt. on May 16, 1864. POW captured at Fort Morgan, Alabama, on August 23, 1864, at New Orleans he was transferred to New York on October 12, 1864.

He was received and confined at Fort Lafayette, New York Harbor, on October 20, 1864, and transferred to Fort Warren, Boston Harbor Massachusetts, on December 17, 1864. Here his place of residence is shown as Randolph, New York. He was released on May 11, 1865. There is considerable paper work in Lt.. Beers file including orders from Colonel Anderson issued at Choctaw Bluff, Alabama, to apprehending deserters from the company.**

Beesley, Edward, Pvt./Corp. Co. E see **Beasley, Edward**

Beets, William H., Sgt./2nd Lt. see **Beers, William H.**

Belantioni, E., Pvt. Co. G
He appears on a register of wounded of the Second Corps of the Army of the Mississippi, at the Battle of Shiloh. Wounded severely in the thigh on April 6th in the A. M. while advancing on attack of 1st Battery. Regimental return for June 1862, reports him wounded and furloughed since April 9, 1862. On a report he appears absent on furlough at Mobile, Alabama, since May 29, 1862.

Belcher, A. (Arthur) M., Pvt. Co. F
Enlisted on September 4, 1862, at Jefferson County, Alabama, by Jas. Tarrant for the war. Drew extra pay as a teamster in February and March 1863. Company muster rolls for March 1, to June 30, 1863, and September/October 1863, report him present. Admitted to Post Hospital at Fort Morgan, Alabama, on December 11, 1863, with dysentery. Sent to general hospital on January 13, 1864. Admitted to Ross General Hospital at Mobile, Alabama, with hemorrhoids and ulcerated bowels on January 13, 1864. He died January 23, 1864, at General Hospital Ross at Mobile, Alabama.

Belcher, J. H., Pvt. Co. F
Enlisted on September 4, 1862, at Jefferson County, Alabama, by Jas Tarrant for the war. Company muster rolls for March 1, to June 30, 1863, and September/October 1863, report him present. He drew clothing on March 31 and June 1, 1864. POW captured at Fort Gaines, Alabama, on August 8, 1864. Received at Ship Island, Mississippi, from New Orleans on October 25, 1864. Exchanged at Ship Island, on January 4, 1865. POW captured at Spanish Fort, Alabama, on April 8, 1865. Received at Ship Island on April 10, 1865, and transferred for exchange to Vicksburg, Mississippi, on May 1, 1865.

Belcher, N., Pvt. Co. F
Enlisted on September 4, 1862, at Jefferson County, Alabama, by Jas Tarrant for the war. His name appears on a receipt roll for extra duty at Choctaw Bluff, Alabama, as a laborer for December 1863. Paid 25 cents per day extra. Company muster rolls for March 1, to June 30, 1863, and September/October 1863, report him present.

Belger, Daniel, Pvt. Co. B
Enlisted on August 25, 1862, at Mobile, Alabama, by Captain DeVaux for three years or the war. Company muster roll for bounty on September 24, 1862, reports him

present and having drawn bounty at time of enlistment. Company muster rolls for March 1, to June 30, 1863, and September/October 1863, report him present. Admitted to Post Hospital at Fort Morgan, Alabama, on January 13, 1864, with int. feb. and returned to duty on January 21. He drew clothing on March 31, 1864, and signed by his mark. POW captured at Fort Gaines, Alabama, on August 8, 1864. Received at Ship Island, Mississippi, from New Orleans on October 25, 1864. Exchanged at Ship Island on January 4, 1865. POW surrendered by Lt. General Richard Taylor at Citronelle, Alabama, on May 4, 1865, and paroled at Meridian, Mississippi, on May 13, 1865. Residence shown as Memphis, Tennessee.

Bell, Edward, Pvt. Co. B
	Enlisted on August 2, 1862, at Mobile, Alabama, by Captain Johnston for the war. Company muster roll for March/April 1863, reports him present. Company muster rolls for May/June 1863, and September/October 1863, report him present sick in quarters. He drew clothing on March 31 and June 1, 1864, and signed by his mark. POW captured at Fort Gaines, Alabama, on August 8, 1864. Received at Ship Island, Mississippi, from New Orleans on October 25, 1864, and exchanged at Ship Island on January 4, 1865. His name appears on a roll of POW's at Elmira, New York, who desire to take the Oath of Allegiance to the US on October 31, 1864. "Was conscripted August 2, 1862. Is an Englishman and has resided in this country since 1859. Was a deckhand on a steamboat on the Alabama River at the outbreak of the war. Desires to remain in the North." His name also appears on an Oath of Allegiance to the USA sworn to at Elmira, New York, May 17, 1865. Released on May 17, 1865. Residence, New Orleans, Louisiana, dark complexion, dark hair, blue eyes, 5 foot 9 inches.

Bell, T. W., Pvt. Co. D
	POW captured at Fort Gaines, Alabama, on August 8, 1864. His name appears on a roll of prisoners exchanged at Ship Island, Mississippi, on January 4, 1865.

Bell, William, Pvt. Co. B
	Enlisted September 3, 1862, at Jefferson County, Alabama, by Captain A. R. Goodwin for three years or the war. Company muster roll for March/April 1983, reports him present and May/June, 1863, roll report him present sick in quarters. Company muster roll for September/October 1863, reports him absent without leave since October 19, 1863. Hospital muster roll July/August 1864, for hospital at Shelby Springs, Alabama, show him attached to the hospital. His name appears on a register of 1st Mississippi, CSA Hospital, Jackson, Mississippi, admitted with chronic diarrhoea on August 19, 1864. He was transferred on October 17.

Bellantoni, Filippe, **(Phil)** Pvt. Co. G
	Paid $22 for service March 1, 1862, to April 30, 1862. Paid $22 for service May 1, 1862, to June 30, 1862. Paid $22 for service July 1, 1862, to August 31, 1862, on detached service. Three pay vouchers are in his file.*

Bence, W. J., Pvt. Co. K

His name appears on a return from 2nd Battalion, 21st Alabama Infantry in December 1862, Fort Morgan enlisted in NC Regiment.

Benley, J. M., Sgt./Pvt. Co. I see **Bentley, J. M.**

Benson, William, Pvt. Co. F

Enlisted October 12, 1863, at Point Clear, Alabama, by Lt. Givian for three years or the war. *There is some obscure paper work in his file that seems to indicate that he requested transfer to the Naval Service, as he is a rigger.* It appears that his request was approved. He was paid $321.50 at Mobile on August 8, 1864, for service rendered from December 19, 1863, to June 9, 1863, = 174 days at $1.25 or 217.50, then from June 10, 1863, to July 31, 1864, = 52 days at $2 or $104.*

Bentley, J. M., Sgt./Pvt. Co. I

Enlisted on October 13, 1862, at Halls Mill, Alabama, by Major Hessee. Company muster roll for bounty on September 24, 1862, reports him present. He is also reported present on company muster rolls for July, August, September and October 1863. POW surrendered by Lt. General Richard Taylor at Citronelle, Alabama, on May 4, 1865, and paroled at Meridian, Mississippi, on May 13, 1865. Residence Mobile County, Alabama.

Benton, Daniel, Co. F

He was captured at Shiloh on April 7, 1862. He died of pneumonia and diarrhoea at USA Prison Hospital at Camp Douglas, Chicago, Illinois, on May 24, 1862.

Benton, Henry, Pvt. Co. F

He enlisted on October 13, 1861, at Baldwin County, Alabama, by Captain McCoy for one year. Severely wounded in the hip at Shiloh on April 6, 1862, at 8:30 A. M. while advancing on the 1st Camp. Regimental return for June 1862 shows him sent to Corinth Hospital May 28, 1862. Company muster roll for bounty on September 24, 1862, reports him present. Company muster roll for March 1, to June 30, 1863, reports him present and on extra duty as commissary butcher since November 29, 1862, by order of Colonel Anderson.

Beretick, Michael, Pvt. Co. H

Severely wounded in leg and ankle on April 6, 1862, at Shiloh 7 A. M. attacking the 1st Battery. "Sent to Mobile." He is paid on detached service from September 1, 1862, to October 31, 1862. He signed by his mark. There is paper work in his file.*

Bernard, Dominick, Pvt. Co. G

Killed at Shiloh, on April 6, 1862, at 4 P. M. at the Old field. Claim filed for $13.20 by attorney.

Beronjon, W. V., Pvt. Co. D/E see **Beryjon, V.**

Berry, Anthony, Pvt. Co. E

Enlisted on October 13, 1861, at Mobile, Alabama, by Captain Chamberlain for the war. Company muster roll for bounty on September 24, 1862, reports him present. Company muster rolls from November 1862; report him detached to work as foundry man as the foundry at Selma, Alabama, by order of Colonel Powell from December 27, 1862. September/October company muster roll reports him detached at Selma Foundry. There are a number of signed pay vouchers in his file.*

Beryjon, V., Pvt. Co. D/E

Enlisted in Co. D, on October 24, 1864, at Mobile, Alabama, by Enrolling Officer for the war. Company muster roll for September/October 1864, reports him absent on detached service by order of General Higgins. POW surrendered by Lt. General Richard Taylor at Citronelle, Alabama, on May 4, 1865, and paroled at Meridian, Mississippi, on May 13, 1865. Residence shown as Mobile, Alabama.

Bethencourt, P., Pvt.

There is only a reference envelope in his file.

Beuliche, M., Pvt. Co. H

Regimental return for June 1862, reports that he was wounded at Shiloh and furloughed.

Biaggini, D., Pvt. Co. G (**Biagino**)

Regimental return for June 1862, reports him sent to interior hospital on May 28, 1862, at the time of evacuation of Corinth, Mississippi.

Bianeo, P., Pvt. Co. G

Regimental return for June 1861, reports him sent to interior hospital on May 28, 1862, at the time of evacuation of Corinth. His name appears on a list of men who returned without arms or with captured arms in Wither's Division 1st Brigade.

Bibby, W. J., Pvt. Co. B (**Ribee**)

He drew clothing in May and June 1864. POW captured at Fort Gaines, Alabama, on August 8, 1864. He was received at Ship Island, Mississippi, from New Orleans on October 25, 1864, and exchanged at Ship Island on January 4, 1865.

Bishop, J. U., Pvt. Co. C see **Bishop, Uriah**

Bishop, Uriah, Pvt. Co. C

Enlisted on October 13, 1861, at Mobile, Alabama, by Captain Rembert for 12 months. Company muster roll for bounty on September 24, 1862, reports him present. Company muster roll for December 31, 1862, to April 30, 1863, reports him absent on detached service since April 28, 1863, at Choctaw Bluff on order of Colonel Wickliff. Company muster roll for May/June 1863, reports him on detached duty with Engineers Department at Choctaw Bluff. Returned to company May 25, 1863, sick in quarters; lost Cartridge box at $2.50, bayonet scabbard at $1, cap pouch at $1, w belt at $75 cts., 10 cartridges and 12 caps at $1. September/October 1863, muster roll reports him present. Drew clothing in March and June 1864. POW captured at Fort Gaines, Alabama, on August 8, 1864. Admitted to USA St. Louis General Hospital at New Orleans on September 7, 1864, with neuralgia. Returned to prison on September 12, 1864, age 24. Received at Ship Island, Mississippi, from New Orleans on October 25, 1864. Exchanged at Ship Island on January 4, 1865. POW captured at Blakeley, Alabama, on April 9, 1865. Received at Ship Island on April 15, 1865. He was transferred to Vicksburg, Mississippi, for exchange on May 1, 1865. There is a signed pay voucher in his file.*

Bishop, William, Pvt. Co. I
Drew clothing on May 31, 1864. POW captured at Fort Gaines, Alabama, on August 8, 1864. Received at Ship Island, Mississippi, from New Orleans on October 25, 1864. Exchanged at Ship Island on January 4, 1865. POW surrendered by Lt. General Richard Taylor at Citronelle, Alabama, on May 4, 1865, and paroled at Meridian, Mississippi, on May 13, 1865. Residence shown as Baldwin County, Alabama.

Biven, D. K., Pvt. Co. K/G see **Bivin, De Kalb**

Bivin, De Kalb, Pvt. Co. K/G
Enlisted on October 18, 1862, at Claiborne, Alabama, by Lt Sewell for the war. His name appears on a hospital muster roll to November 15, 1862, at Concert Hall Hospital in Montgomery, Alabama, as a patient. POW surrendered at Citronelle, Alabama, paroled at Mobile; eyes hazel, hair dark, complexion light, age 36, five foot eight inches, a resident of Monroe County, Alabama.

Blackburn, T. C., Pvt. Co. F
Enlisted on March 15, 1862, at Choctaw Bluff, Alabama, by Captain Dade for the war. Company muster roll for bounty on September 24, 1862, reports him present. Company muster roll for September/October 1863, reports him absent sick in hospital in Mobile since October 25, 1863. Drew clothing on June 1, 1864. POW captured at Fort Gaines, Alabama, on August 8, 1864. Received at Ship Island, Mississippi, from New Orleans on October 25, 1864. He was exchanged at Ship Island on January 4, 1865. POW surrendered by Lt. General Richard Taylor at Citronelle, Alabama, on May 4, 1865, and paroled at Meridian, Mississippi, on May 13, 1865. Residence shown as Perry County, Alabama.

Blackwell, Nathan, Pvt. Co. A
Enlisted on February 1, 1863, at Choctaw Bluff, Alabama, by Captain Cothran for the war. Company muster roll for December 31, 1862, to April 30, 1863, reports him absent on detail with Engineer Department at Choctaw Bluff since February 11, 1863. May/June 1863, muster roll reports him present at Choctaw Bluff by order of Colonel Anderson. September/October 1863, muster roll reports that he died of disease on September 22, 1863, at Quarles Hospital at Point Clear, Alabama. *Note he is buried at Point Clear Cemetery.*

MOBILE CONFEDERATES

Blair, E. J., Pvt. Co. H

Enlisted on August 28, 1862, at Coffee County, Alabama, by Lt. Henry for the war. Company muster roll for September/October 1864 reports him absent having been sent to Hospital Heustis by order of Dr. Armstrong. He drew clothing on March 3, March 31 and June 1, 1864. POW surrendered by Lt. General Richard Taylor at Citronelle, Alabama, on May 4, 1865, and paroled at Meridian, Mississippi, on May 13, 1865. Residence shown as Coffee County, Alabama.

Blackeney, Jos., Pvt. Co. C

His name appears on a register of payments to discharged soldiers. Discharged December 1, 1861. Payment made on February 15, 1864.

Blann, Thomas. W., Pvt. Co. C/A

Enlisted in Co. C on August 2, 1862, at Dallas County, Alabama, by Captain Vass for three years or the war. Transferred to Co. A on March 31, 1863. Company muster roll for December 31, 1862, to April 30, 1863, reports him present as does rolls for May/June 1863 and September/October 1863. He was admitted to Post Hospital at Fort Morgan, Alabama, on December 17, 1863, with int. fever and returned to duty on December 23, 1863. Drew clothing in March and June 1864. POW captured at Fort Morgan, Alabama, on August 23, 1864, sent to New Orleans and was transferred to New York on September 27, 1864. Signed an Oath of Allegiance at Elmira, New York, on June 14, 1865, and released. His place of residence is shown as Bellview Station, Alabama, dark complexion, blue eyes, dark hair, five foot seven inches.

Blount, J., Pvt.

Joined a Mississippi regiment at Corinth on April 9, 1862.

Bnilo, Paul A., Pvt. Co. E

His name appears on a register of payments to discharged soldiers. He was discharged on July 2, 1862.

Boan, F. G., Pvt. Co. B

Drew clothing March and June 1864. POW captured at Fort Gaines, Alabama, on August 8, 1864. His name appears on a morning report as a prisoner confined at Steam Levee Press No. 4 New Orleans on September 29, 2004. Admitted to St. Louis USA General Hospital in New Orleans, on September 29, 1864, with diarrhoea and returned to prison on October 14. He was received at Ship Island, Mississippi, from New Orleans on October 25, 1864. He made application to take the Oath of Allegiance to the USA at Ship Island. He was exchanged at Ship Island on January 4, 1865. Surrendered by Lt. General Richard Taylor at Citronelle, Alabama, on May 4, 1865, and paroled at Meridian, Mississippi, on May 13, 1865. Residence shown as Greenville, Butler County, Alabama.

Boan, S. S., Pvt. Co. B

Drew clothing on May 30, and June 1, 1864. POW captured at Fort Gaines, Alabama, on August 8, 1864. He was admitted to St. Louis USA General Hospital in New Orleans, Louisiana, on September 10, 1864, with diarrhoea and returned to prison on October 20, 1864, age 19. Received at Ship Island, Mississippi, from New Orleans on October 25, 1864, and exchanged at Ship Island on January 4, 1865. Admitted to Ross Hospital at Mobile, Alabama, on January 5, 1865, with diarrhoea and scurvy. Furloughed for 15 days on January 21, 1865. POW surrendered by Lt. General Richard Taylor at Citronelle, Alabama, on May 4, 1865, and paroled at Meridian, Mississippi, on May 13, 1865. Residence shown as Greenville, Butler County, Alabama.

Boan, W., Pvt. Co. B
Surrendered by Lt. General Richard Taylor at Citronelle, Alabama, on May 4, 1865, and paroled at Meridian, Mississippi, on May 13, 1864. Residence shown as Greenville, Butler County, Alabama.

Bodiford, A. G., Pvt. Co. G
Drew clothing on March 3 and 31, 1864. He signed by his mark. His name appears on a register of the Invalid Corps. PACS as retired on November 9, 1864, stationed at Greensboro, Alabama. His name appears on a record of Confederate soldiers paroled at the Headquarters of the US 16th Army Corps at Montgomery, Alabama, in May 1865, five foot seven inches, light hair, blue eyes, fair complexion.

Bodiford, Thomas A., Pvt. Co. F
A claim for a deceased soldier with his name was filed by B. W. Starke on April 20, 1863.

Bollo, William, Pvt. Co. B see **Pollo, John**

Bond, David, Pvt. Co. A
Enlisted at Mobile, Alabama, on October 13, 1861. Discharged by reason of disability on May 4, 1862. Born in Tuscaloosa, Alabama, age 17, five foot four inches, fair complexion, gray eyes, dark hair, by occupation a bookkeeper.

Bond, J. F., 1st Lt. Co. B
Reference envelope only.

Bone, F. G., Pvt. Co. B see **Boan, F. G.**

Bone, S. S., Pvt. Co. B see **Boan, S. S.**

Boner, A., Pvt. Co. F.
His name appears on a muster roll for Captain S. M. Steele's Company B in the Engineer Battalion commanded by Major Meriwether Jackson's Brigade. No Date.

Bones, A. M., Pvt. Co. E
Enlisted on April 29, 1864, at Mobile, Alabama, for the war. His name appears on a roll of detailed men in Quarter Master Department commanded by Major Tom Peters Q. M. captured at Mobile, Alabama. POW surrendered by Lt. General Richard

MOBILE CONFEDERATES

Taylor at Citronelle, Alabama, on May 4, 1865, and paroled at Mobile, Alabama, on May 14, 1865.

Bonestabile, Antonio, Pvt. Co. G
   Discharged on May 17, 1862. Paid by G. W. Holt on May 19.

Bonner, A. R., Pvt. Co. C
   POW captured at Blakeley, Alabama, on April 9, 1865. Received at Ship Island, Mississippi, on April 15. Transferred to Vicksburg, Mississippi, on May 1, 1865, for exchange.

Boon, (Boone) S. D., Pvt. Co. C
   Enlisted on April 3, 1863, at Choctaw Bluff, Alabama, by Captain Smith for three years or the war. May/June 1863, muster roll reports him absent sick in hospital in Mobile since May 1. September/October 1863, muster roll reports him present. Admitted to Fort Morgan Post Hospital on November 9, 1863, with int. feb. Returned to duty on November 14, 1863. He drew clothing on June 1, 1864. POW captured at Fort Gaines, Alabama, on August 8, 1864. Received at Ship Island, Mississippi, on October 25, 1864. He died of dysentery at Ship Island December 29, 1864. He was buried in Grave No. 120.

Boon, (Boone) S. S., Pvt. Co. B see **Boan, S. S.**

Boone, J. C., Pvt. Co. H
   POW captured at Fort Gaines, Alabama, on August 8, 1864. He was received at Ship Island from New Orleans on October 25, 1864 and exchanged on January 4, 1865. POW surrendered by Lt. General Richard Taylor at Citronelle, Alabama, on May 4, 1865, and paroled at Meridian, Mississippi, on May 14, 1864. Residence shown as Sumter County, Alabama.

Boone, T. G., Pvt. Co. B see **Boan, F. G.**

Booth, Pvt. Co. G
   Admitted to Post Hospital at Fort Morgan on November 9, 1863, with neuralgia and returned to duty on January 3, 1864.

Booth, Richard, F., Pvt. Co. G
   He drew clothing March 3, 1864. Paid $107.11 for service and clothing not drawn. In August 30, 1864, transferred to CS Navy.

Borage, W., Pvt. Co. I/D see **Bosage, Victor**

Borden, Levi, Pvt. Co. C
   Enlisted as a substitute for? Steele on April 11, 1863, at Choctaw Bluff, by Captain Smith for three years or the war. Company muster rolls from December 31, 1862, to April 30, 1863, May/June 1863 and September/October 1864, all report him present. Drew clothing on March 31 and June 1, 1864. POW captured at Fort Gaines,

Alabama, on August 8, 1864. He died at St. Louis Hospital in New Orleans, Louisiana, of chronic diarrhoea on September 14, 1864 and was buried in grave No. 350, at Monument Cemetery. He left no effects, age 47, a resident of Marengo County, Alabama. Wife in McKinley. Born in Duplin, North Carolina. His record of death and interment is in his file.*

Bosage, Victor, Pvt. Co. I/D

Enlisted on October 3, 1861, at Halls Mill, Alabama, by Major Hessee for the war. Regimental return for June 1862, reports him wounded and furloughed on April 10. Wounded seriously in the neck at Shiloh on April 6, 1862, at 8 A. M. advancing in attack on the 1st Camp. Furloughed by Dr. Nott on April 9, 1862. He appears present on a company muster roll for September 24, 1862, for bounty. Company muster roll for July/August 1863, reports him present on extra duty in Commissary Department since June 3. On September/October 1863, muster roll he is shown present. There are several receipt rolls for 1864, which show him as a fisherman and detailed transporting. Muster roll for September/October 1864, at Mobile shows him detached at Battery Huger by order of Colonel Fuller. He deserted from Batter Huger on September 6, 1864.

Bosarge, Victor, Pvt. Co. I/D see **Bosage, Victor**

Boswell, J. A., Pvt. Co. I

His name appears on a register of Confederate soldiers who were killed in battle or died of disease at Camp Butler, Illinois. Died March 25, 1862.

Boswell, Robert, Pvt. Co. C

POW captured at Fort Donelson of phtisis pulmonalis on March 8, 1862, at US City General Hospital St. Louis. ? Another entry shows he died same date at Chestnut Street Hospital, Louisville.

Bouchelle, J. E., Pvt. Co. C

Surrendered by Lt. General Richard Taylor at Citronelle, Alabama, on May 4, 1865, and paroled at Meridian, Mississippi, on May 13, 1865. Residence shown as Marengo County, Alabama.

Buden, H. C., Pvt. Co. I see **Burdin, Henry**

Bould, Paul A., Pvt. Co. E

Wounded slightly in the head at Shiloh on April 6, 1862, crossing Old Field at 4:30 P. M. His name appears on a list of men employed at the Military Post of Mobile. He is shown as a conscript with surgeon's certificate employed on June 14, 1864, as a painter in the Ordnance Department.

Bouler, (Bowler) J. W., Pvt. Co. C

Enlisted on September 9, 1862, at Marengo County by Captain DeVaux for three years or the war. He appears present on muster rolls from December 31, 1862, to April 30, 1863, May/June 1863 and September/October 1863. Reference card to see personal papers of **C. C. Williams**, Co. C, 21st Alabama. He drew clothing June 1, 1864. POW captured at Fort Gaines, Alabama, on August 8, 1864. He was received at Ship Island, Mississippi, from New Orleans on October 25, 1864. He died of dysentery at Ship Island on November 30, 1864, and was buried in grave No. 53.

Boullenment, August, Sgt./Pvt. Co. K see **Boullemet, August**

Boullemet, August, Sgt./Pvt. Co. K
Enlisted on October 13, 1861, at Mobile, Alabama, by Captain Stewart for the war. There is some indication that he may have been wounded at Shiloh. He appears on September 24, 1862, muster rolls for bounty as well as November/December 1864. Thereafter on muster rolls until October 1864, he appears absent on detached service with A. Q. M. Department in Mobile by order of General Buckner. He was sent to general hospital on May 28, 1862. A return shows him absent with surgeon's certificate for five days November 25, 1862. A list in July 1864, shows him unfit for field service and a clerk in warehouse for A. Q. M. At one point in June of 1863, he drew expenses ($24.50) to travel to Jackson, Mississippi, as messenger in charge of Government Stores. **

Boun, F. G., Pvt. Co. B see **Boan, F. G**

Boutland, A., Sgt./Pvt. Co. K see **Boullemet, August**

Bowler, W. A., Pvt. Co. H
POW captured at Fort Gaines, Alabama, on August 8, 1864. Received at Ship Island, Mississippi from New Orleans on October 25, 1864, and exchanged at Ship Island on January 4, 1864.

Bowles, J. D., Pvt. Co. D see **Bowles, Joseph**

Bowles, Joseph, Pvt. Co. D
Enlisted on January 15, 1863, at Fort Morgan by Captain Butts for the war. He was reported to have deserted on August 27, 1863. A company muster roll for September/October 1863, report him present under arrest for desertion. Muster roll for November/December 1863, reports him under sentence of General Court Marshal returned from desertion. He drew clothing on August 1864, and signed by his mark. Admitted to Ross Hospital at Mobile, Alabama, on September 22, 1864, with febris intermittens quot. and returned to duty on October 4, 1864. His name appears on a list of patients at Hospital Byrnes, Camp Correction, Mobile, Alabama, dated April 11, 1865. Reference card see personal papers of **George Ashton**, Co.? 21st Ala. Inf.

Box, James R., Pvt. Co. G
Drew clothing on March 3, 1864. POW captured at Fort Gaines, Alabama, on August 8, 1864. Received at Ship Island, Mississippi, from New Orleans on October 25, 1864, and exchanged at Ship Island on January 4, 1865. Surrendered by Lt. General Richard Taylor at Citronelle, Alabama, on May 4, 1865, and paroled at Meridian, Mississippi, on May 14, 1865. Residence shown as Abbeville, Henry County, Alabama.

Bozarge, V., Pvt. Co. I/D see **Bosage, Victor**

Bradberry, W., Pvt. Co. E see **Bradeny, W. W.**

Bradeny, W. W., Pvt. Co. E
Drew clothing on March 3, March 31 and June 1, 1864. POW captured at Fort Gaines, Alabama, on August 8, 1864. Admitted to St. Louis USA General Hospital at New Orleans, Louisiana, on August 18, 1864, with febris remit and acute dysentery. Returned to prison on August 26, 1864, age 34. He was sent to Ship Island, Mississippi, and exchanged on January 4, 1865. Paroled at Talladega, Alabama, by Brevet. Brigadier General M. H. Chrysler on May 23, 1865.

Bradfield, J. R., Pvt. Co. C/K
Enlisted at Shelby County, Alabama, on September 17, 1862, by N. J. Davis for the war. He appears present on company muster rolls for December 31, 1862, to April 30, 1863, and May/June 1863. September/October 1863 muster roll shows him absent without leave since October 12, 1863. He drew clothing on March 31, and June 1, 1864. POW captured at Fort Gaines on August 8, 1864. Admitted to St. Louis USA General Hospital at New Orleans on September 4, 1864, with fever remit. age 24. Returned to prison on September 24. Received at Ship Island, Mississippi, from New Orleans on October 25, 1864, and exchanged at Ship Island on January 4, 1865. POW surrendered by Lt. General Richard Taylor at Citronelle, Alabama, on May 4, 1865, and paroled at Meridian, Mississippi, on May 14, 1864. Residence shown as Shelby County, Alabama. His name appears on a register of refugees and rebel deserters, Provost Marshal General Washington, DC received March 1, 1865, sent from Army of Potomac. Took the Oath (of Allegiance to the USA) and transportation was furnished to Cincinnati, Ohio.

Bradford, A. B., Pvt. Co. A
His name appears on a report near Tupelo, Mississippi, on June 28, 1862. He was sent to Corinth Hospital and from there to interior by order of Surgeon Heustis. Regimental return reports him sent to interior on May 26.

Bradford, John A., Pvt. Co. A
See personal papers of Pvt. **T. A. Foster**, Co. A, 21st Ala. Infantry. Enlisted on February 10, 1863, at Choctaw Bluff, Alabama, by Captain Cothran for 3 years or the war. Company muster roll for December 31, 1862, to April 30, 1863, reports him absent on surgeon's certificate from April 26, 1863. May/June 1863, muster roll reports him present. Company muster roll for September/October 1863, reports him absent sent to General Hospital in Mobile, on October 25, 1863. Admitted to Post Hospital at Fort Morgan, Alabama, on November 22, 1863, furloughed on December 10, 1863. He drew clothing in June 1864. POW captured at Fort Morgan on August 23, 1864. Sent to New York on September 27, 1864. His name appears as a signature to an Oath of Allegiance to the USA at Elmira, New York, on June 14, 1865. Residence shown as Demopolis, AL; florid complexion, auburn hair, hazel eyes, six foot one half inch. Released on June 14, 1865, at Elmira. A descriptive list filed with **T. A. Foster** gives Branford's age as 18.

MOBILE CONFEDERATES

Bradford, M., Pvt. Co. E
　　His name appears on a list of POW's surrendered by Lt. General Richard Taylor at Citronelle, Alabama, on May 4, 1865, and paroled at Demopolis, Alabama, on May 31, 1865. Residence shown as Marengo County, Alabama.

Bradley, E. B., Pvt. Co. D
　　His name appears on a list of POW's paroled by Brevet Brigadier General Chrysler commanding forces at Talladega, Alabama. He was paroled on June 23, 1865, at Talladega.

Brainard, William J., 3rd Lt./1st Lt. Co. K
　　Regimental return reports him present in June 1862, at Tupelo, Mississippi. Returns at Fort Morgan, Alabama, for November and December 1862, show him present. Company muster roll for September 24, 1862, for bounty shows him present. He is reported present on muster rolls for November/December 1862, July/August 1863, September/October 1983 and September/October 1864. Elected and appointed 2 Lt. on May 8, 1862, promoted on July 4, 1863. For the month of May 1864, he filed a requisition from Fort Powell that indicated forces assigned were, 1 officer, 2 subalterns, 54 non-com officers and privates. He signed a Parole of Honor at Meridian, Mississippi, on May 10, 1865. This parole is in his file with much other paperwork. **

Braitlng, John, Pvt. see **Breitling, John**

Brasby, William, Pvt. Co. B
　　Enlisted on October 13, 1861, at Mobile, Alabama, by Major Hessee for 12 months. Company muster roll for September 24, 1862, reports that he is not entitled to bounty due to being over age.

Brassfiled, W. B., Pvt. Co. G see **Brossfiled, W. B.**

Braswell, A. H., Pvt. Co. C see **Braswell, Allen F.**

Braswell, Allen F., Co. C
　　Enlisted on October 13, 1861, at Mobile, Alabama, by Captain Rembert for 12 months. Company muster roll for September 24, 1862, for bounty shows him present. Company muster roll for December 31, 1862, to April 30, 1863, reports him present. Muster roll for May/June 1863, reports him present and lost screw for rammer at $1. Company muster roll for September/October 1863 report him present. Drew clothing on March 31 and June 1, 1864. POW captured at Fort Gaines on August 8, 1864. Received at Ship Island Mississippi, from New Orleans on October 25, 1864, and exchanged at Ship Island on January 5, 1865.

Braswell, H. A., Pvt. Co. C see **Braswell, Allen, F.**

Bray, E. G., Pvt. F
Severely wounded in shoulder at Shiloh on April 6, 1862, at 4 P. M. while advancing at Old Field. Regimental return for June 1862, reports he was sent to Mobile Hospital. Discharged on July 28, 1862. Born Henry County, Alabama, age 21, five foot nine and one half inches, fair complexion, gray eyes, dark hair, by occupation a ? Enlisted in Baldwin County, Alabama, on October 12, 1861, to serve one year.

Brazel, James R., Pvt. Co. A
Enlisted on March 28, 1863, at Choctaw Bluff, Alabama, by Captain Cothran for three years or the war. Company muster roll for December 31, 1862, to April 30, 1863, reports him present and having drawn no pay. Muster roll for May/June 1863, reports him present. Admitted to Post Hospital at Fort Morgan, Alabama, on December 18, 1863, with congestive chill. He died December 19, 1863. See personal papers of **Geo. T. Bailey**, Pvt. Co. A, 21st Ala.

Breckenridge, E., Pvt. Co. C
Enlisted at Choctaw Bluff, Alabama, on October 13, 1862. Born in Marengo County, Alabama, 17 years old, light complexion, blue eyes, light hair, Sent to interior hospital by surgeon at Corinth, Mississippi. Regimental return for June 1862, reports him absent on surgeon's certificate. He was discharged on October 16, 1862, and paid $15.76 for service.

Breckenridge, J. T., Pvt._
His name appears on a register of discharged soldiers. Discharged May 17, 1862.

Breckenridge, R. W., Pvt. Co. C
His name appears on a regimental return reporting that he died at La Grange (GA) Hospital on May 7, 1862? A claim was filed by his father J. T. Breckenridge on January 30, 1863.

Breitling, J., Pvt. Co. E
His name appears on a list of POW's surrendered by Lt. General Richard Taylor at Citronelle, Alabama, on May 4, 1865, and paroled at Meridian, Mississippi, on May 13, 1865. Residence shown as Demopolis, Marengo County, Alabama.

Breitling, John, Pvt._
Enlisted August 4, 1864, (May 9, 1864?) at Fort Gaines, Alabama, by Major Johnson for the war. Drew clothing on June 1, 1864, and signed by his mark. He appears on a hospital muster roll at General Hospital in Marion, Alabama, for July/August 1864, as a patient. He then appears present at Mobile, Alabama, on a company muster roll for September/October 1864.

Bretling, John, Pvt._ see **Breitling, John**

Bridgers, J. W., Pvt. Co. K see **Bridges, John W.**

Bridges, John W., Co. K

Enlisted at Corinth, Mississippi, on March 21, 1862, by Captain Stewart for 12 months. Regimental return for June 1862 shows that he was sent to Mobile hospital on June 6. He appears present on a company muster roll for bounty on September 24, 1862. Regimental return for November 1862 shows him absent with leave at Mobile on November 27, 1862. Company muster rolls for November/December 1862, and July/August 1863, report him present. On muster roll for September/October 1863, he is shown absent with leave until November 3, 1863. Admitted to Ross Hospital at Mobile, Alabama, on August 12, 1864, with acuta dysentaria, returned to duty on September 11. Muster roll for September/October 1864, reports him absent on sick leave for 40 days since October 30, 1864. His name appears on a list of POW's surrendered by Lt. General Richard Taylor at Citronelle, Alabama, on May 4, 1865, and paroled at Meridian, Mississippi, on May 10, 1865. Residence shown as Lumpkin, Stewart County, Georgia.

Bright, Henry, Pvt./Corporal Co. E

Enlisted at Mobile, Alabama, on October 13, 1861, by Captain Chamberlain for the war. Regimental return for June 1862, reports him sent to interior hospital on May 28. He appears present on a company muster roll for bounty on September 24, 1862. Company muster rolls for November/December 1862 and July/August 1863, report him present. He drew clothing on March 16, 1863 and March 31, 1864. Muster roll for September/October 1863, report him absent with leave October 27, to 29, and extended two days in Mobile. Muster roll for September/October 1864, report him present. His name appears on a list of POW's surrendered by Lt. General Richard Taylor at Citronelle, Alabama, on May 4, 1865, and paroled at Meridian, Mississippi, on May 13, 1865. Residence at Yellow Bluff, Alabama. There is paperwork relative to pay roll in his file.*

Broades, [Brodas] H. M., Pvt. Co. I

Enlisted on October 13, 1861, at Halls Mill, Alabama, by Major Hessee for the war. A report dated June 28, 1862, shows he was sent to interior hospital from Corinth, Mississippi, by order of Dr. Heustis. He appears absent on leave since September 23, 1862, on a company muster roll for bounty on September 24, 1862. November and December 1862, regimental returns show him detailed with Commissary Department. Company muster roll for July/August and September/October 1863, reports him present on extra duty with Commissary Department since March 4, 1863, by order of Colonel Forsyth. POW captured at Fort Gaines, Alabama, on August 8, 1864. He was sent to hospital in New Orleans from confinement at Steam Levee Press No. 4 on October 4, 1864. He appears on a roll of POWs received at Ship Island, Mississippi, from New Orleans on October 25, 1864, and exchanged at Ship Island.

Broades. M., Pvt. Co. I

Enlisted on October 13, 1861, at Halls Mill, Alabama, by Major Hessee for the war. He was sent to interior hospital from Corinth, Mississippi, by order of Dr. Heustis. He appears present on a company muster roll for bounty on September 24, 1862. Muster rolls shows him on extra duty as a butcher in November/December 1862, and March/April/May 1863, at Fort Morgan. Muster rolls for July/August 1863, report him absent sick in General Hospital at Mobile, Alabama. He was admitted to Post Hospital at

Fort Morgan, on August 9, 1863, with diarrhoea and returned to duty on August 13. September/October 1863, roll shows him present. POW captured at Fort Gaines, Alabama, on August 8, 1864. He was admitted to St. Louis USA General Hospital at New Orleans on October 4, 1864, with pneumonia and returned to prison on October 15, 1864, age 23. He appears on a roll of POWs received at Ship Island, Mississippi, from New Orleans on October 25, 1864. He was exchanged at Ship Island. His name appears on a list of POW's surrendered by Lt. General Richard Taylor at Citronelle, Alabama, on May 4, 1865, and paroled at Mobile, Alabama, on June 8, 1865. Residence Spring Hill, Alabama. Age 21, red hair, light complexion, gray eyes, five foot 11inches.

Boradous, Moses see **Broades, M.**

Broadas, H. M., Pvt. Co. I see **Broades, H. M.**

Brodus, Alfred, Pvt. Co. I
Enlisted at Halls Mill, Alabama, on October 1, 1861, by Thomas Gleason. Born in Jackson County, Mississippi, age 16, five foot one inch, dark complexion, gray eyes, light hair, by occupation an ox driver. He was discharged at Fort Gaines, Alabama, on December 24, 1861, by surgeon due to youthfulness and disability. His discharge papers are in his file. **

Brodus, M. H., Pvt. Co. I see **Broades, H. M.**

Brooks, J. T., Pvt. Co. G
He was admitted to Post Hospital at Fort Morgan, Alabama, on November 3, 1863, with ty. fever. He died on November 22, 1863.

Brooks, Wm. R., Pvt. Co. K
Discharged November 9, 1864. Born in? Alabama, age 17, five foot seven and one half inches, dark eyes, fair complexion, dark hair.

Brooms, B. H., Pvt. Co. D see **Brooms, D. H.**

Booms, D. H., Pvt. Co. D
Enlisted on October 13, 1861, at Mobile, Alabama, by Captain Butt for one year. He is show as present for company muster roll for bounty on September 24, 1862, and refused to receive bounty. "Deserted since November 8, 1862." Company muster roll for July/August 1863, reports him absent sick in hospital in Mobile returned from desertion on April 11, 1863. Admitted to Post Hospital at Fort Morgan, Alabama, on April 28, 1863, with dysentery, returned to duty on May 7, 1863. He drew clothing June 20, and August 1864.

Brassfield, W. B., Pvt. Co. G
Drew clothing on March 3, March 31 and June 1, 1864. POW captured at Fort Gaines, Alabama, on August 8, 1864. A morning report shows him as a POW confined at Steam Levee Press No. 4 at New Orleans, Louisiana, sent to hospital on September 29,

1864. He was admitted to St. Louis USA General Hospital at New Orleans on September 28, 1864, with inter. fev. and diarrhoea, returned to prison on October 8, age 38. He appears on a roll of POWs received at Ship Island, Mississippi, from New Orleans on October 25, 1864 and exchanged at Ship Island. His name appears on a list of POW's paroled at Montgomery, Alabama, on May 18, 1864. Hair dark, eyes blue, complexion fair, five foot seven inches. His parole is in his file.*

Brothers, Thomas, Pvt. Co. K see **Brothers, T. S.**

Brothers, T. S., Pvt. Co. K
Enlisted on October 6, 1862, at Fort Morgan, Alabama, by Captain Dorgan for the war. Company muster roll for July/August 1863, September/October 1863 and September/October 1864, muster rolls all show him present. He drew clothing on June 10 and 20, and December 19, 1864. He was admitted to Ross Hospital at Mobile, Alabama, on July 19, 1864, with febris intermittens, tert, and returned to duty on August 12, 1864. His name appears on a list of POW's surrendered by Lt. General Richard Taylor at Citronelle, Alabama, on May 4, 1865, and paroled at Meridian, Mississippi, on May 13, 1865. Residence shown as Red Bluff, Wayne County, Mississippi.

Brown, Carl, Pvt. Co. H
Enlisted at Mobile, Alabama, on October 13, 1861, into Captain DeVaux's Company. He was born in Genoa, Italy, 20 years old, five foot two inches, fair complexion, brown eyes, dark hair and a barkeeper by occupation. Discharged in December 1861, by Surgeon Ross. He was paid $28.30 for service. His discharge is in his file.*

Brown, C. R., Pvt. Co. K
Enlisted on August 16, 1864, at Monroe County, Alabama, by Captain Gordon for the war. Company muster roll for September/October 1864, reports that he deserted from Redt. 2 on September 7, 1864.

Brown, Frank, Pvt. Co. B
Enlisted on October 13, 1861, at Mobile, Alabama, by Major Hessee for 12 months. Company muster roll for bounty on September 24, 1862, Muster rolls for March/April 1863, May/June 1863 and September/October 1863, all show him present. Admitted to Ross Hospital in Mobile on November 26, 1863, with gonorrhoea and returned to duty on January 15, 1864. Admitted to 1st Mississippi CSA Hospital in Jackson, Mississippi, with ascitis on June 25, 1864, returned to duty on July 5, 1864. Admitted to Ross Hospital on July 9, 1864, with ascitis and furloughed on September 6, 1864. His name appears on a roll of POW's received at Steam Levee Press No. 4 at New Orleans on October 4, 1864, received from hospital.

Brown, James H., Corporal Co. F
Enlisted at Baldwin [County, Alabama] on October 13, 1861, by Captain McCoy for three years or the war. Reported missing at the Battle of Shiloh and captured at hospital on April 7, 1862. File also shows captured at Pittsburg, Landing. Admitted to

USA Prison Hospital at Camp Douglas, Chicago, Illinois, on June 19, 1862, returned to duty [*prison*] on September 2, 1862. Exchanged from Camp Douglas at Cairo [Illinois] on September 29, 1862. He was transported among 153 Confederate prisoners on board the steamer *Emerald*, which arrived at Vicksburg on November 1. Company muster roll March/June 1863, reports him present.

Brown, J. J., Pvt. Co. E

His name appears on a roll of POW's paroled by General Chrysler at Talladega, Alabama, on June 7, 1864.

Brown, John, Pvt. Co. F

Enlisted at Baldwin County, Alabama, on October 13, 1861, by Captain McCoy for one year. Wounded seriously in the right hip at Shiloh on April 6 at 4 P. M. while charging the Old Field. Sent to Corinth Hospital on May 28. Company muster roll for bounty on September 24, 1862, reports him present. Company muster roll for March/June 1863, reports him present on extra duty QMD [Quarter Master Department] teamster "now sick in hospital" lost two gun screws $1 each.

Brown, Oakely, Pvt. Co. D see **Brown, O. K.**

Brown, O. K., Pvt. Co. D

Enlisted at Selma, Alabama, on February 11, 1863, by Lt. Mims for the war. Company muster rolls for July/August 1863, September/October 1863, November/December 1863, all report him present. Muster roll for September/October 1864, reports him absent on medical furlough for 60 days from October 21. He was admitted to Post Hospital at Fort Morgan, Alabama, on April 26, 1863, to May 16, 1863, with dysentery and on May 16, 1863, to June 23, 1863, with measles and again on January 21 1864, with rheumatism when he was sent to general hospital. He was admitted to Ross Hospital, [Mobile, Alabama] with int. fever quotd, and sent to general hospital. POW captured at Blakeley on April 9, 1865. Received at Ship Island, Mississippi, on April 15, 1865. Transferred to Vicksburg, Mississippi, for exchange on May 1, 1865.

Brown, Ross, Pvt. Co. A

Enlisted at Mobile, Alabama, on October 13, 1861, by Major Hessee. Company muster roll for bounty on September 24, 1862, reports him present where he refused to take the bounty. He was discharged at Choctaw Bluff, Alabama, on October 28, 1862, due to age 28, five foot eight inches, fair complexion, gray eyes, brown eyes, a sailor by profession, born in Ireland. His discharge is in his file.*

Brown, T. G., Pvt. Co. B see **Brown, Frank**

Brown, W. R., Major

POW captured at Fort Gaines, Alabama, on August 8, 1864. He was reported at Ship Island, Mississippi, on November 2, 1864, and exchanged on January 4, 1865.

MOBILE CONFEDERATES

Browning, J., Pvt. Co. D
   POW captured at Fort Gaines, Alabama, on August 8, 1864. Exchanged at Ship Island, Mississippi, on January 4, 1865.

Bruce, William J., Pvt. Co. K
   Enlisted at Mobile, Alabama, on October 12, 1861, by Captain Stewart for the war. Company muster roll for bounty on September 24, 1862, reports him missing since Battle of Shiloh April 7, 1862. POW captured at hospital in ambulance squad at Pittsburg Landing on April 7, 1862. He was sent to Camp Douglas, Illinois, and exchanged at Vicksburg, Mississippi, on November 10, 1862. Prisoners were among 886 POWs transported for exchange on steamer *John H. Done.* Company muster roll for November/December 1862, reports him absent, returned from missing in action but detached by General Forney on December 22, 1862, to AQM Department. Muster rolls for July/August, 1863, September/October 1863 and September/October 1864, report him present. He is assigned on extra duty as a courier and there are pay and expense vouchers in his file associated with these duties. His name appears on a list of POW's surrendered by Lt. General Richard Taylor at Citronelle, Alabama, on May 4, 1865, and paroled at Meridian, Mississippi, on May 13, 1865. Residence Mobile, Mobile County, Alabama.**

Burnson, William A., Pvt. Co. C
   Discharged at Choctaw Bluff, Alabama, on October 19, 1862. Age 16, five foot six inches, light complexion, blue eyes, and a student by occupation, born in Marengo County, Alabama. Signed with an X. His discharge is in his file.*

Bryant, J., Corporal Co. C
   POW captured at Blakeley, Alabama, on April 9, 1865. Received at Ship Island, Mississippi, April 15, 1865. Transferred to Vicksburg, Mississippi, on May 1, 1865.

Bryant, William H., Pvt. Co. F
   Discharged July 4, 1862.

Buck, Henry, Pvt. Co. I
   Enlisted at Halls Mill, Alabama, on October 13, 1863, by Major Hessee for the war. On June 20th his name was on a roll near Tupelo, Mississippi, that was sent to an interior hospital. He was admitted to Post Hospital at Fort Morgan, Alabama, on June 12, 1863, with gonorrhoea and returned to duty on June 18. He was admitted again with the same complaint on June 21, 1863, and returned to duty on June 23, and yet once again on July 25, 1863, to be returned to duty on August 1. Company muster roll for July/August 1863, reports that he transferred to Captain Hutchinson's Company of Engineers on May 20, 1863.

Buckland, Frank, Pvt. Co. I
   His name appears on a regimental return for June 1862, and shows him on detached service as a carpenter.

Buckley, Townsend M., Co. E

Enlisted on October 13, 1861, at Mobile, Alabama, by Captain Chamberlain for the war. Company muster roll for bounty on September 24, 1862, reports him absent sick with surgeon's certificate. Paid on January 22, 1862.

Bull, R. P., Pvt. Co. E

Discharged at Fort Morgan, Alabama, on October 13, 1862. Born in Mobile, Alabama, age 17, five foot ten inches, light hair, dark complexion, and dark eyes. His discharge is in his file.*

Bull, William M., Pvt. Co. E see **Ball, William M.**

Bullock, Allen, Pvt. Co. K

Enlisted at Fort Morgan, Alabama, on August 24, 1862, by Captain Dorgan for the war. Company muster roll for bounty on September 24, 1862, reports him present. Company muster roll for November/December 1862, reports him present.

Bullock, John S., Sgt./2nd Lt.. Co. K

Enlisted October 13, 1861, at Mobile, Alabama, by Captain Stewart for the war. His name appears on a June 28, 1862, report near Tupelo, Mississippi, on furlough since June 18. Company muster roll for bounty on September 24, 1862, reports him present. Muster rolls for November/December 1862, and July/August 1863, report him present. On September/October 1863, roll he is show absent on furlough for two days from October 29. Muster roll for September/October 1864, he is reported absent, sick in hospital since Oct. 10. He signed a parole as having been a POW's surrendered by Lt. General Richard Taylor at Citronelle, Alabama, on May 10, 1865. His parole is in his file.*

Bullock, E. A., Pvt. Co. K

Enlisted on August 24, 1862, at Fort Morgan, Alabama, by Captain Dorgan for the war. Company muster rolls for July/August 1863, September/October 1863 and September/October 1864, all report him present. POW captured at Spanish Fort Alabama, on April 8, 1865. He was received at Ship Island, Mississippi, on April 10, 1865, and transferred from Ship Island to Vicksburg for exchange on May 1, 1865.

Bullock, Thomas S., Corporal Co. K

Enlisted on October 13, 1861, at Mobile, Alabama, by Captain Stewart for the war. His name appears on a list [*not dated – Shiloh?*] of men who returned without arms in Withers Division, 1st Brigade (guns shattered in Battle). Company muster roll for bounty on September 24, 1862, reports him present. Company muster roll for November/December 1862, reports him present. Discharged on April 23, 1863. Age 18, five foot five and one half inches, dark complexion, light hair, gray eyes, born Mobile, Alabama. His discharge is in his file.*

Bunn, J. H., Pvt. Co. F

Captured at Island No. 10 on April 8, 1862. Nurse in hospital at Camp Douglas, Illinois. Sent to Vicksburg among 742 Confederate Prisoners for exchange on September 8, 1862. Prisoners were transported on steamer *Jno. H. Done* which arrived at Vicksburg on September 23, 1863. [Filed with **Brown, James H.**]

Burchke, Peter, Pvt. Co. H

Discharged on June 13, 1862, at Tupelo, Mississippi, for disability.

Burdin, H. C., Pvt. Co. I see **Burdin, Henry**

Burdin, Henry, Pvt. Co. I

Enlisted at Fort Morgan, Alabama, on March 24, 1863, by Lt. Collins for the war. Company muster roll for July/August 1863, reports him present sick in hospital. He was admitted to Fort Morgan Post Hospital with int. fever on July 29, 1863, returned to duty on September 7. Muster roll for September/October 1863, reports him present. POW captured at Fort Gaines, Alabama, on August 8, 1864. Admitted to St. Louis USA General Hospital at New Orleans on September 10, 1864, with measles, returned to prison on September 24, age 19. POW confined at Steam Levee Press No. 4 in New Orleans on October 4, 1864, sent to hospital on October 4. Admitted to St. Louis General Hospital again on October 4, with diarrohea acute and returned to prison on October 17. Received at Ship Island, Mississippi from New Orleans on October 25, 1865, and exchanged at Ship Island on January 4, 1865. His name appears on a list of POW's surrendered by Lt. General Richard Taylor at Citronelle, Alabama, on May 4, 1865, and paroled at Meridian, Mississippi, on May 13, 1865. Residence shown as Marengo County, Alabama.

Buns, R. W., Pvt. Co. E see **Beers, Robert W.**

Burk, Henry, Pvt. Co. F see **Burke, Henry**

Burke, Henry, Pvt. Co. F

Enlisted on October 13, 1861, at Baldwin County, Alabama, by Captain McCoy for one year. His name appears on a regimental return for June 1862, where he is shown as a laborer at Regimental Department ACS. Company muster roll for bounty on September 24, 1862, reports him present. Company muster roll for March 1, to June 30, 1863, reports him present. Muster roll for September/October 1863, reports him absent sick in hospital at Mobile, since October 25. Muster roll for September/October 1864, reports him absent on 15-day furlough granted by the Medical Board from October 25. Admitted to Ross Hospital in Mobile on October 6, 1864, with febris congestion and febris intermittens quot. furloughed on October 26, 1864, for 15 days. His name appears on a muster roll for Sossaman's Detachment of the 21st Alabama Infantry for September/October 1864, shown as absent detailed at Battery Huger by order of Colonel Fuller. POW captured at Spanish Fort, Alabama, on April 7, 1865. He was forwarded by the 16th US Army Corps from Fort Gaines to Ship Island, Mississippi, on April 11, 1865. He is shown as having been confined at New Orleans on April 13, 1863, and released on parole at New Orleans, on May 17. Very nice hand written transfer from US Provost Marshal at Spanish Fort is in his file.*

Burke, J. J., Pvt. Co. G
POW captured at Fort Gaines, Alabama, on August 8, 1864. Received at Ship Island, Mississippi, on October 25, 1864, from New Orleans. Exchanged at Ship Island on January 4, 1865. Paroled by US Provost Marshal at Montgomery, Alabama, on May 30, 1865. Complexion dark, eyes black, hair dark, five foot 11 inches. Signed by his mark.

Burke, Michael, 1 Sgt./Lt. Co. B
Enlisted at Mobile, Alabama, on October 13, 1861, by Major Hessee for 12 months. Company muster roll for bounty on September 24, 1862, reports him absent with leave. Company muster roll for March/April 1863, reports him present. Muster roll for May/June 1863, reports him absent without leave since June 29. Muster roll for September/October 1863, reports him absent with out leave since October 29, and due pay for clothing not drawn, $77.13. His name appears on a descriptive list for pay and clothing at Point Clear, Alabama, on September 23, 1863, age 32, eyes blue, hair brown, complexion light, five ft 11 ¾ inches, born in Ireland. Paid $50 as 1st Sergeant. He was admitted to Post Hospital at Fort Morgan with debility on November 19, 1863, returned to duty on November 21. He was admitted to Ross Hospital at Mobile, Alabama, on February 3, 1864, with intermit fever tert and returned to duty on February 23. He was elected 2nd Lt. on April 5, 1864. POW captured at Fort Gaines, Alabama, on August 8, 1864. Received at Ship Island, Mississippi, on November 25, 1864, from New Orleans. He was admitted to St. Louis USA General Hospital in New Orleans with hoemoptosis (*spitting of blood*) on September 8, 1864, returned to prison on September 17, age 39. Transferred from Ship Island to Vicksburg, Mississippi, on April 28, 1865. At Ship Island he refused to be exchanged and take the Oath of Allegiance to the USA. He was paroled at New Orleans on May 10, 1865, with transportation furnished to Mobile by order of General E. R. S. Canby. A pass dated April 29, 1865, at New Orleans and a signed Parole of Honor is in his file for May 10, 1865.*

Burk, Stephen, Pvt. Co. F
Enlisted at Baldwin County, Alabama, on October 13, 1861, by Captain McCoy for 1 year. Company muster roll for bounty on September 24, 1862, reports him present and "claims to be overage". Paid $66 for service by Major George W. Holt on detached service on July 17, 1862. Signed by his mark.*

Burns, Robert, Pvt. Co. K
He was killed in action at Shiloh on April 6, 1862, at 3 P. M. at Center Field by wound in his head.

Burnett, Joel J., Pvt. Co. E see **Burnett, J. J.**, 31st Alabama Infantry

Burnett, A. L., Pvt. Co. C
   POW among stragglers paroled at Selma, Alabama, during June 1865. Residence shown as Shelby County, Alabama.

Burrell, E. C., Pvt. Co. C
   Enlisted on August 29, 1862, at Jefferson, County, Alabama, by S. Wharton for three years or the war. Company muster roll for May/June 1863, reports him absent in confinement at Mobile, Alabama, for desertion. Muster roll for September/October 1863, reports him present. He was admitted to Ross Hospital in Mobile, Alabama, for anasaria on December 13, 1863, and furloughed for 60 days on December 29. He was admitted to Post Hospital at Fort Morgan, Alabama, on November 17, 1863, with catarrh and sent to general hospital on December 14. Note there is additional information on this man's desertion on January 29, 1863, from Choctaw Bluff, Alabama, in the file of **James. A. Poellnitz.** Special Order No. 62.

Burrell, J. H., Pvt. Co. C
   He enlisted for the war on August 19, 1862, at Jefferson, County, Alabama, by S. Wharton. Company muster rolls for December 31, 1862, to April 30, 1863, May/June and September/October 1863, reports him having deserted at Choctaw Bluff, Alabama, on January 29, 1863. Note there is additional information on this man's desertion on January 29, 1863, from Choctaw Bluff, Alabama, in the file of **James. A. Poellnitz**. Special Order No. 62.

Busby, B., Pvt. Co. I see **Busby, R.**

Busby, C., Pvt. Co. I
   Enlisted on October 13, 1861 at Halls Mill, Alabama, by Major Hessee for the war. Company muster roll for bounty on September 24, 1862, reports him present. Muster roll for July/August 1863, reports him present. Muster roll for September/October 1863, reports him present on extra duty with QMD after September 1, by order of Colonel Williams. A regimental return for June 1862, reports him on extra duty as regimental teamster. POW captured at Fort Gaines, Alabama, on August 8, 1864. He was received at Ship Island, Mississippi, from New Orleans on October 25, 1864, and exchanged at Ship Island on January 4, 1865.

Busby, R (Rossel), Pvt. Co. I
   Enlisted on October 13, 1861 at Halls Mill, Alabama, by Major Hessee for the war. Company muster roll for bounty on September 24, 1862, reports him present. Muster roll for July/August 1863, reports him present on extra duty with Commissary Department since April 9. Muster roll for September/October 1863, reports him absent In general hospital in Mobile, Alabama, since September 24. He was admitted to Ross Hospital in Mobile on September 25, 1863, and sent to Miller Hospital on September 26. His name appears on a list of POW's surrendered by Lt. General Richard Taylor at Citronelle, Alabama, on May 4, 1865, and paroled at Meridian, Mississippi, on May 13, 1865. Residence shown as Mobile County, Alabama.

Buskinoichy, Jap, Pvt. Co. C
Discharged for disability at Corinth, Mississippi, on May 19, 1862.

Buster, R. C., Pvt. Co. B see **Butler, R. C.**

Butler, A., Pvt. Co. K
He was employed on extra duty as a clerk in the AAG office in May 1863. Discharged on July 3, 1862. *There seems to be a mistake in dates in the records.*

Butler, John W., Pvt. Co. A
Discharged on November 27, 1861, at Fort Gaines. Born New York, age 23, five foot four inches, fair complexion, blue eyes, auburn hair, and a clerk by profession. His discharge is in his file.*

Butt, C. W., Captain Co. D
See also 1st Regiment 1st Mobile Volunteers Co. F. Appointed Captain Co. D on October 13, 1861. Wounded severely in left arm at Shiloh April 6, 1862, at 9 A. M. advancing on 1st Camp. Resigned on August 13, 1862. His letter of resignation and a letter from Dr. F. A. Ross as to his condition are in his file *

Butt, Melville, C., Bvd.2nd Lt./Captain Co. D
Wounded seriously in the thigh while retreating crossing Old Field at Shiloh on April 6 at 4:15 P. M. Elected 2nd Lt. on October 13, 1861, promoted May 8, 1862. Promoted to 1st Lt. on August 30, 1862. Regimental return for June 1862, reports him absent due to his wound. November/December muster roll 186_ at Fort Morgan shows him present. On April 3, 1864, he requisitioned the following for his company D, 42 jackets, 28 caps, 30 shirts, 41 pair drawers, and 13 pair shoes as the men lost their clothing in the evacuation of Fort Powell. Muster roll for September/October 1864, reports him absent in hospital in Mobile since October 15. A report of inspection of heavy artillery batteries at Appalachee Batteries on October 17, 1864, reports him absent sick in hospital since September 3, 1864. His name appears on a list of POW's surrendered by Lt. General Richard Taylor at Citronelle, Alabama, on May 4, 1865, and paroled at Meridian, Mississippi, on May 13, 1865. His parole and an unusually large amount of other paperwork are in his file.**

Byrne, M. O., 2nd Lt. Co. B
Elected 2nd Lt. on October 13, 1861, not re-elected on May 8, 1862. Company muster roll for November and December 1861 report him present. He was paid $208 for service on February 24, 1862. A regimental return for June 1862 shows him missing in the march from Corinth since May 30, 1862. Dropped (from rolls) May 8, 1862.

Byrne, Patrick, Pvt. Co. F
POW captured at Pittsburg Landing on April 7, 1862. Sent to Camp Douglas, Illinois. He was admitted to USA Prison Hospital at Camp Douglas near Chicago on June 29, 1862. He died at Camp Douglas on June 30, 1862.

C

Cade, G. M., Corporal. Co. C
 Discharged at Choctaw Bluff, Alabama, on October 13, 1862. Paid $121.63 for service and clothing from March 1, 1862, to October 13.

Cade, W. P., Pvt. Co. H
 POW captured at Fort Gaines, Alabama, on August 8, 1864. He was sent to New Orleans and admitted to USA St. Louis General Hospital on August 29, 1864, with diarrhoea and parotitis. Died in hospital on September 23, 1864. He was buried September 24, 1864, in Monument Cemetery grave No. 369. Left no effects. Residenceshown as Marengo County, Alabama, age 46, wife's name Allie. His record of death is in his file.*

Cagney, Cornelius, Pvt. Co. B
 On detached service. Paid $22 for service in September, and October 1862, on November 20, 1862, at $11 per month.

Cain, Jessie T., Pvt. Co. E
 Enlisted on October 31, 1862, at Fort Morgan, Alabama, by Captain Sossaman for the war. Company muster rolls for November/December 1862, July/August 1863 and September/October 1863, all report him present. On the latter roll he is shown as owed $94.13 for clothing not drawn. POW captured at Fort Gaines, Alabama, on August 8, 1864, sent to New Orleans. He was received from New Orleans at Ship Island, Mississippi, on October 25, 1864, and exchanged at Ship Island on January 5, 1865. His name appears on a list of POW's surrendered by Lt. General Richard Taylor at Citronelle, Alabama, on May 4, 1865, and paroled at Meridian, Mississippi, on May 13, 1865. Residence shown as Mobile, Alabama. * He was a substitute for **T. M. English.**

Cain, S. F., Pvt. Co. E see **Cain, Jessie T.**

Cain, William, Pvt. Co. B
 Discharged for disability at Fort Gaines, Alabama, on December 7, 1861. Age 37, five foot five inches, dark complexion, blue eyes, brown hair, by occupation a tailor, born in Ireland. His handwritten discharge is in his file.*

Cahoon, Wm., Sgt. Co. G
 Wounded slightly in the arm at Shiloh while advancing on the 1st Battery at 8:30 A. M., April 6, 1862. Discharged on July 4, 1862.

Calahan, Jerry, Pvt. Co. B see **Callaghan, Jeremiah**

Caldwell H. M., Pvt. Co. G
 POW captured at Fort Gaines, Alabama, on August 8, 1864, sent to New Orleans. He was received from New Orleans at Ship Island, Mississippi, on October 25, 1864. Died of dysentery at Ship Island on December 22 or 23, 1864. Buried in grave No. 107.

Caldwell, John, Pvt. Co. A

Enlisted on September 21, 1862, at Jefferson County, Alabama, by A. R. Goodwin for three years or the war. Company muster rolls for December 31, 1862, to April 30, 1863, and muster roll for May/June 1863, report him absent on surgeon's certificate since April 23. On muster roll for September/October 1863, he is reported present. POW captured at Fort Morgan, Alabama, on August 23, 1864. Sent from New Orleans to Elmira, New York, on September 27, 1864. Received at Elmira on October 8, 1864. Transferred to Boulware's Wharf James River with 982 other prisoners for exchange on March 14, 1865. His name appears on a roll of paroled and exchanged prisoners at Camp Lee near Richmond, Virginia, where his is reported present. He also appears on a roll of POW's (stragglers) paroled at Selma, Alabama, during the month of June 1865. A resident of Jefferson County, Alabama.

Caldwell, William, Pvt. Co. A

Enlisted on August 21, 1862, at Jefferson, County, Alabama, by J. W. Bass for the war. Company muster roll for December 31, 1862, to April 30, 1863, reports him absent sick at Choctaw Bluff, Alabama. May/June 1863, muster roll reports him present. September/October 1863, muster roll reports him absent sent to General Hospital in Mobile, on October 25. Admitted to Post Hospital at Fort Morgan with diarrhoea on January 25, 1864, returned to duty on January 30. POW captured at Fort Morgan, Alabama, on August 23, 1864. Confined at Steam Levee Press No. 4 New Orleans, on September 21, 1864, sent to hospital on September 21. Admitted to St. Louis USA General Hospital at New Orleans with diarrhoea on 20, 1864, returned to prison September 24, age 22. He was sent from New Orleans to Elmira, New York, on September 27, 1864. Received at Elmira on October 8, 1864. He died at Elmira of chronic diarrhoea on December 29, 1864 and was buried in Grave No. 1293.

Callaghan, Jeremiah, Pvt. Co. B

Enlisted on September 9, 1862, at Mobile, Alabama, by Captain Johnston for the war. Company muster roll for bounty on September 24, 1862, reports him present. Company muster rolls for March/April and May/June 1862, reports him absent sent to General Hospital in Mobile, on December 4, 1862, (on extra duty). His name appears on a hospital muster roll at General Hospital Ross, at Mobile for March/April 1863, as a patient. Company muster roll for May/June 1863, reports him absent sent to General Hospital in Mobile on December 4, 1862. His name appears and shown present on a hospital muster roll for May/June 1863, at General Hospital Miller (also known as Convalescent Hospital, Spring Hill, Alabama. He then appears on a hospital muster roll for July 17, to August 31, 1863, and September/October 1863, at Solder Rest Hospital, Mobile, Alabama. Here he is reported present and paid $18.50 per month as a nurse. . He was transferred to general hospital on September 22, 1863, by order of Brigadier General Comtey. His name appears on a hospital muster roll at General Hospital LeVert, at Mobile for November/December 1863, employed as a nurse at pay of $18.50 per month. Discharge due to disability on April 26, 1864, at Mobile, Alabama. Hazel eyes, five foot ten inches, dark complexion, dark hair, born King County, Ireland, a steamboat man by profession. His name appears September 1864, on a roll of Co. B British Guards 21st Alabama, age 17, employed on extra duty as mechanics and laborers at Mobile by

MOBILE CONFEDERATES

Major Henry St. Paul Chief of River Transportation. Detailed as a ship carpenter under Major Stone. (Detail applied for to Secretary of War). His discharge and several pay vouchers are in his file. He signed by his mark.**

Callametti, Jno., Sgt. Co. H
   Wounded slightly in his knee at Shiloh April 6, 1862, at 7 A. M. while advancing in the attack on 1st Camp. Age 27.

Callange, Charles, Pvt. Co. H
   He appears on a consolidated report near Corinth, Mississippi, on June 28, 1862, as being in hospital at Mobile, Alabama.

Calloway, R. B., Pvt. Co. F
   Captured at Pittsburg Landing, Tennessee, on April 7, 1862, on ambulance squad at hospital. He was received at Camp Chase, Ohio, from Louisville, Kentucky, on August 13, 1862. Age 35, five foot ten inches, blue eyes, dark hair, and light complexion. Exchanged on August 25, 1862, on board the steamer *Jno. H. Done* among 1020 paroled prisoners near Vicksburg, Mississippi, on November 10, 1862.*

Calwell, G., Pvt. Co. B
   His name appears on a roll of POW's paroled at Talladega, Alabama, on May 28, 1865.

Cameron, Alex, Pvt. Co. D
   Enlisted on October 13, 1861, at Mobile, Alabama, by Captain Butt. Wounded slightly in the ankle by a shell at Shiloh in the A. M. on April 6, 1862, at First Camp. Company muster roll for November/December 1861, reports that he was discharged since last muster for being over age. Regimental return for November 1862, reports that he was discharged for being a foreigner and term of service having expired.*

Camp, DeWitt, Pvt. Co. F
   Killed at Shiloh, in the A. M. at 1st Camp, April 6, 1862.

Campa, J. (Guiseppi), Pvt. Co. G
   His name appears on a list of men who returned without arms or with captured arms in Withers' Division, 1st Brigade (at Shiloh). He appears on a consolidated report near Tupelo, as having been sent to interior from Corinth at the time of evacuation. A regimental return for June 1862, reports him sick in hospital since April 18. Paid $7.50 for commutation of rations while on furlough from June 26, to July 26, 1862, and again paid $3.73 for commutation of rations while on furlough from July 24, to August 8, 1862.*

Campbell, A. K., Pvt. Co. E
   POW captured at Fort Gaines, Alabama, on August 8, 1864, and received at Ship Island, Mississippi, from New Orleans on October 26, 1864. Exchanged at Ship Island on January 5, 1865.

Campbell, C. C., Pvt. Co. K

Enlisted at Fort Pillow on March 10, 1862, by Captain Stewart for the war. Company muster roll for bounty on September 24, 1862, reports him present. Company muster roll for November/December 1962, reports that he furnished a substitute **M. Smith** on November 13, 1862.

Campbell, J. A., Pvt. Co. G

Drew clothing on March 21, 1862, signed by his mark. POW captured at Fort Gaines, Alabama, on August 8, 1864, and received at Ship Island, Mississippi, from New Orleans on October 26, 1864, and exchanged at Ship Island on January 5, 1865.

Campbell, John, Pvt. Co. B

Company muster roll for bounty on September 24, 1862, reports him not entitled to bounty as being over age.

Campbell, William B., Sgt. Co. A

Discharged for disability May 11, 1862, Corinth, Mississippi. Born in Norfolk, Virginia, age 26, five foot six and one half inches, fair complexion, hazel eyes, dark hair, and by profession a salesman.

Canaday, E., Pvt. Co. B see **Kennedy, Edward**

Canady, James, Pvt. Co. I

Enlisted on October 13, 1864, at Halls Mill, Alabama, by Major Hessee for the war. Company muster roll for bounty on September 24, 1862, reports him present. Muster rolls for July/August and September/October 1862, all report him present.

Candlish, William, G., Corp./Pvt. Co. A

Enlisted on October 13, 1864, at Mobile, Alabama, by Major Hessee for the war. His name appears on a regimental return for June 1862, as having been sent to the interior at the evacuation of Corinth. Company muster roll for bounty on September 24, 1862, reports him present. Muster roll for December 31, 1862, to April 30, 1863, reports him absent on detached service since November 20, 1862, with Commissary Department at Choctaw Bluff. Muster roll for May/June 1863, reports him present on detached service with Commissary Department at Fort Stonewall, (*near Choctaw Bluff*) by order of Colonel Anderson. Muster roll for September/October 1863, reports him absent and reduced from 1st Corporal to the ranks on Sept. 1, 1863, still on detached service at Choctaw Bluff. He is shown as being paid as a clerk in September 1863, at 25 cents per day. POW captured at Fort Gaines, Alabama, on August 8, 1864. He was admitted to St. Louis USA General Hospital at New Orleans on September 3, 1864, with dysentery, and returned to prison on September 19, 1864, age 29. Received at Ship Island, Mississippi, from New Orleans on October 26, 1864. Exchanged at Ship Island on January 5, 1865. His name appears on a list of POW's surrendered by Lt. General Richard Taylor at Citronelle, Alabama, on May 4, 1865, and paroled at Meridian, Mississippi, on May 13, 1865. Residence shown as Mobile, Alabama.*

MOBILE CONFEDERATES

Canepi, Gusieppi, Pvt. Co. G see **Campa J.**

Cannedy, E., Pvt. Co. B see **Kennedy, Edward**

Canterberry, Walter, Pvt. Co. A
  Enlisted on February 22, 1863, at Marengo, County, Alabama, by Lt. Northrup for 3 years or the war. Company muster roll for December 31, 1862, to April 30, 1863, reports him present. Muster roll for May/June 1863, reports him sick in quarters and September/October roll reports him present. *Note there are some records of a Pvt. Walter Canterberry of the 42nd Alabama, Co. A who was killed on Lookout Mt. Tennessee, November 24, 1863, in this file.*

Canthem, A. W., Pvt. Co. E see **Cawthorn, Alex. W.**

Capelo, Rafael, Pvt. Co. G
  Wounded seriously in the side at Shiloh on April 6, 1862, at 7 A. M. while advancing in the attack on the 1st Battery

Capps, G. W., Pvt. Co. F?
  Enlisted on March 5, 1864, at Selma, Alabama, by G. R. Rassen for the war. Company muster roll for September/October 1864, reports him sent to Hospital Moore, on October 25. Admitted to 1st Mississippi CSA Hospital at Jackson, Mississippi, on March 3, 1865, with feb. cont., transferred on April 24, 1865, to Marion, Alabama.

Capps, J. P., Pvt. Co. B
  Drew clothing June 3, 1864. POW captured at Fort Gaines, Alabama, on August 8, 1864, and received at Ship Island, Mississippi, from New Orleans on October 26, 1864. Exchanged at Ship Island on January 5, 1865. His name appears on a roll of POW's paroled at Talladega, Alabama, on June 15, 1865.

Capps, J. W., Pvt. Co. F
  Enlisted at Selma, Alabama, on March 5, 1864, by Captain Rosser for the war. Hospital muster roll for July/August 1864, reports him present as a patient. POW captured at Champion Hill, Mississippi, May 17, 1863. He appears on a roll of POW's at Fort Delaware where he was discharged (form prison) and joined USA service on August 1, 1863. Mustered into Captain Richard's Battery on July 9, 1863, Pennsylvania Vols.

Capps, William, Pvt. Co. B
  Enlisted at Talladega, Alabama, on September 8, 1862, by George A Carey for the war. Company muster roll for March/April 1863, report him absent detailed as a gardener at Choctaw Bluff, Alabama, since April 18, 1863, by order of Colonel Anderson. Muster roll for May/June 1863, reports that he was discharged for disability June 18, by order of General Maury.

Capps, William J., Pvt. Co. B

Enlisted in Jefferson County, Alabama, August 29, 1862, by M. D. Poole for the war. Company muster roll for March/April 1863, reports him present. May/June 1863, muster roll shows him present, sick in quarters. September/October 1863, muster roll he is reported present and due $39.63 for clothing.

Capps, J., Co. G filed with **Capps, William J.**

He was discharged March 27, 1862. Final payment on February 18, 1864.

Cardin, Harkin, Pvt. Co. D

Enlisted at Talladega, Alabama, on September 11, 1862, for the war. Company muster roll for November/December 1862; report him absent in General Hospital in Mobile. His name appears on a register of deceased soldiers from Alabama. Died at Mobile, Alabama. Claim presented by Elizabeth Cardin, widow on August 10, 1863.

Cardin, L., Pvt. Co. D

His name appears on a return of 2nd Batt'n. 21st Alabama Infantry for December 1862, he is reported sick in General Hospital at Mobile.

Carey, William, Sgt. Co. F see **Carry William**

Carlen, J. B., Pvt. Co. E

Killed at Shiloh April 1862. Shot through head on April 6, 1862, at 7 A. M. during attack on 1st Battery. Filed with **Carlen, John**

Carlen, J. G., Pvt./Corp. Co. E see **Carlen, John**

Carlen, John. G., Pvt./Corp. Co. E

Enlisted October 13, 1861, at Mobile, Alabama, by Capt. Chamberlain for the war. Company muster roll for bounty on September 24, 1862, reports him present. Muster rolls for November/December 1862, July/August 1863 and September/October 1863, report him present. POW captured at Fort Gaines, Alabama, on August 8, 1864, and received at Ship Island, Mississippi, from New Orleans on October 26, 1864. Admitted to St. Louis USA General Hospital at New Orleans with dysentery on September 13, 1864, returned to prison on September 22, 1864, age 22. Exchanged at Ship Island on January 5, 1865. His name appears on a list of POW's surrendered by Lt. General Richard Taylor at Citronelle, Alabama, on May 4, 1865, and paroled at Meridian, Mississippi, on May 13, 1865. Residence shown as Mobile, Alabama.

Carlen, Thomas S., 2nd Lt. Co. B

Elected on July 23, 1862. His name appears on a field report at Brigade Headquarters, Fort Morgan, Alabama, in October 1862, Shown as a loss, transferred to Choctaw Bluff, Alabama, October 6, 1862. He died August 23, 1863. There are several pay vouchers and requisitions in his file.*

Carleton, A. Jr., Pvt. Co. E
Drew clothing on June 1, 1864. POW captured at Fort Gaines, Alabama, on August 8, 1864, and received at Ship Island, Mississippi, from New Orleans on October 26, 1864. Exchanged at Ship Island on January 5, 1865. His name appears on a list of POW's surrendered by Lt. General Richard Taylor at Citronelle, Alabama, on May 4, 1865, and paroled at Meridian, Mississippi, on May 13, 1865. Residence shown as Montgomery, Alabama.

Carlton, J., Pvt. Co. E see **Carlton, A. Jr.**

Carley, John, Pvt. Co. C see **Corley, John**

Carlisle, E. J., Sgt. Co. D,
Reference envelope only in his file.

Carlisle, E. T., Pvt. Co. C
Enlisted on August 22, 1862, at Jefferson County, Alabama, by W. A. Walker for three years or the war. Company muster rolls for December 31, 1862, to April 30, 1863 and May/June 1863, reports him present. He drew rations on May 29, and June 12, 186_, paid at Selma on June 24, 1863. Muster roll for September/October 1863 reports him absent without leave since September 30, 1863. POW captured at Fort Gaines, Alabama, on August 8, 1864, and received at Ship Island, Mississippi, from New Orleans on October 26, 1864. He was admitted to St. Louis USA General Hospital on October 9, 1864, with acute diarrhoea, returned to prison on October 22, 1864, age 25. Died at Ship Island of dysentery on December 3, 1864.

Carlisle, Henry T., Pvt. Co. C
Enlisted on August 22, 1862, at Jefferson County, Alabama, by W. A. Walker for three years or the war. Company muster roll for December 31, 1862, to April 30, 1863, reports him present. Muster roll for September/October 1863, reports him absent without leave since September 4, 1863. He was admitted to Ross Hospital in Mobile, on February 15, 1864, with debililty. POW captured at Fort Gaines, Alabama, on August 8, 1864. He was admitted to St. Louis USA General Hospital at New Orleans on September 9, 1864, with intermit fever, retuned to prison on October 4. He was admitted again on October 23, 1864, the same hospital with chronic diarrhoea, age 20. Died of chronic diarrhoea on November 3, 1864. He was buried in Monument Cemetery grave No. 412 left no effects. He was shown as married and a resident of Jefferson County, Alabama. His death certificate is in his file.*

Carrington, Algernon S., Lt./Captain Co. E/H
Elected 2nd Lt. on September 21, 1861, promoted on May 2, 1862. Elected 1st Lt. on May 8, 1862, promoted to Captain Co. H on March 24, 1864. Company muster roll for December 1861, reports him present and a 2nd Lt.. A regimental return for June 1862 shows him sent to interior hospital by surgeon on May 28. Company muster roll for bounty on September 24, 1862, reports him present. Returns for November and December, shows him present at Fort Morgan, Alabama. Muster rolls for

November/December 1862 and July/August 1863 show him present. On January 13, 1863, he requisitioned 8 muskets and bayonets for Co. E. September/October 1863, roll shows him absent with leave from 29 October, to 31 October. Appointed Captain of Co. H, on March 24, 1864. He requisitioned ordnance on June 20, 1864, at Fort Gaines as follows for his Company H; 67 muskets, bayonets, cartridge boxes, O. B. belts, waist belts, cap pouches, bayonet scabbards, knapsacks, haversacks, canteens, plus 1217 cartridges and caps. POW captured at Fort Gaines, Alabama, on August 8, 1864, and received at Ship Island, Mississippi, from New Orleans on November 5, 1864. He was admitted to St. Louis USA General Hospital at New Orleans on August 20, 1864, with fever intermittent and acute diarrhoea, returned to prison on August 29, age 21. Exchanged at Ship Island on January 4, 1865. His Parole of Honor is in his file showing that he was surrendered by Lt. General Richard Taylor at Citronelle, Alabama, on May 4, 1865, and paroled at Meridian, Mississippi, on May 11, 1865. His appointment, requisitions, and pay vouchers are also in his file.** He was paid $90 per month as Captain.

Carrington, John, Pvt. Co. E/H

Enlisted on August 31, 1862, at Fort Morgan, Alabama, by Capt. Sossaman for the war. Company muster roll for bounty on September 24, 1862, reports him present. Company muster rolls for November/December 1862 and July/August 1863 report him present. Muster roll for September/October 1863, reports him sick in hospital in Mobile. He was admitted to Post Hospital at Fort Morgan on December 20, 1863, with syphilis and sent to general hospital on January 26, 1864. He was admitted to Ross Hospital, Mobile, Alabama, on January 26, 1864, with primary syphilis, deserted on February 2, and admitted again on February 9, 1864, with primary syphilis, and sent to General Hospital in Montgomery, on February 17, 1864. POW captured at Fort Gaines, Alabama, on August 8, 1864, and received at Ship Island, Mississippi, from New Orleans on October 25, 1864. Exchanged at Ship Island on January 4, 1865. He was admitted to Way Hospital in Meridian, Mississippi, on March 10, and transferred. His name appears on a list of POW's surrendered by Lt. General Richard Taylor at Citronelle, Alabama, on May 4, 1865, and paroled at Meridian, Mississippi, on May 13, 1865. Residence shown as Mobile, Alabama.

Carroll, Patrick, Pvt. Co. B

He was paid $44 for detached service March 1, to June 30, 1862. Paid on July 17, 1862. He signed by his mark.

Carroll, R. Thomas, Pvt. Co. G

He was admitted to Post Hospital at Fort Morgan on January 23, 1864, with bronchitis and sent to general hospital on January 26. He drew clothing June 1, 1864. POW captured at Fort Gaines, Alabama, on August 8, 1864, and received at Ship Island, Mississippi, from New Orleans on October 25, 1864. He was exchanged at Ship Island on January 4, 1865.

Carroll, Thomas, Pvt. Co. G see **Carroll, R. Thomas**

Carter, E. L., Pvt. Co. C

. Drew clothing June 1, 1864. POW captured at Fort Gaines, Alabama, on August 8, 1864, and received at Ship Island, Mississippi, from New Orleans on October 25, 1864. He was exchanged at Ship Island on January 4, 1865. His name appears on a list of POW's surrendered by Lt. General Richard Taylor at Citronelle, Alabama, on May 4, 1865, and paroled at Meridian, Mississippi, on May 13, 1865. Residence shown as Marengo County, Alabama.

Carter, J., Pvt. Co. G

His name appears on a June 1862, regimental return. Sent to hospital May 28.

Carter, John, Pvt. Co. E

His name appears on a June 1862, regimental return sent to interior hospital May 28, 1862.

Carter, Thomas, Pvt. Co. C

Enlisted at Saltillo on July 11, 1862, by Captain Clarke for the war. He appears present on the organizational muster roll for bounty on September 24, 1862. Here his name is spelled **Carty**.

Carter, William A., Pvt. Co. E

Enlisted at Mobile, Alabama, on October 13, 1861, by Captain Chamberlain for the war. A regimental return for June 1862 shows him on detached service as Chaplin in Mobile Hospital. Company muster roll for bounty on September 24, 1862, reports him absent detailed December 14, 1861, as hospital Chaplin on order of General Withers. Company muster roll for November/December 1862, reports that he was promoted to post Chaplin by the War Department on November 10, 1862. Discharged on November 10, 1862.

Carter, W. M., Pvt. Co. B see **Curlee, William.**

Carter, W. R., Pvt. Co. C

Enlisted at Mobile, Alabama, on October 13, 1861, by Captain Rembert for 12 months. Company muster roll for bounty on September 24, 1862, reports him present. Muster roll for December 31, 1862, to April 30, 1863, reports him on detached service in Engineer Department at Choctaw Bluff from April 28, 1863, by order of Colonel Wickliff pay stopped from April 26. May/June 1863, muster roll shows him present returned to the company May 25, 1863, lost 10 cartridges and caps at $1. Company muster roll for September/October 1863, reports him present. POW captured at Fort Gaines, Alabama, on August 8, 1864, and received at Ship Island, Mississippi, from New Orleans on October 25, 1864. Admitted to St. Louis USA General Hospital at New Orleans on September 6, 1864, with fever intermit and rupia returned to prison on October 13, 1864, age 26. He was exchanged at Ship Island on January 4, 1865. POW captured at Blakeley, Alabama, on April 9, 1865. Received at Ship Island for second time on April 15, 1865. Transferred to Vicksburg, Mississippi, for exchange on May 1, 1865. There is paperwork in his file.*

Cartright, J. S., Pvt. Co. A see **Cortright, Jerome S.**

Carty, Thomas, Pvt. Co. C see **Carter, Thomas**

Cary, William, Sgt. Co. F
Enlisted at Halls Mill on November 13, 1861, by Capt. McCoy for three years or the war. Company muster roll for March 1, to June 30, 1863, reports him present. Muster roll for September/October 1863, reports him present. Born in Scotland, age 46. Discharged?*

Cassidy, W., Pvt. Co. K see **Cassity, W.**

Cassity, W., Pvt. Co. K
Enlisted by Major Stone on September 1, 1864, at Clarke County, Alabama, for the war. Company muster roll for September/October 1864, reports him absent and temporally attached by Major Stone, Ex. Officer, sick in hospital since October 2, 1864. He was among POW's surrendered by Lt. General Richard Taylor at Citronelle, Alabama, in May 1865, and paroled at Demopolis, Alabama, on June 21, 1865. Residence shown as Clarke County, Alabama.

Cates, W. (William), Pvt. Co. D
Enlisted on August 12, 1864, at Mobile, Alabama, by Major Stone for the war. Company muster roll for September/October 1864, reports him present, assigned to the company by order. He was admitted to Ross Hospital at Mobile on October 12, 1864, with febris intermittens quot. and returned to duty on October 18.

Cawley, J., Pvt Co. C see **Corley, John**

Cawthorn, Alex W., Pvt. Co. E
Enlisted on October 13, 1861, at Mobile, Alabama, by Captain Chamberlain for the war. A regimental return for June 1862 shows him detached as a druggist. Company muster roll for September 24, 1862, for bounty reports him absent detailed as apothecary in Medical Purveyor [office] by order of General Withers since February 1862. Muster roll for November/December 1962, reports him absent detailed in Medical Department. Returns for November and December 1862, report him detached in Medical Department at Okolona, [Mississippi]. His name appears on a hospital muster roll for July 17, to August 31, 1863, at General Hospital, Point Clear, Alabama, present as a steward. Muster rolls for July/August and September/October 1863, report him absent, detailed as hospital steward at Choctaw Bluff. He appears on a hospital muster roll for November/December at Wayside Hospital in Selma, Alabama, present as a steward. There are a number of pay vouchers in his file.**

Cayce, Perry B., Pvt. Co. E
Enlisted on October 13, 1861, at Mobile, Alabama, by Captain Chamberlain for the war. Company muster roll for September 24, 1862, for bounty reports him absent detailed from February 1862, in Commissary Department by General Withers.

MOBILE CONFEDERATES

Regimental returns for November and December 1862, shows him detached at Corinth, Mississippi, in the ACS Department. Muster roll for November/December 1962, reports him absent detailed from April 3, 1862, in Commissary Department. Muster rolls for July/August and September/October 1863, report him absent, detached in Commissary Department. There are a number of pay vouchers in his file.**

Cayce, Stewart. W., Captain/Lt. Colonel/Adjutant
Enlisted on October 13, 1861. Appointed Adjutant July 22, 1861, Promoted on March 31, 1862. A post return from Fort Gaines, Alabama, for November 1861, reports him present as Post Adjutant. A regimental return for December 1961 shows him present as Adjutant. A regimental return for June 1862, shows that he was not reelected Lt. Colonel at reorganization, relieved from duty on May 19, by General Bragg. He makes a $200 claim for his horse killed in action at the Battle of Shiloh on April 6, 1862. Elected Lt Colonel March 31, 1864, not reelected on May 8, 1862. [*Some confusion here.*] There is a considerable amount of paper work in his file.**
This letter in his file on Union paper.

>Headquarters
>21st Alabama Vols.
>April 8, 1862,
>S. W. Cayce
>Lt. Col.
>
>General,
>   As a matter of curiosity I sent you for inspection a mailed vest picked up by one of my men on the field yesterday. Many others were also noticed & some more brought in showing but too conclusively that the dastardly practice of using them was really practiced by the enemy.
>
>I am sir respectfully your obsvt.
>   S. W. Cayce Lt. Col
>
>(back side)
>Having no other paper I write on some that did belong to the enemy.
>*** Copy

Cazalas, Lewis, Pvt. Co. D
Enlisted in Mobile, Alabama, on October 13, 1861, by Captain Butt for one year. A regimental return for June 1862, reports that he was sent to interior hospital at the evacuation [of Corinth]. Company muster roll for September 24, 1862, for bounty reports him present and refused to take the bounty. Company muster rolls for July/August, September/October, November/December 1863, and September/October 1864, all show him present.

Caitan, C. B., Pvt. Co. G. see **Chatain, C. B.**

Chamberlain, John C. Captain Co. E

Enlisted on October 13, 1861. Elected on September 10, 1861. Appointed on October 5, 1861. Regimental returns for November and December 1861, report him present. He was paid $130 per month as a Captain. Resigned for disability May 3, 1862. He died on March 22, 1863. There is paper work in his file.*

Champion, J. S. C., Pvt. Co. B

Enlisted September 1, 1862, at Talladega, Alabama, for the war. Company muster roll for March/April 1863, reports him present, detailed as hospital nurse since March 3, 1863. He died on the night of June 27, 1863, at Choctaw Bluff, Alabama.

Champion, R. W., Pvt. Co. K

Enlisted on September 2, 1864, at Mobile, Alabama, by Major Stone for the war. Company muster roll for September/October 1864, reports him temporarily assigned to the company by Major Stone, Ex. Officer, detailed to report to Capt.? by Major Stone on September 25, 1864.

Chapman, A. J., Pvt. Co. C

Enlisted on September 8, 1862, at Marengo County, Alabama, by Captain DeVaux for three years or the war. Company muster rolls for December 31, 1862, to April 30, 1862, and May/June, 1863, report him present. Muster roll for September/October 1863, report him absent without leave from October 26, 1863. Admitted to Post Hospital at Fort Morgan, Alabama, on November 9, 1863, with icterus [jaundice], returned to duty on January 15, 1864. POW captured at Fort Gaines, Alabama, on August 8, 1864. He was admitted to St. Louis USA General Hospital at New Orleans, on September 8, 1864, with acute diarrhoea, returned to prison on September 22, 1864, age 26. Received at Ship Island, Mississippi, from New Orleans on October 25, 1864. Died of diarrhoea at Ship Island on November 17, 1864. He was buried in grave No. 24.

Chapman, J. P., Pvt. Co. C

Enlisted on September 8, 1862, at Marengo County, Alabama, by Captain DeVaux for three years or the war. Company muster rolls for December 31, 1862, to April 30, 1862, and May/June, 1863, report him present. Muster roll for September/October 1863, reports that he died in hospital at Point Clear, Alabama, on October 15, 1863.

Chapman, P. S. (P. O.), Pvt. Co. D

Enlisted at Montgomery, Alabama, on June 1, 1863, by Enrolling Officer for the war. Company muster rolls for July/August 1863, September/October, and November/December all report him present. He drew clothing in August 1864. Muster roll for September/October 1864, reports him absent, sent to general hospital in Mobile, Alabama, on October 28, 1864.

Chapman, W. P., Pvt. Co. C

Enlisted at Mobile, Alabama, on October 13, 1861, by Captain Rembert for the war his file also shows that he enlisted on September 8, 1862, in Marengo County, by

MOBILE CONFEDERATES

Captain DeVaux for three years or the war. Company muster roll for September 24, 1862, for bounty reports him present. Company muster rolls for December 31, 1862, to April 30, 1862, and May/June, 1863, report him present. Muster roll for September October 1863, reports him present. POW captured at Fort Gaines, Alabama, on August 8, 1864. Received at Ship Island, Mississippi, from New Orleans on October 25, 1864. He died of dysentery at Ship Island on December 27, 1864 and was buried in grave No. 113. There is a pay voucher in his file and he signed by X.*

Chapman, W. T., Pvt. Co. C see **Chapman, W. P.**

Chatain, C. B., Pvt. Co. G
POW captured at Fort Gaines, Alabama, on August 8, 1864. Received at Ship Island, Mississippi, from New Orleans on October 25, 1864, and exchanged at Ship Island on January 5, 1865.

Chathem, J. A., Pvt. Co. G
His name appears on a register of POW's at New Orleans captured at Fort Gaines, Alabama, on August 8, 1864, and exchanged at Ship Island on January 5, 1865.

Chatman, P. S., Pvt. Co. D see **Chapman, P. S.**

Chaudron, Felix, Pvt. Co. H
Enlisted on October 13, 1861, at Mobile, Alabama, to serve one year. Discharged due to disability. Born in Philadelphia, Pennsylvania, age 42, 5 foot 3 inches, dark eyes, dark complexion, gray hair, by profession an agent.

Cherolin, E., Pvt. Co. A
His name appears on a regimental return for June 1862. He is shown being detailed as a druggist at hospital in Mobile, Alabama.

Chester, Matthew, Q. M. Sergeant
His name appears on a regimental return for June 1862. Discharged at Corinth, Mississippi, on May 25, 1862, for disability. He had served in the Governors Guards at Selma. There are several pay vouchers in his file and a letter to Secretary of War CSA seeking appointment.**

Chevalier, Emanuel, Pvt. Co. A
Enlisted at Mobile, Alabama, on October 13, 1861, by Major Hessee for the war. Wounded slightly at Shiloh on April 6, 1861, at 7 A. M. at First Camp. His name appears on a report near Tupelo, Mississippi, on June 26, 1861, detached as druggist and ordered to Mobile by General Bragg. Company muster roll for September 24, 1862, for bounty reports him absent on detached service from June 19, 1862, as a druggist at Mobile hospital. Company muster rolls for December 31, 1862, to April 30, 1863, report him absent detached on June 19, 1862, as a hospital steward by order of Secretary of War. Muster rolls for May/June and September/October 1863, report him absent appointed

hospital steward on October 1, 1863, by Secretary of War. He appears on several Mobile hospital muster rolls. There is paperwork in his file.*

Chichester, William, Pvt. Co. D

His name appears on a regimental return for June 1862. "May 24, Columbus, [*Mississippi*] died hospital, returns furnished."

Chiland, J. H., Pvt. Co. C

His name appears on a regimental return for June 1862. "Absent on Surgeon's Certf."

Child, Frank, Pvt. Co. K

Enlisted at Fort Morgan, Alabama, on Nov. 25, 1862, by Captain Dorgan for the war. His name appears on a regimental return for June 1862, "May 3, Corinth, Miss., discharged for disability." He reenlisted at Fort Morgan on November 24, 1862. Company muster rolls for November/December 1862, July/August 1863, September/October 1863, and September/October 1864, all report him absent, detached with Signal Corps on December 6, 1862, by order of General Forney. Pay vouchers show he was a signal telegraph operator at Mobile. There are a number of pay vouchers in his file.**

Child, G. C., Pvt. Co. K see **Child G. G.**

Child, G. G., Pvt. Co. K

Enlisted on October 13, 1861, at Mobile, Alabama, by Captain Stewart for the war. His name appears on a regimental return for June 1862, "Detached service, Secretary General Hospital". His name also appears on a company muster roll for bounty on September 24, 1862. Company muster roll for November/December 1862, reports him present and detailed as Acting Sgt. Major by order of Col. Stewart. Company muster rolls for July/August 1863, September/October 1863, and September/October 1864, report him absent, detached A. Q. M. Department on December 6, 1862, by order of General Forney. He appears on a list of attaches, etc. employed as a clerk, unfit for field service, at the Military Post of Mobile, Alabama, by order of Brigadier General Macknall. A pay voucher for June 1863 shows he was paid $3 per day for service less rations drawn at 60 cents per day. He is among detached men in Q. M. Department that were surrendered by Lt. General Richard Taylor CSA at Citronelle, Alabama, on May 4, 1865, and paroled at Meridian, Mississippi, on May 11, 1865. There is considerable paperwork in his file.**

Child, W. F., Pvt. Co. K see **Child, Frank**

Childress, J. F., Co. G

There is only a payment record for service March to August 1862, at $11 per month plus $50 bounty, in his file.

Christian, Charles, J., Pvt. Co. C

POW captured at Shiloh on April 7, 1861. He was admitted to USA Prison Hospital at Camp Douglas, Illinois, on April 26, 1862. He died on May 7, 1862, of pneumonia and diarrhoea.

Christian, J. M., Corporal Co. C

Enlisted at Fort Gaines, Alabama, on January 27, 1862, by Captain Rembert for three years or the war. Company muster roll for May/June 1863, reports him present promoted from the ranks on June 6, 1863. Company muster roll for September/October 1863, reports him present. POW captured at Fort Gaines on August 8, 1864. He appears on a list of prisoners received from New Orleans at Ship Island, Mississippi, on October 25, 1864. He was exchanged at Ship Island on January 4, 1865. He was among POW's surrendered by Lt. General Richard Taylor at Citronelle, Alabama, in May 1865, and paroled at Demopolis, Alabama, on May 31, 1865. Residence was shown as Marengo County, Alabama. There is paper work in his file.*

Christian, John, Pvt. Co. C

Enlisted on January 27, 1862, at Fort Gaines, Alabama, by Captain Rembert for three years or the war. His name appears on a company muster roll for bounty on September 24, 1862. Company muster roll for December 31, 1862, to April 30, 1863, reports him present.

Chrockton, B. M., Surgeon

His name appears on a descriptive roll for POW's at Camp Chase, Ohio. He was arrested at Fort Donaldson, Tennessee, on February 16, 1862, and received at Camp Chase on March 1. He was transferred to Johnsons' Island, Ohio, on April 24, 1862.

Cimtee, R., Pvt. Co. G

He was wounded in the thigh severely while advancing in the A. M. at Shiloh on April 6, 1862. A regimental return shows him in hospital since April 9.

Clairin, L. (Lewis) E., Pvt. Co. K

Enlisted on July 4, 1863, at Fort Morgan, Alabama, by Captain Dorgan for the war. Company muster roll for July/August 1863, reports him present. There is a reference card in his file to see personal papers of **J. Albert**.

Clarke, Carter, Pvt. Co. K see **Clarke, C. P.**

Clarke, C. P., Pvt. Co. K

Enlisted on February 13, 1863, at Selma, Alabama, by Captain Dorgan for the war. He was a resident of Marengo County, Alabama. Company muster rolls for July/August 1863, and September/October 1863, report him absent detached in Signal Corps by order of Colonel Powell on February 14, 1863. In October of 1863, he petitioned to be promoted to Lt. in the Alabama Artillery Battalion at Fort Morgan and had several letters of testimony submitted in his behalf. Secretary of War Seddon recommended him but a presidential candidate got the job. The letters are in his file.**

Company muster roll for September/October 1864; show him taken prisoner at Fort Morgan in August 1864. POW captured at Fort Morgan on August 23, 1864, sent to New York on September 27, 1864. He was admitted to St. Louis USA General Hospital at New Orleans on August 26, 1864, with jaundice, age 19, and returned to prison on August 29. He was received at Elmira, New York, from New Orleans on October 8, 1864. Transferred to James River for exchange on February 20, 1865. He was admitted to Receiving and Wayside Hospital or General Hospital No. 9 at Richmond Virginia, on March 3, 1865, and released on March 4, remarks P. P. He appears on a register at General Hospital Howard's Grove at Richmond, Virginia, on March 4 and 7, 1865, with feb. intermittent.

Cleiland, J. H., Pvt./Corp. Co. C see **Clieland, J. H.**

Clemens, R. (Rodriguez), Pvt./Corp. Co. G
POW captured at Shiloh April 8, 1861, while at Pittsburg Landing. His name appears on a roll of POW's at Camp Douglas, Illinois, on August 1, 1862. He was admitted to USA Prison Hospital at Camp Douglas on June 14, 1862, with febris typhoidous, retuned to prison on June 24. He also appears on a roll of POW's at Camp Douglas (captured at Island No. 10 on April 8, 1862,) sent to Vicksburg, Mississippi, on September 8, 1862, for exchange, among 742 prisoners, on board the steamer *John H. Done*. He arrived at Vicksburg on September 28, 1862.

Clement, Charles, Pvt. Co. I see **Clements, Charles**

Clements, Charles, Pvt. Co. I
He drew clothing on June 1, 1864. His name appears on a register of Post Hospital at Fort Morgan, Alabama, as being admitted on July 26, 1864, with int. feb. quar., returned to duty on July 30, 1864. POW captured at Fort Gaines, Alabama, on August 8, 1864. He was sent to New Orleans and confined at Steam Levee Press No. 4 where he was admitted to St. Louis USA General Hospital on October 6, 1864, with morbittis [*morbi cutis, a skin disease?*] and returned to prison on October 22, 1864, age 17. He arrived at Ship Island, Mississippi, from New Orleans on October 25, 1864. He died at Ship Island on December 12, 1864, of dysentery and was buried in grave No. 84.

Clements, Josh, Pvt. Co. I
Enlisted on October 13, 1861, at Halls Mill, Alabama, by Major Hessee for the war. His name appears on a company muster roll for bounty on September 24, 1862. Company muster roll for July/August 1863, reports him present on extra duty in Commissary Department since June 3, 1863. Muster rolls for September/October 1863, and September/October 1864, report him present. His name appears on a list of POW's surrendered by Lt. General Richard Taylor at Citronelle, Alabama, on May 4, 1865, and paroled at Meridian, Mississippi, on May 13, 1865. Residence shown as Mobile County, Alabama.

Clendenin, John, Pvt. Co. F see **Clendenning, John**

Clendenning, John, Pvt. Co. F

Enlisted on October 13, 1861, at Baldwin County, Alabama, by Captain McCoy for one year. His name appears on a company muster roll for bounty on September 24, 1862. Company muster roll for March 1, to June 30, 1863, reports him present. Company muster rolls for September/October 1863, reports him present and on extra duty for AQM, owes for one haversack $1. POW captured at Fort Gaines, Alabama, on August 8, 1864. His name appears on a list of prisoners received from New Orleans at Ship Island, Mississippi, on October 25, 1864. He was exchanged at Ship Island on January 4, 1865.

Cledi, C., Pvt. Co. H

His name appears on a regimental return for June 1862, with the notation "sent to the rear on 28, May".

Clieland, J. H., Pvt./Corp. Co. C.

Enlisted on November 28, 1861, at Fort Gaines, Alabama, by Captain Rembert for 12 months. His name appears on a company muster roll for bounty on September 24, 1862. Company muster rolls for December 31, 1862, to April 30, 1863, and May/June 1863, report him present. Muster roll for September/October 1863, report him present and having lost one haversack at $1 and one canteen at $2. POW captured at Fort Gaines, Alabama, on August 8, 1864. POW captured at Fort Gaines, Alabama, on August 8, 1864. His name appears on a list of prisoners received from New Orleans at Ship Island, Mississippi, on October 25, 1864. He was exchanged at Ship Island on January 4, 1865. His name appears on a list of POW's surrendered by Lt. General Richard Taylor at Citronelle, Alabama, on May 4, 1865, and paroled at Meridian, Mississippi, on May 13, 1865. Residence shown as Marengo County, Alabama. There is a signed pay voucher in his file.*

Cluck, N. M., Pvt. Co. C

Paid $44 on February 16, 1864, on descriptive list for service from September 1, to December 31, 1863.

Cluis, Fredrick V., 1st Lt./Captain Field and Staff

Mustered into State Service on April 1, 1861, mustered into Confederate Service October 13, 1861. Elected 1st Lt. on June 5, 1861. Appointed ACS [*Commissary?*] on March 19, 1862, and transferred to commissary at Fort Morgan. His name appears on a regimental return for December 1861, shown absent "on short leave since the 28th, to return today". On April 8, 1861, he requisitioned subsistence stores for the 21st Alabama at Corinth, Mississippi, as follows; 15 barrels of flour, 750 lbs bulk pork, 1800 lbs salt beef, 150 lbs rice, 300 lbs sugar, 40 lbs crackers adamantine [*very hard*], 100 lbs lard, 1 sack salt (4 bushels), 1 barrel molasses (40 gallons), 250 lbs peas or beans (four pecks, 5 quarts). A regimental return for June 1862, reports him 1st Lt. present at Tupelo, Mississippi, acting Commissary since March 20, 1862. A register of commissioned officers of PACS shows him dropped on May 8, 1862. A field return for October 1862, reports him absent on leave since ? 30, 1862. A field return of Harbor Brigade at Fort Morgan of the 21st Alabama, for November 1862, reports him transferred from Fort Morgan to Choctaw Bluff, Alabama, on special orders of District Headquarters. He signed an Oath of Allegiance to the USA at Meridian, Mississippi, on May 10, 1865. There is paper work in his file.*

Coafers, C. C. R., Pvt. Co. D
Withdrawn and filed with **C. C. R. Cooper**

Cochran, H., Pvt. Co. A
Enlisted on October 6, 1862, at Mobile, Alabama, by Captain DeVaux for the war. His name appears as present on company muster rolls for December 31, 1862, to April 30, 1863, May/June 1863, and September/October 1863. There is a reference card in his file to see personal papers of **Geo. T. Bailey**, Co. A, 21st Alabama Infantry. Transferred to CS Navy on June 2, 1864.

Code, W. P., Pvt. Co. H see **Cade, W. P.**

Coe, William, Pvt. Co. K
Enlisted at Columbia ?, on February 25, 1861, by Lt. Wellborn for three years. Company muster roll for July/August 1863, reports him present. Company muster roll for September/October 1863, reports him present under arrest at this Post.

Cogburn, John D. 2nd Lt. Co. D
Enlisted at Mobile, Alabama, by Captain Butt. Elected 2nd Lt. on July 23, 1862, promoted on August 30, 1862. Returns at Fort Morgan for October, November, and December 1862, report him present. Company muster rolls for November/December 1862, July/August 1862, September/October 1863, November/December 1863 and September/October 1864, report him present. The September/October 1864, roll he signed as commanding the company. His name appears on a register of Ross Hospital at Mobile, Alabama, admitted October 14, 1863, with int. fever tert. Retuned to duty October 21, 1863. His name appears on a register of Ross Hospital at Mobile, Alabama, where he was admitted on February 21, 1864, with a gunshot wound. Retuned to duty on March 8, 1864. He appears on an inspection report of Heavy Artillery stationed near Mobile, Alabama, Department of the Gulf on October 17, 1864, where he is shown stationed at Appalachee Batteries, absent sick in hospital since September 4, 1864. He was paid $80 per month as 2nd Lt. POW surrendered by Lt. General Richard Taylor at Citronelle, Alabama, and paroled at Meridian, Mississippi, on May 13, 1865. He signed a parole at Meridian Mississippi, on May 10, 1865. His parole and a number of pay vouchers are in his file.**

Cogin, Alex, Sgt. Co. H
Enlisted October 13, 1861, at Mobile, by Julius DeVaux. He was born in Anney (Jarorie), France, fifty years old, five foot eight inches, dark complexion, brown eyes, brown hair and by occupation a distiller. Discharged on disability, November 29, 1861.

Colby, John, Pvt. Co. I
His name appears on a regimental return for June 1862, at Mobile. He deserted, was furloughed and missing since.

Cole, William E., Pvt. Co. A

Enlisted on March 20, 1863, at Choctaw Bluff, Alabama, by Captain Cothran for three years or the war. He appears present with company on muster rolls from time of enlistment through May/June 1863. Company muster roll for September/October 1863, reports him absent on detached guard duty at Choctaw Bluff, Alabama, by order of Colonel Anderson. POW captured at Fort Morgan, Alabama, on August 23, 1864. Received from New Orleans at Elmira, New York, on October 8, 1864. He was transferred and forwarded via Point Lookout to James River for exchange on February 13, 1865. Received at Boulwares and Cox Wharf, James River on February 20, 1865 among 3038 paroled Confederate Prisoners of War. He was admitted to Receiving and Wayside Hospital or General Hospital No. 9 Richmond, Virginia, on February 21. Transferred to Howard's Grove Hospital on February 22, 1865, with smallpox. He died at Howard's Grove on March 19, 1865.

Coleman, Lafayettte, W., Pvt. Co. E

Enlisted on October 13, 1861, at Mobile, Alabama, by Captain Chamberlain for the war. His name appears on a register near Tupelo, Mississippi, June 28, 1862, sent to Jackson, Mississippi, from Corinth House by order of Dr. Heustis. His name appears on a company muster roll for bounty on September 24, 1862, where he is shown as absent on surgeon's certificate. Company muster rolls for November/December 1862, and July/August 1863 report him present. Company muster roll for September/October 1863, shows him present and due pay of $67.23 for clothing not drawn. POW surrendered on May 4, 1865, by Lt. General Richard Taylor at Citronelle, Alabama, and paroled at Meridian, Mississippi, May 13, 1865. Residence shown as Madison County, Mississippi.

Coley, J. A., Pvt. Co. F see **Colley, J. A.**

Colley, J. A., Pvt. Co. F

Enlisted at Talladega, Alabama, on August 31, 1862, by W. T. Walthhall for three years. He appears present on company muster roll for December 31, 1862, to June 30, 1863. Company muster roll for September/October 1863, reports him present and charged $1 for haversack. He was admitted to Post Hospital at Fort Morgan, Alabama, on January 6, 1864, with int. fever, returned to duty on January 12. He appears on a hospital muster roll for July/August 1864, at Shelby Springs, Alabama. His name appears on a register of Ross Hospital at Mobile, Alabama, as having been admitted on August 8, 1864, with chronic rheumatism and sent to General Hospital at Selma. He appears on a register of 1st Mississippi CSA Hospital Jackson, Mississippi, admitted on August 13, 1864, with chronic rheumatism, returned to duty on September 29, 1864. Company muster roll for September/October 1864, reports him present. He was admitted again to Ross Hospital at Mobile on January 3, 1865, with acute dysentery and returned to duty on January 17, 1865. He was paroled at Talladega, Alabama, by Brevet Brigadier General M. H. Chrysler on May 22, 1865.

Collin, Celestin, 1st Lt. Co. K see **Collins, C. LeB.**

Collins, C. LeB., 1st Lt. Co. K

Elected 2nd Lt. on October 13, 1861, resigned on November 1, 1861. A regimental return for December 1861, reports him present as 2nd Lt. His resignation accepted by General Bragg on December 15, 1861. Elected 1st Lt. on May 8, 1862. Regimental return at Tupelo, Mississippi, for June 1862, shows him present as 1st Lt. He appears present for company muster for bounty on September 24, 1862. Company muster roll for November/December 1862, reports him absent A. Q. M. of post by order of Colonel Anderson. Company muster rolls for July/August and September/October 1863, report him absent on detached service as AQM. Company muster roll for September/October 1864, reports him absent taken prisoner at Fort Morgan, Alabama, in August 1864. He appears in a register of POW's at New Orleans, Louisiana, captured at Fort Morgan on August 23, 1864, sent to New York on October 1, 1864. He was confined at Fort Lafayette in New York Harbor on October 20, 1864, and released June 12, 1865. Signed and swore an Oath of Allegiance to the USA at Fort Warren Boston Harbor, Massachusetts, June 12, 1865. Residence Mobile, Alabama, light complexion, brown hair, blue eyes, five foot four inches. Reference card to see personal papers of **J. A. Law**, Captain Co. D, 1st Battalion, Alabama Artillery. There is an unusually large amount of paper work in Lt. Collins file.****

Collins, Patrick, Pvt._

Enlisted on August 23, 1864, at Mobile, Alabama, by Major Stone for the war. He appears present on Captain Sossaman's Detachment of the 21st Alabama, Infantry for September/October 1864, at Mobile.

Cometa, C., Pvt. Co. G

Killed at Shiloh April 5, 1862, at 7 A. M. in attack on 1st Battery.

Conden, John, Pvt. Co. D

Enlisted on October 13, 1861, At Mobile, Alabama, by Captain Butt for the war. He appears present on company muster rolls for November/December 1861. He was wounded slightly on April 6, 1862, at 7 A. M. at Shiloh while advancing during attack on 1st Battery. POW captured at Pittsburg Landing at hospital on April 7 or 8, 1862. His name appears on a roll of POW's at Camp Douglas, Illinois, August 1, 1862. He appears present on company muster rolls for July/August 1863, September/October 1863, and November/December 1863. He was admitted to Ross Hospital at Mobile on January 22, 1864, with chronic rheumatism and sent to General Hospital in Montgomery on February 17, 1864. Company muster roll for September/October 1864, reports that he was transferred from General Hospital at Mobile to Greenville [*Alabama*] on October 25, 1864. He was admitted to Ross Hospital at Mobile on December 28, 1864, with chronic diarrhoea and returned to duty on February 26, 1865. POW captured at Blakeley, Alabama, on April 9, 1865. Received at Ship Island, Mississippi, on April 15, 1865 and transferred to Vicksburg, Mississippi, for exchange on May 1, 1865.

Condlich see **Candlish, William G.**, Corporal/Pvt. Co. A

Condon, John see **Conden, John**

Connell, P. F., Pvt. Co. E

Mortally wounded in the breast at Shiloh while advancing and carrying colors at First Camp at 9 A. M., April 6, 1862. He was captured at hospital.

Connells, George, Pvt. Co. G

His name appears on a regimental return during June 1862. On May 12, at Corinth he was reported missing from picket guard.

Connely, James, Pvt. Co. C

He was reported with a broken leg by musket ball [at Shiloh]. His name appears on a regimental return for June 1862, at Tupelo. On June 15, he was transferred to Captain Myers Sharpshooters Battalion.

Conner, L. W.

Only a name card exists in this man's file.

Contra, B., Pvt. Co. H

His name appears on a regimental return for June 1862. He is reported missing on march, cancelled.

Contrelle, M., Pvt. Co. K

Enlisted on July 4, 1863, at Fort Morgan, Alabama, by Captain Dorgan for the war. On company muster rolls for July/August and September/October 1863, he is shown present but also absent without leave for three days in September.

Cook, James B., Pvt. Co. E

Enlisted August 23, 1863, at Gainesville, Alabama, by Colonel Roper for the war. Company muster roll for September/October 1863, reports him present. POW captured at Fort Gaines, Alabama, on August 8, 1864. Pvt. Cook was admitted to St. Louis USA General Hospital at New Orleans with diarrhoea on September 1, 1864, and returned to duty on September 24, 1864, age 40. He was received at Ship Island, Mississippi, on October 25, 1864, from New Orleans. He was exchanged on January 4, 1865, and admitted to Ross Hospital at Mobile, Alabama, on January 7, 1865, with chronic diarrhoea then returned to duty on January 11. POW surrendered on May 4, 1865, by Lt. General Richard Taylor at Citronelle, Alabama, and paroled at Meridian, Mississippi, on May 13, 1865. Residence shown as Greene County, Alabama.

Cook, John, Pvt. Co. D

Paid $32.70 on voucher for service and clothing October 1, to November 3, 1861. He was discharged from the 21st Alabama Infantry on March 10, 1862. Five foot seven inches, gray eyes, sallow complexion, age 24, by profession a teacher, signed by his mark "X". He was admitted to USA General Hospital at Danville, Virginia, on August 7, 1864, with chronic diarrhoea. Here his record shows he was a member of Co. D, 7th Battalion, Alabama and 21st Alabama Infantry. POW surrendered on May 4, 1865, by Lt. General Richard Taylor at Citronelle, Alabama, and paroled at Meridian, Mississippi, on May 13, 1865. Residence shown as Choctaw County, Alabama.

Cook, Nicholas, Pvt. Co. F

Enlisted on October 13, 1861, at Baldwin County, Alabama, by Captain McCoy for one year. His name appears on a regimental, return for June 1862, with the note "sent to interior hospital". A report near Tupelo, Mississippi, shows he was sent from Corinth Hospital on surgeon's certificate May 23, 1862. He appears present on a company muster roll for September 24, 1862, with the notation "not a white man".

Cooper, C. C. R., Pvt. Co. D

Enlisted at Montgomery, Alabama, on July 22, 1863, for the war. Company muster rolls for July/August, September/October and November/December 1863, all show him present. Company muster roll for September/October 1864, reports him absent, sent to General Hospital at Mobile on September 10, 1864. He signed a parole at Headquarters of [US] 16th Army Corps. Provost Marshal's Office at Montgomery, Alabama, on June 9, 1865. He is shown as five foot four inches, black hair, black eyes, and tan complexion.

Cooper, James, Corp./Pvt. Co. F

Enlisted in Baldwin County, Alabama, on October 13, 1861, by Captain McCoy for three years or the war. He appears present on a company muster roll for bounty dated September 24, 1862. Company muster roll for September/October 1863, reports him absent sick in hospital at Mobile since October ?, 1863, reduced to ranks by Colonel Anderson on September 1, 1863. POW captured at Fort Gaines, Alabama, on August 9, 1864. He was received at Ship Island, Mississippi, from New Orleans on October 25, 1864. He was exchanged at Ship Island on January 5, 1865. He deserted at Fort Morgan, on April 7, 1865. Confined as POW at New Orleans on April 13, 1865, and released on April 14, upon taking the Oath of Allegiance to the USA by order of General Canby. His name appears on a roll of prisoners forwarded to New Orleans from Fort Gaines. Here he is show as Joseph S. Cooper who deserted at Spanish Fort, Alabama, on March 21, 1865, arrived at Fort Morgan on April 4, 1865. * [*There may be two soldiers records in this file.*]

Cooper, Joseph, Corp./Pvt. Co. F. see **Cooper, James**

Cooper, W. H., Pvt. Co. E.

His name appears on a list of sick and wounded at General Hospital Howard's Grove at Richmond, Virginia, as having been retired on March 23, 186? His name also appears on a register of claims of deceased soldiers. Claim presented by James M. Martin Attorney on June 11, 1862.

Cople, R. E., Pvt. Co. E

His name appears on a file at USA General Hospital, Camp Dennison, Ohio, wounded in chest. Again at USA General Hospital at Camp Dennison as being admitted on April 18, 1862, with vul. sclopet [*vulnus sclopeticum - gun shot wound*].

Cordray, J., Pvt. Co. ?

Enlisted at Mobile, Alabama, by Major Stone for the war. He appears absent on a company muster roll for September/October 1864, reported to be temporarily attached (to Major Harris at Fort Gaines, by General Gardner?).

Corley, John, Pvt. Co. C

Enlisted on October 13, 1861, at Mobile, Alabama, by Captain Rembert for the war. He appears present on a company muster roll for bounty dated September 24, 1862. Company muster rolls for December 31, 1862, to April 30, 1863, May/June, 1863, September/October 1863, all report him present. POW captured at Fort Gaines, Alabama, on August 8, 1864. He was received at Ship Island, Mississippi, from New Orleans on October 25, 1864, and exchanged at Ship Island on January 8, 1864. POW captured again at Blakeley, Alabama, on April 9, 1865, and received at Ship Island on April 15, 1865. He was transferred to Vicksburg, Mississippi, for exchange on May 1, 1865.

Corly, John, Pvt. Co. C. see **Corley, John**

Cornation, A., Pvt. Co. E

POW captured at Fort Gaines, Alabama, on August 8, 1864. He appears on a list of POW's at New Orleans that were sent to Ship Island, Mississippi, and exchanged on January 4, 1865.

Corri, John, Pvt. Co. H

His name appears on a report near Tupelo, Mississippi, on June 28, 1862, sent to interior from Corinth at the time of evacuation. He also appears on a register of claims of deceased soldiers. Claim filed by Chas. DeVaux Attorney. Born Genoa, Italy, died at Mobile, Alabama.

Cortright, Jerome S., Pvt. Co. A

Enlisted at Mobile, Alabama, on October 13, 1861, by Major Hessee. He appears present on a company muster roll for bounty dated September 24, 1862. Company muster rolls for December 31, 1862, to April 30, 1863, and May/June 1863, report him present. Company muster roll for September/October 1863, reports him absent, sent to General Hospital at Mobile on October 25, 1863. POW captured at Fort Morgan, Alabama, on August 23, 1864, sent to New York on September 27, 1864. He was received at Elmira, New York, on October 8, 1864, from New Orleans. His name appears on a list of POW's at Elmira, New York, who desire to take the Oath of Allegiance to the USA. "Volunteered Oct. 13, 1861, for 12 months, was conscripted at expiration of term of enlistment. Has an uncle in Ingman's Ferry, Pike, Pa. to whom he desires to go." He was released on March 20, 1865, upon taking the Oath of Allegiance to the USA. Resides at Mobile, Alabama, ruddy complexion, auburn hair, blue eyes, five foot ten inches, age 21.

Costa, B., Pvt. Co. H

His name appears on a regimental return for June 1862, May 30, [missing] on march, supposed to be in the hands of the enemy. His name appears on a report near

Tupelo, Mississippi, on June 28, 1862, "lost 1 gun, have not been heard from since May 30, suppose to have fallen into the hands of the enemy". He appears on a register of claims filed for deceased soldiers. Claim filed by Chas. DeVaux, Attorney on Aug. 22. Born Bastia, France.

Costantino, Grano, Pvt. Co. G

Paid $44 for service March 1, to June 30, on a voucher. He signed by his mark "X". The voucher is in his file.

Coswell, J., Pvt. Co. E.

His name appears on a register of Receiving and Wayside Hospital or General Hospital No. 9 at Richmond, Virginia. He was admitted on March 18, 1865, sent to Camp Lee on March 19

Cothran, John, F., 2nd Lt./Captain Co. A

Elected 2nd Lt. on April 2, 1862, promoted on May 8, 1862. His name appears on a regimental return for June 1862. Wounded in his knee, slightly at Shiloh at 3 P. M. on April 6, 1862. He is shown present at his station near Tupelo, Mississippi, elected 1st Lt. on May 8, at reorganization; appointment not yet received. He appears present on a company muster roll for bounty dated September 24, 1862. A field return in October 1862, reports him transferred to Choctaw Bluff, Alabama, on October 6, 1862, from Fort Morgan. Company muster roll for December 31, 1862, to April 30, 1863, reports him present. Muster roll for May/June 1863, reports him present sick in quarters. Company muster roll for September/ October 1863, reports him absent with leave. He was elected Captain on May 8, 1862, and promoted on August 30, 1862. POW captured at Fort Morgan, Alabama, on August 23, 1864, sent to New Orleans and to New York on October 12, 1864. He was confined at Fort Lafayette, New York Harbor on October 20, 1864. He signed an Oath of Allegiance to the USA at Fort Delaware, Delaware, and was released on June 17, 1865. Residence Mobile, Alabama, complexion dark, hair dark, eyes blue, five foot nine inches. He requisitioned 39 pair of shoes for the company as "the men are entirely barefooted" [*not dated*]. Received at Fort Morgan on September 24, 1862, for Co. A, 13 jackets, 18 pair pants, 13 caps, 28 shirts, 42 pair drawers and 32 pair shoes. Received at Choctaw Bluff, on January 19, 1863, 65 pair pants, 65 jackets, 65 caps, 65 blankets and 65 pair drawers "packed in one case". Received at Choctaw Bluff, on January 30, 1863, 8 pair shoes. There are a number of company requisitions and pay vouchers in Captain Cothran's file.***

Cothurn, J. F., Lt./Captain Co. A see **Cothran, John F**

Couch, Henry V., Pvt./2nd Lt. Co. K

Enlisted on February 25, 1863, at Fort Morgan, Alabama, by Captain Dorgan for the war. Company muster rolls for July/August 1863, and September/October 1863, report him present on extra duty as brigade clerk. POW at New Orleans captured at Fort Gaines, Alabama, on August 3, 1864 and escaped on October 22, 1864. *He signed "with a flourish"* his parole on May 10, 1865, at Meridian, Mississippi, as having been surrendered by Lt. General Richard Taylor at Citronelle, Alabama. His parole is in his file.*

Couch, J. E., Pvt. Co. K
Enlisted on August 30, 1862, at Fort Morgan, Alabama, by Captain Dorgan for the war. He appears present on a company muster roll for bounty dated September 24, 1862. Company muster rolls for November/December 1862, July/August 1863, September/October 1863 and September/October 1864, all report him present. POW a member of Co. K. 21st Alabama Regiment, Holtzclaw's Brigade commanded by 1st Lt. Wm. L. Brainard. He was surrendered by Lt General Richard Taylor at Citronelle, Alabama, on May 4, 1865, and paroled at Meridian, Mississippi, on May 10, 1865. Residence shown as Shubuta, Clarke County, Mississippi.

Couch, O. W., Pvt. Co. K.
Enlisted on June 1, 1864, at Fort Powell by Captain Dorgan, for the war. He appears present on company muster roll for September/October 1864. POW surrendered by Lt General Richard Taylor at Citronelle, Alabama, on May 4, 1865, and paroled at Meridian, Mississippi, on May 10, 1865. Residence shown as Shubuta, Clarke County, Mississippi.

Courtney, William P., Pvt. Co. I
He was wounded at Shiloh on April 6, 1862, at 8:30 A. M. while attacking 1st Fort. He was admitted to USA hospital steamer *Empress*, on April 15, 1862, as POW with vul. sclop. [*gunshot wound*], sent to General Hospital at Keokuk, Iowa, on April 20, 1862. His name appears on a list of POW's received at US Hospital, Keokuk, Iowa, on April 20, 1862. Captured at Pittsburg Landing, Tennessee, on April 6, 1862. "Gunshot wound through both thighs." Died at Keokuk, Iowa, on May 25, 1863, of vul. sclopoticum [*gunshot wound*].

Cortwright, Jerome S., Pvt. Co. A see **Cortright, Jerome S.**

Covington, George, Pvt. Co. K
Enlisted on March 10, 1862, at Fort Pillow by Captain Stewart for the war. His name appears on a list of men who returned without arms in Wither's Division, 1st Brigade. "Gun shattered in battle" no date. He appears present on a company muster roll for bounty dated September 24, 1862. Company muster rolls for November/December 1862, July/August 1863, report him present. Company muster roll for September/October 1863, reports him absent with leave on furlough for two days October 29. Muster roll for September/October 1864, reports him absent sick since October "furnished certificate from Medical Board." POW surrendered by Lt General Richard Taylor at Citronelle, Alabama, on May 4, 1865, and paroled at Meridian, Mississippi, on May 13, 1865. Residence shown as Mobile, Mobile County, Alabama.

Cox, ? Pvt. Co. I
This name appears on a regimental return for December 1861.

Cox, F. H., 4th Sgt. Co. K

POW surrendered by Lt General Richard Taylor at Citronelle, Alabama, on May 4, 1865, and paroled at Meridian, Mississippi, on May 13, 1865. Residence shown as Mobile, Mobile County, Alabama.

Cox, J. R., Pvt. Co. ?

Enlisted on October 2, 1864, at Mobile, Alabama, by Major Stone for the war. He appears present on a company muster roll for September/October 1864, as having been temporarily assigned to ? Or. by Major Stone, Exec. Officer.

Coyle, James, Pvt. Co. K

Enlisted on November 25, 1862, at Fort Morgan, Alabama, by Captain Dorgan for the war. He appears present on company muster rolls for November/December 1862, July/August 1863, September/October 1863 and September/October 1864. POW surrendered by Lt General Richard Taylor at Citronelle, Alabama, on May 4, 1865, and paroled at Meridian, Mississippi, on May 13, 1865. Residence shown as Mobile, Mobile County, Alabama.

Craven, John, Pvt. Co. G.

Drew clothing on May 3 and June 1, 1864. POW captured at Fort Gaines, Alabama, on August 8, 1864. He was received at Ship Island, Mississippi, from New Orleans on October 25, 1864, and exchanged at Ship Island on January 4, 1865.

Crawford, James, Colonel Field and Staff

Entered service on July 1, 1861. His name appears on a roster of 21st Regiment of Alabama Volunteers, 3rd Brigade, District of the Gulf, and having been mustered into Confederate service on October 13, 1861, for 12 months. Elected Colonel on July 22, 1861. Resigned on May 1, 1862, successor was **C. D. Anderson.** He drew $195 per month as Colonel.

Crawford, R. L., Pvt. Co. K

His name appears on a regimental return for June 1862, near Tupelo, Mississippi, as having been discharged June 28, 1862, by order of General Bragg. He was discharged to accept a position on the staff of General Ledbetter on SO No. 47-2 dated June 24, 1862. On November 12, 1862, at Mobile, Mr. Samuel A. Roberts and E. L. Dorgan wrote to His Excellency Jefferson Davis a letter which in Pvt. Crawford's file.

                                        Mobile 12, 1864

His Excellency Jefferson Davis
    Dear Sir,

                My young friend Robert Crawford the bearer of this will go to Richmond, as soon as his health has re established to endeavor to get an appointment in the CSA. He is a native of this place, the son of an old and much valued friend of mine for many years. Most al?of the S. Dist. of Alabama as most ?

He volunteered at the beginning of the war & served in the 21st Ala was in the .... at Corinth was in the ranks (I think) and was subsequently on General Ledbetter's' staff where he served through the Campaign in Kentucky. The change in Genl. L's position in the Army has thrown him out of service. The officers with whom he has .... Very Truly, Your Friend and Obt. Svt.
Samuel A. Roberts.

The bearer of this Mr. Robert Crawford I know as a young man of character and worth. His father and mother and all connected with him are all people of truth and honesty. He himself is a person to be relied on at any place he may be placed he will prove the truth of the above statement made in reference to him. I recommend him to the favorable consideration of the Secretary of War for some place of position in the army in which he would be of service. ....not to be found in the county. E. S. Dorgan.

Richmond, 11, Feb. 1863.
Sir,
I beg leave respectfully to recommend Robert Crawford, Eq. of Ala. for the appointment of Judge Advocate for General Forney's Army Corps in place of John Lehle Smith Eq. deceased.
Mr. Crawford is a young lawyer of very respectable ? and is a man of excellent character & I am sure fill the place extremely well.
He is now in the public service as a soldier & entitled to the confidence of the ? Very Respf.
F. S. Lyon

[*Francis Strother Lyon – Confederate Congressman from Alabama*]
Vouchers in his file show that he drew pay, subsistence and commutation for food and clothing on detached service with Commissary Department, clerk in AAG and Signal Corps at Mobile, through March 1, 1864. There is much paperwork in his file.**

Crawford, T. E., Pvt. Co. K
Enlisted on October 10, 1863, at Fort Morgan, Alabama, for the war. He appears present on company muster rolls for September/October 1863 and September/October 1864. POW surrendered by Lt General Richard Taylor at Citronelle, Alabama, on May 4, 1865, and paroled at Meridian, Mississippi, on May 13, 1865. Residence shown as Mt. Pleasant, Clarke County, Alabama.

Crawles, B., Pvt. Co. A
His name appears on a register at Jackson Hospital, Richmond, Virginia. He was admitted on March 8, 1865, with debilities and furloughed on March 9.

Creel, W. C., Pvt. Co. F
There is only a card indicating a reference envelope in his file.

Crenshaw, G. W., Pvt. Co. I

Enlisted on May 6, 1863, at Fort Morgan, Alabama, by Lt. Donoho for the war. He appears present on company muster rolls for July/August 1863 and September/October 1863. POW captured at Fort Gaines on August 8, 1864. He was received at Ship Island, Mississippi, from New Orleans on October 23, 1864, and exchanged at Ship Island on January 5, 1865. He appears on a descriptive list, May 22, 1863, at Fort Morgan. Age 35, gray eyes, dark hair, fair complexion, five foot eight inches, born in Georgia.

Crenshaw, James, Pvt. Co. C

Enlisted on February 18, 1863, at Choctaw Bluff, Alabama, by Captain Smith for the war. He appears present on muster rolls from December 31, 1862, to April 30, 1863, May/June 1863 and September/October 1863. POW captured at Fort Gaines on August 8, 1864. He was received at Ship Island, Mississippi, from New Orleans on October 25, 1864. He died at Ship Island of pneumonia on January 3, 1865, and was buried in grave No. 129. [*Note these graves no longer exist.*]

Crenshaw, M. V. Captain Co. I

Elected 1st Lt. on May 8, 1862, promoted on August 30, 1862. He appears present on a company bounty muster roll September 24, 1862. He was elected Captain on August 30, 1862. In September 1862, he requisitioned fuel at Fort Morgan, for 1 Captain, 2 Subalterns and 51 non-coms, musicians and privates. Regimental returns from Fort Morgan, Alabama, show him present in November and December 1862. Company muster rolls for July/August 1863 and September/October 1863 report him present. He drew $130 per month as Captain. On September 17, 1862, he requisitioned and received for his Company I, 19 Jackets, 38 pants, 16 caps, 35 shirts, 39 pair drawers and 34 pair shoes. He was admitted to Ross Hospital in Mobile, on September 28, 1863, with int. fever tert, and returned to duty on October 6, 1863. On January 30, 1863, he received for his company; 31 muskets, 54 cartridge boxes, 54 waist belts, 56 cap pouches, 56 bayonet scabbards; 56 knapsacks, 56 haversacks, 56 canteens, 1620 ball cartridges and 1944 caps at Fort Morgan. He requisitioned 56 pair of shoes for Co. I "men being entirely barefooted". On May 20, 1864, he requisitioned and received the following ordnance for his 85 officers and men in Co. I; 57 muskets, 57 bayonets, 51 cartridge boxes, 9 C B Belts, 58 waist belts, 53 cap pouches, 55 bayonet scabbards, 83 knapsacks, 74 canteens and 74 canteen straps. POW captured at Fort Gaines on August 8, 1864. He was admitted to St. Louis or USA General Hospital at New Orleans on August 23, 1864, with fever remittent and returned to prison on August 26, 1864, age 24. He was received at Ship Island, Mississippi, from New Orleans on November 25, [*or November 5*] 1864. He was exchanged at Ship Island on January 4, 1865. POW surrendered by Lt General Richard Taylor at Citronelle, Alabama, on May 4, 1865, and paroled at Meridian, Mississippi, on May 10, 1865. His parole is in his file as well as many pay vouchers and material requisitions. **

Crenshaw, Samuel, Pvt. Co. I

Enlisted on October 17, 1861, at Mobile, Alabama, by Major Hessee for the war. Company muster roll for July/August 1863, shows him present. Company muster roll for

September/October 1863, reports him absent sick in general hospital in Mobile, since September 19, 1863. He was admitted to Ross Hospital in Mobile on September 21, 1863, with int. fever quotd. and furloughed on October 26, for 20 days. His name appears on a receipt roll for December 1863, where he was paid $2.40 at Mobile for work as a carpenter.

Crewen, John, 2nd Corporal Co. G

His name appears on a roll of POW's of Co. G, 21st Alabama Volunteers, Holtzclaw's Brigade Confederate States Army commanded by Edw. R Spaulding surrendered by Lt General Richard Taylor at Citronelle, Alabama, on May 4, 1865, and paroled at Meridian, Mississippi, on May 13, 1865. Residence shown as Mobile, Mobile County, Alabama.

Crim, E., Pvt. Co. B.

His name appears on a list of POW stragglers paroled at Selma, Alabama, during the month of June 1865. Residence shown as Shelby County, Alabama.

Crock, C. O., Pvt. Co. A see **Crocker, Charles O.**

Crocker, Charles O., Pvt. Co. A

Enlisted October 13, 1861, at Mobile, Alabama, by Major Hessee for three years or the war. His name appears on a regimental return for June 1862, on detached service as hospital nurse. He appears on a company muster roll for bounty on September 1862, he is reported absent on detached service from April 14, 1862, at Corinth as hospital nurse by order of General Chambers. Company muster rolls for December 31, 1862, to April 30, 1863, May/June 1863 and September/October 1863, report him absent on detached service as a hospital nurse on orders of General Chambers. He appears on a roll in March 1863, of employees at Hospital in Tunnel Hill, Georgia, as ward master. May/June 1863, muster roll reports him detached as nurse at Ringgold, Georgia. He appears on a list of men detached in General Johnston's Department, stationed at Dalton Georgia, detailed as a nurse on April 19, 1863. Company muster roll for September/October 1864, still shows him absent detached at Ross Hospital by order of General Maury. POW surrendered by Lt General Richard Taylor at Citronelle, Alabama, on May 4, 1865, and paroled at Meridian, Mississippi, on May 10, 1865. Residence shown as Mobile, Alabama.

Crony, Jos., Pvt. Co. D

Wounded in the right and left breast at Shiloh on April 6, 1862, at 4:30 P. M. while advancing. POW captured at hospital on April 7, 1862.

Crosby, Daniel, Pvt. Co. D see **Crosby, D. M.**

Crosby, D. M., Pvt. Co. D

Enlisted at DeSoto, Mississippi, on December 13, 1861, by Captain Butt for the war. He appears present on a company muster roll for bounty on September 24, 1862. Company muster roll for November/December 1862, reports him present. July/August

1863, roll reports him on extra duty at Fort Morgan. September/October 1863, roll reports him present and November/December 1863, roll reports him absent detailed at Fort Morgan in Commissary Department. POW captured on August 8, 1864, at Fort Gaines, Alabama. His name appears on a morning report, October 4, 1864, of POW's confined at Steam Levee Press No. 4 in New Orleans, Louisiana. He was admitted to St. Louis USA General Hospital at New Orleans on August 20, 1864, with fever intermittent and returned to prison on September 5, 1864. (Here he is shown as Pvt. **David Crosby**, Co. H., age 26) He was admitted to St. Louis US Army General Hospital on October 4, 1864, by order of the Medical Director, Department of the Gulf, with acute diarrhoea, returned to prison on October 22. [He is shown as Pvt. **Daniel Crosby**, Co. D, age 19.]

Croty, M., Pvt. Co. I

Enlisted August 12, 1862, at Fort Morgan, Alabama, by Lt. Collins. He appears present on a company muster roll for bounty on September 24, 1862. His name appears on a return for November 1862, as having been transferred to 1st Battalion Alabama Artillery.

Crouch, Henry D., Pvt. Co. C

He enlisted at Fort Gaines, Alabama. He was killed while charging at Shiloh on April 6, 1861. His widow Linna C. Crouch was paid for his service time from February 28, 1862, to April 5, 1862.

Crowley, David, Pvt. Co. A

Enlisted on October 13, 1861, at Mobile, Alabama, by Major Hessee for the war. He appears present on a company muster roll for bounty on September 24, 1862. Company muster rolls for December 31, 1862, to April 30, 1863, May/June 1863, and September/October 1863, report him present. POW at New Orleans captured at Fort Morgan on August 23, 1864. He was received at Elmira, New York, on October 8, 1864, from New Orleans. Paroled at Elmira for exchange March 2, 1865, and sent to James River. POW surrendered by Lt General Richard Taylor at Citronelle, Alabama, on May 4, 1865, and paroled at Meridian, Mississippi, on May 13, 1865. Residence shown as Mobile, Alabama.

Cubicke, A. Pvt. Co. K

Enlisted at Fort Morgan, Alabama, on August 11, 1863, by Captain Dorgan for the war. Company muster roll for July/August 1863, reports him present. Company muster roll for September/October 1863, reports him absent detached for special service on October 15, by order of General Maury. Company muster roll for September/October 1864, reports him absent detached for special service on October 15, by order of General Maury.

Cuddigan, John, Pvt. Co. K see **Cuddington, John**

Cuddington, John, Pvt. Co. K

Enlisted on January 5, 1864, at Mobile, Alabama, by Colonel Miller for the war. He was admitted to Post Hospital at Fort Morgan on January 26, 1864, with int. fever, sent to general hospital on January 26, 1864. He was admitted to Ross Hospital in Mobile with a hernia and returned to duty on February 29, 1864, then admitted again to Ross Hospital on April 4, 1864, with rupture and discharged from service on April 15, 1864, (outdoor patient). His name appears on a hospital muster roll for January/February 1864, at General Hospital Ross at Mobile employed as a nurse. Detailed by Hospital Examining Board to be paid $15.50 per month. (Never was paid). His discharge is in his file and his name is spelled **John Cuddigan.** He was conscripted, born in Cork, Ireland, age 46, five foot five and one half inches, light complexion, blue eyes, a gardener by occupation.*

Cummings, W., Pvt. Co. E
   Killed in the A. M. on April 6, 1862, at Shiloh while attacking the 15th Battery. Shot through the head.

Cummins, John, Pvt. Co. A
   His name appears on a regimental return for June 1862, where it was reported that he was sent to interior hospital on June 18. He was discharged on July 7, 1862.

Cummins, Robert H., Pvt. Co. K
   Enlisted at Mobile, Alabama, October 13, 1861. He was discharged on November 20, 1861, at Mobile by order of General Withers as being unfit for duty noted by Dr. Nott. Born in Mobile, Alabama, age 20, five foot nine and one half inches, dark complexion, gray eyes, dark hair and by occupation a clerk. His discharge is in his file.*

Cummins, William, Corporal/Sergeant Co. K
   Enlisted on October 13, 1861, at Mobile, Alabama, by Captain Stewart for the war. He appears present on a company muster roll for bounty on September 24, 1862. Company muster rolls for November/December 1862 and July/August 1863, report him present promoted from 1st Corporal on August 1, 1863. Company muster roll for September/October 1863, reports him absent on surgeon's certificate to November 6, 1863. He was admitted to Ross Hospital at Mobile on October 26, 1863, with acute rheumatism and returned to duty on December 1. Company muster roll for September/October 1864, reports him absent in hospital since October 20, 1864, by order of Assistant Surgeon Armstrong. Admitted to Ross Hospital at Mobile on July 15, 1864, with scabies and retuned to duty on July 22. POW captured at Spanish Fort, Alabama, on April 8, 1865. Received at Ship Island, Mississippi, on April 10, 1865. Paroled at Ship Island and sent to Vicksburg, Mississippi, for exchange on May 1, 1865. There are several pay vouchers in his file.**

Cuney, Colin, Corporal Co. B
   His name appears on a regimental return for June 1862. "Sent to Mobile hospital".

Cupplin, William, Co. G
   His name appears on a slip for USA Post Hospital at Camp Dennison, Ohio, admitted on April 18, 1862, with G S Chest [Gunshot wound].

Curas, Peter, Co. G

He was discharged at Mobile on disability due to a hernia on January 2, 1862. Enlisted at Mobile, Alabama. Born in Catonia, Italy, age 22, five feet eight inches, strong complexion, dark eyes, and dark hair. His handwritten discharge is in his file.*

Curlee, William, Pvt. Co. B.

Enlisted at Rockford, Alabama, by Captain Hancock for the war. Drew clothing on June 1, 1864. He was admitted to Ross Hospital at Mobile on August 8, 1864, with chronic diarrhoea, sent to General Hospital in Selma, Alabama, on August 9. He was admitted to CSA 1st Mississippi Hospital at Jackson, Mississippi, on August 13, 1864, with chronic diarrhoea, deserted on September 13. His name appears on a hospital muster roll dated August 31, 1864, at hospital Shelby Springs, Alabama, for July/August 1864, he is reported as a patient present and never been paid. His name appears on a register of General Hospital, (Soldiers Home Hospital) Shelby Springs, Alabama, August 28, to September 7, 1864. He deserted on September 7. He was paroled at Montgomery, Alabama, on May 22, 1865. Five foot ten inches, black hair, black eyes, and dark complexion. His parole is in his file.*

Curler, William, Pvt. Co. B see **Curlee, William**

Curray, Thomas, Pvt. Co. B see **Curry, Thomas**

Curry, Thomas, Pvt. Co. B

Enlisted on October 13, 1861, at Mobile, Alabama, by Major Hessee for 12 months. He was seriously wounded at Shiloh in the right breast at 8 A. M. on April 6, 1861, while advancing on 1st Camp. He was captured at hospital on April 7. He was admitted to USA General Hospital, Ward 5 at Camp Dennison, Ohio, on April 18, 1862, with vuluns puncture. There is a reference card showing his wound in the back? He is also shown admitted April 24, 1862, to Post Hospital at Camp Dennison with constipation. His name appears on a list of POW's at Camp Chase, Ohio, received from Camp Dennison, Ohio, on June 4, 1862. Five foot seven inches, light complexion, brown hair, light eyes, and age 26. He appears present on a company muster roll for bounty on September 24, 1862. Company muster roll for March/April 1863, reports him present. Company muster roll for May/June 1863, shows him discharged on disability on May 24, 1863. His name appears on a register at Ross Hospital at Mobile from October 1, 1863, to October 12, 1863, with lead colic. [*There may be two men's records contained in this file.*]

Curry, W. L., Pvt. Co. D

Enlisted on May 1, 1864, at Fayette County, Alabama, by Lt. Seay for the war. His name appears on a hospital muster roll at Ladies' Hospital at Montgomery, Alabama, dated November 15, 1864. He is reported present and a patient.

Curtes, W. R., Pvt. Co. C see **Carter, W. R.**

Curtis, T. M., Pvt. Co. D

Enlisted on October 13, 1861, at Mobile, Alabama, by Captain Butt for the war. He appears on a company muster roll for bounty on September 24, 1862, and is reported present and refused to take bounty. He also appears present on company muster roll for November/December 1862.

Curtis, William, Pvt. Co. B

Enlisted on October 13, 1861, at Mobile, Alabama, by Major Hessee for the 12 months. He was wounded in the right thigh at Shiloh on April 6, 1862, at 4 P. M. while charging the Old Field. His name appears on a regimental return for June 1862, "Genl. Hospital, Mobile, April 12." His name appears on a report of June 28, 1862, near Tupelo, Mississippi, "wounded at Shiloh sent to Gen. Hospital Mo. By Dr. Nott. He appears on a company muster roll for bounty on September 24, 1862, and is reported present. Company muster roll for March/April 1863, reports him present. May/June 1863, muster roll reports that he was discharged on disability June 18, 1863, by order of General Maury. His hand written discharge is in his file age 28, five foot six inches, fair complexion, brown eyes, light hair, by occupation a pastry cook. Discharged at Oven Bluff on June 17, 1863. *

Curturight, J. T., Pvt. Co. A see **Cortright, Jerome S.**

Curtis, W. R., Pvt. Co. C see **Carter, W. R.**

Cusby, D., Pvt. Co. D.

His name appears on a regimental return for June 1862, "sent to Interior Hospital after the evacuation." [Of Corinth, Mississippi]

Cuslicke, A., Pvt. Co. K

POW his name appears on a list of divers companies and regiments (detached) of the CSA Army commanded by Colonel R. H. Lindsay that were surrendered by Lt General Richard Taylor at Citronelle, Alabama, on May 4, 1865, and paroled at Meridian, Mississippi, on May 10, 1865. Residence shown as New Orleans, Louisiana.

Cuyer, B., Pvt. Co. E

His name appears on a regimental return for June 1862, "detached service: Clerk I. A. C. S. A. M."

Cuzades, Ed. Pvt. Co. H

His name appears on a regimental return for June 1862, "detached? Ord, Mobile."

D

Dade, B. (Benjamin) Frank, 1st Lt./Captain Co. F

He is reported present on a regimental return for December 1861. He was elected 1st Lt. on October 10, 1861. His name appears on a November 1861, return from Fort Gaines, Alabama, where he is reported absent sick since November 26, 1861. He is also reported present on a regimental return near Tupelo, Mississippi, in June 1862. Elected Captain May 8, 1862. He requisitioned fuel for Company F at Fort Morgan for September 1862, for 1 Captain, 2 subalterns, and 46 men. He requisitioned and received at Fort Morgan on September 17, 1862, the following for Co. F; 29 jackets 50 pair pants, 32 caps, 51 shirts, 70 pair drawers, and 49 pair shoes. His name appears on a field return at Fort Morgan for October 1862, "loss Transferred to Choctaw Bluff Oct. 6, 1862." He requisitioned and received for Co. F at Choctaw Bluff in January 1863, the following; 73 jackets, 73 pants, 73 caps, 73 blankets and 2 pair shoes in two packing cases. He also requisitioned and received 11 pair shoes on January 30, 1863. He appears present on company muster roll from March 1, to June 30, 1863. September/October muster roll shows him absent detached to fish by General Maury on August 15, 1863. An inspection report at Fort Morgan, Alabama, of June 30, 1864, reports that he was detached by order of General Maury on March 19, 1864. On September/October 1864, muster roll he is reported present and temporarily assigned to this Co. (F) by Major General Commanding. POW surrendered by Lt General Richard Taylor at Citronelle, Alabama, on May 4, 1865, and paroled at Mobile, Alabama, on May 12, 1865. He requisitioned, not dated, 55 pair shoes "men being entirely barefooted," He was paid $90 per month as a 1st Lt and $130 as Captain. There a considerable number of pay vouchers and requisitions in his file plus his Parole of Honor.**

Dade, R. H., Sgt./Pvt. Co. F

He enlisted on March 25, 1861, at Mobile, Alabama, by Captain Taylor for one year. He is shown on a report from near Tupelo, Mississippi, June 28, 1862, "wounded at Shiloh, furloughed on surgeon's certificate April 8th sent to Corinth Hospital on surgeon's certificate May 28, 1862." His name appears on a regimental return for June 1862, "sent to Corinth May 28, sick now sick in Mobile." He appears present on company muster roll for bounty on September 24, 1862, "Transferred Nov. 8, 1861, from 2nd to 21st Ala. Reg." Company muster roll for March 1, to June 30, 1863, reports him present. Company muster rolls for September/October 1863 and September/October 1864 report him present. He was due $33.13 for clothing not drawn in October 1864. POW surrendered by Lt General Richard Taylor at Citronelle, Alabama, on May 4, 1865, and paroled at Meridian, Mississippi, on May 13, 1865. Residence show as Baldwin County, Alabama.

Dailey, Daniel, Pvt. Co. F

Enlisted on February 2, 1863, at Choctaw Bluff, Alabama, by Captain Dade for the war. He appears present on a company muster roll for March 1, to June 30, 1863. Company muster roll for September/October 1863, also shows him present. He was admitted to Post Hospital at Fort Morgan, Alabama, on October 30, 1863, with pneumonia where he died on November 2.

Dailey, F., Pvt. Co. E

Drew clothing on June 1, 1864, and signed by his mark "X". POW captured at Fort Gaines, Alabama, on August 8, 1864. He was admitted to St. Louis USA General Hospital at New Orleans on September 9, 1864, with intermit fever, returned to prison on

September 12. He was received at Ship Island, Mississippi, from New Orleans on October 25, 1864, and exchanged at Ship Island on January 4, 1865.

Dailey, W. C., Pvt. Co. G

POW captured at Fort Gaines, Alabama, on August 8, 1864. He was received at Ship Island, Mississippi, from New Orleans on October 25, 1864. Died of pneumonia at Ship Island, Mississippi, on November 27, 1864 and was buried in Grave No. 46.

Dailey, Michael, Pvt. Co. B

His name appears on a regimental return for June 1862, "absent without leave since June 10." He appears on a report near Tupelo, Mississippi, on June 28, 1862, "Sent to Mobile, on surgeon's certificate without notifying the Co." Paid $44 on detached service from March 1, to June 30, 1862.

Daily, Patrick F., Pvt. Co. E

Enlisted October 13, 1861, at Halls Mill, Mobile County, Alabama, by Major Hessee. His name appears on a regimental return for June 1862, "May 23., Corinth, Miss. discharged for disability." Born in the State of Florida? Age 27, light hair, blue eyes, light complexion, five foot three inches, by occupation a grocer. His discharge is in his file.*

Dalton, Perry, Pvt. Co. G

POW captured at Fort Gaines, Alabama, on August 8, 1864. He was received at Ship Island, Mississippi, from New Orleans on October 25, 1864, and exchanged at Ship Island on January 4, 1865. POW surrendered by Lt General Richard Taylor at Citronelle, Alabama, on May 4, 1865, and paroled at Meridian, Mississippi, on May 13, 1865. Residence shown as Henderson Store, Pike County, Alabama.

Damgery, J. N., Corp/2nd Lt. Co. H see **Dangey, John**

Danlenay, William, Pvt. Co. I

"Withdrawn and filed with Wm. McRory."

Dantzler, G. (Gabriel) B., Sgt./2nd Lt. Co. E/I

Enlisted on October 13, 1861, at Mobile, Alabama, by Major Hessee for one year. His name appears on a regimental return for June 1862, "June 12, Tupelo, Mississippi, discharged for disability." His discharge is in his file, age 32, five foot ten and one half, blue eyes, light hair, a machinist by profession, born in Green County, Mississippi. Elected 2nd Lt. on February 19, 1863. Promoted March 24, 1864. He is reported present on a company muster roll for July/August 1863. Muster roll for September/October 1863, reports him absent sick since September 18, 1863. He was admitted to Post Hospital at Fort Morgan, Alabama, with chronic diarrhoea on September 9, 1863, and returned to duty on September 15, 1863. POW captured at Fort Gaines, Alabama, on August 8, 1864. He was received at Ship Island, Mississippi, from New Orleans on October 25, 1864, and exchanged at Ship Island on January 4, 1865. POW surrendered at Citronelle, Alabama, on June 1, 1865, paroled June 2, 1865, at Mobile, Alabama.

Residence Perry County, Mississippi, five foot ten and one half inches, age 35, fair complexion, eyes blue, hair gray.*

Dantzler, Lorenzo N., Pvt. Co. E
Enlisted on October 13, 1861, at Mobile, Alabama, by Major Hessee for one year. Wounded severely in left hand at Shiloh on April 6, 1861, at 4:30 P. M. while crossing the Old Field. His name appears on a regimental return for June 1862, "June 19, Tupelo, Miss. discharged for disability." His discharge is in his file age 28, five foot nine and one half, dark eyes, dark hair, a machinist by profession, born in Green County, Mississippi.*

Danzay, John, Corp./2nd Lt. Co. C/H see **Danzey, John**

Danzey, J. M., Corp./2nd Lt. Co. C/H see **Danzey, John**

Danzey, John, Corp./2nd Lt. Co. C/H
Enlisted on October 13, 1861, at Mobile, Alabama, by Captain Rembert for 12 months. A regimental return for June 1862, reports him absent on sick furlough since April 15. He was discharged on April 6, 1862. Born in Clarke County, Alabama, age 27, five foot nine inches, fair complexion, dark eyes, dark hair, and a farmer by occupation. He appears on a company C muster roll for bounty on September 24, 1862, and is reported present. Company muster roll for December 31, 1862, to April 30, 1863, reports him present. May/June 1863, muster roll reports him present and promoted from 4th to 2nd Sgt. on June 6, 1863. September/October 1863, muster roll reports him absent on sick leave for 15 days from October 17, 1863. Appointed 2nd Lt. Company H on March 4, 1864. POW captured at Fort Gaines, Alabama, on August 8, 1864. He was received at Ship Island, Mississippi, from New Orleans on October 25, 1864, and exchanged at Ship Island on January 4, 1865. There is paperwork in his file.*

Danzey, John W., Corp./2nd Lt. Co. C/H see **Canzey, John**

Danzey, L. R., Corporal Co. H
POW captured at Fort Gaines, Alabama, on August 8, 1864. His name appears on a morning report confined at Steam Levee Press No. 4 at New Orleans, Louisiana, on October 4, 1864, sent to hospital on October 4, 1864. He was admitted to St. Louis, USA General Hospital at New Orleans on October 4, 1864, with acute diarrhoea and returned to confinement on October 22, 1864. He was again admitted to St. Louis, USA General Hospital at New Orleans on September 1, 1864, with dysentery and returned to confinement on September 12, 1864, age 28. He was received at Ship Island, Mississippi, from New Orleans on October 25, 1864, and exchanged at Ship Island on January 4, 1865. POW surrendered at Citronelle, Alabama, on May 4, 1865, paroled May 12, 1865, at Meridian, Mississippi. Residence in Washington County, Alabama.

Danzey, S. W., Corporal Co. H see **Danzey, L. R.**

Davenport, Follin, Corp. Co. E
Wounded in left knee while advancing in ravine at Shiloh on April 6, 1862, at 12 Noon. Paid $26 for service, from March 1, to April 6, 1862. There is paperwork in his file.*

David, V., Pvt. Co. K
Enlisted at Fort Morgan, Alabama, on July 4, 1863, by Captain Dorgan for the war. Company muster rolls for July/August 1863, and September/October 1863, report him present.

Davidson, A. G., Pvt. Co. G
. POW captured at Fort Gaines, Alabama, on August 8, 1864. He was received at Ship Island, Mississippi, from New Orleans on October 25, 1864. He died at Ship Island in December 1864, (in pencil on register). Another card indicates that he was exchanged at Ship Island on January 4, 1865. [*The register of prisoner burials at Ship Island shows a Pvt. Henry Davidson, Co. G, 21st Alabama who died of dysentery on December 30, 1864, and buried in grave No. 56*]

Davidson, A. S., Pvt. Co. G see **Davidson, A. G.**

Davidson, George W., Musician, Co. B
Enlisted on October 13, 1861, at Mobile, Alabama, by Major Hessee for 12 months. He appears on a regimental return for June 1862, where he is reported absent on surgeon's certificate June 8. His name appears on a report dated June 28, 1862, near Tupelo, "Went to Mobile on surgeon's certificate without notifying the Co.". His name appears on a company muster roll for bounty for September 24, 1862, "not entitled to bounty, over age". Discharged at Oven Bluff, Alabama, October 13, 1862, age 47, five foot eight inches, blue eyes, by profession a fifer. His discharge is in his file.*

Davidson, James A., Pvt. Co. E/K
Enlisted on October 13, 1861, at Mobile, Alabama, by Captain Chamberlain for the war. His name appears on a regimental return for June 1862, as forage master clerk. Returns for November and December 1862, report him as detached with Q. M. Company muster roll for bounty on September 24, 1862, reports him absent, detailed March 27, 1862, by order of General Gladden. Company muster rolls for November/December 1862, July/August 1863, and September/October 1863, all show him absent detached in Q. M. Department. September/October 1864, muster roll shows him present and due for clothing not drawn. POW surrendered by Lt General Richard Taylor at Citronelle, Alabama, on May 4, 1865, and paroled at Meridian, Mississippi, on May 13, 1865. Residence shown as Mobile, Mobile County, Alabama.

Davis, A. A., Pvt. Co. F
His name appears on a return for June 1862, " May 5, Columbus, died hospital."

Davis, A (Alfred). B., Pvt Co. K

Enlisted on October 9, 1863, at Grove Hill, Alabama, by Major Mason for the war. He appears present on a company muster roll for September/October 1863, "never paid." He was admitted to Post Hospital at Fort Morgan, Alabama, with diarrhoea on November 22, 1863, sent to general hospital. He was admitted to Ross Hospital in Mobile, on November 29, 1863, and died at Ross Hospital on December 18.

Davis, H. C., Corporal Co. I

POW captured at Fort Gaines, Alabama, on August 8, 1864. He was admitted to St. Louis USA General Hospital, in New Orleans on August 23, 1864, with fever intermittent and returned to confinement on August 29, 1865, and again admitted on September 5, 1865, and returned to confinement on September 16, 1865. He was age 24 at the time. He was received at Ship Island, Mississippi, from New Orleans on October 25, 1864, and exchanged at Ship Island on January 4, 1865.

Davis, Henry G., Pvt. Co. E

He was discharged June 24, 1862. His name appears on a register of deceased soldiers. Claim filed August 20, 1862, and $116.80 paid to Hon. E. S. Dagan. *Much paperwork in his file is unreadable.*

Davis, H. H., Corporal Co. I see **Davis, H. C.**

Davis, H. P., Pvt. Co. K

Enlisted on October 13, 1861, at Mobile, Alabama, by Captain Stewart for the war. Severely wounded in the right lung at Shiloh on April 6 or 7, 1862, at 3 P. M. at Center Field. POW captured at hospital on April 7, 1862. His name appears on a muster roll for bounty on September 24, 1862, "missing – Battle of Shiloh April 7, 1862." His name also appears on a list of Confederate prisoners who have died in the Department of the Ohio. Died May 4, 1862, "Fourth St. Hospt. Cincinnati, Ohio."

Davis, J. C., Sgt. Co. A

His name appears on a list of POW stragglers paroled at Selma, Alabama, in June 1865. Residence shown as Perry County, Alabama.

Davis, J. D., Pvt. Co. H

POW captured at Fort Gaines, Alabama, on August 8, 1864. He was received at Ship Island, Mississippi, from New Orleans on October 25, 1864, and exchanged at Ship Island on January 4, 1865. He signed a parole at Montgomery, Alabama, in May 1865. His parole is in his file. Five foot ten inches, light hair, blue eyes, fair complexion.*

Davis, John D., Pvt. Co. H see **Davis, John D.**

Davis, Joseph, Pvt. Co. C

Enlisted on October 13, 1861, at Mobile, Alabama, by Captain Rembert for the war. Wounded in the calf of left leg slightly while advancing on A. M. attack on 1st Camp at Shiloh April 6, 1862. His name appears on a regimental return for June 1862,

"Wounded at Shiloh, & furloughed. He appears on a report June 28, 1862, "Wounded at Shiloh and sent home on furlough on surgeon's certificate." He appears absent sick on a company muster roll for bounty on September 24, 1862. Company muster roll for December 31, 1862, to April 30, 1863, reports him absent sick. On May/June 1863, muster roll he is reported to be discharged for disability on May 18, 1863, by order of General Slaughter.

Davis, J. W., Pvt. Co. C

Enlisted at Marengo, County, Alabama, on February 9, 1863, by Lt. Northrup for three years or the war. Company muster roll for December 31, 1862, to April 30, 1863, reports him absent sick. On May/June 1863, muster roll he is reported present sick in hospital. Company muster roll for September/October 1863, reports him present. Age 18, gray eyes, dark hair, fair complexion, six foot, Marengo, County, Alabama. A note refers to "see personal papers of **J. Y. Lyles**, Pvt. Co. C. 21st Ala." A descriptive list in Pvt. Lyles file describes Pvt. J. C. Davis as born in Marengo County, Alabama, age 18, gray eyes, dark hair, fair complexion, six foot, occupation a farmer, drew $50 bounty. He signed, J. C. Davis.

Davis, L. C., Pvt. Co. A

Enlisted in August 1863, at Perry County, Alabama, by Captain Night [*Knight?*] for the war. POW captured at Fort Morgan, Alabama, August 23, 1864, "sent to New York Sept. 27/64." Received at Elmira, New York, on October 8, 1864, from New Orleans. His name appears as a signature of POW's paroled at Elmira. New York, and sent to James River for exchange. His parole dated March 14, 1865. Received at Boulware's Wharf, James River on March 18 and 21st, 1865, among 981 POWs. He was admitted to Receiving and Wayside Hospital or General Hospital No. 9, Richmond, Virginia, on March 18, 1865, sent to Camp Lee on March 19.

Dawn, W. N., Pvt. Co. G

He signed a parole at Montgomery, Alabama, on May 19, 1865. Six foot, light hair, yellow eyes, and dark complexion.

Day, Charles, M., Corp. Co. C

Reference card only.

Dayley, Pvt. Co. F see Dailey Daniel

Deakle, T. E., Pvt. Co. H

Enlisted on August 15, 1964, at Mobile, Alabama, by Captain Gordon for the war. His name appears on a company muster roll for September/October 1864, "transferred to Conscript Camp, Notasulga, [Alabama] by order Major ? Enr. Officer, October 18, 1864."

Deakle, James A., Sgt. Co. I

Enlisted on October 13, 1861, at Halls Mill, Alabama, by Major Hessee. Company muster roll on September 24, 1862, for bounty reports him present. His name appears on a register of payments to discharged soldiers. Discharged May 7, 1863. Payment record is in his file.*

Dean, J. J., Pvt. Co. I

POW surrendered by Lt General Richard Taylor at Citronelle, Alabama, on May 4, 1865, and paroled at Meridian, Mississippi, on May 13, 1865. Residence shown as Wilcox County, Alabama.

Deas, H. C., Lt. Co. D see **Deas, H. M.**

Deas, H. M., 1st Lt. Co. D

Enlisted on October 13, 1861. He was elected 1st Lt. on October 14, 1861, and not re-elected May 8, 1862. He appears absent recruiting for the company on a regimental return for December 1861. A return at Fort Gaines, Alabama, November 1861, reports Lt. H. Deas absent with leave since Nov. 22, 1861. A register reports Lt. Henry G. Deas dropped [*from rolls*] on May 8, 1862. A regimental return for June 1862, near Tupelo, Mississippi, reports him present. There are payment vouchers in his file.*

Debrine, (Debirono, Gynogo) J., Pvt. Co. G

His name appears on a regimental return for June 1862, "sent to hospital May 28." Paid $44 for service from March 1, to June 30, 1862.

Deferetes, Manuel, Co. G

Enlisted on October 7, 1861, at Mobile, Alabama, by Major Hessee for twelve months. Discharged July 21, 1862, at Fort Gaines, Alabama, Born Lisbon, Portugal, age 20, five foot eight inches, strong complexion, black eyes, black hair, by occupation a sailor. Disabled due to epileptic fits.

Delouche, S. W., Pvt. Co. H see **Deloach, S. W.**

He was admitted to Post Hospital at Fort Morgan, Alabama, with int. fev. on November 3, 1863, and returned to duty on November 12. POW captured at Fort Gaines, Alabama, on August 8, 1864. He was received at Ship Island, Mississippi, from New Orleans on October 25, 1864. He died of dysentery at Ship Island in December 17, 1864, (in pencil on register) and buried in grave No. 95.

Demeouy, Agustus, Pvt. Co. D

Enlisted by Major Hessee, at Halls Mill, Alabama, on October 13, 1861. Born in Mobile County, Alabama, age 28, five foot eight and three quarter inches, dark complexion, hazel eyes, and black hair. Discharged at Corinth, Mississippi, on April 23, 1862, due to chronic rheumatism of the shoulder. His discharge is in his file.*

Demony, Frank, Pvt. Co. I

Enlisted on October 13, 1861, at Halls Mill, Alabama, by Major Hessee for the war. His name appears on a regimental return for June 1862, "sent to interior hospital on May 28, 1862." He also appears on a report for June 28, 1862, near Tupelo, Mississippi, "Sent to interior hospitals form Corinth, by surgeon on May 28th." He appears present on a company muster roll for bounty on September 24, 1862. Company muster rolls for July/August 1863, and September/October 1863, report him present. He was admitted to Post Hospital at Fort Morgan, Alabama, on April 4, 1863, with ulcer, returned to duty on April 16, 1863.

Demony, Jas., Pvt. Co. I

His name appears on a register at the Battle of Shiloh "In ambulance squad, captured at hospital, April 7 1862."

Demony, Lewis P., Sgt./2nd Lt. Co. K/D

Enlisted on October 13, 1861, at Mobile, Alabama, by Captain Stewart for the war. His name appears on a list of soldiers whose gun was shattered in battle. He appears present on a company muster roll for bounty on September 24, 1862. Company muster roll for November/December 1862, reports him present. Company muster roll for July/August 1863, reports him present and promoted from 2nd Sgt. to 1st Sgt, August 1, 1863. Company muster rolls for September/October 1863 and September/October 1864 report him present. Elected 2nd Lt. Company D on May 28, 1864. He appears on an inspection report of Appalachee Batteries at Mobile, Alabama, for October 15, 1864, absent sick (hosp.) since September 4, 1864. His name appears on a register of wounded POW's at City Hospital, Mobile, Alabama [*no date*]. POW surrendered by Lt General Richard Taylor at Citronelle, Alabama, on May 4, 1865, and paroled at Mobile, Alabama, on May 11, 1865. His parole and payment vouchers in his file.*

Demony, William, Sgt./1st Lt. Co. K/G

Enlisted on October 13, 1861, at Mobile, Alabama, by Captain Stewart for the war. He appears on a regimental return for June 1862, as Acting Sgt. Major 21st Regiment. He appears on a company muster roll for bounty on September 24, 1862, paid $50. His name appears on a Field and Staff muster rolls for July/August 1863, and September/October 1863, reported present. F & S Muster roll for March/April 1864, reports him as having been promoted to 2nd Lt. Company G. on March 24, 1864. POW captured at Fort Gaines, Alabama, on August 8, 1864. He was received at Ship Island, Mississippi, from New Orleans on October 25, 1864, and exchanged at Ship Island on January 4, [1865]. POW surrendered by Lt General Richard Taylor at Citronelle, Alabama, on May 4, 1865, and paroled at Meridian, Mississippi, on May 10, 1865. His parole and payment vouchers in his file.*

Dennaway, J., Pvt. Co. G see **Dunnaway, Jesse W.**

Denham, J. N., 3rd Sgt.. Co. I

Enlisted on October 13, 1861, at Halls Mill, Alabama, by Major Hessee for the war. He appears present on a company muster roll for bounty on September 24, 1862.

Dennis, W. A., Pvt. Co. K

Enlisted on September 1, 1864, at Worcester, Maryland, by Major Stone for the war. He appears absent on a company muster roll for September/October 1864, temporarily attached to the company by Major Stone, "absent on furlough of ? days since October 7, 1864". POW captured at Island No. 10 on April 8, 1862. He was received from Camp Butler, Springfield, Illinois, at Vicksburg, Mississippi, for exchange on September 23, 1862. He was among 1700 POW's aboard the steamer *Jno. A. Done*, exchanged at a landing near Vicksburg on November 10, 1862.

Deshazo, Paul H., Pvt. Co. H

Drew clothing June 1, 1864. POW captured at Fort Gaines, Alabama, on August 8, 1864. His name appears on a register of POW's at New Orleans, Louisiana, "Died in Barracks H". A resident of White Oak Spring, Barbour County, Alabama, married, died October 5, 1864, due to injury of the head and buried October 6, 1864, square 69, grave 18, Monument Cemetery at New Orleans. His death certificate is in his file.*

Desporte, J. A., Pvt. Co. K

Enlisted on October 13, 1861, at Mobile, Alabama, by Captain Stewart for the war. His name appears on a regimental return "sent to general hospital on May 28". He appears on a report near Tupelo, Mississippi, for June 28, 1862, "on furlough since May 29, sent from Corinth." He appears absent on a company muster roll for bounty on September 24, 1862, "absent with leave in Mobile since September 23. Company muster roll for November/December 1862, reports him present. Company muster roll for July/August 1863, reports him absent on surgeon's certificate August 29, 1863. Muster rolls for September/October 1863 and 1864 show him present.

Desporte, V. H., Pvt. Co. K

Enlisted on September 10, 1863, at Enterprise, [*Alabama?*] by Major Berry for the war. Company muster roll for September/October 1863, reports him present and never paid. Drew clothing on December 19, 1863, signed by his mark. Transferred to CS Navy on Special Order No. 100.

DeVaux, C. L. A., Captain Co. H

Elected Captain October 12, 1861. Commissioned October 13, 1861, dismissed October 12, 1863. GCM. [General Court Marshall] He appears present on a return from Post at Fort Gaines, Alabama, for November 1861. A regimental return for December 1861, reports him present. Wounded at Shiloh arm broken while advancing in attack on 1st Battery in the A. M. on April 6, 1862. A regimental return for June 1862, shows him absent, "seriously, wounded April 6, on furlough". He appears on a report near Tupelo, Mississippi, on June 28, 1862, "wounded at Shiloh and on furlough in Mobile." Captain DeVaux file contains considerable paperwork but no indication of reason for his dismissal.*

Develin, Joseph, Pvt. Co. K

Enlisted on October 13, 1861, at Mobile, Alabama, to serve one year. Discharged due to disability on January 27, 1862. Born in Derry County, Ireland, age 27, five foot eight and one quarter, light hair, light complexion, blue eyes, and a florist by occupation.

Devine, L., Pvt. Co. A.

Reference only.

MOBILE CONFEDERATES

Diamond, William, Pvt. Co. H

Paid $6.60 for commutation of rations from October 13, 1863, to November 1, 1863. He drew clothing on June 1, 1864, and signed by his mark. POW captured at Fort Gaines, Alabama, on August 8, 1864. He was admitted to St. Louis USA General Hospital at New Orleans from military prison, on October 15, 1864, with acute diarrhoea, returned to confinement on October 22, age 34. Received at Ship Island, Mississippi, from New Orleans on October 25, 1864. Died at Ship Island December 1, 1864, of dysentery and buried in grave No. 56.

Dickens, Robert, Pvt. Co. I

His name appears on a regimental return for June 1862, "June 14, Tupelo, transferred to Captain Myers sharpshooters."

Dickens, Hampton, Pvt. Co. I

Enlisted on October 13, 1861, at Halls Mill, Alabama, by Major Hessee for the war. His name appears on a regimental return for June 1862, "sent to interior hospital May 28, 1862". He also appears on a report near Tupelo, Mississippi, June 28, 1862, "Sent to interior hospital by surgeon, May 28th. He appears present on a company muster roll for bounty September 24, 1862, "refused to take bounty, claiming to be under age 18." Company muster rolls for July/August 1863 and September/October 1863 report him present. POW surrendered by Lt General Richard Taylor at Citronelle, Alabama, on May 4, 1865, and paroled at Meridian, Mississippi, on May 13, 1865. Residence shown as Jackson County, Alabama.

Dickenson, C. B., Pvt. Co. E

He appears on a regimental return for June 1862, "severely wounded at Shiloh unlimited furlough." His name appears on a register of wounded soldiers at Battle of Shiloh wounded severely in shoulder on April 6, 1862, at 4 P. M. while crossing Old Field advancing. Discharged on July 11, 1862.

Dicks, R. R., Pvt. Co. C see **Dix, R. R.**

Dishough, R. Co. F

Record not complete but it appears likely he was killed at Shiloh. Money left $3.50.

Dismukes, G. W., Pvt. Co. C

Enlisted on February 7, 1863, in Marengo County, Alabama, by Lt. Northrup for three years or the war. Company muster roll for December 31, 1862, to April 30, 1863, reports him present. Company muster rolls for May/June 1863 and September/October 1863 report him present. He was admitted to Post Hospital at Fort Morgan, Alabama, on January 2, 1864, with int. fev., returned to duty on January 12. Drew clothing June 1, 1864. POW captured at Fort Gaines, Alabama, on August 8, 1864. Received at Ship Island, Mississippi, from New Orleans on October 25, 1864. He was exchanged at Ship Island on January 4, 1865.

21ST ALABAMA INFANTRY VOLUNTEERS

Dismukes, J. W., Pvt. Co. C

POW captured at Blakeley, Alabama, on April 9, 1865. Received at Ship Island, Mississippi, on April 15, 1865. Paroled and transferred from Ship Island to Vicksburg, Mississippi, on May 1, 1865, for exchange. [*This is likely the same man as above.*]

Dix, R. R., Pvt. Co. C

He appears on a regimental return for June 1862, "absent on sick furlough". His name appears on a report near Tupelo, Mississippi, June 28, 1862, "sent to interior hospital by Surg. from Corinth." Transferred October 31, 1862. Paid $88 for service. There is a pay voucher in his file.*

Dixon, George E., Pvt./Sgt./1st Lt. Co. A

Wounded severely in the left thigh at Shiloh at 8:30 A. M., April 6, 1862, while advancing on first Camp. Promoted to 2nd Lt. on May 8, and 1st Lt. on August 30, 1862. Paid $80 per month as 1st Lt. His name appears on a consolidated report near Tupelo, Mississippi, on June 28, 1862, leave of absence for 20 days from June 18, by order General Bragg. Field report at Fort Morgan, Alabama, reports him loss, transferred to Choctaw Bluff on October 6, 1862. Company muster roll for bounty on September 24, 1862, report his presence not stated. Muster Rolls for December 31, 1862, to April 30, 1863, report him detached September, 15, 1862, by order of General Forney, May/June 1863, absent on leave, September/October 63, detached October 1, 1863, for 30 days by order of General Maury. Present Dec. 14, 1863, to date, (in) command of the submarine torpedo boat *H. L. Hunley*, proceed to the mouth of Charlestown Harbor, (South Carolina) & destroy any vessel of the enemy. Killed March 1864, "supposed to be on torpedo boat at blowing up the Housatonic." He requisitioned 1 2/6 cords of wood for fuel at Mount Pleasant, South Carolina, in January 1864, he signed as George E. Dixon, Lt. Commanding Submarine Boat. There are a number of requisitions, two letters concerning the Hunley and pay vouchers in his file bearing his signature.**

Alexandria Va, March 5, 1864

General G. T. Beauregard, Camp in Charleston

Sir

Vague dispatches have reached me with reference to investments of the Housatonic and as I am one of the ones of the torpedo boat "H. L. Hunley" and am also the ? of the Capt. Hunley who sacrificed his life in his plans for the destruction of the enemy's vessels. I am increasingly anxious to learn whether **Lt. Dixon** also accomplished his gallant act with our boat or not and whether he had escaped. It will be a source of infinite pride to me to learn this, even in the least ? manner. I have been incidentally of some service to the General who has previously preserved Charleston against the combined attack of the army and ? of the enemy. I would therefore beg to be furnished with the information in this matter. (*Unable to read the remainder*) Signed Henry J. Leroy.

Headquarters Thirty ?

MOBILE CONFEDERATES

        Mt. Pleasant, Feb. 19, 1864.
General [Beauregard]
  Lieunt Col. Dantzler commanding at Battery Marshall reports that on the night of the 17th the torpedo boat went out from Beach Inlet, and has not returned. The signals agreed upon in case she wished to return was observed and answered from this post. Unless she has gone to Charleston, the boat has possibly been lost or captured. I have no reason to believe that the crew would have deserted to the enemy. They ? ? under my directions and ? that it is more likely that she has gone down judging from the past experiences of the machine.
          Very Respectfully
            ?
          R. Ripley
        [Brigadier General] Comm[anding].

Dixon, J. B., Pvt. Co. K
  Enlisted at Camden, Alabama, on August 15, 1864, by Lt. Portis for the war. Company muster roll for September/October 1864, reports him absent sent to hospital, October 13, 1864, by Dr. Armstrong. "Temporarily attached to the company by Major Stone En[rolling]. Officer." POW captured September 29, 1864, at Bridgewater, and appears on a roll of POWs at Harpers' Ferry, Virginia, sent to Point Lookout, Maryland, October 10, 1864. He arrived at Point Lookout from Harpers' Ferry on October 12, 1864. Exchanged on March 17, 1865. His name appears on a report employed at General Hospital Moore at Mobile, Alabama, April 4, 1865, " Detailed by Medl. Exa Board, app'd by Gen. Taylor." Disability hernia and chronic hepatitis. *There are obviously two men's files in this entry.*

Dobbs, William U., Pvt. Co. A
  Enlisted on February 1, 1863, at Choctaw Bluff, Alabama, by Captain Cothran for the war. He appears as present on a company muster roll for December 31, 1862, to April 30, 1863, "drawn no pay." Company muster rolls for May/June 1863, and September/October 1863, report him present. POW captured at Fort Morgan, Alabama, on August 23, 1864, "sent to New York Sept. 27, 1864." Received at Elmira, New York, on October 8, 1864, from New Orleans. He died at Elmira of chronic diarrhoea on November 8, 1864, and was buried in grave No. 870. Reference in his file to see personal papers of **Geo. T. Bailey**, Pvt. Co. A, 21st Alabama Infantry.

Dobson, John B., Hospital Steward
  POW surrendered by Lt General Richard Taylor at Citronelle, Alabama, on May 4, 1865, and paroled at Meridian, Mississippi, on May 13, 1865. Residence Mobile, Alabama.

Dolan, James, Pvt. Co. I
  His name appears on a roll of POW's at Camp Douglas, Illinois, captured at Island 10 on April 8, 1862.

Dominick, Georgio, Pvt. Co. G

Enlisted at Mobile, Alabama, by Major Hessee on October 13, 1861, to serve one year. Wounded slightly in the elbow at Shiloh on April 6th, 1862, 7 A. M. advancing in the charge on 1st Battery. Discharged on disability on February 14, 1863. Born in Dalmitia (Europe), age 31, five foot six inches, light brown complexion, blue eyes, dark hair, and by occupation a laborer. His discharge is in his file.*

Donati, G., Pvt. Co. G

His name appears on a regimental return for June 1862. He also appears on two receipt rolls for commutation of rations.

Donno, J., Pvt. Co. C see **Downey, J.**

Donoho, O. C., 2nd Lt./1st Lt. Co. I

He was discharged as Sergeant on Co. C, on April 2, 1862. He was elected 2nd Lt. on May 3, 1862. His rank is from August 30, 1862. A register indicates that he was dropped [from roll] on May 8, 1862. His name appears on a regimental return from June 1862, "absent sent to interior hospital May 28th from Corinth, [Mississippi] by Surgeon Hustis." Here he is show as 2nd Brevt. He appears present on a company muster roll for September 24, 1862, for bounty. A field return at Fort Morgan, Alabama, for October 1862, reports him present "in arrest." His name appears on a return from Fort Morgan, Alabama, in November and December 1862, where he is shown present. He requisitioned on January 13, 1863, 31 muskets and 31 bayonets of Co. I. July/August 1863, muster roll reports him present. September/October 1863, muster roll reports him absent on furlough from October 30, 1863. Promoted to 1st Lt. on March 24, 1864. An inspection report at Fort Morgan on June 30, 1864, shows him at General Hospital in Mobile since April 28, 1864. POW captured at Fort Gaines, Alabama, on August 8, 1864. . He was admitted from military prison with diarrhoea to St. Louis USA General Hospital at New Orleans, on August 26, 1864, and returned to confinement on August 29. He was admitted from military prison with gastralgia to St. Louis USA General Hospital at New Orleans, on September 1, 1864, and returned to confinement on September 12, 1864, and again admitted with the same complaint on September 28, 1864, and returned to confinement on September 30, age 26. He was received at Ship Island, Mississippi, from New Orleans on November 25, 1864, and exchanged at Ship Island on January 4, 1865. There are a number of pay vouchers and requisitions in his file.*

Donovan, T. T., Pvt. Co. A

He appears on a regimental return for June 1862, " May 11, 1862, Corinth, Miss., discharged for disability." Enlisted at Mobile, Alabama, by Major Hessee on October 13, 1861. Born in Greene County, Alabama, age 18, five foot nine inches, dark complexion, ? hair, dark eyes, by occupation a salesman. He was discharged at Corinth. His discharge is in his file.*

Dorgan, A. P., 1st Lt./Captain Co. K

Elected 1st Lt. on October 13, 1861, and elected Captain on May 8, 1862. He appears present on a regimental return for June 1862, At Tupelo, Mississippi. He appears present on a company muster roll for September 24, 1862, for bounty. He appears present on returns from Fort Morgan, Alabama, in October, November and December 1862. On September 24, 1862, he requisitioned and received the following items: 24 jackets, 24 pants, 16 caps, 20 shirts, 49 pair drawers, 32 shoes. On December 2, 1862, he requisitioned and received for Co. K the following clothing; 52 jackets, 52 pants, 104 shirts, 104 pair drawers, 52 caps, 52 shoes. On January 13, 1863, he requisitioned and received 52 German rifles, 1000 Mississippi rifle cartridges, and 1000 musket caps. Company muster rolls for November/December 1862, and July/August 1863, report him present. Muster roll for September/October 1863, reports him absent, " absent with leave until September 3, 1863. Resigned on August 3, 1864. There are a number of pay vouchers and requisitions in his file.**

Dorgan, L. C., Pvt. Co. K

Enlisted on October 13, 1861, at Mobile, Alabama, by Captain Stewart for the war. His name appears on a list of soldiers that returned (from Shiloh) without arms "sick, turned back gave his gun to a horseman." He appears present on a company muster roll for September 24, 1862, for bounty. Company muster roll for November/December 1862, reports him present. Company muster roll for July/August 1863, reports him absent with leave for two days, "returned and mustered." He was admitted to Ross Hospital in Mobile, on August 25, 1864, with chronic diarrhoea, retuned to duty on September 3. Company muster roll for September/October 1864, shows that he was reduced to rank from 1st Sgt. and assigned to light duty by the Medical Board September 14, 1864, and detached by General Maury on October 15, 1864. He was admitted to Ross Hospital in Mobile with febus intermittens quot, on September 9, 1864, retuned to duty on October 1. POW surrendered by Lt General Richard Taylor at Citronelle, Alabama, on May 4, 1865, and paroled at Mobile on May 23, 1865. Residence shown as Mobile, Alabama.

Dorman, Thomas T., Pvt. Co. K

There is a discharge in his file showing Thomas T. Dorgan of Captain Jewett's Co. A. He joined on October 13, 1861, at Mobile to serve one year. He was born in Greensboro, Alabama, age 18, five foot nine, dark complexion, brown eyes, dark hair and occupation a salesman. Discharged on disability on May 11, 1862, at Corinth, Mississippi. Later muster rolls indicate that he enlisted on September 25, 1862, at Fort Morgan, Alabama, by Captain Dorgan for the war. He appears present on existing muster rolls from November 1862, until October 1864. September/October muster roll reports that he was detailed as Sergeant Major of the 21st Alabama Regiment by Captain Dorgan. His name appears on a register of Post Hospital at Fort Morgan, Alabama, where he was admitted for diarrhoea on September 12, 1863, and sent to general hospital on September 15. POW surrendered by Lt General Richard Taylor at Citronelle, Alabama, on May 4, 1865, and paroled at Meridian, Mississippi, on May 13, 1865. Residence shown as Mobile, Mobile County, Alabama. *

Dortch, L. E., Pvt. Co. H

POW captured at Fort Gaines, Alabama, on August 8, 1864. He was admitted with chronic diarrhoea on November 3, 1864, and died on January 10, 1865, in St. Louis

USA General Hospital at New Orleans, age 34. He was married and a native of Lower Peach Tree, Wilcox County, Alabama. He was buried in grave 456 Cypress Grove Cemetery at New Orleans. There are death records in his file.*

Doss, W. B., 1st Corp. Co. C

Enlisted at Marengo County, Alabama, on October 13, 1861, for one year. Discharged in October 1862, due to being over 35 years old Born in Marengo County, age 36, five foot eight inches, light complexion, blue eyes, light hair and by occupation a planter.

Dougherty, Eneas, Pvt. Co. B

Deserted at Cedar Point (Grant's Pass or Fort Powell) Alabama, on April 22, or 23 1864. He signed an Oath of Allegiance to the USA at New Orleans on April 25, 1864, complexion dark, hair black, eyes blue, five foot nine inches, residence Philadelphia, Pennsylvania.

Douglas, George W., Pvt. Co. C

Enlisted on October 13, 1861, for 12 months. He died on October 12, 1862. His name appears on a register of claims of deceased soldiers that were filed. Claim filed by Sarah Douglas on April 19, 1863. Paid $106.40. Claim returned from Comptroller on September 21, 1864.* [*Buried Okolona, MS Confederate Cem., row 20*]

Douglas, R. B., Pvt. Co. K

His name appears on a regimental return for June 1862, discharged for disability near Corinth, Mississippi, on May 19. Born in South ?, South Carolina, age 25, five foot five and one half inches, gray eyes, fair complexion, by occupation a clerk. Enlisted at Fort Gaines, Alabama, on December 10, 1861.*

Douglas, S., Pvt. Co. K

Drew $21.25 commutation of rations while on furlough from April 1, to June 25, 186?. Discharged, age 21, five foot nine and one half inches.*

Dow, William, Pvt. Co. A.

Information is unreadable.

Downey, Daniel, Pvt. Co. F

Enlisted at Choctaw Bluff, Alabama, by Captain Dade on April 3, 1863, for the war. He appears present on company muster rolls for March 1, to June 30, 1863, and September/October 1863. Discharged by reason of being 45 and transferred to CS Navy. Born in Cork, Ireland, age 47, five foot seven inches, fair complexion, blue eyes, dark hair. Signed by his mark "X."*

Downey, J., Pvt. Co. C

Enlisted at Camden, Alabama, by Lt. Wragg on October 10, 1863, for three years or the war. Company muster roll reports him present for September/October 1863. POW captured at Fort Gaines, Alabama, on August 8, 1864. Received at Ship Island

Mississippi, from New Orleans on October 25, 1864. He died of diarrhoea at Ship Island on November 17, 1864 and was buried in grave 25.

Downs, Andre, Pvt. Co. B

His name appears on a regimental return for June 1862, "May 8, Corinth, Miss., discharged for disability on May 8, 1862." Born in Ireland, age 30, five foot five inches, light complexion, black eyes, brown hair and by occupation a clerk. He was enlisted at Mobile, Alabama, on October 13, 1861, by J. Hessee for one year. His discharge is in his file.*

Downs, William, Sgt. Co. G

POW captured at Fort Gaines, Alabama, on August 8, 1864. Received at Ship Island, Mississippi, from New Orleans on October 25, 1864. Exchanged at Ship Island, on January 5, 1865.

Downs, W. M., Sgt. Co. G see **Downs, William**

Doyle, James, Pvt. Co. E

He appears on a register of wounded at Shiloh. He was wounded severely in the left thigh on April 6, 1862, at 7 A. M. while charging the 1st Battery and captured at the hospital on April 7, 1862.

Doyle, Michael, Pvt. Co. B

His name appears on a report near Tupelo, Mississippi, June 28, 1862, "wounded at Shiloh furlough extended by Dr. Ross to July 1. He appears on a register of discharged soldiers paid on July 28, 1862.*

Doyle, Thomas, Pvt. Co. D

Killed at Shiloh on April 6, 1862, at 9 A. M. Shot through the head.

Draper, P. M., Pvt. Co. D

Enlisted on August 29, 1862, at Jefferson County, Alabama, by W. J. Poole for the war. He appears present on company muster rolls for November/December, 1862, July/August 1862, and September/October 1863. One of these rolls shows him as a conscript. Company muster roll for November/December 1863, reports him absent sick. Company muster roll for September/October 1864, reports him absent sent to General Hospital in Mobile on September 23, 1864. He was admitted to Post Hospital at Fort Morgan, Alabama, on May 31, 1863, with diarrhoea, returned to duty on June 18. He was re-admitted to Post Hospital at Fort Morgan on June 19, 1863, with febris remit., returned to duty on July 12. POW captured at Blakeley, Alabama, on April 9, 1865. Received at Ship Island, Mississippi, on April 15, 1865. Transferred from Ship Island to Vicksburg, Mississippi, for exchange on May 1, 1865.

Drew, M., Pvt. Co. D

His name appears on a regimental return for June 1862, "May, Corinth, deserted just before evacuation."

Driskill, J. A., Pvt. Co. H/G

Enlisted on October 24, 1863, at Camp Watts, Alabama, by Lt. Cummins for the war. He was admitted to Ross Hospital in Mobile, Alabama, on February 17, 1864, with chronic diarrhoea, and sent to General Hospital in Greenville, on February 18. He appears present on a hospital muster roll at General Hospital at Greenville, Alabama, on February 29, 1864. POW paroled in Montgomery, Alabama, on May 30, 1865, five foot eight inches, dark hair, gray eyes, light complexion. His parole and other paperwork is in his file.*

DuBose, C. B., Pvt. Co. C see **DuBose, V. B.**

DuBose, Charles C., Corporal Co. K

Enlisted by Captain Stewart at Mobile, Alabama, on October 13, 1861, for one year. He was discharged May 14, 1862. His name appears on a regimental return for June 1862, near Corinth, Mississippi, "discharged for disability." Born in Mobile, Alabama, age 21, five foot five and one half inches, fair complexion, blue eyes, dark hair and by occupation an engineer. His discharge is in his file.*

DuBose, James, Pvt. Co. K see **DuBose J. O. A.**

Dubose, J. O. A., Pvt. Co. K

Enlisted on August 23, 1862, at Fort Morgan, Alabama, by Captain Dorgan for the war. He appears present on a company muster roll for bounty on September 24, 1862. Company muster roll for November/December 1862, reports that he died of pneumonia at Mobile on December 3, 1862.

DuBose, M. W., Chaplin/Assistant Surgeon, Field and Staff

Regimental return for December 1861, reports him present as Assistant Surgeon. Appointed Chaplin on October 10, 1861. Regimental return for June 1862, reports him present at Tupelo, Mississippi. He is shown present on Field and Staff muster rolls for July/August 1863, September/October 1863 and March/April 1864. POW captured at Blakeley, Alabama, on April 9, 1865. His name appears on a list of hospital Surgeons and Stewards captured at Fort Blakeley, Alabama. He was received at Ship Island, Mississippi, from New Orleans April 16, 1865. Transferred to Vicksburg, Mississippi, for exchange on April 28, 1865. There are a number of requisitions and pay vouchers in his file.**

DuBose, V. B., Pvt. Co. C

Enlisted on October 13, 1861, at Mobile, Alabama, by Captain Rembert for 12 months. He appears present on a company muster roll for bounty on September 24, 1862. Company muster roll for December 31, 1862, to April 30, 1863, reports him absent detached in Engineer Department at Choctaw Bluff on March 25, 1863. May/June 1863, muster roll reports him present sick in quarters detached on March 24, returned to his company on May 15, 1863, lost one canteen strap at 25 cents. September/October 1863, muster roll reports him absent at Choctaw Bluff from July 26, by Colonel Anderson. POW captured at Fort Gaines, Alabama, on August 8, 1864. He was admitted to St.

Louis, USA General Hospital at New Orleans, with dysentery on September 7 1864, and returned to confinement on September 19, age 28. He was re-admitted on September 25, 1864, and returned on October 3. He was received at Ship Island, Mississippi, from New Orleans on October 25, 1864. Exchanged at Ship Island on January 5, 1865. POW surrendered by Lt General Richard Taylor at Citronelle, Alabama, on May 4, 1865, and paroled at Meridian, Mississippi, on May 13, 1865. Residence Sumter County, Alabama.

Duchanfour, J. [Joseph A.], Pvt. Co. K
Enlisted on July 4, 1863, at Fort Morgan, Alabama, by Captain Dorgan for the war. Company muster rolls for July/August and September/October 1863 report him present. He was admitted to Post Hospital at Fort Morgan, Alabama, on August 30, 1863, with ulcer and returned to duty on September 1, 1863. Transferred to Bridges' La. Lt. Artillery on June 24, 1864.

Duegnovich, George, Pvt. Co. H see **Jeyokovich, George**

Duggal, Patrick, Pvt. Co. B see **Duggan, Patrick**

Duggan, P., Pvt. Co. B see **Duggan, Patrick**

Duggan, Patrick, Pvt. Co. B
Enlisted on October 13, 1861, at Mobile, Alabama, by Major Hessee for 12 months. His name appears on a report near Tupelo, Mississippi, on June 28, 1862, "sent away on the evacuation of Corinth about 1st June." He appears present on a company muster roll for bounty on September 24, 1862. He appears present on company muster rolls for March/April 1863 and May/June 1863. Muster roll for September/October 1863, reports him absent "sent to General Hospital at Mobile July 15 / 63 by order of Colonel Anderson." POW captured at Fort Gaines, Alabama, on August 8, 1864. He was received at Ship Island, Mississippi, from New Orleans on October 25, 1864. He was exchanged at Ship Island on January 5, 1865. There is paperwork in his file.*

Dumas, John, Drummer, Co. E
Enlisted on October 13, 1861, at Mobile, Alabama. Discharged at Fort Morgan, Alabama, on October 13, 1862, due to being underage. Born in Mobile, Alabama, age 11, five foot one and one half inches, black hair, black eyes, a drummer by occupation. His discharge is in his file, he signed it with his mark "X". *There may be some records of Joseph Dumas in this file.*

Dumas, John, Corporal Co. D
Enlisted on October 13, 1861, at Mobile, Alabama, by Captain Butt for one year. He appears present on a company muster roll for bounty on September 24, 1862. He appears present on company muster roll for November/December 1862, "promoted from 3rd Corp. to 1st Corp. Dec. 1, 1862." July/August, September/October and November/December 1863, muster rolls all report him present. Muster roll for September/October 1864 shows him absent sent to General Hospital in Mobile on October 10, 1864. POW

surrendered by Lt General Richard Taylor at Citronelle, Alabama, on May 4, 1865, and paroled at Meridian, Mississippi, May 13, 1865. Residence shown as Mobile, Alabama.

Dumony, Angus, Pvt. Co. I

His name appears on a list of payments to discharged soldiers. Discharged on April 26, 1862.

Dumony, F., Pvt. Co. I see **Demony, Frank**

Dunand, John, Pvt. Co. G see file of **Dunnaway, Jesse W.** Pvt. Co. Pvt. Co. G

Enlisted by Major Hessee at Mobile, Alabama, on October 7, 1861, for 12 months. Discharged at Fort Gaines, Alabama, on July 2, 1862. Born Palermo, Italy, age ?, five foot five inches, strong complexion, gray eyes, a sailor by occupation. *His records and discharge are in Dunnaway's file.* *

Dunham, George R., Pvt. Co. A

Enlisted on October 13, 1861, at Mobile, Alabama, by Major Hessee for the war. His name appears on a regimental return for June 1862, "detached service, hospital nurse." He appears present on a company muster roll for bounty on September 24, 1862. Company muster rolls for December 31, 1862, to April 30, 1863, and May/June 1863, report him present. There a payroll vouchers in his file.*

Dunn, F. E., Pvt. Co. D

Enlisted on June 23, 1864, at Camden, Alabama, by Captain Beck for the war. He appears present on a company muster roll for September/October 1864. He was admitted to Ross Hospital at Mobile, Alabama, on April 2, 1865, with febris intermittens quot., returned to duty on April 23.

Dunn, Michael, Pvt. Co. C/B

Enlisted at Choctaw Bluff, Alabama, on April 9, 1863, by Captain Smith for three years or the war. "Enlisted as a substitute for **L. T. Smith** on April 9, 1863, and transferred to Company B Apr." Company muster roll for May/June 1863, reports him present. September/October 1863, muster roll reports him absent sent to General Hospital at Mobile, Alabama, on July 15, by order of Colonel Anderson. His name appears on a register at Ross Hospital in Mobile Oct. 9, 1863. A claim for deceased soldier was filed by Catherine Dunn widow on April 6, 1864.

Dunn, William J., Pvt. Co. D

Enlisted on September 10, 1862, at Mobile, Alabama, by Captain DeVaux for the war. He appears present on a company muster roll for bounty on September 24, 1862. Company muster roll for November/December 1862, reports him present, "promoted from ranks to 2nd Corporal on Dec. 1." He is shown present on rolls for July/August, September/October, 1862, November/December 1863 and September/October 1864. He was admitted to Ross Hospital at Mobile, Alabama, on November 3, 1864, with febris intermittens tert, and returned to duty on November 25. POW captured at Blakeley, Alabama, on April 9, 1865. He was received at Ship Island, Mississippi, from New

Orleans on April 15, 1865 and transferred to Vicksburg, Mississippi, for exchange on May 1, 1865.

Dunnaway, Jesse W., Pvt. Co. G
Enlisted by Major Hessee at Mobile, Alabama, on October 7, 1861, for 12 months. Discharged at Fort Gaines, Alabama, on July 2, 1862. Born Palermo, Italy, age ?, five foot five inches, strong complexion, gray eyes, a sailor by occupation. This discharge is in his file.* [*This first portion of the file may be a man named **John Dunand** as the discharge reads?*] POW captured at Fort Gaines, Alabama, on August 8, 1864. He was received at Ship Island, Mississippi, from New Orleans on October 25, 1864, and exchanged at Ship Island on January 5, 1865. POW surrendered by Lt General Richard Taylor at Citronelle, Alabama, on May 4, 1865, and paroled at Meridian, Mississippi, on May 13, 1865. Residence shown as Shiloh, Marengo County, Alabama.

Durand, Wilson L., Pvt. Co. D
Enlisted on October 13, 1861, at Mobile, Alabama, by Captain Butt for one year. He appears present on a company muster roll for bounty on September 24, 1862. Company muster roll for November/December 1862, reports him present. Muster rolls for July/August 1863, September/October 1863 and November/December 1863, report him present. Roll for September/October 1864, reports him present just returned from General Hospital in Mobile. He was admitted to Mississippi CSA Hospital at Jackson, Mississippi, on October 11, 1864, with febris int. quotidian, discharged ? October 12.

Dyas, R. S., Pvt. Co. D see **Dyis, R. S.**

Dyis, R. S., Pvt. Co. D
Enlisted on October 13, 1861, at Mobile, Alabama, by Captain Butt for the war. His name appears on a regimental return for June 1862, "sent to interior hospital at the evacuation (*of Corinth.*)" He appears present on company muster rolls for July/August 1863, September/October 1863 and November/December 1863. There is paperwork in his file.*

Dyres, S. R., Pvt. Co. D see **Dyris, R. S.**

E

Eadens, J., Pvt. Co. D see **Edins, James**

Eairley, W. G., Sgt. Co. G see **Early, William G.**

Early, William G., 1st Sgt. Co. G
POW captured at Fort Gaines, Alabama, on August 8, 1864. He was received at Ship Island, Mississippi, from New Orleans on October 25, 1864, and exchanged at Ship Island on January 5, 1865. POW he was surrendered by Lt General Richard Taylor at Citronelle, Alabama, on May 4, 1865, and paroled at Meridian, Mississippi, on May 13, 1865. Residence was shown as Elba, Coffee County, Alabama.

Ebel, Joseph, Pvt. Co. H
Enlisted at Mobile, Alabama, on October 13, 1861, by Major Hessee for one year. Discharged at Fort Gaines on January 11, 1862, born in Strasbourg, France, age 34, five foot six inches, blue eyes, brown hair, by profession a cook. His discharge and pay vouchers are in his file.*

Echols, W. P., Pvt. Co. E
His name appears on a muster roll of men paroled by Military Convention on 25th of April 1865, between CSA General Joseph E. Johnston and US General William Sherman. Paroled at Charlotte, North Carolina, on May 6, 1865. "Sharpe's Brigade."

Edens, J, Pvt. Co. D see **Edens, James**

Edington see Eddington, David

Eddington, David, Pvt. Co. B
Enlisted October 13, 1861, at Mobile, Alabama, by Major Hessee for the war. His name appears on a regimental return for June 1862, "detached service laborer M&O RR." He appears absent on a company muster roll for bounty on September 24, 1862, "detailed for M&O RR on June 27, 1862." Company muster roll for March/April and May/June 1863 report him present. Muster rolls for September/October 1863, he is reported absent sent to General Hospital at Mobile on October 27, 1863, by order of Dr. Payne. Transferred to the CS Navy, April 16, 1864. There are pay vouchers in his file.*

Eddins, J. W., Pvt. Co. _
Reference envelope only.

Edins [Eddens], James, Pvt. Co. D
Enlisted on October 13, 1861, at Mobile, Alabama, by Captain Butt for one year. Wounded in left leg while advancing at Shiloh on April 6, 1862, at 5 P. M." Captured at hospital on April 7." POW captured at Island No. 10 (or Pittsburgh Landing) on April 8, 1862. He is on a roll of POW's at Camp Douglas, Illinois, August 1, 1862. His name appears among 7?2 prisoners on board steamer *Jno. H. Dixon* September 2?, 1862, sent to Vicksburg, Mississippi, for exchange. He appears absent on a company muster roll for bounty on September 24, 1862, "Taken prisoner at Battle Shiloh." Company muster roll for November/December, 1862, reports him present with bounty due. July/August and September/October and November/December 1863, muster rolls all show him present. Muster roll for September/October 1864 shows him sent to General Hospital in Mobile, on September 17, 1864.

Edington, Cavid, Pvt. Co. B see **Eddington, David**

Edmondson, J., Pvt. Co. G see **Edmonson, J.**

MOBILE CONFEDERATES

Edmonson, J., Pvt. Co. G/E
On March 23, 1864, he was ordered back to his regiment from detailed service with Ordnance Department at Fort Morgan. See file of **Pvt. F. Basso**. He was admitted to Ross Hospital at Mobile, Alabama, on April 4, 1864, with foot ulcers and returned to duty on April 15, 1864. (Here he is shown in Co. E.) POW captured at Fort Gaines, Alabama, on August 8, 1864. He was received at Ship Island, Mississippi, from New Orleans on October 25, 1864. His name appears on a roll of POW's at Ship Island who applied to take the Oath of Allegiance to the USA. He was exchanged at Ship Island on January 5, 1865. His name appears on a roll of POW's at General Hospital Lauderdale, Mississippi, that were surrendered by Lt General Richard Taylor at Citronelle, Alabama, on May 4, 1865, and paroled at Meridian, Mississippi, on May 13, 1865, resident of Mobile, Alabama. Note to see the personal papers of **Frank Basso**, Pvt. Co. G, 21st Ala.

Edmondson, J. Pvt. Co. G see **Edmonson, J.**

Edwards, Benjamin, Pvt. Co. H (see also 1 Alabama Conscripts)
POW captured at Fort Gaines, Alabama, on August 8, 1864. He was received at Ship Island, Mississippi, from New Orleans on October 25, 1864. He died at Ship Island on December 11, 1864, of dysentery and was buried in Grave No. 78.

Elam, Thomas, Pvt. Co. F
Enlisted on October 13, 1864, at Baldwin County, Alabama, by Captain McCoy for one year. He appears present on a company muster roll for bounty on September 24, 1862. He appears present sick in hospital on a muster roll for March 1, to June 30, 1863. Company muster roll for September/October 1863, reports that he deserted from Point Clear, Alabama, carrying off gun and all equipment and 40 rounds of cartridges. Age 24?, eyes blue, complexion fair, hair light, five foot two inches, residence Baldwin County, Alabama. There is a reference card for a Court Martial. No date. [*From Mobile Register and Advertiser Sunday April 2, 1865*] *Privates Elam and Winn of the 21st Alabama Regiment were shot to death with musketry at Blakeley at 6 o'clock P. M. on Friday – These men deserted to the enemy some time since but were subsequently apprehended, tired, condemned, as suffered the extreme penalty of the law, as above stated.*

Elbert, M., Pvt. Co. H
His name appears on a regimental return for June 1862, "missing on march."

Eldridge, Michael, Pvt. Co. K
Wounded slightly in the neck while crossing field at Shiloh retreating at 4 P. M. on April 6, 1862. Discharged on July 24, 1862.

Elick, Junani, Pvt. Co. G
Killed at Shiloh on April 6, 1862, 2 P. M. at the Old Field.

Elliott, Charles, Pvt. Co. F

Enlisted on October 13, 1861, at Baldwin County, Alabama, by Captain McCoy for one year. His name appears on a regimental return for June 1861, "detached service, carpenter." He appears present on a company muster roll for bounty on September 24, 1862. Company muster roll for March 1, 1863, to June 30, 1863, reports him present on extra duty in QM Department as carpenter from June 28, 1863, by order of Colonel Anderson, "now sick in hospital". September/October 1863, muster roll shows him present detailed on extra duty with AQM. POW captured at Fort Gaines, Alabama, on August 8, 1862. He was received at Ship Island, Mississippi, from New Orleans on October 25, 1864, and exchanged at Ship Island on January 4, 1865.

Elliott, J. M., Pvt. Co. D

POW captured at Blakeley, Alabama, on April 9, 1865. He was confined at Ship Island, Mississippi, on April 15, 1865, and transferred to Vicksburg, Mississippi, for exchange on May 1, 1865.

Elliott, Jeff, Pvt. Co. F.

Enlisted on October 13, 1861, at Baldwin County, Alabama, by Captain McCoy for one year. He appears present on a company muster roll for bounty on September 24, 1862. Company muster roll for March 1, 1863, to June 30, 1863, reports that he died in hospital on June 29, 1863, at Choctaw Bluff, Alabama.

Ellis, A. B., Pvt. Co. I

Enlisted on October 13, 1861, at Halls Mill by Major Hessee for the war. His name appears on a report near Tupelo, Mississippi, on June 28, 1862, "sent to hospital in Mobile from hospital in Corinth by surgeon." He appears present on a company muster roll for bounty on September 24, 1862. Company muster rolls for July/August and September/October 1863 report him present. POW captured at Fort Morgan, Alabama, on August 23, 1864. He was received at Elmira, New York, from New Orleans on October 8, 1864, and transferred for exchange on February 14, 1865.

Ellis, Daniel, Pvt. Co. K

Enlisted on October 13, 1861, at Mobile, Alabama, on October 13, 1864, by Captain Stewart for the war. He appears on a regimental return for June 1862, "sent to Mobile hospital June 6." His name appears on a report June 28, 1862, near Tupelo, Mississippi, "on furlough since May 29th sent from Corinth." He appears present on a company muster roll for bounty on September 24, 1862. Company muster roll for November/December 1862, reports him present "Detailed in Commissary Dept by order of Colonel Anderson." July/August and September/October 1863, muster rolls report him on extra duty in Commissary Department [Issuing clerk] Company muster roll for September/October 1864, reports him detailed ACS Department in Pollard, Alabama, by General Cantry. POW surrendered by Lt General Richard Taylor at Citronelle, Alabama, on May 4, 1865, and paroled at Meridian, Mississippi, on May 9, 1865. Residence shown as Mobile, Alabama.

Ellis, G. K., Pvt. Co. I

Enlisted on July 26, 1863, at Fort Morgan, Alabama, by Lt. Donoho for the war. POW captured at Pittsburg [*Pittsburg landing near Shiloh*] on April 8, 1862. He served on ambulance squad and was captured at hospital. He appears on a roll of POW's at Camp Douglas, Illinois, on August 1, 1862. Company muster roll for July/August 1863, reports him present. Company muster roll for September/October 1863, reports him absent with leave from October 30, 1863. POW captured at Fort Morgan, Alabama, on August 23, 1864. Received at Elmira, New York, from New Orleans on October 8, 1864. He appears on a roll of POW's April 15, 1865, that are desirous to take the Oath of Allegiance to the USA at Elmira and remain North during the war. "He has relatives at New Orleans." Released on June 30, 1865. He appears as signature to an Oath of Allegiance to the USA at Elmira on June 30, 1865. Residence Mobile, Alabama, fair complexion, light hair, blue eyes, five foot eleven inches. There is a card to see the personal papers of Pvt. **Victor Gorlott** of Co. I, 21st Ala.

Ellis, G. R., Pvt. Co. I. see **Ellis, G. K.**

His name appears on a descriptive list and bounty roll August 3, 1862, filed with Pvt. **Victor Gorlott**, Co. I. Age 18, hazel eyes, dark hair, fair complexion, five foot eight inches, born in Mobile County, Alabama, enlisted July 26, 1862, at Fort Morgan, $50 bounty paid.

Ellott, Jeff, Pvt. Co. F see **Elliott, Jeff**

Emerson, George, Pvt. Co. D

Enlisted on October 13, 1861, at Mobile, Alabama, by Captain Butt for one year. Wounded slightly in the breast at Shiloh while advancing on the Center at 11 A. M. on April 6, 1864. His name appears on a regimental return for June 1862, "sent to interior hospital at the evacuation [of Corinth]." He drew a furlough of 20 days from June 10, and signed by his mark "X". He appears present on a company muster roll for bounty on September 24, 1862, and refused to receive bounty. Company muster roll for November/December 1862, reports him present. Company muster roll for July/August 1863, reports that he deserted on August 27, 1863. September/October 1863, muster roll reports him present under arrest for desertion. Muster roll for November/December 1863, reports him present "re? [*returned?*] from desertion." He drew clothing June 20 and in August 1864.

English, T. J. Pvt. Co. A

Drew clothing at Camp Anderson on June 14, 1864. POW captured at Fort Morgan, Alabama, on August 23, 1864, and sent to New York, on September 27, 1864. He was received at Elmira, New York, from New Orleans on October 8, 1864, and released on July 11, 1865. He signed an Oath of Allegiance to the USA at Elmira on July 11, 1865. Residence shown as Demopolis, Alabama, fair complexion, dark hair, hazel eyes, five foot six inches.

English, T. M., Pvt. Co. E

His name appears on a company muster roll for November/December 1862. "Furnished **J. T. Cain** as substitute."

Eppes, J., Pvt. Co. C

Enlisted on September 8, 1862, at Marengo County, Alabama, by Captain DeVoy for three years or the war. Company muster roll for December 31, 1862, to April 30, 1863, reports that he died in hospital at Choctaw Bluff, Alabama, March 8, 1863.

Esturedge, E. T., Pvt. Co. C see **Etheridge, E. T.**

Estruedge, J. W., Pvt. Co. C see **Etheredge, J. W.**

Etherage, S. E., Pvt. Co. C see **Etheridge, S. E.**

Etheredge, E. T., Pvt. Co. C see **Etheredge, S. E.**

Etheredge, J. W., Pvt. Co. C

Enlisted on October 13, 1861, at Mobile, Alabama, by Captain Lambert for 12 months. His name appears on a regimental return for June 1862, "absent on surgeon's certificate". His name appears on a report of June 28, 1862, near Tupelo, Mississippi, "sent to interior hospital by Surgeon from Corinth." He appears present on a company muster roll for bounty on September 24, 1862. Company muster roll for December 31, 1862, to April 30, 1863, reports him present. Company muster roll for May/June 1863, reports him absent without leave [*with furlough is crossed out*]. September/October 1863, muster roll reports him present detached as a teamster on August 5, 1863, by order of Colonel Anderson. POW captured at Fort Gaines, Alabama, on August 8, 1864. He was admitted to St. Louis USA General Hospital in New Orleans on September 5, 1864, with intermit tertian and returned to confinement on September 12, 1864, age 25. He was received at Ship Island, Mississippi, from New Orleans on October 25, 1864, and was exchanged at Ship Island on January 4, 1865. POW surrendered by Lt General Richard Taylor at Citronelle, Alabama, on May 4, 1865, and paroled at Meridian, Mississippi, on May 13, 1865. Residence shown as Marengo County, Alabama.
The records of **Etheridge, J. W.**, Pvt. Co. E, 59th Alabama are filed in error with this man. He was from Autauga County, Alabama and deserted near Washington D. C., in January 65.

Etheredge, N. J., Pvt. Co. C

Enlisted on October 13, 1861, at Mobile, Alabama, by Captain Rembert for 12 months. Seriously wounded through both sides at Shiloh on April 6, at 8:30 A. M. while advancing on 1st Camp. His name appears on a regimental return for June 1862, "wounded at Shiloh and furloughed." He appears on a report near Tupelo, Mississippi, on June 28, 1862, "wounded at Shiloh and sent home on furlough on surgeon's certificate." He appears present on a company muster roll for bounty on September 24, 1862. Company muster roll for December 31, 1862, to April 30, 1863, reports him present. He also appears present on company muster rolls for May/June 1863 and

September/October 1863. POW captured at Fort Gaines, Alabama, on August 8, 1864. He appears on a morning report of POW's at Steam Levee Press No. 4 at New Orleans on September 28, 1864, "sent to hospital on Sept. 28, 64." He was admitted to St. Louis USA General Hospital in New Orleans on September 10, 1864, with fever remit & diarrhoea, returned to confinement on September 24, 1864, age 19. He was re-admitted on September 27, 1864, with chronic diarrhoea and mal fever, returned to confinement on October 22. He was received at Ship Island, Mississippi, from New Orleans on October 25, 1864, and exchanged at Ship Island on January 4, 1865. POW surrendered by Lt General Richard Taylor at Citronelle, Alabama, on May 4, 1865, and paroled at Demopolis, Alabama, on June 15,1865. Residence shown as Clarke County, Alabama.

Etheredge, S. E., Pvt. Co. C

Enlisted on February 9, 1863, at Marengo, County, Alabama, by Lt. Northrup for three years or the war. He appears present on company muster rolls for December 31, 1862, to April 30, 1863, May/June 1863 and September/October 1863. POW captured at Fort Gaines, Alabama, on August 8, 1864. He was admitted to St. Louis USA General Hospital at New Orleans on October 7, 1864, with rubeola, returned to confinement on October 15, age 17. He was received at Ship Island, Mississippi, from New Orleans on October 25, 1864, and was exchanged at Ship Island on January 4, 1865. POW captured at Blakeley, Alabama, on April 9, 1865, received at Ship Island on April 15, 1865.

Etheredge, W. C., [**Etheredge, Columbus W.?**] Pvt. Co. C

Enlisted on October 13, 1861, at Mobile, Alabama, by Captain Rembert for 12 months. His name appears on a regimental return for June 1862, "absent without leave." His name appears on a report near Tupelo, Mississippi, on June 28, 1861, "sent to interior hospital by surgeon from Corinth." He appears present on a company muster roll for bounty on September 24, 1862. He appears present on a company muster roll for December 31, 1862, to April 30, 1863. May/June 1863, muster roll shows him present but lost one bayonet at $5 and haversack at 20 cents. Company muster roll for September/October 1863, reports him present. He was admitted to Post Hospital at Fort Morgan on November 3, 1863, with int. fev. and returned to duty on November 6. He was re-admitted on November 22, 1863, with congestive chill and died on November 22. Pvt. **W. C. Etheridge** Co. E drew clothing on March 31, 1864, signed by his mark. In this file is a payment for deceased soldier to Mary F. Etheredge his widow. **Pvt. Columbus W. Etheredge,** Co. C, who died on September 8, 1862. There is a discharge for disability in this file for Pvt. **Wiley P. Etheredge**, Co. C. who enlisted on October 13, 1861, by Colonel Hessee. He was born in Marengo County, Alabama, age 19, fair complexion, sandy hair, hazel eyes, six foot three inches, and a laborer by occupation. Discharged at Fort Gaines, on December 13, 1861.* [*This file is hopelessly tangled*]

Etheredge, W. J., Pvt. Co. C

Enlisted on February 26, 1863, at Choctaw Bluff, Alabama, by Lt. Poellnitz for three years or the war. Company muster roll for December 31, 1862, to April 30, 1863, reports him absent sick, substitute for **D. B. Thrash**. Company muster roll for May/June 1863 and September/October 1863, report him present. A note is attached that the medical cards filed with **W. C. Etheredge** may belong to this man.

Etheridge, Benjamin S., Pvt. Co. C

Enlisted at Clio, in Marengo County, Alabama, by Captain Rembert on September 20, 1861, to serve one year. Age 22, five foot six inches, black eyes, black hair, by occupation a farmer. Discharged on November 16, 1861, for disability.

Etheridge, E. T., Pvt. Co. C

POW captured at Fort Gaines, Alabama, on August 8, 1864. He was received at Ship Island, Mississippi, from New Orleans on October 25, 1864, and exchanged at Ship Island on January 4, 1865. POW surrendered by Lt General Richard Taylor at Citronelle, Alabama, on May 4, 1865, and paroled at Meridian, Mississippi, on May 13,1865. Residence shown as Marengo County, Alabama.

Etheredge may be spelled Etheridge or Ethridge or even Ethwrge in these files.

Eustis, H. M., Pvt. Co. K

Enlisted on January 29, 1863, at Fort Morgan, Alabama, by Captain Dorgan for the war. He appears present on company muster rolls for July/August 1863, and September/October 1863. On muster roll for September/October 1864, he is shown as absent sick since October 5, 1864, in hospital by order of Dr. Armstrong.

Evanisovich, J., Pvt. Co. G

Wounded slightly in the posterior at Shiloh on April 6, 1862, at 4 P. M. while retreating at The Old Field. His name appears on a report near Tupelo, Mississippi, on June 28, 1862, "wounded at Shiloh and absent since 10th Apl.".

Evans, Wayne, Pvt. Co. C

His name appears on a regimental return for June 1862, "May 16, La Grange, died hospital."

Evans, William, Pvt. Co. H

POW captured at Fort Gaines, Alabama, on August 8, 1864. He was admitted to St. Louis USA General Hospital at New Orleans on August 29, 1864, with diarrhoea and remit fever, returned to confinement on September 12, 1864, age 38. He was admitted to 1st Mississippi, CSA Hospital at Jackson, Mississippi, on March 3, 1865, with feb remit. bill, returned to duty on March 29, 1863. POW surrendered by Lt General Richard Taylor at Citronelle, Alabama, on May 4, 1865, and paroled at Meridian, Mississippi, on May 13,1865. Residence shown as Autauga County, Alabama.

Eurn, Ben, Pvt. Co. F

Enlisted at Point Clear, Alabama, on September 30, 1863. Company muster roll for September/October 1864, reports him absent detached to fish by General Maury September 30, 1863.

Ezell, G. W., Pvt. Co. H

POW captured at Fort Gaines, Alabama, on August 8, 1864. He was received at Ship Island, Mississippi, from New Orleans on October 25, 1864, and exchanged at Ship

Island on January 4, 1865. POW surrendered by Lt General Richard Taylor at Citronelle, Alabama, on May 4, 1865, and paroled at Meridian, Mississippi, on May 13,1865. Residence shown as Sumter County, Alabama.

Ezzell, G. W., Pvt. Co. H see **Ezell, G. W.**

Ezzell, J. W., Pvt. Co. H see **Ezell, G. W.**

F

Fagan, Jefferson, Pvt. Co. I see **Fagan, Thomas**

Fagan, Thomas, Pvt. Co. I
    He drew clothing on March 31, 1864, and signed by his mark. He was admitted to Ross Hospital in Mobile, Alabama, on June 23, 1864, with febris intimit. and returned to duty on July 25, 1864. POW captured at Fort Morgan, Alabama, on August 23, 1864. His name appears among POW's at New Orleans sent to New York on September 7, 1864. He was received at Elmira, New York, on October 8, 1864, then paroled and transferred for exchange to James River on February 13, 1865. His name appears among 3038 Confederate POW's at Boulwares' & Cox Wharf, James River on February 20, 1865. He was admitted to Receiving and Wayside Hospital or General Hospital No. 9 at Richmond, Virginia, on February 20, 1865, and sent to Howard's Grove Hospital on February 21, 1865. He was admitted to Howard's Grove on February 25.

Fagan, T. J., Pvt. Co. I see **Fagan, Thomas**

Falos, James J., Pvt. Co. E
    Enlisted on August 29, 1862, at Jefferson County, Alabama, by W. I. Poole. Company muster roll for November/December 1862, "sick in General Hospital, Mobile."

Farley, P., Pvt. Co. F
    POW captured at Fort Gaines, Alabama, on August 8, 1864. He was admitted to St. Louis USA General Hospital at New Orleans on August 21, 1864, with convalescent of int. fever, returned to confinement on September 9, 1864, age 18. He was received at Ship Island, Mississippi, from New Orleans on October 25, 1864, and exchanged at Ship Island on January 4, 1865. POW captured at Spanish Fort, Alabama, on April 8, 1865. He was confined at Ship Island on April 10, 1865 and sent to Vicksburg, Mississippi, May 1, 1865, on parole for exchange. POW surrendered by Lt General Richard Taylor at Citronelle, Alabama, on May 4, 1865, and paroled at Meridian, Mississippi, on May 12,1865. Residence shown as Jefferson County, Alabama.

Farley, W. Pvt. Co. F
    POW captured at Fort Gaines, Alabama, on August 8, 1864. He was received at Ship Island, Mississippi, from New Orleans on October 25, 1864, and exchanged at Ship Island on January 4, 1865. POW surrendered by Lt General Richard Taylor at Citronelle,

Alabama, on May 4, 1865, and paroled at Meridian, Mississippi, on May 12,1865. Residence shown as Jefferson County, Alabama.

Farmer, E. B., Pvt. Co. B

Enlisted on November 1, 1863, at Tallapoosa County, Alabama, by Captain Slaughter for the war. He drew clothing on June 1, 1864, and signed by his mark. His name appears on a hospital muster roll at Hospital Shelby Springs for July/August 1864, as a patient. He appears on a register at 1st Mississippi, CSA Hospital at Jackson, Mississippi, admitted August 13, 1864, with chronic diarrhoea and transferred on October 13. POW surrendered by Lt General Richard Taylor at Citronelle, Alabama, on May 4, 1865, and paroled at Meridian, Mississippi, on May 13, 1865. Residence shown as Tallapoosa County, Alabama.

Farmer, Loften, Pvt. Co. D

Enlisted on October 13, 1861, at Mobile, Alabama, by Captain Butt for one year. His name appears on a regimental return for June 1862, "sent to interior hospital, at the evacuation." [of Corinth] He appears present on a company muster roll September 23, 1862, for bounty.

Farron, C. S. A., Pvt. Co. E

Enlisted on October 13, 1861, at Mobile, Alabama, by Lt. Chamberlain for 12 months. Captured at hospital on ambulance squad April 7, 1862, [Shiloh] Company muster roll September 23, 1862, for bounty reports that he died since reorganization, "exchange prisoner, died Mobile 22 Sept 1862." Claim filed by Caroline Farrow widow on November 13, 1862. Reference to see the personal paper of Pvt. David Blackman, Co. F, 54th Alabama. The claim is in his file.*

Faulkner, Richard, Pvt. Co. G

POW captured at Fort Gaines, Alabama, on August 8, 1864. He was received at Ship Island, Mississippi, from New Orleans on October 25, 1864, and exchanged at Ship Island on January 4, 1865. POW surrendered by Lt General Richard Taylor at Citronelle, Alabama, on May 4, 1865, and paroled at Meridian, Mississippi, on May 12, 1865. Residence shown as Georgiana, Butler County, Alabama.

Felis, S., 1st Lt. Co. G

Enlisted on October 13, 1861. Elected Lt. on May 2, 1861, appointed October 7, 1861. Discharged by order of General Bragg succeeded by O. C. Donoho. He appears on a return stationed at Fort Gaines, November 1861, shown present. Regimental return for December 1861, reports him present. Regimental return for June 1862, reports him absent on furlough since April 11, for 30 days, since renewed by surgeon. Pay vouchers are included through October 13, 1862.

Fergerson, Joseph, Pvt. Co. A

Enlisted on August 27, 1862, at Jefferson County, Alabama, by William Walker for the war. Company muster roll for December 31, 1862, to April 30, 1863, reports him present. Company muster roll for May/June 1864, reports him present. His name appears on a register of claims for deceased soldiers. Claim presented by E. J. Fergason, widow, on October 31, 1864.

Ferguson, R. A., Pvt. Co. K

Enlisted on October 13, 1861, at Mobile, Alabama, by Captain Stewart for the war. A regimental return for June 1862, reports him on detached service as hospital clerk at Mobile. Hospital muster rolls for General Hospital in Mobile, report him present from November 1, 1861, to February 1864. Company muster roll for September 24, 1862, for bounty reports him absent, "detached in hospital Mobile, Nov. 12/61 by Genl. Withers." Company muster rolls for November/December 1862, July/August 1862, and September/October 1863, report him absent as above. Company muster roll for September/October 1864, reports him absent on steamer *Admiral* (?) September 30, 1864, for 30 days by order of General Maury.

Fergusson, R. H., Pvt. Co. K see **Ferguson, R. A.**

Festorazzi, S., Captain Co. G

Appointed Captain on October 13, 1861. A return from Fort Gaines, Alabama, in November 1861, reports him present. A regimental return for December 1861, reports him present. A regimental return for June 1862, reports him present at Tupelo, Mississippi. Honorably discharged on June 27, 1862, by reason of being without a command as his company was transferred to 1st Regt. Louisiana Infantry.

Feticks, John S., Pvt. Co. G

He was discharged on surgeon's certificate of disability. He appears on a list of personnel at Post Hospital at Fort Morgan, Alabama, from November 4, 1863, in the employ of Dr. Paine.

Fielder, W. M., see **Fields, W. M.**

Fields, James J., Pvt. Co. E

Enlisted on August 27, 1862, at Jefferson County, Alabama, by W. J. Poole for the war. Company muster roll for July/August 1863, report him present. Muster roll for September/October 1863, report him absent sick in hospital. He was admitted to Post Hospital at Fort Morgan, Alabama, on September 16, with rheumatism and died on November 15, 1863.

Fields, W. C., Pvt. Co. D

Enlisted as conscript on August 27, 1862, at Shelby County, Alabama, by W. J. Poole for the war. He appears present on company muster roll for November/December 1862. He was admitted to Post Hospital at Fort Morgan, Alabama, on May 29, 1863, with rubeola and returned to duty on June 24. Company muster roll for July/August 1863, reports him absent sick in General Hospital at Mobile. He was admitted to Post Hospital at Fort Morgan on July 23, 1863, with morbid cutis [a skin disease] and sent to general hospital on August 11. Company muster roll for September/October 1863, still shows him absent in General Hospital at Mobile, and a roll for November/December 1863, reports him absent sick

Fields, William M., Pvt. Co. K/F see **Fields, W. M.**

Fields, W. M., Pvt. Co. K/F

Enlisted August 29, 1862, at Jefferson County, Alabama, by W. J. Poole for the war. Company muster rolls for November/December 1862, July/August 1863 and September/October 1863, all report him present. POW captured at Fort Gaines, Alabama, on August 8, 1864. He was admitted to St. Louis USA General Hospital at New Orleans on September 10, 1864, with fever remit. and returned to confinement on September 16. He was received at Ship Island, Mississippi, from New Orleans on October 25, 1864, and exchanged at Ship Island on January 4, 1865. POW surrendered by Lt General Richard Taylor at Citronelle, Alabama, on May 4, 1865, and paroled at Meridian, Mississippi, May 13, 1865. Residence shown as Jefferson County, Alabama.

Finklea, W., Pvt./Corp. Co. F See **Finkley, Willis**

Finlay, William, Pvt. Co. D. see **Finley, William**

Finley, William, Pvt. Co. D
Only a reference envelope exist.

Finkley, Willis, Pvt. Co. F

Enlisted at Choctaw Bluff, Alabama, on February 26, 1863, by Captain Dade for the war. He appears present on a company muster roll from March 1, to June 30, 1863. Company muster roll for September/October 1863, reports him present, promoted to Corporal on September 1, 1863.

Finley, Partick, Pvt./Corp./Sgt. Co. B

Enlisted on October 13, 1861, at Mobile, Alabama, by Colonel Hessee for 12 months. He appears present on a company muster roll for bounty on September 24, 1862. Company muster roll for March/April 1863, reports him present. Company muster rolls for May/June 1863 and September/October report him present sick in quarters. POW captured at Fort Gaines, Alabama, on August 8, 1864. He was received at Ship Island, Mississippi, from New Orleans on October 25, 1864, applied to take the Oath of Allegiance to the USA at Ship Island and exchanged at Ship Island on January 4, 1865.

Fisher, Henry, Corp./Pvt. Co. D

Enlisted on October 13, 1861, at Mobile, Alabama, by Captain Butt for 12 months. His name appears on a regimental return for June 1862, "sent to interior hospital at the evacuation [of Corinth]." A report from near Tupelo on June 28, 1862, reports him sick in hospital in Mobile sent by surgeon from Corinth. He appears present on a company muster roll for bounty on September 24, 1862. Company muster roll for November/December 1862, reports him present promoted from 2nd Corporal to 5th Sergeant on December 1, 1862. Muster rolls for July/August 1863, September/October

1863, November/December 1863 and September/October 1864, all report him present. He was admitted to the Ross Hospital at Mobile on October 12, 1864, with febris intermittens tert., returned to duty on October 19. The September/October 1864, roll has the notation that he was absent without leave since October 26, 1864, "returned this day October 31."

Flanagan, F. L., Pvt. Co. C

Enlisted on September 28, 1863, at Point Clear, Alabama, by Captain Smith for the war. He appears present on a company muster roll for September/October 1863. POW captured at Fort Gaines, Alabama, on August 8, 1864. He was received at Ship Island, Mississippi, from New Orleans on October 25, 1864, and exchanged at Ship Island, on January 4, 1865.

Flanagan, F. M., Pvt. Co. C see **Flanagan, F. L.**

Flood, Thomas, Pvt. Co. E

Enlisted on October 13, 1861, at Mobile, Alabama, by Captain Chamberlain for the war. His name appears on a regimental return for June 1862, "sent to interior hospital May 27." He appears present on a company muster roll for bounty on September 24, 1862. Company muster roll for November/December 1862, reports him present. Company muster roll for July/August 1863, report him detached in bakery at Point Clear by order or General Maury. Hospital muster roll for General Hospital Miller at Point Clear, Baldwin County, Alabama, for July 17, to August 31, 1863, reports him employed as chief cook since July 25, 1863, employed by Surgeon G. Owen, paid $18.50 per month. Hospital Muster roll at General Hospital Point Clear for September/October 1863, reports him present as chief cook. Company muster roll for September/October 1863, reports him absent detached as baker at Point Clear from July 1, 1863. Hospital muster roll at General Hospital Miller at Greenville, Alabama, shows him present attached to hospital since February 4, 1863, as nurse, "acting as baker for hospital." He appears on a roll of POW captured sick in hospital in Greenville, Alabama, on April 22, 1865, by 16th Army Corp. "paroled & left sick in hospital at Greenville, Alabama."

Flurry, Henry, Pvt. Co. I

Drew clothing May 31, 1864. Claim filed for deceased soldier by Cloe Flurry Mother on November 29, 1864.

Flynn, D. E., Pvt. Co. A

Enlisted on August 8, 1862, at Mobile, Alabama, by Captain DeVaux for three years or the war. He appears present on a company muster roll for bounty on September 24, 1862, for bounty. His name appears on a company muster roll for December 31, 1862, to April 30, 1863. Company muster roll for May/June 1863, reports him absent detached in Medical Department Company muster roll for September/October 1863, reports him detached on February 5, 1863, in Medical Department at Mobile by order General Buckner. His name appears on a list of men employed as a engineer at Military Post of Mobile, Alabama, and as a surgical distiller, medical purveyor, detailed every 30 days by order of Major General Maury. He appears on rolls of privates employed on extra duty in Medical Purveyors Department at Mobile as engineer in the laboratory, from March 1, to April 30, 1864. There are several pay vouchers in his file along with other paperwork.*

Font, Francisco, Pvt. Co. G

His name appears on a regimental return for June 1862, "May 12, Corinth, missing from picket guard."

Forbes, F. F., Pvt. Co. A see **Forbes, Frank T.**

Forbes, Frank T., Pvt. Co. A

Enlisted on October 13, 1861, at Mobile, Alabama, by Major Hessee for three years or the war. Company muster roll for bounty on September 24, 1862, reports him detached in Ordinance Department at Mobile by order of General Withers. Muster rolls for December 31, 1862, to April 30, 1863, May/June 1863, September/October 1863, November/December 1863, May/June 1864, July/August 1864 and September/October 1864, all report him detailed [assigned] January 30, 1862, Ordnance Department One report shows him detailed as clerk to M. L. K Major H. Myers in Ordnance Department at Mobile by order of Major General Maury. POW surrendered by Lt General Richard Taylor at Citronelle, Alabama, on May 4, 1865, and paroled at Columbus, Mississippi, on May 13,1865. Residence shown as Mobile County, Alabama. There are a number of vouchers for repayment to Pvt. Forbes in materials purchased for construction of cartridge bags, tin cans and ordinance stores such as screws, charcoal, hoops, lead, nails, paint, coal, bar iron, flour, lime, boxes of matches, rockets, and many other materials supporting the local shore batteries, Fort Morgan, Montgomery, Selma Armory, Ordnance Warehouse, 3 Mile Magazine, Pollard, Major Boyles Batteries, Choctaw Bluff Battery and Columbus, Mississippi.***

Ford, J. B., Pvt. Co. A

POW captured at Fort Donelson died of pneumonia at City General Hospital at St. Louis, Missouri, on March 5, 1862. He was admitted to City USA General Hospital at St. Louis on February 28, with typhoid pneumonia.

Ford, Peter, Pvt. Co. B

Enlisted on October 13, 1861, at Mobile by Major Hessee for the war. POW captured at Island No. 10 or Pittsburg Landing on April 8, 1862, and sent to Camp Douglas, Illinois. He was admitted to USA Prison Hospital at Camp Douglas near Chicago, Illinois, on April 28, 1862, and returned to confinement on May 10. He was again admitted to USA Prison Hospital at Camp Douglas near Chicago, Illinois, on June 14, 1862, with debilitas and returned to confinement on June 26. He was sent from Camp Douglas to Vicksburg, Mississippi, on September 8, 1862, for exchange. He arrived at Vicksburg among 7?2 Confederate Prisoners aboard the steamer *Jno. H. Done*, on September 28, 1862. Company muster roll for March/April 1863, reports him absent under arrest at Choctaw Bluff. May/June 1863, muster roll reports him present. September/October 1863, muster roll reports him absent, sent to General Hospital at Mobile on July 29, 1863, by order of Colonel Anderson. He drew clothing on May 20,

1864. Company muster roll for September/October 1864, reports him absent sent to Hospital Ross at Mobile on October 10, 1864, by order of Dr. Smith.

Ford, William, Pvt. Co. F see **Fort, William**

Fordick, S. U., Corp. Co. E

His name appears on a regimental return for June 1862, "May 13, 186_, Corinth, Mississippi, discharged for disability." Enlisted on October 13, 1861, by Colonel Hessee to serve one year. Born in Cincinnati, Ohio, age 25, five foot nine and three quarter inches tall, fair complexion, gray eyes, light hair, and by occupation an accountant. Discharged on May 7, 1862. His discharge is in his file.*

Fort, V., Pvt. Co. F see **Fort, William**

Fort, William, Pvt. Co. F

Enlisted on January 31, 1863, at Choctaw Bluff, Alabama, by Capt. Dade for the war. Company muster rolls for March 1, to June 30, 1863, and September/October 1863, reports him present. He was admitted to Post Hospital at Fort Morgan, Alabama, on November 18, 1863, with pneumonia, and returned to duty on December 27. POW captured at Fort Gaines, Alabama, on August 8, 1864. He was received at Ship Island, Mississippi, from New Orleans on October 25, 1864, and exchanged at Ship Island on January 4, 1865.

Foster, Charles, E., Sgt. Co. D

Enlisted on October 13, 1861, at Mobile, Alabama, by Captain Butt for one year. His name appears on a regimental return for June 1862, "sent to interior hospital at the evacuation [of Corinth]." Company muster roll on September 24, 1862, for bounty reports him absent "sick in Gen. Hospital, Mobile, since 20th Sept. 1862." Company muster roll for November/December 1862, reports him present promoted from 4th Sgt. to 2nd Sgt. on December 1, 1862. Company muster rolls for July/August 1862, September/October 1863 and November/December 1863, all report him present. Company muster roll for September/October 1864, reports him absent detached on the river from August 6, 1864. His name appears on a muster roll of detailed men in the O. M. Department at Mobile in July 1864. His name appears on a roll of men at Mobile on extra duty employed by Major Henry St. Paul Chief of River Transportation employed by order of General D. H. Maury as pilot on the *Reindeer*, age 26. There is paperwork in his file.*

Foster, F. A., Pvt. Co. A see **Foster T. A.**

Foster, George, F., Pvt. Co. C

Enlisted on September 28, 1862, at Marengo County, Alabama, by Capt. DeVaux for three years or the war. His name appears on a report for June 1862, "absent on Surgeon's Certif.". He appears on a report June 28, 1862, near Tupelo, Mississippi, furloughed by order of Surgeon Ford to July 1, 1862. Company muster roll on September 24, 1862, for bounty reports him absent sick. Muster roll for December 31, 1862, to April 30, 1863, reports that he is absent sick. Company muster roll for May/June 1863,

21ST ALABAMA INFANTRY VOLUNTEERS

reports that he was discharged for disability on June 28, 1863, by order of General Maury.

Foster, James, Sgt. Co. D

His name appears on a register of Post Hospital at Fort Morgan, Alabama, as having been admitted on April 7, 1863, with int. febris and returned to duty on April 14.

Foster, John, Pvt. Co. I

Enlisted on October 13, 1861, at Halls Mill, Alabama, by Major Hessee for the war. A regimental return for June 1862, reports him sent to interior hospital on May 28, 1862. A report on June 28, 1862, near Tupelo, Mississippi, states that he was sent to interior hospital from Corinth by surgeon on May 28. A return for November, 1862, shows him detailed in Engineering Department. Company muster roll on September 24, 1862, for bounty reports him present in hospital. He was admitted to Post Hospital at Fort Morgan on April 11, 1863, with ulcer, returned to duty on April 15, 1863. Muster rolls for July/August 1863 and September/October 1863, report him present.

Foster, T. A., Pvt. Co. A.

Enlisted on February 1, 1863, at Choctaw Bluff, Alabama, by Captain Cothran for the war. Company muster rolls for December 31, 1862, to April 30, 1863 and May/June 1863, report him present. Muster roll for September/October 1863, reports him absent, sent to General Hospital in Mobile on October 25, 1863. POW captured at Fort Morgan, Alabama, on August 23, 1864. He was received at Elmira, New York, on October 8, 1864, from New Orleans. Transferred at Elmira to James River for exchange on March 2, 1865. He was admitted to Receiving and Wayside Hospital No. 9 at Richmond, Virginia, on March 6, 1865, and sent to Camp Lee on March 7. He was admitted to Jackson Hospital at Richmond Virginia, on March 8, with debilitas and furloughed for 30 days. He appears on a descriptive list as age 18.

Foster, I., Pvt. Co. E

His name appears on a return December 1862, as sick with certificate in general hospital. He drew clothing on June 14, 1864.

Foster, Thomas, R., Pvt. Co. D

POW captured at Fort Morgan, Alabama, on August 23, 1864. He was received at Elmira, New York, on October 8, 1864, from New Orleans. Paroled at Elmira and transferred for exchange to James River on March 2, 1865, "unable to travel." He was admitted to Receiving and Wayside Hospital No. 9 at Richmond, Virginia, on March 7, 1865, and sent to Howard's Grove [Hospital] on March 10, 1865, where he was furloughed for 60 days on March 27.

Foster, T. T.. Pvt. Co. A.

His name appears on a regimental return for June 1862, "detached service, Clerk Ord, Off. Mobile."

Fowler, Ben A., Pvt./Corp. Co. E.

Enlisted on October 13, 1861, at Mobile, Alabama, by Capt. Chamberlain for the war. A return for June 1862, reports that he is clerk for General Withers. Company muster roll on September 24, 1862, for bounty reports him present. Muster roll for November/December 1862, reports him present. Muster roll for July/August 1863, reports him transferred to Capt. Hutchinson's Co. of Engineers on August 1.

Fowler, W. H., Pvt. Co. D

His name appears on a regimental return for June 1862, "May 26, Corinth Mississippi, discharged for disability."

Fowler, William, Pvt. Co. A

Enlisted on January 29, 1863, at Choctaw Bluff, Alabama, by Captain Cothran for the war. He appears present on company muster rolls for December 31, 1862, to April 30, 1863, May/June 1863 and September/October 1863. He was admitted to Post Hospital at Fort Morgan, Alabama, on November 3, 1863, with diarrhoea and returned to duty on November 8. POW captured at Fort Morgan, Alabama, on August 23, 1864. He was received at Elmira, New York, from New Orleans on October 8, 1864. His name appears on a roll of POW's at Elmira, New York, who desire to take the Oath of Allegiance to the USA. "Was conscripted in February of 1863, Is a Scotchman [Scotsman] came to this county in 1849, and is a naturalized citizen of the United States. Removed from New York, to Mobile, Ala. Jany 1, 1860, has friends and relatives in New York, where he desires to go. His health is bad and he prays for a speedy release." He died of chronic diarrhoea on January 3, 1865, and was buried in grave Number 1352.

Fox, James D., Pvt. C

Enlisted on October 31, 1861, at Mobile, Alabama, by Captain Rembert for 12 months. His name appears on a regimental return for June 1862, absent on sick furlough. He appears on a report near Tupelo, Mississippi, June 28, 1862, furloughed on surgeon's certificate June 15th for 20 days. Company muster roll on September 24, 1862, for bounty reports him absent sick. Muster roll for December 31, 1862, to April 30, 1863, reports him present, "pay stopped from 2 Sept. 1862, to 25 Jan. 1863, by sentence of C. Martial." Muster roll for May/June 1863, reports him present, "Lost canteen at 25 cts, strap at 20 cts."

Francisco, L., Pvt. Co. G

His name appears on a regimental return for June 1862, "sent to hospital May 28."

Fredrick, W. B., Pvt. Co. F

Enlisted on February 9, 1863, at Choctaw Bluff, Alabama, by Captain Dade for the war. Company muster roll for March 1, to June 30, 1863, reports him present in arrest. He appears on a register of soldiers of the CSA who were killed in battle, or who died of wounds or disease. Died at Moore Hospital at Mobile, Alabama, effects left – sundries on August 1, 1863, Certificate No. 11.

Fredricks, Alfred, Pvt. Co. A

Enlisted October 13, 1861, at Mobile, by Major J. Hessee for one year. Born Hamburg, age 36, five foot six inches, dark complexion, gray eyes, by occupation a clerk. His name appears on a report near Tupelo, Mississippi, June 28, 1862, "Sent to Corinth Hospital and from there to interior by order of Surgeon Heustis." Discharged due to disability on July 14, 1862, at Camp near Saltillo, Mississippi. His discharge and other paperwork is in his file.*

Freeman, J. F., Pvt. Co. H

Drew clothing May 3, and June 1, 1864, signed by his mark. His name appears on a report of the Medical Examining Board, Dalton, Georgia, under recommendations for extension of furloughs on October 27, 1864. Disability – abscess of lung following attack of pluro pneumonia. Furloughed from Mobile, for 60 days from August 22, 1864, residence Lime Creek, Alabama. Gardner's Brigade. He was admitted to Ross Hospital at Mobile, Alabama, on January 3, 1865, furloughed on January 19, 1865, for 60 days.

Freuing, George, Pvt. Co. A

He appears on a regimental return for December 1961, authorizing discharge of Geo. Freuing, Co. A.

Fulford, J. B., Co. C.

Enlisted at Fort Gaines, Alabama, on February 21, 1862, by Captain Rembert for 12 months. Company muster roll on September 24, 1862, for bounty reports him present. Muster roll for September/October 1863, reports him present. Company muster roll for December 31, 1862, to April 30, 1863, reports him present. May/June 1863, muster roll reports him present lost rammer at $2. POW captured at Fort Gaines, Alabama, on August 8, 1864, received from New Orleans at Ship Island, Mississippi, on October 25, 1864. Died of dysentery on December 31, 1864, buried in grave No. 123. His name appears [*in error?*] on a roll of POW's exchanged at Ship Island on January 4, 1865.

Funomdey, E., Pvt. Co. H.

He appears on a regimental return for June 1862, "sent to the rear on 28 May."

Furchsting, L. G., Pvt. Co. E.

. POW captured at Fort Gaines, Alabama, on August 8, 1864. He appears on a roll of POW's at Ship Island, Mississippi, who refused be exchanged or take the Oath of Allegiance.

Furguson, R. A., Pvt. Co. K see **Ferguston, R. A.**

Fyne, William, Pvt. Co. B see **Tyne, William**

G

Gabel, M. V., Pvt. Co. F

Enlisted on October 13, 1861, at Baldwin County, Alabama, by Captain McCoy for one year. He was elected 2nd Lt. on May 8, 1862, but did not serve due to incompetence. Company muster roll on September 24, 1862, for bounty reports him present. Muster roll for March 1, to June 30, 1863, reports that he was transferred to Captain Barlow's Mounted Men on May 12, 1863, by order of General Slaughter. [*See Co. C, 15th Confederate Cavalry CSA.*]

Galaway, Robert, Pvt. Co. F

He was admitted to USA No. 6, General Hospital, Louisville, Kentucky, on April 17, 1862, with vulnus scolopetucum [*gunshot wound*]. (Sustained at Shiloh, April 6 or 7, 1862) Sent to Provost July 10, 1862.

Gale, E. B. [Jr.], Pvt. Co. K

Enlisted on October 4, 1862, at Fort Morgan, Alabama, by Captain Dorgan for the war. Company muster roll for November/December 1862, reports "absent on Surgeon's certificate." Muster rolls for July/August 1863, September/October 1863 and September/October 1864, report him present. He was admitted to Post Hospital at Fort Morgan, Alabama, on September 23, 1863, with feb con. and returned to duty on October 21. POW surrendered by Lt General Richard Taylor at Citronelle, Alabama, on May 4, 1865, and paroled at Meridian, Mississippi, on May 13,1865. Residence shown as Mobile, Mobile County, Alabama. There are several pay vouchers in his file.*

Gallahen, J. M., Pvt. Co. K

Enlisted on October 1, 1862, at Mobile, Alabama, by Major Stone for the war. Company muster roll for September/October 1862, reports him absent temporarily attached to ? [*company*] by Major Stone.

Gallaway, F. M., Pvt. Co. G see **Gallaway, Francis M.**

Gallaway, Francis M., Pvt. Co. G

POW captured at Fort Gaines, Alabama, on August 8, 1864, received at Ship Island, Mississippi, on October 25, 1864, and exchanged on January 4, 1865. POW surrendered by Lt General Richard Taylor at Citronelle, Alabama, on May 4, 1865, and paroled at Meridian, Mississippi, on May 13, 1865. Residence shown as Curaton's Bridge, Henry County, Alabama.

Gallaway, R. C., Pvt. Co. I

Drew clothing on April 16, 1864. He was admitted to Post Hospital at Fort Morgan, Alabama, on July 29, 1864, with int. feb. quar. and returned to duty on August 4, 1864. POW captured at Fort Gaines, Alabama, on August 8, 1864, received at Ship Island, Mississippi, on October 25, 1864, from New Orleans and exchanged on January 4, 1865. He appears on a register of POW's surrendered at Citronelle, Alabama, on May 4,

1865, paroled May 30, 1865, at Mobile. Residence Jackson County, Mississippi, six foot, age 19, fair complexion, blue eyes, light hair.

Gamble, W. H., Pvt. Co. C see **Gamble, William**

Gamble, William, Pvt. Co. C

His name appears as regimental teamster on a regimental return for June 1862. He was admitted to Post Hospital at Fort Morgan, Alabama, on December 2, 1863, with rheumatism and returned to duty on December 22. Drew clothing June 1, 1864. POW captured at Fort Gaines, Alabama, on August 8, 1864. He died of diarrhoea at St. Louis USA General Hospital at New Orleans on September 2, 1864, age 35 buried grave 327 in Cypress Grove Cemetery no effects left. His death certificate shows him a resident of Clark County, Alabama, single, nearest kin Aunt in Pine Bluff, Alabama. His certificate of death is in his file.*

Gans, Herman, Pvt. Co. B

His name appears on a report from near Tupelo, Mississippi, on June 28, 1862, "sent away on the evacuation of Corinth about 1st June."

Gardner, John D., Pvt. Co. D

Enlisted on February 1861(?) at Montgomery, Alabama, by Lt. Berry for the war. Company muster rolls for July/August 1863, September/October 1863, and November/December 1863, all report him present. Discharged on February 18, 1864.

Gardner, J. J., Pvt. Co. K

Enlisted on March 7, 1861, at Texas, Alabama, by Sgt. Burnett for three years. Company muster rolls for July/August 1863, and September/October 1863, all report him present. He was admitted to Post Hospital at Fort Morgan, Alabama, with gonorrhoea on August 4, 1863, and returned to duty on August 11.

Garner, John, Pvt. Co. K see **Garner, J. J.**

Garner, William J., Pvt. Co. K

POW captured at Vicksburg, Mississippi, on July 4, 1863. Paroled in the City Hospital at Vicksburg, Mississippi, on July 13, 1863.

Garrett, J. F., Pvt. Co. F

Enlisted at Perry County, Alabama, by W. B. Livingston for three years or the war. He appears present on company muster rolls for March 1, to June 30, 1863, and September/October 1863. POW captured at Fort Gaines, Alabama, on August 8, 1864, received at Ship Island, Mississippi, on October 25, 1864, from New Orleans and exchanged on January 4, 1865.

Garrity, Patrick, Pvt. Co. B

Enlisted at Point Clear, Alabama, on October 12, 1863, by Lt. Toumlin for three years or the war. POW captured at Fort Gaines, Alabama, on August 8, 1864, received at

Ship Island, Mississippi, on October 25, 1864, from New Orleans and exchanged on January 4, 1865.

Gazzam, Harry M., Sgt./2nd Lt. Co. A

Enlisted on October 13, 1862, at Mobile, Alabama, by Major Hessee for the war. POW captured at Shiloh April 7, 1862, on the ambulance squad. He is shown as POW at Alton, Illinois, on July 7, 1862, sent from Alton to Vicksburg, Mississippi, for exchange on September 23, 1862, age 19. Company muster roll for December 31, 1862, to April 30, 1863, reports him present, promoted from 4th Corp. to 5th Sgt. on January 1, 1863. Company muster roll for May/June 1863, reports him present. Muster roll for September/October 1863, reports him present, promoted from 5th to 4th Sgt. on September 1, 1863. He was admitted to Ross Hospital at Mobile, Alabama, on November 19, 1863, with scabies and returned to duty on December 21. Elected Lt. on May 16, 1864. POW captured at Fort Morgan, Alabama, on August 23, 1864. He was received at Fort Lafayette, New York Harbor, from New Orleans on October 20, 1864. He appears on a record of POW's at Fort Warren, Massachusetts, as being paroled and transferred for delivery on March 13, 1865. He was received at Boulware's Wharf, James River among 1046 paroled POW's including 11 officers and 70 civilians on March 19, 1865. He was on the paroled list at Citronelle, Alabama, May 10, 1865. His parole is in his file.*

Geary, James, Pvt. Co. _

His name appears on a roll of POW's received at Ship Island, Mississippi, on October 21, 1864. POW captured at St. Joseph, Louisiana, on October 8, 1864, sent to New York on November 5, 1864, by order of Captain M. R. Maiston.

Gee, George L., Pvt./Sgt. Co. B

Enlisted on October 13, 1861, at Mobile, Alabama, by Major Hessee for the war. Company muster roll for March/April 1863, reports him present. POW captured at Island No. 10 (or Pittsburg Landing) on April 8, 1862. He was admitted May 5, 1862, to USA Prison Hospital at Camp Douglas with debilities and returned to confinement on May 9. He appears on a roll of POW's at Camp Douglas, Illinois, on August 1, 1862. He was sent to Vicksburg, Mississippi, and arrived September 28, 1862, among 742 POW's aboard the steamer *Jno. H. Done*. Company muster roll for May/June 1863, reports him absent on sick leave, appointed Sgt. on May 1, 1864. He appears as a patient on the muster roll at General Hospital Ross at Mobile on June 30, 1863. September/October muster roll shows him sent to hospital in Mobile on October 27, 1863, by order of Dr. Payne. POW captured at Fort Gaines, Alabama, on August 8, 1864. He was admitted to St. Louis USA General Hospital at New Orleans on September 2, 1864, with fever remit. and dysentery, and returned to confinement on November 2, 1864, age 24. He is shown as being received at Ship Island, Mississippi, on October 29, 1864, from New Orleans and exchanged on January 5, 1865. *

Gellespie, David, Pvt. Co. A

Enlisted on September 24, 1862, at Jefferson County, Alabama, by Jas, Barrett for the war. Company muster rolls for December 31, 1862, to April 30, 1863 and May/June report him present. He is shown absent sent to general hospital on September 25, 1863, on a muster roll for September/October 1863. POW captured at Fort Morgan, Alabama, on August 23, 1864. He was received at Elmira, New York, from New Orleans on October 8, 1864. He signed the Oath of Allegiance to the USA on July 7, 1865, and was released at Elmira, New York. Residence given as Montevallo, Alabama, gray hair, florid complexion, gray eyes, five foot seven and one half inches.

Genham, Jno., Pvt. Co. B
His name appears on a regimental return for June 1962, "sick furlough."

Genoe, I., Pvt. Co. K
Enlisted September 19, 1864, by Major Stone for the war. Company muster roll for September/October 1864, reports him transferred to Conscript Camp at Notasulga, Alabama, by order of Major Stone, Enrolling Officer on October 18, 1864.

George, Robert B., Pvt./Ord. Sgt. Co. K, F & D
Enlisted in Co. K on March 12, 1861, at Mobile, Alabama, by Captain Wm. Walker for three years or the war. Company K muster roll for September/October 1864, reports him present. Company muster roll for Co. A for July/August 1864, reports him present attached to Regiment from Co. K by order of ? Company muster roll for September/October 1864, reports him transferred to company K. POW surrendered by Lt General Richard Taylor at Citronelle, Alabama, on May 4, 1865, and paroled at Meridian, Mississippi, on May 13, 1865. Residence shown as Cuba Station, Alabama. On his parole he is shown as Ordnance Sergeant.

George, W. J. (Jack), Pvt. Co. C/A
Enlisted at Choctaw Bluff, Alabama, on January 3, 1863, by Colonel Anderson, for three years or the war. Company muster roll for Co. C from December 31, 1862, to April 30, 1863, reports him transferred to Co. A on March 21, 1863. Company muster roll for Co. A December 31, 1862, to April 30, 1863, reports absent him sick in hospital at Choctaw Bluff. Muster roll for Company A for May/June 1863, reports him present. Muster roll for September/October 1863, reports him absent sent to General Hospital at Mobile on July 25, 1863. His name appears on a company muster roll for Co. H, 13th Reg. La. Regiment present, member of the 21st Alabama Regiment temporarily assigned cut off from his command. He appears on a roll of POW's of Co. H, 13th Louisiana Infantry that were surrendered at Citronelle, Alabama, by General Richard Taylor on May 4, 1864, and paroled at Meridian, Mississippi, on May 14. Temporarily assigned by order of General Taylor on April 11, 1865. Note Descriptive list for him and four other soldiers is in **Keane, Edward**, Drummer's file May 21, 1862.
George, William D., age 36, blue eyes, dark hair, light complexion, five foot eleven inches, a farmer, enlisted at Clarke County, Alabama, by Colonel Anderson for the war, $50 bounty received.

Geotrix, Robert, Pvt. Co. B. see **Gratix, Robert**

Gibson, Jno. Major 21st Alabama Infantry

His name appears on a register of commissioned officers of Provisional Army of the Confederate States.

Giddons, P., Pvt. Co. C

POW captured at Blakeley, Alabama, on April 9, 1865. He was received at Ship Island, Mississippi, on April 15, 1865, paroled and transferred to Vicksburg, Mississippi, on May 1, 1865.

Gifford, A., Pvt. Co. G

Drew clothing on March 31, 1864. His name appears on a roll of POW's who entered the lines of the US 16th Army Corps during April 1865. Turned over to Assistant Provost Marshal at Montgomery, Alabama, on May 5, 1865.

Gilbert, C. M., Pvt. Co. K

Enlisted on October 13, 1861, at Mobile, Alabama, by Captain Stewart for the war. His name appears on a regimental return for June 1863, in detached service in Signal Corps. Company muster roll for September 24, 1862, for bounty shows him absent detached on May 25, 1862, in Signal Corps by order or General Beauregard. Company muster roll for November/December 1862, reports the same. A return for November 1862, reports him detached in Signal Corps at Fort Gaines. There are pay vouchers in his file.*

Gill, Charles, Pvt. Co. F

Enlisted on August 28, 1862, at Jefferson County, Alabama, by Jas. Tarrent for the war. Company muster rolls for March 1, to June 30, 1863 and September/October 1863, report him present. He was admitted to Post Hospital at Fort Morgan on November 3, 1863, with int. fever and returned to duty on November 11. He was again admitted to Post Hospital at Fort Morgan on January 10, 1864, with pneumonia and returned to duty on January 19. POW captured at Fort Gaines, Alabama, on August 8, 1864. He was admitted to St. Louis USA General Hospital at New Orleans on August 27, 1864, with fever remittent and returned to confinement on August 31, 1864, age 33. He was again admitted to St. Louis USA General Hospital at New Orleans on October 18, 1864, with hydrops and returned to confinement on January 2, 1865, age 32. He is shown as being received at Ship Island, Mississippi, on January 25, 1864, from New Orleans and exchanged on March 4, 1865. His name appears on a transcript of Hospital Examining Board March 6, 1865, "Maury's command furloughed sixty (60) days general dropsy very recently returned from Ship Island."

Gillard, John, Co. B

His name appears on a register of CSA soldiers who were killed in battle or died of wounds or disease. Left $1.

Gilleland, H. (Hoit), Pvt. Co. D

Enlisted on October 13, 1861, at Mobile, Alabama, by Captain Butt for one year. POW captured at Shiloh (Pittsburg) April 7, or 8, 1862. He appears on a roll of POW's at Camp Douglas, Illinois, on August 1, 1862. He was admitted to USA Prison Hospital at Camp Douglas on May 1, 1862, with pneumonia returned to confinement on June 11, 1862. He was again admitted to USA Prison Hospital at Camp Douglas near Chicago, on August 26, 1862, with chronic diarrhoea. He died at Camp Douglas, Illinois, on September 20, 1862, of diarrhoea.

Gillett. S., Pvt. Co. _
He is reported absent on a muster roll of Sossaman's Detachment, 21st Alabama, Infantry for September/October 1864, at Mobile, Alabama, detailed at Battery Huger by order of Colonel Fuller.

Gillmore, A. A., Pvt./Sgt. Co. C see **Gilmore, A. A.**

Gillott, V., Pvt. Co. D
Enlisted at Mobile, Alabama, by Major Stone for the war. Company muster roll for September/October 1864, reports him absent, sent to General Hospital at Mobile on September 12, 1864, assigned to company by order. He was admitted to Ross Hospital in Mobile on September 13, 1864, with febris intermittes tert, and returned to duty on September 30, 1864.

Gilmore, A. (Allen) A., Pvt./Sgt. Co. C
Enlisted on November 28, 1861, at Fort Gaines, Alabama, by Captain Rembert for 12 months. Company muster roll for bounty on September 24, 1862, reports him present. Muster roll for December 31, 1862, to April 30, 1863, reports him present. May/June 1863, muster roll reports him present promoted from 2nd Corporal to 5th Sergeant on June 6, 1863. Company muster roll for September/October 1863, shows him absent, detached as Sergeant of Guard at Choctaw Bluff, Alabama, on July 24, 1863, by order of Colonel Anderson. POW captured at Fort Gaines, Alabama, on August 8, 1864. His name appears on a morning report of POW's confined at Steam Levee Press No. 4 at New Orleans on September 29, 1864. He was admitted to St. Louis, USA General Hospital, New Orleans on September 20, 1864, and returned to confinement on September 28, age 22. He was received at Ship Island, Mississippi, from New Orleans on October 25, 1864. He died at Ship Island of pneumonia on December 9, 1864, and was buried in grave No. 74.*

Gilsinan, Walter, Pvt. Co. A
Enlisted on November 1, 1861, at Mobile, Alabama, by Major Hessee for three years or the war. He appears on a regimental return for June 1862, "wounded at Shiloh & furloughed since 8th April [1862]". Wounded severely in the hand at Shiloh on April 6, 1862, at 2 P. M. Company muster roll for bounty on September 24, 1862, reports him absent sick. Muster roll for December 31, 1862, to April 30, 1863, reports him absent, detached on March 14, 1862, in Engineering Department by order of General Buckner. Muster rolls May/June and September/October 1863, show him detached in Engineering Department. His name appears on a muster roll of detailed men in the Quarter Master's Department at Mobile to July 31, 1864. He appears on a roll of men at Mobile, Alabama,

in September 1864, employed by Major Henry St. Paul, Chief of River Transportation as a ship carpenter age 28. There are pay vouchers in his file. He signed by his mark.*

Gironi, D., Pvt. Co. G

Wounded severely in the thigh while advancing at Shiloh on April 6, 1862, at 12 noon. He appears on a June report and a report June 28, 1862, near Tupelo, Mississippi, as having been wounded and furloughed since April 9.

Givin, C., see **Givin, C. B**. Co. F

Glass, J. B., Pvt. Co. C

POW surrendered by Lt General Richard Taylor in May 1865, and paroled at Demopolis, Alabama, June 13,1865. Residence shown as Marengo County, Alabama.

Glass, M., Pvt. Co. C

Enlisted on July 10, 1863, at Choctaw Bluff, Alabama, by Lt. Northrup for three years or the war. Company muster roll for September/October 1863, reports him present. POW captured at Fort Gaines, Alabama, on August 8, 1862. He was received at Ship Island, Mississippi, from New Orleans on October 25, 1864, and exchanged on January 4, 1865, "left sick in hospital at Ship Island." Signed by his mark.

Glass, N. C., Pvt. Co. C

His name appears on a transcript of the Hospital Examining Board at Mobile, Alabama, March 9, 1865. He was furloughed for 60 days due to general debility, following small pox and scurvy contracted at Ship Island, Mississippi. POW surrendered by Lt. General Richard Taylor in May 1865, and paroled at Demopolis, Alabama, on June 6,1865. Residence shown as Marengo County, Alabama.

Glass, W. R., Pvt. Co. C

Enlisted on October 13, 1861, at Mobile, Alabama, by Captain Rembert for 12 months. Company muster roll for December 31, 1862, to April 30, 1863, reports him present. Company muster roll for May/June 1863, reports him present, lost bayonet at $1, scabbard at $1, 10 cartridges and 12 caps at $2. Muster roll for September/October 1863, reports him absent in hospital in Mobile since October 21, 1863, lost H. sack at $1. POW captured at Fort Gaines, Alabama, on August 8, 1862, he was received at Ship Island, Mississippi, from New Orleans on October 25, 1864, and exchanged (hospital) on March 4, 1865. POW surrendered by Lt General Richard Taylor in May 1865, and paroled at Demopolis, Alabama, on June 7,1865. Residence shown as Marengo County, Alabama.

Gleason, Thomas, 1st Lt./Captain Co. I

He was elected Lt. on October 13, 1861, and promoted on May 3, 1862. He appears as Captain on a regimental return for June 1862, present at Tupelo, Mississippi. His name appears on a regimental return for December 1861, where he is shown absent on surgeon's certificate since December 28.

21ST ALABAMA INFANTRY VOLUNTEERS

Glespi, D., Pvt. Co. A see **Gellespi, David**

Gnospelius, Gust Ald., Sgt. Co. H

Enlisted on October 13, 1861, at Mobile, Alabama, by Captain DeVaux for 12 months. Discharged on April 18, 1862, by reason of disability. Born Stockholm, Sweden, Europe, age 34, light complexion, gray eyes, light hair, by profession a teacher of music. There is a pay voucher and his discharge in his file.* Note that 21st Ala. Co. H is crossed out and Co. H 1st La. Inf. is written in.

Goddard, William C., Pvt. Co. C

Enlisted on January 18, 1862, at Fort Gaines, Alabama, by Captain Stewart for the war. His name appears on a regimental return for June 1862, on detached service; assigned as hospital steward. He appears on a company muster roll for bounty on September 24, 1962, as present. Company muster roll for November/December 1862, reported him present. Here he is shown as enlisting on October 13, 1861, at Mobile. Muster roll for July/August 1863, reports him absent, detached in Miller Hospital on August 23, 1863, here he is shown as having enlisted at Fort Gaines on July 29, 1862, by Captain Dorgan. Hospital muster roll for July/August 1863, at General Hospital Miller (also known as Convalescent Hospital) Spring Hill, Alabama, reports him present as druggist and enlisted on January 18, 1862. Muster roll for September/October 1863, reports him absent detailed at Miller Hospital. He appears on a Hospital muster roll for January/February, 1864, at General Hospital Miller (also known as Convalescent Hospital) Spring Hill, Alabama, where he is reported present. He appears July 1864, on a list of soldiers employed at Military Post of Mobile as Hospital Steward on authority of Secretary of War.

Godsey, M. M., Pvt. Co. G

POW captured at Fort Gaines, Alabama, on August 8, 1864. He was received at Ship Island, Mississippi, on October 25, 1864, from New Orleans and exchanged at Ship Island on January 4, 1865.

Golden, I., Pvt. Co. K

Enlisted on September 28, 1864, at Mobile, Alabama, by Major Stone for the war. He appears on a company muster roll for bounty on September 24, 1962, as present. He was transferred to Conscript Camp at Notasulga, Alabama, by order of Major Stone on October 18, 1864.

Goldthwaite, Thomas, Pvt. Co. K

Enlisted on October 13, 1861, at Mobile, Alabama, by Captain Stewart for the war. He appears on a regimental return for June 1862, as clerk in General Bragg's Headquarters. He appears on a company muster roll for bounty on September 24, 1962, as present. Returns and muster rolls for November and December 1862, report that he was detached in General Bragg's Office on April 2, 1862, by order of General Bragg. He was discharged on March 9, 1863.

Gonez, Manuel, Pvt. Co. G
POW captured, missing perhaps killed at Shiloh on April 7, 1862.

Goodall, William, S., Pvt./Sgt. Co. E
Enlisted on October 13, 1861, at Mobile, Alabama, by Captain Chamberlain for the war. He was wounded severely in the left leg at Shiloh at 6 P. M. on April 6th 1862, while retreating. He appears on a company muster roll for bounty on September 24, 1962, as present. Company muster rolls for November/December 1862 and July/August 1863, report him present. POW captured at Fort Gaines, Alabama, on August 8, 1864. He was admitted to St. Louis USA General Hospital at New Orleans on October 7, 1864, with acute diarrhoea and returned to confinement on October 11, age 20. He was received at Ship Island, Mississippi, on October 25, 1864, from New Orleans. He was left sick in hospital at Ship Island on January 4, 1865, and exchanged at Ship Island on March 2, 1865. POW as a, 3rd Sergeant, surrendered by Lt General Richard Taylor on May 4, 1865, and paroled at Meridian, Mississippi, on May 13,1865. Residence shown as Mobile, Alabama.

Goode, D. W., Pvt. Co. F
POW captured at Fort Gaines, Alabama, on August 8, 1864. He was admitted to St. Louis USA General Hospital at New Orleans on September 21, 1864, with rubeola and returned to confinement on September 27, age 19. He was received at Ship Island, Mississippi, October 25, 1864, from New Orleans. He died at Ship Island on November 28, 1864, and was buried in grave No. 39.

Goode, Robert, Pvt. Co. F
Enlisted on September 17, 1862, at Talladega, Alabama, by J. Cary for the war. Company muster roll for March 1, 1863, to June 30, 1863, reports him present on extra duty as hospital nurse since February 24, 1863, by order of Colonel Anderson. Company muster roll for September/October 1863, shows him present. Drew clothing on June 1, 1864. POW captured at Fort Gaines, Alabama, on August 8, 1864, and received at Ship Island, Mississippi, on October 25, 1864, from New Orleans and was exchanged at Ship Island on January 4, 1865.

Goodloe, R. H., Pvt. Co. A
His name appears on a list of soldiers employed in the Subsistence Department in the State of Alabama, on May 22, 1864, by order of General Maury for 30 days as clerk at Mill in Mobile. (Yard Clerk) In October 1864, he is shown as age 47 and employed as a clerk in Depot Commissary at Mobile. POW surrendered by Lt General Richard Taylor on May 11, 1865, and paroled at Meridian, Mississippi, on May 13,1865. Residence shown as Mobile, Alabama.

Goodwin, Andrew, Pvt. Co. E
Enlisted on October 13, 1861, at Mobile, Alabama, by Captain Chamberlain for the war. A regimental return for June 1861 shows him on detached service as clerk in Commissary Department. He appears on a company muster roll for bounty on September 24, 1962, as being absent detailed to M&ORR by order of General Withers on March 10,

1862. Company muster rolls for November/December 1862, July/August 1863, and September/October 1863, all show him absent detached with the RR. There are several pay vouchers in his file.*

Goodwin, Jas. H., Pvt. Co. ._
Enlisted on October 13, 1861, age 22, discharged March 10, 1862.

Goodwin, J. J., Pvt. Co. C.
Enlisted on August 9, 1863, at Choctaw Bluff, Alabama, by Colonel Anderson for three years or the war. Company muster roll for September/October 1863, reports him absent detached in A. Q. M. Department on August 9, 1863, by order of General Maury. POW surrendered at Citronelle, Alabama, on May 4, 1865, and paroled at Mobile, Alabama. Residence shown as Mobile, Alabama, age 41, five foot ten inches, dark complexion, dark eyes, gray hair.

Goodwin, Joshua R., Pvt. Co. A
Enlisted on September 21, 1862, at Jefferson County, Alabama, by J. W. Bass for three years or the war. Company muster roll for December 31, 1862, to April 30, 1862, reports him present. Company muster rolls for May/June and September/October 1863, report him present. He was admitted to Ross Hospital at Mobile on January 24, 1864, and sent to General Hospital in Montgomery, on February 17, 1864. POW captured at Fort Morgan, Alabama, on August 23, 1864. He was sent as POW to New Orleans and on to Elmira, New York, on September 27, 1864 He was received at Elmira, New York, on October 8, 1864. His name appears on a roll of POW's desirous to take the Oath of Allegiance to the USA, on May 15, 1865, "was conscripted August 20, 1862, desires to go to his home at Selma, Alabama." Signed an Oath of Allegiance and released on July 7, 1865. residence shown as Greensport, Alabama, florid complexion, dark hair, five foot three inches.

Gorlott, Victor, Pvt. Co. I also **Golatt**
Enlisted on July 9, 1863, at Fort Morgan, Alabama, by Lt. Dorhora for the war. Company muster rolls for July/August and September/October 1863, report him present. He was admitted to Post Hospital at Fort Morgan, Alabama, on September 17, 1863, with abscesses and returned to duty on September 25, 1863. He was again admitted to Post Hospital at Fort Morgan on October 10, 1863, with ulcer and returned to duty on November 5. He appears on a descriptive list and bounty roll on August 3, 1863; age 35, black eyes, black hair, dark complexion, five foot one inch, born Mobile County, Alabama, a planter by occupation, paid $50 bonus. *

Gorman, Michael, Pvt. Co. B
Enlisted on August 28, 1862, at Fort Morgan by Captain Johnston for the war. Company muster roll for bounty on September 24, 1862, reports him present and bounty paid.

MOBILE CONFEDERATES

Gouistabile, Antonio, Pvt. Co. G
Enlisted by J. Hessee at Mobile, Alabama. He was discharged on February 23, 1862. Born in Italy, white complexion, light eyes, light hair, by occupation a painter.

Gouye, Emile, Pvt. Co. A
Enlisted on October 13, 1862, at Mobile, Alabama, by Major Hessee for the war. Company muster roll for December 31, 1862, to April 30, 1863, reports him present. Company muster rolls for May/June and September/October 1863, report him present. Drew clothing at Camp Anderson June 14, 1864. POW captured at Fort Morgan, Alabama, on August 23, 1864. He was sent as POW to New Orleans and on to Elmira, New York, on September 27, 1864, received at Elmira, New York, on October 8, 1864. He took the Oath of Allegiance to the USA on June 14, 1865, and was released. His residence shown as Raleigh, North Carolina, florid complexion, dark hair, blue eyes, five foot six and one half inch.

Gozzan, Harry M., Sgt./2nd Lt. Co. A see **Gazzam, Harry M.**

Gragg, C. W., Pvt. Co. A see **Gregg, C. W.**

Graham, C. G., Sgt./Pvt. Co. F
Enlisted on October 13, 1861, at Baldwin County, Alabama, by Captain McCoy for one year. Wounded severely in the thigh at Shiloh on April 6, 1862, at 4 P. M. while advancing. Company muster roll for bounty on September 24, 1862, reports him present. Company muster rolls for March 1, to June 30 and September/October 1863, show him present. He was transferred to Confederate States Navy.

Grantham, Daniel, Pvt. Co. F
Enlisted on October 13, 1861, at Baldwin County, Alabama, by Captain McCoy for one year. Wounded severely in the arm while advancing on 1st Battery at Shiloh on April 6, 1862, at 7 A. M. Company muster roll for bounty on September 24, 1862, reports him present. Company muster roll for March 1, to June 30, 1863, reports him on extra duty in commissary as a butcher since January 2, 1863, by order of Colonel Anderson. Company muster roll for September/October 1863, reports him present confined in guard house. He was admitted to Ross Hospital in Mobile on October 19, 1863, with remit. fev., returned to duty on November 3. He was admitted to Post Hospital at Fort Morgan on November 17, 1863, with int. fev. and sent to general hospital on January 17, 1864. He was admitted to Ross Hospital at Mobile, on January 16, 1864, with neuralgia and sent to General Hospital in Montgomery on February 17. POW captured at Fort Gaines, Alabama, on August 8, 1864. He was confined at Steam Levee Press No. 4 at New Orleans and admitted to St. Louis USA General Hospital at New Orleans on August 24, 1864, with fever intermittent then returned to confinement on August 29, 1864, age 27. He was again admitted St. Louis USA General Hospital New Orleans on September 21^{st,} with diarrhoea and returned to confinement on October 10. He was received at Ship Island, Mississippi, from New Orleans on October 25, 1864, and exchanged at Ship Island on January 5, 1865.

Gratham, N., Pvt. Co. B/F see **Graham, Walter**

Graham, John (J. P.?), Pvt. Co. B

His name appears on a report from near Tupelo, Mississippi, on June 28, 1862, "sent away on the evacuation of Corinth, about June 1." Company muster roll for bounty on September 24, 1862, reports him present but not entitled to bounty due to age. Company muster roll for March/April 1863, reports him present and having been enlisted at Choctaw Bluff, Alabama, by Captain Anderson on November 21, 1862, for three years or the war. Company muster roll for May/June 1863, reports him present. Company muster roll for September/October 1863, reports him detailed as a nurse at Point Clear Hospital on August 14, 1863. He was admitted to Post Hospital at Fort Morgan on August 3, 1863, with fev. typhoid, and died November 8, 1863. Hospital muster roll for General Hospital at Point Clear, Baldwin County, for September/October 1863, reports him present on extra duty and having been enlisted on August 21, 1861, by Captain Johnson. He appears on a descriptive list at Point Clear on September 23, 1863, born Canada age 46, blue eyes, brown hair, dark complexion, five foot six inches, a sailor by occupation, enlisted at Choctaw Bluff on November 21, 1862, and paid $50 bounty. He appears present on Point Clear Hospital muster roll for November 1, to December 18, 1863, as a nurse. He is shown as having been admitted to Post Hospital at Fort Morgan on December 26, 1863, with diarrhoea and returned to duty on January 9, 1864. Pvt. **J. P. Graham** died of dysentery at Ship Island, Mississippi, on December 29, 1864 and was buried in grave No. 119. Pvt. John Graham age 46 was also shown as being discharged at Choctaw Bluff. *There are more than one man's records in this file.** Note there is additional information on John Graham's desertion on January 29, 1863, from Choctaw Bluff, Alabama, in the File of **James. A. Poellnitz**. Special Order No. 62.

Graham, Walter, Pvt. Co. B/F

Enlisted on October 13, 1861, at Mobile, Alabama, by Major Hessee for 12 months. Pvt. Walter Graham, was discharged at Fort Gaines, Alabama, on January 1, 1862, due to scrofula. He was born in Georgia, age 25, five foot ten inches, light complexion, blue eyes, dark hair, by occupation a farmer. Company muster roll for bounty on September 24, 1862, reports him not entitled to bounty due to age. Company muster roll for March 1, to June 30, 1863, reports him present and lost one haversack at 20 cents. Company muster roll for September/October 1863, shows Pvt. **W. Graham**, enlisted at Choctaw Bluff by Captain Dade for three years or the war, present "confined in Guard House." He was admitted to Post Hospital at Fort Morgan, on October 19, 1863, with remit. fev., and returned to duty on November 2. He was again admitted to the same hospital on November 17, 1863, with int. fever, and returned to duty on December 15. He was admitted to Ross Hospital in Mobile with acute diarrhoea and sent to General Hospital in Montgomery on February 17, 1864. POW captured at Fort Gaines, Alabama, on August 8, 1864. He was received at Ship Island, Mississippi, on October 24, 1865, from New Orleans and applied to take the Oath of Allegiance to the USA. He died of pneumonia at Ship Island on November 23, 1864, and was buried in grave No. 38. There is a copy of a discharge in the file. *There are more than one man's records in this file.**

MOBILE CONFEDERATES

Graham, W. F. and **Graham, William**, Pvt. Co. B/F see **Graham, Walter**

Grandpre, A., Pvt. Co. K
Enlisted on July 4, 1863, at Fort Morgan, Alabama, by Captain Dorgan for the war. Company muster rolls for July/August and September/October 1863, report him present. Note to see personal papers of **J. Albert**, Pvt. Co. K, 21st Ala. Inf.

Grano, C., Pvt. Co. G
His name appears on a report near Tupelo, Mississippi, on June 28, 1862, "sent to interior from Corinth, at the time of evacuation."

Grant, T. W., Pvt. Sossaman's Detachment
Enlisted on August 19, 1862, at Barbour County, Alabama, by Lt. Henry for the war. He appears present on company muster roll for September/October 1864, at Mobile.

Grant, W. G., Pvt. Co. G see **Grant, William**

Grant, William, Pvt. Co. G
He was admitted to Post Hospital at Fort Morgan on November 3, 1863, with int. fev. and returned to duty on November 5. POW captured at Fort Gaines, Alabama, on August 8, 1864. He was admitted as POW to St. Louis USA General Hospital in New Orleans on September 17, 1864, with acute diarrhoea and died on September 29, 1864. He left no effects. He is buried in Monument Cemetery Grave No. 376 and his death certificate is in his file.* Residence shown as Barbour County, Alabama, age 20, mother Mrs. S. A. Grant.

Grantham, G. W., Pvt. Co. H
POW captured at Fort Gaines, Alabama, on August 8, 1864. Received at Ship Island, Mississippi, from New Orleans on October 25, 1864, and exchanged at Ship Island on January 4, 1865. POW surrendered by General Richard Taylor at Citronelle, Alabama, on May 4, 1865, and paroled at Meridian, Mississippi, on May 13. Residence shown as Pike County, Alabama.

Gratrix, Robert, Pvt./Sgt. Co. D
Enlisted on October 13, 1861, at Mobile, Alabama, by Captain Butt for the war. POW captured at Shiloh (Pittsburg or Island No. 10) on April 8, 1864. His name appears on a roll of POW's at Camp Douglas near Chicago, Illinois, on August 1, 1862. On September 8, 1862, he was among 742 prisoners that were sent to Vicksburg, Mississippi, for exchange aboard the steamer *Jno. H. Done*. He appears absent on a company muster roll for bounty on September 24, 1862, "taken prisoner at Shiloh." Company muster rolls for November/December 1862, July/August 1863 and September 1863, all report him present. Company muster roll for November/December 1863, reports him absent on furlough and the roll for September/October 1864, shows him present. POW captured at Blakeley on April 9, 1865, sent to Ship Island, Mississippi, and on to Vicksburg, Mississippi, for exchange on May 1, 1865.*

21ST ALABAMA INFANTRY VOLUNTEERS

Gray, C. B., Pvt. Co. B see **Gray, Charles**

Gray, Charles, Pvt. Co. B
Enlisted on October 13, 1861, at Mobile, Alabama, by Major Hessee 12 months. He appears on a report for June 1862, as being on detached service as a laborer with M & O RR. Company muster roll for bounty on September 24, 1862, reports that him not entitled to bounty due to age. POW captured at Fort Gaines, Alabama, on August 8, 1864. He was received at Ship Island, Mississippi, from New Orleans on October 25, 1864, and exchanged on January 4, 1865. There are pay vouchers in his file.*

Gray, John, Pvt./Corp. Co. D
Enlisted on October 13, 1861, at Mobile, Alabama, by Captain Butt for the war. He was wounded in the left leg while advancing in first charge at Shiloh on April 6, 1862. POW captured in hospital on April 7, 1862 at Shiloh. Pvt. John Gray appears on a undated register of General Hospital, at Savannah Tennessee, with a wound. He was received at Camp Douglas near Chicago, Illinois, on May 26, 1862. His name appears on a roll of POW's at Camp Douglas near Chicago, Illinois, on August 1, 1862. On September 8, 1862, he was among 742 prisoners that were sent to Vicksburg, Mississippi, for exchange aboard the steamer *Jno. H. Done*. He appears absent on a company muster roll for bounty on September 24, 1862, "taken prisoner at Shiloh." Company muster roll for November/December 1862, reports him present and bounty due. Muster rolls for July/August 1863, September/October 1863 and November/December 1863, report him present. September/October 1864, muster roll reports him absent sent to General Hospital in Mobile on October 10. POW captured at Blakeley, Alabama, on April 9, 1865. He was received at Ship Island, Mississippi, on April 15, 1865, and transferred on parole to Vicksburg, Mississippi, for exchange on May 1, 1865.*

Gray, Joshua, Pvt. Co. F
Enlisted on March 16, 1863, at Choctaw Bluff, Alabama, by Captain Dade for the war. Company muster rolls for March 1, to June 30, 1863, and September/October 1863, report him present.

Gray, T. J., Pvt. Co. C
POW captured at Blakeley, Alabama, on April 9, 1865. He was received at Ship Island, Mississippi, on April 15, 1865, and transferred to Vicksburg, Mississippi, on May 1, 1865.

Grayson, John, Co. D
He appears on a register of records of deceased Confederate soldiers on August 30, 1862, at General Hospital at Okolona, Mississippi. Possessions left $5.40.

Grayson, S. W. or **T. W.**, Pvt. Co. I see **Grayson, Y. W.**

Grayson, Y. W., Pvt. Co. I
POW captured at Fort Gaines, Alabama, on August 8, 1864. He was admitted to St. Louis USA General Hospital at New Orleans on September 21, 1864, with rubeola

and returned to confinement on September 30, age 17. He was confined at Steam Levee Press No. 4 at New Orleans on September 30, 1864, received from hospital. He was received at Ship Island, Mississippi, from New Orleans on October 25, 1864, and exchanged on January 4, 1865. POW surrendered on May 4, 1865, by General Richard Taylor at Citronelle, Alabama, and paroled at Meridian, Mississippi, on May 15, 1865. Residence shown as Marengo County, Alabama.

Green, Charles, Pvt. Co. K

Enlisted on February 24, 1864, at Fort Powell, Alabama, by Captain Dorgan for the war. Company muster roll for September/October 1864, reports him absent detached with Engineer Department at Mobile, age 18. There is a letter from Richmond in his file requesting his special assignment dated December 7, 1863. POW captured with Q. M. Department at Mobile and paroled at Mobile on May 14, 1865.*

Green, John George, Corp./Sgt. Major Co. K and NCS.

Enlisted on October 13, 1861, at Mobile, Alabama, by Captain Stewart for the war. He appears present on a company muster roll for bounty on September 24, 1862. Company muster roll for November/December 1862, reports him present as a Corporal. Muster rolls for July/August and September/October 1863, report him present as a 3rd Sgt. Muster roll for March/April 1864, reports him present as Sgt. Major appointed from 3rd Sgt. on April 1, 1864, by order of Colonel Anderson. POW captured at Fort Gaines, Alabama, on August 8, 1864. He was received at Ship Island, Mississippi, from New Orleans on October 25, 1864, and exchanged on January 4, 1865. POW surrendered on May 4, 1865, by General Richard Taylor at Citronelle, Alabama, and paroled at Meridian, Mississippi, on May 15, 1865. Residence shown as Mobile, Alabama.*

Green, Lewis, Pvt. Co. K

Enlisted on October 1, 1861. His name appears on a pay voucher as having served from October 1, to December 31, 1861, and furloughed. He was paid $53.60 on March 1, 1862.*

Green, Thomas R., Pvt. Co. H

Drew clothing on June 1, 1864. POW captured at Fort Gaines, Alabama, on August 8, 1864. He was received at Ship Island, Mississippi, from New Orleans on October 25, 1864, and exchanged on January 4, 1865. He drew clothing on June 1, 1864. It appears that he may have been transferred to CS Navy on June 2, 1864. He was admitted to Ross Hospital at Mobile, Alabama, on January 6, 1865, with debilities and diarrhoea, furloughed on January 14, 1865, for 15 days. POW surrendered on May 4, 1865, by Lt. General Richard Taylor at Citronelle, Alabama, and paroled at Meridian, Mississippi, on May 15, 1865. Residence shown as Marengo County, Alabama.

Gregg, C. W., Pvt. Co. A

POW captured at Fort Morgan, Alabama, on August 23, 1864, (in hospital?). He was admitted to St. Louis USA General Hospital at New Orleans on August 25, 1864, with int. fever and bronchitis, returned to confinement on September 19, 1864, age 27. He was admitted again to St. Louis Hospital on September 25, 1864, with dysentery and returned to confinement on October 5, 1864. Here he was shown as age 29. He may have been in hospital at Ship Island as well. He was received at Elmira, New York, on November 19, 1864, from New Orleans. He was paroled and sent from Elmira to James River on February 20, 1865, shown as belonging to Co. F. He was admitted to Moore Hospital or General Hospital No. 24 at Richmond, Virginia, on February 28, 1865, with chronic diarrhoea and furloughed on March 9 for 60 days. "Took sick on August 3, 1864, PO Charlotte, NC."

Gregg, E. W., Pvt. Co. F/A

POW captured at Fort Morgan, Alabama, on August 23, 1864. He was received at Ship Island, Mississippi, on October 7, 1864, and sent to Elmira, New York, on November 5, 1864. Received at Elmira on November 19, 1864, from Fort Columbus, New York Harbor, transferred from New Orleans to Ship Island, in October 1864, thence to New York, November 5, 1864. He was transferred for exchange on February 20, 1865.

Gregg, J. H., Pvt. Co. F

His name appears on a register of Medical Director's office at Richmond, Virginia, as being in General Hospital No. 15 on October 10, 1862.

Gregor, J. C., Pvt. Co. K

Enlisted on August 30, 1864, at Mobile, Alabama, by Major Stone for the war. He was transferred to Conscript Camp at Notasulga, Alabama, by order of Major Stone on October 18, 1864.

Grice, John, Pvt. Co. B

Enlisted on October 1, 1862, at Talladega, Alabama, by Major Mitchell for the war. He appears present on muster rolls for March/April and May/June 1863. Muster roll for September/October 1863, reports him absent sent to General Hospital at Mobile by order of Dr. Payne. Muster roll of Sossaman's Detachment for September/October 1864, reports him present. POW surrendered on May 4, 1865, by General Richard Taylor at Citronelle, Alabama, and paroled at Meridian, Mississippi, on May 13, 1865. Residence shown Winston County, Alabama.

Griffin, R., Pvt. Co. I

He was admitted with a wound to Way Hospital Meridian, Mississippi, on January 14, 1865.

Griffing, S. Henry, Pvt. Co. E see **Griffing, Stephen H.**

Griffing, Stephen H., Pvt. Co. E

Enlisted on October 13, 1861, at Mobile, Alabama, by Captain Chamberlain for the war. He appears on a regimental return for June 1962, "sent to interior hospital May 27." Company muster roll for bounty on September 24, 1862, reports him present. Company muster rolls for November/December 1862, July/August 1863 and September/October 1863 all report him present. POW captured at Fort Gaines, Ala., on August 8,

1864. He was received at Ship Island, Mississippi, from New Orleans on October 25, 1864, and exchanged on January 4, 1865. POW a member of a detached unit commanded by Colonel R. H. Lindsay that was surrendered on May 4, 1865, by General Richard Taylor at Citronelle, Alabama, and paroled at Meridian, Mississippi, on May 12, 1865. Residence shown as Mobile, Alabama.

Griffiths, James, Pvt. Co. A

Enlisted by Major Hessee at Mobile, Alabama, on October 13, 1861, for 12 months. Discharged on January 18, 1862, at Fort Gaines, Alabama. He was born in London, age 38, five foot six inches, dark complexion, black hair, black eyes, a steamboat man by occupation. Discharged due to disability because of hernia. His discharge is in his file.*

Grimes, J. G., Pvt. Co. I

Enlisted at Halls Mill, Alabama, on October 13, 1861, by Major Hessee for the war. He was wounded severely in the arm while advancing in attack on 1st Battery at Shiloh on April 6, at 7 A. M. He appears on a regimental return for June 1862, "sent to interior hospital on May 28, 1862." He also appears on a report near Tupelo, Mississippi, June 28, 1862, "sent to interior hospital from Corinth, by surgeon on May 28." He appears present on a company muster roll for bounty on September 24, 1862. Company muster rolls for July/August and September/October 1863, report him present. POW captured at Fort Gaines, Alabama, on August 8, 1864. He was received at Ship Island, Mississippi, from New Orleans on October 25, 1864, and exchanged on January 4, 1865.

Groce, D., Pvt. Co. I see **Gross, David**

Groce, George M., Pvt. Co. G

POW captured at Fort Gaines, Alabama, on August 8, 1864. He was received at Ship Island, Mississippi, from New Orleans on October 25, 1864. He died of small pox at Ship Island on December 28, 1864, and was buried in grave 117.

Groce, G. N., Pvt. Co. G see **Groce, George, M.**

Groom, W. E., Pvt. Co. H

POW captured at Fort Gaines, Alabama, on August 8, 1864. He was received at Ship Island, Mississippi, from New Orleans on October 25, 1864. He died of pneumonia at Ship Island on November 21, 1864, and was buried in grave 32.

Gross, David, Pvt. Co. I

Enlisted on October 10, 1863, at Fort Morgan, Alabama, by Lt. McNeil for the war. Company muster roll for September/October 1863, reports him present absent without leave for two days. POW captured at Fort Gaines, Alabama, on August 8, 1864. He was admitted to St. Louis USA General Hospital in New Orleans with bronchitis on September 9, 1864, and returned to confinement on September 12, 1864. He was again admitted to St. Louis USA General Hospital in New Orleans with acute diarrhoea on October 7, 1864, returned to confinement on October 11, 1864, age 42. He was received at Ship Island, Mississippi, from New Orleans on October 25, 1864. He died of dysentery at Ship Island on November 27, 1864, and was buried in grave 47.

Grumbles, J., Pvt. Co. F

There is notation of GO (General Order) No. 29 Court Martial in 1865. POW a member of Holtzclaw's Brigade commanded by Captain Gwin, surrendered on May 4, 1865, by General Richard Taylor at Citronelle, Alabama, and paroled at Meridian, Mississippi, on May 13, 1865. Residence shown as Wilcox County, Alabama.

Gueringer, H. C., Pvt. Co. E see **Hurringer, H. C.**

Gueringer, L. L., Pvt. Co. E

Enlisted on October 13, 1861, at Mobile, Alabama. His name appears on a regimental return for June 1862, "June 26, Tupelo, Miss, discharged for disability." Born in Mobile, Alabama, age 29, five foot five inches, dark complexion, black eyes, black hair, by profession a merchant.

Gueringer, P., Pvt. Co. D

Enlisted on August 2, 1864, at Mobile, Alabama, by Major Stone for the war. Company muster roll for September/October 1864, reports him absent, detached in Ordnance Department by order of General Higgins on August 2, 1864.

Guerit, Victor, Co. H

Discharged due to disability on January 24, 1862. Enlisted in Captain DeVaux's Company H at Mobile, Alabama, on October 13, 1861, by Major Hessee. Born Cayenne, French Guiana, South America, age 27, five foot four inches, dark complexion, black eyes, black hair, by profession a hair dresser. His discharge is in his file.* His name appears only in uncarded records, file case 2192118, GO. August 4, 1914.

Guerringer, H. (Henry) C., Pvt. Co. E

Enlisted on October 13, 1861, at Mobile, Alabama, by Captain Chamberlain for 12 months. He appears on a regimental return for June 1862, "June 3, 1862, Mobile, died at home." Company muster roll for bounty on September 24, 1862, shows, "detailed (since organization) died in Mobile on June 3, 1862." Claim for deceased soldiers filed by Lewis Guerringer his Father. Died unmarried and left neither wife or child. Born in Mobile, Alabama, age 19, five foot six inches, dark complexion, black eyes, brown hair, and a clerk by occupation. There is paperwork in his file including letters his father wrote.**

Guilhelmo, Alexander, Drummer Co. H

Discharged for disability at Fort Gaines, Alabama, on November 19. 1861. Born at F?, Italy, age 26, five foot five, dark complexion, gray eyes, dark hair, by profession a laborer. His discharged is in his file.*

Guillot, M., Pvt. Co. I

He appears on a list of men who returned [*from Battle of Shiloh*] without arms or with captured arms, Withers, Division 1st Brigade. Discharged on July 4, 1862. He drew clothing on March 31, 1864?

Gullidge, H. H., Pvt. Co. F

Enlisted on October 13, 1861, at Baldwin County, Alabama, by Captain McCoy for one year. His name appears on a report near Tupelo, Mississippi, June 28, 1862, "sent to Okolona, June 4, 1862." He appears on a company muster roll for bounty on September 24, 1862, as being present. Muster roll for March 1, to June 30, 1863, reports him present, sick in hospital. September/October 1863, muster roll reports him absent sick since August 19, 1863. File card indicates that on September 28, 1863, he was listed as a deserter. Described as age 22, blue eyes, light hair, dark complexion, five foot eight inches, residence shown as Baldwin County, Alabama.

Gully, N. H., Pvt. Co. F see **Gurley, N.**

Gurley, N., Pvt. Co. F

Enlisted at Camden, [Alabama?] on October 10, 1863, by Major Stone for three years or the war. Company muster roll for September/October 1863, reports him present. Drew clothing on March 31, 1864, and signed by his mark. He was admitted to Ross Hospital at Mobile, Alabama, on June 19, 1864, with dysentery (febris typhoides), sent to General Hospital at Spring Hill. He died on July 13, 1864.

Gustin, Donato, Pvt. Co. G

Wounded in the arm slightly at Shiloh on April 6, at 12 Noon, at the Ravine. His name appears on a report near Tupelo, Mississippi, June 28, 1862, " Wounded at Shiloh and absent since 10th Apl." *

Gwin, C. B., Pvt. Sgt. Co. F

His name appears on a regimental report for June 1862. "Discharged for disability on June 12, 1862."

Gwin, George, B., 2nd Lt./Captain Co. F

A return for November 1861, shows him present and posted at Fort Gaines, Alabama. Elected 2nd Lt. on October 13, 1861, promoted May 8, 1862, and again on August 30, 1862. A regimental return for December, 1861, shows him present. A regimental return for June 1862, shows him absent "Sent to interior hospital, May 28 on surgeon's certificate. A field return on October 1862, shows him transferred to Choctaw Bluff on October 6. Company muster roll for March 1, to June 30, 1863, he is reported absent on sick furlough. Muster roll for September/October 1863, reports him present. Company muster roll for September/October 1864, shows him as Lt. transferred to a detachment of 21st Regiment by order of General Maury. Company muster roll September/October for Sossaman's Detachment of the 21st Regiment Alabama Infantry reports him present a 1st Lt. POW surrendered on May 4, 1865, by Lt. General Richard Taylor at Citronelle, Alabama, and paroled at Meridian, Mississippi, on May 10, 1865.

He signed a requisition [*undated*] for Co. F, for; 14 pair shoes, 18 pair shoes, 19 jackets, 20 pair pants, 9 caps and 74 shirts, "being entirely out." There is considerable paperwork and his Parole of Honor in his file.** See personal papers of **M. C. Burke**.

H

Haden, G. B., Pvt. Co. D see **Hayden, George, B.**

Hadren, B., Pvt. Co. C see **Hudson, B.**

Hair, Joseph, Pvt. Co. F
Enlisted on October 13, 1861, at Baldwin County, Alabama, by Captain McCoy for one year. Company muster roll for bounty on September 24, 1862, reports him present, "Claims to be overage and a alien."

Hariston, P. R. Pvt. Co. G
Enlisted on August 5, 1862, at Macon County, Alabama, by D. Isbell for the war. Company muster roll for September/October 1864, reports him present and last paid on August 31, 1863. He was admitted to Mississippi, CSA Hospital at Jackson, Mississippi, on August 13, 1864, with febris remittens and returned to duty on September 12.

Hale, H. W., Pvt. Co. A see **Hale, William H.**

Hale, William H., Pvt. Co. A
Enlisted on August 27, 1862, at Jefferson County, Alabama, by William Walker for the war. Company muster roll for August 31, 1862, to April 30, 1863, reports him absent sick in hospital at Choctaw Bluff, Alabama. Company muster rolls for May/June 1863 and September/October 1863, report him present. He was admitted to Post Hospital at Fort Morgan, Alabama, with fev. int. on November 9, 1863, and returned to duty on November 14, 1863. He was again admitted to Fort Morgan Post Hospital on November 28, 1863, with int. fever and retuned to duty on December 14, 1863. Once again he was admitted to the same with int. fever on Dec. 30, 1863, and returned to duty on January 9. POW captured at Fort Morgan on August 23, 1864. He was received at Elmira, New York, on October 8, 1864, from New Orleans. He appears on a roll May 15, 1865, of POW's who are desirous to take the Oath of Allegiance "Was conscripted August 27, 1862, Desires to go to his home in Selma, Ala." He signed an Oath of Allegiance to the USA at Elmira, New York, on July 7, 1865, residence Greensport, Alabama, complexion florid, hair light, eyes gray, and five foot seven inches.

Hall, James, Pvt. Co. E
Enlisted on October 13, 1861. *There is a very poor copy of a document in his file.*

Hall, John, Pvt. Co. B.
Enlisted on August 21, 1862, at Jefferson County, Alabama, by W. A. Walker for the war. Company muster rolls for March/April 1863 and May/June 1863, report him present. Company muster roll for September/October 1863, reports him absent sent to

General Hospital at Mobile on October 27, 1863, by order of Dr. Payne. Drew clothing on May 20, 1864. POW captured at Fort Gaines, Alabama, on August 3, 1864. He was received at Ship Island, Mississippi, from New Orleans on October 25, 1864. He died at Ship Island of dysentery on December 12, 1864, and was buried in grave No. 79.

Hall, Joseph, Pvt. Co. A
Confederate POW died of pneumonia in the Department of the Missouri at Fourth Street Hospital in St. Louis, Missouri, on March 15, 1862.

Hall, L., Pvt. Co. K
Enlisted on April 20, 1864, at Mobile, Alabama, by Major Stone, for the war. Company muster roll for September/October 1864, report him absent sick in hospital, since September 29, 1864. Drew $11 pay on August 15, 1864, and signed by his mark.

Hallifiled, W. R., Pvt. Co. F see **Hollifield, W. R.**

Hallmark, C., Pvt. Co. G
Drew clothing on March 31, and June 1, 1864. POW captured at Fort Gaines, Alabama, on August 8, 1864. Received at Ship Island, Mississippi, from New Orleans on October 25, 1864. He was exchanged at Ship Island on January 4, 1865.

Halter, R. M., Pvt. Co. K
POW surrendered by Lt. General Richard Taylor and paroled at Demopolis, Alabama, on June 19, 1865. Residence shown as Clarke County, Alabama.

Hamilton, Benjamin, Corp. Co. I [D?]
Enlisted on October 13, 1861, at Halls Mill, Alabama, by Captain Taylor for one year. Discharged due to disability at Fort Gaines, Alabama, on January 11, 1862. Born Mobile County, Alabama, age 33, five foot seven inches, dark complexion, dark hair, blue eyes, a farmer by occupation.

Hamilton, Franklin, Pvt. Co. I
His name appears on a register of payments to discharged soldiers. Discharged due to neuralgia on April 26, 1862. He was described as thirty years of age, five foot nine and one half inches, fair complexion, gray eyes, auburn hair, by occupation a planter.

Hamilton, F. T., Corp. Co. I
Enlisted on October 13, 1861, at Halls Mill, Alabama, by Major Hessee for the war. Company muster rolls for June/August and September/October1863, report him present. Drew extra duty pay at Fort Morgan, Alabama, for several months and in May 1863, as a fisherman. POW captured at Fort Gaines, Alabama, on August 8, 1864. He was received at Ship Island, Mississippi, from New Orleans on October 25, 1864, and exchanged on January 5, 1865.

Hamilton, James, Pvt. Co. E

Enlisted on October 13, 1861, at Mobile, Alabama, by Captain Chamberlain for twelve months. He was wounded severely in the arm at Shiloh while advancing on April 6, 1862, at 10 A. M. Company muster roll for bounty on September 24, 1862, reports him present. Company muster roll for November/December 1852, shows him present. Company muster roll for July/August 1863, shows that he was transferred to Captain Hutchchins' Company of Engineers on August 1, 1862. Company muster roll for September/October 1863, reports that he re-transferred to Company E on September 1, 1863. He appears on several receipts for extra duty pay at from $2.40 per day to $3 per day, as a carpenter.

Hamilton, John, Pvt. Co. D

Enlisted on October 13, 1861, by Major Hessee at Mobile, Alabama, for one year. Wounded severely in the cheek while advancing on the Old Field at Shiloh on April 6, 1862, at 4 P. M. Discharged due to disability at Corinth, Mississippi, on May 25, 1862. Born in Scotland, age 22, five foot six and one half inches. He signed his pay voucher John Hamilton.*

Hamilton, John C., Pvt. Co. B

Enlisted on June 1862, by Colonel C. D. Anderson at Tupelo, Mississippi, for the war. His name appears on a regimental return for June 1862. Company muster roll for bounty on September 24, 1862, reports him present. Company muster rolls for March/April, May/June and September/October 1863, show him present but detached as a teamster in the Quartermaster's Department on November 1, 1862, by order of Colonel Anderson. He drew clothing on June 1, 1864, and signed by his mark. Muster roll for September/October 1864, shows him absent attached temporarily to the company by Major Stone. He was admitted to Post Hospital at Fort Morgan on January 7, 1864, with int. fever, sent to general hospital on January 17, 1864. He was admitted to Ross Hospital in Mobile, Alabama, on January 16, 1864, with int. fever quotd. and returned to duty on February 1. He was again admitted to Ross Hospital at Mobile on April 1, 1865, with vulnus sclopiticum (gunshot wound), fracture left arm elbow, sent to General Hospital [City Hospital ?] on April 12, 1865.

Hamilton, Robert, Corp. Co. I

Enlisted on October 13, 1861, at Halls Mill, Alabama, by Major Hessee for the war. His name appears on a report on June 28, 1862, near Tupelo, Mississippi, "sent to interior hospital from Corinth by order of Dr. Heustis." Company muster roll for bounty on September 24, 1862, reports him present. Company muster roll for July/August 1863, report him present. Company muster roll for September/October 1863, shows him present, "absent without leave 2 days." He drew clothing on March 31, 1864, and signed by his mark. POW captured at Fort Gaines, Alabama, on August 8, 1864. He was received at Ship Island, Mississippi, from New Orleans on October 25, 1864, and exchanged at Ship Island on January 4, 1865.

Hamilton, Watson, Pvt. Co. K

Enlisted on August 20, 186?, at Fort Morgan, by Captain Dorgan, for the war. His name appears on a report on June 28, 1862, near Tupelo, Mississippi, "sent to interior hospital from Corinth by surgeon on May 28." Company muster roll for bounty on September 24, 1862, reports him present. Paid $22 for detached service September 1, to October 31, 1862. His pay voucher is in his file.*

Hamilton, William, Pvt. Co. I

Enlisted on October 13, 1861, at Halls Mill, Alabama, by Major Hessee for the war. Company muster roll for bounty on September 24, 1862, reports him present. Company muster roll for July/August 1863, reports him present, "absent without leave from 19, to 21 August." Muster roll for September/October 1863, reports him present. A muster roll of Sossaman's Detachment of the 21st Alabama for September/October 1864, shows him present.

Hamilton, Willis, Pvt. Co. I

Enlisted on October 13, 1861, at Halls Mill, Alabama, by Major Hessee for the war. His name appears on a report on June 28, 1862, near Tupelo, Mississippi, "sent to interior hospital from Corinth, by surgeon on May 28." He is paid for extra duty at Fort Morgan, Alabama, in November 1862, as a butcher. Company muster roll for bounty on September 24, 1862, reports him present. Company muster rolls for July/August, September/October 1863 and September/October 1864, all show him present.

Hampt, J. B., Pvt. Co. E. see **Haupt, James P.**

Hancock, G., Pvt. Co. K

His name appears on a regimental return for June 1862, "May 25, 1862, Corinth, Miss. Discharged for disability."

Hand, John, Pvt. Co. B

Enlisted at Oven Bluff, Alabama, on February 1, 1863, by Captain Johnston for the war. Company muster roll for March/April 1863, reports him present. Company muster roll for May/June 1863, reports him present, "sick in qrs." Company muster roll for September/October 1863, reports him absent without leave since October 24, 1863. Transferred to CS Navy.

Hand, W. W., Pvt. Co. F

Enlisted on August 28, 1862, at Talladega, Alabama, by W. T. Walthall for the war. Company muster rolls from March 1, to June 30, 1863, and September/October 1863, report him present. He was admitted to Post Hospital at Fort Morgan, Alabama, on November 1, 1863, with diarrhoea and returned to duty on November 11. He was again admitted to Post Hospital at Fort Morgan with diarrhoea on November 17, 1863, and returned to duty on January 12, 1864. POW captured at Fort Gaines, Alabama, on August 8, 1864. He appears on a morning report of POW's confined in Steam Levee Press No. 4 at New Orleans on October 1, 1864. He was admitted to St. Louis USA General Hospital at New Orleans on October 1, 1864, with diarrhoea and remit. fever and returned to confinement on October 10. He was again admitted to St. Louis USA General Hospital at New Orleans on October 20, 1864, and returned to confinement on October 31, 1864, age 47. He was received at Ship Island, Mississippi, from New Orleans on October 29, 1864, and died of dysentery on November 20, 1864. Some records show he died on December 8, 1864. He was buried in grave No. 73. *Note some dates in his file are in conflict.*

Haney, James, Pvt. Co. A

His name appears on payments to discharged soldiers. He was discharged on July 4, 1862.

Hank, J. M., Pvt. Co. E see **Hawk, J. M.**

Hanley, F. H., Pvt. Co. C

See **F. H. Hanley**, 2nd Confederate Engineer Troops. POW captured at Blakeley, Alabama, on April 9, 1865. He was received at Ship Island, Mississippi, on April 15, 1865, and transferred to Vicksburg, Mississippi, on May 1, 1865.*

Hanley, Francis, Pvt. Co. B

Enlisted on October 13, 1861, at Mobile, Alabama, by Major Hessee for the war. He appears on a report June 28, 1862, near Tupelo, Mississippi, "detached in Quar M Dep Mar 25, 1862, by order of Genl. Gladden." Company muster roll for bounty on September 24, 1862, reports him present. Company muster roll for March/April 1863, reports him absent with leave, reduced to ranks from 5th Sgt. on April 23, 1863. Company muster roll for May/June 1863, report him present detailed in Quartermaster Department on June 22, 1863, by order of Colonel Anderson.

Hannon, P. C., 1st Lt. Co. B see **Harmon, P. C.**

Hanson, John, Pvt. Co. F

Enlisted on October 13, 1861, at Baldwin County, Alabama, by Captain McCoy for one year. He was wounded slightly in the arm by bombshell at Shiloh on April 6, 1862, at 5 P. M. His name appears on a regimental return for June 1862, "interior hospital June 7." Company muster roll for bounty on September 24, 1862, reports him present. Company muster roll for March 1, to June 30, 1863, reports him present. Company muster roll for September/October 1863, reports that he died in hospital at Point Clear, Alabama, on September 3, 1863.

Hanson, Nathan, Pvt. Co. C

POW surrendered by Lt. General R. Taylor, and paroled at Demopolis, Alabama, on June 1, 1865. A resident of Marengo County, Alabama.

Harden, J. R., Pvt. Co. A

POW admitted to City USA General Hospital at St. Louis, Missouri, on March 4, 1862, with vulnus sclopeticum (gunshot). Sent to prison on March 31, 1862.

Harbor, S. J., Pvt. Co. D

Enlisted on January 6. 1862, at Mobile, Alabama, by Major Butts for seven months and seven days. He appears on a regimental return for June 1862, "sent to interior hospital, at evacuation of Corinth." Company muster roll for bounty on September 24, 1862, reports him absent in hospital in Montgomery. Paid $5 for commutation of rations while on 20-day furlough from June 5, to June 25, (*no year shown*).

Hardy, W. J., Pvt. Co. C

His name appears on a register of payments to discharged soldiers, discharged on July 5, 1863.

Hare, T., Pvt. Co. K

Enlisted at Fort Morgan, Alabama, by Captain Dorgan for the war. Company muster roll for September/October 1864, reports him absent, "taken prisoner at Fort Morgan, in August 1864."

Hargrove, W. F., Pvt. Co. H see **Hargroves, W. S.**

Hargroves, W. S., Pvt. Co. H

Drew clothing June 1, 1864. POW captured at Fort Gaines, Alabama, on August 8, 1864. Received at Ship Island, Mississippi, on October 25, 1864, from New Orleans and exchanged at Ship Island on January 4, 1865. He was issued a 60-day furlough at Institute Empire and Bemiss Hospital at Opelika, Alabama, on March 22, 1865, to Society Hill, Alabama. Paroled at Montgomery, Alabama, on May 19, 1865. He was described as five foot eight inches, dark hair, dark eyes, and fair complexion. His parole is in his file.*

Harmon, P. C., Lt. Co. B

Enlisted in state service on April 1, 1861, and into Confederate service on October 13, 1861. He was elected 2nd Lt. on October 8, 1861. His name appears on a regimental return for December 1861, where he is reported absent on short leave since December 28. A return for November 1861, reports him present at Fort Gaines. He appears present on another regimental return for June 1862, at Tupelo, Mississippi. There is some indication that he may have died in service. There are pay voucher in his file.*

Harned, J., Pvt. Co. I

He appears on a regimental return for June 1862, "sent to interior hospital June 28, 1862."

Harnell, E. W., Pvt. Co. K

He appears on a company muster roll for September/October 1864, "taken prisoner at Fort Gaines August 8, 1864." He was received at Ship Island, Mississippi, from New Orleans on October 25, 1864, and exchanged at Ship Island on January 4, 1865. He appears on a list of POW's that were surrendered by Lt. General Richard

Taylor at Citronelle, Alabama, on May 4, 1865, and paroled at Meridian, Mississippi, on May 13, 1865. A resident of Choctaw Bluff, Clarke County, Alabama.

Harper, Daniel C., Pvt. Co. A

Enlisted on August 27, 1862, at Jefferson County, Alabama, by William A. Walker for the war. Company muster roll for December 31, 1862, to April 30, 1863, reports him absent sick in hospital at Choctaw Bluff. Muster rolls for May/June and September/October 1863, report him present. He was admitted to Post Hospital at Fort Morgan, Alabama, on November 9, 1863, with int. fever and returned to duty on November 19. He was admitted again to Post Hospital at Fort Morgan on December 11, 1863, with int. fever, and returned to duty on January 6, 1864. He died at hospital in Mobile, Alabama, on March 29, 1864. He left $51. Claim was filed by Lewis Harper his Father on October 31, 864.

Harper, S. D., Pvt. Co. ?.

Enlisted on February 1, 1864, at Cedar Point, Alabama, by Lt. Tell for the war. Company muster roll for September/October 1964, reports him present. He was admitted to Ross Hospital at Mobile, Alabama, on November 2, 1964, with febris intermittens tert. and returned to duty on November 5, 1864.

Harris, , Pvt. Co. ?

He appears on a regimental return of December 1861, and a register of discharged soldiers. He was discharged on July 4, 1962.

Harris, Jacob, Pvt. Co. E

POW captured at Fort Gaines, Alabama, on August 8, 1864. He appears on a roll of POW's admitted to St. Louis USA General Hospital at New Orleans admitted on September 16, 1964, with diarrhoea.

Harris, James, Pvt. Co. F

On detached service in Mobile, Alabama. A pay voucher is in his file for pay December 18, 1861, to April 28, 1862. Paid $78.60. Paid again $47 for service January 1, to February 28, 1862. He was paid $11 per month plus subsistence and clothing. [Maybe twice?]

Harris, John, Pvt. Co. H

Enlisted on October 13, 1861, at Mobile, Alabama, for one year. He was wounded seriously in the elbow at Shiloh at 4 P. M. at the Old Field on April 6, 1862. Transferred to the 1st Louisiana Regulars on July 4, 1862. He was discharged at Tupelo, Mississippi, on July 19, 1862. Born Gelz, France, age 28, light hair, a merchant by occupation. There is a pay voucher in his file with his discharge. He was paid $34 for service from June 1, 1862, to July 14, 1862.*

Harston, P. R., Pvt. Co. G see **Hairston, P. R.**

Harston, W. T., Pvt. Co. F see **Hurston, W. T.**

MOBILE CONFEDERATES

Hartean, Sam L, Pvt. Co. E see **Hartean, Samuel, W.**

Hartean, Samuel, W., Pvt. Co. E
 Enlisted on October 13, 1861, at Mobile, Alabama, by Captain Chamberlain for the war. He was furloughed from March 1, to April 9, 1862. He appears present on a company muster roll for bounty on September 24, 1862. He appears on a return for November 1862, "Detached to Report to Adm. Buchanan, Mobile Nov. 26, 1862, by order of Gen. Forney." Company muster roll for November/December 1862, report him absent detailed on November 22, 1862, by order of Admiral Buchanan. July/August 1863 and September/October 1863, muster rolls report him absent detailed on gunboat by order of Admiral Buchanan. There are a number of pay vouchers in his file.*

Harter, Charles E., Corp./Pvt. Co. A
 Enlisted on October 13, 1861, at Mobile, Alabama, by Major Hessee for the war. He appears present on a company muster roll for bounty on September 24, 1862. He appears present on muster rolls for December 31, 1862, to April 30, 1863 and May/June 1863. He appears absent on September/October 1863, "detached Aug 15/63 AQM Dept. Mobile order Gen. Maury." "Reduced from 2nd Corp ranks (Hon.) Sept. 1/63". He appears on a muster roll for November/December 1863, of men in the CS Ordinance Department at Mobile. POW captured at Fort Morgan, Alabama, on August 23, 1864. He was sent to New York from New Orleans on September 27, 1864, and received at Elmira, New York, on October 8, 1864. There is a pay voucher in his file.*

Hartnett, William R., Pvt. Co. E
 Enlisted on October 13, 1861, at Mobile, Alabama, by Captain Chamberlain for the war. POW captured at Fort Donelson (one record shows Pittsburg Landing captured on April 8.) on February 16, 1862. His name appears on a register of men missing at Shiloh "on ambulance squad, captured at hospital, April 7/62." He was admitted as a prisoner to Hickory Street USA General Hospital at St. Louis, Missouri, with acute diarrhoea on April 18, 1862, returned to Military Prison on May 17. He appears on a roll of POW's at Camp Douglas, Illinois, on August 1, 1862. He was sent aboard the steamer *Jno. H. Done* to Vicksburg, Mississippi, on September 2, 1862, to be exchanged. He appears absent on a company muster roll for bounty on September 24, 1862, "exchanged prisoner now in Mobile" He appears present on muster rolls for November/December 1862, July/August 1863 and September/October 1863.

Harwell, E. W., Pvt. Co. K see **Harnell, E. W.**

Hatton, T. J., Brevet 2nd Lt./2nd Lt. Co. B
 Mustered into service on October 13, 1861. Elected (appointed) 2nd Lt. on October 8, 1861. He appears present at Fort Gaines, Alabama, on a return for November 1861. Promoted on May 8, 1862. He appears present on a regimental return for June 1862, near Tupelo, Mississippi. He was paid $208 for service from October 13, 1861, to December 3, 1862. The pay voucher is in his file.*

Haupt. James E., Pvt. Co. E see **Haupt, James P.**

Haupt, James P., Pvt. Co. E

Enlisted on November 11, 1862, at Fort Morgan by Captain Sossaman for the war. He appears present on company muster rolls for November/December 1862, July/August 1863, and September/October 1863. POW captured at Fort Gaines, Alabama, on August 8, 1862. He was received at Ship Island, Mississippi, from New Orleans on October 25, 1864, and exchanged at Ship Island on January 5, 1865. He was admitted to St. Louis USA General Hospital at New Orleans on August 25, 1864, with dysentery and returned to military prison on September 2, 1864, age 19. He was surrendered by Lt. General Richard Taylor on May 4, 1865, at Citronelle, Alabama, and paroled at Meridian, Mississippi, on May 13, 1863. Residence Mobile, Alabama.

Haurick, E. G., Pvt. Co. K

His name appears on a payment to discharged soldiers. Discharged on May 26, 1862, for disability due to rheumatism, born in Montgomery, Alabama, age 22, five foot six and one half inches, dark complexion, dark eyes, black hair.*

Hawk, J. M., Pvt. Co. E

Drew clothing June 1, 1864. POW captured at Fort Gaines, Alabama, on August 8, 1864. He was admitted on August 25, 1864, to St. Louis USA General Hospital at New Orleans as military prisoner with typhoid malaria. He died on September 7, 1864, and was buried at Cypress Grove Cemetery at New Orleans grave 337. Age 16, unmarried. Residence Clifton, Alabama, contact R. Bridges.

Hawkins, W. A., Corp. Co. H

Drew clothing on March 3, and May 31, 1864. POW captured at Fort Gaines, Alabama, on August 8, 1862. He was received at Ship Island, Mississippi, from New Orleans on October 25, 1864, and exchanged at Ship Island on January 4, 1865. He was admitted to 1st Mississippi, CSA Hospital, Jackson, Mississippi, on March 3, 1865, with chronic diarrhoea and returned to duty on April 9, 1865. He was admitted to Ocmulgee Hospital at Macon, Georgia, on April 16, 1865, with diarrhoea and transferred on April 18, 1865, residence shown as Monroe County. He was also captured by 1st Brigade 2nd Cavalry Division in April 1865, reported at Macon, Georgia, on April 30, 1865.

Hawkins, William H., Corp. Co. H see **Hawkins, W. A.**

Hawthorn, Pvt. Co. E

His name appears on a regimental return for December 1861.

Hawthorn, A. B., Assistant Surgeon, Field and Staff.

Enlisted on October 13, 1861. Transferred November 15, 1861, successor A. J. Witherspoon.

Hayden, George B., Pvt. Co. D

Enlisted on August 13, 1862, at Fort Morgan, Alabama, by Lt. Carrington for the war. He appears present on a company muster roll for bounty on September 24, 1862, and on a hospital muster roll at Fort Morgan Hospital for September/October 1862, present as druggist. Company muster roll for November/December 1862, reports him present as post druggist. Hospital muster roll for hospital at Fort Gaines in July/August 1863, reports him transferred to Medical Department by order of Secretary of War on May 21, 1863. Hospital muster rolls at Fort Gaines for November/December 1863, and January/February and May/June 1864, report him present. POW, a hospital steward, captured at Fort Blakeley, Alabama, on April 9, 1865. He appears on a list of medical personnel sent from Spanish Fort, Alabama, to Vicksburg, Mississippi, and on to General Hospital at New Orleans.

Hayes, E. R., Pvt, Co. A see **Hayes, Tobias R.**

Hayes, John, Pvt. Co. A
   Enlisted on August 28, 1862, at Fort Morgan, Alabama, by Captain Williams for the war. Company muster roll for December 31, 1862, to April 30, 1863, reports him absent, "arrested for desertion Feb/63, & confined at Mobile." May/June 1863, muster roll shows the same notation except confined at Fort Morgan. Muster roll for September/October 1863, reports him present, absent without leave from October 9, 1862, to March 1, 1863. Paid $177.71 for clothing on November 21, 1863, for service September 1, to November 10, 1863. Transferred to CS Navy on October 31, 1863, by order of the Secretary of War. Discharged at Fort Morgan, Alabama, on November 10, 1863. His discharge is in his file. Born in New Orleans, Louisiana, age 18, five foot six inches, light complexion, brown eyes, S? hair and a tin smith by occupation.*

Hayes, Tobias, R., Pvt. Co. A
   Enlisted on October 13, 1861, at Mobile, Alabama, by Major Hessee for the war. Wounded slightly in the leg at Shiloh at First Camp on April 6, 1862, at 8 A. M. He appears present on a company muster roll for bounty on September 24, 1862. Company muster rolls for December 31, 1862, to April 30, 1863, May/June and September/October 1863, all show him present. Drew clothing on March 31, 1864. POW captured at Fort Morgan, Alabama, on August 22, 1864 and sent from New Orleans to Elmira, New York on September 27, 1864. Received at Elmira, New York, on October 8, 1864. He was released on parole on July 7, 1865. Residence shown as Mobile, Alabama.

Hayman, N., Pvt. Co. I
   Enlisted at Halls Mill, Alabama, on March 1, 1862, by Lt. Cayce. He appears present on a company muster roll for bounty on September 24, 1862, "refused to receive bounty." He appears on a return for November 1862, where he is shown as having deserted November 14.

Haynes, J. D., Pvt. Co. G
   Drew clothing on March 31, 1864, and signed by his mark. He was admitted to Post Hospital at Fort Morgan, Alabama, on January 23, 1864, with pneumonia and sent to general hospital on January 29, 1864. POW captured at Fort Gaines, Alabama, on August 8, 1862. He was received at Ship Island, Mississippi, from New Orleans on October 25, 1864, and exchanged at Ship Island on January 5, 1865. He was surrendered by Lt. General Richard Taylor on May 4, 1865, at Citronelle, Alabama, and paroled at

Meridian, Mississippi, on May 13, 1863. Residence shown as Mobile, Alabama. At one point he was admitted to City Hospital, at Mobile, wounded. No date shown.

Haynes, J. M., Pvt. Co. G see **Haynes, J. D.**

Haynes, Thomas C., Pvt. Co. G

His name appears on a register of Ross Hospital, Mobile, Alabama, where he was admitted on January 28, 1864, with typhoid fever with erysipelas. Returned to duty on February 24, 1864. Name shows as **Tillman Haynes.**

Hayes, Charles C., Pvt. Co. A

Enlisted on November 13, 1861, at Camp Governor Moore for one year. Discharged due to disability on January 14, 1862. He was born in Dallas County, Alabama, age 24, five foot six and one half inches, complexion light, blue eyes, light hair, by occupation a farmer. His discharge and pay voucher is in his file.*

Heard, John F. M., Pvt. Co. C

Enlisted on September 17, 1862, at Fort Morgan, Alabama, by Captain Smith for the war. He appears present on a company muster roll for bounty on September 24, 1862. Company muster rolls for December 31, 1862, to April 30, 1863, May/June and September/October 1863, all show him present. Drew clothing on June 1, and March 31, 1864. POW captured at Fort Gaines, Alabama, on August 8, 1862. He was received at Ship Island, Mississippi, from New Orleans on October 25, 1864, and died of dysentery at Ship Island on November 30, 1864, and was buried in grave No. 54.

Heite, H. A., Pvt. Co. D

POW captured at Fort Blakeley, Alabama, on April 9, 1865. He was received at Ship Island, Mississippi, on April 15, 1865, and transferred to Vicksburg, Mississippi, on May 1, for exchange.

Heiter, Fauldin V., Corporal Co. B

Enlisted on November 1, 1861, at Mobile, Alabama, by Adjutant Cayce for 12 months. He appears present on a company muster roll for bounty on September 24, 1862, "not entitled to bounty under age = refused to take bounty." He was discharged on November 1, 1862. *There is poor quality paperwork in his file.*

Heitman, Pvt. Co. D

He appears on a regimental return of June 1862, "detained by civil authorities in Memphis, for crime."

Helmetag. F. W., Pvt. Co. K

Enlisted on September 9, 1864, at Mobile, Alabama, by Major Stone for the war. He appears on a company muster roll for September/October 1864, "Transferred to Conscript Camp Notasulga, Alabama, by order of Major Stone Enr. [*Enrolling*] Officer, Oct. 18, 1864.

Henderson, W. R., Pvt. Co. F

Enlisted on August 28, 1862, at Jefferson C. [*County, Alabama*], by James Tarrant for the war. Drew clothing on March 31 and June 1, 1864 and signed by his mark. Company muster rolls for March 1, to June 30, 1863 and September/October 1863, report him present. POW captured at Fort Gaines, Alabama, on August 8, 1864. He was admitted to St Louis USA General Hospital at New Orleans with diarrhoea on September 19, 1864, and returned to confinement on October 14, 1864. .He appears on a roll of POW's received at Steam Levee Press No. 4 at New Orleans on October 14, 1864, "received from hospital." He was received at Ship Island, Mississippi, from New Orleans on October 25, 1864. He was to be exchanged in January but instead was left sick in hospital at Ship Island. He died at Mobile, Alabama, on January 26, 1865. Certificate number 281.

Henley, L. (Lewis) L. B., Pvt./Corp. Co. F

Enlisted at Point Clear, Alabama, on August 4, 1863, by Captain Dade for three years or the war. Company muster roll for September/October 1863, reports him present and bounty due. He was paid $50 bounty on December 31, 1863. POW captured at Fort Gaines, Alabama, on August 8, 1862. He was received at Ship Island, Mississippi, from New Orleans on October 25, 1864, and exchanged at Ship Island on January 4, 1865. POW surrendered by Lt. General R. Taylor at Citronelle, Alabama, on May 4, 1865, and paroled at Meridian, Mississippi, on May 13, 1865. He was a resident of Clarke County, Alabama. *Lewis B. Henley was one of four brothers who served in CSA and only one to survive the war. He died April 30, 1924 near Fulton, Alabama see his letters in appendix.*

Henry, Josiah, Pvt. Co. B

Died in service. Left $10.40.

Henry, J. W., Pvt. Co. K

Enlisted on October 13, 1861, at Mobile, Alabama, by C. S. Stewart for 12 months. Drew $50 bounty. Wounded severely in left arm at Shiloh on April 6, 1862, at 9 A. M. during attack while advancing on 1st Camp. Discharged for disability June 17, 1862, born in Mobile, Alabama, age 24, five foot six inches, fair complexion, hazel eyes, dark hair, and a clerk by occupation.

Henson, J. M., Pvt. Co. C see **Hinson, J. M.**

Henson, J. N., Co. C see **Hinson, J. M.**

Henson, John, Corp. Co. D/C

POW captured at Blakeley, Alabama, on April 9, 1865. He was received at Ship Island, Mississippi, on April 15, 1865, and transferred to Vicksburg for exchange on May 1, 1865.

Henson, William, Pvt. Co. C

Enlisted on January 15, 1862, at Fort Gaines, Alabama, by Captain Rembert for the war. He appears present on a company muster roll for bounty on September 24, 1862. Company muster rolls for December 31, 1862, to April 30, 1863, May/June and September/October 1863, all show him present. He drew clothing on March 31 and June 1, 1864. He was received at Ship Island, Mississippi, from New Orleans on October 25, 1864, and exchanged at Ship Island on January 4, 1865. POW captured at Blakeley, Alabama, on April 9, 1865. He was received at Ship Island, Mississippi, on April 15, 1865, and transferred to Vicksburg for exchange on May 1, 1865.*

Henson, W. R., Pvt. Co. C see **Henson, William**

Herbert, T. T., Pvt./2nd Lt. Co. I

Enlisted March 7, 1861, at Montgomery, Alabama, by Captain Thorn for three years. A return for November 1862, reports that he transferred from 1st Batt. Alabama Artillery on November 23, 1862, at Fort Morgan, Alabama, another return in November 1862, reports that he was detailed in Quartermasters Department. Company muster roll for July/August 1863, reports him absent "sick Genl. Hosp. Mobile." He was admitted to Post Hospital at Fort Morgan with ulcer on July 27, 1863, and sent to general hospital on August 25, 1863. He was once again admitted to Fort Morgan Post Hospital on October 21, 1863, with dysentery and returned to duty on November 4, 1863. Company muster roll for September/October 1863, reports him present, sick in hospital. He was elected 2nd Lt. on May 16, 1864. He drew clothing on June 1, 1864. POW captured at Fort Gaines, Alabama, on August 8, 1864. He was received at Ship Island, Mississippi, from New Orleans on November 25, 1864, and exchanged at Ship Island on January 4, 1865.

Herbert, William, W., Pvt. Co. D

Enlisted on May 4, 1861, at Pensacola, Florida, by Captain Cox for the war. Company muster roll for July/August 1863, reports him present, "transferred from Prattville Dragoons, by order General Bragg." A company muster roll for September/October 1863, reports him present. November/December 1863, muster roll reports him absent "Detached in Navy Dept. for 30 days by order of General Maury." Muster roll for September/October 1864, reports him absent detached in the Navy on December 6, 1863.

Herpin, Augustus, Pvt. Co. E

Enlisted on March 19, 1863, at Fort Morgan, Alabama, by Captain Sossaman for the war. Company muster rolls for July/August and September/October 1863, report him present. POW captured at Fort Gaines, Alabama, on August 8, 1864. He was received at Ship Island, Mississippi, on November 25, 1864, and exchanged at Ship Island, on January 4, 1865. POW surrendered by Lt. General R. Taylor at Citronelle, Alabama, on May 4, 1865, and paroled at Meridian, Mississippi, on May 13, 1865. Residence shown as Mobile, Alabama.

Herpin, H., Pvt. Co. E see **Herpin, Augustus**

MOBILE CONFEDERATES

Herpin, John Emile, Pvt. Co. A
    Killed at Shiloh on April 6, 1862, at 8:30 A. M. while advancing on 1st Camp. He was wounded in thigh severing artery and left on the field. A claim of deceased soldier was filed by J. B. Herpin his Father on August 2, 1862.

Herring, E., Sgt. Co. G
    He drew clothing on May 3 and June 1, 1864   POW captured Fort Gaines, Alabama, on August 8, 1864. He was received at Ship Island, Mississippi, from New Orleans on October 25, 1864, and exchanged at Ship Island on January 4, 1865.

Herzey. P., Pvt. Co. D
    POW captured at Blakeley, Alabama, April 9, 1865, and received at Ship Island, Mississippi, April 15, 1865 and transferred to Vicksburg for exchange May 1, 1865.

Heustis, J. M., Sgt. Co K
    Paid $69.20 for service from October 13, 1861, to December 31, 1861, sick.

Hewett, John W., Pvt./Sgt. Co. A
    Enlisted on October 13, 1861, at Mobile, Alabama, by Major Hessee for the war. He appears present on a muster roll for bounty on September 24, 1862. Company muster rolls for December 31, 1862, to April 31, 1863, May/June 1863, September/October 1863 and a muster roll for Sossaman's Detachment September/October 1864, all show him present. He was admitted to Post Hospital at Fort Morgan on November 4, 1863, with remit. fever and returned to duty on November 13. He was again admitted to Post Hospital at Fort Morgan on December 17, 1863, with int. fever and returned to duty on December 24. He was again admitted to Post Hospital at Fort Morgan on December 31, 1863, and sent to general hospital on January 17, 1864. He was admitted to Ross Hospital on January 17, 1864, with int. fever tert., then sent to Montgomery on February 17, 1864. He drew clothing on May 31, 1864. He was admitted to Ross Hospital on October 14, 1864, with febris intermittins quot. and returned to duty on October 24, 1864.

Hewitt, David M., Pvt./Sgt. Co. E/K
    Enlisted on October 13, 1864, at Mobile, Alabama, by Captain Chamberlain for the war. He appears present on a muster roll for bounty on September 24, 1862. Company muster rolls for November/December 1862, July/August 1863 and September/October 1864, all report him present. He was admitted to Post Hospital at Fort Morgan, Alabama, on September 14, 1863, with diarrhoea and returned to duty on September 21, 1863. He drew clothing on June 1, 1864. He was admitted to Ross Hospital in Mobile, Alabama, on September 3, 1864, with febris intermittens tert. and returned to duty on October 16, 1864. He was again admitted to Ross Hospital with the same complaint on October 18, 1864, and furloughed on November 29, for 60 days. POW surrendered by Lt. General R. Taylor at Citronelle, Alabama, on May 4, 1865, and paroled at Meridian, Mississippi, on May 13, 1865. Residence shown as Mayhew Station, Lowndes County, Mississippi.

Hewitt, James E., Pvt. Co. E

Enlisted at Mobile, Alabama, on August 18, 1864, by Captain DeVaux for the war. He appears present on a muster roll for bounty on September 24, 1862. Company muster rolls for November/December 1862, July/August 1863 and September/October 1863, all show him absent detached to work on the floating Battery on October 20, 1862, by order of General Forney. He drew clothing on May 16, 1863.*

Hewitt. J. W., Pvt./Sgt. Co. A see **Hewett, John W.**

Hewitt, William, N., Pvt. Co. E

Enlisted at Mobile, Alabama, on August 18, 1864, by Captain DeVaux for the war. He appears present on a muster roll for bounty on September 24, 1862. Company muster rolls for November/December 1862, July/August 1863 and September/October 1863, all show him absent detached to work on the floating Battery October 20, 1862, by order of General Forney. He was admitted to Ross Hospital at Mobile, Alabama, on December 15, 1863, with debility and sent to General Hospital in Montgomery, Alabama, on February 17, 1864. He died at St Mary's Hospital, Alabama, on July 8, 1864. Left $93.20.*

Hicks, John, Pvt. Co. B

Enlisted on September 2, 1862, at Jefferson, County, Alabama, by W. A. Walker for the war. Company muster roll for March/April 1863, reports him present. May/June 1863, muster roll he is shown present sick in quarters. Company muster roll for September/October 1863, reports him present detailed as nurse for sick in quarters. He was admitted to Post Hospital at Fort Morgan, Alabama, on December 22, 1863, with abscess and returned to duty on January 17, 1864. He was admitted to Ross Hospital at Mobile, Alabama, on January 16, 1864, with ulcer, sent to General Hospital in Montgomery on February 17, 1864. *There may be two men in this file.*

Hicks, John T., Pvt. Co. B

Enlisted on September 17, 1862, at Lawrence [*County?*] by D. C. Kennard for three years or the war. He appears present on company muster roll for March/April 1863, detailed as a teamster in Q. M. Department on April 7, 1862. May/June 1863, muster roll reports him present sick in quarters and September/October 1863, roll reports him present but due pay for clothing not drawn in kind. He drew clothing on June 1, 1864. POW captured at Fort Gaines, Alabama, on August 8, 1864. He was received at Ship Island, Mississippi, from New Orleans on November 25, 1864, and exchanged at Ship Island on January 4, 1865. He was admitted to Ross Hospital at Mobile, Alabama, on January 6, 1865, with bronchitis and furloughed for 15 days on January 19.

Hill, G. B., Pvt. Co. C

Enlisted at Mobile, Alabama, on October 13, 1861, by Captain Rembert for twelve months. A regimental return for June 1862, reports him absent on sick furlough. A report near Tupelo, Mississippi, on June 28, 1862, shows him as having been sent to interior hospital by surgeon near Corinth. He appears present on a muster roll for bounty on September 24, 1862. Company muster rolls for December 31, 1862, to April 1863,

May/June 1863 and September/October 1863, report him present. On the last roll he is shown as having lost a canteen and charged $2. He drew clothing on May 31 and June 1, 1864. POW captured at Fort Gaines, Alabama, on August 8, 1864. He was received at Ship Island, Mississippi, from New Orleans on October 25, 1864, and exchanged at Ship Island on January 4, 1865. POW surrendered by Lt. General R. Taylor at Citronelle, Alabama, and paroled at Demopolis, Alabama, on June 22, 1865. Residence shown as Marengo County, Alabama.

Hill, G. P., Pvt. Co. C see **Hill, G. B.**

Hill, W. H. (Henry) Pvt. Co. H

Was paid for commutation of rations while on sick furlough July 4, to July 29, 1863. Drew clothing on March 3 and June 1, 1864. POW captured at Fort Gaines, Alabama, on August 8, 1864. He was received at Ship Island, Mississippi, from New Orleans on October 25, 1864, and exchanged at Ship Island on January 4, 1865.

Hill, Jesse, Pvt. Co. D

Enlisted on October 13, 1861, at Mobile, Alabama, by Major Hessee for one year. Discharged on July 22, 1862, by reason of being a minor, five foot five inches, fair complexion, gray eyes, auburn hair, age 17, a student when enlisted. His discharge is in his file.*

Hill, S. A., Pvt. Co. I

Enlisted on March 24, 1863, at Fort Morgan, Alabama, by Lt. Collins for the war. Company muster rolls for July/August and September/October 1863, report him present. Drew clothing on May 31 and December 8, 1864. POW captured at Blakeley, Alabama, on April 9, 1865. He was received at Ship Island, Mississippi, on April 15, 1865, and transferred to Vicksburg, Mississippi, for exchange on May 1, 1865. POW surrendered by Lt. General R. Taylor at Citronelle, Alabama, in May 1865, and paroled at Demopolis, Alabama, on June 3, 1865. Residence shown as Marengo County, Alabama.

Hilton, Thomas, Musician Co. C see **Hylton, Thomas S.**

Hinson, J. M., Pvt. Co. C

Enlisted on January 3, 1863, at Choctaw Bluff, Alabama, by Captain Smith for three years or the war. Company muster rolls for December 31, 1862, to April 30, 1863, May/June 1863 and September/October 1863, all report him present. On the September/October 1863, roll he is shown as having lost one trigger at $1. He was admitted to Post Hospital at Fort Morgan, Alabama, on November 9, 1863, with bronchitis and sent to general hospital on January 26, 1864. POW captured at Fort Gaines, Alabama, on August 8, 1864. He was received at Ship Island, Mississippi, from New Orleans on October 25, 1864, and exchanged at Ship Island on January 4, 1865. POW captured at Blakeley, Alabama, on April 9, 1865. He was admitted to St. Louis USA General Hospital at New Orleans on September 25, 1864, with acute diarrhoea, and returned to confinement on September 30, 1864. He appears on a list of CSA prisoners at Steam Levee Press No. 4 in New Orleans received from hospital on September 30, 1864. He was received at Ship Island, Mississippi, on April 15, 1865, and transferred to Vicksburg, Mississippi, for exchange on May 1, 1865.

Hinson, William, Pvt. Co. D

His name appears on a roll of POW's captured by the Army of the Tennessee (US) and sent to Memphis, Tennessee, May 23, 1863. Roll dated Headquarters Department of Tennessee, in the field near Vicksburg, Mississippi, on June 29, 1863. Captured at Big Black [*Mississippi*] on May 17, 1863.

Hinson, W. R., Pvt. Co. C see **Hinson, William**

Hoban, John, Pvt. Co. B

Enlisted on October 13, 1861, at Mobile, Alabama, by Major Hessee for twelve months. He appears on a company muster roll for bounty on September 24, 1862, as not being entitled to bounty, underage.

Hiver, John, Pvt. Co. H

Enlisted on October 13, 1861, at Mobile, Alabama, by Major Hessee for twelve months. Discharged at Fort Gaines, Alabama, due to disability on November 19, 1861, but paid to February 6, 1862. He is described as; age 36, five foot six inches, dark complexion, black eyes, dark hair, born in Florence Italy, a watchmaker by profession. He signs as Giovanni Hiver. His discharge and pay voucher are in his file.*

Hodgen, William, Pvt. Co. B

Enlisted on September 9, 1862, at Mobile, Alabama, by Captain Johnson for the war. He appears present on a company muster roll on September 24, 1862, for bounty. Company muster rolls for March/April and May/June 1863, report him present.

Hodges, Henry Lee., Pvt. Co. E

Enlisted on October 13, 1861, at Mobile, Alabama, by Captain Chamberlain for the war. He was wounded in thigh during attack on 1st Battery at Shiloh on April 6, 1862, at 7 A. M. while advancing. His name appears on a regimental return for June 1862, "clerk Gen'l Court Marshal." He appears absent on a company muster roll on September 24, 1862, for bounty. He was detailed with Signal Corps on September 8, 1862, on order of Colonel Powell. Company muster rolls for November/December 1862, July/August 1863 and September/October 1863, continue to show him absent detailed with Signal Corps. He appears on a receipt pay roll January 10, 1863, at Mobile, Alabama, as signal operator. Other receipts for pay show him as a signal and telegraph operator. He was transferred to Signal Corps on April 13, 1864. There are a number of pay vouchers in his file.*

Holcombe. L. L, Co. K

His name appears on a regimental return for December 1861.

Holdsmith, William, Pvt. Co. B see **Holdsworth, William**

Holdsworth, William, Pvt. Co. B

Enlisted on October 13, 1861, at Mobile, Alabama, by Major Hessee for twelve Months. He appears on a report near Tupelo, Mississippi, on June 28, 1862, "sent to Hazelhurst Hospital by Dr. Heustis." He appears present on a company muster roll on September 24, 1862, for bounty "refuses to take bounty." Company muster roll for March/April 1863, shows him a Corporal and present. A company muster roll for May/June 1863, reports him present and reduced to ranks on May 1, 1863, from 3rd Corporal, sick in quarters. September/October muster roll shows him absent sent to General Hospital in Mobile on July 15, 1863, by order of Colonel Anderson. POW captured at Fort Gaines, Alabama, on August 8, 1864. He was received at Ship Island, Mississippi, from New Orleans on October 25, 1864, and exchanged at Ship Island on January 4, 1865.

Holifield, William, Pvt. Co. F see **Hollifield, W. R.**

Hollandsworth, S. M., Pvt. Co. I see **Hollingsworth, S. M.**

Hollifield, W. R., Pvt. Co. F

Enlisted on September 12, 1862, at Perry County, [*Alabama?*] by W. B. Livingston for three years or the war. Company muster roll for March 1, to June 30, 1863, reports him present. Muster roll for September/October 1863, report him absent, "sick in hospital in Mobile, since July 16, 186." He appears on a hospital muster roll for General Hospital at Mobile, Alabama, for March/April 1864, present as patient. He appears on a hospital muster roll for Hospital Shelby Springs, Alabama, July/August 1864, present as patient. He was admitted to 1st Mississippi, CSA Hospital at Jackson, Mississippi, with acute diarrhoea on August 13, 1864, and transferred on October 13.

Hollingsworth, J. C., Pvt. Co. A see **Hollingsworth, J. G.**

Hollingsworth, J. G., Pvt. Co. A

He appears on a roll of POW's at Camp Morton, Indiana, in June 1862, captured at Fort Donelson February 16. 1862. He appears on a roll of POW's sent from Camp Morton on August 24, 1862, to Vicksburg, Mississippi, to be exchanged. Exchanged November 10, 1862, at Atkins Land[*ing*].

Hollingsworth, S. M., Pvt. Co. I

He was due clothing on March 31, 1864. POW captured at Fort Gaines, Alabama, on August 8, 1864. He was received at Ship Island, Mississippi, from New Orleans on October 25, 1864, and applied to take the Oath of Allegiance to the USA. Exchanged at Ship Island on January 4, 1865.

Holley, J. D., Pvt. Co. G

POW captured at Fort Gaines, Alabama, on August 8, 1864. He was admitted to St. Louis USA General Hospital at New Orleans on August 29, 1864, with diarrhoea. He died at St. Louis USA General Hospital at New Orleans of diarrhoea on September 10, 1864. He was buried on September 11, 1864, in grave 344, Monument Cemetery, New

21ST ALABAMA INFANTRY VOLUNTEERS

Orleans. Age 36, next of kin his Mother in Buena Vista, Monroe County, Alabama. He left no effects.

Holleyman, Aaron, Pvt. Co. A

POW captured at Fort Donelson on February 16, 1862. He appears on a roll of POW's at Fort Monroe, Indiana, in June 1862. He appears on a roll of POW's sent from Fort Monroe to Vicksburg, Mississippi, on August 24, 1862, to be exchanged and was exchanged at Atkens Landing on November 10, 1862.

Holmes, B. R., Sgt. Co. H

Drew clothing on March 1 and 31, 1864. POW captured at Fort Gaines, Alabama, on August 8, 1864. He was received at Ship Island, Mississippi, from New Orleans on October 25, 1864, and exchanged at Ship Island on January 4, 1865. POW straggler surrendered by Lt. General R. Taylor in May 1865, and paroled at Selma, Alabama, on May 29, 1865. Residence shown as Autauga County, Alabama.

Holmes, Hamilton, R., Pvt. Co. K

Enlisted on October 13, 1861, at Fort Morgan, Alabama, by Captain Dorgan for the war. Muster rolls for November/December 1862, July/August 1863, September/October 1863 and September/October 1864, all show him present. He drew clothing on July 10, December 19, 1863 and June 30, 1864. POW a straggler surrendered by Lt. General R. Taylor at Meridian, Mississippi, in May 1865, and paroled at Mobile, Alabama, on May 19, 1865. Residence shown as Mobile County, Alabama.

Holmes, James W., Pvt. Co. K

Enlisted on October 13, 1861, at Mobile, Alabama, by Captain Stewart for the war. He appears present on a company muster roll for bounty on September 24, 1862. Company muster roll for November/December 1862, reports him present. Company muster roll for July/August 1863, reports that he was transferred to Seldon's Battery on August 1, 1863. There are pay vouchers in his file.*

Holmes, William H., Pvt. Co. ?

He appears on a March/April 1863, company muster roll as Inspector and Enrolling Officer and 1st Lt. C. S. Artillery. He drew supplies for two horses at Fort Stonewall, Alabama, for month of July 1863.*

Holstein, W. J., Pvt. Co. D

He was wounded seriously in the left thigh at Shiloh on April 6, 1862, at 4 P. M. crossing Old Field while retreating. He appears on a report near Tupelo, Mississippi, June 28, 1862, "badly wounded at Shiloh unlimited Surgeon's Certif." Discharged on September 15, 1862. Born in North Carolina, age 23, five foot eight inches, dark complexion, dark hair, dark eyes, by occupation a student. His discharge is in his file.*

Holston, Pvt. Co. G

He was admitted to Post Hospital at Fort Morgan, Alabama, on November 3, 1863, with constipates and returned to duty on November 5.

MOBILE CONFEDERATES

Holt, A. D., Pvt. Co. E see **Holt, H. D.**

Holt, Anthony, Pvt. Co. _
His name appears on a signature to an Oath of Allegiance to the USA signed at Nashville, Tennessee, on March 10, 1865. Resident of Madison, County, Tennessee, fair complexion, brown hair, blue eyes, five foot eight inches. Deserted on January 11, 1865.

Holt, E. A., Pvt. Co. K
Enlisted on October 13, 1861, at Mobile, Alabama, by Captain Stewart for one year. His name appears on a regimental return in June 1862, where he is shown as clerk for Division Medical Director. He appears on a register of payments to discharged soldiers discharged July 5, 1863, paid on July 7. He drew $50 bounty on July 10, 1862. Born Mobile, Alabama, age 25, five foot eight and one half inches, fair complexion, gray eyes, light hair, by occupation a clerk. His discharge and pay vouchers are in his file.*

Holt, H. D., Pvt. Co. E
He drew clothing on March 31, 1864, and signed by his mark. POW captured at Fort Gaines, Alabama, on August 8, 1862. He was received at Ship Island, Mississippi, from New Orleans on October 25, 1864, and exchanged at Ship Island on January 4, 1865. He was admitted to Post Hospital at Fort Morgan, Alabama, on January 18, 1864, with int. fever and returned to duty on January 30, 1864.

Hooker, Lee, Pvt. Co. D
Enlisted on September 4, 1862, at Fort Morgan, Alabama, by Captain Butt for the war. Company muster roll for bounty on September 24, 1862, reports him present. Company muster roll for November/December 1862, shows him in the guardhouse under sentence of Court Marshal. He appears on a return for November 1862, as absent without leave. Muster rolls for July/August, September/October and November/ December 1863, all report him present. He was admitted to Ross Hospital in Mobile on January 24, 1864, with anasaica [*edema or dropsy*] and returned to duty on February 16, 1864. Company muster roll for September/October 1864, report him absent in arrest in Mobile since October 25, 1864. POW surrendered by Lt. General Richard Taylor at Citronelle, Alabama, on May 4, 1865, and paroled at Meridian, Mississippi, on May 13, 1865. Residence shown as Berkeley County, Virginia.

Hoover, William L., Pvt. Co. F
POW captured at Port Gibson, Mississippi, on May 1, 1863. He was paroled at Alton Military Prison at Alton, Illinois, until exchanged. He was sent to City Point, Virginia, among over one thousand Confederate prisoners for exchange.

Hopper, H. H., Pvt. Co. K
Enlisted on October 13, 1861, at Mobile, Alabama, by Captain Butt for the war. He appears on a regimental return for June 1863, "sent to hospital June 4." He appears on a report near Tupelo, Mississippi, on June 28, 1862, "on furlough since May 29, sent from Corinth." Company muster roll for bounty on September 24, 1862, reports him present. He appears present on muster rolls for November/December 1862, July/August,

September/October 1863 and September/October 1864. POW surrendered by Lt. General Richard Taylor at Citronelle, Alabama, on May 4, 1865, and paroled at Meridian, Mississippi, on May 13, 1865. Residence shown as Mobile, Mobile County, Alabama.

Hopper, Hugh L., 2nd Lt. Co. K

He appears on a regimental return for June 1862, shown present at Tupelo, Mississippi, acting A. A. Q. M. since June 16, 1862. Company muster roll for bounty on September 24, 1862, reports him present. He appears present on a company muster roll for November/December, 1862. Elected 2nd Lt. on May 8, 1862, and resigned on July 4, 1863. He appears on a field return from Brigade Headquarters at Fort Morgan, Alabama, for October 1862, "absent with leave, since Oct. 30, 1862, for four days." He appears on a field return from Brigade Headquarters at Fort Morgan, Alabama, for November 1862, "absent with leave, from November 25, 1862." On June 4, 1863, Doctor J. C. Nott at Mobile certifies that Lt. Hopper cannot stand the exposure of camp life due to eye inflammation. His infirmary report and pay vouchers are in his file.*

Horber, L. J., Pvt. Co. D see **Harber, L. J.**

Horlock, John, Pvt. Co. D

Enlisted on October 13, 1861, at Mobile, Alabama, by Major Hessee for one year. Wounded slightly in the forehead at Shiloh on April 6th at 5 P. M. Discharged for disability. Born in Mobile, Alabama, age 18, five foot five and one half inches, dark complexion, black eyes, dark hair. His discharge and pay voucher are in his file.*

Horn, William, Pvt. Co. D

Enlisted July 22, 1863, at Montgomery, Alabama, by Enrolling Officer for the war. Muster rolls for July/August, September/October and November/ December 1863, report him present. He drew clothing on June 20 and August 1, 1864. Company muster roll for September/October 1864, reports him absent, "sent to Genl. Hospital Mobile, Oct. 25, 1864." He was admitted to Ross Hospital in Mobile on October 26, 1864, with febris continua and furloughed for 20 days on November 10. POW captured at Blakeley, Alabama, on April 9, 1865. He was received at Ship Island, Mississippi, on April 15, 1865, and transferred to Vicksburg, Mississippi, on May 1, 1865.

Horne, W. H., Pvt. Co. D see **Horn, William**

Horney, James, Pvt. Co. A

His name appears on a regimental return for June 1862, "Tupelo Hospital June 16."

Horta, Peter, 2nd Lt. Co. G

Enlisted and appointed 2nd Lt. on October 13, 1861. Elected 2nt Lt. on July 1, 1861. His name appears on a regimental return for December 1861, and he is shown present. He was wounded seriously in the knee at Shiloh on April 6, 1862, at 3:30 P. M. while advancing in the center. A regimental return for June 1862, reports him absent "Wounded at Shiloh, absent on furlough." He appears on a report near Tupelo,

Mississippi, on June 28, 1862, "absent on furlough since April 10, 1862, in Mobile." There are several pay vouchers in his file.*

Horton, Frank, S., Pvt. Co. K

Enlisted on October 13, 1861, at Mobile, Alabama, by Captain Stewart for the war. Company muster roll for bounty on September 24, 1862, reports him absent, detached on June 12, 1862, A. C. S. Department by General Bragg. There is a pay voucher in his file for detached pay at 25 cents per day while on service at Selma, Alabama, with Captain Z. W. Woodruff, A. C. S. for 92 days. Company muster rolls for November/December 1862, July/August 1863, September/October 1863 and September/October 1864, all show him absent and detached in A. C. S. Department. His name appears on a list of soldiers employed in the Subsistence Department in the State of Alabama, at Montgomery, Alabama, on May 22, 1864. Employed by Captain Z. W. Woodruff Post Commander as clerk at Gainesville on medical certificate. He appears on a return from Gainesville, Alabama, in May 1864, as bookkeeper at commissary. POW captured the night of April 8, 1865, by US Forces before Blakeley, Alabama, "clerk for Gen. Thomas." There are a number of vouchers for pay for commutation of clothing and detached service in his file.**

Horton, T. S., Pvt. Co. K see **Horton. F. (Frank) S.**

Hosea, S. L., Pvt. Co. C

Enlisted on February 17, 1863, at Marengo County, Alabama, by Lt. Northrup for three years or the war. He appears present on a company muster roll for December 31, 1862, to April 30, 1863, "never been paid." Discharged May 3, 1863. Born in Marengo County, Alabama, age 17, five foot ten inches, fair complexion, gray eyes, light hair, by occupation a farmer.

Houston, W. T., Pvt. Co. G

Died at Mobile, Alabama, on January 18, 1865.

Hovell, W. D., Pvt. Co. H

Confederate soldier paroled at Headquarters of the 16th US Army Corps., Montgomery, Alabama, on May 23, 1865.

Howel, P. N., Pvt. Co. I see **Howell, Phil**

Howell, James, Pvt. Co. I

Enlisted on October 13, 1861, at Halls Mill, Alabama, by Major Hessee for the war. He appears present on a company muster roll for bounty on September 24, 1862. Returns for November 1862 and for December 1862, show him detailed with Q. M. Department. Company muster roll for July/August 1863, shows him present on extra duty with Q. M. Department since October 6, 1862. Company muster roll for September/October 1863, reports him present. Drew clothing on March 31, 1864. POW captured at Fort Gaines, Alabama, on August 8, 1864. He was received at Ship Island,

Mississippi, from New Orleans on October 25, 1864, and exchanged at Ship Island on January 4, 1865.

Howell, J. D., Pvt. Co. K

Enlisted on August 29, 1864, at Mobile, Alabama, by Major Stone for the war. His name appears on a company muster roll for September/October 1864, where he is shown absent temporarily attached to the company by Major Stone Enrolling Officer. "Detached to report to Major Harris at Dog River by Genl. Gardner Aug. 29, 64."

Howell, Phil, Pvt. Co. I

POW captured at Fort Gaines, Alabama, on August 8, 1864. His name appears on a morning report of prisoners confined at Steam Levee Press No. 4 at New Orleans on August 15, 1864, "sent to hospital on August 15, 1864. He was admitted to St. Louis, USA General Hospital Ward K at New Orleans with fever intermittent quot. on August 15, 1864, and returned to confinement on August 20, 1864. He was again admitted to St. Louis, USA General Hospital, at New Orleans with measles on September 24, 1864, and returned to confinement on October 6, 1864, age 18. He was received at Ship Island, Mississippi, from New Orleans on October 25, 1864. He died at Ship Island, Mississippi, on December 15, 1864. *Note the service records show that he died of dysentery and was buried in grave 90 but a listing of burials at Ship Island, state that he was shot by sentry.*

Howell, P. M., Pvt. Co. I see **Howell, Phil**

Howell, W. D., Pvt. Co. H

Enlisted on October 2, 1862, at Montgomery, Alabama, by Captain Stone for the war. A receipt roll for pay shows that he drew extra pay at Fort Gaines, Alabama, from May 1, to June 30, 1864, on boat crew. He appears on a hospital muster roll at General Hospital Moore at Mobile, Alabama, for November/December 1863, as a patient. Drew clothing on March 3, March 31 and June 1, 1864. POW captured at Fort Gaines, Alabama, on August 8, 1864. He was admitted to St. Louis USA General Hospital at New Orleans on August 24, 1864, with intermit. fever and returned to confinement on August 30, 1864. He was again admitted to St. Louis USA General Hospital on September 18, 1864, with the same complaint and returned to confinement on October 20, 1864, age 26. He was received at Ship Island, Mississippi, from New Orleans on October 25, 1864, and exchanged at Ship Island on January 4, 1865. He signed a parole at the Headquarters of the 16th US Army Corps. in Montgomery, Alabama, on May 23, 1865. He was described as five foot eight inches, light hair, gray eyes, and fair complexion.

Howell, William D., Pvt. Co. H see **Howell, W. D.**

Howland Jr., J., Pvt. Co. E

POW surrendered by Lt. General Richard Taylor at Citronelle, Alabama, on May 4, 1865, and paroled at Meridian, Mississippi, on May 13, 1865. Residence shown as Mobile, Alabama.

Hubbard, M. A., Pvt. Co. G see **Hubbard, M. O.**

Hubbard, M. O., Pvt. Co. G
Drew clothing on March 3, March 31 and June 1, 1864. POW captured at Fort Gaines, Alabama, on August 8, 1864. He was received at Ship Island, Mississippi, from New Orleans on October 25, 1864. He refused to be exchange on January 4, 1865. He was released upon taking the Oath of Allegiance to the USA on April 14, 1865, and returned to New Orleans on orders from Headquarters Military Division of West Mississippi. His name appears on a return of Military and Political prisoners in confinement at Ship Island, Mississippi, commanded by Colonel Ernest W. Holmesrh. He signed an Oath of Allegiance at New Orleans on April 14, 1865, by permission of the Secretary of War. Residence shown as Mobile, Alabama, with ruddy complexion, brown hair, brown eyes, five foot seven inches.

Huckabee, G. J., Pvt. Co. C/H
Enlisted on August 24, 1962, at Fort Morgan, Alabama, by Captain Smith for the war. He appears present on a company muster roll for bounty on September 24, 1862. Company muster rolls for December 31, 1862, to April 30, 1863, May/June 1863 and September/October 1863, all show him present. Drew clothing on June 1, 1864, and signed by his mark. He appears on a receipt roll for extra duty pay as a laborer from January 1, to February 10, 1862, and at Point Clear as a carpenter for September 1863. POW captured at Fort Gaines, Alabama, on August 8, 1864. He was received at Ship Island, Mississippi, from New Orleans on October 25, 1864, and exchanged at Ship Island on January 4, 1865. He was admitted to Ross Hospital at Mobile, Alabama, on January 6, 1865, with scurvy and furloughed for 15 days from January 23. 1865.

Huckabee, R., Pvt. Co. C/H
Enlisted on February 26, 1863, at Choctaw Bluff, Alabama, by Lt. Pollnitz for three years or the war. Company muster roll for December 31, 1862, to April 30, 1864, shows him present and enlisted as a substitute for **C. McPhaul**. Muster roll for May/June 1863, shows him present but sick in quarters. Muster roll for September/October 1863, shows him present and lost one haversack at $1. He drew clothing on March 31 and June 1, 1864, and signed by his mark. POW captured at Fort Gaines, Alabama, on August 8, 1864. He was received at Ship Island, Mississippi, from New Orleans on October 25, 1864, and exchanged at Ship Island on January 4, 1865. POW surrendered by Lt. General Richard Taylor at Citronelle, Alabama, in May 1865, and paroled at Demopolis, Alabama, on June 19, 1865. His residence was shown as Marengo County, Alabama.

Huckabee, R., Pvt. Co. C/H
Enlisted on December 26, 1862, at Choctaw Bluff, Alabama, by Captain Smith for three years or the war. Company muster roll for December 31, 862, to April 30, 1864, shows him absent "Detached in Engr. Dept. at Choctaw Bluff, Mch 25, '63, by order of Gen. Buckner, pay stopped Mch 25/63." Company muster roll for May/June 1863, shows him present "Detached in Engr. Dept. at Choctaw Bluff, Mch 25, '63, Retd. to Co. May 23/63, sick in quarters." September/October 1863, muster roll reports him present. He appears on a receipt roll for extra duty pay as a carpenter at Point Clear for September

1863, and for March 1, to March 15, 1864, at Mobile and Pollard. POW captured at Fort Gaines, Alabama, on August 8, 1864. He was received at Ship Island, Mississippi, from New Orleans on October 25, 1864, and exchanged at Ship Island on January 4, 1865. POW surrendered by Lt. General Richard Taylor at Citronelle, Alabama, in May 1865, and paroled at Demopolis, Alabama, on June 19, 1865. Residence shown as Marengo County, Alabama.

Huckabee, W. B., Pvt. Co. C/H

Enlisted on November 28, 1861, at Fort Gaines, Alabama, by Captain Rembert for 12 months. He appears present on a company muster roll for bounty, September 26, 1862. Company muster roll for December 31, 1862, to April 30, 1863, reports him present. Company muster roll for May/June 1863, reports him present but having lost one canteen at 24 cents and strap at 20 cents, plus six cartridges and 12 caps at 60 cents. September/October 1863, muster rolls shows him present. He drew clothing on April 14 May 31 and June 1, 1864, and signed by his mark. POW captured at Fort Gaines, Alabama, on August 8, 1864. He was received at Ship Island, Mississippi, from New Orleans on October 25, 1864, and exchanged at Ship Island on January 4, 1865. He was surrendered by Lt. General Richard Taylor in May 1865, and paroled at Demopolis, Alabama, on June 19, 1865, a resident of Marengo County, Alabama.

Huckaby, R., Pvt. Co. C/H see **Huckabee, R.**

Huckaby, R. P., Pvt. Co. C/H see **Huckabee, R. P.**

Huckaby, W. B., Pvt. Co. C/H see **Huckabee, W. B.**

Huckaby, G. J., Pvt. Co. C/H see **Huckabee, G. J.**

Hudson, B., Pvt. Co. C

Enlisted on July 29, 1863, at Linden, Alabama, by Lt. McLeod for three years or the war. Company muster roll for September/October 1863, reports him present, detailed as regimental shoe maker on September 25, 1863, by order of Colonel Anderson. Drew clothing on June 1, 1864. He appears on a descriptive list of pay and clothing at Point Clear, Alabama, on October 12, 1863. Born Marengo County, Alabama, age 36, blue eyes, black hair, dark complexion, five foot ten inches, and a farmer by occupation. POW captured at Fort Gaines, Alabama, on August 8, 1864. He was admitted to St. Louis, USA General Hospital at New Orleans on August 26,m 1864, with diarrhoea, and retuned to confinement on September 5. He was received at Ship Island, Mississippi, from New Orleans on October 25, 1864, and died at Ship Island of dysentery on December 21, 1864. He was buried in grave 105.

Hudson, Burrell, Pvt. Co. C see **Hudson, B.**

Hughes, Asa, Pvt. Co. D

Enlisted on October 13, 1861, at Mobile, Alabama, by Captain Butt for one year. His name appears on a regimental return for June 1862, "sent to interior hospital at the evacuation of Corinth, Mississippi." His name appears on a report near Tupelo, Mississippi, on June 28, 1862, " Sent to hospital in Mobile from hospital at Corinth by Surgeon." Company muster roll for bounty on September 24, 1862, reports him absent without leave. Company muster rolls for July/August 1863, September/October 1863 and November/December 1863, report him present. He drew clothing on June 20, 1864. He was admitted to Post Hospital at Fort Morgan, Alabama, on August 9, 1863, with remit. fever and returned to duty on August 20, 1863.

Hunt, William, Pvt. Co. B

Enlisted on October 13, 1864, at Mobile, Alabama, by Major Hessee for twelve months. He appears present on a company muster roll for bounty on September 26, 1862. Company muster roll for May/June 1863, reports him present, "sick in quarters." Company muster roll for September/October 1863, reports him present "due for clothing not drawn in kind $58.13." His name appears on a roll of soldiers on extra duty at Fort Morgan, Alabama, from November 3, to November 20, 1863, on boat crew. Drew clothing May 10 and June 1, 1864. POW captured at Fort Gaines, Alabama, on August 8, 1864. He was received at Ship Island, Mississippi, from New Orleans on October 25, 1864, and exchanged at Ship Island on January 4, 1865.

Hurtel, A. F., 1st Sgt/2nd Lt. Co. K see **Hurtel, Amedu**

Hurtel, Amedu, 1st Sgt../2nd Lt. Co. K

Enlisted at Mobile, Alabama, on October 13, 1861, by Captain Stewart for the war. He was discharged ?, and paid $36.16 for his service as 1st Sgt., born Mobile, Alabama, age 24, five foot eight and one half, hazel eyes, dark hair, dark complexion, a student by occupation. He appears present on a company muster roll for bounty on September 26, 1862. Company muster roll for November/ December 1862, reports him present. His name appears on a return for November 1862, "absent with leave Mobile Nov. 27, 1862." He drew clothing on July 10, 1863. Company muster roll for July/August 1863, reports him absent with leave for two days." Promoted from 1st Sergeant to Jr. 2nd Lieut. July 24, 1863." Elected 2nd Lt. on July 25, 1863. Company muster rolls for September/October 1863 and September/October 1864, report him present. Note in his file to see personal papers of **M. C. Burke**. His Parole of Honor is in his file signed on May 10, 1865, at Meridian, Mississippi. There are a number of pay vouchers and requisitions in his file.*

Hurston, W. T., Pvt. Co. G

He drew clothing on April 16, March 3 and June 1, 1864. POW captured at Fort Gaines, Alabama, on August 8, 1864. He was received at Ship Island, Mississippi, from New Orleans on October 25, 1864, and exchanged at Ship Island on January 4, 1865.

Huton, F. S., Pvt. Co. K

His name appears on a regimental return for June 1862, on detached service as clerk Subsistence Department in Selma.

Hutto, R. M., Pvt. Co. K.
Enlisted on August 15, 1864, at Henry County, Alabama, by Captain Gordon for the war. Company muster roll for September/October 1864, reports him absent, temporarily attached to camp by Major Stone, Enrolling Officer. "Absent sick in Hosp. since Oct. 2/64." He was admitted to Ross Hospital at Mobile, Alabama, with debilities chromia hepatitis on September 12, 1864, and sent to General Hospital in Greenville.

Hutto, W. J., Pvt. _
His name appears on a roll of POW's at Camp Chase, Ohio, captured at Fort Donelson on February 16, 1862, and exchanged on August 25, 1862.

Hylton, Thomas, S., Musician Co. C
Enlisted on January 7, 1862, at Fort Gaines, Alabama, by Captain Rembert for 12 months. He was seriously wounded in the face at Shiloh while advancing on the attack of the 1st Camp at 8:30 A. M. on April 6, 1862, age 23. His name appears on a regimental return for June 1862, wounded at Shiloh and furloughed. His name appears on a report filed near Tupelo, Mississippi, on June 28, 1862, "Wounded at Shiloh, and sent home on furlough on surgeon's certificate. He appears present on a company muster roll for bounty on September 26, 1862. Company muster roll for December 31, 1862, to April 30, 1863, reports him present. Company muster roll May/June 1863, reports him present, sick in quarters. Muster roll for September/October 1863, reports him present. He drew clothing on March 31 and June 1, 1864. POW captured at Fort Gaines, Alabama, on August 8, 1864. Admitted to St. Louis USA General Hospital at New Orleans from military prison on October 5, 1864, with a[cute] diarrhoea, returned to confinement on October 13, 1864, age 20. He was received at Ship Island, Mississippi, from New Orleans on October 25, 1864, and exchanged at Ship Island on January 4, 1865.

*[It is reported by descendants that **Thomas S. Hylon** from the 21st Alabama Infantry (Witherspoon Guards) is buried in Boligee, Alabama, his gravestone lists him as "Drummer Boy of Shiloh." He enlisted as a drummer. He was wounded on his 18th Birthday while attacking the first union camp in at Peter Spain's field (Prentis's camp. He was shot through the mouth and lost three teeth and a piece of his jaw. The 1860 census list him as a clerk in the Planter's Hotel in Boligee, AL]*

I

Ingersoll, A. J., Lt. Colonel, F&S
Entered state service July 1861. Elected Lt. Colonel on July 22, 1861, appointed on October 3, 1861, resigned on May 27, 1862. He was succeeded by S. W. Cayce. His name appears as present on a return for troops stationed at Fort Morgan for November 1, 1861. He was appointed Provost Marshal of Mobile, Alabama, on May 26, 1862, S. O. 121.

Ingraham, T. C. R., Pvt. Co. I
POW captured at Fort Gaines, Alabama, on August 8, 1864. He was received at Ship Island, Mississippi, from New Orleans on October 25, 1864, and exchanged at Ship

Island on January 4, 1865. His name appears on a roll of POW's who applied to take the Oath of Allegiance to the US.

Ingrum, T. D., Sgt. Co. G

His name appears on a register of General Hospital at Howard's Grove at Richmond, Virginia, on December 29, 1863.

Irner, Mathew, Pvt. Co. B/D

Enlisted on August 26, 1862, at Fort Morgan, Alabama, by Captain Johnson for the war. He appears present on a company muster roll for bounty on September 26, 1862. Company muster roll for March/April 1863, reports him present. Muster roll for May/June 1863, reports him present under arrest. A company B muster roll for September/October 1863, reports him present and due pay for clothing not drawn in kind. Company D muster roll for September/October 1864, reports him absent sent to General Hospital at Mobile on October 27, 1864, "assigned to Company D by order." Muster roll of Captain Sossaman's Detachment of the 21st for September/October 1864, reports him absent detached at Battery Huger by order of Colonel Fuller "lost canteen and haversack at $5.00." POW captured at Spanish Fort, Alabama, on April 8, 1865. He was received at Ship Island, Mississippi, on April 10, 1865, and transferred to Vicksburg, Mississippi, for exchange on May 1, 1865.

Irvins, William, Pvt. Co. H see **Irwin, William**

Irwin, M., Pvt. Co. B/D see **Irner, Mathew**

Irwin, William, Pvt. Co. H

He drew clothing March 31 and May 5, 1864, and signed by his mark. POW captured at Fort Gaines, Alabama, on August 8, 1864. He was received at Ship Island, Mississippi, from New Orleans on October 25, 1864, and exchanged at Ship Island on January 4, 1865.

J

Jackson, B. A., Pvt. Co. K

He drew clothing July 10, 1863. He was admitted to Post Hospital at Fort Morgan, Alabama, on December 9, 1863, with int. fev. and returned to duty January 1, 1864. He was again admitted on January 6, 1864, and returned to duty on January 12.

Jackson, J. F., Pvt. Co. H

He drew clothing on June 1, 1864. POW captured at Fort Gaines, Alabama, on August 8, 1864. He was received at Ship Island, Mississippi, from New Orleans on October 25, 1864, and exchanged at Ship Island on January 4, 1865. POW surrendered in May 1865, by Lt. General Richard Taylor and paroled at Demopolis, Alabama, on June 12, 1864. He was shown as a resident of Marengo County, Alabama.

Jackson, Jordan, Pvt. Co. D see **Jordon, J. T.**

Jackson, J. W., Pvt. Co. C

Enlisted at Camden, Alabama, on October 12, 1863, by Lt. Wragg for three years or the war. He drew clothing on March 31 and June 1, 1864. Company muster roll for September/October 1863, reports him present. POW captured at Fort Gaines, Alabama, on August 8, 1864. He was received at Ship Island, Mississippi, from New Orleans on October 25, 1864, and exchanged at Ship Island on January 4, 1865.

Jackson, M. H., Pvt. Co. C

He drew clothing on March 31 and June 1, 1864. Company muster roll for September/October 1863, reports him present. POW captured at Fort Gaines, Alabama, on August 8, 1864. He was received at Ship Island, Mississippi, from New Orleans on October 25, 1864, and exchanged at Ship Island on January 4, 1865. POW surrendered at Citronelle, Alabama, by Lt. General R. Taylor and paroled at Meridian, Mississippi, on May 13, 1865. A resident of Marengo County, Alabama. He was admitted to Yandell Hospital at Jackson, Mississippi, on April 10, 1865, with ascites. [*A serious accumulation of fluid in the abdominal cavity.*]

Jackson, R., Pvt. Co. C

Enlisted on February 16, 1863, at Marengo County, Alabama, by E. Morgan for three years or the war. Company muster roll for December 31, 1862, to April 30, 1863, reports him present. Muster roll for May/June, 1864, shows him absent sick since May 20, at Selma Alabama. Company muster roll for September/October 1863, reports him deserted at Mobile on October 27, 1863. He drew clothing on April 14 and June 1, 1864.

Jackson, R. A., Pvt./Corp. Co. K

Enlisted on October 13, 1861, at Mobile, Alabama, by Captain Stewart for the war. POW captured at Pittsburg Landing, Tennessee, on April 7, 1862. He was received at Camp Douglas, Illinois, on April 14, 1862, and discharged from there on June 15, 1862. He was received at Gratiot Street Military Prison at St. Louis, Missouri, in June 1862, and discharged to Alton, Illinois, on July 19, 1862. He was admitted to Hickory Street USA General Hospital at St. Louis on April 29, 1862, with acute diarrhoea and paroled for one week at Mrs. R. W. Seris' from June 20, returned to prison on July 5, 1862. His name appears on a roll of POW's who joined, escaped, discharged and died at Alton, Illinois, in July 1862. He appears absent on a company muster roll on September 24, 1862, for bounty, "Missing Battle of Shiloh on April 7, 1862." He appears present on muster rolls for July/August and September/October, 1863. He drew clothing on December 19, 1863, and June 10, 1864. He was admitted to Post Hospital at Fort Morgan, Alabama, on April 3, 1864, with ulcer and returned to duty on May 11. Muster roll for September/October 1864, reports him absent "sick in hospital since October 28, 1864, by order of Asst. Surgeon Armstrong." *There is some confusion in his file.*

Jackson, Robert, Pvt. Co. D

Enlisted on October 13, 1861, at Mobile, Alabama, by Captain Butt for one year. He was discharged due to age at Fort Morgan on October 1, 1862. Age 45, five foot seven inches, fair complexion, blue eyes, light hair, by occupation a gardener. He was paid $15.76 for his service.

Jackson, S. [Shields], Pvt. Co. C/H

Enlisted on February 16, 1863, at Monroe County, Alabama, by E. Moran for three years or the war. Company muster rolls for December 31, 1862, to April 30, 1863, May/June and September/October 1863, report him present. He was admitted to Ross Hospital at Mobile, Alabama, on February 17, 1864, with pneumonia and returned to duty on March 7. He drew clothing on March 31 and June 1, 1864. POW captured at Fort Gaines, Alabama, on August 8, 1864. He was received at Ship Island, Mississippi, from New Orleans on October 25, 1864, and exchanged at Ship Island on January 4, 1865. POW surrendered on May 4, 1865, at Citronelle, Alabama, by Lt. General R. Taylor and paroled at Meridian, Mississippi, on May 13, 1865. A resident of Marengo County, Alabama.

Jackson, Thomas, Pvt. Co. K

Enlisted by Captain Stewart at Fort Gaines, Alabama, on February 20. POW captured at Pittsburg Landing, Tennessee, on April 7, 1862. He was sent to Gratiot Street Prison at St. Louis, Missouri, arriving in June 1862. He was admitted to Hickory Street USA General Hospital at St. Louis on April 29. 1862, with acute diarrhoea, [furloughed] Mrs. R. W. Sires' house. Died June 13, 1862, [at Mrs. Sires?]. Claim filed by A. J. Jackson, widow, of Louisville, Winston County, Mississippi. Her affidavit and paper work is in his file.* He was born Kemper County, Mississippi, age 30, six foot two inches, fair complexion, blue eyes, light hair, a merchant by occupation.

Jackson, W. E., Pvt. Co. C

His name appears on a register of Yandell Hospital at Meridian, Mississippi, as having been admitted on April 1, 1865.

Jackson, J. S., Sgt./Pvt. Co. D

Enlisted on October 13, 1861, at Mobile, Alabama, by Captain Butts for one year. He appears present on a company muster roll on September 24, 1862, for bounty. Company muster roll for November/December 1862, reports that he was transferred to Co. C. 14th Battery Alabama Artillery on December 1, 1862, at Fort Morgan.

James, David, Pvt. Co. A

A company muster roll for December 31, 1862, to April 30, 1863, reports that he deserted on January 30, 1863, from Choctaw Bluff. Note there is additional information on this man's desertion on January 29, 1863, from Choctaw Bluff, Alabama, in the file of James. A. Poellnitz. Special Order No. 62.

James, Frank L., Pvt. Co. E

He enlisted on October 13, 1861, by Captain Chamberlain at Mobile, Alabama, for twelve months. Discharged for disability (inguinal hernia) on January 2, 1862, at Fort Gaines, Alabama. Born at Mobile, Alabama, age 20, five foot and three quarter inch, fair complexion, gray eyes, light hair and by occupation a student. He wrote several letters in

December 1863, to John C. Campbell, Assistant Secretary of War to offer his services as interpreter as he speaks and writes French and German very well. These letters and his discharge are in his file.*

Jarvis, Moses, R., Pvt. Co. A

Conscript discharged on April 28, 1862. "There is due him transportation from Corinth to Mobile, Ala." He was paid $21.26 for service March 1, to April 28, 1862. Enlisted on October 13, 1861, at Mobile by Major Junkns for one year. Born at City of New York, age 25, five foot eight inches, dark complexion, dark hair, black eyes a jeweler by occupation. He was paid $109.50 for services as clerk in the Intelligence Office at Mobile for August 1862 for three months and $8.75 from November 26, to December 31, 1863. He was paid $35.40 for commutation of rations while on duty in the Army Intelligence Office at Mobile from January 1 to February 28, 1863. He was also paid in the same capacity in September 1863. His discharge and pay vouchers are in his file.* See also papers filed with Co. C 12 Alabama Infantry case of **Jno. McGowan**.

Jemason, N., Pvt. Co. H

He drew clothing on March 3, and June 1, 1864, and signed by his mark. He was surrendered by Lt. General Richard Taylor at Citronelle, Alabama, on May 4, 1865, and paroled at Meridian, Mississippi, on May 13, 1865. Residence Wilcox County, Alabama.

Jerry, Pvt. Co. D

Captured at the hospital at Shiloh on April 7, 1862.

Jewett, John F., Captain Co. A

He entered service in April 26, 1861, was elected Captain on October 13, 1861, and was not re-elected on May 8, 1862. His successor was Captain J. M. Williams. His name appears on a return from Fort Gaines, Alabama, for November 1861, where he is shown absent on detached service since November 24, 1861. His name appears on a regimental return for December 1861, "Detached service by order #54 by Genl. Withers dated Nov. 28." His name appears on a regimental return for June 1863, "Resigned May 12, 1862." Dropped from the rolls on May 8, 1862. Rate of pay was $130 per month. . There are pay vouchers in his file.*

Jeyokovich, Giorgio, Pvt. Co. H

Enlisted on October 13, 1861, at Mobile, by Julius Hessee for one year. Born in Dalmatia (Europe) [*Bosnia-Herzegovina*], age 32, five foot four, brown complexion, dark eyes, brown hair, by occupation a laborer. Discharged at Camp Moore due to inguinal hernia on November 14, 1861. His discharge and Pay vouchers are in his file. *

John, R. N., Pvt. Co. D

His name appears on a regimental return for June 1861, "sent to interior hospital, at evacuation of Corinth [*Mississippi*]."

Johnson, Charles, Captain/Major see **Johnston, Charles B.**

MOBILE CONFEDERATES

Johnson, Edward, Pvt. Co. H

His name appears on a list of Confederate prisoners who have died in general hospitals in the Department of the Ohio. POW captured at Shiloh gunshot wound in shoulder. He died April 30, 1862, at General Hospital at Camp Dennison, Ohio.

Johnson, F. [Frank P.], Pvt. Co. K

Wounded slightly in the thigh at Shiloh while advancing at the center of the field at 3 P. M. on April 6, 1862. He appears on a report near Tupelo, Mississippi, on June 28, 1862, "wounded at Shiloh and furloughed since Apl 8th." Discharged on July 21, 1862.

Johnson, Hampton, Pvt. Co. D

Enlisted by Major Hessee at Mobile, Alabama, on October 13, 1861, for one year. Discharged at Halls Mill, Alabama, due to disability on November 13, 1861. Born in Anderson County, North Carolina, age 43, six foot, sallow complexion, blue eyes, gray hair, carpenter by occupation. Paid $36 for service. There is a receipt in his file that reads. "For value received I transfer my interest in the writers certificate to Cap C. W. Bush." Signed H. Johnson and witnessed by two. His discharge is also in his file.*

Johnson, James, W., Pvt. Co. A

POW captured at Jonesboro, Georgia, September 4, 1864, and died at Camp Douglas, Illinois, of small pox on December 21, 1864.

Johnson, John, Pvt. Co. K

Enlisted on October 13, 1861, at Mobile, Alabama, by Captain Stewart for the war. His name appears on a regimental return for June 1862, "on sick furlough since April 4." His name appears on a report near Tupelo, Mississippi, on June 28, 1862, "Absent on furlough in Mobile since April 2." He appears present on a company muster roll for bounty on September 24, 1862. Company muster roll for November/December 1862, reports him present. He was discharged by furnishing a substitute on March 26, 1863, at Fort Morgan, Alabama. Born in Mobile, Alabama, age 20, five foot six and one half inch, dark complexion, black eyes, black hair, a clerk by profession. His discharge and pay voucher are in his file.*

Johnson, M., Pvt. Co. I

His name appears on a regimental return for June 1862, " sent to interior hospital from Clark Creek."

Johnson, N., Pvt. Co. I

Enlisted on October 13, 1861, at Halls Mill, Alabama, by Major Hessee for the war. His name appears on a report near Tupelo, Mississippi, on June 28, 1862, "Sent to interior hospital from Corinth by Surgeon May 28." He appears present on a company muster roll for bounty on September 24, 1862. Company muster rolls for July/August and September/October 1863, reports him present on extra duty in Quarter Master's Department since March 63. Rolls of extra duty soldiers in July, September and November 1863, shows him on extra duty as a teamster. Drew clothing March 31, 1864, signed by his mark. POW captured at Fort Gaines, Alabama, on August 8, 1864. He was received at Ship Island, Mississippi, from New Orleans on October 25, 1864, and exchanged at Ship Island on January 4, 1865.

Johnson, R., Pvt. Co. K

POW surrendered on May 4, 1865, at Citronelle, Alabama, by Lt. General R. Taylor and paroled at Meridian, Mississippi, on May 13, 1865. A resident of Mobile, Mobile County, Alabama.

Johnson, T. H., Pvt. Co. D see **Johnson, Thomas, J.**

Johnston, Charles B., Captain Co. B/Major Field and Staff

Entered state service on April 1, 1861. Elected Captain on October 8, 1861. His name appears as present on a return from Fort Gaines, Alabama, in November 1861. A regimental return for June 1862, reports him present stationed at Tupelo, Mississippi. On September 24, 1862, he requisitioned for Co. B stationed at Fort Morgan the following; 26 jackets, 34 pants, 28 caps, 41 shirts, 74 pair drawers, and 30 pair shoes. He appears on a field return at Fort Morgan, Alabama, transferred to Choctaw Bluff, Alabama, on October 6, 1862. On January 19, 1863, he requisitioned for Co. B, stationed at Oven Bluff, Alabama, the following; 76 pair pants, 76 jackets; 76 caps; 76 blankets, 41 pair drawers. Promoted on May 1, 1863, to senior Captain successor Jno. F. O'Conner. "Major McCoy failed to pass Board Examination." Company muster roll for March/April, 1863, reports him present. May/June 1863, muster roll reports him absent on sick furlough until July 1, 1863. September/October muster roll reports him absent sick. Company muster roll for March/April 1864, reports him present, "Promoted to Major from Captain of Co. B, April 30, 1864, appointment just received since last muster." POW captured August 8, 1864, at Fort Gaines, Alabama. He was admitted to St. Louis USA General Hospital at New Orleans on August 20, 1864, with fever remittent and diarrhoea and returned to confinement on September 24, 1864, age 32. He refused to be exchanged at Ship Island, Mississippi, on January 5, 1865. He was transferred from Ship Island, to Vicksburg on April 28, 1865. He appears on a roll of rebel POW's paroled at New Orleans during May 1865. He was paroled at New Orleans, on May 10, 1865, and transportation furnished to Mobile, Alabama. He drew $130 per month as Captain and $150 per month as Major. There are a considerable number of pay vouchers and requisitions in his file.*

Johnston, N., Pvt. Co. D see **Johnson, N.**

Johnston, Thomas A., Pvt. Co. D. see **Johnston, Thomas J.**

Johnston, Thomas J., Pvt. Co. D

Enlisted January 6, 1862, at Mobile, Alabama, (Fort Gaines) by Captain Butt for 9 months and 7 days. A company muster roll for bounty on September 24, 1862, reports him present. Company muster roll for November/December 1862, reports him present and that he was promoted from the ranks to 3rd Corporal on December 1, 1862. Company muster rolls for July/August and September/October 1863, report him present. Muster roll for November/December, 1863, shows that he was reduced to ranks from Corporal on December 5, 1863. He drew clothing on June 30, 1864, and again on August 1, 1864, and signed by his mark. Muster roll for September/October 1864, reports him absent sent to General Hospital in Mobile on October 25, 1864. He was admitted to Ross Hospital in Mobile on September 3, 1864, with febris intermittens quot. and returned to duty on September 9. He was on a sick furlough from hospital examining board from November 12, 1864. Born Autauga County, Alabama, age 22, fair complexion, blue eyes, auburn hair, and six foot one inch. POW captured at Macon, Georgia, on April 20 or 21st by 1st Brigade 2nd Cavalry Division. There are signed pay vouchers in his file.*

Johnston, Thomas T., Pvt. Co. D. see **Johnston Thomas, J.**

Johnston, T. M., Pvt. Co. D see **Johnston, Thomas J.**

Jones, Albert, Sgt. Co. K
Wounded in the knee mortally at Shiloh on April 6, 1862, 4 P. M. crossing field while protecting battery.

Jones, Francis J., Pvt. Co. E
Enlisted on October 5, 1862, at Fort Morgan, Alabama, by Captain Sossaman for the war. His name appears on a descriptive list for bounty on October 6, 1862 Age 15, blue eyes, dark hair, fair complexion, five foot four inches, born in Mobile, Alabama, a clerk by profession, paid $50 bounty. His name appears on a return for November 1862, where he is show absent with leave from December 1, for 4 days at Mobile. He appears present on company muster rolls for November/December 1862, July/August 1863 and September/October 1863. He drew clothing on March 31, April 14 and June 1, 1864. POW captured at Fort Gaines, Alabama, on August 8, 1864. He appears on a register of POW's at New Orleans in hospital from September 10, 1864. He was admitted to St Louis USA General Hospital at New Orleans on August 17, 1864, with intermitten fever and acute diarrhoea and returned to confinement on September 12, 1864. He was admitted again in Ward K on October 11, 1864, with chronic diarrhoea and returned to confinement on November 2, 1864, age 17. He was received at Ship Island, Mississippi, on October 29, 1864, and exchanged at Ship Island on January 4, 1865.

Jones, Frank J., Pvt. Co. E see **Jones, Francis J.**

Jones, Henry M., Pvt. Co. D
Enlisted on October 13, 1861, at Mobile, Alabama, by Captain Butt for one year. He appears present on a company muster roll for bounty, on September 24, 1862, "refused to take bounty" Company muster rolls for November/December 1862, July/August 1863, September/October 1863, November/December 1863, and September/October 1864, all report him present. He drew clothing on April 14, 1864, June 30, 1864, and in August 1864. POW captured at Blakeley, Alabama, on April 9, 1865. He was received at Ship Island, Mississippi, on April 15, 1865, and transferred on parole to Vicksburg for exchange.

Jones, J., Pvt. Co. G

He drew clothing on May 3 and June 1, 1864. POW captured at Fort Gaines, Alabama, on August 8, 1864. He was received at Ship Island, Mississippi, from New Orleans on October 25, 1864, and exchanged at Ship Island on January 4, 1865.

Jones, James, Pvt. Co. C.

He was killed in action at the Battle of Shiloh on April 6, 1862, shot through the head at 7 A. M. attacking the 1st Battery and left on the field.. Claim for deceased soldier filed by R. M. Jones.

Jones, J. B., Pvt. Co. G see **Jones, T. B.**

Jones, J. F., Pvt. Co. E see **Jones Francis J.**

Jones, J. P., Pvt./Sgt. Co. D

Enlisted on October 13, 1861, at Mobile, Alabama, by Captain Butt for one year. He appears present on a company muster roll for bounty on September 24, 1862. Company muster rolls for November/December 1862, reports him present and promoted from the ranks to 1st Sgt. on December 1, 1862. POW captured at Shiloh Hospital on April 7, 1862, reported as sick. His name appears on a roll of POW's at Camp Douglas, Illinois, on August 1, 1862, captured at Pittsburg Landing. There is a hand written letter filed at Dalton, Georgia by Lt. Col J. B. Bibb of 23rd Alabama, on April 1, 1864. The letter is a request that Lt. **Jones** be appointed Chaplain of 23rd Regiment Alabama Infantry. Lt. **J. P. Jones**, of the 32nd or 38th Alabama Infantry who had served in the 21st Alabama until about 20th of January 1863. It states that he was elected 3rd Lt. in Co. K of the 23rd Alabama, on the above date. He is a resident of Prattville, Alabama. The letter is indorsed clearly approved by **Bush Jones**, Col Commanding, **Alex P. Stewart** Major General and **J. B. Hood**, Gen. Commanding.*

Jones, P. R. I.

His name appears on a hospital report at Hickory Street USA General Hospital at St. Louis, Missouri, as having been admitted on April 22, 1862, with vulnus sclopeticum (gun shot wound). He was returned to military prison on May 17, 1862.

Jones, S. A., Pvt. Co. D

His name appears on a regimental report for June 1862, "May 23, Corinth, Miss., Discharged for disability."

Jones, T. B., Pvt. Co. G

Paid for commutation of rations on December 19, 1863. Drew clothing on March 31, May 3 and June 1, 1864. POW captured at Fort Gaines, Alabama, on August 8, 1864. He was admitted to St. Louis USA General Hospital at New Orleans on September 1864, with gastric fever, age 38. One hospital card shows chronic diarrhoea. He died in hospital on October 15, 1864, buried in Monument Cemetery in grave No. 394. Contact Mark C. Jones, Plantersville, Alabama PO. A resident of Autauga, County. His death certificate is in his file.*

MOBILE CONFEDERATES

Jones, William, Pvt. Co. C
He drew clothing on June 31, 1864, and signed by his mark. Paroled by 16th US Army Corp. Provost Marshal at Montgomery, Alabama, in 1865. He was described as five foot 10 inches, dark hair, blue eyes, and dark complexion. His parole is in his file.*

Jordan, Jackson, Pvt. Co. D see **Jordan, J. T.**

Jordan, Josiah, Pvt. Co. G. (see also 1st Alabama Conscripts)
Drew clothing on March 3, 1864, signed by his mark. POW captured at Fort Gaines, Alabama, on August 8, 1864. He was received at Ship Island, Mississippi, from New Orleans on October 25, 1864, and exchanged at Ship Island on January 4, 1865.

Jordan, J. T., Pvt. Co. D
He appears on a register of payments to discharged soldiers, discharged on June 20, 1863. Enlisted on December 7, 1863, at Orrville, Alabama, (Or December 11, 1863, at Selma, Alabama, for the war.) by enrolling officer for the war. He appears present on a company muster roll for November/December 1863. He was admitted to Post Hospital at Fort Morgan, Alabama, on June 14, 1863, with consumption, and discharged on June 20. Jack Jordan was admitted to Post Hospital at Fort Morgan on December 12, 1863, with debility and returned to duty on December 13, 1864. Jackson Jordan was admitted to Post Hospital at Fort Morgan, on January 21, 1864, with diarrhoea and sent to General Hospital on January 26, 1864. Jack Jordan was admitted to Ross Hospital at Mobile, Alabama, on January 26, 1864, with int. fever quotd. He was sent to General Hospital in Montgomery, Alabama, on February 13, 1864. Discharged due to consumption at Fort Morgan on June 20, 1863. Born Wahlough? District, South Carolina, age 25, five foot eleven inches, fair complexion, blue eyes, light hair, by occupation a farmer. His discharge and pay vouchers are in his file.*

Jordon, Jackson, Pvt. Co. D see **Jordan, J. T.**

Jordon, J. T., Pvt. Co. D see **Jordan, J. T.**

Julian, A., Pvt. Co. K see **Jullian, Arthur**

Julian, Arthur, Pvt. Co. K see **Jullun, Arthur**

Julien, Arthur, Pvt. Co. K see **Jullien, Arthur**
Jullien, Arthur, Pvt. Co. K
Enlisted on October 13, 1861, at Mobile, Alabama, by Captain Stewart for the war. A regimental return for June 1861, reports him on detached service: clerk in hospital at Mobile. Returns for November and December 1862, shows him on detached medical service at Mobile. He appears absent on a company muster roll for bounty on September 24, 1862, "Detached Hospl. Nurse Dec. 28, 1861, by Genl Withers." Company muster rolls for November/December 1862, July/August 1863, September/October 1863 and September/October 1864, all show him absent and detached as hospital

nurse. He appears on hospital muster rolls at General Hospital Moore, General Hospital Nott and General Hospital Ross all in Mobile. There is a signed pay voucher in his file.*

K

Kanard, _, Pvt. Co. B

His name appears on a register at Post Hospital at Fort Morgan, Alabama, as having been admitted on January 18, 1864, with pneumonia. Returned to duty on January 29, 1864.

Kane, William, Pvt. Co. B

Enlisted on October 13, 1861, at Mobile, Alabama, by Major Hessee to serve one year and discharged on December 20, 1861. He was born in Ireland, age 47, five foot five inches, dark complexion, gray eyes, black hair, and by profession a tailor. He signed by his mark. His discharge and a pay voucher in the amount of $49.93 are in his file.*

Kates, Wiley, Pvt.

Enlisted on August 10, 1864, at Mobile, Alabama, by Major Stone for the war. He appears on a muster roll for Sosserman's Detachment for September/October 1864, "absent, det. Battery Huger order Col. Fuller."

Keane, Edward, Drummer, Co. A

Enlisted on October 5, 1862, at Mobile, Alabama, by Captain DeVaux for the war. He appears present on muster rolls for December 31, 1862, to April 30, 1863 and May/June 1863. He appears on a descriptive payroll for pay on May 21, 1863, age 18, gray eyes, dark hair, fair complexion, five foot four inches, born Mobile, Alabama, occupation a clerk, drew $50 bounty. Company muster roll for September/October 1863, reports him absent sent to Spring Hill Hospital on October 25, 1863. Drew clothing March 31, 1864, and was at Camp Anderson on June 14, 1864. POW captured at Fort Morgan, Alabama, on August 23, 1864, sent to New York on September 27, 1864. He was received at Elmira, New York, from New Orleans on October 8, 1864. He died on January 5, 1865, of chronic diarrhoea. Descriptive list for he and four other 21st Ala. soldiers is in his file.*

Kearns, David, Pvt. Co. B

Wounded seriously in his left thigh advancing at Shiloh, April 6, 1862, at 8 A. M. while attacking 1st Camp. His name appears on a regimental register for June 1862, "May 20, Corinth, died of wounds in action." A claim for a deceased solder was filed by J. R. Eastburn, Att. paid $104.70.

Keating, Michael, Pvt. Co. A

Appears on a register of payments on descriptive list June 21, 1863. $50 bounty.

Keene, E., Drummer, see **Keane, Edward**

MOBILE CONFEDERATES

Keenan, B. M., Pvt. Co. D

His name appears on a roll of POW's that were surrendered at Citronelle, Alabama, by Lt. General Richard Taylor on May 4, 1865 and paroled at Meridian, Mississippi, on May 13, 1865. Residence shown as Walker County, Georgia.

Keeth, John, N., Pvt. Co. A

Enlisted on October 13, 1861, at Mobile, Alabama, by Major Hessee for the war. He appears present on a company muster roll for December 31, 1862, to April 30, 1863. Company muster roll for May/June 1863, reports him present and detailed on June 10, to Commissary Department at Fort Stonewall by order of Colonel Anderson. Muster roll for September/October 1863, reports him present. He drew clothing on March 31 and in June 1864. POW captured at Fort Morgan, Alabama, on August 23, 1864. He was received from New Orleans as POW at Elmira, New York, on October 8, 1864. He signed an Oath of Allegiance to the USA at Elmira and was released on June 21, 1864. Residence St. Stephens, Alabama, complexion dark, hair dark, eyes hazel, five foot 10 inches. There are records of **Kieth, John W.**, Pvt. Co. A on November 10, 1862, at Atkins Landing. See personal papers of **Pvt. T. A. Foster**, Co. A. filed with this man's records. **Pvt. John W. Kieth** was wounded severely in the forehead and knee at the Center Field on April 6, 1862, 2:30 P. M. at Shiloh. He was captured at hospital on April 7, 1862. He appears on a roll of POW's at Camp Douglas, Illinois, August 1, 1862. He then appears on a roll of POW's at Camp Douglas, sent September 8, 1862, to Vicksburg, Mississippi, aboard the steamer *John H. Done* to be exchanged. He was exchanged on November 10, 1862, at Atkins Landing. See personal papers of **Pvt. T. A. Foster**, Co. A.

Keeth, William, Pvt. Co. A

His name appears on a muster roll for bounty on September 24, 1862, where he is reported present and refused to take bounty.

Keith, J. W., Pvt. Co. A see **Keeth, John N.**

Keller, John, Pvt. Co. A

Enlisted on October 13, 1861, at Mobile, Alabama, by Major Hessee. His name appears on a regimental register for June 1862, on detached service as a harness maker. He appears on a company muster roll for bounty on September 24, 1862, where he is shown absent, detached to Ordinance Department by order of General Withers. He is shown in a similar fashion on a muster roll for December 31, 1862, to April 30, 1863, May/June 1863 and September/October 1863. There are a number of signed pay vouchers in his file.*

Kelley, C. D., Pvt. Co. C see **Kelly, E. D.**

Kelly, E. D., Pvt. Co. C

POW captured at Blakeley, Alabama, on April 9, 1865. His name appears on a roll of POW's transferred on parole from Ship Island, Mississippi, to Vicksburg on May 1, 1865.

Kelly, G. P., Pvt. Co. C

Enlisted on October 13, 1861, at Mobile, Alabama, by Captain Lambert for three years or the war. POW captured at Island No. 10, on April 8, 1861, and sent to Camp Douglas, Illinois. He appears on a roll of POW's at Camp Douglas on August 1, 1862, and was sent to Vicksburg, Mississippi, on September 8, 1862, aboard the steamer *John H. Done*. He appears present on a company muster roll for bounty on September 24, 1862. May/June 1863, muster roll reports him absent sick in hospital in Mobile since May 5, 1863. September/October 1863, muster roll reports him present and lost one haversack. Drew clothing March 31 and June 1, 1864. POW captured at Fort Gaines, Alabama, on August 8, 1864. He was received at Ship Island, Mississippi, on October 25, 1864, from New Orleans and exchanged on January 4, 1865. POW captured at Battle of Blakeley on April 9, 1865, and received at Ship Island on April 15, 1865. He was transferred to Vicksburg, Mississippi, on May 1, 1865. *Note this man was POW on three separate occasions.*

Kelly, Peter, Pvt. Co. C

Enlisted on October 12, 1863, at (Fort Gaines) Point Clear, Alabama, by Captain Smith for three years or the war. He appears present on a company muster roll for September/October 1863. A March/April 1864, hospital muster roll for Hospital at Fort Morgan, Alabama, reports him attached to hospital as a nurse on November 4, 1863, "Returned to his Co. Dec. 24, 1863...." Drew clothing on March 31 and June 1, 1864.

Kelly, P. P., Pvt. Co. C see **Kelly, G. P.**

Kelly, William M., Pvt. Co. G

He drew clothing March 3, March 31, and June 1, 1864. A claim was filed for deceased soldier by Sarah J. Kelley, widow on August 13, 1864.

Kemp, W. (Uriah), Pvt. Co. F

Enlisted at Baldwin County, Alabama, on October 13, 1861, by Captain McCoy for year. His name appears on a report near Tupelo, Mississippi, on June 28, 1861, wounded at Shiloh furloughed on surgeon's certificate April 8, 1861, and sent from Corinth, Mississippi, on May 28, 1861. A regimental return shows he was sent to a Mobile hospital on May 28. Discharged due to being over age on October 13, 1862, at Choctaw Bluff, Alabama. Born Savannah, Georgia, age 46, five foot eight and one half, dark complexion, gray eyes, gray hair, by profession a farmer.

Kennedy, Daniel, Corp./Pvt. Co. B

Enlisted on October 13, 1861, at Mobile, Alabama, by Major Hessee for 12 months. He appears present on a company muster roll for bounty September 23, 1864. Company muster rolls for March/April 1863, show him as 2nd Corporal and present. Company muster roll for May/June 1863, show him absent with leave for four days from June 27, 1863. Muster roll for September/October 1863, report him absent, sent to general hospital on October 29, 1863, by order of Dr. Payne. Drew clothing on June 1, 1864, and signed by his mark. POW captured at Fort Gaines, Alabama, on August 8, 1864. He was received at Ship Island, Mississippi, on October 25, 1864, from New

Orleans and was exchanged at Ship Island on January 4, 1865. Reference to see medical card filed with **Edward Kennedy**, Co. B 21st Ala. Infantry.

Kennedy, Edward, Pvt. Co. B
Enlisted on November 1, 1862, at Oven Bluff, Alabama, by Captain Johnston for the war. Company muster roll for March/April 1863, reports him present, to forfeit one months pay by order of Regiment CM [*Court Marshal*]. May/June 1863, muster roll shows him present sick in quarters. September/October 1863, roll shows him present, lost one knapsack. He drew clothing on March 31, 1864, signed by his mark. POW captured at Fort Gaines, Alabama, on August 8, 1864. He was received at Ship Island, Mississippi, on October 25, 1864, from New Orleans and was exchanged at Ship Island on January 4, 1865. POW captured at Spanish Fort, Alabama, on April 8, 1865. He was transferred on parole from Ship Island to Vicksburg, Mississippi, on May 1, 1865. Medical Card for the name **Kennedy**, Pvt. Co. B reports that he was admitted on January 18, 1864, to Post Hospital at Fort Morgan, Alabama, with int. fev. and returned to duty on January 19, 1864.

Kennedy, Edward, Pvt. Co. F
Enlisted on August 27, 1862, at Talladega, Alabama, by J. A. Cary for the war. He appears present on company muster rolls for March 1, to June 30, 1863, and September/October 1863. He was admitted to Post Hospital at Fort Morgan, Alabama, on October 30, 1863, with int. fever and returned to duty on November 4. He was admitted to Post Hospital at Fort Morgan on November 19, 1863, with debility and returned to duty on November 25. He was again admitted to Post Hospital at Fort Morgan with int. fev. on January 19, 1864, and sent to general hospital on January 26. He was admitted to Ross Hospital at Mobile with anasarca on January 26, 1864, then sent to General Hospital in Montgomery on February 17, 1864. He was admitted to Ross Hospital at Mobile, Alabama, with intermit. fever on March 12, 1864, furloughed for 60 days on March 31. POW captured at Fort Gaines Alabama, on August 8, 1864. He was received at Ship Island, Mississippi, on October 25, 1864, from New Orleans and made application to take the Oath of Allegiance to the USA. He died of dysentery at Ship Island on December 13, 1864 and was buried in grave No. 85.

Kennedy, E. W., Pvt. Co. F see **Kennedy Edward**

Kennedy, John, Pvt. Co. A
POW captured at Fort Morgan, Alabama, on August 13, 1864, sent to New York on September 27, 1864. He was received at Elmira, New York, on October 8, 1864, from New Orleans and released on June 30, 1865. He signed the Oath of Allegiance to the USA at Elmira on June 30, 1865. Residence, Louisville, Kentucky, dark complexion, dark hair, hazel eyes, five foot seven. Signed by his mark.

Kennedy, S. R., Pvt. Co. F
Enlisted at Talladega, Alabama, on August 27, 1862, by J. A. Cary for the war. He appears present on company muster rolls for March 1, to June 30, 1863, and September/October 1863. Drew clothing on June 1, 1864. POW captured at Fort Gaines,

Alabama, on August 8, 1864. He was received at Ship Island, Mississippi, on October 25, 1864, from New Orleans. He applied to take the Oath of Allegiance to the USA at Ship Island. He died of dysentery at Ship Island on December 20, 1865, and was buried in grave No. 104.

Keyser, G., Pvt. Co. C

POW captured at Blakeley, Alabama, on April 9, 1865. He was received at Ship Island, Mississippi, on April 15, 1865, and transferred on parole for exchange to Vicksburg, Mississippi, on May 1, 1865.

Kirnman, F., Pvt. Co. K

Enlisted on September 18, 1862, at Fort Morgan, Alabama, by Captain Dorgan for the war. He appears present on a company muster roll for bounty on September 24, 1862. Company muster rolls for November/December 1862, July/August 1863, September/October 1863 and September/October 1864, all report him present. He drew clothing on July 10, 1863, June 10, 1864, and December 19, 1864. He was surrendered by Lt. General Richard Taylor at Citronelle, Alabama, on May 4, 1865, and paroled at Meridian, Mississippi, on May 13, 1865, and was shown as a resident of Mobile, Mobile, County, Alabama.

Killebrew, J. C., Pvt. Co. D. see **Killebrew, John**

Killebrew, John, Pvt. Co. D

Enlisted at Fort Gaines, Alabama, on December 8, 1861, by Captain Butt for the war. Company muster rolls for November/December 1862, July/August 1863, September/October 1863, November/December 1863 and September/October 1864, all report him present. He drew clothing on August 1, 1864, and signed by his mark.

King, George, D., Pvt. Co. G

He drew clothing on March 2, March 31 and June 1, 1864. POW captured at Fort Gaines Alabama, on August 8, 1864. He was received at Ship Island, Mississippi, on October 25, 1864, from New Orleans and exchanged at Ship Island on January 5, 1864. He was surrendered by Lt. General Richard Taylor at Citronelle, Alabama, on May 4, 1865, and paroled at Meridian, Mississippi, on May 13, 1865. A resident of Abbeville, Henry County, Alabama.

King, J. A., Pvt. Co. K

Enlisted on May 2, 1864, at Mobile, Alabama, by Captain Beebe for the war. Company muster roll for September/October 1864, reports that he was transferred to Conscript Camp at Notasulga, Alabama, by order of Major? Enrolling Officer on October 18, 1864.

King, J. W., Pvt. Co. C

He was surrendered by Lt. General Richard Taylor in May 1865, and paroled at Demopolis, Alabama, on June 22, 1865. A resident of Clarke County, Mississippi.

King, John A., Pvt. Co. A

Wounded in the mouth severely at 8:30 A. M. on April 6, 1862, at Shiloh First Camp. He appears on a regimental return for June 1862, wounded at Shiloh and on furlough since 9th April. A report dated June 28, 1862, near Tupelo, Mississippi, reports him wounded at Shiloh and at Mobile, Alabama, hospital. There are two signed pay vouchers in his file.*

King, S. S., Pvt. Co. C

Enlisted on March 13, 1862, at Fort Pillow by Captain Rembert for 12 months. Wounded in the left side slightly while advancing crossing Old Field at 4 P. M. on April 6, 1862. He was discharged on July 18, 1862, born in Madison, County, Alabama, age 38, six foot, fair complexion, blue eyes, dark hair, and a planter by occupation. His signed discharge is in his file.*

King, W. D., Pvt. Co. E

His name appears on a list dated July 1864, of clerks and etc. employed in the various offices and bureaus at the Military Post at Mobile with certificate of light duty. POW of Co. F. 2nd regiment Mississippi Cavalry Reserves commanded by Colonel E. A. Chase surrendered at Meridian Mississippi, by Lt. General Richard Taylor on May 4, 1865, and paroled at Mobile, Alabama, on May 22, 1865. A residence Wilcox County, Alabama.

King, W. D., Pvt. Co. K

POW of Co. K, 21st Alabama Regiment, Holtzclaw's Brigade commanded by 1st Lt. William I. Brainard surrendered at Citronelle, Alabama, by Lt. General Richard Taylor on May 4, 1865, and paroled at Meridian, Mississippi, on May 13, 1865. A residence of Kings Landing, Monroe County, Alabama.

Kinnard, W. H., Pvt. Co. C

Enlisted on October 24, 1862, at Choctaw Bluff, by Captain Smith for three years or the war. Company muster rolls for December 31, 1862, to April 30, 1863, and May/June 1863, report him present. Company muster roll for September/October 1863, reports him present, lost one canteen at $2. He was admitted to Post Hospital at Fort Morgan, Alabama, on December 7, 1863, with icterus and returned to duty on December 15. He drew clothing March 31 and June 1, 1864. POW surrendered by Lt. General Richard Taylor in May 1865, and paroled at Demopolis, Alabama, on June 8, 1865. A resident of Dallas County, Alabama.

Kirby, Robert F., Pvt. Co. G

Enlisted at Greenwood, Montgomery County, Alabama, on December 14, 1862, for three years. He was discharged due to disability on July 27, 1863, at Montgomery, Alabama. Born in Stokes County, North Carolina, age 41, five foot nine, dark eyes, dark complexion, dark hair, by occupation a harness maker. His discharge and pay voucher is in his file.*

21ST ALABAMA INFANTRY VOLUNTEERS

Kirk, William, Pvt. Co. E

Enlisted on August 19, 1862, at Mobile, Alabama, by Captain DeVaux for the war. He appears present on a company muster roll for bounty on September 24, 1862. Company muster rolls for November/December 1862, July/August 1863 and September/October 1863, all show him present. On the latter roll he is shown as having enlisted On August 17, 1862, at Fort Morgan, Alabama, by Captain Sossaman. Muster rolls for May/June 1864, July/August 1864 and September/October 1864 for detailed men in the CS Ordnance Department report him present and detailed from Co. E 21st Alabama, Special Order 181 on June 29, 1864. He drew clothing on September 24, 1864. POW surrendered by Lt. General Richard Taylor at Citronelle, Alabama, on May 4, 1865, and paroled Meridian, Mississippi, May 13, 1865. Residence shown as Mobile, Alabama.

Kizer, William D., Pvt. Co. A

POW captured at Fort Donelson on February 16, 1862. His name appears on a roll of POW's at Camp Morton, Indiana, in June 1862. He was sent from Camp Morton to Vicksburg, Mississippi, to be exchanged on August 24, 1862. Exchanged at Atkins Landing on November 10, 1862.

Klie, George A., Sgt./Pvt. Co. C

Enlisted on October 13, 1861, at Mobile, Alabama, by Captain Rembert for the war. He appears present on a company muster roll for bounty on September 24, 1862. Company muster roll for December 31, 1862, to April 30, 1863, reports him absent detailed in Engineering Department at Choctaw Bluff, Alabama, from March 25, 1863, by order of General Buckner. Pay stopped from March 25, 1863 [*in the Company*]. May/June muster roll reported him present in the Engineering Department at Choctaw Bluff on June 15, 1863, appointed 4th Sgt. on August 1, 1862, reduced to ranks on January 1, 1863. A reference card indicated he was transferred from the 21st to the CS Navy on August 22, 1863. POW captured at Blakeley, Alabama, on April 9, 1865, received at Ship, Island, Mississippi, on April 13, 1865. Transferred on parole to Vicksburg, Mississippi, on May 1, 1865. There is a signed pay voucher in his file dated September 29, 1862, indicating he was detached sick at that time.* *May be two men's files here.*

Kline, G. A., Sgt./Pvt. Co. C see **Klie, George A.**

Knight, A., Pvt. Co. C

Enlisted on October 30, 1862, at Choctaw Bluff, Alabama, by Captain Smith for three years or the war. POW captured at Fort Donelson in February and sent to Camp Butler at Springfield, Illinois. He was transferred from Camp Butler to Vicksburg, Mississippi, aboard the steamer *John H. Done* on September 23, 1862. He appears present on a company muster roll for December 31, 1862, to April 30, 1863. Died of disease in hospital at Choctaw Bluff on May 31, 1863. A claim for deceased soldier, Andrew Knight, was made by J. B. Knight his Father. [*There is date conflict in this file.*]

MOBILE CONFEDERATES

Knight, J. J., Pvt. Co. I

He drew clothing on March 3 and March 31, 1864. POW captured at Fort Gaines, Alabama, on August 8, 1864. He arrived at Ship Island, Mississippi, on October 25, 1864, from New Orleans and was exchanged at Ship Island on January 4, 1865.

Knox, D. W., Pvt. Co. F

Enlisted on October 31, 1861, at Baldwin County, Alabama, by Captain McCoy for one year. He appears on a regimental return for June 1862, sent to interior hospital on May 28, 1862. His name appears on a consolidated report of deserters of the Reserve Corps Army of the Mississippi, Brigadier Withers Commanding near Tupelo, Mississippi, June 28, 1862, "sent from Tupelo, June 14." He appears present on a company muster roll for bounty on September 24, 1862. Company muster roll for March 1, to June 30, 1863, reports him present. Company muster roll for September/October 1863, reports him absent detached on duty at Choctaw Bluff by Colonel Anderson. He drew clothing on March 31, and June 1, 1864. POW captured at Fort Gaines, Alabama, on August 8, 1864. He was received at Ship Island, Mississippi, from New Orleans on October 25, 1864, and exchanged at Ship Island on January 5, 1965. He was admitted to Ross Hospital at Mobile, Alabama, on April 3, 1865, with scabies and sent to General Hospital in Meridian, Mississippi, on April 9, 1865. His name appears on a list of POW's at Lee Hospital at Lauderdale, Mississippi, commanded by Surgeon Henry Yandell that were surrendered by Lt. General Richard Taylor at Citronelle, Alabama, on May 4, 1865, and paroled at Meridian, Mississippi, on May 13. Residence shown as Mobile, Mobile County, Alabama.

Knox, Joseph, Sgt. Co. B

Enlisted on October 13, 1861, at Mobile, Alabama, by Major Hessee for twelve months. His name appears on a company muster roll for bounty on September 24, 1862. He was not entitled to bounty as he was over age. Discharged at Oven Bluff, Alabama, on October 13, 1862. Born in Ireland, age 39, five foot six and one half inches, dark complexion, black eyes, brown hair, a boat maker [?]. His discharge is in his file.

Koln, John, Pvt. Co. K

Enlisted on April 22, 1863, at Fort Morgan, Alabama, by Captain Dorgan for the war. Company muster rolls for July/August and September/October 1863, report him present. He drew clothing July 10, December 19, 1863, and again on June 19, 1864. He signed in December 63, by his mark. He transferred to CS Navy in 1864.

Kucher, J., Pvt. Co. H

His name appears on a regimental return for June 1862, "sent to rear 28th May." His name appears on a report near Tupelo, Mississippi, on June 38, 1862, "sent to the interior from Corinth, Mississippi, at the time of evacuation."

L

Ladd, J. N., Pvt. Co. ?

Enlisted on August 20, 1864, at Mobile, Alabama, by Major Stone for the war. He appears on a company muster roll for September/October 1864, as absent sent to hospital by order of Dr. Armstrong.

Ladell, Pvt. Co. C see **Liddell R. F.**

Ladonna, D., Pvt. Co. G

His name appears on a regimental return for June 1862, "sent to hospital May 28."

Lagala, Guisice, Sgt. Co. G

Lagala, Joseph, Sgt. Co. G filed with Lagala, Guisice

Enlisted on October 13, 1861, at Mobile, Alabama, by Major Hessee for twelve months. Discharged at Camp near Corinth, Mississippi, on surgeon's certificate of disability on April 13, 1862, with transportation to Mobile, Alabama. Born in Italy, age 31, five foot eight inches, dark complexion, brown eyes, dark hair, and a fruit merchant by occupation. His discharge and pay voucher is in his file.*

Lagorne, J. G., Pvt. Co. F see **Lagrone, J. H.**

Lagrone, J. H., Pvt. Co. F

Enlisted on September 12, 1862, at Mobile, Alabama, by W. B. Livingston, for the war. He appears present on a company muster roll for March 1, to June 30, 1863. Company muster roll for September/October 1863, reports him absent sick in hospital at Mobile, Alabama, since July 16, 1863. Drew clothing on June 1, 1864. POW captured at Fort Gaines, Alabama, on August 8, 1864. He was received at Ship, Island, Mississippi, on October 25, 1864, from New Orleans and exchanged at Ship Island on January 4, 1865. He died at Mobile on January 9, 1865. Certificate No. 101. [*Not in his file*]

Lagroon, J. H., Pvt. Co. F see **Lagrone, J. H.**

Lagrove, J. G., Pvt. Co. F see **Lagrone, J. H.**

Lagrow, J. H., Pvt. Co. F see, **Lagrone, J. H.**

Laine, [Lane] G., Pvt. Co. I

He appears on a report near Tupelo, Mississippi, on June 28, 1862, "sent to interior hospitals from Corinth by Surgeon May 28." His name appears a register of soldiers in November 1862, detailed in Quartermaster's Department.

Laine, Alexander, Pvt. Co. I

Enlisted on February 19, 1863, at Fort Morgan, Alabama, by Lt. McNeil for the war. He was admitted to Post Hospital at Fort Morgan on March 18, 1863, with int. febris and returned to duty on April 1, 1863. He was again admitted to Post Hospital at Fort Morgan on August 31, 1863, with diarrhoea and returned to duty on August 25, 1863.

Company muster rolls for July/August and September/October 1863, report him present. Drew clothing on March 31, 1864, signed by his mark. POW captured at Fort Gaines, Alabama, on August 8, 1864. He was received at Ship, Island, Mississippi, on October 25, 1864, from New Orleans and exchanged at Ship Island on January 4, 1865. He was surrendered by Lt. General Richard Taylor at Citronelle, Alabama, on May 4, 1865, and paroled at Meridian, Mississippi. Residence shown as Mobile, County, Alabama.

Laine, William, Pvt. Co. I see **Lane William**

Lake, John, T., Pvt. Co. G
Drew clothing on March 2, 1863. Discharged on August 31, 1864. Age 22, born in Monroe, County, Alabama, five foot seven inches, dark complexion, hazel eyes, dark hair, a farmer by occupation. Transferred to CS Navy.

Lamar, J. S., Pvt. Co. I
His name appears on a roll of POW's (stragglers) paroled at Selma, Alabama, during June 1864. Residence shown as Bibb County, Alabama,

Lamas, J., Pvt. Co. I see **Lamas, S. N.**

Lamas, S. H., Pvt. Co. I see **Lamas, S. N.**

Lamas, S. N., Pvt. Co. I
Enlisted on October 15, 1863, at Mobile, Alabama, by Colonel Miller for the war. Company muster roll for September/October 1863, reports him present. He drew clothing on June 1, 1864. A muster roll of Sossaman's detachment of the 21st Alabama, for September/October 1864, reports him present. He was surrendered by Lt. General Richard Taylor at Citronelle, Alabama, on May 4, 1865, and paroled at Meridian, Mississippi. Residence shown as Selma, Alabama.

Lambert, F., Pvt. Co. H
Drew clothing on March 2 and June 1, 1864, signed by his mark. POW captured at Fort Gaines, Alabama, on August 8, 1864. He was received at Ship, Island, Mississippi, on October 25, 1864, from New Orleans and exchanged at Ship Island on January 4, 1865. He was surrendered by Lt. General Richard Taylor at Citronelle, Alabama, on May 4, 1865, and paroled at Meridian, Mississippi. Residence Monroe County, Alabama.

Lambert, Frank, Pvt. Co. H see **Lambert, F.**

Lambert, J., Pvt. Co. ?
Enlisted on January 1, 1863, at Monroe, County, Alabama, by Lt. Sewell for the war. He drew clothing on March 3, 1864. He appears present on a company muster roll for September/October 1864.

Lambert, William, Pvt. Co. H
POW captured at Fort Gaines, Alabama, on August 8, 1864. He was received at Ship Island, Mississippi, on October 25, 1864, from New Orleans and exchanged at Ship Island on January 4, 1865. He drew clothing on March 3, 31 and June 1, 1964.

Lancaster, R. A., Pvt. Co. K
Referenced envelope only.

Landy, George, Pvt. Co. I see **Lundy, G. W.**

Lane, Alexander, Pvt. Co. I see **Laine, Alexander**

Lane, George, Pvt. Co. E
Detached sick. Paid $66 on July 9, 1862, for service from January 1, 1862, to June 30, 1862. He signed by his mark. His pay voucher is in his file.*

Lane, W., Pvt. Co. E
He drew clothing on March 31, 1864, and signed by his mark. He was paid 40 cents per day extra as a carpenter for June 1864, and admitted to Ross Hospital at Mobile, Alabama, on November 2, 1864, with febris intermittens tert. and returned to duty on November 7.

Lane, William, Pvt. Co. I
Enlisted on October 13, 1861, at Halls Mill, Alabama, by Major Hessee for the war. A regimental return for June 1862, shows him on detached service as a carpenter. A return for December 1862, shows him detached in Q. M. Department as carpenter. Company muster roll for bounty on September 24, 1862, reports him present. Company muster rolls for July/August and September/October 1863, report him present on extra duty in Q. M. Department from September 10, 1862. He appears on a roll of soldiers on extra duty at Fort Morgan, Alabama, in November 1863, as a carpenter, Sundays deducted [*from pay*]. A muster roll for Captain Sossaman's Detachment of the 21st Alabama, for September/October 1864, reports him present. He was admitted to Ross Hospital at Mobile, Alabama, on September 5, 1864, with ascites and sent to General Hospital at Greenville, Alabama, on September 13, 1864. He was surrendered by Lt. General Richard Taylor at Citronelle, Alabama, on May 4, 1865, and paroled at Meridian, Mississippi. Residence shown as Mobile County, Alabama. Note there is a discharge in his file for Pvt. **George W. Lane**, discharged at Fort Morgan, Ala., on September 23, 1862, for disability. He enlisted in Co. I on October 13, 1861, born Wayne County, North Carolina, age 30, five foot six and three quarter inches, dark complexion, gray eyes, light hair, by profession a planter. He signed by his mark. His discharge is in his file.*

Laney, M. M., Sgt./Pvt. Co. I
Enlisted on October 13, 1861, at Halls Mill, Alabama, by Major Hessee (Captain Taylor ?) for 12 months. He was wounded slightly by accident by bayonet on April 6, 1862, at Shiloh. He was paid $73.49 for service as 4th Sergeant, from March 1, to June 31, 1862. He appears present on a company muster roll for bounty on September 24,

1862, "Detached by Genl. ordered to report to enrolling officer July 28, /62, Returned to duty Oct. 30." Company muster roll for November/December 1862, reports him present. Company muster roll for July/August 1863, reports him present, "absent without leave from 11, to 14 July." Drew clothing July 10, 1863. Muster roll for September/October 1863, reports him present. There are pay vouchers in his file.*

Langdon, C. C., Pvt. Co. K

Enlisted on October 13, 1861, at Mobile, Alabama, by Capt. Stewart for one year. He appears on a regimental return for June 1862, on May 3, [62] near Corinth, Mississippi, he was discharged for disability. He was discharged on April 29, 1862, at Corinth, Mississippi, due to being unfit for duty. Born Mobile, Alabama, age 21, five foot nine and one half inch, dark complexion, black eyes, black hair, by occupation a farmer. His name appears on a list of attaches etc. employed by authority of Lt. General Hardee, at the Military Post of Mobile, Alabama, on July 16, 1863, "unfit for field duty." His name appears on a hospital muster roll for General Hospital Miller, (also know as Convalescent Hospital) Spring Hill, Alabama, employed on July 16, 1863, as a nurse, "Present clerk." (He is also shown as having enlisted on July 16, 1863, by Captain Dorgan.) He appears absent on furlough on a hospital muster roll for General Hospital Miller at Greenville, Alabama, for July/August 1864. A roll of men on extra duty at Greenville for July 1, to August 31, 1864, shows him as Ward Master. His discharge and pay vouchers are in his file.*

Langdon, C. C. Jr., Pvt. Co. K

Enlisted on July 25, 1863, at Fort Morgan, Alabama, by Captain Dorgan for the war. Company muster rolls for July/August and September/October 1863, show him "Absent detached in Miller Hosp. July 25/63, by Gen. Maury." Hospital muster roll for General Hospital Miller at Spring Hill, Alabama, for July/August 1863, shows him present employed as a nurse, acting clerk. Muster roll for September/October 1864, shows him "Absent, detached in A. Q. M. Mobile, on Med. Certificate." Hospital muster rolls for General Hospital Miller at Spring Hill, Alabama, for September/October and November/December 1864, report him present employed as a nurse.

Lappington, George W., Pvt. Co. A

Enlisted in Co. A at Mobile, Alabama, October 13, 1861, by Major Hessee for one year. He was discharged October 13, 1862, for being underage, Age 17, born Mobile, Alabama, five foot five inches, fair complexion, gray eyes, light hair, a mechanic by profession. He appears present on a company muster roll for bounty on September 24, 1862, shown present but refused to take bounty. He was paid $40.76 for his service. His discharge and pay voucher is in his file.*

LaRosa, Ignacia., Pvt. Co. G

Wounded slightly in the knee at Shiloh while advancing during attack on 1st Camp at 7 A. M. on April 6th 1862. His name appears on a regimental return for June 1862, "wounded & furloughed since April 9." Paid for commutation of rations on March 15, 1862 and June 27, 1862, signed by his mark.

Latham, A. R., Pvt. Co. F

His name appears on a register of payments to discharged soldiers. He was discharged on July 4, 1862.

Latham, J. B., Pvt. Co. F

Wounded severely in the head at Shiloh while advancing at the Old Field on April 6, 1862, at 4 P. M. POW captured at Shiloh hospital on April 7, 1862.

Laudumay C., Pvt. Co. K see **Kaudumey, C.**

Launay, Charles, Corp. Co. H

Enlisted on October 13, 1861, at Mobile, Alabama, by Major Hessee for one year. His name appears on a register of payments to discharged soldiers. Discharged on November 19, 1861, at Fort Gaines, Alabama, due to disability (?). Born New Orleans, age 26, five foot 6 inches, light complexion, gray eyes, light hair, by profession a bookkeeper. His discharge is in his file.*

Laudumey, C., Pvt. Co. K

Enlisted on July 4, 1863, at Fort Morgan, Alabama, by Captain Dorgan for the war. Company muster rolls for July/August and September/October 1863, report him present. He drew clothing on July 10, 1863.

LaVesgy, Lorenzo, Pvt. Co. E

Discharged on May 3, 1862, at Corinth, Mississippi, due to disability. Born in Tuscaloosa, Alabama, age 18, five foot five and one quarter inches, fair complexion, gray eyes, black hair, by profession a clerk. His discharge is in his file.*

Law, William, Pvt. Co. C

A regimental return for June 1862, reports him absent on sick furlough. A claim for deceased soldier was filed by F. S. Lyon Attorney on February 5, 1863 on behalf of Ann T. Hylton the mother of William Law. There are several poor copies of documents referring to this claim. He died leaving neither wife nor children.*

Lawless, H., 21st Alabama Infantry

His name appears on a register of soldiers who were killed in battle or who died of wounds or disease.

Lawrence, Henry, Pvt. Co. A

Enlisted on September 2, 1862, at Mobile, Alabama, by Captain DeVaux for the war. He appears present on company muster rolls for September 24, 1862, (*for bounty*), December 31, 1862, to April 30, 1863, May/June 1863 and September/October 1864. He appears absent on muster roll for September/October 1863, sent to General Hospital at Mobile on October 25, 1863.

Lawson, W., Pvt. Co. F

POW captured at Champion Hill, Mississippi, on May 10, 1862, and sent to Memphis, Tennessee. He drew clothing in 3rd quarter of 1864.

Lay, E. C., Pvt./Corp. Co. F

Enlisted on October 5, 1862, at Fort Morgan, Alabama, by Captain Dade for the war. He appears present on a company muster roll for March 1, to June 30, 1863. Company muster roll for September/October 1863, reports him present promoted to 4th Corporal on September 1, 1863, with bounty due. He was admitted to Post Hospital at Fort Morgan on November 11, 1863, with catarrh and returned to duty on November 16, 1863. He drew clothing on March 31 and June 1, 1864, and signed by his mark. POW captured at Fort Gaines, Alabama, on August 8, 1864. Confined at Steam Levee Press No. 4 at New Orleans on September 25, 1864, "sent to hospital on September 25, 1864." He was admitted to St. Louis USA General Hospital at New Orleans with fever intermit. on September 10, 1864, and returned to confinement on September 16, and again admitted on September 24, and returned to confinement on October 22, 1864, age shown as 22. Received at Ship Island, Mississippi, from New Orleans on October 25, 1864 and exchanged at Ship Island on January 4, 1865. There is a pay voucher in his file.*

Lay, N. A., Pvt./QM Sgt. Co. K/Field and Staff see **Layet, Adolphe**

Layet, Adolphe, Pvt./QM Sgt. Co. K/Field and Staff

Enlisted on October 13, 1863, at Mobile, Alabama, by Captain Stewart for the war. He was wounded slightly in the hand at Shiloh while advancing on attack on the First Camp on April 6, 1862, at 8 A. M. He was appointed QM Sgt. from Pvt. on May 28, 1862. He appears on regimental return at Corinth, Mississippi, for June 1862, "transfd' Q. M. Sergeant." He appears present on company muster rolls for July/August, September/October 1863 and March/April 1864, as QM Sgt. POW captured at Fort Gaines, Alabama, on August 8, 1864. He was admitted to St. Louis USA General Hospital at New Orleans with fever intermittent on August 21, 1864, and returned to confinement on August 24, 1864, age shown 22. He was received at Ship Island, Mississippi, on October 25, 1864, from New Orleans and exchanged at Ship Island on January 4, 1865. POW surrendered by Lt. General Richard Taylor on May 4, 1865, at Citronelle, Alabama, and paroled at Meridian, Mississippi, on May 13, 1865. There are pay vouchers in his file.*

Leafeaver, J., Pvt. Co. I see **Lefever, John**

Leap, William, E., Corp./Sgt. Co. B

Enlisted on October 13, 1861, at Mobile, Alabama, by Major Hessee for one year. His name appears on a regimental return for June 1862, "Sent to interior Hospital May 28." In July 1861, he appears on a list of soldiers employed at General Hospital at Okolona, Mississippi, as a nurse June 1862. He appears present on a company muster roll for bounty on September 24, 1862. Company muster roll for March/April 1863, reports him present as 1st Corp. Company muster roll for May/June 1863, reports him present "Appointed 4th Sgt. May 1st, 1863, sick in quarters." September/October 1863, roll reports him present " sick in quarters, due for clothing not drawn in kind $59 63/100." He was admitted to Post Hospital at Fort Morgan, Alabama, with int. fever on December 23, 1863, and returned to duty on January 28, 1864. He drew clothing on March 31 and June 1, 1864. POW captured at Fort Gaines, Alabama, on August 8, 1864.

He was received at Ship Island, Mississippi, on October 25, 1864, from New Orleans, and exchanged on January 4, 1865. A duplicate set of data cards for **L. A. Long** (crossed out and Wm. E. Leap written in) indicate POW captured at Fort Gaines, Alabama, on August 8, 1864, and received at Elmira, New York, on October 8, 1864, from New Orleans. "This correction made November 29, 1864." Released on January 12, 1865, per orders from QGP, dated January 1, 1865. His name (William E. Leap, Sgt. Co. B 21st Alabama Inf.) appears on a roll of POW's at Elmira, New York, desirous to take the Oath of Allegiance to the USA, roll dated October 31, 1864. Captured at Fort Gaines on August 8, 1864, "Volunteered Oct. 13, 1861, for one year, was conscripted at the expiration of his enlistment. Is a native of Rochester, New York, but was in Mobile, Ala. at the outbreak of war could not well get away. Was forced to enlist from mere force of public opinion. His father lives at Rochester and he prays to be released and allowed to return to him. His only brother is in the US Navy."

Leas, Pvt. Co. B see **Lees, Thomas**

Leathergood, B. F., Pvt. Co. E
His name appears on a regimental return for June 1862, "Clerk at A. A. G. O. Brig. Hdqrs."

Leavens, A., Pvt. Co. C/F see **Leavens, John**
Leavens, E. B., Pvt. Co. F
Enlisted at Baldwin County, on October 13, 1861, by Captain McVoy for one year. He appears present on a company muster roll for bounty on September 24, 1862. Company muster roll for March 1, to June 30, 1863, reports him present sick in hospital. He appears on a roll of extra duty men at Fort Stonewall & Sidney Johnston, Alabama River as a butcher for July 1863. Muster roll September/October 1863, reports him present, confined in G. [*Guard*] House. [*Lost*] haversack $1, canteen $2. POW captured at Fort Gaines, Alabama, on August 8, 1864. He arrived at Ship Island, Mississippi, from New Orleans on October 25, 1864, and applied to take the Oath of Allegiance to the USA. He was exchanged at Ship Island on January 5, 1865.

Leavens, James, Pvt. Co. F
He enlisted at Fort Gaines, Alabama, on February 7, 1862, by Captain McCoy for one year. His name appears on a report near Tupelo, Mississippi, on June 28, 1862, "wounded at Shiloh furloughed on Surgn's certif. Apl. 8th sent from Corinth Hospital Surgeons certif. May 28, 1862". His name appears on a regimental return for June 1862, "sent to Mobile Hospital on May 28". He appears present on a company muster roll for bounty on September 24, 1862. Company muster roll for March 1, to June 30, 1863, reports him present sick in hospital "lost one haversack 20 cents", here he is shown as having enlisted on January 11, 1862. Muster roll September/October 1863, reports him absent, detached to fish by General Maury August 23, 1863. He drew clothing on March 31, 1864, and signed by his mark. POW captured at Fort Gaines, Alabama, on August 8, 1864. He arrived at Steam Levee Press No. 4 at New Orleans, Louisiana, on October 14, 1864, and was sent to hospital. He arrived at Ship Island, Mississippi, from New Orleans

on October 25, 1864, and applied to take the Oath of Allegiance to the USA. He was exchanged at Ship Island on January 5, 1865.

Leavens, John, Pvt. Co. C/F

Enlisted in Co. C on January 31, 1862, at Choctaw Bluff, Alabama, by Captain Smith for three years or the war. Company muster roll for December 31, 1862, to April 30, 1863, reports him transferred to Co. F April 4, 1863, never paid. Company muster roll for March 1, to April 31, 1863, reports him present, sick in hospital, lost one lock screw at $1.00. Company muster roll for September/October 1863, reports him has having deserted from hospital at Point Clear, Alabama, on September 14, 1863, carrying off haversack and canteen. September 28, 1863, he was advertised as dark eyes, dark hair, dark complexion, 5 foot 8 inches, age 25, resident of Baldwin County. He drew clothing on March 31 and June 1, 1864, signed by his mark. He was admitted to Post Hospital at Fort Morgan, Alabama, with abscess on December 27, 1863, and returned duty on January 6, 1864, also he is show as having deserted on Jan 3, 1864. POW came in at Fort Morgan on April 4, 1865, deserted at Spanish Fort, Alabama. He was confined on April 13, 1865, at New Orleans and took the Oath of Allegiance to the USA and was released on April 14, 1865. Here he is shown as light complexion, brown hair, 5 foot 8 inches, blue eyes, and a resident of Baldwin County. In this same file **John Leavens**, Pvt. Co. F was admitted to St. Louis, USA General Hospital, at New Orleans with acute diarrhoea on October 14, 1864, and returned to confinement on October 17, 1864, age 18.

Leavens, Richard, Pvt. Co. F

He enlisted on March 12, 1862, at Choctaw Bluff, Alabama, by Captain Dade for the war. Company muster roll for March 1, to January 30, 1863, reports him present sick in hospital. Company muster roll for September/October 1863, reports him has having deserted from hospital at Point Clear, Alabama, August 11, 1863, carrying off gun, knapsack, haversack and canteen and 40 cartridges.

Leavens, W. B., Sgt. Co. F

He enlisted on October 13, 1861, at Baldwin County by Captain McCoy for one year. Wounded slightly in the leg at Shiloh on April 6, 1862, at 7 A. M. advancing on attack on 1st Battery. He appears present on a company muster roll for bounty on September 24, 1862. Company muster roll for March 1, to June 30, 1863, reports him present sick in quarters, lost one haversack at 20 cents. Company muster roll for September/October 1863, reports him present. He drew clothing on March 31, 1864.

Leavens, William, Pvt. Co. F see **Leavins, William H.**

Leavins, E. B. Pvt. Co. F see **Leavens, E. B.**

Leavins, James, Pvt. Co. F see **Heavens, James**

Leavins, W. B., Sgt. Co. F see **Leavens, W. B.**

Leavins, William H., Pvt. Co. F

Enlisted at Fort Gaines, Alabama, on February 16, 1862, by Captain McCoy for one year. He appears on a report near Tupelo, Mississippi, wounded at Shiloh, and furloughed on surgeon's certificate April 8, then sent from Corinth, Mississippi Hospital on surgeon's certificate May 28, 1862. He appears on a regimental return for June 1862, "sent to Mobile Hospital, May 28." He appears present on a company muster roll for bounty on September 24, 1862. Company muster roll for March 1, to June 30, 1862, reports him present, lost one haversack at 20 cents. Company muster roll for September/October 1863, reports him present confined in guard house, [*lost*] one haversack at $1.00 and one canteen at $2.00. Admitted to Post Hospital at Fort Morgan, Alabama, on November 18, 1863, with int. fev., returned to duty on November 25. He was again admitted to Post Hospital at Fort Morgan with pneumonia on January 18, 1864, and returned to duty on January 26, 1864. Drew clothing March 31, 1864, and signed by his mark.

LeBaron, Alexander S., Pvt. Co. A

. There is a certificate of disability for Co. A, 3rd Alabama Infantry in his file dated August 14, 1862. He was born in Mobile, Alabama, age 19, five foot three inches, florid complexion, hazel eyes, auburn hair, and a clerk by occupation. There is a reference card in his file for Alexander LeBaron, Co. A, 3rd Alabama Infantry and Co. K 21st Alabama Infantry, "see **Fleetwood Foster**." Enlisted on September 3, 1863, at Fort Morgan, Alabama, by Captain Dorgan for the war. Company muster roll for September/October 1863, reports him absent on surgeon's certificate to November 5, 1863. He was admitted to Post Hospital at Fort Morgan on September 13, 1863, with int. fev. and returned to duty on September 18, 1863. He appears present on a company muster roll for September/October 1864. POW surrendered at Citronelle, Alabama, by Lt. General Richard Taylor on May 4, 1865, and paroled at Meridian, Mississippi, on May 13, 1865. He was a resident of Mobile, Mobile County, Alabama There are pay vouchers and a payment on descriptive list in his file.**

LeBlane, Pvt. Co. ?

There is a card showing "Official Communications, Dec. S. O. [Special Order] 256, date Dec. 5, Richmond, Dec. 2, Dec. 5 detaching Private LeBlank. Woodruff Rifles, 21st La. Vols. Detailed."

LeCount, Pvt. Co. K see **Lecount, O.**

Lecount, O., Pvt. Co. K

Enlisted on July 4, 1863, at Fort Morgan, Alabama, by Captain Dorgan for the war. Company muster rolls for July/August, September/October 1863 and September/October 1864, all show him present. He was admitted to Post Hospital at Fort Morgan on October 2, 1863, with fev. con. and sent to general hospital on October 9, 1863. He was admitted to Ross Hospital at Mobile, Alabama, on October 9, 1863, and returned to duty on October 12. He drew clothing on July 10, 1863, December 1863, (here he signs by his mark) June 20, 1864 and August 14, 1864.

Ledford, John, Pvt. Co. A

He is buried in the Raphael Semmes Camp 11 UCV plot at Magnolia Cemetery in Mobile, Alabama. There is not a CSR file on this man.

Ledyard, Henry A., Pvt. Co. K

He was killed by a shot through the head at Shiloh at First Camp on April 6, 1862, at 7 A. M.

Lee, George D., Pvt. Co. B

He was detached sick from March 1, 1862, to August 31, 1862. He drew clothing March 31, 1864. A pay voucher is in his file.*

Lee, John, Pvt. Co. D/B

Enlisted on October 13, 1861, at Mobile, Alabama, by Captain Butt for one year. He was wounded at Shiloh on April 6, 1862, at 7 A. M. while attacking 1st Battery. He was received on board steamer *Charles* at Vicksburg, Mississippi, on December 14, 1862, among 114 exchanged Confederate Prisoners of War. He appears present on a company muster roll for bounty on September 24, 1862, but refused to take bounty. He appears present on company D muster rolls for November/December 1862, July/August 1863, September/October 1863, November/December 1863 and September/October 1864. He was admitted to Ross Hospital at Mobile, Alabama, on August 8, 1864, with acute diarrhoea and returned to duty on August 10, 1864. Company muster roll for Co. D September/October 1864, reports him absent detailed to Battery Huger by order of Colonel Fuller. He drew clothing on March 31, 1864, and signed by his mark.

Lee, Lewis W., Pvt. Co. D

Enlisted on October 13, 1861, at Mobile, Alabama, by Captain Butt for one year. His name appears on a report near Tupelo, Mississippi, on June 28, 1862, "sent to hospital in Mobile from hospital in Corinth, by Surgeon." A report for June 1862, reports that he was sent to interior hospital at the evacuation of Corinth. He appears present on a company muster roll for bounty on September 24, 1862. Company muster rolls for November/December 1862, July/August 1863, September/October 1863 and November/December 1863, all show him present. He drew clothing on June 30, 1864, and in August 1864. A company muster roll for September/October 1864, reports him absent sent to General Hospital in Mobile on October 6, 1864. POW a detailed man captured at Mobile and paroled at Mobile on May 14, 1865. Residence shown as Mobile, Alabama.

Leeland, William P., see Neeland, William Pvt. Co. B.

Lees, Thomas, Pvt. Co. B

Enlisted on October 13, 1861, at Mobile, Alabama, by Major Hessee for one year. His name appears on a report near Tupelo, Mississippi, on June 28, 1862, "detached in Quar. M. Dep. March 26, 1862, by order of General Gladden." A report for June 1862, reports that he is on detached service in Q. M. Department at Mobile. He appears present on a company muster roll for bounty on September 24, 1862, but refused to take bounty. He appears on a receipt roll for pay in November 1862, as a carpenter at Oven and

Choctaw Bluffs, Alabama. Company muster roll for March/April 1863, reports him present and detailed in Engineering Department at Oven Bluff, Alabama, on April 20, 1863, by order of Colonel Anderson. Muster roll for May/June 1863, reports him present and detailed in Quarter Master Department since June 22. Muster roll for September/October 1863, reports him present sick in quarters. He appears on a roll employed at Fort Morgan, Alabama, as a carpenter, pay for Sundays deducted. He appears on a descriptive list for pay and clothing at Point Clear, Alabama, on September 23, 1863, born in England, age 30, blue eyes, light hair, light complexion, five foot eight inches, and a carpenter by occupation. He drew clothing on June 1, 1864. POW captured at Fort Gaines, Alabama, on August 8, 1864. He was received at Ship Island, Mississippi, from New Orleans on October 25, 1864, and exchanged at Ship Island on January 4, 1865.

Lefever, John, Pvt. Co. I. **LaFerer, John**
He drew clothing on June 1, 1864. He was admitted to Post Hospital at Fort Morgan, Alabama, with int. fev. quiar. on July 28, 1864, and returned to duty on August 4, 1864. POW captured at Fort Gaines, Alabama, on August 8, 1864. He was received at Ship Island, Mississippi, from New Orleans on October 25, 1864, and exchanged at Ship Island on January 4, 1865. He was admitted to Ross Hospital at Mobile on January 6, 1865, with febris remittens and died on January 28, 1865. He left no effects.

Lefevre, John, Pvt. Co. I see **Lefever, John**

Legner, J. M., Pvt. Co. G
He was admitted to Ross Hospital at Mobile, Alabama, on January 6, 1865, with diarrhoea and scurvy and furloughed for 60 days on January 19, 1865.

Lemmons, James, Pvt. Co. A
POW captured at Fort Donelson on February 16, 1862. He appears on a roll of POW's at Camp Morton, Indiana, in June 1862. He was sent from Camp Morton Indiana, to Vicksburg, Mississippi, among 983 POW's and exchanged at Atkens Landing on November 10, 1862.

Leonard, Thomas, Pvt. Co. B
He enlisted at Talladega, Alabama, on September 10, 1862, by Geo. A. Harvey for the war. Company muster rolls for March/April, May/June and September/October 1863, report him present. He drew clothing on March 31 and June 1, 1864. POW captured at Fort Gaines, Alabama, on August 8, 1864. He was received at Ship Island, Mississippi, from New Orleans on October 25, 1864, and exchanged at Ship Island on January 4, 1865.

Leroy, James E., Pvt. Co. K see **Leroy, J. E.**

Leroy, J. E., Pvt. Co. K
Enlisted on March 18, 1863, at Mobile, Alabama, by Captain Seldon for the war. He appears present on a Co. K muster roll for July/August 1863, reported present, "transferred to this company in exchange for **J. W. Holmes Jr.** on August 1/63." He

was admitted to Post Hospital at Fort Morgan, Alabama, on August 27, 1863, with syphilis and returned to duty on September 4, 1863. Company muster roll for September/October 1863, reports him absent "detached in Engineer Department, by order of General Maury Oct. 22/63." Company muster roll for September/October 1864, reports him "detached in Engineer Dept, by order of Gen. Maury, Oct. 7/64 for 30 days." He appears in October and December 1863, on receipt rolls for pay as a boatman at Mobile paid $2.40 per day. He appears in February, March and April, 1864, on receipt rolls for pay as overseer at Mobile, Alabama, at $3 per day, signed by his mark. There are pay vouchers in his file.*

Leslie, Henry, Pvt./Sgt. Co. D
Enlisted on November 18, 1862, at Fort Morgan, Alabama, by Captain Butt for the war, as a substitute for **John Fowler**. Company muster roll for July/August 1863, reports him present. Company muster roll for September/October 1863, reports him absent on furlough. November/December 1863, muster roll reports him present. He drew clothing on April 16, 1864. September/October 1864, he is shown absent sent to hospital in Mobile on August 17, 1864. He was admitted to Ross Hospital at Mobile, Alabama, on October 26, 1864, with chronic rheumatimus and discharged from service on December 7, 1864. Born in Virginia, age 44, six foot two inches, fair complexion, blue eyes, light hair, a builder by occupation. His discharge is in his file. His certificate of disability on November 14, 1864, (in his file also) shows he was born in Norfolk, Virginia, age 52, five foot nine, light complexion, blue eyes, light hair, a mason by occupation.**

Levens, John, Pvt. Co. C/F see **Leavens, John**

Leverett, S., Pvt. Co. D
POW surrendered by Lt. General Richard Taylor at Citronelle, Alabama, on May 4, 1865, and paroled at Meridian, Mississippi, on May 13, 1865. He was a resident of Greenville, Alabama.

Levers, William, Pvt. Co. F see **Leavins, William K.**

Leivins, John, Pvt. Co. C/F see **Leavens, John**

Levines, John, Pvt. Co. C/F see **Leavens, John**

Lewis, George, Pvt. Co. I
His name appears on a register of payments to discharged soldiers on April 9, 1862. His name then appears on a roll of POW's at Military Prison, Alton, Illinois, received on May 18, 1863, captured at Port Gibson, Mississippi, on May 1, 1863, and exchanged on June 12, 1863.

Lewis, John Y., Pvt. Co. I
POW wounded severely in right breast at Shiloh, on April 6, 1862, at 7 A. M. while attacking 1st Battery. He was captured at hospital on April 7, 1862.

Lewis, Sylvester C., Pvt. Co. K

Enlisted on October 13, 1861, by Captain Stewart to serve one year. He was born in Sumter County, Alabama, age 24, five foot six and three quarter inches, fair complexion, blue eyes, light hair, a student when enlisted. Discharged due to disability at Corinth, Mississippi, on April 29, 1862. His discharge and a pay voucher is in his file.*

Lewis, W. H., Pvt. Co. I

Enlisted on October 17, 1863, at Madison, County, Alabama, by Capt. Ravisies for the war. He appears absent on a company muster roll for September/October 1863, "detached in Engineers Department on Oct. 25/ by Gen. Maury." He received a 90-day furlough [*detail?*] at Demopolis, Alabama, on February 22, 1864, (expires on June 28) with 30-day extension from June 26, 1864, as his services are necessary for the completion of the railroad connection "near this place". POW surrendered by Lt. General Taylor in May 1865, and paroled at Demopolis, Alabama, on June 10, 1865. His handwritten furlough? and extension are in his file.*

Liddell, R. F., Pvt. Co. C

Enlisted on August 21, 1862, at Dallas County, Alabama, by R. H. Dawson for three years or the war. He appears present on a company muster roll for December 31, 1862, to April 30, 1863. Company muster roll for May/June 1863, reports him absent sick in Selma, Alabama, since May 20, 1863, lost cartridge box at $2.50, cap pouch at $1.00, W belt at $75 cts., bayonet scabbard at $1.00, plate at $1.00, 10 cartridges and 12 caps at $1.00. Company muster roll for September/October 1863, reports him absent in hospital at Mobile, Alabama, since October 25, 1863. He was admitted to Post Hospital at Fort Morgan, Alabama, with int. fev. on January 19, 1864, and sent to general hospital on January 26, 1864. He was admitted at Ross Hospital at Mobile, Alabama, with int. fever tert. on January 26, 1864, and sent to General Hospital at Montgomery, Alabama, on February 17, 1864. He was paid as a teamster for May 20, to June 30, 1864, at 25 cents per day. He drew clothing on June 1, 1864. POW captured at Fort Gaines, Alabama, on August 8, 1864. He was admitted to St. Louis USA General Hospital at New Orleans with fever remit. on September 10, 1864, and returned to confinement on September 15, 1864, age 35. He was received at Ship Island, Mississippi, on October 25, 1864, from New Orleans and exchanged on January 4, 1865.

Liddell, Robert F., Co. C see **Liddell, R. F.**

Liddell, William, Pvt. Co. H

He drew clothing on March 3 and June 1, 1864, and signed by his mark. POW captured at Fort Gaines, Alabama, on August 8, 1864. He was received at Ship Island, Mississippi, on October 25, 1864, from New Orleans and exchanged on January 4, 1865. POW surrendered by Lt. General Richard Taylor at Citronelle, Alabama, on May 4, 1865, and paroled at Meridian, Mississippi, on May 13, 1865. He was shown as a resident of Clairborne, Alabama,

Liffner, A., Pvt. Co. G see **Lifford, A.**

MOBILE CONFEDERATES

Lifford, A., Pvt. Co. G

He drew clothing on March 3 and signed his name and on June 1, 1864, he signed by his mark. POW captured at Fort Gaines, Alabama, on August 8, 1864. He was received at Ship Island, Mississippi, on October 25, 1864, from New Orleans and exchanged at Ship Island on January 4, 1865.

Liftner, A., Pvt. Co. G see **Liffnord, A.**

Lightner, J. M., Pvt. Co. G

He drew clothing on March 3, March 31 and June 1, 1864. POW captured at Fort Gaines, Alabama, on August 8, 1864. He was received at Ship Island, Mississippi, on October 25, 1864, from New Orleans and exchanged at Ship Island on January 4, 1865.

Lineahan, J., Pvt. Co. D see **Linnihan, Jerry**

Linehan, Jerry, Pvt. Co. D see **Linnihan, Jerry**

Ling, B., Pvt. Co. I see **Lingo, B.**

Ling, T. A., Pvt. Co. I

His name appears on regimental return for June 1862, "sent to interior hospital May 28, 1862."

Lingo, B., Pvt. Co. I

Enlisted at Halls Mill, Alabama, on March 2, 1862 by Major Hessee (Lt. Cayce) for the war. Company muster roll for bounty on September 24, 1862, reports him present. He was admitted to Post Hospital at Fort Morgan, Alabama, with rubeola on March 13, 1863, and returned to duty on April 3, 1863. He is reported present on a company muster roll for July/August 1863 and September/October 1863, but absent without leave for 14 days on the last roll. He drew clothing on March 31, 1864. POW captured at Fort Gaines, Alabama, on August 8, 1864. He was received at Ship Island, Mississippi, on October 25, 1864, from New Orleans and exchanged on January 4, 1865. POW surrendered by Lt. General Richard Taylor at Citronelle, Alabama, on May 4, 1865, and paroled at Meridian, Mississippi, on May 13, 1865. He was shown as a resident of Marengo County, Alabama.

Linihan, Jerry, Pvt. Co. D see **Linnihan, Jerry**

Linnihan, Jerry, Pvt. Co. D

Enlisted on October 13, 1861, at Mobile, Alabama, by Captain Butt for one year. He appears present on a company muster roll for bounty on February 24, 1862, "refused to take bounty." Company muster rolls for November/December 1862, July/August 1863, September/October 1863 and November/December 1863, all report him present. A claim for a deceased soldier was filed on May 4, 1864, by Catherine Linnihan his widow.

21ST ALABAMA INFANTRY VOLUNTEERS

Littlejohn, William, Pvt. Co. D
POW captured at Blakeley, Alabama, on April 9, 1865. He was received at Ship Island, Mississippi, and was transferred for exchange on parole to Vicksburg, Mississippi, on May 1, 1865.

Littlejohn, James, Pvt. Co. B
Enlisted on October 13, 1861, at Mobile, Alabama, by Major Hessee for the war. Company muster roll for bounty on September 24, 1862, reports him present. He was found not to be entitled to bounty. He was discharged on October 17, 1862, and paid for one-month service from September 1, 1862. Muster roll for March/April 1863, shows him present but having enlisted at Oven Bluff on January 1, 1863, by Captain Johnston for the war. May/June 1863, muster roll reports him absent on sick leave for 15 days from June 15, 1863. He appears on a descriptive list for pay on September 23, 1864, at Point Clear, Alabama, born in Ireland, age 48, gray eyes, gray hair, dark complexion, five foot seven and one half inches, and a gardener by occupation, paid $50. (Here he is shown as having enlisted at Oven Bluff on January 21, 1863, by Captain Johnson for three years or the war.) Muster roll for September/October 1863, reports him present but absent without leave for 4 days since last muster. He drew clothing on March 31, 1864. Muster roll for Captain Sossaman's Detachment of the 21st for September/October 1864, reports him present at Mobile.

Livermord, John H., Pvt. Co. A see **Livermore, John W.**

Livermore, John W., Pvt. Co. A
Enlisted on August 7, 1862, at Mobile, Alabama, by Captain DeVaux for three years or the war. He appears present on a company muster roll for bounty on September 24, 1862. Company muster rolls for December 31, 1862, to April 30, 1863, May/June 1863 and September/October 1863, all report him absent, detached as a carpenter on January 6, 1863, by order of General Buckner. He was paid on January 1, 1963, at Choctaw Bluff, Alabama, for service in December as a carpenter.

Livingston, J. P., Pvt. Co. K
Reference envelope only.

Lockhart, E., Pvt. Co. C
Enlisted on January 9, 1862, at Tupelo, Mississippi, by Lt. Luther for the war. He appears absent sick on a company muster roll for bounty on September 24, 1862. Claim for deceased soldier filed by E. A. Lockhart on March 16, ?

Lockhart, R. H., Pvt. Co. C
Wounded at Shiloh on April 6, 1862, at 4 P. M. while advancing crossing Old Field. He appears on a report June 28, 1862, near Tupelo, "wounded at Shiloh and sent home on Fur. on surg. certificate."

Lofton, M. H., Pvt. F

Enlisted on April 21, 1863, at Choctaw Bluff, Alabama, by Captain Dade for the war. He appears present on a company muster roll for March 1, to June 30, 1863. POW captured at Fort Gaines, Alabama, on August 8, 1864. He was admitted to St. Louis USA General Hospital at New Orleans with remit. fever on August 23, 1864, and died September 9, 1864, left no effects. He was buried in Monument Cemetery grave 343 on September 10. His death certificate is in his file, age 19, born Georgia, single, a resident of Monroe County, Alabama. Remarks Mrs. Lofton, Clabrorn, [*Claiborne*] Alabama.

Long, J. W., Pvt. Co. I

Enlisted at Halls Mill, Alabama, on October 13, 1861. Wounded seriously in the elbow and passing through the body on April 7, in the morning. Died of wounds and typhoid fever at Mobile about May 12, 1862. Claim for deceased soldier filed by Nancy R. Long on April 7, 1863. Found due $51.40. There is paperwork in his file.*

Long, Thomas, A., Corp./Sgt. Co. I.

Enlisted on October 13, 1861, at Halls Mill, Alabama, by Major Hessee for the war. His name appears on a report near Tupelo, Mississippi, on June 28, 1862, "Sent to interior hospital from Corinth by Surgeon May 28th." He appears absent with leave since September 23, 1862, on a company muster roll for bounty dated September 24, 1862. Company muster rolls for July/August 1863 and September/October 1863, report him present. He is shown absent without leave for two days on the latter roll. He drew clothing on June 1, 1864. He was admitted to Post Hospital at Fort Morgan, Alabama, on July 24, 1864, with int. fev. quar. and returned to duty on July 31, 1864. POW captured at Fort Gaines, Alabama, on August 8, 1864. He was received at Ship Island, Mississippi, on October 25, 1864, from New Orleans and exchanged on January 4, 1865.

Looney, John F., Corporal Co. F

He appears May 18, 1863, on a roll of POW's at Military Prison at Alton, Illinois. Captured at Port Gibson, Mississippi, on May 3, 1863. Exchanged June 12, 1863.

Looney, John T., Corp. Co. F see **Looney, John F.**

Lorengo, M., Pvt. Co. G

His name appears on a report near Tupelo, Mississippi, on June 28, 1862, "Sent to interior hospital from Corinth at the time of evacuation." He appears on a regimental return for June 1862, "sent to hospital, May 21."

Lorlock, L., Pvt. Co. D

He appears on a regimental return for June 1862, "sent to hospital, at evacuation of Corinth."

Lott, James, P., Pvt. Co. A

Enlisted on October 13, 1861, at Mobile, Alabama. Discharged due to having syphilis on December 25, 1861, at Fort Gaines, Alabama. Born New Orleans, Louisiana, age 19, five foot eight inches, dark complexion, black eyes, and black hair.

Loughry, E. R., Pvt. Co. E
Discharged?

Lovering, Arthur, Pvt. Hospital Steward, Co. A
Enlisted on October 13, 1861, at Mobile, Alabama, by Major Hessee. He appears absent on a company muster roll for September 24, 1862, for bounty, detached on April 14, 1862, as hospital nurse at Corinth by order of General Chambers. Hospital muster rolls at Post Hospital at Dalton, Georgia, for September, October, November, and December 1862, reports him present employed by Surgeon F. H. Evans. Hospital muster rolls for January, February and March, 1863, report him present at Oliver Hospital at Dalton. Hospital muster rolls for April, May, June and July 1863, report him present at Cannon Hospital at Dalton. A hospital muster roll at Medical Directors Office, Columbus, Georgia, reports him present to October 31, 1864. Company muster rolls for the 21st Alabama from December 31, 1862, to April 30, 1863, May/June 1863 and September/ October 1863, all report him absent detached as hospital steward by order of Secretary of War. There is paperwork in his file including the Special Order No. 34 appointing him Hospital Steward.*

Lowan, H. H., Pvt. Co. E see **Lowary, Henry H.**

Lowary, Henry H., Pvt. Co. E
POW captured at Fort Gaines, Alabama, on August 8, 1864. He was admitted to St. Louis USA General Hospital at New Orleans, on September 5, 1864, with diarrhoea and returned to confinement on October 22, 1864, age 17. He was received at Ship Island, Mississippi, from New Orleans on October 25, 1864. He made application to take the Oath of Allegiance and refused to be exchanged on January 5, 1865. He was transferred back to New Orleans on February 15, 1865, per request of US Captain M. R. Marston, Com. of prisoners for Military Division of Mississippi. He claimed to be a conscript and took the Oath of Allegiance to the USA at New Orleans on February 31, 1865, by order of Major General Canby. There is a testimonial from a Notary Public in New Orleans for John Lowary of No. 111 Front Levee Street, New Orleans.*

Lowenthal, Edward, Drum Major
Enlisted on October 13, 1861, at Mobile, Alabama, by Major J. Hessee for one year. Discharged at Corinth, Mississippi, due to disability due to (Rakenmadis – Ralemadis or rattle while breathing?), age 39, born Russia? Europe, five foot four inches, gray eyes, ruddy complexion, back hair, a musician by profession. Examined and discharged by J. F. Heustis Surgeon and Medical Director.

Luchlin, Rocco, Pvt. Co. H
Enlisted on October 13, 1861, at Mobile, Alabama, in Co. H, French Guards by Major Hessee for one year. Discharged at Fort Gaines, Alabama, on December 6, 1861. Born Dalmatia, Europe, age 25, five foot seven inches, dark complexion, gray eyes, dark hair, a laborer by occupation.

Lucas, J. N., Pvt. Co. F

Enlisted at Shelby, County, on September 19, 1862, by W. J. Davis. Company muster rolls for March 1, to June 30, 1863 and September/October 1863, report him present. He was admitted to Post Hospital at Fort Morgan, Alabama, on November 9, 1863, with int. fev. and returned to duty on November 23. He drew clothing on March 31, 1864. POW captured at Fort Gaines, Alabama, on August 8, 1864, received at Ship Island, Mississippi, on October 25, 1864, from New Orleans and exchanged at Ship Island on January 5, 1865. POW captured again at Spanish Fort, Alabama, on April 8, 1865. Received at Ship Island on April 10, 1865, and transferred on parole to Vicksburg, Mississippi, on May 1, 1865.

Lucas, N., Pvt. Co. F see **Lucas, J. N.**

Luke, Henry, Pvt. Co. D

Re-enlisted at Fort Morgan, Alabama, on November 18, 1862.

Luker, S. D., Pvt. Co. K

Reference envelope only.

Lundy, G. W., Pvt. Co. I.

Enlisted on October 13, 1864, at Halls Mill, Alabama, by Major Hessee for the war. POW captured at Pittsburg [*Landing*], on April 8, 1864. A register reports that he was on ambulance squad and captured at hospital. His name appears on a roll of POW's at Camp Douglas, Illinois, on August 1, 1862. Company muster rolls for July/August 1863 and September/October 1863, report him present. He was admitted to Ross Hospital at Mobile, Alabama, on. September 23, 1863, with fev. con. and returned to duty on October 2, 1863. He drew clothing on March 31, 1864, and signed by his mark. He was admitted to Ross Hospital at Mobile, Alabama, on August 3, 1864, with fev. remit. and returned to duty on August 9, 1864. Company muster roll for September/October 1864, reports him absent under civil arrest since October 19, 1864. He was admitted to Ross Hospital with anasaica [*edema or dropsy*] on January 3, 1865, and sent to general hospital on February 9, 1865, (pest house).

Lundey, [Lundy] Pinkney, Pvt. Co. I

Enlisted on October 13, 1861, at Halls Mill, Alabama, by Major Hessee for one year. His name appears on a report near Tupelo, Mississippi, June 28, 1862, "Sent to interior hospitals from Corinth by surgeon May 28th." He was discharged at Tupelo, Mississippi, on 24, 1862, born Pike County, Mississippi, age 31, five foot nine and one quarter inches, fair complexion, blue eyes, light hair, a shingle maker by occupation. Paid $70.46 for service.

Lundy, S. E. W., Pvt. Co. I see **Lundy, G. W.**

Lundy, T. J., Pvt. Co. I

Enlisted on October 13, 1861, at Halls Mill, Alabama, by Major Hessee for one year. His name appears on a report near Tupelo, Mississippi, June 28, 1862, "Sent to interior hospitals from Corinth by surgeon May 28th." He appears present on a company muster roll for bounty on September 24, 1862. He appears present on company muster rolls for July/August 1863 and September/October 1863. He was admitted to Post Hospital at Fort Morgan, Alabama, on August 6, 1863, with dysentery and returned to duty on August 16.

Luther, E. J. M., 2nd Lt./Hospital Steward Co. C/Field and Staff see **Luther J. G. M.**

Luther, J. G. M., 2nd Lt./Hospital Steward Co. C/Field and Staff
Elected 2nd Lt. Co. C on October 13, 1861. He requisitioned and drew armament at Corinth, Mississippi, cartridge boxes and cartridges. At Corinth, on April 30, 1862, he requisitioned and drew 5000 buck and ball cartridges. At Corinth, on May 3, 1862, he requisitioned and drew 10000 ball cartridges with caps. He appears present on a Regimental Return for Co. C, 21st Ala. at Tupelo, Mississippi, in June 1862. He appears present as Hospital Steward on a F & S muster rolls for July/August 1863 and September/October 1863, having joined at Choctaw Bluff, Alabama, on December 28, 1862, by Captain Small for the war. F & S muster roll for March/April 1864, reports him absent with leave on 40-day furlough from April 5, 1864. POW captured at Fort Gaines, Alabama, on August 8, 1864. He was received at New Orleans during the five days ending August 20, 1864. Released at New Orleans and sent through the lines by order of US Major General E. R. S. Canby. Surrendered at Citronelle, Alabama, by Lt. General Taylor on May 4, 1865, and paroled at Meridian, Mississippi, on May 13, 1864. Residence Marengo County, Alabama. Requisitions and pay vouchers are in his file.*

Lyghtner, J. M., Pvt. Co. G see **Lightner, J. M.**

Lyles, John, Pvt. Co. C/H see **Lyles, J. Y.**

Lyles, J. Y., Pvt. Co. C/H
Enlisted at Choctaw Bluff, Alabama, on October 30, 1862, by Captain Smith for three years or the war. He is reported absent sick on a company muster roll for December 31, 1862, to April 30, 1863. Company muster roll for May/June, 1863, reports him absent on sick leave for 15 days since June 29, 1863. Company muster roll for September/October 1863, reports that he deserted at Mobile, Alabama, on October 27, 1863, lost one canteen at $2. He drew clothing on March 31 and June 1, 1864. POW captured at Fort Gaines, Alabama, on August 8, 1864, and received at Ship Island, Mississippi, from New Orleans on October 25, 1864. He was exchanged at Ship Island on January 4, 1865. His name appears on a roll of POW's of hospital attendants and patients at Hinkley Hospital at Demopolis, Alabama, commanded by Surgeon Hinkley surrendered by Lt. General R. Taylor on May 4, 1865, and paroled at Meridian, Mississippi, on May 14, 1865. There is a descriptive list in his file that describes him as age 34, black eyes, black hair, dark complexion, 5 foot 6 inches, born in Clark County, Alabama, a farmer by occupation, paid $50 bounty. The descriptive list also includes Privates; **G. Raley, J. W. Davis, R. A. Smith, and H. Northrup**.*

MOBILE CONFEDERATES

Lyon, Lee K., Pvt. Co. K

Enlisted by C. S. Stewart at Fort Pillow, Tennessee, on March 10, 1862. Discharged on October 13, 1862, at Fort Morgan, Alabama. He was born in Demopolis, Marengo County, Alabama, age 17, five foot nine inches, fair complexion, blue eyes, sandy hair, a clerk by occupation. (Discharged due to nearsighted? illegible) His discharge is in his file.*

Lyon, Thomas F. A., Captain Co. D. and A. C. S.

Elected A. C. S. of the 21st Alabama, on October 13, 1861. He was detached on March 19, 1862. F. J. Cluis became A. C. S. He appears on a regimental return for December 1861, reported present at Depot Commissary. He again appears on a regimental return for June 1962, "Permanently detached as Division A. C. S." He appears on a register of commissioned officers on November 14, 1861. A return for November 1, 1861, reports him present at Post Commissary.

Lyon, W. H. Jr., Pvt. Co. C

Enlisted on October 16, 1862, at Marengo County, Alabama, by Capt. DeVaux for three years or the war. He appears present on a company muster roll for December 31, 1862, to April 30, 1863. He drew his $50 bounty on February 2, 1863. May/June 1863, muster roll shows him present, lost cartridge box at $2.50, cap pouch at $1, waist belt at. 75 cents, bayonet scabbard plate at $1, plus 10 cartridges and 12 caps at $!. Company muster roll for September/October 1863, reports him absent in hospital in Mobile, Alabama, since October 25, 1863. He drew clothing on March 31 and June 1, 1864. POW captured at Fort Gaines, Alabama, on August 8, 1864. He was admitted to St. Louis USA General Hospital at New Orleans on August 30, 1864, with dysentery and returned to confinement on September 6, 1864, age 36. He was received at Ship Island, Mississippi, from New Orleans on October 25, 1864, and exchanged at Ship Island on January 4, 1985. POW surrendered by Lt. General Richard Taylor in May 1865, and paroled at Demopolis, Alabama, on May 30, 1865.

Lyons, C., Pvt. Co. G/C

POW captured at Fort Gaines, Alabama, on August 8, 1864. He was received at Ship Island, Mississippi, from New Orleans on October 25, 1864, and exchanged at Ship Island on January 4, 1865.

Lyons, Patrick, Pvt. Co. B

He enlisted on October 13, 1861, at Mobile, Alabama, by Major Hessee for the war. He appears present on a company muster roll for bounty on September 24, 1862, and was paid his $50 bounty. He appears present on company muster rolls for March/April, May/June and September/October 1863. He drew clothing on March 31, April 14 and June 1, 1864, and signed by his mark. His name appears as signature on an Oath of Allegiance to the USA at New Orleans, Louisiana. Residence St. Louis, Missouri, light complexion, sandy hair, brown eyes, and five foot nine inches.

M

Macartney, Edwin, 2nd Lt. Co. F

He appears present on a company muster roll for March 1, to June 30, 1863. He also appears present on a company muster roll for September/October 1863, "detached in A. Q. M. by Col. Anderson." He was paid $80 per month as 2nd Lt. There is a pay voucher in his file.*

Macartney, M. E., Pvt./2nd Lt. Co. F/K

Enlisted on October 13, 1861, at Mobile, Alabama, by Captain Stewart for one year. He appears on a regimental return in June 1862, as clerk in Adjt. Office. Promoted to 2nd Lt. Co. F on August 30, 1862. He appears present on a company muster roll for bounty on September 24, 1862, "Promoted from private Co. K July 23, 1862." On June 20, 1864, at Fort Gaines, Alabama, he commanded Co. F and requisitioned and drew allowances of 5 blankets to make total of 49, 5 bayonets to make a total of 49, 5 cartridge boxes to make a total of 50, 5 c box belts to make a total of 50, 5 waist belts to make a total of 50, 50 cap pouches to make a total of 50, 5 bayonets scabbards to make a total of 50, 1 canteen strap to make a total of 50, 100 cartridges to make a total of 1009, and one haversack to make a total of 58. On July 25, 1864, he drew 14 new conversion tents. POW captured at Fort Gaines, Alabama, on August 8, 1864. He was received at Ship Island, Mississippi, from New Orleans on October 25, 1864, and exchanged at Ship Island on January 4, 1865. POW surrendered by Lt. General R. Taylor and paroled at Meridian, Mississippi, on May 14, 1865. There are a number of requisitions, pay vouchers, monthly summary statements, and his Parole of Honor in his file.**. There is a letter written at Choctaw Bluff, Alabama, on April 28, 1863, and signed by three officers as to stores and condition of same. Note 1st Lt. E. Macartney, Co. F is shown as a loss on Co. E field return at Fort Morgan, Alabama, "Transferred to Choctaw Bluff." [*This is filed under* **Thomas N. Macartney**.]

Macartney, Thomas N., Bvt.2nd Lt./2nd Lt. Co. F

He was elected 2nd Lt. of Co. F on November 25, 1862, (**M. V. Gabel** failed to pass the Board of Examiners). He appears present on company muster rolls for March 1, to June 30 and September/October 1863. He requisitioned and received the following for the 78 men in his Co. F; x muskets, x bayonets, x cartridge boxes, x waist belts, 46 on hand required 5 cap pouches, x bayonet scabbards, x knapsacks, 57 on hand required 1 haversack, 54 on hand required 6 canteens, x cartridges. POW captured at Fort Gaines, Alabama. He was received at Ship Island, Mississippi, from New Orleans on October 25, 1864 and exchanged at Ship Island on January 4, 1865. POW surrendered by Lt. General R. Taylor and paroled at Meridian, Mississippi, on May 10, 1865. There are letters of testimonial and his parole in his file.* "Lt. Mcartney served in the 3rd Regiment Mobile Cadets in the early part of the war and was in all the Battles about Richmond." There is note to see the personal papers of **M. C. Burke**. There are requisitions, testimonial letters, and pay vouchers in his file plus his Parole of Honor.** He was appointed Judge Advocate (place not named) on February 6, 1865, by Secretary of War. The appointment letter is also in his file.*

Macartney, N. E., Pvt./2nd Lt. see **Macartney, M. E.**

Maddison, A., Sgt. Co. I see **Madison, Alexander**

Maddison, James, Pvt. Co. I see **Madison, J. S.**

Maddison, N. W., Pvt. Co. I see **Madison, N. W.**

Madison, Alexander, Sgt. Co. I
    Enlisted on March 1, 1862, at Halls Mill, Alabama, by Lt. Cayce for the war. He appears present on company muster rolls for July/August and September/October 1863. He drew clothing on March 31, 1864. POW captured at Fort Gaines, Alabama, on August 8, 1864, and received at Ship Island, Mississippi, from New Orleans on October 25, 1864. He was exchanged at Ship Island on January 4, 1865. POW appears on a roll of POW's of Co. I 21st Alabama Infantry commanded by Captain M. V. Crenshaw, surrendered by Lt. General Richard Taylor at Citronelle, Alabama, on May 4, 1965, and paroled at Meridian, Mississippi, on May 13, 1865. His residence is shown as Marengo County, Alabama.

Madison, James, Pvt. Co. I see **Madison, J. S.**

Madison, J. S., Pvt. Co. I
    He drew clothing on April 14 and June 1, 1864. POW captured at Fort Gaines, Alabama, on August 8, 1864, and received at Ship Island, Mississippi, from New Orleans on October 25, 1864. He was exchanged at Ship Island on January 4, 1865. POW appears on a roll of POW's of Co. I, 21st Alabama Infantry commanded by Captain M. V. Crenshaw, surrendered by Lt. General Richard Taylor at Citronelle, Alabama on May 4, 1965, and paroled at Meridian, Mississippi, on May 13, 1865. Residence shown as Burleson County, Texas.

Madison, N. W., Pvt. Co. I
    He drew clothing on June 1, 1864. POW captured at Fort Gaines, Alabama, on August 8, 1864, and received at Ship Island, Mississippi, from New Orleans on October 25, 1864. He was exchanged at Ship Island on January 4, 1865. POW appears on a roll of POW's of Co. I, 21st Alabama Infantry commanded by Captain M. V. Crenshaw, surrendered by Lt. General Richard Taylor at Citronelle, Alabama, on May 4, 1965, and paroled at Meridian, Mississippi, on May 13, 1865. Residence shown as Marengo County, Alabama.

Madison, W. G., Pvt. Co. I
    He enlisted at Fort Morgan, Alabama, on March 24, 1863, by Lt. Collins for the war. Company muster roll for July/August 1863, reports him present, "sick in hospital." He was admitted to Post Hospital at Fort Morgan, Alabama, on August 30, 1863, with fev thypoid and died of disease on September, 25, 1863.

Madkins, R., Pvt. Co. I see **Matkins, R.**

21ST ALABAMA INFANTRY VOLUNTEERS

Magginson, D. A., Pvt. Co. C see **Megginson, D. A.**

Maguire, John P., Pvt. Co. E see **McGuire, John P.**

Mahoney, John, Pvt. Co. B
    Enlisted on September 10, 1862, at Mobile, Alabama, by Captain Johnston for the war. He appears present on a company muster roll for bounty on September 24, 1862. Company muster roll for March/April 1863, report him absent "under arrest at Choctaw Bluff. To forfeit three months pay by sentence of G. C. M. [*General Court Marshal*]" Company muster rolls for May/June and September/October 1863, report him present. He is due $60.63 for clothing. He drew clothing on March 31, April 14 and June 1, 1864 (signed by his mark). POW captured at Fort Gaines, Alabama, on August 8, 1864. He was received at Ship Island, Mississippi, on October 25, 1864, where he applied to take the Oath of Allegiance to the USA. He appears on a roll of POW's at Elmira, New York, on November 30, 1864, captured at Fort Gaines, on August 8, 1864, and who are desirous to take the Oath of Allegiance, "was conscripted August 1, 1862, came to Elmira on the name of **William Welch**, 21st Ala. Inf. Co. A, having exchanged places with him for the purpose of getting north. Desires to go to Stillwater, Minn." Signed the Oath of Allegiance at Elmira, New York, on May 19, 1865, and released, residence Huntsville, Alabama, light complexion, light hair, blue eyes, and five foot eight inches. Pvt. John Mahoney is shown as having been exchanged at Ship Island, Mississippi, on January 4, 1865. [*Was this his partner William Welch?*]

Mahony, John, Pvt. Co. B see **Mahoney, John**

Maines, Albert, Pvt. Co. H
    His name appears on a regimental return for June 1862. He was taken prisoner, May 13, at Farmington.

Majors, Edward, Pvt. Co. F
    He enlisted on February 2, 1862, at Choctaw Bluff, Alabama, by Capt. Dace for the war. He is recorded present on a company muster roll for March 1, to June 30, 1863. Muster roll for September/October 1863, shows him absent "absent sick in hospital at Mobile since July 16, 63." He drew clothing on March 3 and June 1, 1864. POW captured at Fort Gaines, Alabama, on August 8, 1864. He was admitted to St. Louis USA General Hospital in New Orleans on September 25, 1864, with int. quot and acute diarrhoea and returned to confinement on October 5, 1864. He was again admitted to St. Louis Hospital with pneumonia on October 11, 1864, and returned to confinement on November 2, 1864, age 39. He was received at Ship Island, Mississippi, on October 29, 1864, from New Orleans and died of dysentery at Ship Island on December 10, 1864. He was buried in grave No. 75. [*Note he must have not been among the prisoners received at Ship Island on October 29.*]

Maley, Edward, Pvt. Co. B see **Mealey, Edward**

Malone, Patrick, Pvt. Co. B

Enlisted on October 13, 1861, by Major Hessee for one year. He was discharged due to disability on June 25, 1862, at Tupelo Mississippi. Born in Ireland, age 29, five foot seven and one half inches, light complexion, blue eyes, light hair and by occupation a laborer. His discharge is in his file.*

Maloney, Ennis, Pvt. Co. B

Enlisted on October 13, 1861, at Mobile, Alabama, by Major Hessee for the war. He appears present September 24, 1862, on a company muster roll for bounty, "Not entitled to bounty, under age." He was paid $1.25 on March 11, 1862, for commutation of rations out of hospital at Mobile, Alabama, going to join his regiment at Memphis, Tennessee, five days at 25 cents.

Maloney, T. T., Pvt. Co. A

His name appears on a regimental return for June 1862, "May 4, at Corinth, Deserted from camp probably to enemy."

Mandick, John, Pvt. Co. H

Enlisted on October 13, 1861, at Mobile, Alabama, by Major Hessee for one year. He was discharged due to disability at Camp Moore on November 14, 1861. Born Dalmatia, Europe, age 28, five foot five inches, dark complexion, blue eyes, black hair and by occupation when enlisted a laborer. His discharge is in his file signed by F. A. Ross, Surgeon.

Mann, John, 2nd Lt. Co. A

Enlisted on October 13, 1861, elected 2nd Lt. on May 26, 1861, resigned on March 30, 1862. He appears present on a return at Fort Gains, Alabama, in November 1861. A regimental return for December 1861, reports him absent on account of sickness in his family since December 28. There is paperwork in his file.*

Manning, Dennis, Pvt. Co. B

Enlisted on October 13, 1861, at Mobile, Alabama, by Major Hessee for one year. He was wounded slightly in the right foot at Shiloh on April 6, 1862, while charging the 1st Camp at 8 A. M. A report near Tupelo, Mississippi, on June 28, 1862, reports him wounded at Shiloh joined his regiment, shortly afterwards his wound reopened and he was sent to general hospital in Mobile. He appears present on a company muster roll for September 24, 1864, for bounty, "sick in quarters in Garrison Hospital." Company muster roll for March/April 1863, reports him absent sent to general hospital in Mobile on January 4, 1863. He was discharged by medical director on May 10, 1863, at Mobile due to gunshot wound of abdomen received at Shiloh yet unhealed. Born in Ireland, age 22, five foot nine inches, fair complexion, blue eyes, light hair and a laborer by occupation. His discharge and pay vouchers are in his file.* *There are some L. Manning documents in this file.*

Manning, James, Pvt. Co. A.

Enlisted on October 13, 1861, at Mobile, Alabama, by Major Hessee for one year. He was discharged due to syphilis ?? and enlargement of knee joint, on December 24, 1861, at Mobile. Born in Lowndes County, Alabama, five foot nine and one half inches high, fair complexion, blue eyes, light hair, a steamboat man by occupation. His discharge is in his file.*

Manning, Reeder, Sgt./Pvt. Co. K.

Enlisted on October 13, 1861, at Mobile, Alabama, by Captain Stewart for the war. His name appears on a regimental return for June 1862, as being in detached service as clerk for Medical Purveyor, W. H. Anderson. He appears absent on company muster roll for bounty on September 24, 1862, "Detached in Med. Dept. Dec. 5/61 by Genl. Withers." Company muster rolls for November/December 1862, July/August and September/October 1863, all show him absent with the same explanation.

Manning, Thomas, Pvt. Co. A

Enlisted on September 3, 1862, at Jefferson County by A. R. Goodwin for the war. His name appears on a company muster roll for December 31, 1862, to April 30, 1863, as having deserted on January 30, 1863, from Choctaw Bluff. Note there is additional information on this man's desertion on January 29, 1863, from Choctaw Bluff, Alabama, in the file of **James. A. Poellnitz**. Special Order No. 62.

Manning, William, Pvt. Co. A

Enlisted on August 28, 1862, at Jefferson County, by A. R. Goodwin for the war. His name appears on a company muster roll for December 31, 1862, to April 30, 1863, as having deserted on January 30, 1863, from Choctaw Bluff. Note there is additional information on **H. Manning** desertion on January 29, 1863, from Choctaw Bluff, Alabama, in the File of **James. A. Poellnitz**. Special Order No. 62.

Maples, Simon, Pvt. Co. I.

POW captured at Fort Gaines, Alabama, on August 8, 1864. He was admitted to St. Louis USA General Hospital at New Orleans on September 25, 1864, with intmit fever (rubeola) and returned to confinement on September 30, 1864. His name appears on a morning report as a prisoner received from hospital at Steam Levee Press No. 4 at New Orleans on September 30, 1864. He was received at Ship Island, Mississippi, from New Orleans on October 25, 1864 and died of dysentery at Ship Island on December 26, 1864, and was buried in grave No. 112.

Marion, G., Pvt. Co. C see **Marion, Jerome**

Marion, Jerome, Pvt. Co. C

Enlisted on October 13, 1861, at Mobile, Alabama, by Captain Rembert for one year. He appears present on a company muster roll for bounty on September 24, 1862. Company muster rolls for December 31, 1862, to April 30, 1863, May/June and

September/October 1863, all show him present. He drew clothing on March 31 and June 1, 1864, and signed by his mark. POW captured at Fort Gaines, Alabama, on August 8, 1864, he was received at Ship Island, Mississippi, on October 25, 1864, from New Orleans and exchanged on January 4, 1865. POW surrendered by Lt. General Richard Taylor CSA at Citronelle, Alabama, on May 4, 1865, and paroled at Meridian, Mississippi, on May 13, 1863. He was shown as a resident of Marengo County, Alabama. There is a pay voucher in his file.*

Markham, J. P., Pvt. Co. E

He drew clothing on March 31 and June 1, 1864. POW captured at Fort Gaines, Alabama, on August 8, 1864, he was received at Ship Island, Mississippi, on October 25, 1864, from New Orleans and exchanged on January 4, 1865.

Markham, P., Pvt. Co. E see **Markham, J. P.**

Marshall, Robert, Pvt. Co. K

He was killed on April 6, 1862, at 3 P. M. at the Center Field at Battle of Shiloh. Wounded in shoulder.

Marxhall, W., Pvt. Co. K.

Enlisted on August 29, 1864, at Mobile, Alabama, by Major Stone for the war. A company muster roll for September/October 1864, reports him absent, temporarily attached to company by Major Stone, enrolling officer. Detached to report to Major Harris at Dog River by General Gardner on August 29, 1864.

Martin, Edward, Drummer

Enlisted on September 5, 1863, at Mobile, Alabama, by Captain Blacker for three years. He appears present on a company muster roll for September/October 1863. He appears on a descriptive list on September 18, 1863, age 15, gray eyes, sandy hair, light complexion, five foot four inches, born New Orleans, Louisiana, a newsboy by occupation. Paid $50 bonus. He drew clothing on March 31 and June 1, 1864, and signed by his mark. POW captured at Fort Gaines, Alabama, on August 8, 1864, he was received at Ship Island, Mississippi, on October 25, 1864, from New Orleans and exchanged on January 4, 1865.

Martin, J., Corp. Co. G

His name appears on a report near Tupelo, Mississippi, June 28, 1862, "absent on furlough since May 29, 1862, in Mobile." A regimental return for June 1862, shows that he was sent to the rear on May 28.

Martin, James N., Pvt. Co. F

Enlisted on January 9, 1863, at Choctaw Bluff, Alabama, by Captain Dade for the war. He was paid on extra duty as a butcher at Choctaw Bluff in February 1863. He drew clothing on March 31, 1863, and signed by his mark. Company muster rolls for March 1, to June 30 and September/October 1863, report him present. He died on April 27, 1864. Born Georgia, age 48, five foot one inch, light complexion, gray eyes, light hair, and a farmer by occupation. Final settlement paid to Eliza Martin widow filed on June 11, 1864, returned on November 11, 1864, $60.97 found due. His discharge due to death was issued at Fort Gaines, Alabama. It and other documents are in his file.*

Martin, Jules, Pvt. Co. H

He enlisted on October 13, 1861, at Mobile, by Major Hessee. He was discharged at Fort Gaines, Alabama, due to disability on February 21, 1862. Born, Paris, France, age 29, dark complexion, gray eyes, black hair, five foot eight inches by profession a gunmaker. There are several copies of his discharge in his file.*

Martin, P., Pvt. _

Enlisted August 12, 1864, in Captain Sossaman's Detachment of the 21st Alabama Infantry at Mobile, Alabama, by Major Stone for the war. Muster roll for September/October 1864, at Mobile shows that he was sent to Hospital Canty on October 5, 1864, by order of Dr. Smith.

Martin, Ransom, H., Sgt./2nd Lt. Co. G

He drew clothing on March 3, March 31 and June 1, 1864. POW captured at Fort Gaines, Alabama, on August 8, 1864, he was received at Ship Island, Mississippi, on October 25, 1864, from New Orleans and was exchanged on January 4, 1865. POW surrendered by Lt. General Richard Taylor at Citronelle, Alabama, and paroled at Meridian, Mississippi, on May 10, 1865. His parole is in his file.*

Martin, R. R., Pvt. Co. K

Enlisted on September 27, 1862, at Fayette County, Alabama, by M. J. Davis for the war. He appears present on a company muster roll for November/December 1862.

Martin, William B., Pvt. Co. K

Enlisted on September 27, 1862, at Fayette County, Alabama by Captain Dorgan, for the war. He drew clothing on July 10, 1863. He appears present on a company muster roll for July/August 1863. Company muster roll for September/October 1863, reports him present detailed in hospital at the post by order of Colonel Williams. He was admitted to Post Hospital at Fort Morgan, Alabama, with diarrhoea on September 15, 1863. Muster roll at Fort Morgan Hospital for September/October 1863, reports him present as a nurse. He drew clothing on December 19, 1863. He appears on a hospital muster roll at Fort Morgan, Alabama, for March/April 1864, attached to hospital as a nurse, returned to his company on January 25, 1864. (Here he is shown as having enlisted in Shelby County on September 18, 1862.) He drew clothing on June 20, 1864. He appears on a muster roll of Co. A, 1st Regiment Louisiana Heavy Artillery (Regulars) for July and August 1864, absent attached to the regiment from Co. K, 21st Alabama by orders from Dist. Headquarters, sick in hospital at Mobile since August 30, 1864. Company muster roll for Co. A, 1st Reg. Louisiana Heavy Artillery for September/October 1864, shows him transferred to his Co. K, 21st Alabama on October 17, 1864. Muster roll for September/October 1864, reports him absent detached in Q. M. Department at Mobile by General Maury on October 27, 1864, for 10 days. POW surrendered among a group of stragglers by Lt. General R. Taylor on May 4, 1865, and paroled at Selma, Alabama, in June 1865.

Martin, William M., Corporal Co. E

Enlisted on October 13, 1861, at Mobile, Alabama, by Captain Chamberlain for the war. He appears present on a company muster roll for bounty on September 24, 1862. He is reported present on company muster rolls for November/December 1862, July/August and September/October 1863. He drew clothing on March 31 and June 1, 1864. POW captured at Fort Gaines, Alabama, on August 8, 1864, he was received at Ship Island, Mississippi, on October 25, 1864, from New Orleans and exchanged on January 4, 1865.

Mask, D. (Dudley) Pvt. Co. C

Enlisted on July 29, 1863, at Linden, Alabama, by Lt. McLeod for three years or the war. He appears present on a company muster roll for September/October 1863. He appears on a descriptive list at Point Clear, Alabama, on October 12, 1863, born in Richmond County, North Carolina, age 35, hazel eyes, light hair, dark complexion, five foot eleven inches, a farmer by occupation. He drew clothing on June 1, 1864. POW captured at Fort Gaines, Alabama, on August 8, 1864. He was admitted to St. Louis USA General Hospital at New Orleans on September 2, 1864, with dysentery and returned to confinement on September 9, 1864. He was received at Ship Island, Mississippi, on October 25, 1864, from New Orleans and exchanged on January 4, 1865.

Mask, P. (Phil), Pvt. Co. C

Enlisted on July 29, 1863, at Linden, Alabama, by Lt. McLeod for three years or the war. He appears present on a company muster roll for September/October 1863. He appears on a descriptive list at Point Clear, Alabama, on October 12, 1863, born in Richmond County, North Carolina, age 37, blue eyes, dark hair, fair complexion, five foot ten inches, a farmer by occupation. He drew clothing on March 31 and June 1, 1864. POW captured at Fort Gaines, Alabama, on August 8, 1864. He was received at Ship Island, Mississippi, on October 25, 1864, from New Orleans and exchanged on January 4, 1865. He was surrendered by Lt. General R. Taylor and paroled at Demopolis, Alabama, on June 15, 1865. He was a resident of Marengo, County, Alabama.

Mason, E. A., Pvt. Co. C

He appears on a report near Tupelo, Mississippi, June 28, 1862, "sent to interior hospital by Surg. from Corinth." Regimental return for June 1862, reports him absent on sick furlough. There are research notes in his file.*

Mately, E., Pvt. Co. G.

POW captured at Fort Gaines, Alabama, on August 8, 1864. POW died at Ship Island, Mississippi, on December 20, 1864.

Mathers, P. E., Pvt. Co. C. see **Mathews, J. E.**

Mathews, J. E., Pvt. Co. C

He appears on a regimental return for June 1862, as detached service with Pioneer Corps. His name appears on the muster roll (no date) of Captain S. M. Steele's Co. B in the Pioneer Battalion commanded by Major Merriwether, Jackson's Brigade. He appears on a pay receipt roll for June 1864.

Mathews, Jesse W., Pvt. Co. G

POW surrendered by Lt. General Richard Taylor at Citronelle, Alabama, on May 4, 1865, and paroled at Meridian, Mississippi, on May 13, 1865. Residence shown as Prattville, Autauga, County, Alabama.

Mathews, J. H., Pvt. Co. K

Enlisted on August 30, 1864, at Mobile, Alabama, by Major Stone for the war. He appears on a company muster roll for September/October 1864, as having been transferred to Conscript Camp at Notasulga, Alabama, by order of Major Stone on October 18, 1864.

Matkins, R., Pvt. Co. I

Enlisted on March 1, 1862, at Halls Mill, Alabama, by Lt. Cayce for the war. A regimental return for June 1, 1862, shows him on extra duty as regimental teamster. A return for December 1862, reports him absent without leave on December 27, 1862. He appears present on a company muster roll for bounty on September 24, 1862. Company muster roll for July/August 1863, reports him present. Company muster roll for September/October 1863, report him present but absent without leave for four days. POW captured at Fort Gaines, Alabama, on August 8, 1864. He was received at Ship Island from New Orleans on October 25, 1864, and exchanged on January 4, 1865.

Maton, R., Pvt. Co. C. see **Mayton, Robert**

Mattocks, James, Pvt. Co. B

Enlisted on September 9, 1862, at Randolph (County?) by O. P. Knight for the war. He appears on a company muster roll for March/April 1863, where he is shown as absent on sick furlough for 30 days from April 15, 1863. Muster roll for May/June 1863, has similar note from June 1. Company muster roll for September/October 1863, reports him deserted absent without leave since June 1, 1863.

Maxwell, M. F., Pvt. Co. B

Enlisted on September 3, 1862 at Jefferson (County?) Alabama, by A. R. Goodwin for the war. Company muster roll for March/April 1863, reports him present. Muster roll for May/June 1863, reports him present sick in hospital. Company muster roll for September/October 1863, reports him present and due $59.63 for clothing not drawn in kind. He was admitted to Post Hospital at Fort Morgan, Alabama, with intermitten fever on November 9, 1863, and returned to duty on November 13. He drew clothing on March 31, 1864, and signed by his mark.

May, Benjamin, Pvt. Co. D

Enlisted June 6, 1862, at Mobile, Alabama, by Captain Butt for the war. He appears present on a company muster roll for bounty on September 24, 1862. Company muster roll for November/December 1862, reports him present. Company muster roll for July/August 1863, reports that he was transferred to the Engineer Corps by order of General Maury. POW captured at Blakeley, Alabama, on April 9, 1865. He was received at Ship Island, Mississippi, on April 15, 1865, (age 29) and transferred to Vicksburg, Mississippi, on May 1. He was received at Vicksburg on parole on May 6.

May, B. H., Pvt. Co. D. see **May, Benjamin**

May, J. D., Corp. Co. H

Drew clothing May 3, and June 1, 1864. POW captured at Fort Gaines, Alabama, on August 8, 1864, arrived at Ship Island, Mississippi, from New Orleans on October 25, 1864. He was admitted to St. Louis USA General Hospital at New Orleans on August 19, 1864, with intermitten fever and acute diarrhoea (age 21) and returned to confinement on August 26. He was again admitted to St. Louis Hospital on September 25, 1864, with diarrhoea and returned to confinement on October 17, 1864. He was exchanged at Ship Island on January 4, 1865. He was admitted to Ross Hospital at Mobile on January 6, 1865, with scurvy and furloughed on January 21, 1865, for 15 days. POW surrendered by Lt. General Richard Taylor at Citronelle, Alabama, on May 4, 1865, and paroled at Meridian, Mississippi, on May 13, 1865. He is shown as a resident of Pike County, Alabama.

May, Peter D., Pvt./1st Sgt. Co. C

Enlisted on November 22, 1861, at Fort Gaines, Alabama, by Captain Rembert for one year. A regimental return for June 1862, reports him absent on sick furlough. He appears on a report near Tupelo, Mississippi, on June 28, 1864, "sent to interior hospital by Surg. from Corinth." He appears present on company muster roll for bounty on September 24, 1862. A company muster roll for December 31, 1862, to April 30, 1863, reports him present. Company muster roll for May/June 1863, reports that he was transferred to 1st Battalion Alabama Artillery on June 6, 1863. He drew clothing on June 1, 1864. POW captured at Fort Gaines on August 8, 1864. He was received at Ship Island, Mississippi, from New Orleans on October 25, 1864, and exchanged at Ship Island on January 4, 1865. POW surrendered by Lt. General Richard Taylor at Citronelle, Alabama, in May 1865, and paroled at Demopolis, Alabama, on June 15, 1865. He was a resident of Marengo County, Alabama.

Mayton, Robert, Pvt. Co. C

Enlisted on October 13, 1861, at Mobile, Alabama, by Captain Rembert for twelve months. He appears present on company muster roll for bounty on September 24, 1862. Company muster rolls for December 31, 1862, to April 30, 1863, May/June 1863 and September/October 1863, report him present. POW captured at Fort Gaines, Alabama, on August 8, 1864. He appears on a list of prisoners at New Orleans confined at the Steam Levee Press No. 4 on September 29, 1864, and sent to hospital. He was admitted to St. Louis USA General Hospital, at New Orleans with diarrhoea on

September 29, and returned to confinement on September 30, 1864, age 22. He appears on a morning report as having been received at Steam Levee Press No. 4 from hospital on September 30, 1864. He was received at Ship Island, Mississippi, from New Orleans on October 25, 1864, and exchanged at Ship Island on January 4, 1865. POW captured at Blakeley, Alabama, on April 9, 1865. He was received at Ship Island on April 15, 1865, and was transferred to Vicksburg, Mississippi, on May 1, 1865. POW surrendered by Lt. General Richard Taylor at Citronelle, Alabama.

McAfee, George, Pvt. Co. B.
Enlisted on August 6, 1862, at Fort Morgan, Alabama, by Captain Johnston for the war. He appears present on company muster roll for bounty on September 24, 1862. Company muster rolls for March/April, May/June and September/October 1863, all show him present. In October 1863, he is show as due $46.63 for clothing not drawn in kind. He drew clothing on March 31, 1864, signed by his mark and on June 1, 1864. Deserter came into the Federal lines with the fleet before the capture of Fort Gaines and took the Oath of Allegiance to the USA on August 3, 1864.

McAffee, George, Pvt. Co. B see **McAfee, George**

McBoy, M., Pvt. Co. E see **McVoy, M. W.**

McBride, Patrick, Pvt. Co. B
Enlisted at Mobile, Alabama, on August 16, 1862, by Captain DeVaux for the war. He appears present on company muster roll for bounty on September 24, 1862, "Recruit received Bounty at time of enlistment, bounty paid." Company muster rolls for March/April, May/June, and September/October 1863, report him present. In October he is due $46.63 for clothing not drawn in kind. Drew clothing March 31 and June 1, 1864, and signed by his mark. POW captured at Fort Gaines on August 8, 1864. He was received at Ship Island, Mississippi, from New Orleans on October 25, 1864, and exchanged at Ship Island on January 4, 1865. POW surrendered by Lt. General Richard Taylor at Citronelle, Alabama, on May 4, 1865, and paroled at Meridian, Mississippi, on May 13, 1865. He was shown as a resident of Marengo County, Alabama. He also shown as a resident of Memphis, Tennessee.

McBride, W., Pvt. Co. K
He enlisted at Mobile, Alabama, on September 10, 1864, by Major Stone for the war. A company muster roll September/October 1864, reports that he was transferred to the Conscript Camp at Notasulga, Alabama, by order of Major Stone, Enrolling Officer on October 18, 1864.

McCabe, Pvt. Co. D
A company muster roll for September/October 1864, reports him absent, "Sent to Gen. Hospital (Mobile August 17/64. Assigned to Company by order."

McCabe, John, Pvt. Co. B

Enlisted at Fort Morgan, Alabama, on September 11, 1862, by Captain Johnston, for the war. He is reported present on a company muster roll for bounty on September 24, 1862. He appears absent in Mobile on sick furlough on a company muster roll for March/April 1863. Muster roll for May/June 1863, reports him present sick in quarters. Company muster roll for September/October 1863, reports him present, detailed by order of Colonel Anderson, due $92.63 for clothing not drawn in kind. He was admitted to Ross Hospital, Mobile, Alabama, on September 10, 1864, with ascites, febris intermittens quot and sent to General Hospital at Greenville, on September 13, 1864. He drew clothing at General Hospital at Greenville, Alabama, on September 25, 1864.

McCabe, M., Pvt. Co. H

He was enlisted on October 13, 1861, at Mobile, Alabama, by Captain DeVaux to serve twelve months. He was born in Tulemone, Kings County, Ireland, age 28, five foot eight and one half inches, light complexion, blue eyes, dark hair and by occupation a laborer. Discharged due to disability (broken down constitution and fistula in ?) on April 26, 1862. His discharge is in his file.*

McCarron, Neill, Sgt. Co. B

Enlisted on October 13, 1861, at Mobile, Alabama, by Major Hessee for twelve months. He appears present on a company muster roll for bounty on September 24, 1862. Wounded in right foot slightly, at Shiloh, on April 6, 1862, at 7 A. M. charging in attack on 1st Battery. He was discharged on November 1, 1862. His discharge is in his file but unreadable.*

McCartney, T. N., Bvt. 2nd Lt./2nd Lt. Co. F see **Macartney, Thomas N.**

MaCauley, F. H., Sgt. Co. E

POW admitted to St. Louis USA General Hospital at New Orleans on October 11, 1864, with rubeola and pneumonia, transferred October 15. Returned to prison on October 15, rubeola struck through on page. Age 27.

McCordy, William, Pvt. Co. E

Enlisted on May 2, 1861, at Corinth, by Captain Chamberlain for twelve months. A regimental return for June 1862, reports him in hospital in Mobile. He appears present on company muster roll for bounty on September 1862. November/December 1862, July/August 1863 and September/October 1863, muster rolls report him absent detached as pilot on Alabama, River on orders of Gen. Buckner on October 28, 1862. There are a number of pay vouchers in his file.*

McCormack, James, Pvt. Co. B

Enlisted on September 18, 1862, at Fort Morgan, Alabama, by Lt. Vidmer for the war. He appears present on company muster roll for bounty on September 24,1862. Company muster roll for July/August 1862 and September/October 1862, report him present. A death benefit claim was filed by his widow Clarendal McCormack on May 3, 1864.

21ST ALABAMA INFANTRY VOLUNTEERS

McCoy, F. J., Captain/Major Co. F & Field and Staff

A regimental return for December 1861, shows him absent on 10 day leave signed by General Withers from December 19. Elected Captain on October 10, 1861, elected Major on May 8, 1862. Wounded slightly in the side at Shiloh April 6, 1862, at 4 P. M. at Old Field. A regimental return for June 1862, reports that he was sent to interior hospital on May 28, on surgeon's certificate this is also shown on a report June 28, 1862, near Tupelo, Mississippi. Dropped from the roll on May 8, 1862. There are several pay vouchers in his file with other paperwork.*

McCrary, Edward, Pvt. Co. D

Enlisted at Mobile, Alabama, on October 13, 1861, by Captain Butt for one year. He appears absent without leave on company muster roll for bounty on September 1862. Drew clothing on March 31 and June 10, 1864. Transferred to Co. B, 6th Alabama, Cavalry on July 23, 1864.

McCraw, William M., Pvt. Co. A

Enlisted on September 21, 1862, in Jefferson County, Alabama, by A. R. Goodwin for the war. Company muster roll for December 31, 1862, to April 30, 1863, reports him present. Muster rolls for May/June 1863 and September/October 1863, report him present. Drew clothing April 14, 1864, and at Camp Anderson on June 14, 1864, signed by his mark. POW captured at Fort Morgan, Alabama, on August 28, 1864. Sent to Elmira, New York, from New Orleans on September 27, 1864. He arrived at Elmira, New York, on October 8, 1864, and died of pneumonia at Elmira on February 2, 1865. He was buried in grave No. 1810.

McCrory, R., Pvt. Co. I see **McRory, William**

McCrory, William, Pvt. Co. I see **McRory, William**

McCullough, David S., Sgt./2nd Lt. Co. A/B

Enlisted on October 13, 1861, at Mobile, Alabama, by Major Hessee for the war. He appears present on company muster roll for bounty on September 24, 1862. Company muster rolls for December 31, 1862, to April 30, 1863, May/June 1863 and September/October 1863, all report him present. He was elected 2nd Lt. on January 22, 1864. He requisitioned arms and supplies at Fort Gaines on June 21, 1864; to fill the company requirements; 58 muskets, 58 bayonets, 58 cartridge boxes, 8 C. B. belts, 58 waist belts, 58 bayonet scabbards, 58 cap pouches, 57 knapsacks, 57 haversacks, 57 canteens and 57 canteen straps. (*Much was already on hand*). POW captured at Fort Gaines on August 8, 1864. He was received at Ship Island, Mississippi, from New Orleans on November 25, 1864, and exchanged at Ship Island on January 4, 1865. POW surrendered by Lt. General Richard Taylor at Citronelle, Alabama, on May 4, 1865, and paroled at Meridian, Mississippi, on May 10, 1865. His Parole is in his file with other paper work including his commission to 2nd Lt.**

McCollough, D. M., Sgt./2nd Lt. see **McCullough, David S.**

McCurdy, William, Pvt. Co. E see **McCordy, William H.**

McDurmott, M., Pvt. Co. F
Enlisted on October 13, 1861, at Baldwin County, Alabama, by Captain McCoy for one year. He appears present on company muster roll for bounty on September 24, 1862, "claims to be overage." He appears on a regimental return for June 1862, "on detached service: Nurse in hospital." He signed by his mark. There is a pay voucher in his file.*

McDonald, Cornelius, Pvt. Co. B
Enlisted at Mobile, Alabama, on October 8, 1861, by Major Hulse for one year. Born in Ireland, age 37, five foot four and three quarters inch, light complexion, blue eyes, light hair, a laborer by occupation. Discharged due to disability on December 3, 1861, approved by General Withers. His discharge is in his file. He signs by his mark.*

McDonald, F. M., Pvt. Co. H
He drew clothing on March 31, May 3 and June 1, 1864. POW captured at Fort Gaines on August 8, 1864. He was received at Ship Island, Mississippi, from New Orleans on October 25, 1864, and exchanged at Ship Island on January 4, 1865. POW captured at Greenville, Alabama, on April 25, 1865. There is paperwork in his file.*

McDonald, H., Pvt. Co. H see **McDonald, F. M.**

McDonald, Thomas W., Pvt. Co. A
Enlisted on August 8, 1863, at Mobile, Alabama, by Captain DeVaux for the war. He appears present on company muster roll for bounty on September 24, 1862. Company muster rolls for December 31, 1862, to April 30, 1863 and May/June 1863, report him present.

McDuffee, C. F., Pvt. Co. C
His name appears on a regimental return for June 1862, "June 19, 1862, Columbus (Mississippi?) died hospital." Claim filed by Catherine McDuffee his widow on March 5, 1863. She was paid $114.96. There is a signed letter from Catherine E. McDuffy with direction that duplicate be sent to her at Clio, PO Marengo County, Alabama, February 16, 1868. There is other paperwork in his file that is unreadable.*

McDuffee, W. K., Pvt. Co. C see **McDuffie, W. K.**

McDuffie, W. K., Pvt./Sgt. Co. C
Enlisted on October 13, 1861, at Mobile, Alabama, by Captain Rembert for 12 months. He appears present on company muster roll for bounty on September 24, 1862. Company muster rolls for December 31, 1862, to April 30, 1863, May/June 1863 and September/October 1863, report him present. He was promoted from 3rd Corporal to 1st Corporal on June 6, 1863. He drew clothing on May 21, and June 1, 1864. POW captured at Fort Gaines on August 8, 1864. He was admitted to St. Louis USA General Hospital at New Orleans on September 6, 1864, with dysentery and returned to

confinement on September 9, 1864, age 22. He was received at Ship Island, Mississippi, from New Orleans on October 25, 1864, and exchanged at Ship Island on January 4, 1865. POW surrendered by Lt. General Richard Taylor at Citronelle, Alabama, on May 4, 1865, and paroled at Meridian, Mississippi, on May 13, 1865. Here he is shown as 2nd Sgt. Co. C a resident of Marengo County, Alabama.

McEhaney, W. T., Pvt. Co. F

Enlisted on March 11, 1863, at Choctaw Bluff, Alabama, by Captain Dade for the war. Company muster roll for March 1, to June 30, 1863, shows him present, never been paid and lost one haversack at 20 cents. Muster roll for September/October 1863, shows him present paid on August 31, 1863, and lost one haversack at $1 and one canteen at $2. He drew clothing on May 21 and June 1, 1864. He drew clothing on March 31 and June 1, 1864, and signed by his mark. POW captured at Fort Gaines on August 8, 1864. He was received at Ship Island, Mississippi, from New Orleans on October 25, 1864, and exchanged at Ship Island on January 4, 1865. He appears on a roll of detached men at Columbus, Mississippi, on May 19, 1865, a POW surrendered by Lt. General Richard Taylor in May 1865.

McFee, George, Pvt. Co. B see **McAfee**

McGahey, W. T., Pvt. Co. F

Enlisted on October 15, 1862, at Talladega, Alabama, by W. T. Whathall for the war. Company muster roll for March 1, 1863, to June 30, 1863, reports him present, on extra duty in A. Q. M. Department since June 28, 1863, as carpenter by order of Colonel Anderson. Paid 25 cents per day for extra duty as laborer at Choctaw Bluff for the month of December 1862. POW surrendered by Lt. General Richard Taylor at Citronelle, Alabama, on May 4, 1865, and paroled at Meridian, Mississippi, on May 13, 1865. He is reported to be a resident of Perry County, Alabama.

McGAlier, W. T., Pvt. Co. F see **McGahey, W. T.**

McGinty, B. F., Pvt. Co. F

Enlisted at Choctaw Bluff, Alabama, on February 2, 1863, by Captain Dade for the war. Company muster roll for March 1, to June 20, 1863, reports him present. He is reported present on a company muster roll for September/October 1863. His name appears on a list of soldiers employed at Mobile as a mechanic in July 1864, and as a blacksmith in September 1864. POW surrendered as a nurse or patient of Moore Hospital, at Citronelle, Alabama, by Lt. General Richard Taylor on May 4, 1865, and paroled at Meridian, Mississippi, on May 16, 1864. He is reported to be a resident of Chambers County, Alabama. There is paperwork in his file.*

McGraw, E., Pvt. Co. D

His name appears on a regimental return for June 1862, "Sent to interior Hospital at the evacuation of Corinth."

McGuire, John P., Pvt. Co. E

Enlisted on August 4, 1863, at Fort Morgan, Alabama, by Captain Sossaman for the war. He appears present on a company muster roll for July/August 1863, (never paid). Muster roll for September/October 1863, reports him present. He drew clothing on March 31 and June 1, 1864. POW captured at Fort Gaines, Alabama, on August 8, 1864. He was received at Ship, Island, Mississippi, from New Orleans on October 25, 1864, and exchanged on January 4, 1865. POW surrendered by Lt. General Richard Taylor at Citronelle, Alabama, on May 4, 1865, and paroled at Meridian, Mississippi, on May 13, 1865. He is reported to be a resident of Mobile County, Alabama.

McGuire, Joseph, Pvt. Co. E

Killed at Shiloh on April 6, 1862, in 7:30 A. M. in attack on 15 (1st?) Battery. Shot in the groin. His data is filed with **Pvt. John P. McGuire.**

McInnis, M., Pvt. Co. E

His name appears on a regimental return for June 1862, "Sent to interior Hospital from Corinth."

McInnis, M., 1st Lt. Co. E

He appears present on a company muster roll for bounty on September 24, 1862. He appears absent without leave for four days since October 30. 1862, on a field return for October 1862. He appears present at Harbor Brigade Headquarters at Fort Morgan, Alabama, on a field return for November 1862. By requisition he filled his company's requirements at Alabama Port on May 6, 1864; 60 muskets, 60 bayonets, 60 cartridge boxes, 9 CB belts, 60 waist belts, 60 cap pouches, 60 bayonet scabbards, 84 knapsacks, 84 haversacks, and 84 canteens and shaps. He received by requisition 3000 cartridges at Fort Gaines on May 22, 1864. He was elected 1st Lt. on August 30, 1864. Muster rolls for July/August and September/October 1863, report him present. POW captured at Fort Gaines, Alabama, on August 8, 1864. He was admitted to St. Louis USA General Hospital at New Orleans on September 2, 1864, with intermit fever, age 36. Returned to military prison on September 9, 1864. He was received at Ship, Island, Mississippi, from New Orleans on October 25, 1864, and exchanged on January 4, 1865. He was surrendered by Lt. General Richard Taylor on May 10, 1865, and paroled at Meridian, Mississippi,. His signed Parole of Honor is in his file with other misc. pay vouchers, requisitions and other paperwork.*

McIntosh, John R. B., Pvt. Co. E

He was enlisted at Mobile, Alabama, on October 13, 1861. He was born in Baltimore, Maryland, age 42, five foot seven and one half inches, fair complexion, blue eyes, black hair and by occupation a pilot. He was wounded slightly in the knee at Shiloh on April 6, 1862, at 7 A. M. while advancing on the 1st Battery. He was discharged at Tupelo, Mississippi, on July 2, 1862. His discharge is in his file.*

McIntosh, Neal, Pvt. Co. F. also **Neal M. , N. M. & N. W. McIntosh**

Neal M. McIntosh enlisted at Choctaw Bluff, Alabama, on February 2, 1863, by Captain Dade for the war. Company muster rolls for March 1, to June 30, 1863 and

September/October, 1863, report him present. **N. W. McIntosh** drew clothing on March 31 and June 1, 1864. POW captured at Fort Gaines, Alabama, on August 8, 1864. He was received at Ship Island, Mississippi, from New Orleans on October 25, 1864. **N. W. McIntosh died** at Ship Island on November 16, 1864. **N. W. McIntosh** is also shown as exchanged on January 4, 1865. He is further shown as having been surrendered at Citronelle, Alabama, by General Richard Taylor on May 4, 1865, and paroled at Meridian, Mississippi, on May 13, 1865. His residence was shown as Wilcox County, Alabama.

McIver, A. M., Pvt. Co. D

Enlisted at Mobile, Alabama, on September 10, 1864, by Major Stone for the war. Company muster roll for September/October 1864, reports him absent on furlough for 30 days granted by Medical Board on October 11, 1864.

McKinley, H., Pvt. Co. K

Enlisted at Marion, Alabama, on August 15, 1864, by Captain Gordon for the war. Company muster roll for September/October 1864, reports that he deserted from Redoubt 2, on September 7, 1864.

McKnight, James, Corp./Sgt. Co. E

Enlisted October 13, 1861, at Mobile, Alabama, by Captain Chamberlain for the war. Company muster roll for bounty on September 24, 1862, reports him present. Company muster rolls for November/December 1862 and July/August 1863, report him present. Company muster roll for September/October 1863, reports him transferred as Sgt. to Captain Richardson's Company of Engineers on September 1, 1863. There is some unreadable paper work in his file.*

McKnight, James P., Corp/Sgt. Co. E see **McKnight, James.**

McKnight, John K., Pvt. Co. D

Enlisted October 13, 1861, at Mobile, Alabama, by Captain Butt for one year. He appears present on a company muster roll for bounty on September 24, 1862. Company muster roll for November/December 1862, reports him absent in General Hospital at Mobile. He was admitted to Post Hospital at Fort Morgan, Alabama, on April 29, 1863, with rheumatism and returned to duty on April 29. He was again admitted on May 28, 1863, with diabetes and returned to duty on June 21. On June 30, 1863, he was admitted to Fort Morgan Post Hospital with diabetes and discharged on July 21. Company muster roll for July/August 1863, reports that he was discharged due to disability by order of General Maury. He was born in State of Illinois, age 20, five foot, dark complexion, blue eyes, light hair and by occupation a laborer. Copies of his disability and discharge are in his file.*

McKnight, William, Pvt. Co. E

Enlisted on October 13, 1861, at Mobile, Alabama, by Capt. Chamberlain for the war. He appears present on a company muster roll for bounty on September 24, 1862.

MOBILE CONFEDERATES

Company muster rolls for November/December 1862, July/August 1863, and September/October 1863, report him present. He drew clothing on March 16, 1863.

McSain, A., Pvt. Co. E see **McSean, Andrew, C.**

McLaney, F. H., Pvt. Co. E see **McLarney, Frank H.**

McLarney, Frank. H., Pvt. Co. E
    Enlisted on October 13, 1861, at Mobile, Alabama, by Captain Chamberlain for the war. A regimental return for June 1861, reports him as a guard with Colonel Stewart. He appears present on a company muster roll for bounty on September 24, 1862. Company muster rolls for November/December 1862, July/August 1863 and September/October 1863, report him present. He drew clothing on March 31 and June 1, 1864. POW captured at Fort Gaines, Alabama, on August 8, 1864. He was received at Ship Island, Mississippi, from New Orleans on October 25, 1864, and exchanged at Ship Island on January 4, 1865.

McLean, Andrew C., Pvt. Co. E.
    Enlisted on October 13, 1861, at Mobile, Alabama, by Captain Chamberlain for twelve months. A company muster roll for November/December 1862, shows that he was discharged on orders from General Forrest. A return for November 1862, reports "being a foreigner, discharged, term of service having expired."

McLean, S. J., Pvt. Co. G see **McLean, S. S.**

McLean, S. S., Pvt. Co. G
    He drew clothing on March 3 and June 1, 1864. POW captured at Fort Gaines, Alabama, on August 8, 1864. He was received at Ship Island, Mississippi, from New Orleans on October 25, 1864, and died at Ship Island of dysentery on November 25, 1864. He was buried in grave 42.

McLellan, C. W., Pvt. Co. K
    His name appears on a regimental return for June 17, 1861, near Tupelo, Mississippi, "transf Q. M. Sgert, 17' Ala. Regt."

McLeod, A. D., Pvt. Co. C see **McLeod, Alexander**

McLeod, Alexander, Sgt/Bvt. 2nd Lt. Co. C
    Enlisted November 4, 1861, at Mobile, Alabama, by Captain Rembert for twelve months. He appears on a report near Tupelo, Mississippi, for June 28, 1862, "sent to int. hospital May 29, by Dr. Heard." He appears present on a company muster roll for bounty on September 24, 1862. Elected 2nd Lt. on November 23, 1862. Company muster rolls for December 31, 1862, to April 30, 1863 and May/June 1863, report him present sick in quarters. Company muster roll for September/October 1863, reports that he died in hospital at Point Clear on October 9, 1863. There are a number of pay vouchers in his file.*

McMahon, Patrick, Pvt. Co. D see **McMahon, Patrick**, Pvt. Co. D, 1st Ala. Infantry

McMillan, J. A., Pvt. Co. C

Enlisted November 4, 1861, at Mobile, Alabama, by Captain Rembert for twelve months. He appears absent sick on a company muster roll for bounty on September 24, 1862. Company muster rolls for December 31, 1862, to April 30, 1863, report him present. Company muster roll for May/June 1863, shows him present sick in quarters. September/October 1863, roll shows him absent detached at Choctaw Bluff July 26, 1863, by order of Colonel Anderson. He drew clothing on June 1, 1864. POW captured at Fort Gaines, Alabama, on August 8, 1864 and was received at Ship Island, Mississippi, from New Orleans on October 25, 1864. He was exchanged at Ship Island on January 4, 1865. He appears on a roll of POW's of divers companies and regiments (detached) commanded by Lt. Colonel R. H. Lindsay that was surrendered at Citronelle, Alabama by Lt. General Richard Taylor on May 4, 1865, and paroled at Meridian, Mississippi, on May 13, 1864. He was a resident of Marengo County, Alabama. There is a pay voucher in his file.*

McNab, Robert, Pvt. Co. E

Enlisted November 4, 1861, at Mobile, Alabama, by Captain Chamberlain for twelve months. He appears present on a company muster roll for bounty on September 24, 1862. Company muster rolls for November/December 1862, July/August 1863 and September/October 1863, show him present. He drew clothing on March 16, 1863, March 31, 1864 and June 1, 1864. POW captured at Fort Gaines, Alabama, on August 8, 1864. He was admitted to St. Louis USA General Hospital at New Orleans from military prison, on August 22, 1864, with dysentery and returned to confinement on August 31, 1864, age 23. He was received at Ship Island, Mississippi, from New Orleans on October 25, 1864, and exchanged at Ship Island on January 4, 1865. POW surrendered at Citronelle, Alabama, by Lt. General Richard Taylor on May 4, 1865, and paroled at Meridian, Mississippi, on May 13, 1865. He was a resident of Mobile, Alabama. There is a pay voucher in his file.*

McNay, M., Pvt. Co. E see **McVoy, M. W.**

McNeill, A., Pvt. Co. C

Enlisted on September 1, 1862, at Fort Morgan, Alabama, by Captain Smith for the war. He appears present on a company muster roll for bounty on September 24, 1862.

McShane, C., Pvt. Co. C

Enlisted on September 12, 1862, at Jefferson County, Alabama, by Captain R. A. Gorinon for the war. Company muster roll for December 31, 1862, to April 30, 1864, shows he was discharged by reason of substitute.

McRory, William, Pvt. Co. I.

Enlisted on September 30, 1862, at Butler County, Alabama, by Lt. Freeman for the war. Company muster roll for July/August 1863, reports him present, "Exchanged for

McDonald." Company muster roll for September/October 1863, reports him present but absent with out leave for 2 days. POW captured at Fort Gaines, Alabama, on August 8, 1864. He was received at Ship Island, Mississippi, from New Orleans on October 25, 1864, and exchanged at Ship Island on January 4, 1865. His parole at Montgomery, Alabama, on June 1, 1862, shows him as five foot five inches, light hair, blue eyes, fair complexion and the parole is made out to Wm. McRoy it is signed **Wm. Debnony**? His parole is in his file.*

McRory, W. J., Pvt. Co. I see **McRory, William**

McSpeed, James, Pvt. Co. C. see **Speed, James M.**

McVoy, John K., Sgt. Co. D
Enlisted on October 13, 1861, by Captain Chamberlain for one year. Born in Mobile, Alabama, age 19, five foot eight, fair complexion, hazel eyes, dark hair and by occupation a pilot. Discharged due to disability on January 1, 1862, at Fort Gaines. He had lost three fingers of his right hand plus a gunshot wound and had retention of urine. He is indebted to the Captain who advanced him. His discharge and a letter by the surgeon is in his file.*

McVoy, M. W., Pvt. Co. E
Enlisted on September 22, 1863, at Fort Morgan, Alabama, by Captain Sossaman for the war. Company muster roll for September/October 1863, reports him present and never having been paid. He drew clothing on June 1, 1864. POW captured at Fort Gaines, Alabama, on August 8, 1864. He was admitted to St. Louis USA General Hospital at New Orleans on August 17, 1864, with fever remittens and returned to military prison on August 24, age 19. He was again admitted on September 5, with diarrhoea and returned to confinement on September 16, 1864. Here he is shown as age 18. He was received at Ship Island, Mississippi, from New Orleans on October 25, 1864, and exchanged at Ship Island on January 4, 1865. POW surrendered at Citronelle, Alabama by Lt. General Richard Taylor on May 4, 1865, and paroled at Meridian, Mississippi, on May 13, 1865. He was shown as a resident of Mobile, Alabama.

Mealey, Edward, Pvt. Co. B
Enlisted at Oven Bluff, Alabama, on March 19, 1863, by Captain Johnston for the war. Company muster rolls for March/April 1863, May/June 1863 and September/October 1863, all report him present. On September/October, 1863, roll he is shown as being sick in quarters and absent without leave for four days since last muster. He was admitted to Post Hospital at Fort Morgan, Alabama, on December 2, 1863, with an ulcer and returned to duty on December 5, 1863, he was admitted again on December 6, 1863, with an ulcer and sent to general hospital on January 26, 1864. He was admitted to Ross Hospital at Mobile on January 26, 1864, and sent to General Hospital at Montgomery on February 17, 1864. He was paid $50 bounty on December 31, 1863. He appears as a patient on a hospital muster roll for July/August 1864, at Shelby Springs, Alabama. His name appears on a register of 1st Mississippi CSA Hospital at Jackson, Mississippi, with abscesses admitted August 1, 1864, and returned to duty on November 3, 1864. On April

4, 1865, he was recommended to light duty due to ulceration of leg of one year duration by doctors at Hospital Moore in Mobile. His certificate is in his file.* He was detailed as a nurse at Hospital Moore.

Mealey, Thomas, Musician Co. B

Enlisted at Mobile, Alabama, on October 13, 1861, by Major Hessee for the war. He appears on a company muster roll for bounty September 24, 1862, "Not entitled to bounty, underage, Refuses to take bounty."

Meggerson, E. T., Pvt. Co. C

POW wounded in left hip at Shiloh on April 6, 1862, at 4:30 P. M. at Old Field. Captured at hospital on April 7, 1862.

Meggingon, D. A., Pvt. Co. C see **Megginson, D. A.**

Megginson, D. A., Pvt. Co. C

Enlisted at Choctaw Bluff, Alabama, on February 9, 1863, by Colonel Anderson for three years or the war. He appears on a company muster roll for December 31, 1862, to April 30, 1863, as present and never having been paid. Company muster rolls for May/June 1863 and September/October 1863, report him present. He was admitted to Post Hospital at Fort Morgan, Alabama, on December 6, 1863, with int. fev. and returned to duty on January 4, 1864. He was again admitted to the same hospital on January 21, 1864, with debilitas and sent to general hospital, on January 26, 1864. He was admitted to Ross Hospital in Mobile on January 26, 1864, and sent to General Hospital at Montgomery, Alabama, on February 17, 1864. He drew clothing on March 31 and June 1, 1864. POW captured at Fort Gaines, Alabama, on August 8, 1864. He was received at Ship Island, Mississippi, from New Orleans on October 25, 1864, and exchanged at Ship Island on January 4, 1865. POW surrendered at Citronelle, Alabama by Lt. General Richard Taylor in May 1865, and paroled at Demopolis, Alabama, on June 3, 1865. He was a resident of Marengo County, Alabama.

Megginson, J. A., Pvt. Co. C

Enlisted on February 9, 1863, at Choctaw Bluff, Alabama, by Colonel Anderson for three years or the war. He appears on a company muster roll for December 31, 1862, to April 30, 1863, as present and never having been paid. Company muster rolls for May/June 1863 and September/October 1863, report him present. September/October roll reports that he lost a canteen at $2. Company muster roll for September/October 1864, reports him paid last on June 30, 1864, and due $69.13 for clothing. He drew clothing on March 31 and June 1, 1864. He was admitted to Ross Hospital at Mobile for februs intermittens quot, on August 14, 1864, and returned to duty on August 20, 1864. See personal papers for **C. C. Williams**, Pvt. Co. C, 21st Alabama. There is a reference to a **James H. Megginson**, Pvt. Co. C in this file; POW surrendered at Citronelle, Alabama, on May 4, 1865, paroled at Mobile, Alabama, on May 30, 1864, a resident of Clarke County, Alabama, age 36, five foot 8 inches, florid complexion, gray eyes, dark hair.

Megginson, J. S., Pvt. Co. C see **Megginson, J. A.**

Meggison, J. A., Pvt. Co. C see **Megginson, J. A.**

Menziel, F. J., Pvt. Co. K see **Menzie, Frank**

Menzie, Frank, Pvt. Co. K
    Enlisted on September 15, 1863, at Fort Morgan, Alabama, by Captain Dorgan for the war. Company muster roll for September/October 1863, reports him present and never paid. Company muster roll for September/October 1864, reports him absent sick in hospital since October 30, 1864, paid on June 30, 1864, by Captain St. Paul. Drew clothing on June 30, 1864 and December 19, 1864. POW surrendered at Citronelle, Alabama, by Lt. General Richard Taylor on May 4, 1865, at paroled at Meridian, Mississippi, on May 13, 1865. He was shown as a resident of Mobile, County, Alabama.

Meredith, J. D., Pvt. Co. F see **Merideth, J. B.**

Merideth, J. B., Pvt. Co. F
    He drew clothing on March 31 and June 1, 1864. POW captured at Fort Gaines, Alabama, on August 8, 1864. He was received at Ship Island, Mississippi, from New Orleans on October 25, 1864, and exchanged at Ship Island on January 4, 1865. His parole at Montgomery, Alabama, on June 1, 1862, shows him as five foot five inches, light hair, blue eyes, and fair complexion. He was admitted to Ross Hospital on April 8, 1865, with vulnus sclopiticum (gunshot wound) flesh wound to his left thigh and sent to General Hospital in Montgomery. His name appears on a list of stragglers surrendered by Lt. General Richard Taylor on May 4, 1865, and paroled at Selma, Alabama, in June 1865. He was shown as a resident of Shelby County, Alabama.

Merrideth, J. B., Pvt. Co. F see **Merideth, J. B.**

Merrill, Chapman, Drummer, Co. K.
    Enlisted at Mobile, Alabama, on August 29, 1863, by Captain Blocker for the war. Company muster rolls for September/October 1863 and September/October 1864, report him present. He drew clothing on December 19, 1863, April 14, 1864 and June 20, 1864. He appears on a descriptive list dated September 18, 1863, at Mobile, Alabama; Age **13**, blue eyes, dark hair, light complexion, four foot seven inches, a newsboy by occupation. He signed the roll C. R. Merrill. POW surrendered at Citronelle, Alabama, by Lt. General Richard Taylor on May 4, 1865, at paroled at Meridian, Mississippi, on May 13, 1865. He was a resident of Mobile, County, Alabama.
Merrill, C. R. Drummer, Co. K see **Merrill, Chapman.**

Metzger, George, Pvt. Co. A
    Enlisted on October 13, 1861, at Mobile, Alabama, by Major Hessee for the war. Company muster roll for bounty on September 24, 1862, reports him present. Company muster rolls for December 31, 1862, to April 30, 1863 and May/June 1863, show him present. On muster roll for May/June 1863, he is reported present but sick in hospital and September/October 1863, he is reported present. Drew clothing May 20, 1864, and again

at Camp Anderson on June 14, 1864. POW captured at Fort Morgan, Alabama, on August 23, 1864, received at Elmira, New York, on October 8, 1864, from New Orleans and released on May 17, 1865. He signed a roll of POW's desirous to take the Oath of Allegiance to the USA in November 1864, "He was conscripted Apl., 16, 1864. Is a Frenchman has lived in this county about five years. At outbreak of war he was in Mobile, Ala. had French protection paper which exempted him from the army until this year. He tried to leave the south but could not get away. While at Fort Morgan he attempted to desert but was caught and Court Marshaled but acquitted. Has friends in Buffalo and Cincinnati." Note that none of his service records confirm his statements. *The Yanks didn't believe him either as he was not released until May 17, 1865.*

Middleton, Robert, Bvt. 2nd. Lt./ 1st Lt. Co. E

Enlisted on October 13, 1861, for 12 months. His name appears on a roster for April, May, June, July, August and September 1861. Elected 2nd Lt. on May 8, 1862, promoted May 1, 1863, and promoted to 1st Lt. on May 18, 1864. He appears on a company muster roll for bounty on September 24, 1862. Company muster rolls for November/December 1862, July/August 1863 and September/October 1863, report him present. Inspection report for June 30, 1864, at Fort Morgan reports him detached as AAQM by order of General Higgins since January 25, 1864. A reference in his file to see personal papers of **M. C. Burks**. A roster of Engineer Troops at Mobile on January 1, 1865, reports him assigned on temporary duty with Co. C by Maury on October 25, 1864. Recommended at 2nd Lt. of Co. C 2nd Engineer Regiment. There are a number of pay vouchers in his file.**

Millard, Joseph, A., Pvt. Co. I

POW surrendered at Citronelle, Alabama, by Lt. General Richard Taylor on May 4, 1865, at paroled at Mobile, Alabama, on May 22, 1865. He was shown as a resident of Mobile, County, Alabama.

Miller, C. A., Pvt. Co. K

Enlisted on October 13, 1861, at Mobile, Alabama, by Major S. Stewart. Discharged on May 12, 1862, due to disability by chronic rheumatism. Born New York, New York, age 29, eyes blue, five foot five inches, light hair, fair complexion. His discharge is in his file.*

Miller, Charles, Pvt. _

He appears on a regimental return for December 1861, filed with **W. S. Cameron** of the 29th Mississippi Co. C. At Lauderdale Springs Hospital on April 18, 1864, he was temporarily detailed to light duty due to asthma of two months duration. A medical certificate and a pay voucher are in his file.*

Miller, Charles F., Pvt. Co. E see **Miller, Charles H.**

Miller, Charles, H., Pvt. Co. E

Enlisted at Fort Morgan on January 24, 1863, by Captain Sossaman for the war. Company muster roll at Mobile, Alabama, for September/October 1864, reports him absent sent to Ross Hospital on October 9, by order of Dr. Smith. Muster roll for July/August 1863, reports him present while September/October 1863, roll reports him absent sick in hospital at Mobile since October 1. He appears on a hospital muster roll at Hospital Nott, for September/October 1863. His name appears on a list of men for the month of July 1864, employed as a nurse under Surgeon William Henderson since June 23, 1864. He was admitted to Post Hospital at Fort Morgan, on May 12, 1863, with syphilis and returned to duty on June 30, 1864. He was again admitted to Post Hospital at Fort Morgan on July 4, 1863, with asthma and returned to duty on July 10, and again on July 13, 1863, sent to general hospital, on July 14, 1863. He was back at Fort Morgan Post Hospital on July 31, 1863, and sent back to general hospital on August 11. September 1, 1863, he was admitted to Post Hospital at Fort Morgan and sent back to general hospital, on September 5. November 25, 1863, he is back in Fort Morgan Post Hospital still with asthma and returned to general hospital, on November 26. He was admitted to Ross Hospital at Mobile on March 6, 1864, with asthma and returned to duty on April 14, 1864. He was once again admitted to Ross Hospital on April 23, 1864, with syphilis primitira and returned to duty on May 27, 1864. He was admitted to Ross Hospital on October 9, 1864, with asthma and returned to duty on January 14, 1865, (complaint was chronic rheumatism). He is shown as being admitted to Ross Hospital with debility on November 28, 1863, and returned to duty on February 1, 1864. It appears that two Charlie Miller's files are combined in these records.

Miller, Charles W., Pvt. Co. B.

Enlisted at Randolph ? Co.? by O. P. Knight for the war. Muster rolls for March/April 1863 and May/June 1863 report him present. Muster roll for September/October 1863, reports him absent "Sent to Genl. Hospital in Mobile, Oct 27, 1863, by order Dr. Payne." Died at General Hospital Spring Hill on November 5, 1863. He left 55 cents that was turned over to the Quartermaster.

Miller, Jacob H., Pvt./Musician Co. A

Enlisted on September 30, 1862, at Mobile, Alabama, by Captain DeVaux for the war. Company muster rolls for December 31, 1862, to April 30, 1863, May/June 1863 and September/October 1863, all report him present. Transferred to CS Navy on Special Order 48/6 February 27, 1864. Reference card in his file to see personal papers of **T. A. Foster**, Pvt. Co. A.

Miller, Jack

A descriptive list filed with **Foster, T. A**. reports him as age 20.

Miller, R. B., Pvt. Co. F

He drew clothing on June 1, 1864. POW captured at Fort Gaines, Alabama, on August 8, 1864. Confined at Steam Levee Press No. 4 New Orleans on September 25, 1864. Admitted to St. Louis USA General Hospital on September 24, 1864, with measles and returned to prison on October 25, 1864, age 18. He was received at Ship Island, Mississippi, on October 28, 1864, and exchanged on January 4, 1865. He appears on a roll of POW's of Co. F., 21st Alabama commanded by Captain G. B. Gwin that was surrendered at Citronelle, Alabama, on May 4, 1865, by Lt. General Richard Taylor and paroled at Meridian, Mississippi.

Milligan, John, Corporal/Sgt. Co. A

Enlisted on October 13, 1861, at Mobile, Alabama, by Captain Hessee for the war. He was wounded in the arm slightly at Shiloh on April 6, 1862, at 3 P. M. while advancing in the center. He appears present on a company muster roll for bounty on September 24, 1862. Company muster rolls for December 31, 1862, to April 30, 1863, May/June 1863 and September/October 1863, all report him present. Promoted from the ranks to 4th Corporal on September 1, 1863. He was admitted to Post Hospital at Fort Morgan on November 28, 1863, with int. fever and returned to duty on December 7, 1863. He drew clothing on March 31, May 20 and June 20, 1864. POW captured at Fort Morgan on August 23, 1864. He was received at Elmira, New York, from New Orleans on October 8, 1864, and transferred to James River for exchange on March 14, 1865. He was received at Bolware's Wharf on the James River between March 18 and 21, 1865, among 982 paroled Confederate POW's. He was admitted to Receiving and Wayside Hospital or General Hospital No. 9, Richmond, Virginia, on March 18, 1865, and sent to Camp Lee on March 19. POW surrendered by Lt. General Taylor at Citronelle, Alabama, on May 4, 1865, and paroled at Meridian, Mississippi, on May 13, 1865. His residence was shown as Mobile, Alabama.

Millwood, John, Pvt. Co. B

Enlisted on September 9, 1862, at Blount, [County?] by M. A. Fryer for three years or the war. Company muster roll for March/April 1863, reports him present. May/June 1863, muster roll reports him present but sick in quarters. Company muster roll for September/October 1863, reports that he died of disease in Jefferson County on August 29, 1863.

Mimms, James M., Sgt./Lt./Adjutant see **Mims, James M.**

Mims, F. J., Pvt. Co. G/D

He drew clothing on March 3, March 31 and June 1, 1864. POW captured at Fort Gaines, Alabama, on August 8, 1864. He was confined at Steam Levee Press No. 4 in New Orleans and sent to hospital on September 24, 1864. He was admitted to St. Louis USA General Hospital at New Orleans on September 23, 1864, with acute pneumonia (left) and returned to confinement on November 25, 1864, age 27. He was received at Ship Island, Mississippi, from New Orleans on December 13, 1864, and exchanged on January 5, 1865.

Mims, James M., Sgt./Lt./Adjutant, Co. D and Field and Staff

Enlisted on October 13, 1861, at Mobile, Alabama, by Captain Butt for one year. He was wounded in the arm slightly at Shiloh at 9 A. M. on April 6, 1862, while advancing. His name appears on a return for December 1862, present at Fort Morgan, Alabama, "Elected Jr 2nd Lt. Nov. 26, assigned to duty Dec. 1, 1862, Sgt. Co. D, assigned to duty by spc. Order No – from Brigade H'd Qrs as Jr. 2nd Lt. Co. D." Company muster roll for bounty on September 24, 1862, reports him present. Company muster roll for

November/December 1862, reports him present and promoted from 3rd Sgt. to Lt. on December 1, 1862. He was elected Jr. 2nd Lt. of Co. D on November 30, 1862. Muster roll for July/August 1863, shows on recuperation that he is absent sick. Muster roll for September/October 1863, on recuperation shows him present for duty. Company muster roll for November/December 1863, reports him present. He was admitted to Post Hospital at Fort Morgan August 19, 1863, with feb. con. and returned to duty on August 27, 1863. He was promoted to Sr. 2nd Lt. of Co. H on March 24, 1864. POW captured at Fort Gaines, Alabama, on August 8, 1864. He was received at Ship Island, Mississippi, on November 25, 1864, and exchanged at Ship Island on January 4 1865. Paroled at US 16th Headquarters at Montgomery, Alabama, on May 16, 1865; dark hair, hazel eyes, fair complexion, five foot seven and one half inches. There are a number of pay vouchers in his file.**

Minge, C. H., Pvt. Co. K
His name appears on a regimental return for December 1861.

Minich, S., Pvt. Co. H
His name appears on a report near Tupelo, Mississippi, on June 28, 1862, "Sent to the interior from Corinth, at the time of evacuation."

Minis, J. M., Sgt./Lt./Adjutant see **Mims, James M.**

Mins, F. J., Pvt. Co. G/D **see Mims F. J.**

Miranda, S., Pvt. Co. H
His name appears on a report near Tupelo, Mississippi, on June 28, 1862, "Sent to the interior from Corinth, at the time of evacuation."

Mitchell, J. J., Pvt. Co. F
Enlisted at Baldwin County, on October 13, 1861, by Captain McCoy for one year. A regimental return for June 1862, reports him on detached service as blacksmith. He drew one pair of shoes from Quartermaster at Selma on June 23, 1862. He appears present on a company muster roll for bounty September 24, 1862. Company muster roll for March 1, to June 30, 1863, reports him absent detached in Mobile as blacksmith on October 20, 1862, by order of General Maury. September/October 1863, muster roll reports him absent detached as a blacksmith on August 4, 1863. There are a number of pay vouchers in his file.**

Modawell, M. V., Pvt. Co. C
Enlisted on November 4, 1861, at Fort Gaines by Captain Rembert for twelve months. He appears present on a company muster roll for bounty September 24, 1862. There are pay vouchers and other paper work in his file.*

Mon, Edmand, Pvt. Co. I
Enlisted at Fort Morgan on October 10, 1863, by Lt. McNeil for the war. He drew clothing on March 31, 1864, and signed by his mark. He was admitted to Post

Hospital at Fort Morgan on July 24, 1864, with int. feb. and returned to duty on July 31, 1864. POW captured at Fort Gaines, Alabama, on August 8, 1864. He was received at Ship Island, Mississippi, on November 25, 1864, and exchanged at Ship Island on January 4 1865.

Mongin, John, Pvt. Co. G

His name appears on a regimental return at Corinth in June 1862, "missing from picket guards."

Mongin, R., Pvt. Co. G. (**Monjo, Rofala**)

Wounded slightly in the wrist at Shiloh at 3 P. M. on April 6, 1862, while advancing. His name appears on a regimental return for June 1862, "Wounded and furloughed since April 9." He drew $5 of commutation of rations while on furlough from May 23, to June 11, 1862. Signed **Rofala Monjo**.

Monju, R., Pvt. Co. G see **Mongin, R.**

Montgomery, F., Pvt. Co. F

Enlisted by Captain McCoy at Baldwin County, Alabama, on October 13, 1861, for one year. His name appears on a regimental return for June 1862. "May 8, Corinth, Miss. Discharged for disability." He was born in New York, New York, age 59, dark complexion, blue eyes, dark hair, a boatman. He was injured by a fall from a horse.

Moon, Henry, G., 2nd Lt. Co. I

Enlisted on October 13, 1861, elected 2nd Lt. on October 7, 1861, resigned on March 28, 1862. There are pay vouchers in his file.*

Moon, H. J., 2nd Lt. Co. I see **Moon Henry G.**

Moore, G. W., Pvt. Co. C

His name appears on a regimental return for June 1862, "May 8, Corinth died hospital." Claim for deceased soldier was filed by W. F. Moore his father on January 26, 1863, and was paid $99.93.

Moore, James J., Pvt. Co. E

Enlisted at Fort Morgan, Alabama, on April 8, 1863, by Captain Sossaman for the war. Company muster rolls for July/August and September/October 1863, report him present. He drew clothing on March 16, 1863. He was admitted to Post Hospital at Fort Morgan, Alabama, with diarrhoea on May 9, 1863, and returned to duty on June 2, 1863. On November 23, 1863, he was issued Special Order No. 30 detailing him to Q. M. Department by order of Brigadier General Higgins.

Moore, Thomas, Pvt. Co. F

Enlisted on January 31, 1862, at Choctaw Bluff, Alabama, by Captain Dade for three years or the war. He appears present on a company muster roll for March 1, to June 30, 1863. Company muster roll for September/October 1863, reports that he deserted from Choctaw Bluff on July 15, 1863, carrying off haversack, knapsack and canteen. Advertised as a deserter, age 16, blue eyes, dark hair, fair complexion, five foot eight inches, born in Clarke County, Alabama.

Moore, W. J., Pvt. Co. D

Enlisted on October 13, 1861, at Mobile, Alabama, by Major Hessee for one year. He was discharged at Mobile by order of Brigadier General Withers on February 19, 1862. He was born in Mississippi, age 19, five foot nine inches, fair complexion, gray eyes, light hair and by occupation a carpenter. He was paid $79.60 for service and transferred his interest to pay to F. R. Foster Jr. His name appears on a register of the Medical Director's Office, Richmond, Virginia, at 2nd Alabama Hospital sent to Farmville on October 22, 1862. His discharge and transfer of pay voucher is in his file.*
[*Note his file is out of place on the microfilm. Filed after* **Mims, F. J.***]*

Morali, Felice, Pvt. Co. G

Enlisted at 6 A. M. by Major Hessee at Mobile, Alabama, on September 27, 1861, for twelve months. He was discharged January 21, 1862, at Fort Gaines due to disability caused by syphilis ogoena?. Born at Messina, Italy, age 25, five foot six inches, strong complexion, black eyes, black hair and by profession a shoemaker. His discharge is in his file.*

Morali, Lewis, Pvt. Co. G see **Morali, Fleice**

Morgan, John, Pvt. Co. H, Musician detached (fifer)

He was paid $56.20 at Mobile, Alabama at the rate of $12 per month plus subsistence and clothing for service from October 13, 1861, to December 31, 1861. He was again paid $73 for service from March 1, to June 30, 1862. His name appears on a report June 28, 1862, near Tupelo, Mississippi, "absent on furlough in Mobile." His pay vouchers are in his file.*

Morgan, J. S., Pvt. Co. C/D

Enlisted on November 22, 1861, at Fort Gaines, Alabama, by Captain Rembert for twelve months. He appears present on a company muster roll for bounty September 24, 1862. Company muster rolls Co. C for December 31, 1862, to April 30, 1863, May/June 1863 and September/October 1863, all show him present. His name appears on a return at Fort Morgan in Co. D for December 1862? "G(?) transferred." He is shown in Co. C and was admitted to Post Hospital at Fort Morgan, Alabama, on December 30, 1863, with int. feb. and returned to duty on January 2, 1864. He drew clothing in Co. C on June 1, 1864.

Morgan, Thomas T., Pvt. Co. D

Enlisted at Mobile on February? (*on roll*) 13, 1861, at Mobile, Alabama, by Captain Wilkins for the war. He appears present on a company muster roll for November/December 1862, "transferred from Co. H, 1st Bat. Ala. Arty."

Moris, J. S. (Morris J. L.), Pvt. Co. F

Enlisted on October 13, 1861, at Mobile, Alabama by Captain McCoy for one year. His name appears on a register of payments to discharged soldiers discharged on December 14, 1862, paid February 12, 1862. He was born in the State of Georgia, age 22, five foot nine inches, dark complexion, dark eyes, black hair, and a shoemaker by occupation. He was discharged due to disability caused by phthisis. There is a Oath of Allegiance to the USA in his file signed at Montgomery, Alabama, on June 9, 1865.* Here he is shown as having hazel eyes.

Morris, Andrew, Pvt. Co. A

His name appears on a roll of POW's at Camp Butler, Springfield, Illinois, captured at Fort Donalson on February 16, 1862. He was transferred among 1777 POW's from Camp Butler to Vicksburg, Mississippi, on board the steamer *John H. Done*, September 23, 1862 to be exchanged.

Morris, John, Pvt. Co. I

He drew clothing on April 16, 1864. POW captured at Fort Gaines, Alabama, August 8, 1864, received at Ship Island, Mississippi, from New Orleans on October 25, 1864, and exchanged at Ship Island on January 4, 1865. He applied to take the Oath of Allegiance to the USA at Ship Island.

Morris, John E., Pvt. Co. G

He drew clothing on March 3, March 31 and June 1, 1864, and signed by his mark. POW captured at Fort Gaines, Alabama, August 8, 1864, received at Ship Island, Mississippi, from New Orleans on October 25, 1864, and exchanged at Ship Island on January 4, 1865. He was admitted to St. Louis USA General Hospital at New Orleans on August 23, 1864, with fever, intermittent and returned to confinement on August 28, 1864, age 27.

Morris, Stephen H., Pvt. Co. G

Enlisted on April 4, 1864, at Coffee County, Alabama, by Captain Kinney for the war. He drew clothing on March 3? and June 1, 1864, signed by his mark. He appears present and never having been paid on company muster roll for September/October 1864, at Mobile. POW surrendered by Lt. General Richard Taylor at Citronelle, Alabama, on May 4, 1865, and paroled at Meridian, Mississippi, on May 13, 1865. He was shown as a resident of Elba, Coffee County, Alabama.

Morris, W., 2nd Lt. Co. I

This man filed in error as he was appointed 2nd Lt. of 21st Regiment Infantry Tennessee, Vols.

Morrison, James, Pvt./Sgt. Co. A

Enlisted on November 13, 1861, at Halls Mill, Alabama, by Captain Jewett for the war. He appears present on company muster roll for bounty on September 24, 1862. Company muster rolls for December 31, 1862, to April 30, 1863 and May/June 1863, report him present. He served on extra duty as a butcher at Fort Stonewall II, Sidney

Johnston, and Choctaw Bluff Alabama River, in February and July 1863. He drew clothing on March 31, 1864. He was promoted from the ranks to 2nd Corporal on September 1, 1863. He appears present as 3rd Sgt. on company muster roll for September/October 1864. POW surrendered by Lt. General Richard Taylor and paroled at Demopolis, Alabama, on June 1, 1865. He was shown as a resident of Marengo County, Alabama.. There is a pay voucher in his file.*

Morrison, Joseph, Pvt./Corp. Co. E

Enlisted on October 13, 1861, at Mobile, Alabama, by Captain Chamberlain for the war. He was wounded severely in the thigh at Shiloh on April 6, 1862, at 8 A. M. while advancing during attack on 1st Camp. His name appears on a regimental return for June 1882, "wounded unlimited furlough." He appears present on company muster roll for bounty on September 24, 1862. Company muster rolls for November/December 1862, July/August, 1863 and September/October 1863, report him present. He was paid on extra duty at Choctaw Bluff, Alabama, as a butcher during March 1863. (See James Morrison above, there may be some confusion in these two men's files.) He drew clothing on March 16, 1864. He was admitted to Post Hospital at Fort Morgan, Alabama, on August 11, 1863, with an ulcer and returned to duty on August 31, 1863.

Moseley, George W., Pvt. Co. B

He enlisted on February 23, 1864, at Greenville, Alabama, by Colonel Murphy to serve three years. He drew clothing on March 31, 1864, and signed by his mark. He was discharged due to disability caused by rheumatism on July 27, 1864. He served three weeks on active duty. Born in Edgefield District, South Carolina, age 45, five foot eleven inches, dark complexion, dark eyes, black hair, and a farmer by occupation. He was stationed at General Hospital at Greenville, Alabama. His discharge is in his file.*

Moseley, Robert, Pvt. Co. B

He drew clothing on June 1, 1864. POW captured at Fort Gaines, Alabama, on August 8, 1864. He was received at Ship Island, Mississippi, from New Orleans on October 25, 1864, and exchanged at Ship Island on January 4, 1865. POW captured at Greenville, Alabama, on April 16, 1864, and paroled at Greenville.

Moses, Robert, Pvt. Co. F

He enlisted on September 28, 1862, at Jefferson (*County Alabama*?) by John Bass for three years. He appears present on a company muster roll for March 1, 1863, to June 30, 1863, but lost one haversack at 20 cents. Company muster rolls for September/October 1863 (one haversack $1) and September/October 1864, report him present. He is reported on a hospital muster roll as a nurse for March/April 1864. He is shown as having joined the hospital on January 2, 1864, and having enlisted at Talladega, Alabama, on September 5, 1862. He drew clothing on June 1, 1864, and signed by his mark. POW captured at Spanish Fort, Alabama, on April 8, 1865. He was received at Ship Island, Mississippi, on April 10, 1865, and transferred to Vicksburg, Mississippi, on May 1, 1865.

Mothershead. G. A., Pvt. Co. F.

He was captured at Shiloh Hospital while serving on ambulance squad on April 7, 1862. He was admitted to USA Prison Hospital at Camp Douglas near Chicago, Illinois, on May 15, 1862, with typhoid fever. He died on May 23, 1862. His certificate for undertaker is in his file.* He was shown as being five foot 10 inches tall.

Motley, Edwin, Pvt. Co. G

He drew clothing on March 3, March 31 and June 1864. POW captured at Fort Gaines, Alabama, on August 8, 1864. He was received at Ship Island, Mississippi, on October 25, 1864, and died of dysentery on December 20, 1864. He was buried in grave No. 101.

Mulligan, John, Corp./Sgt. Co. A see **Milligan, John**

Muntz, Joseph, Pvt. Co. H

His name appears on a report near Tupelo, Mississippi, June 28, 1862, "Wounded at Shiloh and sent to Mobile." There are several pay vouchers in is file. The last voucher is for $22, detached sick from September 1, to October 31, 1862.*

Murphy, B., 21st Alabama

His name appears on a register of soldiers who were killed or died. Died at Kingston, Hospital, Georgia. Effects of $4 were received on October 1, 1863.

Murphy, David, Pvt. Co. B

He enlisted on October 13, 1861, at Mobile, Alabama, by Major Hessee for one year. He was discharged at Tupelo, Mississippi, on July 2, 1862, due to imperfect vision. He was born in Ireland, age 20, five foot eight inches, light complexion, black eyes, light hair and by occupation a laborer. His discharge and pay vouchers are in his file.*

Murphy, George, W., 1st Sgt. Co. H

He drew clothing on June 1, 1864. POW captured at Fort Gaines, Alabama, on August 8, 1864. He was received at Ship Island, Mississippi, from New Orleans on October 25, 1864, and exchanged at Ship Island on January 4, 1865. POW surrendered by Lt. General Richard Taylor, at Citronelle, Alabama, on May 4, 1865, and paroled at Meridian, Mississippi, on May 12, 1865. He was shown as a resident of Mobile, Alabama.

Murphy, George, W., Pvt. Co. E

Enlisted on September 11, 1861, at Mobile, Alabama, by Captain Sossaman for twelve months. His name appears on a regimental return for June 1862, as a clerk for Surgeon Foard. He appears absent on company muster roll for bounty on September 24, 1862, "detached Apl 20, 62, by Genl. Bragg." Company muster roll for November/December 1862, reports him detached with Dr. Foard by order of Gen. Bragg. Company muster rolls for July/August and September/October 1863, report him present. His name appears on a roll for November 1863, as a brigade clerk at Fort Morgan. There are a number of pay vouchers and commutation documents in his file.*

Murphy, James W. Pvt. Co. G

He drew clothing on March 2 and June 1, 1864. POW captured at Fort Gaines, Alabama, on August 8, 1864. He was received at Ship Island, Mississippi, from New Orleans on October 25, 1864, and exchanged at Ship Island on January 4, 1865. POW surrendered by Lt. General Richard Taylor, at Citronelle, Alabama, on May 4, 1865, and paroled at Meridian, Mississippi, on May 13, 1865. He was shown as a resident of Camden, Wilcox County, Alabama.

Murphy, Martin, Pvt. Co. D

He enlisted on October 13, 1861, at Mobile, Alabama, by Captain Butt for one year. His name appears on a regimental return in June 1862, "Sent to Interior Hospital at the evacuation of Corinth." He appears absent without leave on a company muster roll for bounty on September 24, 1862. Company muster roll for November/December 1862, report him present with bounty due.

Murry, Thomas, Pvt. Co. B

He enlisted on October 13, 1861, at Mobile, Alabama, by Major Hessee for the war. His name appears on a regimental return in June 1862, "Absent without leave since June 10." He also appears on a report near Tupelo, Mississippi, June 28, 1862, as absent without leave since June 11. He appears present and refuses to take bounty on a company muster roll for bounty on September 24, 1862. There is a discharge in his file dated October 13, 1862, at Oven Bluff, Alabama. He was born in Ireland, age 42, dark complexion, blue eyes, brown hair, five foot six inches and by occupation a laborer. He appears on a descriptive list on November 23, 1863, where it was stated that he was capable in mind and body of serving as a soldier. Enlisted November 21, 1862, at Choctaw Bluff by Colonel Anderson, born in Ireland, age 42, gray eyes, black hair, dark complexion, five foot eight inches, and a sailor by occupation, paid $50 bounty. Company muster rolls for March/April 1863, May/June 1863 and September/October 1863, all show him present. He appears on a roll of extra duty men employed as signalman at Fort Morgan in November 1863. His discharge, descriptive list and a pay voucher are in his file.*

Muths, George, 1st Lt. Co. H

Enlisted on October 13, 1861, elected 1st Lt. on October 23. His name appears on a return at Fort Gaines, Alabama, in November 1861, shown present. He appears on a regimental return for June 1862, as present at Tupelo, Mississippi. He was honorably discharged by order of General Bragg. There is a signed sworn statement in his file as to $351 owed him for service. The paper is dated July 21, 1862.*

Myers, William, Pvt. Co. _

POW captured at Corinth, Mississippi, June 1, 1862. His name appears on a roll of POW's at St. Louis Gratiot Street Prison on June 27, to be sent to Alton, Illinois, in July 1862. He is shown at Alton, Illinois, in July 1862, sent to Vicksburg, Mississippi, to be exchanged on September 23, 1862. He was exchange at Alken's Landing near Vicksburg on November 11, 1862.

N

Napier, John, C., Pvt. Co. C

Captured at Shiloh April 7, 1862, at Pittsburg Landing. He was on the ambulance squad and captured at hospital. He appears on a list of POW's sent to Alton, Illinois, in June 1862. His name appears as a patient at Hickory Street, USA General Hospital at St. Louis, Missouri on parole at Mrs. H. Clay Harts since June 18, 1862, complaint fev typhoid. He was discharged and received at Gratiot Street Military Prison at St. Louis, Missouri, during the week of July 27, 1862, discharged on July 21, 1862. He died July 22, 1862, in prison hospital with chronic diarrhoea, and febris typhoids. His death certificate shows him as five foot nine inches. His death certificate is in his file.*

Narimore, Joseph, Pvt. Co. A

POW died at Fourth Street Hospital, St. Louis, Missouri, of typhoid fever on June 12, 1862. Twenty-four years old, five foot seven inches. His death certificate is in his file.*

Narthert, (Northcut) T. M., Pvt. Co. C

POW signed the Oath of Allegiance to the USA at Montgomery, Alabama, on May 29, 1865. Five foot eleven inches, black hair, dark eyes, fair complexion, he signed by his mark.

Nash, Thomas, E., Pvt. Co. F

He enlisted on February 11, 1861, at Choctaw Bluff, Alabama, by Captain Dade for the war. He appears present on a company muster roll for March 1, to June 30, 1863.

Natals, B., Pvt. G

His name appears on a list without remarks of men who returned (at Shiloh) without arms or with captured arms, Wither's Division, 1st Brigade.

Nealy, Edward, Pvt. Co. B

His name appears on a report of furloughs granted by the Medical Examining Board at Disabled Camp Lauderdale, Mississippi, during the week of March 14, 1865. Residence shown as Mobile, Alabama, sixty-day furlough with osticits. (*likely ostitis inflammation of a bone*)

Nedmer, George Field and Staff, 1st Lt./Adjutant (See **Vidmer, George**, 1st Lt./Adjutant)

POW captured at Fort Gaines on August 8, 1864, exchanged at Ship Island, Mississippi, on January 4, 1865.

Neeland, William P., Pvt. Co. B

POW captured at Pittsburgh Landing, Tennessee, on April 6, 1862. He was admitted to USA Hospital steamer *Empress* with vulnus sclopeticum (*gunshot*) on April 10, 1862. He was admitted to USA General Hospital at Keokuk, Iowa, on April 20, 1862, with congestion of lungs and died May 10, 1862. Death claim filed by Catherine Leelan his widow on November 5, 1862.

Neille, James, Pvt. Co. B

He enlisted on August 13, 1862, at Mobile, Alabama, by Captain DeVaux for the war. He appears present on a company muster roll for bounty on September 24, 1862, with the note that the recruit was paid bounty at time of enlistment. Company muster roll for March/April 1863, reports him present. Company muster roll for May/June 1863, reports that he was discharged on disability on June 16, 1862, by order of General Maury. There are pay vouchers in his file.*

Nelson, John B., Corp. Co. F

Enlisted at Baldwin County, Alabama, by Captain McCoy on October 13, 1861, for one year. He was discharged on October 13, 1862, at Choctaw Bluff age 16, five foot four inches, dark eyes, dark complexion, black hair, and a schoolboy by occupation. His discharge is in his file.*

Netti, Francisco, Sgt. Co. G

POW captured April 7, 1862. He was paid $19 per month for March and April 1862. A pay voucher is in his file.*

Nettles, J. R., Pvt. Co. C

He was discharged and paid for service from October 13, 1861, to December 31, 1861. There is a pay voucher in his file.*

Newel, J. K., Pvt. Co. I see **Newell, J. R.**

Newell, J. R., Pvt. Co. I

He enlisted on October 13, 1861, at Halls Mill, Alabama, by Major Hessee for the war. He appears on regimental return for June 1862, on detached service with Pioneer Corps. His name appears on a muster roll of Captain S. M. Steele's Co. B in the Pioneer Battalion commanded by Major Meriwether, Jackson' Brigade. He appears present on a company muster roll for bounty on September 24, 1862. Company muster rolls for July/August and September/October 1863, report him present. He drew clothing on March 31, 1864. POW captured at Fort Gaines, Alabama, on August 8, 1864. He was received at Ship Island, Mississippi, from New Orleans on October 25, 1864, and exchanged at Ship Island January 5, 1865. POW surrendered by Lt. General Richard Taylor at Citronelle, Alabama, on May 4, 1865, and paroled at Meridian, Mississippi, on May 13, 1865. He was a resident of Mobile, County, Alabama.

Nicolan, Jose, Pvt. Co. G

He was wounded at Shiloh on April 6, 1862, at 7 A. M. in a charge on the 1st Battery. He was paid $22 on May 16, 1863, for service from March 1, to April 30, 1862. He signed by his mark.*

Nichols, W. N., Pvt. Co. C/D

Enlisted on October 13, 1862, at Choctaw Bluff, Alabama, by Captain Smith for three years or the war. Company muster roll for December 31, 1862, to April 30, 1863, and May/June 1863, report him present. Muster roll for September/October 1863, reports him absent on furlough for 10 days from October 28, 1863. He drew clothing on March 31 and June 1, 1864. POW captured at Fort Gaines on August 8, 1864. He was received at Ship Island, Mississippi, from New Orleans on October 25, 1864, and exchanged at Ship Island on January 5, 1865. POW captured at Blakeley, Alabama, on April 9, 1865, received at Ship Island on April 15, 1865, and sent to Vicksburg, Mississippi, on May 1, 1865, for exchange. He was received at Vicksburg, Mississippi, on parole on May 6.

Nicholas, G., Pvt. Co. G

His name appears on a regimental return in June 1862, "Wounded and furloughed since April 9." He was paid on May 15, 1862.

Niscon, Williams, Pvt. Co. B see **Nixon, Williams**

Nicholas, Nisuis, Bugler Co. H

Enlisted at Mobile, Alabama, on October 13, 1861, to serve one year. Born in Kirsch, France, age 26, five foot six inches, fair complexion, brown eyes, brown hair, and a shoemaker by occupation. Discharged at Fort Gaines on November 10, 1861, by Dr. Nott due to having epilepsy. His discharge and pay voucher are in his file.*

Niscom, William, Co. B

His name appears on a register of POW's at New Orleans Register No. 4, page 1, or carded? Auxiliary Register No. 4. This information is filed with **Nixon, William**.

Nixon, Samuel, Pvt. Co. B

Enlisted at Mobile, Alabama, on October 13, 1861, for 12 months by Major Hessee. He appears on a regimental return in June 1862, "Detached service: Hospital Nurse." He also appears on a report on June 28, 1862, near Tupelo, Mississippi, "Detached a nurse for genl. hospital at Corinth April 27." He appears on a company muster roll for bounty on September 24, 1862, (not stated if present or absent, not entitled to bounty – over age). He was discharged due to disability on September 22, 1862, born England?, age 32, five foot 11 inches, fair complexion, blue eyes, light hair, a gardener by profession. Paid $99 for service on October 7, 1862. His discharge is in his file.*

Nixon, William, Pvt. Co. B

Enlisted on September 9, 1862, at Mobile, Alabama, by Captain Johnson for the war. He appears present on company muster rolls for September 24, 1862, March/April 1863, May/June 1863 and September/October 1863. On the May/June roll he is shown sick in quarters. He drew clothing on March 31 and June 1, 1864, and signed by his mark. POW captured at Fort Gaines, Alabama, on August 8, 1864. He was received at Ship Island, Mississippi, from New Orleans on October 25, 1864, and exchanged at Ship Island on January 4, 1865. See also **Niscom, William**.

Nobles, William B., Pvt. Co. G

He drew clothing on March 5 and June 1, 1864, and signed by his mark. POW captured at Fort Gaines, Alabama, on August 8, 1864. He was received at Ship Island, Mississippi, from New Orleans on October 25, 1864, and exchanged at Ship Island on

January 4, 1865. POW surrendered by Lt. General R. Taylor at Citronelle, Alabama, on May 4, 1865, and paroled at Meridian, Mississippi, on May 13, 1865. He was a resident of Prattville, Autauga County, Alabama.

Noel, J. R., Pvt. Co. I see **Newell, J. R.**

Nolan, William, Pvt. Co. H
He drew clothing on March 5, March 31 and June 1, 1864, and signed by his mark. POW captured at Fort Gaines, Alabama, on August 8, 1864. He was received at Ship Island, Mississippi, from New Orleans on October 25, 1864, and exchanged at Ship Island on January 4, 1865.

Nored, J. S., or **Nored,** John, Pvt. Co. C see **Norred, J. S.**

Norman, G. W., Pvt. Co. A/B/D see **Norman, W. G.**

Norman, W. G., Pvt. Co. A/B/D
Enlisted at Choctaw Bluff, Clarke County, Alabama, on March 28, 1863, by Captain Cottran for the war. He appears present on company muster roll for December 31, 1862, to April 30, 1862. Muster roll for May/June 1863, reports him transferred to Company B on June 30, 1963, by order of Colonel Anderson. He appears present in Company B on September/October 1863, muster roll. Muster roll for September/October 1864, reports him absent sent to General Hospital in Mobile on October 20, 1864. He drew clothing on June 20, 1864, in Co. D. See personal papers of **T. A. Foster**, Co. A, 21st Alabama. A descriptive list filed with Foster reports Norman, W. G. as age 36.

Norred, J. S., Pvt. Co. C
Enlisted at Mobile, Alabama, on October 13, 1861, by Captain Rembert for 12 months. He appears on a regimental return for June 1862, absent on sick furlough. He appears present on a company muster roll for bounty on September 24, 1862. He appears present on a company muster roll for December 31, 1862, to April 30, 1863. Muster roll for May/June 1863, reports him present and detailed on extra duty with AQM Department from June 10, 1863, by order of Colonel Anderson. Muster roll for September/October 1863, reports him absent on furlough for 15 days from October 17, 1863. He drew clothing May 31 and June 1, 1864, and signed his name. He appears on several receipt rolls for pay as a teamster from March to June 1864. Muster roll for September/October 1864, reports him absent, "Temporarily attached to the camp by Maj. Stone, En. Officer." "Sick in hospital since Oct.1/64." His name appears on a register of Ross Hospital at Mobile, Alabama, admitted on September 21, 1864, with dysenteria, acuta and sent to General Hospital at Greenville on September 26, 1864. POW surrendered by Lt. General Richard Taylor at Citronelle, Alabama, on May 4, 1865, and paroled at Meridian, Mississippi, on May 13, 1865.

Norred, Wesley, Corp. Co. C
His name appears on a regimental return for June 1862, "May 2, 1862, Corinth, died in hospital." Claim filed and paid to M. Norred, F. (father) for $51.73. His claim

account is in his file but almost illegible. Born Marengo County Alabama, age 31, dark complexion, hazel eyes, black hair, five foot ten and one half inches high, by occupation a laborer. Enlisted by Captain Rembert in Marengo County, Alabama, on October 13, 1861, to serve for twelve months.*

Norred, John, Pvt. Co. C see **Norred, J. S.**

Norride, J. S., Pvt. Co. C see **Norred, J. S.**

Northcut, F. M. Pvt. Co. C see **Northeut, F. M.**

Northrup, Albert, 1st Sgt./1st Lt. Co. C
    Elected 1st Lt. on July 23, 1862, promoted August 30, 1862. He appears present on a company muster roll for bounty on September 24, 1862, as present and promoted from 1st Sgt. on July 28, by election. He was transferred to Choctaw Bluff, Alabama, on October 2, 1862. He appears present on a company muster roll for December 31, 1862, to April 30, 1863. On a company muster roll for May/June 1863, he is reported present, sick in quarters. He requisitioned 80 pair of shoes for Co. C at Mobile, Alabama, on May 25, 1863. September/October 1863, muster roll reports him absent on sick leave for 20 days from October 11, 1863. He was ordered to take 40 days leave from Fort Morgan by General Maury on June 3, 1864. POW captured at Fort Gaines, Alabama, on August 8, 1864. He was received at Ship Island, Mississippi, from New Orleans on November 5, 1864, and exchanged at Ship Island on January 4, 1865. See personal papers of **M. C. Burk**. 1stLt. A. Northrup signed a Parole of Honor at Meridian, Mississippi, on May 10, 1865. His parole and a number of requisitions and pay vouchers are in his file.**

Northrup, B. F., Pvt. Co. C
    POW surrendered by Lt. General Richard Taylor at Citronelle, Alabama, on May 4, 1865, and paroled at Meridian, Mississippi, on May 13, 1865. His residence was shown as Marengo County, Alabama.

Northrup, F., Pvt. Co. C
    He enlisted on February 11, 1863, at Marengo County, Alabama, by Lt. Northrup for three years or the war. He is shown present on company muster rolls for December 31, 1862, to April 30, 1863 and May/June 1863. Company muster roll for September/October 1863, reports him present in arrest absent without leave from September 1, to September 17, 1863, "lost one haversack at $1 and canteen at $2." He drew clothing on May 31, 1864. POW captured at Fort Gaines, Alabama, on August 8, 1864. He was admitted to St. Louis USA General Hospital at New Orleans on October 10, 1864, with rubeola and returned to confinement on October 25, age 19. He was received at Ship Island, Mississippi, from New Orleans on October 27, 1864, and exchanged at Ship Island on January 4, 1865.

Northrup, H., Pvt. Co. C.
    Enlisted on February 11, 1863, at Marengo County, Alabama. By Lt. Northrup for three years or the war. He is reported absent sick on a company muster roll for

December 31, 1862, to April 30, 1863. May/June 1863, muster roll he is reported present sick in quarters. He was admitted to Post Hospital at Fort Morgan, Alabama, on November 16, 1863, with debilitas and returned to duty on December 2, 1863. He was admitted again on December 7, 1863, with dysentery and furloughed on December 30, 1863. He was discharged on surgeon's certificate July 29, 1863. Born in Marengo County, Alabama, age20, five foot eight inches, fair complexion, blue eyes, dark hair, and a planter by occupation. (*Note the dates of discharge do not match hospital records.*) His discharge is in his file.*

Norwood, A. L., Pvt. Co. C

He was enlisted on February 10, 1863, at Choctaw Bluff, Alabama, by Lt. Northrup for three years or the war. He is reported present on company muster roll for December 31, 1862, to April 30, 1863. May/June 1863, muster roll reports him absent on furlough for four days from June 27, 1863. Muster roll for September/October 1863, reports that he died in hospital at Point Clear, on October 5, 1863. He appears on a descriptive list for bounty paid at Mobile on May 2, 1863. Pvt. A. L. Norwood, age 25 blue eyes, dark hair, dark complexion, five foot ten inches, born in Dallas County, Alabama, a farmer by occupation. The descriptive list contains the names of Pvt. **T. J. Rawls, Pvt. A. S. Partin, Pvt. G. P. Oakley, and Pvt. John Rentz** see their files for description.*

Norwood, W. N., Pvt. Co. C

Enlisted at Point Clear, Alabama, on October 6, 1863, by Captain Smith for three years or the war. He is shown on a descriptive list for bounty on October 12, 1863, at Point Clear, Alabama, age 18, hazel eyes, dark hair dark complexion, five foot five inches, and a farmer born in Marengo County, Alabama. Paid $50 bounty. He appears present on a company muster roll for September/October 1863. He was admitted to Post Hospital at Fort Morgan, Alabama, on November 3, 1863, with int. feb. and returned to duty on November 4, 1863. He drew clothing March 31 and June 1, 1864. POW captured at Fort Gaines, Alabama, on August 8, 1864. He was admitted to St. Louis USA General Hospital in New Orleans on October 9, 1864, with dysentery, age 19. He died in St. Louis USA General Hospital on October 30, 1864. He was buried in Monument Cemetery grave 411. I. G. Norwood, Father listed as next of kin Shiloh, Marengo County, Alabama. His death certificate is in his file.*

Nowland, James, Pvt. Co. ?

His name appears on a roll of POW's at Alton, Illinois, in July 1862, Captured at Fort Henry on February 6, 1862. He was sent from Alton, Illinois, to Vicksburg, Mississippi, on September 23, 1862, to be exchanged. Exchanged at Alken's Landing near Vicksburg on November 11, 1862.

Nugent, William, Pvt. Co. B.

He was enlisted at Mobile, Alabama, on October 13, 1861, by Major Hessee for twelve months. He appears present on company muster roll for bounty on September 24, 1862, "refused to take bounty." There is a pay voucher and unreadable document in his file.*

O

Oakley, A. P., Pvt. Co. C see **Oakly G. P.**

Oakley, J. P., Pvt. Co. C see **Oakly, G. P.**

Oakly, G. P., Pvt. Co. C

Enlisted February 16, 1863, at Marengo, County, Alabama, by Lt. Northrup for three years or the war. His name appears on a descriptive list for bounty pay at Mobile on May 2, 1863, list is filed with Pvt. **A. L. Norwood. Oakley, G. P.**, Pvt. enlisted at Mobile age 18, dark eyes, dark hair, dark complexion, five foot five inches, born in Marengo County, Alabama, a farmer by occupation. He appears present on company muster rolls for December 31, 1862, to April 30, 1863, May/June 1863 and September/October 1863. On the latter roll he is reported missing one haversack at $1. He drew clothing on June 1, 1864. POW captured at Fort Gaines, Alabama, on August 8, 1864, received at Steam Levee Press No 4. at New Orleans on October 14, 1864, and sent to hospital. He was admitted to St. Louis USA General Hospital twice from military prison. Sent once on August 18, 1864, with fever remit. and acute diarrhoea and again on October 14, 1864, with acute diarrhoea. He was returned to confinement after the second admission on October 22, 1864, age 19. He was received at Ship Island, Mississippi, on October 25, 1864, and died at Ship Island of dysentery on December 10, 1864. Grave Number 76.

Oats, Arch, Pvt. Co. G

He drew clothing on March 31, May 1, and June 1, 1864, and signed by his mark. POW captured at Fort Gaines, Alabama, on August 8, 1864. He died at St. Louis USA General Hospital in New Orleans of typhoid fever on October 29, 1864. He left no effects and was buried in grave number 399 at Monument Cemetery. He was reported as age 41, a resident of Autauga County, Alabama, born in South Carolina. Ms. Nancy Oats, Prattville, Alabama, was his wife and next of kin. His death certificate is in his file.*

O'Brien, Peter, Pvt. Co. B.

He was enlisted at Fort Morgan, Alabama, on August 20, 1862, by Captain Johnston for the war. He appears present on a company muster roll for bounty on September 24, 1862. Company muster roll for March/April 1863, reports him absent with leave. Muster roll for May/June 1863, reports that he deserted from Oven Bluff, Alabama, on June 1, 1863.

O'Conner, R. E., Pvt. Co. K see **O'Connor, R. E.**

O'Connor, R. E., Pvt. Co. K

He was enlisted at Fort Morgan, Alabama, on August 18, 1862, by Captain Dorgan for the war. He appears absent with leave on a company muster roll for bounty on September 24, 1862, in Mobile, since September 23, 1862. Company muster roll for November/December 1862, reports him present. He drew clothing on July 10, 1863.

Company muster roll for July/August 1863, reports him absent sick. He was admitted to Ross Hospital at Mobile, Alabama, on October 27, 1863, with debility and sent to general hospital on December 1, 1863. September/October 1863, roll reports him absent on surgeon's certificate to November 10, 1863. He appears on a hospital muster roll for General Hospital Canty at Mobile, Alabama, for November/December 1863. He drew clothing in April 14 and June 10, 1864. He was admitted to Ross Hospital in Mobile on August 12, 1864, with acute diarrhoea and returned to duty on August 15, 1864. September/October 1864, roll reports him absent sick in hospital since October 15, 1864, by Dr. Armstrong. POW surrendered by Lt. General Richard Taylor at Citronelle, Alabama, on May 4, 1865, and paroled at Meridian, Mississippi, on May 13, 1865. Residence shown was New Orleans, Louisiana.

O'Conner, John, Pvt. Co. B, 1st Lt./ Captain
He appears on a field return for October 1862, as having been transferred to Choctaw Bluff, Alabama, on October 6, 1862. He was elected 1st Lt. on May 8, 1862, and promoted on May 1, 1863. He is reported present on company muster rolls March/April, May/ June and September/October 1863. He requisitioned and received for his company at Pollard, Alabama, April 16, 1864, the following items; 4 muskets, 7 cartridge boxes, 6 waist belts, 3 bayonet scabbards, all required to make at total of each of 57, of each and 1 knapsack, 0 haversacks, and 7 canteens all required to make a total of 60 each. POW captured August 8, 1864, at Fort Gaines, Alabama. It appears he was temporarily confined at Ship Island, Mississippi, on August 10, 1864, before being sent to New Orleans where he was hospitalized on November 2, 1864. He was admitted to Barracks USA General Hospital at New Orleans with small pox on November 1, 1864, and transferred to prison on November 9, 1864. Transferred back to Ship Island on December 18, 1864, and exchanged at Ship Island on January 4, 1865. POW surrendered by Lt. General Richard Taylor at Citronelle, Alabama, and paroled at Meridian, Mississippi, on May 10, 1865. There are a number of requisitions, pay vouchers and his Parole of Honor in his file.* There is a note to see the file of **M. C. Burk** in his file.
O'Connor, Robert, Pvt. Co. K see **O'Connor, R. E.**

Odom, James, Pvt. Co. B
Enlisted at Mobile, Alabama, on October 13, 1861, by Major Hessee for the war. He appears on a regimental return for June 1862, "Detached Service, Laboratory M & O RR." He appears on a company muster roll for bounty on September 24, 1862, reported absent detached for M & O RR on June 27, 1862. Company muster rolls for March/April, May/June and September/October 1863, report him absent detached for M & O RR January 1862, by order of General Bragg, descriptive list furnished. There are several signed pay vouchers in his file.*

O'Farrell, Pvt. Co. D/K see **O'Farrell, J. S.**

O'Farrell, J. C. Pvt. _
Enlisted on August 12, 1864, at Mobile, Alabama, by Major Stone for the war. He is reported absent on a company muster roll for September/October 1864, detached to Battery Huger, by order of Colonel Stone.

O'Farrell, Patrick, Co. B. Drummer/Musician see **Poellnitz, S. C.**, Pvt. Co. C.

Enlisted on April 18, 1863, at Mobile, Alabama, by Captain Johnston for the war. He appears present on a company muster roll for March/April 1863. A company muster roll for May/June 1863, reports him absent on 10-day sick leave from June 20, 1863. September/October 1863, muster roll reports him absent sent to hospital in Mobile on October 27, 1863, by order of Dr. Payne. He appears on a descriptive list for bounty at Point Clear, Alabama, September 23, 1863, age 18, blue eyes, light hair, fair complexion, five foot five, born in Ireland, paid $50. He drew clothing on March 31 and June 1, 1864, and signed by his mark. POW captured at Fort Gaines, Alabama, on August 8, 1864. He was received at Ship Island, Mississippi, from New Orleans on October 25, 1864, and applied to take the Oath of Allegiance to the USA. He was exchanged at Ship Island on January 4, 1865. He also appears on a roll of POW's at Elmira, New York, on November 30, 1864, "Captured at Fort Gaines, October 8, 1864, volunteered on April 17, 1863, to avoid conscription. Exchanged places with **S. C. Pollnitz**, 21st Ala. Inf. Co. C at Ship Island, and came to Elmira in his name. This he did to get North where he desires to stay. He has relatives at Woonsocket, R. I." (*He died of pneumonia on December 21, 1864, and is buried in Grave 1163 which is marked Pvt. S. C. Poellnitz.*)

O'Farrell, J. S., Pvt. Co. D/K.

Enlisted on August 19, 1864, at Mobile, Alabama, by Major Stone for the war. A company muster roll for September/October 1864, reports him absent "Temporarily attached by Maj. Stone, En (enrolling) Officer. Sick in Hospital since August 19/64,"

Oldham, Bennet, Pvt. Co. D

Enlisted on March 30, 1861, at Montevallo, Alabama, by Captain Gee for three years. A company muster roll for November/December 1862, reports him present transferred from Co. G, 1st Bat. Ala. Arty. Muster roll for July/August 1863, reports him present. He is reported present on extra duty on muster roll for September/October 1863. Muster roll for November/December 1863, he is reported present, detached in Engineering Department by order of General Maury. In July 1863, he was on extra duty at Fort Morgan as a carpenter. In October 1863, he was paid $2.40 per day as a carpenter and in December 1863, he was paid $2.40 per day as a carpenter at Mobile, Alabama. In February and March 1864, he drew extra duty pay of $3 per day as a carpenter. He signed by his mark. POW surrendered by Lt. General Richard Taylor on May 4, 1865, at Citronelle, Alabama, and paroled at Selma, Alabama, in May 10, 1865. He was shown as a resident of Shelby County, Alabama.

O'Neill, Alex, Pvt. Co. E

His name appears on a regimental return June 1862, "June 24, at Tupelo, (Mississippi) Transf: Capt. Myers Sharpshooters."

O'Neill, John, 1st Corporal/4th Sergeant Co. B

Enlisted on October 13, 1861, at Mobile, Alabama, by Major Hessee for twelve months. His name appears on a register of men in the 2nd Corps, Army of Mississippi, at the Battle of Shiloh missing since April 7, 1862, supposed captured. He appears present as 1st Corporal on a company muster roll for bounty on September 24, 1862. A company muster roll for March/April 1863, reports him as 4th Sergeant. May/June 1863, muster roll reports him present sick in quarters as does muster roll for September/October 1863. He drew clothing May 20 and June 1, 1864. POW captured at Fort Gaines on August 8, 1864. He was received at Ship Island, Mississippi, from New Orleans on October 25, 1864, and exchanged on January 4, 1865. POW surrendered by Lt. General Richard Taylor on May 4, 1865, at Citronelle, Alabama, and paroled at Meridian, Mississippi, on May 13, 1865.

O'Reilly, Charles, Pvt. Co. D see **O'Riley, Charles**

O'Reilly, Ignatius, Pvt. Co. H
POW captured at Fort Gaines on August 8, 1864. A morning report for September 28, 1864, shows him as a prisoner confined at Steam Levee Press No. 4 at New Orleans, Louisiana, sent to hospital on September 21, 1864. He was admitted to St. Louis USA General Hospital at New Orleans on August 22, 1864, with fever intermittens and returned to prison on September 9, 1864. He is shown as age 15. He was again admitted to the same hospital on September 27, 1864, with diarrhoea, and returned to prison on October 10, 1864. He was received at Ship Island, Mississippi, from New Orleans on October 25, 1864, and exchanged on January 4, 1865. POW surrendered by Lt. General Richard Taylor on May 4, 1865, at Citronelle, Alabama, and paroled at Meridian, Mississippi, on May 13, 1865.

O'Riley, Charles, Pvt. Co. D
Enlisted for the war on July 28, 1864, at Mobile, Alabama, by Enrolling Officer. He drew clothing in August 1864. A company muster roll for September/October 1864, reports him absent "Sent to Genl. Hospt at Mobile, Oct. 13, 1864." He was admitted to Ross Hospital at Mobile, Alabama, on September 11, 1864, with febris intermittens quot and returned to duty October 4, 1864. He was again admitted to Ross Hospital on October 19, 1864, with acute dysentery and sent to general hospital on December 6, 1864. POW surrendered by Lt. General Richard Taylor on May 4, 1865, at Citronelle, Alabama, and paroled at Meridian, Mississippi, on May 13, 1865. He is shown as a resident of Mobile, Alabama.

Orrell, William, Pvt. Co. F
Enlisted in Baldwin County, Alabama, on October 13, 1862, by Captain McCoy for one year. Company muster roll for bounty on September 24, 1862, reports him present. His is reported present on a company muster roll for March 1, to June 30, 1863. Muster roll for September/October 1863, reports him absent detached to fish by General Maury on August 23, 1963. He drew clothing on March 31, 1864. POW captured at Fort Gaines on August 8, 1864. He was received at Ship Island, Mississippi, from New Orleans on October 25, 1864, and exchanged on January 4, 1865.

Ortelli, John B., Pvt. Co. E
Killed at Shiloh on April 6, 1862, at 8 A. M. in attack on 1st Camp. Wound in the back of his neck.

Osborne, A. B., Pvt. Co. A

POW captured at Fort Donaldson on February 16, 1862. He appears on a roll of several hundred POW's at Camp Morton, Indiana, that were sent to Vicksburg, Mississippi, and exchanged at Atkins' Landing on November 10, 1862. He appears on a parole of POW's at Office of the Provost Marshal General, Army of the Potomac on May 4, 1863.

Osborne, Frank R. Pvt. Co. A

Enlisted on October 13, 1861, at Mobile, Alabama, by Major Hessee for twelve months. He was discharged at Fort Gaines due to disability by Dr. Nott on December 24, 1861. Born in Ireland, age 21, six foot, dark complexion, gray eyes, brown hair, and a clerk by occupation. His certificate of disability is in his file.*

Osburn, A. B., Pvt. Co. A see **Osborne, A. B.**

Osbum, R., Pvt. Co. K

Paid $34 for service from March 29, to June 30, 1862, on descriptive list.

Osburne, A. V., Pvt. Co. A see **Osborne, A. B.**

Osteen, Thomas A., Pvt. Co. E

Claim paid for deceased soldier to Mary Osteen on November 24, 1862.

Oston, Pvt. Co. C/A see **Austin, W. A.**

Oswaltz, P., Pvt. Co. H

His name appears on a regimental return for June 1862, where he is shown as missing on march, this entry canceled. He was wounded in the right arm slightly while advancing at Shiloh on April 6, 1862, at 2 P. M. at the center.

Overstreet, _, Pvt. Co. F

His name appears on a register at Post Hospital at Fort Morgan, Alabama, where he was admitted on December 30, 1863, with int. feb and returned to duty January 18, 1864.

Owen, F. A., Pvt. Co. K

Enlisted on April 22, 1861(?), at Mobile, Alabama, by Captain St. Paul for the war. He drew clothing on June 10, 1864. A company muster roll for September/October 1864, reports him absent in hospital since October 10, 1864, by Dr. Armstrong. POW surrendered by Lt. General Richard Taylor on May 4, 1865, at Citronelle, Alabama, and paroled at Meridian, Mississippi, on May 10, 1865. He is shown as a resident of Mobile County, Alabama.

Owen, George, Pvt. Co. K

He was wounded slightly in the left arm on April 6, 1862, at Shiloh at 7 A. M. while advancing on the 1st Battery.

MOBILE CONFEDERATES

Owen, W. C., Pvt. Co. D
Enlisted on September 1, 1864, at Mobile, Alabama, by Major Stone for the war. A company muster roll for September/October 1864, reports him present. His name appears on a register of POW's surrendered at Citronelle, Alabama, on May 4, 1865, and paroled at Mobile, Alabama, on June 7, 1865. A resident of Monroe County, Alabama, six foot one inch, age 37, florid complexion, gray eyes, brown hair.

Owen, William C., Pvt. Co. D see **Owen, W. C.**

Owen, William, Pvt. Co. B
Enlisted on September 7, 1862, at Mobile, Alabama, by Captain Johnston for the war. He appears present on a company muster roll for bounty September 24, 1862. A company muster roll for September/October 1863, reports him present. He drew clothing on March 31 and June 1, 1864. His name appears on an Oath of Allegiance to the USA at New Orleans, Louisiana. "Deserter, came into the Federal lines with the fleet before the capture of Fort Gaines August 3, 1864." Signed the oath on August 13, 1864. A resident of Mobile, Alabama, dark complexion, dark hair, gray eyes, five foot seven inches. There is an enquiry in this file for William H. Owen from Judge of Probate at Escambia, County, Brewton, Alabama in 1921.*

P

Packer, George, T., Pvt. Co. A
His name appears on a regimental return for June 1862, "sent to Columbus Hospital."

Paine, Bailey C., Pvt. Co. K see **Paine, B. C.**

Paine, Bailey C., Pvt. Co. K
Enlisted on November 22, 1863, at Fort Morgan by Captain Dorgan for the war. He drew clothing on December 19, 1863, and signed by his mark and drew clothing again on June 20, 1864. He was admitted to Post Hospital at Fort Morgan with debility on December 25, 1863, and returned to duty on December 30. He was admitted to Post Hospital at Fort Morgan with int. feb. on January 1, 1864, and returned to duty on January 30. He appears absent on a company muster roll for September/October 1864, "Detailed in Hospital Ross 30 days by Genl. Maury Sept. 23/64." He was admitted to Ross Hospital on October 31, 1864, with meningitis and died October 31, 1864.

Paine, J. F. Y., Surgeon Field and Staff see **Payne John F. Y.**

Palmer, John, Pvt. Co. I
His name appears on a regimental return for June 26, 1862, Memphis, died. "Was left at Memphis heard of his death June 26." Claim of $139.53 for deceased soldier paid on April 22, 1864, to J. R. Eastburn, attorney at Mobile for Elisa Palmer his widow. Voucher and paperwork for payment of claim is in his file.** Descriptive list shows him as age 34, blue eyes, light hair, fair complexion, five foot nine and one half inches, born

in Mississippi, a planter by profession. Enlisted at Halls Mill, Alabama, on October 13, 1861, for one year.

Paris, Benjamin, Pvt. Co. F
He was killed at Shiloh on April 6, 1862, at 8:30 A. M. at First Camp. "Wound not known."

Parish, T. M., Pvt. Co. C/A see **Parrish. T. M.**

Parish, William R., Pvt/Corp. Co. B
Enlisted on October 13, 1861, at Mobile, Alabama, by Major Hessee for twelve months. POW captured at the hospital. He was on the ambulance squad at Shiloh on April 7, 1862. He appears present on a company muster roll for bounty on September 24, 1862. March/April 1863, muster roll reports him present and detailed in Quarter Master Department on March 18, 1863. Muster roll for May/June 1863, reports him absent on sick leave from June 13, 1863. On the September/October 1863, roll he is shown as present as a 2nd Corporal. Appointed 2nd Corporal by order of Colonel Anderson on September 1, 1863. He drew clothing on March 31 and June 1, 1864. POW captured at Fort Gaines, August 8, 1864. He was received at Ship Island, Mississippi, from New Orleans on October 25, 1864, and exchanged on January 4, 1865.

Parker, George T., Pvt. Co. A
Discharged on July 5, 1862, at Camp near Tupelo. He enlisted on October 13, 1861, by Major Hessee at Mobile, Alabama. Born in Mobile, Alabama, dark complexion, dark eyes, five foot five and one half inches, age 34. His discharge is in his file.*

Parker, G. M., 1st Lt. Co. E/Adjutant Field and Staff
He was elected 1st Lt. Co. E on September 10, 1861. He was not re-elected on May 8, 1862, due to his absence because of capture. He appears on a return as present at Fort Gaines, Alabama, for November 1861. He appears on a regimental return for December 1861, and is shown absent by verbal order of General Withers for duty in Mobile since December 19, 1861. His name appears on a return from Shiloh as missing since 10 A. M. on April 7, 1862, "supposed captured." POW captured at Pittsburg Landing on April 7, 1862. He was received at Camp Chase, Ohio, on April 18, 1862, and transferred to Johnson's Island, Ohio, on April 26, 1862. He was sent to Vicksburg, Mississippi, for exchange on September 1, 1862. He was received on board the steamer *John H. Done* among 1104 POW's at Atkins' landing near Vicksburg on September 20, 1862. He was paid $140 on December 17, 1862, at Mobile, Alabama, he signed as Provost Marshal. There is correspondence, requisitions and vouchers in his file.**
Parker, J. M., Lt. Co. E & Adjutant Field and Staff see **Parker, G. M.**

Parker, William M., Pvt. Co. B
His name appears on a roll of POW's paroled at Alton, Illinois, until exchanged. Captured May 1, 1863, at Port Gibson, Mississippi. He was received at City Point, Virginia, among one thousand and ??? prisoners for exchange on June 12, 1863. He was

admitted to USA General Hospital at Pittsburgh, Pennsylvania, on June 17, 1863, with variola (small pox) and died July 1, 1862.

Parker, William N., Pvt. Co. B see **Parker William M.**

Parris, Jacob, Pvt. Co. F/E

Enlisted October 13, 1861, at Baldwin County, Alabama, by Captain McVoy for one year. He appears present on company muster roll for bounty on September 24, 1862. He appears present on company muster rolls for March 1, to June 30, 1863 and September/October 1863. He was admitted to Post Hospital at Fort Morgan on January 7, 1864, with int. fev. and returned to duty on January 10, 1864. He drew clothing on March 31 and June 1, 1864, and signed by his mark. POW captured at Fort Gaines, Alabama, on August 8, 1864. He was admitted to St. Louis USA General Hospital at New Orleans on September 16, 1864, with diarrhoea and returned to confinement on October 28, 1864, age 22. He was received at Ship Island, Mississippi, from New Orleans on October 29, 1864, and exchanged at Ship Island on January 4, 1865.

Parrish, T. M., Pvt. Co. C/A

Enlisted in Co. C on January 3, 1863, at Choctaw Bluff, Alabama, by Colonel Anderson for two years or the war. He was transferred to Co. A on March 31, 1863. He appears present on a company muster roll for December 31, 1862, to April 30, 1863, "has drawn no pay". Muster rolls for May/June 1863 and September/October 1863, report him present. He drew clothing on March 31, 1864, and at Camp Anderson on June 14, 1864. POW captured at Fort Morgan, Alabama, on August 23, 1864. He applied to take the Oath of Allegiance to the USA at Elmira, New York, on May 15, 1865, and go to his home in Randolph County, Alabama. He arrived at Elmira, New York, on October 8, 1864, from New Orleans and died of pneumonia June 17, 1865. He is buried in grave 2915. A descriptive list filed with **Foster, T. A.** reports Parrish as age 28.

Parsons, W., Pvt. Co. B see **Parsons, Malchi**

Parsons, Malchi, Pvt. Co. B

Enlisted on January 10, 1864, at Elyton, Alabama, by Capt. Gruss for the war. He was admitted to Post Hospital at Fort Morgan with pneumonia on January 22, 1864, and sent to general hospital on January 26, 1864. He appears present on a company muster roll for September/October 1864, at Mobile. He appears on a hospital muster roll to February 1864, at General Hospital at Greenville, Alabama, where he is shown as present and enlisted January 9, 1864, at Ellington, Alabama, by Captain Moore for the war. He was admitted to 1st Mississippi, CSA Hospital at Jackson, Mississippi, on March 20, 1865, with debilitas and returned to duty on April 4, 1865. His name appears on a roll of POW's who were paroled June 17, 1865, at Talladega, Alabama.

Parson's, Marion, Pvt. Co. B

Enlisted on September 4, 1862, at Jefferson, County, Alabama, by Captain Vass for three years or the war. He appears present on company muster rolls for March/April 1863, and May/June 1863, (sick in quarters in May/June). Muster rolls for

21ST ALABAMA INFANTRY VOLUNTEERS

September/October 1863 and September/October 1864, report him present. He drew clothing on May 30, 1863, and signed with his mark X.

Parson's, M. B., Pvt. Co. B

Enlisted on September 12, 1862, at Jefferson County, Alabama, by A. R. Goodwin for three year or the war. Company muster rolls for March/April 1863, May/June 1863, September/October 1863 and September/October 1864, all report him present. He was admitted to Ross Hospital at Mobile, Alabama, on January 26, 1864, with int. fever quotd. and returned to duty on February 28, 1864. (register shows him as **Miltyri Pearsons** and complaint was dysenteria) He drew clothing on March 31, 1864, and signed by his mark. POW surrendered at Citronelle, Alabama by Lt. General Richard Taylor on May 4, 1865, and paroled at Meridian, Mississippi, on May 13, 1865. Residence shown as Jefferson County, Alabama.

Parson's, Miltyne or Miltyri see **Parson's M. B.**

Parten, A. J., Pvt. Co. C see **Parton, A. J.**

Parten, James M., Pvt. Co. C see **Parton, James M.**

Parten, John F., Pvt. Co. C see **Parton, J. M.**

Parten, John M., Pvt. Co. C see **Parton, J. M.**

Parton, A. J., Pvt Co. C

Enlisted on February 9, 1863, at Marengo County, Alabama, by Lt. Northrup for two years or the war. Company muster rolls for May/June 1963 and September/October 1863, (lost one canteen at $2), report him present. He was admitted to Post Hospital at Fort Morgan, Alabama, on November 9, 1863, with feb. int. and returned to duty on November 5, 1863. He was admitted to Ross Hospital at Mobile, Alabama, on February 9, 1864, with remt. fever and sent to General Hospital at Greenville on February 24, 1864. POW captured at Fort Gaines, Alabama, on August 8, 1864, and received at Ship Island, Mississippi, on October 25, 1864, from New Orleans. He died of ascites at Ship Island on December 21, 1864, (one reports shows December 31). Buried in grave 122. Note says see personal papers of **A. G. Norwood**, Pvt. Co. C, 21st Alabama Infantry. Here is found data from a descriptive list filed with Norwood that shows A. J. Parton, Pvt. Enlisted at Mobile, Alabama, age 37, blue eyes, dark hair, light complexion, six foot two, born in Sumter, South Carolina, a farmer by occupation.

Parton, James, W., Pvt. Co. C

Enlisted at Point Clear, Alabama, on October 9, 1863, by Captain Smith for three years or the war. He is reported present on a company muster roll for September/October 1863. He drew clothing on June 1, 1864. POW captured at Fort Gaines, Alabama, on August 8, 1864. James M. Parten was received at Ship Island, Mississippi, from New Orleans on October 25, 1864, and died at Ship Island on December 31, 1864. File also

MOBILE CONFEDERATES

shows James M. Parton was surrendered at Citronelle and paroled at Demopolis on June 2, 1865. He was shown as a resident of Marengo County, Alabama.

Parton, James M., Pvt. Co. C

Enlisted at Camp Moore on November 7, 1861, by Captain Rembert for twelve months. He appears present on a company muster roll for bounty September 24, 1862. Company muster roll for December 31, 1862, to April 30, 1863, reports him detached in Engineering Department. at Choctaw Bluff on March 25, 1863, by order of General Buckner, "pay stopped from March 25, 1863." Company muster roll for May/June 1863, reports him present detached in Engineering Department on March 25, 1863, returned to company on May 21, 1863. Company muster roll for September/October 1863, reports him absent detached at Choctaw Bluff on September 22, 1863, by order of Colonel Anderson. He drew clothing March 31, 1864, and signed by his mark. POW captured at Fort Gaines, Alabama, on August 8, 1864, received at Ship Island, Mississippi, from New Orleans on October 25, 1864, and **John F. Parton** was exchanged on January 4, 1865. POW surrendered at Citronelle, Alabama, by Lt. General Taylor in May 1865 and paroled at Demopolis on June 2, 1865. A resident of Marengo County, Alabama.

Note the last three men's files are jumbled and have conflicting data.

Partridge, James, Pvt. Co. K

Enlisted on April 10, 1863, at Fort Morgan, Alabama, by Captain Dorgan for the war. He appears present on company muster rolls for July/August and September/October 1863. He drew clothing on July 10 and December 19, 1863.

Partridge, Thaddius, Pvt./Sgt. Co. K

Enlisted on October 13, 1861, at Mobile, Alabama, by Captain Stewart for the war. He appears present on a company muster roll for bounty September 24, 1862. He appears on a return for November 1862, as absent with leave (at) Mobile on November 22, 1862. Company muster roll for November/December 1862, reports him present as a private. Company muster rolls for July/August and September/October 1863, report him present as 1st Corporal. He drew clothing on December 19, 1863, and June 20, 1864. Company muster roll for September/October 1864, reports him absent at 4th Sergeant, "Absent on furlough of 15 days since October 27/64." POW surrendered at Citronelle, Alabama, by Lt. General R. Taylor on May 4, 1865, and paroled at Meridian, Mississippi, on May 10, 1865 He was shown as a resident of Mobile County, Alabama.

Pasqual, Sanfileqie T., Pvt. Co. G

Wounded severely in the shoulder while advancing at Shiloh on April 6, 1862 10 A. M. Paid $22 for service March and April, 1862. He signed by his mark X. His pay voucher is in his file.*

Pate, David, (E.) Pvt. Co. Co. B

Enlisted October 13, 1861, at Mobile, Alabama, by Major Hessee for the war. POW captured on ambulance squad and taken prisoner at the hospital on April 7, 1862, at the Battle of Shiloh. US records show him captured at Island 10 and sent to Camp

Douglas near Chicago, Illinois. He was admitted to USA Prison Hospital at Camp Douglas on May 27, 1862, with icterus (jaundice) and returned to confinement on June 16, 1862. He was sent to Vicksburg, Mississippi, to be exchanged on September 8, 1862, He arrived at Vicksburg among 742 POW's on board the steamer *John H. Done* on September 23, 1862, and exchanged at Atkins Landing on November 10, 1862. Company muster rolls for March/April, May/June and September/October 1863, all show him present. He drew clothing on March 31, 1864, and signed by his mark. Company muster roll for September/October 1864, reports him present. There is a pay voucher in his file.*

Pate, D. E., Pvt. Co. B see **Pate, David**

Patterson, James, Pvt. Co. E
He was wounded slightly in the hand while advancing on April 6, 1862, 8 A. M. in the attack on the First Camp at Shiloh. He was discharged on July 2, 1862. His name appears on a register of payments to discharged soldiers on July 28, 1862.

Patton, William, Sergeant Co. I
His name appears on a roll of POW's captured at Champion Hill, Mississippi, on May 16, 1863.

Payne, Isaac, Pvt. Co. A
His name appears on a roll of POW's captured at Fort Donaldson, on February 16, 1862, and sent to Camp Morton, Indiana. He was sent from Camp Morton, to Vicksburg, Mississippi, on August 24, 1863, to be exchanged. He arrived at Vicksburg, among 983 POW's on September 11, 1862, and was declared exchanged at Atkins Landing on November 10, 1862.

Payne, John F. Y., Surgeon Field and Staff
He appears present on muster rolls for July/August, September/August 1863 and March/April 1864. His name appears on a register of Inspector of Hospitals Office, Richmond, Virginia, from Pollard Alabama, for April 12, to July 18, 1864. There are a number of pay vouchers at $162 per month in his file with a requisition for clothing.

Pearson, J. M., Pvt. Co. C
Enlisted on October 13, 1861, at Mobile, Alabama, by Captain Rembert for 12 months. He appears present on a company muster roll for bounty on September 24, 1862. Company muster roll for December 31, 1862, to April 30, 1863, reports him present. Company muster roll for May/June 1863, reports him present, sick in quarters, lost one canteen at 25 cents, one strap at 20 cents and haversack at 20 cents. Company muster roll for September/October 1863, reports him absent in hospital in Mobile since October 25, 1863. He was admitted to Post Hospital at Fort Morgan on January 15, 1864, and sent to Ross Hospital in Mobile, with int fever quot and on to General Hospital in Montgomery on February 17, 1864. He drew clothing on June 1, 1864. POW captured at Fort Gaines, Alabama, on August 8, 1864. He was received at Ship Island, Mississippi, from New Orleans on October 25, 1864, and exchanged at Ship Island on January 4, 1865. POW

surrendered at Citronelle, Alabama, by Lt. General Taylor on May 4, 1865, and paroled at Meridian, Mississippi, May 13, 1864. Residence shown as Marengo County, Alabama.

Pearson, R. E., Pvt. Co. C

POW surrendered at Citronelle, Alabama, by Lt. General Taylor on May 4, 1865, and paroled at Meridian, Mississippi, on May 13, 1864. Residence shown as Marengo County, Alabama.

Peary, C. W., Pvt. Co. C see **Peavy, C. W.**

Peavy, C. W., Pvt. Co. C

Enlisted on March 21, 1862, at Monroe County, Alabama, by Captain Campbell. He appears present on company muster roll for December 31, 1962, to April 30, 1863. Company muster roll for May/June 1863, reports him present, lost canteen at 25 cents and one strap at 20 cents. Muster rolls for September/October 1863 and September/October 1864, report him present. He drew clothing on May 31 and June 1, 1865. POW captured at Blakeley, Alabama, on April 9, 1864, sent to Ship Island, Mississippi, and on May 1, 1865, to Vicksburg, Mississippi, for exchange.

Peckham, William, J., Pvt. Co. A

Enlisted on October 13, 1862, at Mobile, Alabama, by Major Hessee for the war. His name appears on a regimental return for June 1861, detached as clerk in A.A.Q.M. Department at Mobile. He appears absent on a company muster roll for bounty on September 24, 1862, detached as clerk in Ordnance Office at Mobile, on December 26, 1861, by order of General Withers. Company muster rolls show the same for Dec. 31, 1862, to April 30, 1863, May/June 1863 and September/October 1863. He appears present on a muster roll for detailed men in the C. S. Ordnance Department at Mobile, Alabama, for November/December 1863, May/June 1864, July/August 1864 and September/October 1864. POW surrendered at Citronelle, Alabama, among detailed men in Ordnance Department at Macon, Mississippi, by Lt. General Richard Taylor and paroled at Columbus, Mississippi, on May 18, 1864. There are several signed pay vouchers in his file.*

Peden, John H., Pvt. Co. H

He drew clothing on June 1, 1864. POW captured at Fort Gaines, Alabama, on August 8, 1864. He was admitted to St. Louis USA General Hospital at New Orleans, on August 20, 1864, with fever, intermitten, and returned to confinement on August 26, 1864, age 19. He was received at Ship Island, Mississippi, from New Orleans on October 25, 1864, and exchanged at Ship Island on January 4, 1865. POW surrendered at Citronelle, Alabama, by Lt. General Taylor on May 4, 1865, and paroled at Meridian, Mississippi, on May 13, 1864. Residence shown as Mobile, Alabama.

Pennington, John, Pvt. Co. A

Enlisted on February 1, 1863, at Choctaw Bluff, Alabama, by Captain Cothran for the war. He appears present on company muster rolls for December 31, 1862, to April 30, 1863 and May/June 1863. Company muster roll for September/October 1863, reports that he died of disease at Point Clear, Alabama, on September 24, 1863. He appears on a descriptive list along with five other soldiers on May 26, 1863. Age 19, gray eyes, light hair, fair complexion, five foot ten and one half inches, born Cherokee County, Georgia, a farmer by occupation, drew $50 bounty.*

Penny, F. T., Pvt. Co. K

. POW surrendered at Citronelle, Alabama, by Lt. General Taylor on May 4, 1865, and paroled at Meridian, Mississippi, on May 13, 1864. Residence shown as Mobile, Mobile County, Alabama.

Penwell, William A., Pvt. Co. B

His name appears on a register of payments of deceased soldiers. Payment made to L. J. Penwell his widow on February 27, 1863.

Perkins, J. M., Pvt. Co. C

Enlisted on January 7, 1862, at Fort Gaines, Alabama, by Captain Rembert for twelve months. He was wounded slightly in the left thigh on April 6, 1862, while advancing at 7 A. M. attack on the First Battery at Shiloh. His name appears on a regimental return for June 1862, as regimental wagon master. He appears present on a company muster roll for bounty on September 24, 1862. Company muster roll for December 31, 1862, to April 30, 1863, reports him absent detached as wagon master at Choctaw Bluff, Alabama. May/June 1863, muster roll reports that he was detached as wagon master at Choctaw Bluff by order of Colonel Anderson on October 7, 1862, and lost canteen at 25 cents. September/October 1863, muster roll reports him absent detached as wagon master on August 5, 1863, by order of General Maury. Drew clothing on March 31 and June 1, 1864. POW captured at Fort Gaines, Alabama, on August 8, 1864. He was received at Ship Island, Mississippi, from New Orleans on October 25, 1864, and exchanged at Ship Island on January 4, 1865. POW surrendered at Citronelle, Alabama, by Lt. General Taylor on May 4, 1865, and paroled at Meridian, Mississippi, on May 13, 1864. Residence shown as Marengo County, Alabama. There is a signed pay voucher in his file.*

Perkins, S. C., Pvt. Co. C

Enlisted on January 7, 1862, at Fort Gaines, Alabama, by Captain Rembert for twelve months. He appears present on a company muster roll for bounty on September 24, 1862. Company muster roll for December 31, 1862, to April 30, 1863, reports him present. Company muster roll for May/June 1863, reports him present detailed as a teamster June 10, 1863, by Colonel Anderson. September/October 1863, muster roll reports him present detailed in A. Q. M. Department from August 5, 1863, by Colonel Anderson. Company muster roll for September/October 1864, reports him absent temporarily attached by Major Stone En. Officer, detailed as teamster by Captain Dade. Drew clothing on June 1, 1864. POW surrendered at Citronelle, Alabama, by Lt. General Taylor on May 4, 1865, and paroled at Gainesville, Alabama, on May 11, 1864. Residence shown as Marengo County, Alabama.

MOBILE CONFEDERATES

Perkins, Thomas, A., Pvt. Co. A.
POW captured at Fort Donaldson on February 16, 1862, and sent to Camp Morton, Indiana. He was sent from Camp Morton, to Vicksburg, Mississippi, for exchange on August 24, 1862. He was received near Vicksburg on September 11, 1862, and exchanged at Atkins Landing on November 10, 1862.

Perry, Joseph, Pvt. Co. K
Enlisted on August 22, 1864, at Mobile, Alabama, by Major Stone for the war. Company muster roll for September/October 1864, reports him absent temporarily attached to the camp by Major Stone sick in hospital since October 20, 1864. A second muster roll for September/October 1864, reports him being discharged on account of being a minor by General Maury. "Illegally conscripted."

Perry, W. S., Pvt. Co. K
Enlisted on September 22, 1864, at Clarke County, Alabama, by Major Stone for the war. Muster roll for September/October 1864, reports him absent temporarily attached to the camp by Major Stone detailed for 10 days in Q. M. Department by General Maury on October 27, 1864.

Pettus, John A., Pvt. Co. K
Enlisted on October 13, 1861, at Mobile, Alabama, by Captain Stewart for the war. He appears absent on a company muster roll for bounty on September 24, 1862, detached in M & O Railroad on April 2, 1862, by General Gladden. Company muster rolls for November/December 1862, July/August 1863, September/October 1863 and September/October 1864, all show him absent on detached service with the Mobile and Ohio Railroad. There is a note in his file to see the personal papers of **H. Harding** CSA Superintendent of Repairs for M & O RR detailed as a conductor. There are pay vouchers in his file.*

Phifer, J., Pvt. Co. D
Enlisted on October 2, 1864, at Mobile, Alabama, by Major Stone for the war. Company muster roll for September/October 1864, reports that he was sent to hospital at Mobile on October 14, 1864. He was admitted to Ross Hospital at Mobile on October 15, 1864, with febis intermittens quot. and returned to duty on November 20, 1864. Never paid.

Philbrook, Walter, Pvt. Co. K.
Enlisted on October 13, 1861, at Mobile by Captain Stewart for the war. He was wounded slightly in the right shoulder on April 6, 1862, at 9 A. M. while advancing in the attack on the First Camp at Shiloh. His name appears on a report for June 1862, wounded at Shiloh, and on furlough. He appears absent on surgeon's certificate from July 15, 1862, on a company muster roll for bounty on September 24, 1862. A return for November 1862, shows him absent on surgeon's certificate. Company muster rolls for November/December 1862, July/August 1863, September/October 1863 and September/October 1864, all report him absent detached as Government expert by order of Secretary of War. A document in his file indicates that he was paid for service August 31, 1862, to

October 28, 1862, in the amount of $20.90, "October 28, 1862, private Walter Philbrook Co. K, 21st Ala; was detached by Adj. Genl. for duty in the Treasury Department on which day his army pay stopped." There is a card in his file indicating Philbrook, Walter, clerk in charge of notes see personal papers of H. Hareford, VA regiment. There is the following letter and pay vouchers in his file.*

> Honorable C. G. Memminger
> Sec'y of Treasury
> The undersigned is an applicant for a position in the Treasury Dep't. He is a private in Co. K 21st Reg't Alabama Vols. Incapacitated for active duty by reason of wound. He has had eight years experience as bank clerk, and is particularly conversant with the duties of Teller.
> H solicits employment which will enable him to support a widowed mother.
> Walter Philbrook

> References
> Hon. E. S. Dorgan M. C.
> W. A. Stother Esq.
> Cashers of the Mobile Bank.

Philen, W. S., Pvt. Co. G see **Phillan, W. S.**

Philipps, Henry. T., Pvt. Co. C
Enlisted November 3, 1861, at Marengo County, Alabama, to serve twelve months. He as discharged due to severe disability on October 2, 1862, at Fort Morgan. He was born in Jones County, Georgia, age 46, five foot eight inches, fair complexion, blue eyes, sandy hair and by occupation a planter. He was paid $39 for service on November 20, 1862.

Phillan, W. S., Pvt. Co. G
There is a signed voucher for payment of rations while on sick furlough, signed at Montgomery, Alabama, August 18, 1863. He drew clothing on March 31, May 3 and June 1, 1864. POW captured at Fort Gaines, Alabama, on August 8, 1864. He was admitted to St. Louis USA General Hospital at New Orleans from military prison on September 5, 1864, with chronic diarrhoea and returned to confinement on September 15, 1864, age 37. He was received at Ship Island, Mississippi, from New Orleans on October 25, 1864, and died of pneumonia at Ship Island on December 22, 1864. He is buried in grave 108.

Phillips, Tully, Pvt Co. A
Enlisted at Choctaw Bluff, Alabama, on February 1, 1863, by Captain Cothran, for the war. He appears present on company muster rolls for December 31, 862, to April 30, 1863, May/June 1863 and September/October 1863. He drew clothing on March 31, 1864, and signed by his mark and on June 14, 1864, at Camp Anderson. POW captured at Fort Morgan, Alabama, on August 23, 1864. He appears on a register of prisoners of

war at New Orleans, which were sent to New York on September 27, 1864. He was received at Elmira, New York, on October 8, 1864, from New Orleans. He signed as being desirous to take the Oath of Allegiance to the USA and go to his home in Benton County, Alabama. He was released on July 27, 1865. Residence shown as Rome, Georgia, sallow complexion, dark hair, gray eyes, six foot. This data is from a descriptive list on May 26, 1863, list is filed with **Pvt. John Pennington**, Co. A.

Pvt. **Tuly Phillips**, age 37, blue eyes, dark hair, fair complexion, six foot, born in North Carolina, a farmer by occupation, enlisted at Clarke County, Alabama, by Captain Cothran for the war, paid $50 bounty.

Phillpot, R., Pvt. Co. D. see **Philpot, R. A.**

Philpot, R. A., Pvt. Co. D

Enlisted at Greenville, Alabama, on November 4, 1863, by Lt. Barton for the war. He appears present on company muster rolls for November/December 1863 and September/October 1864. He drew clothing on June 20, 1864. POW surrendered at Citronelle, Alabama, by Lt. General Taylor on May 4, 1865, and paroled at Meridian, Mississippi, on May 13, 1864. Residence shown as Greenville, Alabama.

Piel, William, Pvt.

Paid $144.40 for service on July 21, 1863. Enlisted by Captain Arrington in Co. A of Arrington's City Troop, Third Brigade on October 1862, at Camp Withers. Born in Mobile, Alabama, age 23, five foot eight inches, fair complexion, gray eyes, dark hair. He was discharged on April 28, 1862, as unfit for action, disability. Copies of his discharge and other paperwork are in his file.*

Pike, Thomas, Pvt. Co. B

His name appears on a report of sick and wounded for the quarter ending September 30, 1862, at Gratiot Street Prison Hospital at St. Louis, Missouri, under deaths from debilitas on August 13. (*See information on Gratiot Street Prison at* http://www.civilwarstlouis.com/Gratiot/gratiotfaq.htm)

Pillett, Julian, Pvt. Co. B

Enlisted on October 13, 1861, at Mobile, Alabama, by Major Hessee for three years or the war. His name appears on a register of missing at the Battle of Shiloh "taken prisoner Apl 62." His name appears on a roll of POW's at Camp Douglas, Illinois, August 1, 1862, captured April 8, 1862, at Pittsburg (Landing). Company muster rolls for March/April and May/June 1863, report him present. He appears absent on a company muster roll for September/October 1863, "Sent to Genl Hospital Mobile July 13, 1863, by order of Col Anderson." He was reported to be in Ross Hospital at Mobile, Alabama, October 1, 1863, with typhoid fever, returned to duty December 1, 1863. A claim of deceased soldier was filed by **Madeline Pillet** his mother on November 5, 1864.

Pinkney, J., Pvt. Co. D.

Enlisted at Choctaw Bluff, Alabama, on January 12, 1863, by Colonel Anderson, for the war. Company muster roll for September/October 1864, reports him present assigned to the commissary by order. Pvt. John Pickney was admitted to Ross Hospital at Mobile on September 29, 1864, with febris intermittens quot. and sent to General Hospital at Lauderdale Springs on October 6, 1864. There is additional card for Pvt. J. Pickney that shows him enrolling on August 12, 1863, at Choctaw Bluff, Alabama, by Captain Dade and reports him absent on company muster roll for September/October 1864, detached at Battery Huger by order of Colonel Fuller.

Pinkney, John, Pvt. Co. F.
Enlisted on January 27, 1863, at Choctaw Bluff, Alabama, by Captain Dade for the war. Company muster roll for March 1, to June 30, 1863, reports him present. Muster roll for September/October 1863, reports him absent sick in hospital at Mobile since October 25, 1863. He appears on a hospital muster roll for General Hospital Moore at Mobile, Alabama, as a patient. Roll is dated November/December 1863. He drew clothing on March 31, 1864.

Pitts, John, T., Pvt. Co. G
He drew clothing on March 3, March 31 and June 1, 1864. POW captured at Fort Gaines, Alabama, on August 8, 1864. He was received at Ship Island, Mississippi, on October 25, 1864, from New Orleans and died of dysentery on December 15, 1864. He was buried in Grave No. 88. There is a commutation of ration form in his file signed by John Pitts.*

Plum, Henry, L., Pvt. Co. A/K
Enlisted on October 13, 1861, at Mobile, Alabama, by Major Hessee for the war. He was wounded in the left side at Shiloh on April 6, 1862, at 4 P. M. while crossing The Old Field and captured at the hospital at Pittsburg Landing on July 7. He was admitted to No. 4 USA General Hospital at Louisville, Kentucky, Ward No. 1 on April 17, 1862, with wound in the right side and sent to General Hospital at Camp Chase, Ohio. He was admitted to USA Post Hospital at Camp Chase, on May 13, 1862, with gunshot wound, and returned to prison on May 26, 1862. He appears on a list of wounded prisoners received at Camp Chase, Ohio, from Louisville, Kentucky, on May 13, 1862, having been received on May 12. He was sent from Camp Chase to Vicksburg, Mississippi, for exchange on August 25, 1861. He was among 1020 prisoners aboard the steamer *John H. Done* that were exchanged at Atkins' Landing, on November 10, 1862. He appears absent sick captured by the enemy on a company muster roll for bounty on September 24, 1862. Company muster roll for December 31, 1862, to April 30, 1863, reports him absent detached on January 30, 1863, to Com. Department at Fort Morgan by order of General Macknall. Muster roll for May/June 1864, reports the same. September/October roll reports him present but detached similarly. His name appears on a list of clerks employed in various offices and bureaus at Mobile for July 1864, a clerk, for Captain T. Clewis Asst. Chief C. G., unfit for field service. POW surrendered at Citronelle, Alabama, by Lt. General R. Taylor on May 4, 1865, and paroled at Meridian, Mississippi, a resident of Mobile, Alabama. There are a number of pay vouchers and record of receipt in his file.**

Pockham, W. J., Co. A

His name appears on a list for July 1864, as a clerk for M. L. K. Major H. Myers Ordinance Department by order of Major General Maury, unfit for field service.

Poellnitz, B., Pvt. Co. C

(*This filed with B. B. Poellnitz below I believe should be a separate entry AEG.*) Enlisted on August 21, 1863, at Marengo County, Alabama, by Lt. Poellnitz for three years or the war. Company muster roll for September/October 1863, reports him present and never been paid

Poellnitz, Bruno B., 2nd Lt./Pvt. Co. C

Enlisted on October 13, 1861, and elected 2nd Lt. on October 3, 1861, resigned July 6, 1862. His name as 2nd Lt. appears as present on a regimental return for December 1861. He again appears on a regimental return for June 1862, "absent on furlough since April 4, for 30 days, extended by surgeon." His name appears on a return of troops present and stationed at Fort Gaines, Alabama, in November 1861. He was paid $335.96 cents at $80 per month for service March 1, to July 6, 1862, on October 28, 1862. He appears on descriptive list for pay on October 12, 1863, at Point Clear, Alabama, born in Marengo County, Alabama, age 41, eyes hazel, dark hair, dark complexion, five foot eleven inches, a farmer by occupation, born in Marlboro District, South Carolina.

Poellnitz, Edwin A., 2nd Lt. Co. C

Enlisted on October 13, 1861, and elected 2nd Lt. Co. C on August 30, 1862. He appears present on a company muster roll for bounty on September 24, 1862, "Promoted from 1st Sgt. Aug. 30, by election." Field return for October 1862, reports him transferred to Choctaw Bluff, Alabama, on October 6, 1862. He appears present on company muster roll of December 31, 1862, to April 30, 1863. He is reported absent on a company muster roll for May/June 1863, "absent on four day furlough from the 25 June 1863, and Leave extended." Company muster roll for September/October 1863, reports him present. On June 2, 1864, Lt. Poellnitz requisitioned ordnance stores for his 97 non-commissioned officers and privates of Co. C to make up the following required issue: 85 muskets, 85 bayonets, 85 cartridge boxes, 18 shoulder straps, 85 waist belts, 85 cap pouches, 85 bayonet scabbards, 97 haversacks, 97 canteens, 97 knapsacks, 0 cartridges, 0 caps. POW captured at Fort Gaines, Alabama, on August 8, 1864, received at Ship Island, Mississippi, from New Orleans on November 25, 1864, and exchanged at Ship Island on January 4, 1865. There are a number of signed pay vouchers and the ordnance requisition in his file.**

Poellnitz, James, Pvt./2nd Lt. Co. C

Enlisted on April 27, 1862, at Corinth, Mississippi, by Lt. Luther for three years or the war. His name appears on a regimental return for June 1862, "May 1, Corinth, Miss. gain mustered in camp." He appears present as Sgt. on company muster roll for bounty on September 24, 1862. Company muster roll for December 31, 1862, to April 30, 1863, reports him present as 3rd Sgt. May/June 1863, muster roll reports him present, promoted from 3rd Sgt. to 1st Sgt. on June 6, 1863. Company muster roll for September/October 1863, reports him present. Elected 2nd Lt. on November 20, 1863,

"Lt. Luther failed to pass Board of Examiners after election." He was issued a discharge at Fort Morgan upon being elected 2nd Lt.. Born in Marengo County, Alabama, age 24, five foot eight inches, fair complexion, blue eyes, light hair, a student by occupation. POW captured at Fort Gaines, Alabama, on August 8, 1864. He was received at Ship Island, Mississippi, from New Orleans on November 25, 1864, and exchanged at Ship Island on January 4, 1865. The items below and other paper work are in his file.**

Headquarters Choctaw Bluff
January 30, 1863

Special Order

No. 62   II Sergt. James A. Poellnitz, Co. C, 21st Ala. Regt. will proceed fortwith to Montevallo, Ala. at the termination of the Selma, Rail Road for the purpose of apprehending privates Thos Manning, H. Manning, W. T. Reid, David James – John Graham, E. Burrell & J. H. Burrell who deserted from this post on the 29th day of Jany / 63. The A. Q. M. will furnish transportation.

By order of Col Anderson
Geo Vidmer
1st G & Post Adjutant

1863 from 30 of Jany to the 10th of Feby, 1863

For one day board in Selma @ $4.00
Six days board at Montevallo @ $2.00 per day
Traveling expenses from Montevallo to Selma $2.00
"   "   "   Selma to Montevallo $3.00
…………Received payment at Choctaw Bluff, February 11, 1863

Poellnitz, S. C., Pvt. Co. C (*see also O'Farrell, Patrick*)

Enlisted on June 26, 1862, at Tupelo, Mississippi, by Lt. Luther for twelve months. His name appears on a report June 28, 1862, near Tupelo furloughed on surgeons certificate. He appears absent detached in the Signal Corps on a company muster roll for bounty on September 24, 1862. Company muster rolls for December 31, 1862, to April 30, 1863, May/June 1863 and September/October 1863 reports him detached at Fort Morgan with the Signal Corps by order of General Forney since September 8, 1862. His name appears on a roll of non-commissioned officers and privates employed on special duty during July 1863, as a signal operator. (*filed with B. Poellnitz above*). He drew clothing on June 1, 1864. POW captured at Fort Morgan, Alabama, on August 23, 1864. He was admitted to St. Louis USA General Hospital at New Orleans on September 21, 1864, with fev. remittent and diarrhoea and returned to confinement on September 20, 1864. His name appears on a list of POW's confined at Steam Levee Press No. 4, at New Orleans on September 30, 1864. He was sent to Ship Island, Mississippi. His identity was stolen at Ship Island by Patrick O'Farrell who wanted to go north. Records show that he was sent to New York, on November 5, 1864, by order of Captain Marston. (*This order is unusual, was the Captain in on the ruse?*) He (O'Farrell) was received at Fort Columbus, New York Harbor, on November 16, 1864, and received at Elmira, New York, on October 8, 1864, in hospital. Patrick O'Farrell died of pneumonia on December 21, 1864, and is buried in Grave No. 1163. The official records will show Pvt. S. C. Poellnitz buried in grave 1163. There are several signed pay vouchers in his file.*

Poelmitz, Sidney, Pvt. Co. C see **Poellnitz, S. C.**

Poelwith, W. A. C., Pvt. Co. C see **Poellnitz, S. C.**

Poelwitz, W. A. C., Pvt. Co. C see **Poellnitz, S. C.**

Polk, James R., Pvt. Co. F
    Enlisted on October 13, 1861, by Captain McCoy to serve for one year. Discharged December 20, 1861, at Fort Gaines, Alabama. Born in Georgia, age 15, five foot four inches high, fair complexion, blue eyes, light hair, by occupation a laborer. He was discharged for want of proper physical development. His discharge and pay voucher is in his file.*

Pollard, J. R., Pvt. Co. C
    Enlisted on September 7, 1862, at Fort Morgan, Alabama, by Captain Smith for the war. He appears present on company muster roll for bounty on September 24, 1862. Company muster rolls for December 31, 1862, to April 30, 1863, May/June 1863 and September/October 1863, all show him present. Drew clothing March 31 and June 1, 1864, and signed by his mark. POW captured at Fort Gaines, Alabama, on August 8, 1864. He was received at Ship Island, Mississippi, on October 25, 1864, and exchanged on January 4, 1865, at Ship Island. He was admitted to Ross Hospital in Mobile, Alabama, on January 6, 1865, with debilitas and returned to duty on January 17, 1865. POW captured again at Blakeley, Alabama, on April 9, 1865. He was received at Ship Island on April 15, 1865, and transferred to Vicksburg, Mississippi, on May 1, 1865, for exchange.

Pollard, V., Pvt. Co. D see **Pollard, William J.**

Pollard, William, Pvt. Co. D
    Enlisted on October 13, 1861, at Mobile, Alabama, by Captain Butt for one year. A regimental return for June 1862, reports him on detached service in Pioneer Corps. A muster roll shows him a member of Captain Steele's Company B in the Pioneer Battalion commanded by Major Meriwether, Jackson's Brigade. He appears present on company muster roll for bounty on September 24, 1862. Company muster rolls for November/December 1862 and July/August 1863, report him present. Company muster roll for September/October 1863, reports him absent, in guardhouse at Fort Morgan. He was admitted to Post Hospital at Fort Morgan on October 31, 1863, with diarrhoea and returned to duty on November 13, 1863. November/December 1863, muster roll reports him present. He was discharged from the 21st Alabama on April 24, 1864, at Cedar Point, Alabama, born in Tennessee, age 24, five foot seven inches, fair complexion, gray eyes, light hair. Transferred to CS Navy on June 2, 1864. His discharge and a pay voucher are in his file.*

Pollo, John, Pvt. Co. B

Enlisted at Mobile, Alabama, on October 13, 1861, by Major Hessee for one year. He appears present in arrest on company muster roll for bounty on September 24, 1862. Company muster rolls for March/April 1863 and May/June 1863, report him present. September/October 1863, he is reported present sick in quarters, due $48.63. Drew clothing on March 31 and June 1, 1864, signed by his mark. POW captured at Fort Gaines, Alabama, on August 8, 1864. He was received at Ship Island, Mississippi, on October 25, 1864, and exchanged on January 4, 1865, at Ship Island.

Polo, John, Pvt. Co. B see **Pollo, John**

Pondere, Charles, Pvt. Co. C

He was admitted to St. Louis USA General Hospital in New Orleans on September 11, 1864, with fever remitten, returned to military prison on September 27, 1864, age 17.

Pope, C. H., Pvt. Co. K

He was wounded in the left arm slightly at Shiloh on April 6, 1862, at 9 A. M. while advancing on First Camp. His name appears on a regimental return for June 1862, June 18, at Tupelo. "Transf'd to Sharpshooters."

Pope, Charles, Pvt. Co. K see **Pope C. H.**

Porcaso, John, Pvt. Co. G

His name appears on a regimental return for June 1862, "Sent to hospital, May 28." He also appears on a report near Tupelo, Mississippi, on June 28, 1862, "Sent to interior from Corinth at the time of the evacuation."

Post, Sylvanus, Pvt. Co. A

Enlisted on October 13, 1861, at Mobile, Alabama, by Major Hessee for one year. He was discharged on January 1, 1862, at Fort Gaines, Alabama, due to disability caused by variocele (*enlargement of the veins of the spermatic cord*) of two years standing. Born in Essex, Connecticut, age 29, five foot seven inches, dark complexion, hazel eyes, dark hair, by occupation a sailor. His discharge is in his file.*

Post, Ward, Pvt. Co. F

Enlisted October 13, 1861, at Baldwin County, by Captain McCoy. Discharged on October 25, 1862, at Choctaw Bluff, Alabama, due to advance age. Born in Essex, Connecticut, age 42, five foot eight inches, dark complexion, blue eyes, dark hair and by occupation a carpenter. There is a voucher for pay in his file for $78.60 while working on gunboats at Mobile from December 18, 1861, to April 25, 1862. His discharge is in his file.*

Post, Wind, Pvt. Co. F

His name appears on a report filed near Tupelo, Mississippi, on June 28, 1862, "Sent from Tupelo, June 14." He appears on a regimental return for June 1862, "Sent to Interior Hospt. May 28."

Powell, Colonel, Field and Staff

His name appears in an Order and Letter book of Post Hospital at Fort Morgan, Alabama.

Powell, J. W., Pvt. Co. C see **Privett, J. W.**

Powell, W. G., Pvt. Co. G see **Powell, William J.**

Powell, William J., Pvt. Co. G

Enlisted at Pike County, Alabama, by Lt. Henry on August 12, 1862, for the war. He drew clothing on March 3, 1864. POW surrendered at Citronelle, Alabama, by Lt. General Richard Taylor on May 4, 1865, and paroled at Meridian, Mississippi, May 13, 1865. He was shown as a resident of Troy, Pike County, Alabama.

Powers, O. B., Corp./Pvt. Co. D

Enlisted October 13, 1864, at Mobile, Alabama, by Captain Butt for one year. His name appears on a regimental return for June 1862, "sent to Interior Hospital at the evacuation."(of Corinth) He appears on a report for June 28, 1862, near Tupelo, Mississippi, "sick in hospital in Mobile sent by surgeon from Corinth." He appears as 1st Corporal present on a company muster roll for bounty on September 24, 1862. Company muster roll for November/December 1862, reports him absent promoted from 1st Corporal to 4th Sergeant on December 1, 1862, and detached by order of General Forney for 30 days, to get no pay. Muster roll for July/August 1863, reports him detached on Alabama River as pilot by order of General Macknall on February 3, 1863. Company muster roll for September/October 1863, reports him absent detached as pilot on Alabama River. Company muster roll for November/December 1863, reports him detached by order of General Forney on December 5, 1862, as engineer and muster roll for September/October 1864, reports him absent detached as pilot on December 5, 1862. There are two signed pay vouchers in his file.*

Pradera, Louis, Pvt. Co. G

Enlisted on October 13, 1861, at Mobile, Alabama, by Major Hessee to serve one year. He was discharged on April 21, 1862, near Corinth, Mississippi, due to disability caused by varicose veins of the leg. His discharge is in his file.*

Prados, Arthur A., Pvt. Co. K

Enlisted on January 24, 1862, at Fort Gaines, Alabama, by Captain Stewart for twelve months. Wounded in the breast severely at Shiloh on April 6, 1862, on Center Field and captured at hospital on April 7, 1862. Company muster roll for bounty on September 24, 1862, reports him present. Company muster roll for November/December 1862, reports him present. Muster roll for July/August 1863, report him transferred to

Captain Hutchinson's Company of Engineers. He drew clothing on July 10, 1864. There is one pay voucher in his file.*

Premo, Alfred, Pvt. Co. A

Enlisted on October 13, 1861, at Mobile, Alabama, by Major Hessee. His name appears on a report on June 28, 1862, near Tupelo, Mississippi, "discharged from Hazelhurst hospital ordr'd to report to his company never appeared rep. as a deserter." Company muster roll for bounty on September 24, 1862, reports him present refused to take bounty.

Price, Benjamin M., Pvt./Corp. Co. E

Enlisted on October 13, 1861, at Mobile, Alabama, by Captain Chamberlain. His name appears on a report June 28, 1862, near Tupelo, Mississippi, "sent to interior hospital by Surgeon." He received payment for commutation of rations while on furlough from June 9, to July 18, 1862. Company muster roll for bounty on September 24, 1862, reports him present. Company muster rolls for November/December 1862, July/August 1863 and September/October 1863, all report him present. He drew clothing on March 31 and June 1, 1864. POW captured at Fort Gaines, Alabama, on August 8, 1864. He was sent to New Orleans and was in confinement at Steam Levee Press No. 4 on September 29, 1864. He was admitted to St. Louis USA Hospital at New Orleans on September 28, 1864, with acute diarrhoea and returned to confinement on September 30, 1864, age 28. He arrived at Ship Island, Mississippi, from New Orleans on October 25, 1864, and was exchanged at Ship Island on January 4, 1865. POW surrendered at Citronelle, Alabama, by Lt. General Richard Taylor on May 4, 1865, and paroled at Meridian, Mississippi, on May 13, 1865. He was shown as a resident of Mobile, Alabama.

Price, Thomas, Sgt./Pvt. Co. B/A

Enlisted on October 13, 1864, at Mobile, Alabama, by Major Hessee for the war. He appears present as 1st Sgt. on a company muster roll for bounty on September 24, 1862. Company muster roll for March/April 1863, reports him present as 1st Sgt. Company muster roll for May/June 1863, reports him transferred to Co. A as a Private by Colonel Anderson on May 25, 1863. Muster roll for September/October 1863, reports him present as Private. He was admitted to Post Hospital at Fort Morgan, Alabama, on January 24, 1864, with debitilas and sent to general hospital on January 24, 1864. He was transferred to CS Navy on Special Order No. 46, (February 1864?)

Pritchard, A., Pvt. Co. K

Enlisted on May 2, 1864, at Mobile, Alabama, by Major Stone for the war. He was discharged on disability on October 18, 1864. Born in Dublin, Ireland, age 32, five foot five and one half inches, light complexion, gray eyes, dark hair and by occupation a clerk. Discharged due to phthisis pullmonalis (*tuberculosis*). His discharge is in his file.*

Pritchett, R. Hobbs, Pvt. Co. C

Enlisted on October 13, 1861, at Mobile, Alabama, by Captain Rembert for the war. His name appears on a regimental return for June 1862, "absent on sick furlough."

He appears on a report for June 28, 1862, near Tupelo, Mississippi, "Sent to interior Hospital by Surg. from Corinth." He appears present on a company muster roll for bounty on September 24, 1862. Muster roll for December 31, 1862, to April 30, 1863, reports him present. Muster roll for May/June 1863, reports him present, lost canteen at 25 cents and strap at 20 cents. Muster roll for September/October 1863, reports him present. He drew clothing on May 31, and June 1864. POW captured at Fort Gaines, Alabama, on August 8, 1864. He was admitted to St. Louis USA General Hospital at New Orleans from military prison on August 29, 1864, with diarrhoea and returned to confinement on October 22, 1864, age 20. He was received at Ship Island, Mississippi, on October 25, 1864, and exchanged on January 4, 1865. POW captured at Blakeley, Alabama, on April 9, 1865, and received at Ship Island on April 15, 1865. He was transferred from Ship Island, to Vicksburg, Mississippi, on parole for exchange on May 1, 1865.

Pritchett, W. G., Pvt. Co. C
Enlisted on January 11, 1862, at Fort Gaines, Alabama, by Captain Rembert for twelve months. His name appears on a regimental return for June 1862, "absent without leave." He appears on a report for June 28, 1862, near Tupelo, Mississippi, "on furlough April 9, for 20 d now in Marengo County." He was discharged on January 20, 1863, at Choctaw Bluff, born in Marengo County, Alabama, age 47, five foot nine inches, fair complexion, blue eyes and light hair. Discharged due to being over 45 years of age. There is a handwritten document cover endorsed "I hereby transfer the sutlers certificate to J. D. Bridges, with witness" signed W. G. Pritchett. His discharge, a pay voucher and the transfer document is in his file.*

Pritchett, R. H., Pvt. Co. C see **Pritchett, Hobbs**

Privett, George W., Pvt. Co. C see **Privett, J. W.**

Privett, J. M., Pvt. Co. C see **Privett, J. W.**

Privett, J. M., Pvt. Co. C
Enlisted on September 21, 1863, at Marengo, County, Alabama, by Lt. Northrup for three years or the war. Company muster roll for December 31, 1862, to April 30, 1863, reports him present. A company muster roll for May/June 1863, reports him present, sick in quarters. September/October muster roll reports him absent in hospital in Mobile since October 26, 1863. Private Privett was admitted to Post Hospital at Fort Morgan, Alabama, on January 8, 1864, with int. feb. and sent to general hospital on January 17, 1864. John W. Privett was admitted to Ross Hospital at Mobile, Alabama, on January 16, 1864, with chronic rheumatism and sent to general hospital at Montgomery on February 17, 1864. He drew clothing on June 1, 1864. POW captured at Fort Gaines, Alabama, on August 8, 1864. He was received at Ship Island, Mississippi, from New Orleans on October 25, 1864, and exchange at Ship Island on January 4, 1865. POW surrendered at Citronelle, Alabama, by Lt. General Richard Taylor on May 4, 1865, and paroled at Meridian, Mississippi, on May 13, 1865. He was shown as a resident of Marengo County, Alabama. There is a pay voucher is his file.*

Prudeau, Louis, Pvt. Co. G
His name appears on a register of payments to discharged soldiers. Discharged on April 25, 1862.

Pullintz, E. A., 2nd Lt. Co. C see **Poellnitz, Edwin, A.**

Purvis, A., Pvt. Co. A
His name appears on a regimental return for June 1862, "May 25, hospital, Deserted ordered to report – not done so."

Q

Quillan, E. R., Pvt. Co. G see **Quillen, Edgar R.**

Quilllen, Edgar R., Pvt. Co. G
Drew clothing on May 3, and June 1, 1864. POW captured at Fort Gaines, Alabama, on August 8, 1864. He was received at Ship Island, Mississippi, from New Orleans on October 25, 1864, and exchange at Ship Island on January 4, 1865. POW surrendered at Citronelle, Alabama, by Lt. General Richard Taylor on May 4, 1865, and paroled at Meridian, Mississippi, on May 13, 1865, a resident of Abbeville, Henry County, Alabama.

Quillin, E. R., Pvt. Co. G see **Quillen, Edgar, R.**

Quinn, John, Pvt. Co. B/E
Enlisted on August 25, 1862, at Mobile, Alabama, by Captain DeVaux for the war. He appears present on a company muster roll for bounty on September 24, 1862, "recruit received bounty at the time of enlistment. Bounty paid." Company muster roll for May/June 1863, reports him deserted from Oven Bluff on January 12, 1863. POW a member of Co. E, 21st Alabama surrendered at Citronelle, Alabama, by Lt. General Richard Taylor on May 4, 1865, and paroled at Meridian, Mississippi, on May 13, 1865, a resident of Mobile, Alabama.

Quinn, J. T., Pvt. Co. B/E see **Quinn, John**

Quinn, Peter, Pvt. Co. D/E
Enlisted on October 13, 1861, at Mobile, Alabama, by Captain Butt for the war. He appears on a company muster roll for Co. D in November/December 1862, "transferred to Co. B, 1st Batt. 21st Al Regt." He appears present on a company muster roll for bounty on September 24, 1862. Here he is shown as having enlisted on September 14, 1862, at Fort Morgan, Alabama, by Captain Johnston for the war. His name is on a return for November 1862, as detached in Ordnance Department. Company muster rolls for March/April 1863 and May/June 1863, reports him present, detached in Ordnance Department on January 25, 1863, at Oven Bluff. He appears on two receipt rolls for pay at Choctaw, (*Bluff*) and Oven Bluff, in December and January 1863, paid 40 cents (*per day extra*) as Artificer. There is also a pay voucher in his file.*

R

Rabby, Peter, Jr., 2nd Lt. Co. E

Wounded in the cheek slightly at Shiloh while advancing on First Battery, on April 6, 1862, at 7 A. M. Elected 2nd Lt. May 8, 1862, resigned May 1, 1863. His name appears on a return reported present at Fort Morgan, Alabama, in November 1862. He is reported present at Brigade Headquarters on a field return for November 1862. He also appears on a return for December 1962, where he is reported absent with leave. There are very poor copies of some paper work in his file.*

Rafield, Lewis R. G., Drummer, Co. K

Discharged. A poor copy of his discharge is in his file.*

Rafail, Capella, Co. G

His name appears on a register for payment for claims filed for settlement for deceased soldiers. Filed January 6, 1863, by Attorney J. R. Eastburn.

Railey, Green, Pvt. Co. C

Enlisted on October 13, 1861, at Mobile, Alabama, by Captain Rembert for three years or the war. He was captured at Shiloh Pittsburg Landing at hospital while serving on ambulance squad on April 8, 1862. He also shown as captured at Island 10 and sent to Camp Douglas, Chicago, Illinois, where he is reported on a roll of POW's, August 1, 1862. He was sent to Vicksburg, Mississippi, on September 8, 1862, on board the steamer *John H. Done* among other prisoners for exchange. A company muster roll for December 31, 1862, to April 30, 1863, reports him absent detailed as hospital nurse at Choctaw Bluff, Alabama. May/June 1863 and September/October 1863, muster rolls reports him present at Choctaw Bluff as a hospital nurse since March 7, 1863, by order of Colonel Anderson. He appears on a hospital muster roll for March/April 1864, from Post Hospital at Fort Morgan transferred to his company January 25, 1864. He appears on a hospital muster roll at Fort Gaines, Alabama, for May/June 1864, present as a nurse. POW captured at Fort Gaines, Alabama, on August 8, 1864. He was received at Ship Island, Mississippi, from New Orleans on October 25, 1864. and exchanged at Ship Island on January 4, 1865. POW a nurse at Moore CSA Hospital surrendered at Citronelle, Alabama, by Lt. General Richard Taylor on May 4, 1865, and paroled at Meridian, Mississippi, on May 16, 1865, a resident of Marengo County. There is a card in his file to see the personal papers of **J. Y. Lyles** of Co. C. 21st Alabama. This data obtained from a descriptive list on June 15, 1862, for payment of $50 bounty. Filed with **Lyles, J. Y.**

Raley, G., Pvt., age 38, blue eyes, dark hair, dark complexion, six foot and one half inch, born Green County, Mississippi, a farmer by occupation. Enlisted November 22, 1862, by Captain Rembert for the war.

Rainsford, John A., Pvt. Co. A

Enlisted on October 13, 1861, at Mobile, Alabama, by Major Hessee, for one year. Discharged on May 11, 1862, at Corinth, Mississippi, due to disability with chronic hepatitis and ?. Born in Glasgow, Scotland, age 32, five foot eight and one half inches, light complexion, hazel eyes, brown hair and by occupation a clerk. His discharge is in his file.*

Raley, Green, Pvt. Co. C see **Railey, Green**

Raley, Jackson, Pvt. Co. C
Enlisted on November 22, 1861, at Fort Gaines, Alabama, by Captain Rembert for twelve months. Discharged on January 2, 1862, at Fort Gaines due to disability caused by weak constitution, apoplexy and various nervous afflictions. Born in Green County, Mississippi, age 34 years of age, five foot nine and one half inches, dark complexion, blue eyes, dark hair and by occupation a planter. His discharge and a pay voucher is in his file.*

Two A. Rankin files are combined in the CSR.

Rankin, A. (Anthony), Pvt. Co. K
Enlisted on October 13, 1861, at Mobile, Alabama, by Captain Stewart for the war. He appears absent on a company muster roll for bounty on September 24, 1862, absent missing at the battle of Shiloh on April 7, 1861. Pvt. A. Rankin, Co. C is reported at Camp Douglas, POW prison, having been captured at Fort Donaldson on February 16, 1862. He was sent to Vicksburg from Camp Douglas on September 5, 1862, to be exchanged. Pvt. A. Rankin, Co. K was captured (*at Shiloh?*) on April 7, 1862. Company muster roll for November/December 1862, reports him absent with surgeon's certificate. Company muster roll for July/August reports him absent detached at hospital in Marion, Alabama, enlisted on January 29, 1862. Company muster roll for September/October 1863, reports the same enlistment and detached hospital service at Marion since June 16, 1863, by order of General Buckner. Hospital muster roll for Breckinridge's Division Hospital at Marion, Alabama, January 12, 1864, reports him as ward master present by order of General Maury. There are several poor copies of pay vouchers in this file.*

Rasimi, Joseph E., Pvt. Co. E
Discharged on December 9, 1861. Enlisted on October 13, 1861, at Mobile, Alabama, by Captain Chamberlain for twelve months. Born at Fort Gaines, Georgia, age 23, five foot seven, dark complexion, blue eyes, dark hair, by occupation a steamboat clerk. Discharged at Fort Gaines due to disability caused by inguinal hernia. He is indebted to Captain Chamberlain for 25 dollars due to clothing and he is not indebted to the laundress. There are two discharges in his file. No. 2 is for discharge from Captain J. B. Webbers, Co. F, B. W. H Regiment of Calvary. Enlisted by Lt. Gibbons, at Knoxville, Tennessee, August 21, 1862, age 24. He was indebted to the CSA for $5.25. He was discharged due to disability on October (?) 1, 1862, at Fayetteville, Tennessee. Both discharges and a pay voucher are in his file.*

Ravisies, E. P., Pvt. Co. K
He was mortally wounded in the spine at Shiloh on April 6, 1862, at 10 A. M. while retreating from First Camp.

Rawls, T. G., Pvt. Co. C

His name appears on a regimental return for June 1862. Discharged May 24, 1862, at Corinth, Mississippi, due to disability.

Rawls, T. J., Pvt. Co. C

Enlisted on October 13, 1861, at Mobile, Alabama, by Captain Rembert for twelve months. He appears present on a company muster roll for bounty on September 24, 1862. Company muster roll for December 31, 1962, to April 30, 1863, reports him present. May/June 1862, muster roll reports him present and having lost 12 caps. Company muster roll for September/October 1863, reports him transferred to CS Navy on June 9, 1863, by order of General Maury. He is shown as having been admitted to Post Hospital at Fort Morgan on November 5, 1863, with pneumonia, and returned to duty on November 11, 1863. POW (shows him in Co. A) captured at Fort Morgan on August 23, 1864, and sent to New York on September 27, 1864.
This data is from a descriptive list for bounty pay at Mobile of May 2, 1863, the list is filed with Pvt. **A. L. Norwood.**
Rawls, T. J., Pvt. Enlisted at Mobile, Alabama, age 22, blue eyes, light hair, fair complexion, five foot seven and one half, born in Marengo County, Alabama, an overseer by occupation.

Raysdelly, A. A., Pvt. Co. D

POW captured at Blakeley, Alabama, on April 9, 1865. He was received at Ship Island, Mississippi, on April 15, 1865, and transferred to Vicksburg, Mississippi, on May first on parole for exchange.

Read, Charles, Pvt. Co. A

He enlisted on October 13, 1861, at Mobile, Alabama, by Major Hessee. He appears present on a company muster roll for bounty on September 24, 1862.

Read, James, T., Pvt. Co. A

Enlisted at Jefferson County, Alabama, on August 8, 1862, by James Tarrens for the war. Company muster roll for December 31, 1962, to April 30, 1863, reports him deserted on January 30, 1863, at Choctaw Bluff, Alabama.

Read, (Reid) William T., Pvt. Co. A

Enlisted at Jefferson County, Alabama, on August 28, 1862, by James Tarrens for three years or the war. He appears present on a company muster roll for September/October 1863, "absent without leave from January 30, to Sept." He was admitted to Post Hospital at Fort Morgan on November 24, 1863, with int. fever and returned to duty on December 3, 1863. He was admitted to Post Hospital again on December 15, 1863, with the same complaint and sent to general hospital on January 17, 1864. He was admitted to Ross Hospital in Mobile, Alabama, on January 16, 1864, with debility and sent to General Hospital in Montgomery on February 17, 1864. There was a death claim paid to E. J. Reid his widow on February 8, 1863, **Reid, W. T.**
Note there is additional information on this man's desertion on January 29, 1863, from Choctaw Bluff, Alabama, in the File of James. A. Poellnitz. Special Order No. 62.

There are obviously two men's data in this file.

Reader, Newton S., Pvt. Co. B

Enlisted on September 3, 1863, at Jefferson County, Alabama, by A. R. Goodwin, for three years or the war. He appears present, sick in quarters, on company muster roll for May/June 1863. Company muster roll for September/October 1863, reports him absent, "Appd. 4th Corpl. By order of Colonel Anderson Sept. 1/63, as guard at Choctaw Bluff." A hospital muster roll for July/August 1864, at General Hospital at Marion, Alabama, reports him present as a patient. POW surrendered at Citronelle, Alabama, by Lt. General R. Taylor on May 4, 1865, and paroled at Meridian, Mississippi, on May 13, 1865. He is shown as a resident of Jefferson County, Alabama.

Reaves, (Rives) McDaniel, Pvt. Co. F

Enlisted on February 26, 1863, at Choctaw Bluff, Alabama, by Captain Dade for three years or the war. He appears present on a company muster roll for March 1, to June 30, 1863. Company muster roll for September/October 1863, reports him present. He was admitted to Post Hospital at Fort Morgan, Alabama, on December 22, 1863, with cold and pneumonia and returned to duty POW captured at Fort Gaines, Alabama, on August 8, 1864. He was received at Ship Island, Mississippi, from New Orleans on October 25, 1864, and exchanged at Ship Island on January 4, 1865. POW surrendered at Citronelle, Alabama, by Lt. General R. Taylor on May 4, 1865, and paroled at Meridian, Mississippi, on May 13, 1865. He was shown as a resident of Wilcox County, Alabama.

Redwood, Robert H., Chaplin/ Surgeon/Major, Field and Staff

Enlisted October 13, 1861. He was appointed Chaplin on October 10, 1861, and promoted on December 1, 1861. **M. W. Dubose** was his successor as Chaplin. A return for November at Fort Morgan reports him present as Assistant Surgeon. He appears on a return, "captured at hospital, wounded April 7, 1862." His name appears on a return, "taken prisoner on April 6, 1862." He signed a Parole of Honor at St Louis, Missouri, on April 15, 1862, that he will render professional service to the CSA (prisoners?) at McDowell College and will report each week to authority. He signed another on April 20, 1862, at St. Louis to proceed as a POW to without delay proceed to Camp Douglas. He appears on a list of POW's unconditionally discharged from Camp Douglas near Chicago, Illinois, on June 25, 1862. Charges and specifications were brought against Surgeon Redwood at Holley Springs, Mississippi, in October 1862. The copies of particulars of these charges are too poor to read. POW he signed a Parole of Honor at Columbus, Mississippi, on May 16, 1865, surrendered by Lt. General Richard Taylor.

Redwood, ?. H. Jr., Pvt. Co. K

His name appears on a regimental return for June 1862, at having been killed in action. Farmington May 9.

Reed, F. T., Pvt./Corp. Co. C

POW captured at Fort Donalson on February 16, 1862. He appears on a roll of prisoners of war at Camp Butler at Springfield, Illinois. He was sent from Camp Butler to Vicksburg, Mississippi, on September 23, 1862, to be exchanged. He was received among 1777 prisoners on board the steamer *John H. Done*, near Vicksburg in September and exchanged at Atkins Landing on November 10, 1862.

Reed, James B., Co. C.
He was admitted to the City USA General Hospital at St. Louis, Missouri, on February 28, 1862, and sent to prison on April 7, 1862.

Reeder, N. S., Pvt./Sgt. Co. B see **Reader, Newton S.**

Reese, W. D., Pvt. co. D, 2nd Alabama.
His name appears on a register of the Medical Directors Office at Richmond, Virginia, transferred on January 19, 1863, to Howard's Grove Hospital. *This card filed in error. Should be with 2nd Alabama.*

Reeves, Peter, Pvt. Co. I see **Rieves, Peter**

Rembert, J. M., Captain Co. C
Elected Captain on October 13, 1861. Mortally wounded at Shiloh in the left side in A. M. attack on the 1st Battery. Captured at hospital on April 7, 1862. Died at Fourth Street Hospital at St. Louis, Missouri, on April 20, 1862. Claim on deceased soldier filed by James P. Rembert on May 2, 1863. There are poor copies of paper work in his file.*

Reneau, John Pvt. Co. A
His name appears on a regimental return for June 1862, "sent to the interior at the evacuation of Corinth (Mississippi)."

Rener, Daniel, Pvt./Corp. Co. B
Enlisted on October 13, 1864, at Mobile, Alabama, by Major Hessee for twelve months. He appears present on a company muster roll for bounty on September 24, 1862, "not entitled to bounty under age." Paid $52 for service March 1, to June 30, 1862. A pay voucher is in his file.*

Rentz, J., Pvt. Co. C
Enlisted at Monroe County, Alabama, on February 9, 1863, by Lt. Northrup for three years or the war. He appears present on company muster roll for December 31, 1862, to April 30, 1863. May/June 1863, muster roll reports him present sick in quarters. Company muster roll for September/October 1863, reports him absent in hospital at Mobile since October 25, 1863. He was admitted to Post Hospital at Fort Morgan, Alabama, on November 24, 1863, with remit. fever and returned to duty on December 12, 1863. POW captured at Fort Gaines on August 8, 1864. He was received at Ship Island, Mississippi, from New Orleans on October 25, 1864, and exchanged at Ship Island on January 4, 1865. POW captured at Blakeley, Alabama, on April 9, 1865, and transferred to Vicksburg, Mississippi, on parole for exchange on May 1, 1865.
This data is from a descriptive list for bounty pay at Mobile of May 2, 1863, list is filed with Pvt. **A. L. Norwood**.

Rentz, John, Pvt. Enlisted at Mobile, Alabama, age 18, blue eyes, light hair, fair complexion, five foot nine inches. Born in Marengo County, a farmer by occupation.

Reves, M. D., Pvt. Co. F see **Riaves, M. D.**

Reynolds, Alfred, C., Pvt. Co. K
Enlisted on October 13, 1861, at Mobile, Alabama, by Captain Stewart for the war. Company muster roll for bounty on September 24, 1862, reports him absent detached May 1, 1862, in Signal Corps by order of General Bragg. Company muster roll for November/December 1862, shows him absent detached in Signal Corps. His name appears on regimental return for June 1862, as being detached in the Signal Corps. *Some data cards and paperwork in this file is not readable.* There is a notice to see the personal papers of **Carlo Patti**. (*Carlo Patti was brother to the famous opera singer Angelina Patti) Carlo Patti served in the Signal Corps at Dauphin Island at one time during the war and later became famous himself as an orchestra conductor.*) There are a number of pay vouchers in his file.**

Reynolds, Francis H., Pvt. Co. A
Paid $47.40 for detached service at S Kates & Co. foundry at Mobile from November 1861, through January 1862. Paid $18.60 per month on detached service in foundry at Mobile, Alabama, in March 1862. *Much of the data in his file is not readable.**

Reynolds, F. H., Pvt. Co. A see **Reynolds, Francis H.**

Reynolds, W. C., Pvt. Co. K
Enlisted on October 13, 1861, at Mobile by Captain Stewart for the war. A regimental return for June 1862, reports him on detached service with the Signal Corps. Company muster roll for bounty on September 24, 1862, reports him absent detached April 15, 1862, in Signal Corps by order of General Bragg. Company muster rolls for November/December 1862, July/August 1863 and September/October 1863, all report him absent on detached service with Signal Corps. *Some data cards and paperwork in this file is not readable.* There are a number of pay vouchers in his file.**

Riberon, A., Pvt. Co. G
His name appears on a regimental return in June 1862, "sent to interior hospital." His name also appears on a report near Tupelo, Mississippi, on June 28, 1862, "Sent to interior from Corinth at the time of the evacuation."

Rice, W. H., Pvt. Co. A
He appears on a list of wounded admitted into US Prison Hospital at Champion, Hill, Mississippi, from May 17, to May 23, 1863. "Penetrate wound right knee joint, amputation lower third to thigh."

Richard, D. I., Pvt. Co. G
POW surrendered at Citronelle, Alabama, by Lt. General Richard Taylor on May 4, 1864, and paroled at Meridian, Mississippi. He was a resident of Mobile, Alabama.

Richards, C. R., Pvt. Co. K

POW surrendered at Citronelle, Alabama, by Lt. General Richard Taylor on May 4, 1864, and paroled May 13, 1865, at Meridian, Mississippi. He was a resident of Mobile, Alabama.

Richards, Thomas, Pvt. Co. G

Enlisted October 15, 1862, at Wilcox County, Alabama, by Lt. Sewall for the war. He appears present on a company muster roll for September/October 1864, at Mobile. POW surrendered at Citronelle, Alabama, by Lt. General Richard Taylor on May 4, 1864, and paroled May 13, 1865, at Meridian, Mississippi. He was a resident of Camden, Wilcox County, Alabama.

Richards, W. W., Pvt. Co. K

Enlisted on January 24, 1863, at Fort Morgan, Alabama, by Captain Dorgan for the war. He was admitted to Post Hospital at Fort Morgan on May 6, 1863, with diarrhoea and returned to duty on May 14, 1863. He appears present on company muster rolls for July/August, September/October 1863 and September/October 1864. POW surrendered at Citronelle, Alabama, by Lt. General Richard Taylor on May 4, 1864, and paroled May 13, 1865, at Meridian, Mississippi. He was a resident of Mobile, Alabama.

Richardson, J. P., Pvt. Co. H

Enlisted on May 20, 1864, at Mobile, Alabama, by H. J. Bache for the war. His name appears on muster rolls for men in the C. S. Ordnance Department at Mobile, Alabama, for July/August and September/October 1864, shown present and detailed by enrolling officer, Co. A, 21st Ala., Special Order. He appears on a list of men employed at Mobile in July 1864, employed on December 26, 1863, by order of Major General Maury, Special Agt. Ordn. Department H Myers, Ordn. Department, detailed. (Here he is shown in Co. H) POW surrendered at Citronelle, Alabama, by Lt. General Richard Taylor on May 4, 1864, and paroled May 18, 1865, at Columbus, Mississippi. He was a resident of Mobile County, Alabama.

Richardson, J. P., Pvt. Co. H/A see **Richardson, J. P.**

Richardson, William, Pvt. Co. I

Enlisted on January 10, 1864, at Point Clear, Alabama, by Captain Crenshaw for the war. He appears present on a company muster roll for September/October 1864. He was admitted to Ross Hospital at Mobile, Alabama, on June 23, 1864, with debilities and returned to duty on July 1, 1864. He was admitted to Ross Hospital with the same complaint on July 4, 1864, and returned to duty on July 19, 1864.

Ricker, Henry, A., Pvt. Co. E

Enlisted on October 13, 1861, at Mobile, Alabama, by Captain Chamberlain for the war. His name appears on a regimental return for June 1862, "Detached Service Yardmaster Mob. & Ohio RR." He appears absent on company muster rolls for November/December 1862, July/August 1863 and September/October 1863, detailed on

M & O RR in March 1862, by order of General Withers. Detached March 16, 1862. There is a pay voucher in his file.*

Rickman, A. P., Pvt. Co. K

POW surrendered by Lt. General Richard Taylor in May 1865, and paroled at Columbus, Mississippi, on May 19, 1865. A resident of Pickens County, Alabama.

Ried, William, Pvt. Co. A see **Read, William T.**

Rieves, Peter, Pvt. Co. I

Enlisted on October 13, 1861, at Halls Mill, Alabama, by Major Hessee for the war. Wounded in the foot slightly April 6, 1862, at Shiloh at 6 A. M. while advancing on First Battery. POW captured at Battle of Shiloh on April 7, 1862. He was treated and discharged at Gratiot Street Military Hospital in St. Louis, Missouri, on July 14, 1862. He appears on a roll of POW's at Alton, Illinois, in August 1862. His name appears on a roll of POW's at Military Prison, Alton, Illinois, transferred to Vicksburg, Mississippi, for exchange on September 23, 1862. A return for November 1862, reports him missing in action. A return for December 1862, reports him absent sick since December 12, 1862, for 30 days. He was admitted to Post Hospital at Fort Morgan on June 11, and sent to general hospital on June 11, 1863, with syphilis. He appears absent on a company muster roll for July/August 1863, sent to general hospital June 12, 1863. September/October 1863, company muster roll reports him absent sick in General Hospital, at Mobile since June 12, 1863. POW captured at Fort Morgan, Alabama, on August 23, 1864. He was sent to New York from New Orleans on September 1864. He was received at Elmira, New York, on October 8, 1864. He was released July 7, 1865. A resident of Mobile, Alabama, sallow complexion, light hair, blue eyes, six foot. There is a pay voucher in his file.*

Riggins, James E., Pvt. Co. C

His name appears on a register of discharged soldiers in June 1862.

Riley, G., Pvt. Co. I see **Railey, Green**

Riley, George, Pvt. Co. I

Enlisted on March 10, 1862, at Fort Pillow, Tennessee, by Captain Dorgan for the war. POW wounded severely in the abdomen at Shiloh on April 6, 1862, 3 P. M. in the field and captured at hospital. He was received at Camp Chase, Columbus Ohio, on June 3, 1862, from Pittsburg, PA. (*Could have meant Pittsburg Landing?*). He was transferred to Vicksburg, Mississippi, for exchange on August 25, 1862. He was received among 1020 prisoners aboard the steamer *John H. Done* in September 1862, near Vicksburg. He appears missing in Battle of Shiloh on a company muster roll for September 24, 1862, for bounty. Company muster roll for November/December 1862, reports him present, returned from missing in action December 29, 1862. Company muster roll for July/August 1863, reports him present. September/October 1864, muster roll reports him absent sick in hospital since October 25, 1864, Dr. Armstrong.

Riley, G. P., Pvt. Co. K see **Riley, George**

Riley James, Pvt. Co. C
His name appears on a register of POW's of the US Department of the Cumberland, "Deserter, Paroled and allowed to return home." He appears on a list of deserters paroled and released at Tullahoma, Tennessee, by US Office of Provost Marshal General at Tullahoma on July 9, 1863. Residence near Little Brown Creek, Jackson, County.

Riley, M. E., Pvt. Co. A
His name appears on a roll of POW's released at Fort McHenry, Maryland, during the five days ending June 5, 1865, pursuance to instructions from Commanding General of Prisons at Washington on May 3, 1865. He is reported to be a resident of Hillsboro, Illinois. Captured at Port Gibson, Mississippi, on May 1, 1863.

Ripley, F. H., Pvt./1st Sgt. Co. E
Enlisted April 30, 1864, at Mobile, Alabama, by Captain Bebee for the war. Company muster roll for September/October 1864, reports him present, promoted from ranks Sept 1. He was admitted to Ross Hospital at Mobile on June 13, 1864, with diarrhoea and returned to duty on June 20, 1864.

Rivers, E. R., Pvt. Co. K
Enlisted October 13, 1861, at Mobile, Alabama, by Captain Stewart for the war. His name appears on a regimental return for June 1862, on detached service with A.Q. M. at Mobile. Company muster roll for bounty on September 24, 1862, reports him present. Company muster roll for November/December, 1862, reports him present. There are several pay vouchers in his file for pay while in the employ of Quarter Master at Mobile.*

Rivers, John, Pvt. Co. D
Enlisted on September 1, 1864, at Mobile, Alabama, by Major Stone for the war. A company muster roll for September/October 1864, reports him present.

Rives, M. D., Pvt. Co. F see **Raves, M. D.**

Ribbards, John L., Pvt. Co. C see **Roberds, John L.**

Robbins, Albert, A., Pvt. Co. E
Enlisted on October 13, 1861, at Mobile, Alabama, by Captain Chamberlain for twelve months. A regimental return for June 1862, reports him on detached service as conductor on M. & O. RR. A company muster roll for bounty on September 24, 1862, reports him absent detached March 13, 1862, on M & O. RR by order of General Withers. Company muster rolls for November/December 1862, July/August 1863 and September/October 1863, all report him absent on detached service with RR. There are pay vouchers in his file.* He was paid $11 per month.

Roberts, A., Pvt. Co. I

Enlisted on October 13, 1861, at Halls Mill, Alabama, by Major Hessee for the war. His name appears on a regimental return for June 1862, sent to interior hospital April 24. He appears on a report near Tupelo, Mississippi, on June 28, 1862, sent to interior hospitals from Corinth by surgeons on May 28th. A company muster roll for bounty on September 24, 1862, reports him present, refused to receive the bounty claiming to be under the age of 18. Company muster roll for July/August 1863, reports him present. Company muster roll for September/October 1863, reports him present, lost one bayonet. POW Austin Roberts was captured at Fort Gaines, Alabama, on August 8, 1864. He was received at Ship Island, Mississippi, from New Orleans on October 25, 1864, and exchanged at Ship Island on January 4, 1865.

Roberts, Austin, Pvt. Co. I see **Roberts, A.**

Roberts, J. G., Pvt. Co. K

Pvt. J. G. Roberts, Co. D. 3rd Alabama was confined at Knoxville, Tennessee, on November 16, 1863, (?) and released on November 4, 1863, upon taking the Oath of Allegiance to the USA on November 4, 1863. Pvt. J. C. Roberts of Confederate Cavalry appears on a list of deserters who took the Oath to the USA at the Office of the Provost Marshal General of East Tennessee on December 16, 1863, and was sent to Kentucky. He was shown as a resident of Walker County, Alabama. Enlisted on August 16, 1864, at Mobile, Alabama, by Captain Gordon, for the war. He appears on a company muster roll for September/October 1864, transferred to Conscript Corps at Notasulga on October 18, 1864.

Roberds, John L., Pvt. Co. C * *as recorded on microfilm*

Enlisted on October 13, 1861, at Mobile, Alabama, by Captain Rembert for one year. Discharged at Fort Gaines, Alabama, due to dislocated hip and general debility on January 21, 1862. Born in Marengo County, Alabama, thirty years old, five foot ten and one half inches, sallow complexion, blue eyes, dark hair and a farmer by occupation His discharge is in his file.*

Roberts, Richard, Pvt. Co. I

POW captured at Fort Gaines, Alabama, on August 8, 1864. He was admitted to St. Louis USA General Hospital at New Orleans on September 21, 1864, with rubeola and returned to confinement on October 10, 1864, age 17. He was received at Ship Island, Mississippi, from New Orleans on October 25, 1864, and exchanged at Ship Island on January 4, 1865.

Robertson, D. G., Pvt. Co. I

Enlisted on March 10, 1863, at Fort Morgan, Alabama, by Lt. Collins for the war. He was admitted to Post Hospital at Fort Morgan, with tonsillitis on April 17, 1863, and returned to duty on May 31. A company muster roll for July/August 1863, shows him present but absent without leave July 1, to July 5. Company muster roll for September/October 1863, reports him present. POW captured at Fort Gaines, Alabama, on August

8, 1864. He was received at Ship Island, Mississippi, from New Orleans on October 25, 1864, and exchanged at Ship Island on January 4, 1865.

Robertson, Dan, Pvt. Co. I. Filed with Pvt. D. G. Robertson above.
He was discharged April 9, 1862.

Robins, A. K., Pvt./Corp. Co. C see **Robinson, A. K.**

Robinson, A. A., Pvt. Co. F
Enlisted on October 13, 1861, at Baldwin County, Alabama, by Captain McCoy for one year. He was wounded slightly at Shiloh in the arm while advancing on the 1st Camp on April 6, 1862, at 8 A. M. His name appears on a regimental return for June 1862, sent to interior hospital. He appears on a report near Tupelo, Mississippi, June 28, 1862, wounded at Shiloh furloughed on surgeon's certificate on April 8., and sent to Corinth Hospital, surgeons certificate April 28, 1862. He appears present on a company muster roll for bounty September 24, 1862. Company muster roll for March 1, to June 30, 1862, reports him present. September/October 1863, muster roll reports him absent, detached to fish by General Maury on August 21, 1863. Company muster roll for September/October 1864, reports that he deserted in August 1865.

Robinson, A. K., Pvt./Corp. Co. C see Robison, A. K.
[*This material provided by Sons of Confederate Veterans:* **Robison, Alonzo King**, *Pvt. Co. C. Alabama Penison No. 15814, Marengo County. Name of Pensioner A. K. Robinson, witnesses; L. M. Trawick and J. S. Nored, Address Clay Hill, Ala.*]

Robinson, G.?, Pvt. Co. H
His name appears on a regimental return for June 1862, sent to the rear May 28. He appears on a report near Tupelo, Mississippi, June 28, 1862, sent to the interior from Corinth at the time of evacuation.

Robinson, James B., Pvt. Co. K
Enlisted on October 13, 1861, at Mobile, Alabama, by Captain Stewart to serve for one year. He was certified disabled and discharged May 6, 1862, due to rheumatism. Born Lancaster County, Virginia, twenty-two years of age, five foot ten inches, fair complexion, blue eyes, fair hair, and a merchant by occupation. His discharge is in his file.*

Robinson, J. L., Pvt. Co. D
Enlisted on February 2, 1863, at Prattville, Alabama, by Lt. Mims for the war. Company muster roll for July/August 1863, reports him present. Muster roll for September/October 1863, reports him absent in hospital at Fort Gaines. Muster roll for November/December 1863, reports him present. Muster roll for September/October 1864, reports him absent sent to General Hospital at Mobile on October 10, 1864. He was admitted to Ross Hospital at Mobile on October 10, 1864, with febris intermittens quot., sent to General Hospital at Greenville, on October 25, 1864.

[*The following is from a member of Sons of Confederate Veterans in the Prattville, Alabama, area in 2009.* **Robinson,** *men members of the Robinson Springs United Confederate Veterans Camp 396 as described from memory, cira 1902-1910, by W. D. Whetstone, Camp Adjutant.*

J. L. (Jacob L.) – *Brother of W. L and Dr. J. A. was in Co. D, 21st Alabama Infantry Regiment and served until the close, and died at Deatsville, Ala., and is buried at the old home. Has two sons living Milton and DuBose.*]

Robinson, J. W., Pvt. Co. D

Enlisted August 12, 1864, at Mobile, Alabama, by Major Stone for the war. Company muster roll for September/October 1864, reports him present assigned to the company by order. A second muster roll for September/October 1864, reports him absent detailed to Battery Huger on order of Colonel Fuller. He was admitted to Ross Hospital at Mobile on October 26, 1864, with febris intermittens quot and returned to duty on October 28. He was again admitted to Ross Hospital with the same complaint on November 2, 1864, and returned to duty on December 15.

Robinson, M., Pvt. Co. D

His name appears on a company muster roll for September/October 1864, where he is reported absent without leave since October 15, 1864, assigned to company by order.

Robinson, R., Pvt. Co. D

POW captured at Blakeley, Alabama, on April 9, 1865. He was received at Ship Island, Mississippi, on April 15, 1865, and transferred to Vicksburg, Mississippi, on May 1, 1865.

Robinson, R. N., Pvt. Co. C

POW captured at Blakeley, Alabama, on April 9, 1865. He was received at Ship Island, Mississippi, on April 15, 1865, and transferred to Vicksburg, Mississippi, on May 1, 1865.

[*This material furnished by Sons of Confederate Veterans;* **Robert Neil Robinson**, *Pvt. Co. C. Pension record card Clarke County, Alabama Pension Number 27090. Pension application witnessed by G. W. Dismukes and J. S. Nored. Address, 1921, Thomasville, Clarke County, Alabama.*]

Robinson, William, Corp./Pvt. Co. F

Enlisted at Baldwin County, Alabama, on October 13, 1861, by Captain McCoy for one year. His name appears on a report June 28, 1862, near Tupelo, Mississippi, "Wounded at Shiloh furloughed on surgeon's certif. April 8, sent from Corinth Hospital surgeon's certif. May 28, 1862." He appears on a regimental return for June 1862, "Interior Hospital June 7." He appears present on a company muster roll for bounty on September 24, 1862. Company muster roll for March 1, to June 30, 1863, reports him present sick in quarters. Muster roll for September/October 1863, reports him absent detached to fish by General Maury from August 23, 1863. Company muster roll for September/October 1864, reports that he deserted on October 16, 1864.

MOBILE CONFEDERATES

Robinson, W. L., Pvt. Co. D

Enlisted on July 22, 1863, at Montgomery, Alabama, by Enrolling Officer for the war. He appears present on muster rolls for July/August and September/October 1863. Company muster roll for November/December 1863, reports him present on daily duty in Commissary Department. Muster roll for September/October 1864, reports that he was absent sent to General Hospital at Mobile on September 30, 1864.

[The following is from a member of Sons of Confederate Veterans in the Prattville, Alabama, area in 2009. **Robinson,** *men members of the Robinson Springs United Confederate Veterans Camp 396 as described from memory, cira 1902-1910, by W. D. Whetstone, Camp Adjutant.* **W. L. (W. Lawrence)** *Son of L. G. Robinson, lived four miles southwest of Robinson Springs. Was in Co. D, 21st Alabama Regiment until the close of war. Died several years ago, and is buried at the family cemetery at his old home. May have served also in the 8th Alabama Infantry Regiment Co. B]*

Robison, A. K., Pvt./Corp. Co. C

Enlisted on November 22, 1861, at Fort Gaines, Alabama, by Captain Rembert for twelve months. He appears present on a company muster roll for bounty on September 24, 1862. Company muster roll for December 31, 1862, to April 30, 1863, report him present. Muster roll for May/June 1863, reports him present, promoted to 4th Corporal on June 6, 1863. September/October 1863, muster roll reports him present, lost one canteen at $2.00. POW captured at Fort Gaines, Alabama, on August 8, 1862. He was received at Ship Island, Mississippi, from New Orleans on October 25, 1864, and exchanged at Ship Island on January 4, 1865. POW captured at Blakeley, Alabama, on April 9, 1865. He was received at Ship Island, Mississippi, on April 15, 1865, and transferred to Vicksburg, Mississippi, on May 1, 1865.

Roblet, J. W., Pvt. Co. C

His name appears on a roll of POW's at Camp Butler, Illinois, captured February 16, 1862, at Fort Donalson.

Rodgers, B. A., Pvt. Co. D

Enlisted in August 1863, at Grove Hill, Alabama, by Captain Daily, for the war. He appears present on a company muster roll for September/October 1864.

Rodgers, F. W., Pvt. Co. D

He enlisted on August 23, 1863, at Marengo County, Alabama, by Lt. Poelintz for the war. He appears absent on a company muster roll for September/October 1864, sent to General Hospital at Mobile on September 9, 1864, assigned to the company by order.

Rodgers, John, Pvt. C/A

Enlisted on October 5, 1862, at Talladega, Alabama, by W. L. Watthorth for three years or the war. He appears on a company C muster roll for December 31, 1862, to April 30, 1863, as having been transferred to Co. A on March 31, 1863. He appears on company A muster roll for the same period as absent detailed November 1, 1862, in Medical Department at Choctaw Bluff. May/June 1863, muster roll for Co. A reports him present detached November 1, 1862, as hospital nurse at Fort Stonewall by order of

Colonel Anderson. Muster roll for company A for September/October 1863, reports him present. His name appears on a Post Hospital at Fort Morgan listed as assistant cook for November 7, to November 27, 1863. He was admitted to Post Hospital at Fort Morgan on January 25, 1864, with rheumatism and returned to duty on January 30, 1864. He was admitted to Ross Hospital at Mobile on August 10, 1864, with rheumatism and returned to duty on August 26, 1864. He was again admitted to Ross Hospital with acute diarrhoea on October 28, 1864, and returned to duty on October 23, 1864. Muster roll for company A for September/October 1864, reports him present. There is paperwork in his file that is not readable.*

Rodgers, Thomas, Pvt. Co. E see **Rogers, Thomas**

Rodgers, T. (Thomas) J., Pvt. Co. A
    He drew clothing on March 31, 1864, and again at Camp Anderson on June 14, 1864, and signed by his mark. POW captured at Fort Morgan, Alabama, on August 23, 1864, sent to New York on September 27, 1864. Received at Elmira, New York, from New Orleans on October 8, 1864. He is on a roll of prisoners who desires to take the Oath of Allegiance May 15, 1865, "volunteered December 1, 1863, and desires to go to his home in Selma, Alabama." His name appears on a Oath of Allegiance to the USA on June 1, 1865, residence Montevallo, Alabama, dark complexion, dark hair, hazel eyes, five foot ten and one half inches, signed by his mark.

Rodgers, T. W., 1st Lt. Cop. Co. I see **Rogers, T. W.**

Rogers, B. D., Pvt. Co. C
    POW surrendered at Citronelle, Alabama, by Lt. General Richard Taylor on May 4, 1865, and paroled at Meridian, Mississippi, on May 13, 1865. A resident of Marengo County, Alabama.

Rogers, E. T., Pvt. Co. K
    Enlisted on October 13, 1861, at Mobile, Alabama, by Captain Stewart for the war. His name appears on a return for November and December 1862, detached in Mobile on October 16, 1862. He appears present on company muster roll for bounty on September 24, 1862. Company muster rolls for November/December 1862, July/August 1863, September/October 1863 and September/October 1864, report him absent detached in the ordnance department by orders in October 1862. On April 21, 1865, an official of the Cotton Exchange Agent request that Pvt. E. T. Rogers of the Invalid Corps be assigned to him. POW surrendered at Citronelle, Alabama, by Lt. General Richard Taylor on May 4, 1865, and paroled at Meridian, Mississippi, on May 9, 1865. A resident of Mobile, Alabama. There is considerable paperwork in his file.**

Rogers, J. H., Pvt. Co. A see **Rodgers, John**

Rogers, John, Pvt. Co. A see **Rodgers, John**

Rogers, Samuel, Pvt. Co. K

Enlisted on August 23, 1862, at Jefferson County, Alabama, by James Tarrant for the war. Company muster rolls for November/December 1862 and July/August 1863, report him present. He was admitted to Post Hospital at Fort Morgan, Alabama, on May 20, 1863, with dysentery and retuned to duty on May 25, 1863. He was admitted to Ross Hospital at Mobile, Alabama, on February 27, 1864, with int. fever quot. and returned to duty on March 9, 1864. Company muster roll for September/October 1864, reports him present sick in quarters. He drew clothing on June 20, 1864. There is a Special Order No. 85 by General Bragg at Tullahoma, Tennessee, allowing Pvt. S. A. Rogers of Co. K 21st Alabama Regiment to exchange places with Charles Hurtel of Co. G, 24th Alabama Regiment and transfer to Co. G of the 24th Alabama, Regiment.*

Rogers, T. D., Pvt. Co. E see **Rogers, Thomas**

Rogers, Thomas, Pvt. Co. E

He drew clothing on June 1, 1864, and signed by his mark. POW captured at Fort Gaines, Alabama, on August 8, 1864. He was received and imprisoned at Steam Levee Press No. 4 at New Orleans and sent to hospital on October 14, 1864. He was admitted to St. Louis USA General Hospital on October 14, 1864, with morbilla (measles) and returned to confinement on October 25, 1864, age 17. He was received at Ship Island, Mississippi, on October 28, 1864, and died there on November 29, 1864, of dysentery He was buried in grave No. 50.

Rogers, T. W., 1st Lt. Co. C

Enlisted on October 13, 1861. Elected Lt. on October 3, 1862, resigned on July 6, 1862, succeeded by A. Northrup. He appears on a regimental return present for November, 1861, at Fort Gaines, Alabama, and present on a return for December 1861. His name appears on a report near Tupelo, Mississippi, June 28, 1862, furloughed on surgeons certificate April 25, 1862, for 25 days. Regimental return for June 1862, reports him absent on furlough for 25 days since April 26, since renewed by surgeon. There are pay vouchers in his file.*

Rogers, T. W., Pvt. Co. C

Enlisted on August 31, 1863, at Marengo County, Alabama, by Lt. Poellnitz for three years or the war. He appears present on a company muster roll for September/October 1863. POW surrendered at Citronelle, Alabama, by Lt. General Richard Taylor on May 4, 1865, and paroled at Meridian, Mississippi, on May 13, 1865. He is shown as a resident of Marengo County, Alabama.

Rolins, A. K., Pvt./Corp. Co. C see Robison, A. K

Roonan, Patrick, Pvt. Co. B

Enlisted on August 26, 1862, at Mobile, Alabama, by Captain DeVaux for the war. He appears present on a company muster roll for bounty on September 24, 1862, with the note that he received bounty at his enlistment. Company muster roll for March/April 1863, reports him absent under arrest at Choctaw Bluff, Alabama.

Company muster roll for May/June 1863, reports him present sick in quarters. September/October 1863, muster roll reports him present and due for clothing not drawn in kind $64.63. He was admitted to Post Hospital at Fort Morgan, Alabama, on December 26, 1863, with abscess and returned to duty on January 3, 1864. He was admitted to Ross Hospital in Mobile with chronic rheumatism on July 5, 1864, and returned to duty on July 30, 1864. He appears present in Captain Sossaman's Detachment for September/October 1864.

Rooney, James, Sgt./ Pvt. Co. B

Enlisted on October 13, 1861, at Mobile, Alabama, by Major Hessee for twelve months. He appears present of company muster roll for bounty on September 24, 1862. March/April 1863, company muster roll reports him present. May/June 1863, muster roll reports him absent on sick leave for 20 days from June 25, 1863. He was shown as 2nd Sgt. on September/October 1863, muster roll that reported him present and due $17.63 for clothing not drawn in kind. POW captured at Fort Gaines, Alabama, on August 8, 1864. He was received at Ship Island, Mississippi, from New Orleans on October 25, 1864, and exchanged at Ship Island on January 4, 1865. POW surrendered at Citronelle, Alabama, by Lt. General Richard Taylor on May 4, 1865, and paroled at Meridian, Mississippi, on May 13, 1865. He was shown as a resident of Mobile, Alabama.

Rooney, James E., Co. A

His name appears on a register of claims for deceased soldiers. Claim filed on October 2, 1862, by J. T. Jewett, attorney. This data filed with James Rooney above.

Root, John, Pvt. Co. C

He was killed by a wound to the abdomen and left on the field at the Battle of Shiloh April 6, 1862, at 8:30 A. M. at First Camp. His name appears on a register of Claims for deceased soldiers. Claim filed on April 21, 1864, by Emeline Root his widow. $38.20 found due. There is paperwork in his file that is not readable.*

Roper, Dick A., Pvt. Co. E

Enlisted on March 13, 1862, at Mobile, Alabama, by J. C. Chamberlain for one year. Wounded severely in the left thigh April 7, 1861, at the Battle of Shiloh at 8 A. M. while retreating at the 1st engagement. Discharged on July 20, 1862, at Tupelo, Mississippi, due to disability born at Carrolton, Alabama, age 19, five foot eight and one half inches, fair complexion, blue eyes, light hair, a clerk by occupation. His discharge is in his file.*

Rosette, John, Pvt./Corp./Sgt. Co. A

Enlisted on October 13, 1861, at Mobile, Alabama, by Major Hessee for the war. His name appears on a report near Tupelo, Mississippi, on June 28, 1862, sent to Corinth Hospital and from there to interior hospital by order of Surgeon Heustis. He appears present on a company muster roll for bounty on September 24, 1862. Company muster roll for December 31, 1862, to April 30, 1863, reports him present, promoted to 2nd Corporal from the ranks on January 1, 1863. Company muster roll for May/June 1863, reports him present. Company muster roll for September/October 1863, reports him present promoted from 2nd Corporal to 5th Sergeant on September 1, 1863. He was admitted to Post Hospital at Fort Morgan on November 1, 1863, with int. fever and returned to duty on November 3, 1863. POW captured at Fort Morgan, Alabama, on August 23, 1864, sent to New York on September 27, 1864, from New Orleans. He was received at Elmira, New York, on October 8, 1864, and transferred for exchange on March 14, 1865. He was received at Boulware's Wharf on James River among 982 paroled prisoners of war on March 19 and 21, 1865.

Ross, H. William, Pvt. Co. H

He drew clothing March 31 and June 1, 1864, and signed by his mark. POW captured at Fort Gaines, Alabama, on August 8, 1864. He was received at Ship Island, Mississippi, from New Orleans on October 25, 1864, and exchanged at Ship Island on January 4, 1865.

Ross, J. F., Pvt. Co. H see **Ross, J. T.**

Ross, J. P., Pvt. Co. H see **Ross, J. T.**

Ross, J. T., Pvt. Co. H

He drew clothing on June 1, 1864. POW captured at Fort Gaines, Alabama, on August 8, 1864. He was received at Ship Island, Mississippi, from New Orleans on October 25, 1864, and exchanged at Ship Island on January 4, 1865. There was a request for information from Texas Com. of Pensions in September 1915, with a response from Montgomery that he went blind at Ship Island and was allowed to go home.*

Ross, R. A., Pvt. Co. C

Enlisted on October 13, 1861, at Mobile, Alabama, by Captain Rembert for twelve months. He appears present on a company muster roll for bounty on September 24, 1862. Company muster rolls for December 31, 1862, to April 30, 1863 and May/June 1863, report him present. POW captured at the Battle of Blakeley on April, 9, 1865. He was received at Ship Island, Mississippi, on April 15, 1865, and transferred on parole to Vicksburg, Mississippi, on May 1, 1865, for exchange.

Ross, Thomas S., Pvt. Co. C

Enlisted on October 13, 1861, at Mobile, Alabama, by Captain Rembert for one year. He was discharged December 31, 1861. Born in Fairfield County, North Carolina, age 45, dark complexion, blue eyes, dark hair, and a planter by profession. Paid $28.39 for service and subsistence from January 1, 1862, to March 1, 1862.

Ross, T. M., Pvt. Co. C

Enlisted on February 9, 1863, at Marengo County, Alabama, by Lt. Northrup for three years or the war. He appears on a descriptive list with four other men on May 2, 1863, as having received $50 bounty, born Marengo County, age 18, blue eyes, light hair, light complexion, five foot five inches, a farmer by occupation. Company muster rolls for December 31, 1862, to April 30, 1863, May/June 1863 and September/October 1863, all report him present. He was admitted to Post Hospital at Fort Morgan, Alabama, on

January 19, 1864, with int. fev. and sent to general hospital on January 26. He was admitted to Ross Hospital at Mobile on January 26, 1864, with debility and returned to duty on February 1, 1864. He drew clothing on March 31 and June 1, 1864, and signed by his mark. POW captured at Fort Gaines, Alabama, on August 8, 1864. His name appears on a morning report September 25, 1864, from New Orleans where he was confined at Steam Levee Press No. 4 and sent to hospital September 24. He was admitted to St. Louis USA General Hospital at New Orleans from Military Prison on September 24, 1864, with fever intermimit. and returned to confinement on September 28, 1864, age 19. He was received at Ship Island, Mississippi, from New Orleans on October 25, 1864, and exchanged at Ship Island on January 4, 1865. The descriptive list is in his file.*

Ross, William, Pvt. Co. H see **Ross, H. William**

Ross Joseph, Pvt. Co. G
His name appears on a regimental return for June 1862, sent to hospital on May 28.

Rowell, Joseph, Musician
Enlisted on October 13, 1861, at Baldwin County, Alabama, by Captain McCoy. He was discharged due to being overage at Choctaw Bluff, Alabama, on October 13, 1862. Born in Hopkinton, New Hampshire, age 49, five foot six and one half inches, fair complexion, blue eyes, light hair. He was paid $17.20 at time of discharge for service and travel from Choctaw Bluff to Mobile. *Note this man is likely the same Joseph Rowell musician that served with the 38th Alabama Infantry. He is mentioned in news articles of the musicians of the 38th Alabama.* His discharge is in his file.*

Rourke, Henry S., Pvt. Co. E
Enlisted on November 11, 1862, at Fort Morgan, Alabama, by Captain Sossaman for the war. Company muster roll for November/December 1862, reports him present. July/August 1863, muster roll reports him present confined in guard house. Company muster roll for September/October 1863, reports him present but absent without leave from October 20, to October 22. He drew clothing on March 31, 1864.

Royals, G. H., Sgt. Co. E
His name appears on a regimental return for June 1862, "May 19, Corinth, Miss., transferred: Reclaimed Captain."

Royals, J. M., Pvt. Co. D
His name appears on a regimental return for June 1862, " Corinth, Discharged for disability." Born in Butler County, Alabama, age 22, fair complexion, gray eyes, black hair, and a blacksmith by occupation. He was examined at camp near Corinth on April 26, 1862. His discharge is in his file.*

MOBILE CONFEDERATES

Rudd, Leon, Pvt. Co. _
POW captured at Fort Gaines, Alabama, on August 8, 1864. He appears on a register of POW's at New Orleans transferred to Ship Island, Mississippi, on December 10, 1864, and exchanged at Ship Island on January 4, 1865.

Rucker, Henry, A., Pvt. Co. E see **Ricker, Henry A.**

Ruez, Thomas, Pvt. Co. _
Referenced envelope only.

Russell, G. A., Pvt. Co. K see **Russell, George**

Russell, G. C., Pvt. Co. K
Enlisted at Fort Morgan, Alabama, on October 6, 1863, by Captain Dorgan for the war. He appears present on a company muster roll for September/October 1863, "never been paid." Company muster roll for September/October 1864, reports him absent detailed in Quarter Master Department in Mobile by General Maury on October 27, 1864, for 10 days. POW a straggler surrendered at Citronelle, Alabama, by Lt. General R. Taylor on May 4, 1865, and paroled at Mobile, Alabama, on May 21, 1865. He is shown as a resident of Mobile.

Russell, George, Pvt. Co. K
Enlisted September 10, 1862, at Fort Morgan, Alabama, by Captain Dorgan for the war. He appears present on a company muster roll for bounty on September 24, 1862. He is reported present on muster rolls for July/August 1862, September/October 1863 and November/December 1863. He drew clothing on June 20, 1864. Muster roll for September/October 1864, reports him absent sick in hospital since October 26, by Dr. Armstrong. POW surrendered at Citronelle, Alabama, by Lt. General R. Taylor on May 4, 1865, and paroled at Meridian, Mississippi, on May 13, 1865. He is shown as a resident of Mobile, Mobile County, Alabama.

Russell, J. A., Pvt. Co. C/D?
His name appears on a regimental return for June 1862, "Died, No Returns furnished from Hospital." Claim for deceased soldier filed by J. R. Eadbin on March 23, 1863.

Ruter, H., Pvt. Co. E see **Ricker, Henry A.**

Ruyer, David, Co. B
He appears on a report near Tupelo, Mississippi, on June 28, 1862, detached as nurse for General Hospital at Corinth April 17, 1862. His name appears on a regimental return for June 1862, on detached service hospital nurse.

Ryan, Dennis, Pvt. Co. B
Enlisted on September 9, 1862, at Mobile, Alabama, by Captain Johnson for the war. He appears present on a company muster roll for bounty on September 24, 1862.

He is reported absent on a muster roll for March/April 1863, under arrest at Choctaw Bluff. Company muster roll for May/June 1863, reports him present. September/October 1863, muster roll reports him present sick in quarters, due for clothing not drawn in kind $75.63. POW captured at Fort Gaines, Alabama, on August 8, 1864. He was received at Ship Island, Mississippi, from New Orleans on October 25, 1864, and exchanged at Ship Island on January 4, 1865. He was admitted to Lee Mississippi CSA Hospital at Jackson, Mississippi, on March 3, 1865, with bronchitis and returned to duty on March 10, 1865. POW of Lee Hospital at Lauderdale, Mississippi, surrendered at Citronelle, Alabama, by Lt. General R. Taylor on May 4, 1865, and paroled at Meridian, Mississippi, on May 13, 1865. He is shown as a resident of New Orleans, Louisiana.

S

Sackoff, John C., Pvt. Co. A
Enlisted at Mobile, Alabama, on October 13, 1861 by Major Hessee for one year. His name appears on a regimental return for June 1862, discharged for disability due to phthisis and feeble health at Corinth, Mississippi, on May 3, 1862. Born in Prussia, five foot six and one half inches, age 23, fair complexion, gray eyes, black hair and by occupation a cabinetmaker. His disability discharge is in his file.*

Sale, R. A., Pvt. Co. G
POW captured at Fort Gaines, Alabama, on August 8, 1864. He was admitted to St. Louis USA General Hospital at New Orleans on August 29, 1864, with diarrhoea and returned to confinement on November 2, 1864, age 26. He was received at Ship Island, Mississippi, on October 29, 1864, from New Orleans. (*This date must be incorrect*) He died at Ship Island on November 22, 1864, of diarrhoea (one report states pneumonia). He was buried in grave No. 34.

Sale, J. T., Pvt./Corporal Co. D see **Sales, John**

Sales, **J. T.**, Pvt./Corporal Co. D see **Sales, John**

Sales, R. A. , Pvt Co. G see **Sale, R. A.**

Sales, John, Pvt./Corporal Co. D
Enlisted on February 25, 1863, at Mobile, Alabama, by Lt. Mims for the war. He appears present on company muster rolls for July/August 1863, September/October 1863 and November/December 1863. Company muster roll for September/October 1864, reports him absent sent to General Hospital in Mobile on October 10, 1864.

Sallwhite, John, Pvt. Co. A see **Satterwhite, John**

MOBILE CONFEDERATES

Sally, John, Corporal Co. C/D

POW captured at Blakeley, Alabama, on April 9, 1865. He was received at Ship Island, Mississippi, on April 15, 1865, and transferred to Vicksburg, Mississippi, on parole for exchange on May 1, 1865.

Salter, L. C., Pvt. Co. E

His name appears on a regimental return for June 1862, at hospital at Mobile. He is shown on a report near Tupelo, Mississippi, on June 24, 1862, sent to interior hospital.

Salter, L. W., Pvt. Co. F see **Salter, Z. W.**

Salter, Z. W., Pvt. Co. E

Enlisted on January 31, 1863, at Choctaw Bluff, Alabama, by Captain Dade for the war. He appears present on a company muster roll for March 1, to June 30, 1863. He appears absent on company muster roll for September/October 1863, sick in hospital in Mobile since October 22, 1863. He was admitted to Ross Hospital at Mobile, Alabama, on June 19, 1864, with dysentery and sent to General Hospital at Spring Hill on June 20, 1864. Company muster roll for September/October 1864, reports him present and due for clothing $111.13. POW captured at Spanish Fort, Alabama, on April 8, 1865. He was received at Ship Island, Mississippi, on April 10, 1865, and transferred to Vicksburg, Mississippi, on parole for exchange May 1, 1865.

Sanders, (Saunders) J. M., Sgt. Co. H

POW captured at Fort Gaines, Alabama, on August 8, 1864. He was received at Ship Island, Mississippi, from New Orleans on October 25, 1864, and exchanged at Ship Island on January 4, 1865. POW a member of Co. H, 21st Alabama Infantry, Holtzclaw's Brigade CSA commanded by Captain A. B. Carrinton surrendered at Citronelle, Alabama, by Lt. General R. Taylor on May 4, 1865, and paroled at Meridian, Mississippi, on May 13, 1865. He is shown as a resident of Chambers County, Alabama.

Sane, A., Pvt. Co. K

His name appears on a register of payments to discharged soldiers. Discharged on July 3, 1862.

Sanpilipo, D. P., Pvt. Co. G

He appears on a regimental return for June 1862, wounded and furloughed since April 9, (1862). His name appears on a report June 28, 1862, near Tupelo, Mississippi, absent on furlough since April 29, 1862, in Mobile. Paid $22 on July 21, 1862. His pay voucher is in his file.*

Sarre, H. W., Pvt. Co. K

Paid $9.25. at Mobile, Alabama, for commutation of rations while on furlough for 37 days from January 23, 1862, to March 1, 1862.

21ST ALABAMA INFANTRY VOLUNTEERS

Satterwhite, Philip, Pvt. Co. A
Enlisted on August 28, 1862, at Jefferson County, Alabama, by W. T. Poole for the war. He appears present on company muster rolls for December 31, 1862, to April 30, 1863 and May/June 1863. Company muster roll for September/October 1863, reports him present in confinement. He drew clothing on June 14, 1864. POW captured at Fort Morgan, Alabama, on August 23, 1864, and sent to New York from New Orleans on September 27, 1864, and confined at Elmira on October 8, 1864. He died of chronic diarrhoea, at Elmira, New York, on April 5, 1865. He is buried in grave 2615.

Satterwhite, John, Pvt. Co. A
Enlisted September 23, 1862, at Jefferson County, Alabama, by A. R. Goodwin for the war. He appears present on company muster rolls for December 31, 1862, to April 30, 1863, May/June 1863 and September/October 1863. POW captured at Fort Morgan, Alabama, on August 23, 1864, and sent to New York from New Orleans on September 27, 1864, and confined at Elmira on October 8, 1864. He died of pneumonia at Elmira, New York, on March 19, 1865. He is buried in grave 1531.

Saulter, G. W., Pvt. Co. F see **Salter, Z. W.**

Saulter. J. W., Pvt. Co. F see **Salter, Z. W.**

Saunders, J. M., Sgt. Co. H see **Sanders, J. M.**

Savage, Thomas, J., 2nd Lt./1st Lt. Co. D
Enlisted at Mobile, Alabama, on October 13, 1861. Elected 2nd Lt. on October 14, 1861. He appears present on a regimental return for December 1861. He appears on a regimental return for June 1862, absent sent from Corinth to interior hospital by order of Surgeon Heustis. His name appears on a report June 28, 1862, near Tupelo, Mississippi, "on sick furlough in Mobile, since April 9, 1862." A register shows him dropped on May 8, 1862? He was promoted to 2nd Lt. on August 30, 1862. He appears present on a company muster roll for bounty on September 24, 1862. He appears present at Fort Morgan on returns for November and December 1862. Company muster rolls for November/December 1862, (signs roll as commanding company) July/August 1863, September/October 1863 and November/December 1863, all show him present. Company muster roll for September/October 1864, reports him absent detached by order of Lt. Colonel Sterling on August 31, 1864. *There is considerable paperwork in his file that is not readable.* *

Savom, J. T., Pvt. Co. _
There is a reference envelope in his file only.

Sayre, M. A., Pvt. Co. K
Enlisted on October 13, 1861, at Mobile, Alabama, by Captain Stewart for twelve months. He appears present on a company muster roll for bounty on September 24, 1862. Company muster rolls for November/December 1962, July/August 1863 and September/October 1863, all report him present. Muster roll for September/October 1864, reports

him absent sick in hospital since October 22, 1864. POW surrendered at Citronelle, Alabama, by Lt. General R. Taylor on May 4, 1865, and paroled at Meridian, Mississippi, on May 13, 1865. He is shown as a resident of Mobile, Mobile County, Alabama.

Scafin, L., Pvt. Co. G

His name appears on a report on June 28, 1862, near Tupelo, Mississippi, sent to interior from Corinth at the time of evacuation. He appears on a report for June 1862.

Scarber, M., Pvt. Co. I see **Scarbrough, M.**

Scarborough, J., Pvt. Co. I see **Scarbrough, M.**

Scarbrough, E. S., Pvt. Co. I

Enlisted on October 13, 1861, at Halls Mill, Alabama, by Major Hessee for the war. He appears present on a company muster roll for bounty on September 24, 1862. He appears present on muster rolls for July/August 1863 and September/October 1863. POW captured at Fort Gaines, Alabama, on August 8, 1864. He was received at Ship Island, Mississippi, from New Orleans on October 25, 1864, and exchanged at Ship Island on January 4, 1865.

Scarbroough, M., Pvt. Co. I

Enlisted on October 13, 1861, at Halls Mill, Alabama, by Major Hessee for the war. He appears present on a company muster roll for bounty on September 24, 1862. His name appears on two reports for November and December 1862, as being detailed in Commissary Department. He appears present on muster rolls for July/August 1863 and September/October 1863, where both rolls report him detailed on extra duty in Commissary Department from May 20, 1863. POW captured at Fort Gaines, Alabama, on August 8, 1864. He was received at Ship Island, Mississippi, from New Orleans on October 25, 1864, and exchanged at Ship Island on January 4, 1865.

Scattergood, B. L., Sgt. Co. E

Enlisted on October 13, 1861, at Mobile, Alabama, by Captain Chamberlain for the war. He appears present on a company muster roll for bounty on September 24, 1862. He appears present on a company muster roll for November/December 1862. *There is paperwork in his file that is not readable.*

Schmit, ?, Pvt. Co. H.

His name appears on a regimental return for June 1862. He is shown on a report for June 28, 1862, near Tupelo, Mississippi, sent to hospital in Mobile.

Schrimer, ?, Pvt. Co. K

Enlisted on September 20, 1864, at Mobile, Alabama, by Captain Stone for the war. He appears present on a company muster roll for September/October 1864. It appears he was transferred to Conscripts at Talladega, on October 18, 1864.

Schwartz, Edward, Co. H

His name appears on a register of payments for soldiers who are deceased. Payment made on August 18, 1862, at Mobile, Alabama. Born in France?

Scott, Jeremiah, Pvt. Co. B

Enlisted on August 17, 1862, at Fort Morgan, Alabama, by Captain Johnston for the war. He appears present on a company muster roll for bounty on September 24, 1862. He appears present on company muster rolls for March/April 1863, May/June 1863 and September/October 1863. POW captured at Fort Gaines, Alabama, on August 8, 1864. He was received at Ship Island, Mississippi, from New Orleans on October 25, 1864, and exchanged at Ship Island, on January 4, 1865. He made application to take the Oath of Allegiance to the USA at Ship Island. He appears to sign (by mark) to an Oath of Allegiance to the USA at Elmira, New York, on June 16, 1865. Residence Mobile, Alabama, fair complexion, dark hair, blue eyes, five foot eight and one half inches, released June 16, 1865.

Scranton, Lewis, Pvt. Co. K

Wounded slightly at Shiloh in the left breast, on April 6, 1862, at 11 A. M. on the center battlefield.

Seabrok, D. O., Pvt. Co. D/C

POW captured at Blakeley, Alabama, on April 9, 1865. He was sent to Ship Island, Mississippi, and transferred to Vicksburg, Mississippi, on parole for exchange on May 1, 1865.

Seabrok, A. (Isaac) H., Pvt. Co. C

Enlisted on October 13, 1861, at Marengo County, By Captain Rembert. He appears on a report for June 1862, died at hospital on May 17. His name appears on a register of payments for soldiers who are deceased. Payment of $103.23 made on March 23, 1863, for his service February 28, to May 17, 1862, plus bonus and commutation of clothing to Bowen Seabrok his father. He was born in Marengo County, Alabama, age 19, five foot two inches, light complexion, brown eyes, auburn hair, by occupation a clerk. His claim payment voucher and a certificate of service is in his file.*

Seale, Benjamin B., Pvt. Co. C.

Enlisted by Captain Rembert at Mobile, Alabama, on October 13, 1861. He was discharged due to disability due to the effects of typhoid fever at Fort Gaines on December 9, 1861, age 22, six foot and one half inch, dark complexion, hazel eyes, a dentist by occupation, born in Sumter County, Alabama. He was paid $45.90 for service on April 28, 1862.

*His pension file furnished by a descendant shows he enlisted at Rembert Hills, Alabama, and continued until discharged due to bad health in December 1861. He then re-enlisted in Co. F, 40th Alabama Infantry at Mobile and continued until captured at Vicksburg, Mississippi, detailed as brigade wagon master. He was wounded at Bentonville, North Carolina and captured March 19, 1865. POW at David Island, North Carolina. He arrived home on July 5, 1865. His name is reported here as **Benjamin Bluford Seale**.*

MOBILE CONFEDERATES

Seale, L (Littleton?) B. (Bluford), Pvt. Co. C

Enlisted on October 13, 1861, at Mobile, Alabama, by Captain Rembert for three years or the war. He appears present on a company muster roll for bounty on September 24, 1862. Company muster rolls report him present for December 31, 1862, to April 30, 1863, May/June 1863 and September/October 1863. He was admitted to Post Hospital at Fort Morgan, Alabama, on November 9, 1863 with int. fev. and returned to duty on November 16. He was again admitted to Post Hospital at Fort Morgan on November 22, 1863, with chills int. and furloughed on January 9, 1864. He drew clothing March 31, 1864. POW captured at Fort Gaines, Alabama, on August 8, 1864. He was admitted to St. Louis USA General Hospital at New Orleans on August 21, 1864, from military prison with diarrhoea and returned to confinement on August 26, 1864, age 21. He was again admitted to St. Louis USA Hospital on September 11, 1864, with fev. remit and hemorrhoids and returned to confinement on September 17. He was received at Ship Island, Mississippi, on October 24, 1864, and exchanged at Ship Island on January 4, 1865. POW surrendered at Citronelle, Alabama, by Lt. General R. Taylor on May 4, 1865, and paroled at Meridian, Mississippi, on May 13, 1865. He is shown as a resident of Sumter County, Alabama.

Seale, T. B., Pvt. Co. C see **Seale, L. B.**

Segula, Contanstien, Pvt. Co. G

Wounded slightly at Shiloh on April 6, 1862, 8 A. M. while advancing on First Camp. He appears on a regimental return for June 1862, furloughed. He was paid $22 on July 17, 1862. His pay voucher is in his file.*

Seiffert, John, Co. H

He was killed at Shiloh shot through the head on April 6, 1862, at Center Field. Born in Germany. Mobile Polaski Rifles, Alabama Infantry was entered and struck out on his file.

Self, Elijah, Pvt. Co. F

Enlisted August 26, 1862, at Jefferson County, Alabama, by W. A. Walker (one card shows by Captain Brewster) for the war. He appears present on company muster rolls for March 1, to June 30, 1863, and September/October 1863. POW captured at Fort Gaines, Alabama, on August 8, 1864. He was sent to New Orleans and admitted to St. Louis USA General Hospital at New Orleans from military prison on August 23, 1864, with diarrhoea and returned to confinement on November 2, 1864, age 21. He was received at Ship Island, Mississippi, on October 29, 1864, from New Orleans. He died of pneumonia on November 23, 1864, and was buried in grave No. 38 (37?).

Self, William, Pvt., Co. F

Enlisted at St Clair County, Alabama, on December 20, 1861, by Captain Brewster for three years or the war. He appears present on company muster rolls for March 1, to June 30, 1863 and September/October 1863. POW captured at Fort Gaines, Alabama, on August 8, 1864. He was received at Ship Island from New Orleans on

October 25, 1864, and exchanged at Ship Island on January 4, 1865. He was paroled at Talladega, Alabama, on June 17, 1864.

Self, W. W., Pvt. Co. F see **Self, William**

Sellers, Abram, Sgt. Co. A
Discharged on January 14, 1862.

Simmes, Charles, Pvt. Co. K/F see **Simms, Charles**

Segui, Joaquin, 2nd Lt. Co. G
Enlisted on October 13, 1861, and elected 2nd Lt. on October 7, 1861. His name appears on regimental returns for November and December 1861, present. He appears on a regimental return for June 1862, present at Tupelo, Mississippi. Discharged by General Bragg? *There is unreadable paperwork in his file.**

Serafin, Castro, Pvt. Co. G
He appears on a regimental return for June 1861.

Sessions, C. C., Pvt. Co. E
Enlisted on October 13, 1861, at Mobile, Alabama, by Captain Chamberlain for the war. He was wounded slightly in his thumb at Shiloh on April 6, 1862, at 4 P. M. His name appears on a regimental return for June 1862, sent to interior hospital from Corinth. His name appears on a report made June 28, 1862, near Tupelo, Mississippi, sent to interior hospital by surgeon. He appears absent on a company muster roll for bounty on September 24, 1862, detached on August 5, as hospital steward on order of General Bragg. Returns for November and December 1862, report him detached in Medical Department. Company muster rolls for November/December 1862, and July/August 1863, report him absent and detached as before. He appears on a hospital rolls at Hospital at Tunnel Hill, Georgia, March and April 1863, as hospital steward.

Sessions, Columbus C., Pvt. Co. E see **Sessions C. C.**

Sexton, G. W., Pvt. Co. D
POW captured at Blakeley, Alabama, on April 9, 1865. He was sent to Ship Island, Mississippi, and transferred on parole to Vicksburg, Mississippi, for exchange on May 1, 1865.

Shaw, A., Pvt. C/F
Enlisted Baldwin County, Alabama, on October 13, 1861. He appears on a regimental return for June 1862, discharged May 8, 1862, for disability at Corinth, Mississippi. Born in Georgia, age 56, light complexion, gray eyes, light hair, and a farmer by occupation. A poor copy of his discharge is in his file.*

Shay, Martin, Pvt. Co. A

Enlisted on October 13, 1861, at Mobile, Alabama, by Major Hessee for the war. He was wounded severely in left leg on April 6, 1862, at Center field and captured at hospital. [*may be error as he appears in a Mobile, hospital*?] He appears on a regimental return for June 1862, wounded at Shiloh and furloughed since April 11. He appears on a report on June 28, 1862, near Tupelo, Mississippi, wounded at Shiloh and at a Mobile, Hospital. He appears present on a company muster roll for bounty on September 24, 1862. He appears present on company muster rolls for December 31, 1862, to April 30, 1863, May/June 1863 and September/October 1863. POW captured at Fort Morgan, Alabama, on August 23, 1864. He was received at Elmira, New York, on October 8, 1864, from New Orleans. He signed an Oath of Allegiance to the USA and was released on July 7, 1865. Residence Mobile, Alabama, dark complexion, dark hair, gray eyes, five foot nine inches. There is unreadable paperwork in his file.*

Shearrer, E. W., Sgt. see **Sherrer, E. W.**

Sheey, Martin, Pvt. Co. A see **Shay, Martin**

Sheeler, O. E., Pvt. Co. C

There is a pay voucher possibly a discharge in his file. Too difficult to read.*

Sheffield, J. R., Sgt./Pvt. _
Reference envelop only.

Sheffiled, N., Sgt./Pvt.
Reference envelop only.

Sheffield, Thomas L., Pvt. Co. K

Enlisted on March 10, 1862, at Fort Pillow by Captain Stewart for the war. He appears absent on a company muster roll for bounty on September 24, 1862, detached in Quarter Master Department on March 24, 1862, by General Gladden. He is shown absent in a similar fashion on muster rolls for November/December 1862, July/August 1863 and September/October 1863. Muster roll for September/October 1864, reports him absent sent to general hospital October 20, 1864. He was admitted to Ross Hospital at Mobile, Alabama, on October 2, 1863, with acute dysentery and returned to duty on October 14. He was again admitted to Ross Hospital on July 16, 1864, with acute dysentery and returned to duty on July 22. POW surrendered at Citronelle, Alabama, by Lt. General Richard Taylor on May 4, 1865, and paroled at Meridian, Mississippi, on May 13, 1865. He is shown as a resident of Mobile, Alabama. There are vouchers for payment for service and commutation of rations while on detached service in his file.*

Sheffield, William H., Pvt. Co. K

Enlisted on March 10, 1862, at Fort Pillow, by Captain Stewart for the war. He was wounded slightly in the head at Shiloh on April 6 at 4 P. M. while advancing on Old Field. He appears present on a company muster roll for bounty on September 24, 1862, He appears present on company muster rolls for November/December 1862, July/August

1863 and September/October 1863. Muster roll for September/October 1864, reports him absent sent to hospital on October 29. POW surrendered at Citronelle, Alabama, by Lt. General Richard Taylor on May 4, 1865, and paroled at Meridian, Mississippi, on May 13, 1865. He is shown as a resident of Mobile, Alabama.

Sheffield, W. L., Pvt. Co. K see **Sheffield, W. H.**

Shelton, William, Pvt. Co. A
Enlisted on September 3, 1862, at Jefferson County, by A. R. Goodwin for three years or the war. He appears absent on a company muster roll for December 31, 1862, to April 30, 1863, sick in hospital at Choctaw Bluff. May/June 1863, muster roll reports him absent sent to Springhill Hospital at Mobile on June 4, 1863. Muster roll for September/October 1863, reports him absent sent to Springhill Hospital on April 25, 1863. He appears present as a nurse in September/October and November/December 1863 and January/February 1864, at General Hospital Miller at Springhill, Alabama. He appears present in July and August 1864, on a hospital muster roll at General Hospital Miller at Greenville, Alabama, as a nurse. His name appears on a roll of POW's paroled at Talladega, Alabama, on June 5, 1865.

Shepherd, J. J., Sgt./Pvt. Co. E see **Sheppard, John J.**

Sheppard, John, J., Sgt./Pvt. Co. E
Enlisted on October 13, 1864, at Mobile, Alabama, by Captain Chamberlain for the war. He appears present on a company muster roll for bounty on September 24, 1862. Company muster roll for November/December 1862, reports him present and reduced to ranks from November 11, 1862, by Court Marshal. Company muster rolls for July/August and September/October 1863, report him as a Private absent detached from June 25, 1863, by order General Maury. POW captured at Fort Gaines, Alabama, on August 8, 1864. He was received at Ship Island from New Orleans on October 25, 1864, and exchanged at Ship Island on January 4, 1865. POW surrendered at Citronelle, Alabama, by Lt. General Richard Taylor on May 4, 1865, and paroled at Meridian, Mississippi, on May 13, 1865. He is shown as a resident of Mobile, Alabama, age 20, blue eyes, dark brown hair, fair complexion, five foot ten inches, born at ? Court House, Virginia, a clerk by occupation. *His paperwork copy is not readable.*

Sheppard, Thomas M., 1st Lt. Co. K
Enlisted on October 13, 1861. Elected 1st Lt. April 29, 1861. Killed at Shiloh on April 6, 1862, at 3 P. M. *The remainder of his file is not readable.*

Sheppherd, B., Pvt. Co. H
Enlisted 10, 1863, at Camden, Alabama, by Lt. Wragg for three years or the war. POW captured at Fort Gaines, Alabama, on August 8, 1864. Died suddenly of heart disease in Steam Press No. 4 at New Orleans on August 29, 1864.

Sherdon, T., Pvt. Co. C see **Sheridan, Thomas**

MOBILE CONFEDERATES

Sheridan, Borney, Pvt. Co. D
His name appears on a register at Ross Hospital at Mobile, Alabama, admitted January 2, 1864, with acute dysentery and returned to duty on January 23, 1864.

Sheridan, Thomas J., Pvt. Co. D
Enlisted on October 13, 1861, at Mobile, Alabama, by Captain Butt for the war. His name appears on a regimental return for June 1862, "May 29, on march suppose to have been captured." He appears on a roll of POW's at St. Louis to be sent to Alton, Illinois. He arrived at Alton, Illinois, on June 27, 1862. He appears on a roll of POW's at Alton, Illinois, captured at Corinth, Mississippi, on June 1, 1862. He appears on a roll at Alton, Illinois, on September 23, 1862, to be exchanged. He appears absent on a company muster roll for bounty on September 24, 1862, "taken prisoner at Corinth." Company muster roll for November/December 1862, he is reported present. Muster roll for July/August 1862, he is reported in guardhouse at Fort Morgan under General Court Marshal. September/October 1863, muster roll reports him present. Muster roll for November/December 1863, reports him absent detached for 20 days by order of General Maury. He was admitted to Ross Hospital at Mobile, Alabama, on January 11, 1864, with acute dysentery and returned to duty on February 1, 1864. He was admitted to Post Hospital at Fort Morgan with syphilis on June 4, 1864, and returned to duty on June 16, 1864. He was admitted to Post Hospital at Fort Morgan with the same complaint on June 17, 1864, and returned to duty on June 28, 1864. POW captured at Mobile Bay on August 5, 1864, and sent to New Orleans. He was admitted to St. Louis USA General Hospital at New Orleans on October 4, 1864, with acute diarrhoea and returned to confinement on October 10, 1864. He was received at Ship Island, Mississippi, on October 28, 1864, and exchanged on March 4, 1865. There is a prison transfer and a pay voucher in his file .*

Sheridan, T. J., Pvt. Co. D see **Sheridan, Thomas**

Sherley, E., Pvt. Co. C
His name appears on a regimental return for June 1862.

Shearer, E. W., Pvt. Co. H

Sherrer, E. W., Sgt. Co. H
POW captured at Fort Gaines, Alabama, on August 8, 1864; He was received at Ship Island, Mississippi, from New Orleans on October 24, 1864, and exchanged at Ship Island on January 4, 1865. He appears on report of Medical Examining Board at Selma, Alabama, April? 28, 1865, furlough for 60 days, diarrhoea. POW surrendered at Citronelle, Alabama, by Lt General Richard Taylor in May 1865, and paroled at Selma on May 25, 1865. A resident of Autauga, County, Alabama.

Shetzinger, John, Pvt. Co. H
His name appears on a regimental return for June 1862.

Shiney, T. N. or Shiney, F. M., Pvt. Co. C/K see **Shirey, F. M**

Shirey, F. M., Pvt. Co. K

Enlisted on November 22, 1861, at Fort Gaines, Alabama, by Captain Rembert for three years or the war. He appears present on a company muster roll for bounty on September 24, 1862. Company C muster rolls for December 31, 1862, to April 30, 1863, May/June 1863, (lost 1 canteen at 25 cents and one strap at 20 cents) and September/October1863, all report him present. He was admitted to Post Hospital at Fort Morgan on November 17, 1863, with int. feb. and returned to duty on November 29, 1863. He was again admitted to Post Hospital at Fort Morgan on November 30, 1863, with chills and fever and returned to duty on January 13, 1864. Company K muster roll for July/August 1864, reports him present attached by headquarters. Muster roll for September/October 1864, "transferred to this company K by SO 291, on October 17, 1864." POW surrendered at Citronelle, Alabama, by Lt General Richard Taylor on May 4, 1865, and paroled at Meridian, Mississippi, on May 13, 1865. A resident of Shiloh, Marengo County, Alabama.

Shiry, F. M., Pvt. Co. C/K see **Shirey, F. M.**

Shoemaker, J. W., Pvt. Co. E

Enlisted on August 6, 1862, at Jefferson, County, Alabama, by W. J. Poole for the war. He appears present on company muster rolls for November/December 1862, and July/August 1863. Company muster roll for September/October 1863, reports him absent sick since October 7, 1863, $70,22 due him for clothing. POW captured at Fort Gaines, Alabama, on August 8, 1864, died on board steamer on way to New Orleans. He then appears on a morning report at New Orleans confined at Steam Levee Press No. 4 on September 25, 1864, sent to hospital on September 25, 1864. Jas. Shoemaker was admitted to St. Louis USA General Hospital at New Orleans on September 24, 1864, with diarrhoea and returned to prison on October 8, 1864, age 34. He was received at Ship Island, Mississippi, on October 25, 1864, and exchanged at Ship Island on January 4, 1865.

Shoemaker, Robert, Pvt. Co. I

He appears on a report at USA Prison Hospital at Camp Douglas, Illinois, for June 18, 1863, with typhoid fever. Returned to prison on July 2, 1863.

Shropshire, M. L., Pvt. Co. A

Enlisted on October 13, 1861, at Mobile, Alabama, by Major Hessee. He appears absent on a company muster roll for bounty on September 24, 1862.

Sichleman, William, Pvt. Co. D

He appears on a medical card at USA General Hospital at Camp Dennison, Ohio, April 20, 1862.

Siddell, Pvt. Co. G

He was admitted to Post Hospital at Fort Morgan, Alabama, on November 3, 1863, with dysentery and returned to duty on November 5, 1863.

Sigale, Constantine, Pvt. Co. G

He appears on a report for June 1862, near Tupelo, Mississippi, on June 28, 1862, wounded at Shiloh and absent since April 10, 1862. He was paid $4.25 for rations while on furlough from June 25, 1862, to July 12, 1862.

Sigmands, J., Pvt. Co. G

He appears on a report near Tupelo, Mississippi, on June 28, 1862, sent to interior from Corinth at the time of evacuation. He also appears on a regimental return for June 1862.

Silva, Pvt. Co. G

POW captured April 7, 1862.

Simmons, B. F., Pvt._

Reference envelope only.

Sims, B. P., Pvt. Co. H

POW captured at Fort Gaines, Alabama, on August 8, 1862. He was confined at Steam Levee Press No. 4 at New Orleans and sent to the hospital on September 29, 1864. He was admitted to St. Louis USA General Hospital at New Orleans, on September 29, 1864, with fever remit. and returned to prison on October 8, 1864, age 42. He was received at Ship Island, Mississippi, on October 25, 1864, from New Orleans and exchanged at Ship Island on January 4, 1865.

Simmons, W. M., Pvt. Co. I

Data unreadable.

Simms, Charles, Pvt./Sgt. Co. K/F.

Enlisted on July 26, 1862, at Saltillo, Mississippi, by Captain Dorgan for the war. He appears present on a company muster roll for bounty on September 24, 1862. Company muster roll for November/December 1862, reports him present. Company F muster roll for March 1, to June 30, 1863, reports him present as Sgt., sick in quarters.

Simms, Reuben, Pvt. Co. I

Enlisted February 24, 1863, at Fort Morgan, Alabama, by Lt. Donoha, for the war. He appears present on a company muster roll for July/August 1863. Muster roll for September/October 1863, no remark. He was admitted to Post Hospital at Fort Morgan, Alabama, with rubella on March 15, and returned to duty on April 11, 1863. POW captured at Fort Gaines, Alabama, on August 8, 1864. He was received at Ship Island, Mississippi, from New Orleans on October 25, 1864, and exchanged at Ship Island on January 4, 1865.

Simms, W. R., Pvt. Co. H/I

He was admitted to Post Hospital at Fort Morgan, Alabama, with fev. con. on July 26, and returned to duty on July 29, 1863. POW captured at Fort Gaines, Alabama, on August 8, 1864. He was admitted to St. Louis USA General Hospital at New Orleans on

August 20, 1864, with fever remittent and diarrhoea and returned to prison on August 31, 1864, age 35. He was received at Ship Island, Mississippi, from New Orleans on October 25, 1864, and exchanged at Ship Island on January 4, 1865. He was admitted to 1st Mississippi, CSA Hospital at Jackson, Mississippi, on March 20, 1865, and returned to duty on April 4, 1865.

Simpson, J. S., Pvt. Co. D
Enlisted in Monroe County, Alabama, on August 1, 1864, by Lt. Foster for the war. He died in hospital in Mobile, Alabama, on October 26, 1864. Never paid.

Simpson, Lewis, Pvt./Sgt. Co. E/H
Enlisted on October 13, 1864, at Mobile, Alabama, by Captain Chamberlain for the war. He appears on a regimental return for June 1862, a nurse sick. He appears present on a company muster roll for bounty September 24, 1862. Company muster rolls for November/December 1862, July/August 1863 and September/October 1863, all report him present. He appears on a receipt roll for extra duty pay as a boatman in September 1863. He drew clothing on May 16, 1863 and March 31, 1864. POW captured at Fort Gaines, Alabama, on August 8, 1864. He was received at Ship Island, Mississippi, from New Orleans on October 25, 1864, and exchanged at Ship Island on January 4, 1865. POW surrendered at Citronelle, Alabama, by Lt. General Richard Taylor on May 4, 1865, and paroled at Meridian, Mississippi, on May 13, 1865.

Sims, B. P., Pvt. Co. H see **Simms, B. P.**

Sims, M., Pvt. Co. G
His name appears on a regimental return for June 1862, sent to hospital May 28.

Sims, P. P. Pvt. Co. H
He was admitted to Ross Hospital at Mobile, Alabama, on January 6, 1865, with chronic diarrhoea. He died January 13, 1865.

Sims, Reuben, Pvt. Co. I see **Siumms, Reubin.**

Simms, Will, Pvt. Co. H/I see **Simms, W. R.**

Sims, W. R., Pvt. Co. H/I see **Simms, W. R.**

Sinclair, Alexander C., Pvt. Co. G
POW captured at Port Gibson, Mississippi, May 1, 1863. He appears on a list of POW's at Military Prison, Alton, Illinois, May 18, 1863. He was received at City Point, Virginia, in June 1863, for exchange.

Skates, Edward, Pvt. Co. K
Killed at Shiloh shot in left lung on April 6, 1862, at 8 A. M.

Skinner, W. B., Pvt. Co. C.
He was admitted to Yandell Hospital at Meridian, Mississippi, on April 5, 1862.

Skinner, Erasimus D., Pvt. Co. C
He was discharged from Company A of the 43rd Alabama Infantry on January 25, 1863, Enlisted on July 29, 1863, at Linden, Alabama, by Lt. McLeod for three years or the war. He appears present on a company muster roll for September/October 1863. *His discharge is in the file but too dark to read.*

Skipper, B., Pvt. Co. C. see **Skipper, J. B.**

Skipper, J. S., Pvt. Co. C. see **Skipper J. B.**

Skipper, J. B., Pvt. Co. C
Enlisted on December 6, 1862, at Marengo County, Alabama, by Lt. Northrup for three years or the war. He appears present on a company muster roll for December 31, 1862, to April 30, 1863. Company muster roll for May/June 1863, reports him present, detailed as ambulance driver on March 25, 1863, returned to the company in June 1863. Muster roll for September/October 1863, reports him present in hospital at Fort Morgan. He was admitted to Post Hospital at Fort Morgan, Alabama, with asthma on October 30, 1863, and returned to duty on November 23, 1863. POW captured at Fort Gaines, Alabama, on August 8, 1864. He was admitted to St. Louis USA General Hospital at New Orleans on August 20, 1864, with remtt. fever and returned to confinement on September 30, 1864, age 28. He was again admitted to St. Louis USA General Hospital at New Orleans on October 23, 1864, with pneumonia and returned to confinement at Steam Levee Press No. 4 on November 2, 1864. He was received at Ship Island, Mississippi, from New Orleans on November 5, 1864, and exchanged on January 4, 1865. He died at Mobile on January 25, 1865. Pvt. J. A. Skipper was surrendered at Citronelle by Lt. General R. Taylor and paroled at Demopolis, Alabama, on May 29, 1865. *Likely two files combined here.* See personal papers of Pvt. **T. M. Ross**, Co. D. This data from a descriptive list on May 2, 1863, for bounty and clothing. Filed with **Ross, T. M.**

Skipper, J. B., Pvt. age 26, dark eyes, dark hair, dark complexion, five foot eight inches, born Coweta County, Georgia?, paid $50 bounty.

Slade, William (Wiley) F., Pvt. Co. A
Enlisted on February 1, 1863, at Choctaw Bluff, Alabama, by Captain Cothran for three years or the war. Company muster rolls for December 31, 1862, to April 30, 1863, May/June 1863 and September/October 1863, all report him present. He was admitted to Post Hospital at Fort Morgan, Alabama, with diarrhoea on January 8, 1864, and returned to duty on January 17, 1864. He drew clothing on March 31, 1864. POW captured at Fort Morgan, Alabama, on August 27, 1864. He was confined at Steam Levee Press No. 4 at New Orleans and sent to hospital on September 25, 1864. He was admitted to St. Louis USA General Hospital at New Orleans with diarrhoea on September 24, 1864, and returned to confinement September 27, 1864, age 36. His name appears on a list of

POW's at New Orleans sent to New York, on September 27, 1864. He was received at Elmira, New York, on October 8, 1864, and died of chronic diarrhoea on January 1, 1865. He is buried in grave 1342.

This data is from a descriptive list on May 26, 1863, list is filed with Pvt. **John Pennington,** Co. A.

Pvt. **W. G. Slade,** age 34, brown eyes, black hair, five foot ten inches, born in SC, a farmer by occupation, enlisted at Clarke County, Alabama, by Captain Cothran, paid $50 bonus.

Slaton, William, Corporal, Co. H

He drew clothing on June 1, 1864. POW captured at Fort Gaines, Alabama, on August 8, 1864. He was received at Ship Island, Mississippi, on October 25, 1864, from New Orleans and exchanged at Ship Island on January 4, 1865.

Slatter, H. H., Pvt. Co. E

His name appears on a regimental return for June 1863, detailed to Division A.Q.M. He was paid $69 for service from March 1, to June 30, 1862.

Slatter, S. F., Pvt. Co. K

Enlisted on October 13, 1861, at Mobile, Alabama, by Captain Stewart for the war. He is reported present on a company muster roll for bounty on September 24, 1862. Muster roll for November/December 1862, also reports him present. He was paid $44 on July 19, 1862, for detached service from March 1, 1862, to June 30, 1862. There is a pay voucher in his file.*

Smethley, David, Co. H

Died August 18, 1862, at Fort Gaines, Alabama. He was born in Mayence, Georgia.

Smith, Pvt. Co. I

He was admitted to Post Hospital at Fort Morgan, Alabama, on May 5, 1863, with int. fev. and returned to duty on May 12.

Smith, A. A., Pvt. Co. D

He was surrendered at Citronelle, Alabama, by Lt. General Richard Taylor on May 4, 1865, and paroled at Meridian, Mississippi, on May 13, 1865. He was a resident of Mobile, Alabama.

Smith, Abb W., Pvt. Co. E see **Smith A. W.**

Smith, A. J., Pvt. Co. K

He appears present on a muster roll for Company A 1st Regiment Louisiana Artillery in July and August 1864. He appears present on a Company A muster roll for September/October 1864, 1st Regiment of Louisiana Heavy Artillery Regulars where he enlisted at Mobile, Alabama, on August 15, 1864. This muster roll reports him attached to his Co. K, 21st Alabama on Special Order 291. Enlisted on August 16, 1864, in Company K of the 21st Alabama Infantry at Mobile, Alabama, by Captain Gordon for the war. Company muster roll for September/October 1864, reports that he was transferred to Conscript Corp at Notasulga, (Alabama) by order of Enrolling Officer on October 18, 1864.

Smith, A. W., Pvt. Co. E
　　　　Enlisted on November 25, 1862, at Fort Morgan, Alabama, by Captain Sossaman for the war. Substitute for D. H. Herms. Company muster roll for November/December 1862, reports him present sick in hospital. Company muster roll for July/August 1863, reports him present. Muster roll for September/October 1863, reports him absent sick in Mobile on October 27, 1863. Abb Smith was admitted to Ross Hospital at Mobile with debility on January 16, 1864, and returned to duty on February 1, 1864, name shows Asalim? Smith. POW captured at Fort Gaines, Alabama, on August 8, 1864. He was confined at Steam Levee Press No. 4, New Orleans and sent to hospital on October 28, 1864. He was admitted to St. Louis USA General Hospital at New Orleans on August 19, 1864, with chronic diarrhoea and returned to confinement on August 22, 1864, age 50. He was again admitted to St. Louis USA General Hospital on September 2, 1864, with rheumatism and returned to prison on September 12, 1864. He was received at Ship Island, Mississippi, from New Orleans on October 25, 1864, and died of dysentery on December 13, 1864. He was buried in grave 86.

Smith, A. W., Pvt. Co. I/K
　　　　Enlisted on October 13, 1861, at Halls Mill, Alabama, by Major Hessee for the war. He appears present on a company muster roll for bounty on September 24, 1862. Company muster rolls for July/August 1863 and September/October 1863, report him present. On muster roll for September/October 1864, he is reported absent, sent to hospital October 26, 1864. POW surrendered at Citronelle, Alabama, by Lt. General Richard Taylor on May 4, 1865, and paroled at Meridian, Mississippi, on May 13, 1864. He is shown as residing in Mobile, Mobile County, Alabama,

Smith, D. J., Pvt. Co. B
　　　　POW surrendered at Citronelle, Alabama, by Lt. General Richard Taylor on May 4, 1865, and paroled at Meridian, Mississippi, on May 13, 1864. He is shown as residing in Port Hudson, Louisiana.

Smith, F., Pvt. Co. I/K
　　　　Enlisted on October 13, 1861, at Halls Mill, Alabama, by Major Hessee for the war. He appears present on a company muster roll for bounty on September 24, 1862. Company muster rolls for Company I, July/August 1863 and September/October 1863, report him present. On muster roll for Company D September/October 1864, he appears absent, sent to General Hospital in Mobile on October 3, 1864, assigned to Company D on order. J. F. Smith of Co. D. Was admitted to Ross Hospital at Mobile on October 4, 1864, with febris intermittens quot. and returned to duty on November 19, 1864. He also appears on a muster roll for Captain Sossaman's detachment for September/October 1864, absent detailed at Battery Huger on order of Colonel Fuller. POW surrendered at

Citronelle, Alabama, by Lt. General Richard Taylor on May 4, 1865, and paroled at Meridian, Mississippi, on May 13, 1864. He is shown as residing in Mobile County, Alabama.

Smith, F. N., Lt./Captain Co. C

Enlisted on October 13, 1861, elected 2nd Lt. October 10, 1861, elected April 30, 1862, promoted May 8, 1862. He appears present on a regimental returns for November and December 1861. His name appears on a regimental return at Tupelo, Mississippi, for June 1862. He appears present on a company muster roll for bounty on September 24, 1862. A company muster roll for December 31, 1862, to April 30, 1863, reports him present and he signs roll as Captain, inspecting, mustering officer. He is reported present on a company muster roll May/June 1863. Muster roll for September/October 1863, reports him absent in hospital at Mobile since October 29, 1863. He was given 190 days leave at Fort Morgan, Alabama on June 24, 1864, by order of General Maury. POW captured at Fort Gaines, Alabama, on August 8, 1864. He was admitted to St. Louis USA General Hospital at New Orleans on August 27, 1864, with diarrhoea and returned to prison on August 30, 1864, age 25. He was received at Ship Island, Mississippi, from New Orleans on November ?, 1864, and exchanged at Ship Island on January 4, 1865. There are a number of requisitions and pay vouchers in his file**. *Most are too dark to read.* He drew $180 per month as Captain.

Smith, ?, Co. C

Killed at Shiloh on April 6, 1862. Filed with **F. N. Smith**.

Smith, George, Pvt. Co. D

POW captured at Blakeley, Alabama, on April 9, 1865. He was received at Ship Island, Mississippi, on April 15, 1865, and transferred to Vicksburg, Mississippi, on parole for exchange on May 1, 1865.

Smith, George W., Co. E

Wounded in the wrist severely at Shiloh on April 6, 1862, at 8:30 A. M. during attack on First Camp. He was discharged July 2, 1862.

Smith, H., Pvt. Co. D.

His name appears on a regimental return for Jun 1862. Died at hospital on May 24, 1862, Mobile.

Smith, James, J., Pvt. Co. H

POW captured at Fort Gaines, Alabama, on August 8, 1864. He was admitted to St. Louis USA General Hospital at New Orleans on August 20, 1864, with diarrhoea and fever remit. He was returned to prison on August or October? 21, 1864, age 29. He was received at Ship Island, Mississippi, from New Orleans on October 25, 1864, and exchanged at Ship Island, on January 4, 1865. He was admitted to Ross Hospital at Mobile, Alabama, on January 10, 1865, with acute diarrhoea and furloughed for 60 days. His parole was issued by the 16th US Army Corps, Provost Marshal at Montgomery,

Alabama, on June 13, 1865. The parole describes him as five foot seven, dark hair, blue eyes, dark complexion, he signed by his mark "x". His parole is in his file.*

Smith, Joseph, W., Corp. Co. G

There is a voucher for payment on November 27, 1863, of $13.20 for commutation of rations while on furlough for 40 days. POW captured at Fort Gaines, Alabama, on August 8, 1864. He was received at Ship Island, Mississippi, from New Orleans on October 25, 1864, and exchanged at Ship Island on January 4, 1865. POW surrendered at Citronelle, Alabama, by Lt. General Richard Taylor on May 4, 1865, and paroled at Meridian, Mississippi, on May 13, 1864. He is shown as residing at Mt. Andrew, Barbour County, Alabama.*

Smith, J. T., Pvt. Co. E

He was admitted to Post Hospital at Fort Morgan, Alabama, on September 27, 1863, with chronic dysentery and sent to general hospital on October 28, 1863. He was again admitted to Fort Morgan Post Hospital on January 13, 1864, with diarrhoea and sent to general hospital on January 17, 1864. He was admitted as POW to St. Louis USA General Hospital at New Orleans on September 27, 1864, with fever remit. and returned to prison on October 22, 1864, age 49.

Smith, L. T., Sgt. Co. C

Enlisted on October 13, 1861, at Mobile, Alabama, by Captain Rembert for three years or the war. He was wounded in the left thigh at Shiloh April 6, 1862, while advancing during the A. M. attack on First Camp. His name appears on a report near Tupelo, Mississippi, June 28, 1862, "Wounded at Shiloh and sent home on fur. (furlough) on surg. certification." He appears present on a company muster roll for bounty on September 24, 1862. Company muster roll for December 31, 1862, to April 30, 1863, reports him discharged by reason of furnishing a substitute on April 9, 1863. "See case of **Michael Dunn** substitute."

Smith, ? M., Pvt. Co. K

Enlisted on November 13, 1862, at Fort Morgan, Alabama, by Captain Dorgan for the war. He appears present on a company muster roll for November/December 1862, never paid, a substitute for **C. C. Cruifiled**? ?, 13, 1862. *File is difficult to read.*

Smith, N. L., Pvt. Co. H

His name appears on a list of prisoners captured at Iuka and Corinth, Mississippi, and brought to the Post of Columbus, Kentucky, with orders to have them reported to General Sherman at Memphis, Tennessee, November 15, 1862. Attachment to the list indicates he was among prisoners received near Vicksburg, Mississippi, for exchange.

Smith, R. A., Pvt. Co. C/H

Enlisted at Choctaw Bluff, Alabama, on February 3, 1863, by Captain Smith for three years or the war. Company muster roll for December 31, 1862, to April 30, 1863, reports him absent detached in Engineering Department at Oven Bluff by order of General Buckner. Company muster rolls for May/June, and September/October 1863,

report him absent, detached March 25, 1863. First pay on June 30, 1863. POW captured at Fort Gaines, Alabama, on August 8, 1864. He was admitted to St. Louis USA General Hospital at New Orleans on September 11, 1864, with intermit. (tertian) and returned to prison on September 20, 1864, age 35. He was received at Ship Island, Mississippi, on October 25, 1864. He died of typhoid fever at Ship Island on December 2, 1864. He was buried in grave No. 58. Note one report shows he died of dysentery on December 2, 1864. "See personal papers of **Y. Lyles**, Co. C" (for descriptive list)
This data obtained from a descriptive list on June 15, 1862, for payment of $50 bounty. Filed with **Lyles, J. Y.**

Smith, R. A., Pvt. Age 35, blue eyes, dark hair, dark complexion, 5 foot 8 inches, born in Clarke County, Alabama, a farmer by occupation. Enlisted on February 3, 1863, at Oven Bluff by Colonel Anderson for the war.

Smith, W. B., Pvt. Co. I/D
Enlisted on August 12, 1864, at Mobile, Alabama, by Major Stone for the war. Company D muster roll for September/October 1864, reports him absent, sent to General Hospital at Mobile, Alabama, on October 10, 1864, assigned to the company by order. Another muster roll for September/October 1864, reports him transferred, "returned to enrolling officer by order of Captain Beebe."

Smith, W. T., Co. I/D
Enrolled on October 13, 1861, at Halls Mills, Alabama, by Major Hessee for the war. Company muster roll for bounty on September 24, 1862, reports him present. Muster rolls for company I in July/August and September/October 1863, report him present. Muster roll for company D September/October 1864, reports him sent to General Hospital at Mobile on September 13, 1864, assigned to company D by order. There is an additional muster roll for Captain Sossaman's detachment for September/October 1863, which shows him absent detailed to Battery Huger. He was admitted to Ross Hospital at Mobile, on September 13, 1864, with fever remittens and furloughed for 20 days on September 24.

Smithey, R., Pvt. Co. C/E see **Smithy, R.**

Smithy, R. (Robert), Pvt. Co. C
Enlisted on September 9, 1862, at Marengo County, Alabama, by Captain DeVaux for three years or the war. Company muster roll for December 31, 1862, to April 30, 1863, reports him present. Muster roll for May/June 1863, reports him present. Company muster roll for September/October 1863, reports him absent in hospital at Mobile since October 25, 1863, lost one canteen at $2.00. He was admitted to Post Hospital at Fort Morgan, Alabama, on December 16, 1863, with int. fever and returned to duty on January 2, 1864. POW captured at Fort Gaines, Alabama, on August 8, 1864. Robert Smithy Company E was admitted to St. Louis USA General Hospital at New Orleans on August 21, 1864, with diarrhoea and returned to prison on August 25, 1864, age 26. He was again admitted to St. Louis Hospital on September 26, 1864, with diarrhoea and returned to prison on October 3, 1864. He was received at Ship Island,

MOBILE CONFEDERATES

Mississippi, from New Orleans on October 25, 1864, and exchanged at Ship Island on January 4, 1865. POW surrendered at Citronelle, Alabama, by Lt. General Richard Taylor on May 4, 1865, and paroled at Meridian, Mississippi, on May 13, 1864. He is shown as residing at Linden, Marengo County, Alabama.

Snider, A. J., Pvt. Co. I

He was paid $69 for service March 1, to June 30, 1862. His name appears as a deserter on a return for November 1862.

Snoody, J. M., Pvt. Co. C

His name appears on a list of exchanged prisoners sent to their commands by order of Captain J. H. Campbell. 50 Ala.?

Snow, William A., Pvt. Co. F

Enlisted on September 31, 1862, at Jefferson County, Alabama, by W. T. Pool for the war. Company muster roll for March 1, to June 30, 1863, reports him present sick in hospital. Company muster roll for September/October 1863, reports him present POW captured at Fort Gaines, Alabama, on August 8, 1864. He was received at Ship Island, Mississippi, from New Orleans on October 25, 1864, and exchanged at Ship Island on January 4, 1865. POW paroled at Talladega, Alabama, on June 15, 1865.

Sole, J. D., Pvt. Co. G

POW captured at Fort Gaines, Alabama, on August 8, 1864. He was sent to Ship Island, Mississippi, from New Orleans on November 5, 1864.

Solley, Seaborn, Pvt. Co. C

Enlisted on October 13, 1861, at Mobile, Alabama, for one year. He was discharged on January 31, 1862, due to disability. He was born in Lincoln County, Georgia, age 52, six feet three quarter inch, light complexion, blue eyes, gray hair, a farmer by occupation. His discharge is in his file.*

Soloman, James A., Pvt. Co. F

Enlisted on October 13, 1861, at Baldwin County, Alabama, by Captain McVoy for three years or the war. Company muster roll for bounty on September 24, 1862, reports him present. Muster roll for March 1, to June 30, 1863, reports him present sick in hospital. Company muster roll for September/October 1863, reports him absent sick in hospital in Mobile since October 26, 1863. Drew clothing on June 1, 1864. There is a receipt for one shirt and one pair pants for J. A. Solomon, Co. F, 18th Alabama Regiment on July 22, 1863, filed in error. POW captured at Fort Gaines, Alabama, on August 8, 1864. He was received at Ship Island, Mississippi, from New Orleans on October 25, 1864, and exchanged at Ship Island on January 4, 1865.

Solomon, James A., Pvt. Co. F see **Soloman, James A.**

Sossaman, Blount, Sgt./Pvt. Co. E

Enlisted on October 13, 1861, at Mobile, Alabama, by Captain Chamberlain for the war. Company muster roll for bounty on September 24, 1862, reports him present. Muster roll for November/December 1862, reports him present as 1st Sgt. Muster roll for July/August 1863, reports him absent detached on February 25, by order of General Buckner. September/October 1863, muster roll reports him absent detached on February 20, 1863, by General Buckner. Pvt. Blount Sossaman, was surrendered as a straggler at Meridian, Mississippi, in May 1865, by Lt. General Richard Taylor and paroled at Mobile, Alabama, on May 19, 1865. There are several signed pay vouchers in his file.*

Sossaman, Henry, Co. E. Lt./Captain.

He enlisted on October 13, 1861 and elected 2nd Lt. on September 21, 1861, then promoted on May 8, 1862. His name appears as 2nd Lt. on a regimental return for June 1862, present at Tupelo, Mississippi. He appears on a company muster roll for bounty on September 24, 1862, and signed roll as commanding company. He appears as Captain on a field return for October 1862, as absent with leave since October 20, for four days. His name appears on returns for November, and December 1862, as present at Fort Morgan, Alabama. He appears present on a company muster roll for November/December 1862. Muster roll for July/August 1863, reports him in arrest. Muster roll for September/October 1863, reports him present. Muster roll for Sossaman's Detachment for September/October 1864, reports him absent sick from September 14, 1864. POW surrendered by Lt. General Richard Taylor and paroled at Meridian, Mississippi, on May 10, 1865. He was paid $130 per month as Captain. There are a number of vouchers, requisitions and one Board of Survey on which he served at Fort Morgan on December 29, 1862, in his file.* *He led Sossaman's Detachment that served at Battery Huger for a time.*

Southworth, Charles, Pvt. Co. K

Enlisted on August 18, 1862, at Fort Morgan, Alabama, by Captain Dorgan for the war. He appears present on a company muster roll for bounty on September 24, 1862. Muster roll for November/December 1862, reports him present. Muster roll for July/August 1863, reports him transferred to Captain Hutchinson's Company of Engineers. There is a pay voucher in the amount of $11 for service July 1863.

Southworth, James, Pvt./Sgt. Co. K

Enlisted on October 13, 1861, at Mobile, Alabama, by Captain Stewart for the war. Wounded slightly in the left arm at Shiloh April 6, 1862, at 2 P. M. while advancing on Center Field. He appears present on a company muster roll for bounty on September 24, 1862. Muster rolls for July/August 1863, September/October 1863 and September/October 1864, all report him present. He was admitted to Post Hospital at Fort Morgan, on April 16, 1863, with diphtheria and furloughed to April 21, 1863. POW surrendered as a straggler at Meridian, Mississippi, in May 1865, by Lt. General Richard Taylor and paroled at Mobile, Alabama, on May 19, 1865.

Spaulding, E. R. Captain Co. G

Enlisted October 13, 1861. Appointed Captain March 24, 1864. POW captured at Fort Gaines, Alabama, on August 8, 1864. He was admitted to St. Louis USA General Hospital at New Orleans on August 27, 1864, with diarrhoea and retuned to prison on August 30, 1864, age 28. He was received at Ship Island, Mississippi, from New Orleans on November 25, 1864, and exchanged on January 4, 1865. He appears on a list of POW's captured by 1st Div C. C., M. D. M. on April 19, 1865, at Forsyth, (*Georgia*?) by Scouts 2 Brigade. He also appears on a report of Confederates captured at Macon, Georgia, April 20 and 21, 1865, by the 1st Brigade, 2nd Cav. Div. There are requisitions for clothing and shoes for Co. G in his file.*

Spange, L. D., Pvt. Co. C see **Sproud. L D.**

Spann, ?, Pvt. Co. A

Enlisted at Choctaw Bluff, Alabama, on February 1, 1862. *His microfilm file is not readable.*

Spaulding, E. C., Pvt. Co. C

His name appears on a register of discharged soldiers on March 13, 1862.

Spear, ? M., Pvt. Co. E

Killed at Shiloh at Old Field, shot through the head at 4:30 P. M.

Speed, James, M., Pvt. Co. C

He was admitted to Post Hospital at Fort Morgan, Alabama, on December 26, 1863, with abscess and returned to duty on January 9, 1864. He was again admitted to Post Hospital at Fort Morgan on January 17, 1864, with int. feb. and sent to general hospital on June 22, 1864. He appears on a register of General Hospital, (Soldiers Home Hospital) Shelby Springs, Alabama, April 25, to June 26, 1864, with chronic debilitas, discharged (from hospital?) June ?, 1864. He also appears on a register of Mississippi CSA Hospital at Jackson, Mississippi, admitted April 4, 1864, and returned to duty June 29, 1864. He appears on a register of Ross Hospital at Mobile, Alabama, admitted August 8, 1864, with ascites and sent to General Hospital at Selma on August 9, 1864.

Spence, William, Pvt. Co. A

He was admitted to No. 2 USA General Hospital (Marine) Evansville, Indiana, on April 15, 1862, with vulnus sclopeticum (gunshot wound). He appears on a list of prisoners who have died in General Hospital Department of Ohio at Hospital No. 2 Evansville, Indiana, on August 16, 1862. Captured at Shiloh vulnus sclopeticum. (gunshot wound).

Spigener, M., Pvt. Co. D see **Spigner, M.**

Spigner, M., Pvt. Co. D

He appears present on a company muster roll for July/August, 1863, shown as enrolled at Montgomery, Alabama, on July 22, 1863, by Enrolling Officer. Company muster roll for September/October 1863, reports him present and shows that he enlisted at Prattville, Alabama, on February 22, 1863, by Lt. Mims for the war. Muster rolls for November/December 1863 and September/October 1864, report him present with enrolling date of July 22, at Montgomery. Record shows M. Spinner, Pvt. Co. D, POW captured at Blakeley, Alabama, on April 9, 1865, transferred to Vicksburg, Mississippi, on May 1, 1865.

Sproud, L. D., Pvt. Co. C

He appears on a roll of POW's at Camp Butler, Springfield, Illinois, captured at Fort Donaldson on February 16, 1862, sent from Camp Butler to Vicksburg, Mississippi, on September 23, 1862, to be exchanged.

Stabler, Malachi L., Pvt. Co. G

POW captured at Fort Gaines, Alabama, on August 8, 1864, he was received at Ship Island, Mississippi, from New Orleans on October 25, 1864, and exchanged at Ship Island on January 4, 1865. POW he was surrendered at Citronelle, Alabama, by Lt. General Richard Taylor on May 4, 1865, and paroled at Meridian, Mississippi, on May 13, 1865. Residence shown as Bells Landing, Monroe County, Alabama.

Material furnished by descendants. Malachi Lamar Stabler was born February 8, 1843 near Finchburg, Monroe County, Alabama. He joined the Confederate Army, and served in Holtzclaus' Brigade, Maurice's Division, Company G, 21st Alabama. After the war he moved to Lower Peachtree, where he operated a prosperous mercantile business and plantation. He also served as postmaster, and made an unsuccessful attempt to change the name of the town from "Lower Peachtree" to "Stabler". Malachi was charter member of the local Baptist Church. He was married five times, however, had children only by his third wife, the former Lucy Portis; Lucy and he had six children. He died February 21, 1925 and is buried in the Portis Cemetery near Lower Peachtree, Alabama.

Stacks, (Stocks) E., Pvt. Co. F

Enlisted at Shelby County, Alabama, on September 16, 1862, by W. I. Davis for three years or the war. Company muster roll for March 1, to June 1863, reports him absent on sick furlough from June 27, 1863. Company muster rolls for September/October 1863 and September/October 1864, report him present. He was admitted to Ross Hospital at Mobile, Alabama, on January 19, 1864, with syphilis and sent to general hospital on January 26, 1864. He was again admitted to Ross Hospital at Mobile on October 21, 1864, with febris intermittens quot. and returned to duty on October 23, 1864. POW he was surrendered at Citronelle, Alabama, by Lt. General Richard Taylor on May 4, 1865, and paroled at Meridian, Mississippi, on May 13, 1865. Residence shown as Shelby County, Alabama.

Stagall, R., Pvt. Co. C. see **Stegall, Ralph**

Standard, Charles LaB., Corp./Sgt. Co. K

Enlisted on October 13, 1861, at Mobile, Alabama, by Captain Stewart for the war. He appears present on a company muster roll for bounty on September 24, 1862. Company muster rolls for November/December 1862, July/August 1863, September/October 1863 and September/October 1864, all report him present. POW he was surrendered at Citronelle, Alabama, by Lt. General Richard Taylor on May 4, 1865, and paroled at Meridian, Mississippi, on May 13, 1865. Residence shown as Mobile, Mobile County, Alabama.

Stannard, William, Pvt. Co. K

Enlisted on January 29, 1862, at Fort Gaines, Alabama, by Captain Stewart for twelve months. He appears on a regimental return for June 1862, sent to Mobile hospital May 28. His name appears on a report near Tupelo, Mississippi, on June 28, 1863, "on furlough." Company muster rolls for November/December 1862 and July/August 1863, report him present. Company muster roll for September/October 1863, reports him absent on furlough for two days. Company muster roll for September/October 1864, reports him absent sick in hospital. POW he was surrendered at Citronelle, Alabama, by Lt. General Richard Taylor on May 4, 1865, and paroled at Meridian, Mississippi, on May 13, 1865. Residence shown as Mobile, Mobile County, Alabama.

Stanley, F., Co. B

His name appears on a regimental return for June 1862.

Stannard, Charles LaB., Corp./Sgt. Co. K see **Stanard, Charles. Le B.**

Stannard, William, Pvt. Co. K see **Stanard, William**

Starr, William, Pvt. Co. B

Enlisted on October 26, 1862, at Mobile, Alabama, by Captain DeVaux for three years or the war. He appears on a descriptive list at Point Clear, Alabama, on September 23, 1863, five foot six inches, brown hair, blue eyes, dark complexion, born in Ireland, a laborer by occupation. Company muster roll for March/April 1862, reports him present. Muster roll for May/June 1863, reports him present, sick in quarters. Muster roll for September/October 1863, reports him present, due $51.63 for clothing not drawn in kind. POW captured at Fort Gaines, Alabama, on August 8, 1864, he was received at Ship Island, Mississippi, from New Orleans on October 25, 1864, and exchanged at Ship Island on January 4, 1865.

Staunton, F., Pvt. Co. K

Enlisted on April 15, 1864, at Alabama Port by Lt. Touluren for the war. Company muster roll for September/October 1864, reports him present. POW he was surrendered at Citronelle, Alabama, by Lt. General Richard Taylor on May 4, 1865, and paroled at Meridian, Mississippi, on May 13, 1865. Residence shown as Mobile, Mobile County, Alabama.

Steel, Henry, Pvt. Co. F.
It is not possible to read his short file due to poor microfilm copy.

Steele, W. B., Pvt. Co. H
POW captured at Fort Gaines, Alabama, on August 8, 1864. He was admitted to Ward K, St. Louis, USA General hospital at New Orleans on August 12, 1864, with gunshot (Minnie Ball) wound to right shoulder, returned to prison on September 15, 1864, age 17. He was again admitted to St. Louis USA Hospital on September 26, 1864, with fever intermit and returned to prison on October 22, 1864. He was received at Ship Island, Mississippi, from New Orleans on October 25, 1864, and exchanged at Ship Island on January 4, 1865.

Stegall, Ralf, Pvt. Co. C
Enlisted on October 13, 1861, at Mobile, Alabama, by Captain Rembert for three years or the war. Wounded slightly at Shiloh on April 6, 1862, 7 A. M. while advancing on First Battery. POW captured at Pittsburgh Landing on April 7, 1862, and received from Louisville, Kentucky, at Camp Chase, Ohio, on May 13, 1862. He was reported aboard the USA Hospital steamer *Empress* on May 2, 1862 with vul. sclop. He was admitted to USA Camp Chase Post Hospital on May 7, 1862, with vulnus sclopeticum (gunshot wound). He was again admitted to USA Camp Chase Post Hospital on May 13, 1862, with erysipelas and returned to prison in June 11, 1862. He was transferred to Vicksburg, Mississippi, for exchange on August 25, 1862. Company muster roll for December 31, 1862, to April 30, 1863, reports him present. Muster roll for May/June 1863, reports him present detailed on extra duty with Engineering Department. Muster roll for September/October 1863, reports him present. Hospital muster rolls at Fort Gaines and Fort Morgan show him on duty at a nurse during first half of 1864. POW captured at Fort Gaines, Alabama, on August 8, 1864, he was received at Ship Island, Mississippi, from New Orleans on October 25, 1864, and exchanged at Ship Island on January 4, 1865. He was admitted to Ross Hospital at Mobile, Alabama, on January 6, 1865, with scurvy and debilitas and on January 17, 1865, was furloughed for 60 days. POW he was surrendered by Lt. General Richard Taylor in May 1865, and paroled at Demopolis, Alabama, on May 31, 1865. Residence shown as Marengo County, Alabama.
This data from a descriptive list on May 2, 1863, for bounty and clothing. Filed with **Ross, T. M.**

Stegall, R., Pvt. Enlisted at Fort Gaines in 1861, age 28, dark eyes, dark hair, dark complexion, five foot ten inches, born Marengo County, a planter by occupation, paid $50 bounty.

Steiner, J., Pvt. Co. I see **Steiner, John**

Steiner, John, Pvt. Co. I

Enlisted on October 13, 1861, at Halls Mill, Alabama, by Major Hessee for the war. POW captured at Shiloh, on April 8, 1862, at Pittsburg Landing. His name appears on a roll of POW's at Camp Douglas, Illinois, on August 1, 1862, and to Cairo, Illinois, to be exchanged on September 29, 1862. He was admitted to USA Prison Hospital at Camp Douglas near Chicago, with pneumonia on April 30, 1862, and returned to prison on May 1, 1862. He appears on a return at Fort Morgan for November 1862, November 28, 1862, from missing in action. Company muster rolls for July/August and September/October 1863, report him present. Transferred to C. S. Navy, 1864.

Steinwinder, J. R., Pvt. Co. D

Enlisted October 13, 1861, at Mobile, Alabama, by Major Barnwell for one year. His name appears on a regimental return for June 1862, sent to interior hospital at the evacuation of Corinth (Mississippi). His name appears on returns for November and December 1862, detailed as a carpenter. He appears present on a company muster roll for bounty on September 24, 1862. Company muster roll for November/December 1862, reports him present. muster roll for July/August 1863, shows that he was transferred. He was named on a register of payments to a discharged soldier April 30, 1862? *There is unreadable paperwork in his file.**

Stenson, S. T., Pvt. Co. H see **Stinson, S. T.**

Stephens, John, Pvt. Co. I

POW captured at Fort Gaines, Alabama, on August 8, 1864, he was received at Ship Island, Mississippi, from New Orleans on October 25, 1864, and exchanged at Ship Island on January 4, 1865.

Stephenson, H., Pvt. Co. E

Killed shot in head at Shiloh, on April 5, 1862, at First Camp.

Sterling, Daniel, Corp. Co. A.

Enlisted on October 13, 1861, at Mobile, Alabama, by Major Hessee. He appears on a regimental return for June 28, 1862, near Tupelo, Mississippi, furloughed for five days from June 25, 1862, by General Bragg. He also appears on a regimental return for June 1862. He appears present on a company muster roll for bounty on September 24, 1862, he refused to take bounty.

Stevens, John, Pvt. Co._ see **Stephens, John**

Stephenson, James E., Co. B

POW captured at Missionary Ridge, on November 25, 1863, and forwarded to Nashville, Tennessee, then on to Knoxville, Tennessee, December 5, 1863. *Likely an error.*

21ST ALABAMA INFANTRY VOLUNTEERS

Stewart, C. A., Pvt. Co. D
POW he was surrendered by Lt. General Richard Taylor in May 1865, and paroled at Meridian, Mississippi, on May 31, 1865. Residence shown as Mobile, Alabama.

Stewart, Carroll, Pvt. Co. C
He appears on a regimental return for June 1862, "June 13, 1862, Tupelo, furloughed."

Stewart, Charles, S., Captain/Lt. Colonel Co. K
Entered CSA service in April 1861. Enlisted in the 21st Alabama Infantry on October 13, 1861, for twelve months. Elected Captain on April 29, 1861. Elected Lt. Colonel of Regiment and promoted on May 8, 1862, successor A. P. Dorgan. He appears present on returns for Fort Gaines, Alabama, November 1861. He appears on a regimental return for June 1862, absent on detached service S. O. 25, General Bragg. Returns for November and December 1862, show him present at Fort Morgan in command of Battalion. Lt. Colonel Stewart was killed by explosion of gun at Fort Morgan on April 30, 1863, successor James. M. Williams. *Much of his file is to poor a microfilm copy to read. Lt. Colonel Charles Somerville Stewart is buried in Square 7 Lot 48, Magnolia Cemetery, Mobile, Alabama.*

Stewart, Fredrick, Major
Enlisted on October 13, 1861. Elected July 22, 1861, resigned on March 31, 1862. His name appears on a register for October 3, 1861, and a return for November 1861, at Fort Gaines, Alabama, where he is shown present. His resignation is in his file.*

Stewart, S. M., Pvt. Co. D
Enlisted on October 13, 1861, at Spanish River (Battery), Alabama, by Captain Hall for the war. Company muster roll for September/October, 1863, report him absent on sick furlough. Company muster rolls for July/August 1863, November/December 1863 and September/October 1864, all report him present. He signed a Parole of Honor at Montgomery, on May 27, 1865. five foot four inches, dark hair, and blue eyes. *A poor copy of his parole is in his file.* *

Stiener, John, Co. I see **Steiner, John**

Still, W. B., Pvt. Co. H see **Steele, W. B.**

Stikes, Ephram, Pvt. Co. I
He was admitted to Ross Hospital at Mobile, Alabama, on January 26, 1864, with icterus (jaundice) and sent to General Hospital at Montgomery on February 17, 1864.

Stiner, John, Pvt. Co. I see **Steiner, John**

MOBILE CONFEDERATES

Stinson, John H., Pvt. Co. E

Enlisted at Fort Gaines, Alabama, on January 21, 1862, by Captain Chamberlain for the war. He appears present on a company muster roll for bounty on September 24, 1862. Company muster rolls for November/December 1862, July/August 1863 and September/October 1863, all report him present. In October 1863, the roll notes that he is due $5 for clothing not drawn in kind. POW surrendered by Lt. General Taylor in May 1865, and paroled at Columbus, Mississippi, on May 17, 1865.

Stinson, S. T., Pvt. Co. H

POW captured at Fort Gaines, Alabama, on August 8, 1864. He was received at Ship Island, Mississippi, from New Orleans on October 25, 1864. He died at Ship Island of dysentery on January 1, 1865, and was buried in grave 127.

Stinson, Willliam, Pvt. Co. A

Enlisted on February 1, 1863, at Choctaw Bluff, Alabama, by Captain Cothran for the war. Company muster rolls for December 31, 1862, to April 30, 1863 and May/June 1863. Muster roll for September/October 1863, reports him absent, sent to General Hospital at Mobile, on October 25.

This data is from a descriptive list on May 26, 1863, list is filed with **Pvt. John Pennington,** Co. A.

Pvt. **Stinson, William**, age 34, blue eyes, light hair, fair complexion, five foot eleven and one half inches, born Hall County, Georgian, a farmer by occupation, enlisted at Clarke County, Alabama, by Captain Cothran for the war, paid $50 bonus.

Sterling, Daniel, Corp. Co. A

He drew $52 for service March 1, to June 30, 1862. There is a pay voucher in his file.

St. John, James C., Pvt. Co. B

Enlisted on September 25, 1862, at Talladega, Alabama, by Geo. A. Carry for the war. He was discharged by reason of disability on April 23, 1863.

Stobaugh, L. G, drummer Co. I

POW surrendered at Citronelle, Alabama, by Lt. General Richard Taylor on May 4, 1865, and paroled at Meridian, Mississippi, on May 17, 1865. His residence is shown as Marengo County, Alabama.

Stockman, F., Pvt. Co. F

Enlisted in Perry County, Alabama, on September 12, 1862, by W. B. Livingston, for the war. Company muster rolls for March 1, to June 30, 1863, and September/October 1863, report him present. POW captured at Fort Gaines, Alabama, on August 8, 1864. He was received at Ship Island, Mississippi, from New Orleans on October 25, 1864. He died at Ship Island of dysentery on November 28, 1864, and was buried in grave 49.

Stone, Sherman, Pvt. Co. K

Killed in an attack at Shiloh on April 7, 1862, at 7 A. M. Shot in the head.

Stone, Thomas, D., Pvt. Co. F

Wounded slightly at Shiloh on April 6, 1862, while advancing on First Camp.

Stouts, William, Corp. Co. H

His name appears on a report for June 1862, detailed service in Ordnance at Mobile.

Stringer, A. R., Pvt. Co. F/E/K

Enlisted on March 11, 1863, at Choctaw Bluff, Alabama, by Captain Dade for three years or the war. Muster rolls for Co. F March 1, to June 30, 1863 and September/ October 1863, report him present. Company K muster roll for September/ October 1864, reports him present. There is a card in his file for Co. F September 28, 1863, "Deserter". He was shown in Co. F and admitted to Post Hospital at Fort Morgan on November 26, 1863, with cong feb. and furloughed on December 30, 1863. He was shown in Co. E and admitted to Ross Hospital at Mobile on April 6, 1865, with scorbutus (scurvy) and sent to General Hospital at Columbus, (Mississippi) on April 23, 1865. POW of Co. E. surrendered at Citronelle, Alabama, on May 4, 1865, and paroled at Mobile, Alabama, on June 5, 1865, age 19, six foot, fair complexion, blue eyes, brown hair, a resident of Clarke County, Mississippi.

Stringer, A. L., Pvt. Co. K see **Stringer, A. R.**

Stritzinger, John, Pvt. Co. H

Wounded in the right thigh at Shiloh on April 7th in the evening while retreating. He appears on a report near Tupelo, Mississippi, on June 28, 1862, wounded at Shiloh and sent to Mobile. He was paid $22 for service in May and June 1862. A pay voucher is in his file.*

Stroud, Mark A., Pvt. Co. A

Enlisted on September 16, 1862, at Blount County, Alabama, by William A. Walker for the war. Company muster roll for December 31, 1862, to April 30, 1863, reports that he died March 17, 1863, at Choctaw Bluff. Claim for deceased soldier filed and paid to Joshua Stroud his father in the amount of $51.98.

Stuart, S. M., Pvt. Co. D see **Stewart, S. M.**

Sturdevant, John Marion, Pvt. Co. D

Company muster roll for September/October 1863, reports that he enlisted at Gainesville, by Major Russer for the war and shows him absent. Company muster roll for September/October 1864, reports that he enlisted on June 17, 1863, at Fort Morgan, Alabama, by Captain Dorgan for the war and absent as superintendent of Government work at Sumter County, Alabama, by order of General Polk.

Livingston, Alabama, October 8, 1863,

> General Jos, E. Johnston
>   Dear Sir My brother John Sturdevant a member of Mobile Cadets of 21st Ala. desires a detail as his own Bo cruor (?) on his plantation Sumter Cty, Ala. not being able procure the services of a competent man. My brother is 44 yrs of age, very feeble health, not able to perform the duties of a soldier. You will please let me hear from you. I can give any information you may desire.
>   Yours Respectfully,
>   B. T. Sturdevant

He was certified disabled at Demopolis, Alabama, on March 19, 1864 by Medical Examining Board. His certificate of disability and the letter from his brother are in his file.*

Suggs, W. A., Pvt. Co. F/D see **Suggs, William**

Suggs, William, Pvt. Co. F/D
  Enlisted on October 13, 1861, at Baldwin County, Alabama, by Captain McCoy for the war. Company muster roll for bounty September 24, 1862, reports him present. Muster roll for March 1, to June 30, 1863, reports him present in arrest, lost one canteen at 25 cents and one haversack at 20 cents. Muster roll for Co. F September/October 1863, reports him absent, detached to fish by General Maury on August 23, 1863. Muster roll for Co. D September/October 1864, reports him recently assigned to Commissary by order. A second muster roll for September/October 1864, reports him absent assigned to Battery Huger. He was admitted to Ross Hospital, Mobile, Alabama, on October 14, 1864, with febris intermittens tert. and returned to duty on October 20, 1864.

Sullivan, Murphy, Pvt. Co. B
  Enlisted on October 13, 1861, at Mobile, Alabama, by Major Hessee for the war. His name appears on a report June 28, 1862, near Tupelo, Mississippi, sent away on the evacuation of Corinth about June 1. Company muster roll for bounty on September 24, 1862, reports him present and refused to take bounty. Paid $15 for commutation of rations while on 60day furlough from May 28, to July 28, 1862. There is a pay voucher in his file.*

Sumrall, T. M., Pvt. Co. K
  Enlisted on August 30, 1864, at Mobile, Alabama, by Captain Gordon for the war. Company muster roll for September/October 1864, reports him transferred to Conscripts at Notasulga, Alabama, on October 18, 1864.

Suthron, William, Pvt. Co. B
  His name appears on a regimental return for June 1862, on sick furlough.

Sutton, I., Pvt. Co. K

Enlisted on August 28, 1864, at Mobile, Alabama, by Major Stone for the war. Company muster roll for September/October 1864, reports him transferred to Conscripts at Notasulga, Alabama, October 18, 1864.

Swann, Lewis, B., Pvt. Co. K

He was paid $44 for two months service for May and June on July 1, 1862. There is a pay voucher in his file.*

Swearingen, J. W., Sgt. Co. G

POW captured at Fort Gaines, Alabama, on August 8, 1864. He was received at Ship Island, Mississippi, from New Orleans on October 25, 1864. He died at Ship Island of dysentery on December 21, 1864 and was buried in grave 106.

Swearingen, J. W., Sgt. Co. G see **Swearinger**

Sweeney, P., Pvt. Co. D. see **Sewieny, Patrick**

Sweeney, Timothy, Pvt. Co. C see **Sweeny, Timothy**

Sweeny, Patrick, Pvt. Co. D

Enlisted on March 3, 1862, at Mobile, Alabama, by Lt. Deas for the war. Wounded at Shiloh severely in the hand while advancing in the Center on April 6, 1862, in the A.M. His name appears on a regimental return for June 1862, sent to interior hospital at the evacuation of Corinth. Company muster roll for bounty on September 24, 1862, reports him present. Company muster roll for November/December 1862, reports him present. He appears on a report for November 1862, sick at General Hospital at Mobile. There are pay vouchers in his file.*

Sweeny, Timothy, Pvt. Co. D

Enlisted on October 13, 1864, at Mobile, Alabama, by Captain Butt for one year. His name appears on a regimental return for June 1862, sent to interior hospital at evacuation of Corinth. Company muster roll for bounty on September 24, 1862, reports him present. Muster rolls for November/December 1862, July/August 1863, September/October 1863 and November/December 1863, all report him present. He drew clothing on June 20, 1864. He was on extra duty at Fort Powell in 1864, with boats. Muster roll for September/October 1864, reports him absent, sent to General Hospital at Mobile on September 9, 1864.

Sykes, Lewis M., Pvt. Co. C

Enlisted at Fort Gaines, Alabama, on February 13, 1862. His name appears on a report for June 1862, near Tupelo, Mississippi, sent to interior hospital at the evacuation of Corinth. His name appears on a regimental return for June 1862, absent on sick furlough. Company muster roll for bounty on September 24, 1862, reports him absent.

T

Taggars, T. J., Pvt. Co. I see **Fagan, Thomas**

Talbert, J. Pvt. Co. C see **Tolbert, John M.**

Talbert, J. M., Pvt. Co. C
Enlisted on January 1, 1862, at Choctaw Bluff, Alabama, by Captain Smith for three years or the war. Company muster roll for December 31, 1862, to April 30, 1863, reports him present and never paid. May/June 1863, muster roll reports him present, paid on April 30. September/October 1863, muster roll reports him absent on 15-day furlough from October 17, 1863. James M. Talbert was POW captured at Fort Gaines, Alabama, on August 8, 1864. He was confined at Steam Levee Press No. 4 at New Orleans and admitted to St. Louis USA Hospital at New Orleans with fever inter. on September 22, 1864, and returned to prison on October 4, 1864, age 41. He was received at Ship Island, Mississippi, from New Orleans on October 25, 1864. He died at Ship Island of chronic diarrhoea on November 15, 1864, and was buried in grave No. 20.

Talbert, John Pvt. Co. C see **Talbert, John M.**

Talley, Horace, 1st Lt. Co. I
Enlisted on October 13, 1861. Elected Lt. on October 7, 1861, resigned April 12, 1862. A return for November 1861, reports him present at Fort Gaines. He appears present on a regimental return for December 1861. There are pay vouchers in his file.*

Taney, J., Pvt. Co. B see **Tansey, John**

Tansey, John, Pvt. Co. B
Enlisted on October 13, 1861, at Mobile, Alabama, by Major Hessee for the war. He appears present on a company muster roll for bounty on September 24, 1862, refused to take bounty. Company muster roll for March/April 1863, reports him present. Muster roll for May/June 1863, reports him present sick in quarters. September/October 1863, muster roll reports him present and due $59.63 for clothing not drawn in kind. He was admitted to Post Hospital at Fort Morgan, on November 28, 1863, and sent to general hospital on December 14, 1863. He was admitted to Ross Hospital in Mobile, Alabama, on December 14, 1863, with debility and sent to general hospital on February 17, 1864. He was admitted again to Ross Hospital on February 24, 1864, with int. fever quot. and sent to general hospital (Demopolis) May 6, 1864. He appears on a descriptive list for bounty, pay and clothing at Point Clear, Alabama, September 23, 1863, born Ireland, blue eyes, light hair, light complexion, five foot ten inches. He was once again admitted to Ross Hospital on May 11, 1864, with debilities and returned to duty on May 31, 1864. POW captured at Fort Gaines, Alabama, on August 8, 1864. He was confined at Steam Levee Press No. 4 at New Orleans and admitted to St. Louis USA Hospital at New Orleans with conval. of fev. inter. on September 20, 1864, then returned to prison on October 22, 1864, age 32. He was received at Ship Island, Mississippi, from New Orleans on October 25, 1864, and exchanged on January 4, 1865. John Tansey (or Peter

Doroughty) stole the identity of a Southern prisoner who was captured at Fort Morgan to gain transportation to New York. Pvt. John Tansey appears on a roll of POW's at Elmira, New York, November 30, 1864, who desires to take the Oath of Allegiance to the USA. "Captured at Fort Gaines August 8, 1864, Was conscripted on October 8, 1862, came to Elmira in name of Peter Doroughty (Not found in the CS records of the 21st Alabama Infantry) of (maybe Barbour?) County. I having exchanged places with him to have a chance to come North. I have relatives at Cincinnati, is where he desires to go." He signed an Oath of Allegiance to the USA on May 29, 1865, resident of Cincinnati, Ohio, dark complexion, dark hair, blue eyes, and five foot seven inches. *Could this man be related to Pvt. Eneas Dougherty, Co. B that the CS records report deserted from the 21st at Grant's Pass on April 22 or 23, 1864, and claimed Philadelphia as his residence? There are pay vouchers in his file.*

Tanaley, John, Pvt. Co. B see **Tansey, John**

Tanzy, John, Pvt. Co. B see **Tansey, John**

Tate, George W., Pvt. Co. H
POW captured at Fort Gaines, Alabama, on August 8, 1864. He was admitted to St. Louis USA General Hospital at New Orleans from Steam Levee Press No. 4 with fever remittent on September 23, 1864, and returned to prison on October 5, 1864, age 23. He was received at Ship Island, Mississippi, from New Orleans on October 25, 1864. He died of chronic diarrhoea at Ship Island on November 12, 1864, and was buried in grave No. 17.

Tate, J., Pvt. Co. C/H/A
Enlisted in Co. C on February 16, 1863, at Marengo County, Alabama, by Lt. Northrup for three years or the war. Company muster rolls for Co. C from December 31, 1862, to April 30, 1863, May/June 1863 and September/October 1863, all report him present. Private J. A. Tate, Co. A was a POW captured at Fort Gaines, Alabama, on August 8, 1864. Pvt. J. A. Tate, Co. H was admitted to St. Louis USA Hospital New Orleans with fever remittent on August 23, 1864, and returned to prison on August 29, 1864, age 19. Pvt. J. A. Tate Co. A was admitted to St. Louis USA General Hospital on October 15, 1864, with dysentery and returned to prison on October 25, 1864. Pvt. J. R. Tate Co. C was received at Ship Island, Mississippi, from New Orleans on October 25, 1864, and Private James A. Tate Co. H was exchanged on January 4, 1865. Private James A. Tate Co. H was a POW surrendered in May by Lt. General Richard Taylor and paroled at Demopolis on May 31, 1865, a resident of Marengo County. *Confusing records.*

Tate, James A., Pvt. C/H see **Tate J. A.**

Tate, Norvell, F. H., Pvt. Co. H
He drew clothing on June 1, 1864, and signed by his mark. POW captured at Fort Gaines, Alabama, on August 8, 1864. He was admitted to St. Louis USA General Hospital at New Orleans with rubeola (measles) and fever intermitten from military

prison on September 10, 1864, age 17. Died November 21, buried November 22, 1864, in grave 425 Monument Cemetery, age 17, a resident of Marengo County, Alabama, born in Georgia, single, next of kin David Tate, Father. His death certificate is in his file.*

Tate, J. R., Pvt. Co. H see **Tate, J. A.**

Tate, Robert B., Pvt. Co. C
Killed at Shiloh on April 6, 1862, shot through the head at 7 A. M. at First Battery and left on the field. Claim for deceased soldier filed by James Tate his father on April 30, 1864.

Tatum, Henry, Pvt. Co. I
Drew clothing on May 31, 1864. POW captured at Fort Gaines, Alabama, on August 8, 1864. He was received at Ship Island, Mississippi, on October 25, 1864, from New Orleans. He died at Ship Island of pneumonia December 4, 1864 and was buried in Grave 64.

Taylor, Albert, Pvt./Sgt. Co. A
Enlisted on October 13, 1864, at Mobile, Alabama, by Major Hessee for the war. Promoted from the ranks on January 1, 1863. He appears present on company muster roll for bounty on September 24, 1862. Company muster roll for December 31, 1862, to April 30, 1863, reports him present and promoted to Sgt. from the ranks on January 1, 1863. Company muster roll for May/June 1863, reports him present. Muster roll for September/October 1863, reports him present and promoted from 4th to 3rd Sgt. on September 1, 1863. POW captured at Fort Morgan, Alabama, on August 23, 1864. He was sent from New Orleans to New York on September 27, 1864, and received at Elmira, New York, on October 8, 1864. He was released on June 21, 1865. There is paper work in his file.*
Taylor, Albert – *Mobile Press of March 25, 2007 (1907) has lived 92 years; has seen the Blue the victor over the Gray and has seen all of the other 500 men who surrendered Fort Morgan pass to the Great Beyond." He had served at Shiloh as well as at the Battle of Mobile Bay.*

Taylor, Benjamin, F., Pvt. Co. G
His name appears on a descriptive list of Swanson's Guards for service March 1, to March 25, 1863. POW surrendered at Citronelle, Alabama, by Lt. General Richard Taylor on May 4, 1865, and paroled at Meridian, Mississippi, on May 13, 1865. He was a resident of Elba, Coffee County, Alabama.

Taylor, Henry, B., Pvt. Co. E
Enlisted on October 13, 1861, at Mobile, Alabama, by Captain Chamberlain for 12 months. His name appears on a regimental return for June 1864, on detached service as a telegraph operator at Fort Morgan. He appears on a company muster roll for November/December 1862, discharged by General Forney. He appears on a register as having been paid for service November 17, to November 24, 1862.

Taylor, J. M., Pvt. Co. C

Enlisted on January 1, 1863, at Choctaw Bluff, by Captain Smith for three years or the war. He appears on a company muster roll for December 31, 1862, to April 30, 1863, as having never been paid and died in hospital at Choctaw Bluff on ? 17, 1863.

Taylor, Reuben, Pvt./Corp. Co. K

Enlisted on October 13, 1861, at Mobile, Alabama, by Captain Stewart for the war. He appears present on company muster roll for bounty on September 24, 1862. Company muster rolls for November/December 1862, July/August 1863 and September/October 1863, all report him present. He was promoted to 4th Corporal on August 1, 1863. Muster roll for September/October 1864, reports him absent sick in hospital since October 26, by order of Assistant Surgeon Armstrong. POW surrendered at Citronelle, Alabama, by Lt. General Richard Taylor on May 4, 1865, and paroled at Meridian, Mississippi, May 13, 1865. He was a resident of Leakesville, Green County, Mississippi.

Taylor, S. S., Captain Co. I

Enlisted on October 13, 1862, for twelve months. Elected Captain October 7, 1861. He appears present on a return for November 1861, at Fort Gaines. He also appears present on a return for December 1861, post not noted. He died on April 17, 1862. His successor was **Thomas S. Gleason**. *Confusion in dates.*

Taylor, W. W., Pvt. Co. A

Enlisted on February 1, 1863, at Choctaw Bluff, Alabama, by Captain Cothran, for three years or the war. Company muster roll for December 31, 1862, to April 30, 1863, reports him present and drawn no pay. Company muster rolls for May/June 1863 and September/October 1863, report him present. He was admitted to Post Hospital at Fort Morgan on December 26, 1863, with int. fever and returned to duty on December 27, 1863. POW captured at Fort Morgan, Alabama, on August 23, 1864. He was sent to New York from New Orleans on September 27, 1864. He was received at Elmira, New York, on October 8, 1864. He died of diarrhoea at Elmira on March 10, 1865, and was buried in grave number 1889.

This data is from a descriptive list on May 26, 1863, list is filed with Pvt. **John Pennington,** Co. A.
Pvt. **W. W. Taylor**, age 18, black eyes, dark hair, ruddy complexion, five foot nine and one half inches, born Cherokee County, Alabama, a farmer by occupation, enlisted at Clarke County, Alabama, by Captain Cothran for the war, paid $50 bonus.

Taylor, W. J. N., Pvt. Co. I

Enlisted on September 6, 1862, at Tuscaloosa, Alabama, by A. Kain for the war. Company muster rolls for July/August and September/October 1863, report him present. POW captured at Fort Gaines, Alabama, on August 8, 1864. He was received at Ship Island, Mississippi, on October 25, 1864, from New Orleans and exchanged at Ship Island on January 4, 1865. POW surrendered at Citronelle, Alabama, by Lt. General Richard Taylor on May 4, 1865, and paroled at Meridian, Mississippi, on May 13, 1865. He was shown as a resident of Tuscaloosa County, Alabama.

MOBILE CONFEDERATES

Tell, Charles, L., Sgt./1st Lt. Co. A
Enlisted on October 13, 1861, at Mobile, Alabama, by Major Hessee for the war. He appears as Sergeant present on company muster roll for bounty on September 24, 1862. He was elected December 12, 1862, and promoted on May 16, 1864. Company muster rolls for December 31, 1862, to April 30, 1863, report him as 2nd Lt. and present. Muster rolls for May/June 1863 and September/October 1863, report him as 2nd Lt. and present. Muster roll for September/October 1864, in Mobile reports him present and he signed roll as commanding company as 1st Lt. POW (resident of ?) New Orleans paroled on May 10, 1865, at Meridian, Mississippi, age 23, light hair, fair complexion, hazel eyes, and five foot six inches. His parole is in his file.* Reference card in his file to see personal papers of **M.C. Burke**. *Paper work in his file too poor a copy to read.*

Thigpen, S. W., Pvt. Co. E
POW captured at Fort Gaines, Alabama, on August 8, 1864. He was received at Ship Island, Mississippi, on October 25, 1864, from New Orleans and exchanged at Ship Island on January 4, 1865. POW paroled on May 15, 1865, by V. D. Vroom, Major 2nd N. J. Cav., and A. A. Inspector General C. F. M. D. W. M.

Thigpen, L. G., Pvt. Co. E
POW captured at Fort Gaines, Alabama, on August 8, 1864. He was received at Ship Island, Mississippi, on October 25, 1864, from New Orleans and exchanged at Ship Island on January 4, 1865. POW surrendered at Citronelle, Alabama, by Lt. General Richard Taylor on May 4, 1865, and paroled at Meridian, Mississippi, on May 13, 1865. He was shown as a resident of Greenville, Butler County, Alabama.

Thomas, Edward, Pvt. Co. A
Enlisted on February 1, 1863, at Choctaw Bluff, Alabama, by Captain Cothran for three years or the war. Company muster roll for December 31, 1862, to April 30, 1863, reports him absent in confinement at Choctaw Bluff. Muster roll for May/June 1863, reports him present in confinement at Choctaw Bluff, "drawn no pay". Discharged at Mobile in July 1863, born in Clarke County, Alabama, dark complexion, five foot eight inches, dark hair. His discharge is in his file but not readable.*

Thomas, William G., Pvt. Co. K
Enlisted on August 1, 1862, at Fort Morgan, Alabama, by Captain Randolph for the war. Company muster roll for September/October 1864, reports him absent sent to hospital on September 5, 1864. He was admitted to Ross Hospital at Mobile, Alabama, on August 12, 1864, with febris remittens and returned to duty on August 25, 1864. He was again admitted to Ross Hospital at Mobile, Alabama, on September 4, 1864, with febris intermittens quot. and returned to duty on September 12, 1864.

Thomas, W., Pvt. Co. K see **Thomas, William**

Thomas W. J. R., Pvt. Co. K
Enlisted October 5, 1863, at Camden, Alabama, by Lt. Wragg for the war. Company muster roll for September/October 1863, reports him present sick in quarters

and never paid. Muster roll for September/October 1864, reports him absent sent to hospital on October 30, 1864. This 1864 roll shows he enlisted on October 8, 1863, at Fort Morgan, Alabama, by Captain Dorgan. POW captured at Spanish Fort, Alabama, on April 8, 1865. He was confined on May 1, 1865, at New Orleans. He was admitted to Barracks USA General Hospital at New Orleans on April 11, 1865, with shell wound of right arm. Treatment was amputation of arm shoulder joint on the field with flap, age 42. He was paroled on June 28, 1865.

Thompson, C., Pvt. Co. E

POW surrendered at Citronelle, Alabama, by Lt. General Richard Taylor on May 4, 1865, and paroled at Meridian, Mississippi, on May 13, 1865. He was a resident of Mobile, Alabama.

Thompson, Robert M., Pvt. Co. E

Enlisted on October 13, 1861, at Mobile, Alabama, to serve one year. Discharged due to disability because of hernia on April 19, 1862. Born in Antique, West Indies, age 22, five foot one inch, light complexion, blue eyes, light brown hair, and a clerk by occupation. A good copy of his certificate of disability is in his file.*

Thompson, Samuel, Sgt. Co. I

Enlisted on October 13, 1861, at Halls Mill, Alabama, by Major Hessee for the war. He appears present on company muster roll for bounty on September 24, 1862. He refused bounty. Company muster roll for July/August 1863, reports him present, absent without leave from June 29, to July 3. Muster roll for September/October 1863, reports him present. POW captured at Fort Gaines, Alabama, on August 8, 1864. He was admitted to St. Louis USA General Hospital at New Orleans on August 24, 1864, with fever intermitten and returned to prison on September 12, 1864. He was confined at Steam Levee Press No. 4 in New Orleans and sent to St. Louis USA General Hospital on September 27, 1864, with diarrhoea, age 32, then returned to confinement on October 5, 1864. He was again admitted to St. Louis Hospital on October 20, 1864, with acute dysentery and returned to prison on November 2. He was received at Ship Island, Mississippi, from New Orleans on November 2, 1864, and died at Ship Island of dysentery on January 1, 1865. He was buried in Grave No. 125.

Thompson, Uriah, Pvt. Co. F

Enlisted on October 13, 1864, at Baldwin County, Alabama, by Captain McCoy to serve one year. He was discharged due to disability with broken down constitution caused by a long life of hard drinking and hemorrhoids on April 27, 1862, at Corinth, Mississippi. Born in Bridgeport, Ohio, age 49, six foot, dark complexion, gray eyes, dark hair, and a laborer by occupation. His certificate of disability is in his file.*

Thompson, William, Pvt. Co. H

POW admitted to St. Louis USA General Hospital at New Orleans, with bronchitis on August 29, 1864, and returned to prison on September 12, 1864, age 17.

Thrash, D. B., Pvt. Co. C

Enlisted on February 26, 1863, at Choctaw Bluff, Alabama, by Captain Smith for three years or the war. Discharged by reason of substitute on February 26, 1863.

Threadgill, H. D. W., Pvt. Co. F

His name appears on a regimental return for June 1862, sent to interior hospital on May 28. He was paid $15.76 for travel from Choctaw Bluff, Alabama, to Mobile.

Tilghman, (Tillman),William, Pvt. Co. I

Wounded seriously in right leg at Shiloh on April 6, 1862, at 7 A. M. in attack on First Battery while advancing. He was admitted to USA Post Hospital at Camp Dennison, Ohio, on April 18, 1865, with gunshot wound to ankle, secuh. Died on April 27, 1862, at General Hospital Camp, Dennison, Ohio. He is buried at Camp Dennison, Ohio.

Tillery, V. (Virgil), Pvt. Co. G

He drew clothing in 1864. POW captured at Fort Gaines, Alabama, on August 8, 1864. He was received at Ship Island, Mississippi, on October 25, 1864, from New Orleans, and exchanged at Ship Island, on January 4, 1865.

Tillman, James P., Pvt. Co. I

He drew clothing on June 1, 1864. POW captured at Fort Gaines, Alabama, on August 8, 1864. He was admitted to St. Louis USA General Hospital at New Orleans, Ward K on August 14, 1864, with fever intermitten quot and returned to prison on August 24, 1864, age 21. He was received at Ship Island, Mississippi, on October 25, 1864, from New Orleans. He died of pneumonia at Ship Island on November 23, 1864 and was buried in grave No. 40.

Tillman, Willis, Drummer Co. I

He enlisted on October 13, 1861, at Halls Mill, Alabama, by Major Hessee for the war. He appears present on a company muster roll for bounty September 24, 1862, refused to receive bounty due to being under 18 years of age. Company muster rolls for July/August 1863 and September/October 1863, report him present. POW captured at Fort Morgan, Alabama, on August 23, 1864, and imprisoned at New Orleans. He was sent to New York on September 27, 1864. He was received at Elmira, New York, from New Orleans on October 8, 1864. He was paroled for exchange at Elmira, New York, on March 2, 1865, and sent to James River. He was admitted to Jackson Hospital, Richmond, Virginia, with debilities on March 6, 1865, and furloughed for 30 days on March 9.

Tillman, James, C., Pvt./Sgt. Co. I

He enlisted on October 13, 1861, at Halls Mill, Alabama to serve one year. James C. Tillman was discharged due to disability at Fort Gaines, Alabama, on January 28, 1862, because of injury to the right shoulder when the carriage of a sawmill passed over it.. He was born in Jackson County, Mississippi, blue eyes, light hair, fair complexion, five foot seven and one half inches, by occupation an ox driver. His discharge is in his file.* James Tillman 21st Alabama Regiment appears on a parole of POW at Provost Marshal Office, Army of the Potomac, near Sharpsburg, Maryland, on September 21, 1862. (filed in error?) He is shown as having enlisted at Fort Morgan, Alabama, on September 18, 1862, by Lt. Vidmer for the war. He appears present on a company muster roll for bounty September 24, 1862. Company muster rolls for July/August 1863, September/October 1863 and September/October 1864, (at Mobile) report him present. He was shown Corp. and admitted to Post Hospital at Fort Morgan on August 31, 1863, with gonorrhoea and returned to duty on September 19, 1863. POW a straggler surrendered by Lt. General Richard Taylor at Meridian, Mississippi, and paroled at Mobile on May 19, 1865, shown as Sgt. of Company I.

Tillman, G., Pvt. Co. D

Enlisted on October 13, 1861, at Halls Mill, Alabama, by Major Hessee for the war. He appears present on a company muster roll for bounty on September 24, 1862. He was admitted to Post Hospital at Fort Morgan, Alabama, on April 23, 1863, with dysentery and returned to duty on April 26. Company muster roll for September/October 1863, reports him present. Muster roll for July/August 1863, reports him present, absent without leave July 5 to 8. Company muster roll for September/October 1864, reports him absent sent to General Hospital in Mobile in September 1864, "He was assigned to the company by order." A second muster roll for September/October 1864, reports him absent detailed at Battery Huger, by order of Colonel Fuller. He was admitted to Yandell Hospital at Jackson, Mississippi, on April 1, 1865.

Tillman, James, Pvt./Sgt. Co. I see **Tillman, James C.**

Tipton, William K., Pvt. Co. B

Enlisted on October 13, 1861, at Halls Mill, Alabama, by Major Hessee for the war. He appears present on a company muster roll for bounty on September 24, 1862, he was not entitled to bounty the reason not stated.

Tolbert, John M., Pvt. Co. C

Enlisted November 4, 1861, at Fort Gaines, Alabama, by Captain Rembert for twelve months. He appears present on a company muster roll for bounty on September 24, 1862. Company muster roll for December 31, 1862, to April 30, 1863, reports him present. Muster roll for May/June 1863, reports him present, lost canteen at 25 cents, strap at 20 cents and haversack at 20 cents. Muster roll for September/October 1863, reports him present. POW captured at Fort Gaines, Alabama, on August 8, 1864. He was received at Ship Island, Mississippi, on October 25, 1864, from New Orleans and exchanged on January 4, 1865, at Ship Island. POW captured at Blakeley, Alabama, on April 9, 1865, received at Ship Island on April 15, 1865, and transferred to Vicksburg, Mississippi, for exchange on May 1, 1865. Note is in his file to see the personal papers of **T. M. Ross.**
This data is from a descriptive list on May 2, 1863, for bounty and clothing. Filed with **Ross, T. M.**

MOBILE CONFEDERATES

Tolbert, James, Pvt. Enlisted at Choctaw Bluff, age 39, dark eyes, dark hair, dark complexion, six foot one inch, born North Carolina, a farmer, paid $50 bounty.

Tomisick, Vincent, Pvt. Co. A
  Enlisted November 1, 1861, at Mobile, Alabama, by Major Hessee. He appears present on a company muster roll for bounty on September 24, 1862, "refused to take the bounty". His name appears on a report near Tupelo, Mississippi, for June 1862, sent to Corinth Hospital and from there to interior by order of Surgeon Heustis.

Tonor, John, Pvt. Co. B
  Enlisted October 13, 1861, at Mobile, Alabama, by Major Hessee for twelve months. He appears present on a company muster roll for bounty on September 24, 1862, "not entitled to bounty due to age, refused to take the bounty." He appears on a regimental return for June 1861, sent to interior hospital May 28. Paid for service September 1, to October 13, 1862. Detached service. There is a pay voucher in his file.*

Toomy, David, Pvt./Corp. Co. A
  Enlisted October 13, 1861, at Mobile, Alabama, by Major Hessee for twelve months. He appears present on a company muster roll for bounty on September 24, 1862. Company muster roll for December 31, 1862, to April 30, 1863, reports him present, promoted from the ranks on January 1, 1863. Muster roll for May/June 1863, reports him present. Muster roll for September/October 1863, reports him present promoted from 4th Corporal to 1st Corporal September 1, 1863. He was admitted to Post Hospital at Fort Morgan, Alabama, with int. fev. on January 15, 1864, and returned to duty on January 18. Payment for deceased soldier filed by his mother Brigit Toomy on August 25, 1864.

Tortoricei, Guissippi, Pvt. Co.G
  Enlisted at Mobile in 1861, by Major Hessee to serve twelve months. He was discharged due to disability on January 18, 1862. Born Palermo, Italy, age 19, five foot five inches, blue eyes, by occupation a sailor. His discharge is in his file.*

Touart, Joseph, Sgt. Co. E
  His name appears on a regimental return for June 1862, June 13, 1862, Tupelo, Mississippi, discharged due to disability. A poor copy of his discharge is in his file.*

Touart, Louis, Pvt. Co. A/K
  Discharged from Co. A on April 28, 1863, a poor copy of his discharge is in his file.* Enlisted in Co. K on July 20, 1864, at Fort Powell by Captain Dorgan for the war. A company muster roll for September/October 1864, reports him absent detached with Quartermaster Corps at Mobile. Discharged due to disability on April 28, 1863, age 26, five foot ten inches, florid complexion, gray eyes, dark hair, and a merchant by profession.

Touchstone, L. J., Pvt. Co. E
  POW captured at Fort Gaines, Alabama, on August 8, 1864. He was confined at Steam Levee Press No. 4 at New Orleans on October 6, 1864, and sent to hospital. He

was admitted to St. Louis USA General Hospital at New Orleans on October 6, 1864, with acute diarrhoea, age 27, and returned to prison on October 13, 1864. He was admitted to St. Louis USA Hospital September 5, to September 12, 1864, for diarrhoea and on September 23, to September 24, 1864, with general debility. He was received at Ship Island, Mississippi, on October 25, 1864, and applied to take the Oath of Allegiance to the USA. He was exchanged on January 4, 1865, at Ship Island but refused to be exchanged.

Toulmin, John F., Sgt./1st Lt. Co. K/B

Enlisted in Co. K on October 13, 1862, at Mobile, by Captain Stewart for the war. He appears present on a company muster roll for bounty on September 24, 1862. Company muster roll for November/December 1862, reports him present, reduced to the ranks from Sgt. by Captain Stewart on December 20, 1862. Company muster roll for Co. B for May/June 1863, reports him transferred to Co. B on June 21, 1863, for promotion. Muster roll for May/June 1863, Co. B. reports him present as 2nd Lt. September/October muster roll Co. B reports him present as Jr. 2nd Lt. Appointed 2nd Lt. Co. B on May 20, 1863, promoted August 18, 1863. POW captured at Fort Gaines, Alabama, on August 8, 1864. He was received at Ship Island, Mississippi, on November 25, 1864, from New Orleans and exchanged at Ship Island on January 4, 1865. There is paperwork in his file.*

Travis, William, Fifer/Drum Major Co. E

Enlisted on October 13, 1861, at Mobile, Alabama, by Captain Chamberlain for the war. He appears present on a company muster roll for bounty on September 24, 1862. Company muster roll for November/December 1862, reports him present confined in guard house. Muster roll for July/August 1863, reports him present. Company muster roll for September/October 1863, reports him present, absent without leave from September 23, to September 30, 1863, due $56.18 for clothing not drawn in kind. Muster roll for March/April 1864, reports him present appointed principal musician on March 2, 1864, by order of Colonel Anderson. POW captured at Fort Gaines, Alabama, on August 8, 1864. He was admitted to St. Louis USA General Hospital at New Orleans, Louisiana, on August 12, 1864, with fever remittent and returned to prison on August 29, 1864. He was received at Ship Island, Mississippi, on October 25, 1864, from New Orleans and exchanged at Ship Island on January 4, 1865. POW surrendered at Citronelle, Alabama, on May 4, 1865, by Lt. General Richard Taylor and paroled at Meridian, Mississippi, on May 13, 1864. Residence was shown as Mobile, Alabama.

Treadwell, C. D., Pvt. Co. C

Enlisted on February 19, 1863, at Marengo County, Alabama, by Lt. Northrup for three years or the war. Company muster roll for December 31, 1862, to April 30, 1863, reports him present and never been paid. He appears present on a company muster roll for December 31, 1862, to April 30, 1863. Company muster roll for May/June 1863, reports him absent sick on 30-day sick leave from June 19, 1863, and lost one belt and plate at 75 cents. Company muster roll for September/October 1863, reports him present, lost one haversack at $1. POW captured at Fort Gaines, Alabama, on August 8, 1864. He was admitted to St. Louis USA General Hospital at New Orleans on September 11,

1864, with fever remit and returned to prison on September 15, 1864, age 17. He was received at Ship Island, Mississippi, on November 25, 1864, from New Orleans and exchanged at Ship Island, on January 4, 1865.
This data from a descriptive list on May 2, 1863, for bounty and clothing. Filed with **Ross, T. M.**

Treadwell, C. D., Pvt. age 19, gray eyes, light hair, fair complexion, five foot eight inches, enlisted in Marengo County, Alabama, paid $50 bounty.
Tredwell, Charles D., Pvt. Co. C is buried in Cem No. 2 at the Confederate Soldiers Home Marbury Ala.

Treat, ?win M., Pvt. Co. A
Captured at Shiloh on April7, 1862.

Trescutt, A. A., Pvt. Co. A
His name appears on a register at Receiving and Wayside Hospital or General Hospital No. 9, Richmond, Virginia, on May 24, 1864, sent to Howard's Grove Hospital on May 25, 1864.

Trosclair, L. A., Pvt. Co. K
Enlisted on July 4, 1862, at Fort Morgan, Alabama, by Captain Dorgan for the war. Company muster roll for July and August 1863, reports him present and never paid. Muster roll for September/October 1863, reports him present and paid August 31, 1863.

Troy, Jerry, Pvt. Co. E
Enlisted at Mobile, Alabama, on October 13, 1861, by Captain Chamberlain for the war. His name appears on a regimental return for June 1862, as being on detailed service as conductor with Mobile and Ohio Railroad. He drew pay at Mobile on September 5, 1862, for detached service from March 1, to September 31, 1862, in the amount of six months at $11 per month for $66, plus clothing not drawn in kind $25 for a total of $91. Company muster roll for bounty on September 24, 1862, reports him detailed on M & O RR on March 19, 1862, by order of General Withers. Muster rolls for November/ December 1862, July/August 1863 and September/October 1863, all report him absent detailed with the M & O RR. There are pay vouchers in his file.*

Trumbull, T., Pvt. Co. F
His name appears on a regimental return for June 1862, discharged on May 8, 1862, for disability at Corinth, Mississippi.

Trennelly, C. D., Pvt. Co. C
POW captured at Blakeley, Alabama, on April 9, 1865. He was received at Ship Island, Mississippi, on April 15, 1865, and transferred to Vicksburg on parole on May 1, 1865.

Tubbs, D. S., Musician Co. A

His name appears on a regimental return for June 1862, discharged on May 27, 1862, for disability at Corinth, Mississippi.

Tubbs, William, Pvt. Co. F

Enlisted on September 12, 1862, at Perry County, Alabama, by W. B. Livingston for three years or the war. Company muster roll for March 1, to June 30, 1863, reports him present. Muster roll for September/October 1863, reports him present. He was admitted to Post Hospital at Fort Morgan, Alabama, with int. fever on November 19, 1863, and returned to duty on November 27, 1863.

Tucker, F. M. (F. N.), Pvt. Co. G see **Tucker, Pleasant M.**

Tucker, J. L., Pvt. Co. C

Enlisted on February 16, 1863, at Marengo County, Alabama, by Lt. Northrup for three years or the war. Company muster roll for December 31, 1862, to April 30, 1863, reports him present. Muster roll for May/June 1863, reports him present sick in quarters, lost gun tube at $1. He was paid on April 30, 1863. He appears present on a muster roll for September/October 1863. He was admitted to Post Hospital at Fort Morgan, Alabama, on November 5, 1863, with fever remit. and returned to duty on November 19, 1863. POW captured at Fort Gaines, Alabama, on August 8, 1864. He was received at Ship Island, Mississippi, on November 25, 1864, from New Orleans and exchanged at Ship Island on January 4, 1865. POW surrendered at Citronelle, Alabama, by Lt. General Richard Taylor on May 4, 1865, and paroled at Meridian, Mississippi, on May 13, 1865. Residence shown as Marengo County, Alabama. There is a very poor copy of a descriptive list in his file.*

Tucker, James, Pvt. Co. B

Enlisted on October 13, 1861, at Mobile, Alabama, by Major Hessee for twelve months. He appears present on a company muster roll for bounty on September 24, 1862. Company muster roll for March/April 1863, reports him present, detailed to Quartermaster Department on March 18, 1863. Muster rolls for May/June 1863 and September/October 1863, report him present. He was admitted to Post Hospital at Fort Morgan on January 3, 1864, and returned to duty on January 8, 1864. POW captured at Fort Gaines, Alabama, on August 8, 1864. He was received at Ship Island, Mississippi, from New Orleans on October 25, 1864, and sent to Elmira, New York, Prison. He was received at Elmira on October 8, 1864, "Entry taken from remarks with name of **G. H. Scott Co. F. 1st Regt. Ala.** thus – James T. Tucker Pvt. Co. B, 21st Ala. came in Scott's name and was released December ? by order of C. S. P. dated ?" At Elmira he applied to take the Oath of allegiance to the USA on October 31, 864. "Was conscripted Oct. 13, 1862. Is a native of Siubeck, Maine, but was in Mobile at outbreak of the war, was sick and destitute and could not get away. Claims to have been a Union man and kept out of the Army as long as possible. His parents live in Rockland, Maine, where he desires to go." He signed an Oath of Allegiance to the USA on December 21, 1864, at Elmira, New York. Residence Mobile, County, Alabama, fair complexion, dark brown hair, black eyes, five foot nine inches. "Released on his taking the Oath as proscribed in the Presidents Proclamation of Dec. 8, 1863, of Special Orders No. 38, Par. IV from the

Office of the Comm. Genl. of Prisoners, Washington. D. C." Note some of these dates do not match and he is also shown as being exchanged at Ship Island on January 4, 1865.

Tucker, L. D., Pvt. Co. K

His name appears on a register of Ross Hospital at Mobile, Alabama, admitted September 12, 1864, with acute diarrhoea and returned to duty on September 18, 1864.

Tucker, Peasant M., Pvt. Co. G

POW captured at Fort Gaines, Alabama, on August 8, 1864. He was transported to Ship Island, Mississippi, from New Orleans, December 10, 1864, and exchanged on January 4, 1865. There is some correspondence on November 17, 1864, from Office of Commissary of Prisons at New Orleans relating to **F. W. Tucker**. *There may be two men's file combined here.* POW Pvt. Pleasant M. Tucker was surrendered at Citronelle, Alabama, by Lt. General Richard Taylor on May 4, 1865, and he was paroled on May 13, 1865, at Meridian, Mississippi. Residence shown at Shiloh, Marengo County, Alabama. There is paper work in his file.*

Tucker, U. ?, Pvt. Co. A

Wounded by breaking his right leg at Shiloh on April 6, 1862, at 7 A. M. advancing on 1st Battery.

Tulley, P., Pvt. Co. E

His name appears at USA Transit Hospital, New York City, on July 8, 1865. ? July 10, 1865, ? David's Island.

Turbenville, J., Pvt. Co. J

POW captured at Blakeley, Alabama, on April 9, 1865, and sent to Ship Island, Mississippi. He was transferred on parole from Ship Island to Vicksburg, Mississippi, on May 1, 1865.

Turnbull, F. F., Pvt. Co. F

Enlisted on October 13, 1861, at Baldwin County, Alabama, by Captain McVoy for one year. He appears present on a company muster roll for bounty on September 24, 1862. Company muster roll for March 1, to June 30, 1863, reports him present. Muster roll for September/October 1863, reports him absent detached to fish by General Maury on August 23, 1863. He appears on a company D muster roll for September/October 1864, present and assigned to company by order. He also appears on a muster roll for Sossaman's Detachment of the 21st Alabama, for September/October 1864, shown absent detached to Battery Huger by Colonel Fuller. He was admitted to Ross Hospital at Mobile, Alabama, on October 26, 1864, with fever intermittens, tert. and returned to duty on October 28, 1864.

Turnbull, G. W., Pvt. Co. F

Enlisted on October 13, 1861, at Baldwin County, Alabama, by Captain McVoy for one year. He appears present on a company muster roll for bounty on September 24, 1862. Company muster roll for March 1, to June 30, 1863, reports him present, lost one canteen at 25 cents. Muster roll for September/October 1863, reports him absent, detached to fish by General Maury on August 23, 1863.

Turnbull, J. W., Pvt. Co. F

Enlisted on October 13, 1861, at Baldwin County, Alabama, by Captain McVoy for one year. He appears present on a company muster roll for bounty on September 24, 1862. Company muster roll March 1, to June 30, 1863, reports him present. Company muster roll for September/October 1863, reports him absent detached in A. C. S. on August 22, 1863. Muster roll for September/October 1864, reports him present in Captain Sossaman's Detachment.

Turnbull, William, Pvt. Co. F

Discharged on May 3, 1862, at Corinth, Mississippi, due to disability from shortage of one leg, age 31, five foot nine inches, light hair, fair complexion, and blue eyes. Enlisted on February 1, 1863, at Choctaw Bluff, Alabama, by Captain Dade for three years or the war. He appears present on a company muster roll for September/October 1863. He appears on a register of soldiers who died, date of death April 12, 1864, at Pollard, Alabama.

Turner, Arthur J., Pvt. Co. K

Discharged age 18years. 10th Confederate Cavalry. He was paid for service March and April 1862. His discharge is in his file.* *His record is very difficult to read.*

Turner, Austin, H., Pvt. Co. H

POW captured at Fort Gaines, Alabama, on August 8, 1864. He was received at Ship Island, Mississippi, from New Orleans on October 25, 1964, and exchanged at Ship Island on January 4, 1865.

Turner, George W., Pvt. Co. A

Enlisted on October 13, 1861, at Mobile, Alabama, by Captain Jewett for one year. Company muster roll for November 1, 1861, to January 31, 1862, reports him present detailed as a nurse on November 16. He was discharged due to disability at Fort Gaines, Alabama, on January 11, 1862, born in Green County, Mississippi, age 40, five foot ten inches, light complexion, black eyes, a clerk by occupation. His discharge is in his file.*

Turner, Henry, Pvt. Co. I

Enlisted on October 13, 1861, at Halls Mill, Alabama, by Major Hessee for the war. He appears on a regimental return for June 1862, detached as regimental butcher. Company muster roll for bounty on September 24, 1862, reports him present. Muster roll for September/October 1863, reports him present on extra duty at Commissary Department August 28, 1862. Company returns for November and December report him on detail with Commissary Department as butcher. Muster roll for July/August 1863, reports him present on extra duty with Comsy. Dept. POW captured at Fort Gaines, Alabama, on August 8, 1962. Received at Ship Island, Mississippi, on October 25, 1864, from New Orleans. He was exchanged at Ship Island on January 4, 1865.

Turner, O. W., Pvt. Co. E

POW captured at Fort Gaines, Alabama, on August 8, 1962. He was admitted to St. Louis USA General Hospital at New Orleans on September 10, 1864, with diarrhoea and returned to prison on September 16, 1864, age 24. He was received at Ship Island, Mississippi, on October 25, 1864, from New Orleans. He died of dysentery at Ship Island and is buried there in grave No. 128.

Turner, Whitfield, Pvt. Co. K

Enlisted on August 20, 1862, at Fort Morgan, Alabama, by Captain Dorgan for the war. Company muster roll for bounty on September 24, 1862, reports him present. Muster roll for November/December 1862, reports him present.

Turner, ?, Regimental Band, Co. E

His name appears on a regimental return for June 1862.

Turnham, J. C., Pvt. Co. G

POW captured at Fort Gaines, Alabama, on August 8, 1962. He was received at Ship Island, Mississippi, on October 25, 1864, from New Orleans and exchanged at Ship Island on January 4, 1865. *There is unreadable paperwork in his file.**

Tylton, T. T., Musician, Co. C

A resident of Marengo County, Alabama. POW he was surrendered at Citronelle, Alabama, by Lt. General Richard Taylor on May 4, 1865, and paroled at Meridian, Mississippi, on May 13.

Tyne, William, Pvt. Co. B

Enlisted at Fort Morgan, Alabama, on September 6, 1862, by Captain Johnston, for the war. Company muster roll for bounty on September 24, 1862, reports him present. Company muster roll for March/April 1863, reports him present to forfeit one months pay by sentence of General Court Marshal. Muster roll for May/June 1863, reports him present under arrest to forfeit one months pay by sentence of G. C. M. September/October 1863, roll reports him present with same note. He appears on a Federal list as a deserter that came into the Federal lines with the fleet before the capture of Fort Gaines on August 3, 1864. He took the Oath of Allegiance to the USA on August 13, 1864, at New Orleans. A resident of Mobile, light complexion, brown hair, gray eyes, five foot ten inches.

U

Uhler, Napoleon, Pvt. Co. H

Enlisted on October 13, 1861, at Mobile, Alabama, by Major Hessee for one year. Discharged on January 2, 1862, at Fort Gaines, Alabama due to general disability. He was born in Moayona, Germany, age 45, five foot ten inches, dark complexion, gray eyes, light hair, by occupation a laborer. There are pay vouchers and his discharge in his file.*

V

Vail, L., Pvt. Co. K

Enlisted on July 4, 1862, at Fort Morgan, Alabama, by Captain Dorgan for the war. He was admitted to Post Hospital at Fort Morgan with asthma on July 24, 1863, and returned to duty on July 30, 1863. Company muster rolls for July/August 1863 and September/October 1863, report him present. Muster roll for September/October 1864, reports him absent detailed for 30 days in Ordnance Department by order of General Maury. POW surrendered at Citronelle, Alabama, on May 4, 1865, by Lt. General Richard Taylor and paroled at Meridian, Mississippi, on May 10, 1864. A resident of Mobile, Mobile County, Alabama.

Vail, Lovick, 4th Corporal Co. D

Enlisted on October 13, 1861, at Mobile, Alabama, by Captain Butt for one y ear. He appears present on a company muster roll for bounty on September 24, 1862, "refuses to receive bounty."

Van Antwerp, George, Pvt. Co. A

Enlisted on October 13, 1861, at Mobile, Alabama, by Major Hessee for the war. His name appears on a regimental return for June 1862, detached as druggist. He appears absent on a company muster roll for bounty on September 24, 1862, detached on November 8, 1861, as druggist at Mobile Hospital by order of General Withers. Company muster rolls for December 31, 1862, to April 30, 1863, May/June, 1863, and September/October 1863, all report him absent and detached as druggist at Mobile. He appears on a number of hospital muster rolls at General Hospital, and Ross Hospital at Mobile, Alabama. There are a number of pay vouchers in his file.*

Van Horn, R. E., Pvt. Co. I

Enlisted on October 13, 1861, at Halls Mill, Alabama, by Major Hessee for the war. He appears present on a company muster roll for bounty on September 24, 1862. Company muster rolls for July/August 1863, and September/October 1863, report him present. He was admitted to Post Hospital at Fort Morgan, Alabama, on July 25, 1864, with int. feb. quar. and returned to duty on July 29, 1864. POW captured at Fort Gaines, Alabama, on August 8, 1962. He was received at Ship Island, Mississippi, on October 25, 1864, from New Orleans and exchanged at Ship Island on January 4, 1865. He was admitted to Ross Hospital at Mobile, Alabama, on January 6, 1865, with chronic diarrhoea and furloughed for 60 days on January 18, 1865. POW surrendered at Citronelle, Alabama, on May 4, 1865, by Lt. General Richard Taylor, and paroled at Meridian, Mississippi, May 13, 1864. A resident of Mobile, Mobile County, Alabama.

Vaughan, R. E., Pvt. see **Van Horn, R. E.**

Vass, Douglas, Captain/Quarter Master

Enlisted October 13, 1861. Appointed Depot Quartermaster on September 16, 1861. A regimental return for June 1861, reports him permanently disabled and detached to Division A. Q. M. A return for November 1861, from Post at Fort Gaines, Alabama,

MOBILE CONFEDERATES

reports him present as Post Quartermaster. A regimental return for December 1861, reports him Depot Quartermaster. Field and Staff Muster roll for March/April 1864, reports him absent under orders connected with his Department. There is a considerable amount of paperwork in his file.**

Vass, H. Pen?, 1st Sgt. Co. K
His film data is too poor to read.

Verbuke, ?, Pvt. Co. H
His name appears on a regimental return for June 1862.

Verner, Aug, Pvt. Co. K
His name appears on a regimental return for June 1862, missing on march, suppose to be in the hands of the enemy.

Vidmer, George, Corporal Co. E/Sgt. Major/Adjutant, Field and Staff
Wounded seriously in the thigh at Shiloh on April 6, 1862, advancing on First Battery. He appears on a regimental return for June 1862, as having been advanced to Sgt. Major on May 4, 1862, at Corinth, Mississippi. He was appointed Adjutant on June 20, 1862. Field and Staff muster rolls for July/August 1863, September/October 1863 and March/April 1864, all report him present. POW captured on August 8, 1964, at Fort Gaines, Alabama. He was received at Ship Island, Mississippi, from New Orleans on November 25, 1864, and exchanged on January 4, 1865. His signed Parole of Honor is in his file. He signed it at Mobile on May 11, 1865. *There is a considerable amount of paperwork in his file but much is not readable.**

Vidmer, George, Field and Staff, 1st Lt./Adjutant see **Nedmer, George**

Vierd, Antoine, Pvt. Co. B
He appears as **A. Vieva** on a report for June 28, 1862, near Tupelo, Mississippi, sent to interior from Corinth at the time of the evacuation. Enlisted on January 7, 1864, at Mobile, Alabama, by Colonel Miller for the war. Hospital muster roll for July/August 1864, reports him present as a patient, never been paid. Muster roll for Sossaman's Detachment for September/October 1864, reports him absent sent to the hospital. He was admitted to Post Hospital at Fort Morgan, Alabama, on January 14, 1864, with diarrhoea and returned to duty on June 19, 1964. He was admitted with chronic diarrhoea to 1st Mississippi USA Hospital at Jackson, Mississippi, on August 13, 1864, and returned to duty on September 29, 1864.

Vilra, Antoine, Pvt. Co. B see **Vierd, Antoine**

Vigner, George, Pvt. Co. G
His name appears on a regimental return for June 1862. He appears on a report for June 28, 1862, near Tupelo, Mississippi, absent on furlough since May 29, 1862, in Mobile.

Vines, W. A. J., Pvt. Co. F

Enlisted on October 13, 1861, at Baldwin County, Alabama, by Captain McVoy for one year. His name is on a regimental return for June 1862, on detached service as a carpenter. He appears present on a company muster roll for bounty on September 24, 1862. He died November 21, 1862, at Choctaw Bluff, Alabama. Claim filed for deceased soldier by Evaline Vines his widow on April 20, 1863. She was paid $49.35. He claim is in his file.* He was born in Georgia, age 26, five foot seven inches, fair complexion, gray eyes. dark hair by occupation a carpenter.*

Vinet, J., Pvt. Co. K

Enlisted on July 4, 1862, at Fort Morgan, Alabama, by Captain Dorgan for the war. He appears present on muster rolls for July/August and September/October 1863.

Volkart, John, Pvt. Co. B

Enlisted in Co. B, 21st Alabama, October 13, 1861, at Mobile by Major Hessee. He was discharged at Fort Gaines, Alabama, on November 20, 1861, due to blindness in his right eye. Born Switzerland, age 33, five foot ten inches, fair complexion, blue eyes, light hair, and a sailor by occupation. His discharge is in his file.*

Vuscovich, P., Pvt. Co. H

He appears on a regimental return for June 1862, sent to hospital on May 2. His name appears on a report for June 28, 1862, near Tupelo, Mississippi, sent to interior hospital in May. There is a pay voucher in his file for service March 1, to August 31, 1862. He was paid $66 for service plus $25 for clothing for a total of $91 on October 29, 1862. His pay voucher is in his file.* He signed by his mark "X".

W

Wade, Francis, M. Pvt. Co. A

POW captured at Fort Donaldson on February 16, 1862. His name appears on a roll of POW's at Fort Morton, Indiana, June 1862. He was admitted to City USA General Hospital at Indianapolis, Indiana, on February 22, 1862, with bilious fever and returned to prison on March 31, 1862. He was sent from Camp Morton to Vicksburg, Mississippi, for exchange on August 25, 1862. Exchanged at Atkins Landing near Vicksburg, on November 10, 1862.

Wade, J. W., Pvt. Co. C

Enlisted on February 10, 1863, at Marengo County, Alabama, by Lt. Northrup for three years or the war. He appears present on company muster roll for December 31, 1862, to April 30, 1863. Company muster roll for May/June 1863, reports that he died in Hospital at Selma, Alabama, on May 21, 1863, of disease. There is additional description upon a descriptive list filed with **J. L. Tucker**, which is not readable.

Wade, W. T., Pvt. Co. C

Enlisted on February 10, 1863, at Marengo County, Alabama, by Lt. Northrup for three years or the war. He appears present on company muster roll for December 31,

1862, to April 30, 1863. Company muster roll for May/June 1863, reports him present, sick in quarters. Muster roll for September/October 1863, reports him present, lost one canteen at $2. POW captured at Fort Gaines, Alabama, on August 8, 1864. He was confined in New Orleans at Steam Levee Press No. 4 on September 29, 1864. He was admitted to St. Louis USA General Hospital at New Orleans on August 28, 1864, with diarrhoea and returned to prison on September 17, 1864, age 36. He was admitted once again to St. Louis USA Hospital on September 29, 1864, with chronic diarrhoea and died on October 18, 1864. He was buried in grave No. 396 Monument Cemetery, and left no effects. Residence shown as Marengo County, Alabama. There is additional description upon a descriptive list filed with **J. L. Tucker** that is not readable. His death certificate is in his file.*

Wadsworth, William W., Pvt. Co. D
He was admitted to Post Hospital at Fort Morgan, Alabama, on April 8, 1863, with rheumatism and returned to duty on May 12, 1863.

Waggenson, J. A., Pvt. Co. C see **Megginson, J. A.**

Walker, A. J., Pvt. Co. F
Enlisted at Choctaw Bluff, Alabama, on February 23, 1863, by Captain Dade for the war. Company muster roll for March 1, to June 30, 1863, reports him absent without leave since June 28, 1863. Muster roll for September/October 1863, reports that he died at Choctaw Bluff on September 20, 1863. "Never been paid." Due $97.63.

Walker, C. W., Pvt. Co. A
His name appears on a regimental return for June 1862. He was discharged for disability on June 13, 1862, at Tupelo, Mississippi.

Walker, E. (Eugene) B., Pvt. Co. F/C
He was severely wounded at Shiloh in the right shoulder while advancing on the 1st Battery at 8 A. M. on April 6, 1862, and captured at the hospital. He was admitted to USA Post Hospital at Camp Dennison, Ohio, in April 1862. He was admitted to USA General Hospital, Camp Dennison, Ohio, on April 20, 1862, wounded in right shoulder. Residence Mobile, Alabama. He was discharged from the CSA Army on March 14, 1863.

Walker, H., Pvt. Co. F
His name appears on a regimental return for June 1862, sent to interior hospital. Discharged from CSA Army on March 4, 1863.

Walker, J. A., Pvt. Co. I see **Walker James**

Walker, James, Pvt. Co. I
Enlisted March 1, 1862, at Halls Mill, Alabama, by Lt Cayce for the war. He appears present on company muster roll for bounty on September 24, 1862. Muster rolls for July/August 1863 and September/October 1863, report him present. POW captured at

Fort Gaines, Alabama, on August 8, 1864. He was received at Ship Island, Mississippi, from New Orleans on October 25, 1864, and exchanged at Ship Island on January 5, 1865. POW surrendered at Citronelle, Alabama, by Lt. General Taylor on May 4, 1865, and paroled at Meridian, Mississippi, May 13, 1865. Residence shown as Marengo County, Alabama. His name appears on a register of paroled Confederate Soldiers on June 15, 1865. His parole is in his file, five foot two inches, dark eyes, dark hair, dark complexion.* He signed by his mark "X".

Walker, James K., Pvt. Co. A
Discharged on March 1, 1862.

Walker, J. C., Pvt. Co. F.
Enlisted on February 23, 1863, at Choctaw Bluff, Alabama, by Captain Dade for three years or the war. Company muster roll for March 1, to June 30, 1863, reports him present. Muster roll for September/October 1863, reports him absent, detached to fish by General Maury on August 23, 1863. POW captured at Fort Gaines, Alabama, on August 8, 1864. He was received at Ship Island, Mississippi, from New Orleans on October 25, 1864, and exchanged at Ship Island on January 5, 1865. POW surrendered at Citronelle, Alabama, by Lt. General Taylor on May 4, 1865, and paroled at Meridian, Mississippi, May 13, 1865. Residence shown as Conecuh County, Alabama.

Walker, J. L., Pvt. Co. F
His name appears on a consolidated report near Tupelo, Mississippi, on June 26, 1862, musician absent on furlough.

Walker, J. P., Pvt. Co. I see **Walker, James**

Walker, Sim, Pvt. Co. F
Enlisted September 30, 1863, at Point Clear, Alabama, by Captain Dade for three years or the war. Company muster roll for September/October 1863, reports him absent detailed to fish by General Maury on September 30, 1863. There is paperwork in his file.*

Walker, R. H., Pvt. Co. K
Enlisted on October 29, 1863, at Fort Morgan, Alabama, by Captain Dorgan for the war. Company muster rolls for September/October 1863 and September/October 1864, report him present. POW surrendered at Citronelle, Alabama, by Lt. General Taylor on May 4, 1865, and paroled at Meridian, Mississippi, May 13, 1865. Residence shown as New Orleans, Louisiana.

Walkly, Nelson, Pvt. Co. E
Killed at Shiloh by gunshot to head on April 6, 1862, at 7 A. M.

Wall, John H., Pvt. Co. F
Enlisted at Choctaw Bluff, Alabama, on February 21, 1863, by Captain Dade for the war. Company muster roll for March 1, to June 30, 1863, shows him present sick in hospital, lost one canteen at 25 cents. Muster roll for September/October 1863, reports

him present. He was admitted to Ross Hospital at Mobile, Alabama, on February 12, 1864, with remit. fever and returned to duty on March 6, 1864. Data card also indicates typhoid fever.

Wall, Thomas, Pvt. Co. F

He was admitted to Ross Hospital Mobile, Alabama, on November 11, 1863, with pneumonia and returned to duty on December 4, 1863. *Filed with **Wall, John H.***

Waller, J. M., Pvt. Co. C

Enlisted on March 10, 1862, at Fort Pillow by Captain Rembert for three years or the war. A regimental return for June, 1862, shows him as regimental teamster. He appears present on a company muster roll for bounty on September 24, 1862. Muster roll for December 31, 1862, to April 30, 1863, reports him present and enlisted on November 10, 1862. Muster roll for May/June 1863, reports him present and detailed as a teamster on June 10, 1863, by order of Colonel Anderson. Muster roll for September/October 1863, reports him absent detailed as a teamster in Mobile on August 5, 1863, by order of General Maury. Muster roll for September/October 1864, of Sossaman's detachment reports him absent on five days leave. POW surrendered by Lt. General Taylor in May 1865, and paroled on May 15, 1865, at Demopolis, Alabama. Residence given as Marengo County, Alabama.

Walls, A., Pvt. Co. C

Enlisted on September 17, 1862, at Shelby County, Alabama, by N. J. Davis for three years or the war. Company muster roll for December 31, 1862, to April 30, 1863, reports him present. Muster roll for May/June 1863, reports him present, lost canteen at 25 cents, strap at 20 cents and haversack at 20 cents. Muster roll for September/October 1863, reports him present.

Walls, J. A., Pvt. Co. C

POW captured at Fort Gaines, Alabama, on August 8, 1864. He was received at Ship Island, Mississippi, from New Orleans on October 25, 1864, and exchanged at Ship Island on January 5, 1865. POW surrendered at Citronelle, Alabama, by Lt. General Taylor on May 4, 1865, and paroled at Meridian, Mississippi, May 13, 1865. Residence shown as Shelby County, Alabama.

Walsh, Richard, Pvt. Co. A

His name appears on a regimental return for June 1862. sent to interior hospital on June 7. He appears on a report June 28, 1862, near Tupelo, Mississippi, sent to hospital at Baldwin. There is paper work in his file.*

Walters, Burwell, Pvt. Co. D

Enlisted on October 13, 1861, at Mobile, Alabama, by Captain Butt for one year. His name appears on a regimental return for June 1862, sent to interior hospital at the evacuation of Corinth. He appears on returns in November and December 1862, as a butcher. Company muster roll for bounty on September 24, 1862, reports him absent with leave. Company muster rolls for November/December 1862 and July/August 1863, report him present. Muster roll for September/October 1863, reports him as a deserter, September.

Ward, Charles, Corporal Co. G

Died of small pox at Ship Island Prison, on December 27, 1864. He was buried in grave 114.

Ward, Robert H., Pvt. Co. A

Enlisted on October 13, 1862, at Mobile, Alabama, by Major Hessee for three years or the war. Wounded at Shiloh in the foot slightly on April 6, 1862, while attacking First Battery. POW captured at Shiloh Hospital on April 7, 1862, and sent to Camp Morton Indiana, August 26, 1862. He was admitted to No. 2 USA General Hospital (Marine) at Evansville, Indiana, on April 15, 1862, with vulnus sclopitium (gunshot) and sent to Indianapolis on April 29. He appears on a roll of POW's at Depot of Prisoners at Sandusky, Ohio, that were sent to Vicksburg, Mississippi, September 1, 1862. He was among 1100 Prisoners aboard the steamer *John H. Done* that were received at Atkins Landing near Vicksburg, Mississippi, on September 20, 1862. Company muster roll for bounty on September 24, 1862, reports him present captured April 7, 1862, and exchanged. Company muster roll for December 31, 1862, to April 30, 1863, reports him absent detached on January 23, 1863, to A. Q. M. Department at Mobile by order of General Slaughter. Company muster rolls for May/June and September/October 1863, report him detached January 23, 1863, to A. Q. M. Department at Mobile by order of General Slaughter. He was paid $108.40 on September 4, 1863, for expenses to Atlanta, and back to Mobile as messenger in charge of Government stores. POW captured at Fort Morgan, Alabama, on August 23, 1864. He was sent to New York from New Orleans on September 27, 1864, and received at Elmira, New York, on October 8, 1864, then released in June 1865.. He signed an Oath of Allegiance to the USA at Elmira, New York, on June 14, 1865. Residence reported as New Orleans, fair complexion, dark hair, blue eyes, five foot four inches, age 19. There is considerable paperwork in his file.**

Ward, Thomas, Corporal Co. G/A

POW captured at Fort Gaines, Alabama, on August 8, 1864. He was admitted to St. Louis USA General Hospital at New Orleans on September 29, 1864, with jaundice and returned to prison on October 14, 1864. He appears on a roll of POW's confined at Steam Levee Press No. 4 at New Orleans on October 14, 1864, received from hospital. He was received at Ship Island, Mississippi, on October 25, 1864, and died on December 27, 1864, at Ship Island.

Ward, W. J., Pvt. Co. D

POW surrendered at Citronelle, Alabama, by Lt. General Taylor on May 4, 1865, and paroled at Meridian, Mississippi, May 13, 1865. Residence shown as Mobile, Alabama.

Ware, Elijah S., Pvt. Co. C

Enlisted on August 26, 1862, at Jefferson County, Alabama, by J. Walker for three years or the war. Company muster rolls for December 31, 1862, to April 30, 1863,

May/June 1863 and September/October 1863, all show him present. He was admitted to Post Hospital at Fort Morgan, Alabama, on December 13, 1863, with int. feb. and sent to General Hospital Ross at Mobile on January 16, 1864, then furloughed for 30 days on February 9. POW captured at Fort Gaines, Alabama, August 8, 1864. He was received at Ship Island, Mississippi, from New Orleans on October 25, 1864, and exchanged at Ship Island on January 5, 1865.

Ware, George, Pvt. Co. B

Enlisted on September 8, 1862, at Jefferson County, Alabama, by A. R. Goodwin for three years or the war. Company muster roll for March/April 1863, reports him present. Muster roll for May/June 1863, reports him present sick in quarters. Muster roll for September/October 1863, reports him absent without leave since October 22, 1863. September/October 1864, muster roll reports him absent detailed at Battery Huger on orders of Colonel Fuller. He was admitted to Ross Hospital at Mobile on August 17, 1864, with chronic diarrhoea and sent to General Hospital in Selma on August 26, 1864. He appears on a July/August 1864, hospital muster roll as patient at General Hospital at Marion Alabama. POW surrendered at Citronelle, Alabama, by Lt. General Taylor on May 4, 1865, and paroled at Meridian, Mississippi, May 13, 1865. His residence was shown as Jefferson County, Alabama.

Ware, H. M., Pvt. Co. C

Enlisted on August 28, 1862, at Jefferson County, Alabama, by J. Walker for three year or the war. Company muster rolls for December 31, 1862, to April 30, 1863, May/June 1863 and September/October 1863, all report him present. POW captured at Fort Gaines, Alabama, on August 8, 1864. He was received at Ship Island, Mississippi, from New Orleans on October 25, 1864, and exchanged at Ship Island on January 5, 1865.

Ware, J. D., Pvt. Co. C

Enlisted on March 11, 1863, at Choctaw Bluff, Alabama, by Captain Smith for three years or the war. Company muster rolls for December 31, 1862, to April 30, 1863, May/June 1863 and September/October 1863, all report him present. He appears on a muster roll for Sossaman's Detachment for September/October 1864, at Mobile, sent to Hospital Ross on October 23, 1864. There is further description of J. D. Ware on a descriptive list filed with **J. L. Tucker**.

Ware, J. H., Pvt. Co. F.

Enlisted on September 27, 1862, at Jefferson County, Alabama, by W. A. Walker for three years or the war. Company muster roll for March 1, 1863, to June 20, 1863, reports him present detailed in Q. M. Department as teamster since June 20, 1863. Company muster roll for September/October 1863, reports him present. There is a pay voucher in his file.*

Waring, M. M., Pvt. Co. K

Enlisted on May 14, 1864, at Fort Powell, Alabama, by Captain Dorgan for the war. Company muster roll for September/October 1864, reports him present and paid on

June 30, 1864. POW surrendered at Citronelle, Alabama, by Lt. General Taylor on May 4, 1865, and paroled at Meridian, Mississippi, May 13, 1865. Residence shown as Mobile, Mobile County, Alabama.

Warner, Theodore, A., Pvt./Sgt. Co. E/F

Enlisted May 2, 1862, at Corinth, Mississippi, by Captain Chamberlain for the war. He appears on a regimental return for June 1862, sent to interior hospital from Corinth. His name appears on a report for June 28, 1862, near Tupelo, Mississippi, Furloughed for 30 days from June ?, 1862. He appears present on a company muster roll for bounty on September 24, 1862. Muster rolls for November/December 1862, July/August 1863, September/October 1863 and September/October 1864, all report him present. POW surrendered at Citronelle, Alabama, by Lt. General Taylor on May 4, 1865, and paroled at Meridian, Mississippi, May 13, 1865. Residence was shown as Mobile, Alabama. He is shown here as 1st Sgt. Co. F.

Warren, Charles, R., Pvt. Co. A

Enlisted on October 13, 1861, at Mobile, Alabama, by Major Hessee for the war. He appears present on a Company muster roll for bounty on September 24, 1862, refused to take the bounty. Muster roll for December 31, 1862, to April 30, 1862, reports him present pay stopped while detailed in Engineering Department from March 26, to April 26, 1863. Muster roll for May/June 1863, reports him absent under orders from General Slaughter, witness in a case in Civil Court.

Waters, B., Pvt. Co. D see **Walters, Burwel**

Watkins, C. C., Pvt. Co. C

Enlisted on September 1, 1862, at Marengo County, by Captain Dorgan for three years or the war. Muster rolls for December 31, 1862, to April 30, 1862, May/June 1863 and September/October 1863 all report him present. POW captured at Fort Gaines, Alabama, on August 8, 1864. He was received at Ship Island, Mississippi, from New Orleans on October 25, 1864, and exchanged at Ship Island on January 5, 1865. POW surrendered at Citronelle, Alabama, by Lt. General Taylor on May 4, 1865, and paroled at Meridian, Mississippi, May 13, 1865. Residence shown as Marengo County, Alabama. He is shown on a descriptive list filed with **J. L. Tucker**, Co. C.

Watson, Richard, Pvt. Co. D.

Enlisted on October 13, 1864, at Mobile, Alabama, by Captain Butt for one year. His name appears on a regimental return for June 1862, sent to interior hospital at the evacuation of Corinth.

Walt, John, Pvt. Co. A

Enlisted on October 13, 1864, at Mobile, Alabama, by Major Hessee for one year. Company muster rolls for December 31, 862, to April 30, 1863, May/June 1863 and September/October 1863, report him absent detached January 8, 1862, druggist at Mobile by order of General Withers. He appears on several muster rolls at General Hospital in Mobile as a nurse. A list in July 1864, reports him as a druggist.

Watts, ?, Pvt. Co. F

He was admitted to Post Hospital at Fort Morgan on November 5, 1863, with icterus (*jaundice*) and returned to duty on December 9, 1863.

Watts, C. J., Pvt. Co. C/A

Enlisted on February 1, 1863, at Choctaw Bluff, Alabama, by Captain Cothran for three years or the war. Company muster roll Co. C for December 31, 862, to April 30, 1863, reports him transferred to Co. A on March 31, 1863. Company A muster rolls for December 31, 1862, to April 30, 1863 and May/June 1863, report him present. Muster roll for September/October 1863, reports that he died on October 5, 1863, at Point Clear, Alabama.

This data is from a descriptive list on May 26, 1863, list is filed with **Pvt. John Pennington**, Co. A.

Pvt. **C. J. Watts**, age 18, blue eyes, dark hair, light complexion, five foot nine inches, born in Alabama, a farmer by occupation, enlisted at Clarke County, Alabama, by Captain Cothran for the war, paid $50 bonus.

Watts, T. J., Pvt. Co. A see **Watts, C. J.**

Wattwood, P. J., Pvt. Co. C/A

Enlisted on January 31, 1863, at Choctaw Bluff, Alabama, by Colonel Anderson for the war. Company muster roll Co. C for December 31, 1862, to April 30, 1863, reports him transferred to Co. A on March 31, 1863. Company muster roll Co. A for December 31, 1862, to April 30, 1863, reports him absent in hospital at Choctaw Bluff. Company A muster roll for May/June 1863, reports him present, "drawn no pay". He appears on a register of deceased soldiers at Mobile. Died August 4 1863, in general hospital.

Weatherly, L. F., Corporal/Pvt. Co. D

Enlisted on October 13, 1861, at Mobile, Alabama, by Captain Butt for one year. His name appears on a regimental return for June 1862, sent to interior hospital at the evacuation of Corinth. He appears present on a Company muster roll for bounty on September 24, 1862, refused to take the bounty. Muster rolls for November/December 1862, July/August 1863, and September/October 1983, all report him present. Company muster roll for November/December 1863, reports him absent "went on furlough." Muster roll for September/October 1864, reports him present. POW captured Blakeley, Alabama, on April 9, 1865. He was received at Ship Island, Mississippi, on April 15, 1864, and sent to Vicksburg, Mississippi, for exchange on May 1, 1864.

Weatherly, ?, Pvt. Co. C

He appears on a regimental return for June 1862.

Weatherly, W. H., Pvt./Corporal see **Weaterly, William**

Weatherly, William, Pvt./Corporal Co. D

Enlisted on October 13, 1861, at Mobile, Alabama, by Captain Butt for one year. His name appears on a regimental return for June 1862, sent to interior hospital at the evacuation of Corinth. He appears present on a company muster roll for bounty on September 24, 1862, refused to take the bounty. Company muster rolls for November/December 1862, July/August 1863 and September/October 1863, all report him present. Muster roll for November/December 1863, reports him absent went on furlough. Muster roll for September/October 1864, reports him present.

Webb, A. T., Pvt. Co. C

Enlisted September 21, 1863, at Point Clear, Alabama, by Captain Smith for three years or the war. Company muster roll for September/October 1864, reports him absent at hospital in Mobile since October 25, 1863. He was admitted to Post Hospital at Fort Morgan, Alabama, on January 14, 1864, with erysipelas and returned to duty on January 21, 1864. POW captured at Fort Gaines, Alabama, on August 8, 1864. He was admitted to St. Louis USA General Hospital at New Orleans on August 25, 1865, with fever and diarrhoea and returned to prison on September 13, 1864, age 18. He was received at Ship Island, Mississippi, from New Orleans on October 25, 1864, and exchanged at Ship Island on January 5, 1865. POW surrendered at Citronelle, Alabama, by Lt. General Taylor on May 4, 1865, and paroled at Meridian, Mississippi, May 13, 1865. His residence was shown as Marengo County, Alabama.

Webb, B., Pvt. Co. C

Enlisted on March 21, 1863, at Choctaw Bluff, Alabama, by Captain Smith for three years or the war. Muster rolls for May/June 1863 and September/October 1863, report him present.

Webb, E. P., Pvt. Co. K

Enlisted on October 13, 1861, at Mobile, Alabama, by Captain Stewart for twelve months. He appears present on a company muster roll for bounty on September 24, 1862. Company muster roll for November/December 1862, reports him present. There is a pay voucher in his file.*

Webb, John, Pvt. Co. B

Enlisted on October 13, 1861, at Mobile, Alabama, by Captain Stewart for twelve months. His name appears on a regimental return for June 1863. He appears on a report for June 28, 1863, near Tupelo, Mississippi, sent away on the evacuation of Corinth, Mississippi, around June 1. He appears present on a company muster roll for bounty on September 24, 1862. Company muster roll for March/April 1863, reports him absent under arrest at Choctaw Bluff, Alabama. Muster roll for May/June 1863, reports him present. Muster roll for September/October 1863, reports him present sick in quarters. He is on a list of soldiers at Post Hospital at Fort Morgan as an assistant cook for November 6, 1683, to January 2, 1864. He returned to his company on January 2, 1864. He was admitted to Post Hospital at Fort Morgan on January 7, 1864, with int. fev. and returned to duty on January 12, 1864. There are poor reproductions of legal documents and testimony in his file.*

Webb, Mahon, Pvt. Co. F

Enlisted on February 27, 1864, at Selma, Alabama, by J. D. Burke for the war. He appears on a register and a list of wounded POW's at City Hospital at Mobile, Alabama. He was surrendered by Lt. General Richard Taylor on April 12, 1865, and paroled on May 11, 1865, at Mobile. He was admitted to Marine General Hospital at Mobile, Alabama, on June 7, 1865, with int. fever and released on June 18, 1865. His residence shown as Marengo County, Alabama.

Weeks, D. A., Pvt. Co. K

Enlisted May 20, 1862, at Fort Morgan, Alabama, by Captain Dorgan for the war. Company muster roll July/August 1864, for Co. A 1st Regiment Louisiana Heavy Artillery (Regulars) reports, attached to Co. K, 21st Alabama. Company muster roll for September/October 1864, reports him present attached to Regiment Co. K, 21st Alabama.

Weeks, Noah H., Pvt. Co. A

Enlisted on September 17, 1862, at (Hillsboro) Shelby County, Alabama, by N. J. Davis for three years or the war. Company muster roll for December 31, 1862, to April 30, 1863, reports him present as does May/June 1863, roll. Muster roll for September/October 1863, reports him absent sent to General Hospital in Mobile on July 25, 1863. Muster roll for September/October 1864, reports him present. He appears on a hospital muster roll as a patient for July 1, to December 31, 1863, admitted to French's Division Hospital at Shelby Springs, Alabama, on December 7, 1863. He also appears on a register of 1st Mississippi, CSA Hospital at Jackson, Mississippi, admitted on December 7, 1863, febris inter. tert. and returned to duty on September 11, 1864. POW surrendered at Citronelle, Alabama, by Lt. General Taylor on May 4, 1865, and paroled at Meridian, Mississippi, May 13, 1865. Residence shown as Shelby County, Alabama.

Weemes, Lewis H., Pvt. Co. E

Enlisted on October 13, 1861, at Mobile, Alabama, by Captain Chamberlain for the war. His name appears on a report June 28, 1862, near Tupelo, Mississippi, sent to interior hospital by surgeon. He appears present on a company muster roll for bounty on September 24, 1862. Muster roll for November/December 1862, reports that he furnished **A. W. Smith** as a substitute.

Welch, R. W., Pvt. Co. A

His name appears on a regimental return for June 1862, discharged for disability at Corinth, Mississippi, on May 3, 1862.

Wells, Dan C., Pvt. Co. F

His name appears on a regimental return for June 1862, "Tupelo, transferred to Captain Myers Sharpshooters."

Wells, John, Pvt. Co. I

Enlisted on October 13, 1861, at Halls Mill, Alabama, by Major Hessee for the war. POW captured at Pittsburg Landing on April 7, 1862. He appears on a roll of POW's at Camp Douglas, Illinois, on August 1, 1862. J. R. Wells' name appears on a regimental return for June 1862, as company cook. Company muster roll for July/August 1863, reports him present on extra duty with Commissary Department since March 28, 1863. Muster roll for September/October 1863, reports him present. He was admitted to Ross Hospital at Mobile on September 20, 1864, with febris remittens and returned to duty on September 25, 1864. Muster roll for September/October reports him absent sent to Hospital Canty by Doctor on October 30, 1864. *Some confusing data in this file.*

Wells, J. R., Pvt. Co. I see **Wells, John**

Welsh, Maurice, Pvt. Co. B
Enlisted on October 13, 1861, at Mobile, Alabama, by Major Hessee for twelve months. He appears present on a company muster roll for bounty on September 24, 1862, "not interested in bounty." His name appears on a regimental return for June 1862, Surgeon's Certificate. He appears on a report June 28, 1862, near Tupelo, Mississippi, sent away on the evacuation about June 1, 1862. He was paid $44 for service. His pay voucher is in his file.*

Welsh, William H., Pvt. Co. A
Enlisted on March 4, 1862, at Mobile, Alabama, by Captain Jewett for the war. His name appears on a regimental return for June 1862, sent to hospital at Mobile, Alabama, on May 26. He appears on a report for June 28, 1862, near Tupelo, Mississippi, sent to Corinth Hospital from there to interior. He appears absent sick on a company muster roll for bounty on September 24, 1862. Company muster rolls for December 31, 1862, to April 30, 1863 and May/June 1863, report him absent on Surgeon's Certificate April 11, 1863. Muster roll for September/October 1863, reports him present. He was admitted to Post Hospital at Fort Morgan on January 17, 1864, with int. fev. and returned to duty on January 5, 1864. POW captured at Fort Morgan, Alabama, on August 23, 1864. He was admitted to St. Louis USA General Hospital at New Orleans on September 10, 1864, with scurvy and returned to prison on October 5, 1864. He was received at Ship Island, Mississippi, from New Orleans on October 7, 1864. He was sent to New York on November 5, 1864. He was received at Fort Columbus, New York Harbor, from Ship Island on November 16, 1864. He was received at Elmira, New York, on November 19, 1864. Released in May 1865. There is paperwork in his file.*

Wearners, Auguste, Pvt. Co. H
He appears on a report for June 28, 1862, near Tupelo, Mississippi, "lost one gun, not been heard from for a time, supposed to have fallen into hands of the enemy." He appears on a register as having been discharged due to disability on August 22, 1862. Born in Germany.

Werthman, John E., Pvt. Co. A
Enlisted on October 13, 1861, at Mobile, Alabama, by Major Hessee. Wounded in left thigh at Shiloh on April 6, 1862, at 8:45 A. M. at camp. His name appears on regimental return for June 1862, wounded at Shiloh and furloughed since April 9, 1862. Company muster roll for September 24, 1862, reports him absent sick. His name appears on a report for June 28, 1862, near Tupelo, Mississippi, wounded at Shiloh and is at

MOBILE CONFEDERATES

Mobile Hospital. Paid $17.50 for rations while on furlough from May 22, to July 30, 1862.

Wertmeyer, Samuel E., Pvt. Co. E
Wounded in the abdomen at Shiloh on April 6, 1862, at 8:30 A. M. at 1st Camp. Claim filed for deceased solder on August 4, 1862, at Mobile, Alabama, by May Wertmeyer his widow.

Wetherford, J. D., Pvt. Co. K
Enlisted on October 2, 1863, at Camden, Alabama, by Major Stone for the war. Discharged on October 21, 1863, by Major General Maury. Company muster roll for September/October 1863, reports him never paid and discharged.

Wheatley, William, Pvt. Co. F
POW captured at Spanish Fort, Alabama, on April 8, 1865. He was received at Ship Island, Mississippi, on April 10, 1865, and transferred to Vicksburg, Mississippi, for exchange on May 1, 1865.

Wheatley, W. J., Pvt. Co. F
POW captured at Fort Gaines, Alabama, on August 8, 1864. He was received at Ship Island, Mississippi, on October 25, 1864, from New Orleans and exchanged at Ship Island on January 4, 1865.

Wheelas, W. A., Pvt. Co. C see **Wheeles, W. A.**

Wheeler, Christopher, Pvt. Co. I
Enlisted on October 7, 1861, at Halls Mill, Alabama, by Captain Taylor to serve twelve months. Discharged due to disability from a inguinal hernia on January 28, 1862, at Fort Gaines, Alabama. Born in Perry County, Mississippi, age 39, five foot nine inches, light complexion, gray eyes, brown hair, in coal business when enlisted.

Wheeler, Simson, Pvt. Co. I
Enlisted on October 13, 1861, at Halls Mill, Alabama, by Major Hessee for the war. Wounded slightly in the cheek at Shiloh on April 6, 1862, at 2 P. M while advancing. He appears present on a company muster roll for bounty on September 24, 1862, refused to take the bounty claiming to be over age. His name appears on a return for November 1862, sent with leave November 27, 1862, four days at Mobile. A return for December, 1862, shows him detailed as clerk to Chaplin. Muster rolls for July/August 1863 and September/October 1863, report him present, detailed as Assistant to Post Chaplin on December 8, 1862. He was admitted to Post Hospital at Fort Morgan on July 31, 1864, with int. feb. tert. and returned to duty on August 6, 1864. POW captured at Fort Morgan, Alabama, on August 23, 1864. He was sent to New York from New Orleans in September 1864. He was received at Elmira, New York, on October 8, 1864. *It is not possible to read part of copy of his record.*

Wheeles, M. A., Pvt. Co. C see **Wheeles, W. A.**

Wheeles, W. A., Pvt. Co. C

Enlisted on February 17, 1863, at Marengo County, Alabama, by Lt. Northrup for the war. Company muster roll for December 31, 1862, to April 30, 1863, reports him present. Company muster rolls for May/June 1863 and September/October 1863, report him present. POW captured at Fort Gaines, Alabama, on August 8, 1864. He was received at Ship Island, Mississippi, on October 25, 1864, from New Orleans and exchanged at Ship Island on January 4, 1865. POW surrendered by Lt. General Richard Taylor in May 1865, and paroled at Demopolis, Alabama, on May 10, 1865. He was shown as a resident of Clarke County, Alabama.

Whitstone, William D., Sgt. Co. D

Enlisted on October 13, 1861, at Mobile, Alabama, by Captain Butt for one year. He appears present on a company muster roll for bounty on September 24, 1862. Company muster roll for November/December 1862, July/August 1863 and September/October 1863, all report him present. He was promoted from 5th to 3rd Sergeant in December 1862. Muster roll for September/October 1864, reports him absent sent to general hospital on October 10, 1864. He was admitted to Ross Hospital at Mobile on October 10, 1864, with febris intermittens tert. and sent to General Hospital at Greenville on October 25, 1864, He appears on a muster roll at Ladies' Hospital at Montgomery, Alabama, in November, 1864, as a patient. POW he was paroled at Headquarters of the 16th US Army Corps at Montgomery on May 23, 1865. Hazel eyes, five foot nine inches, dark hair, light complexion. His parole is in his file.*

Whitacre, S., Pvt. Co. F

He was killed at Shiloh on April 6, 1862, at 4 P. M.

Whitbeck, Henry, Pvt. Co. K

Enlisted on October 13, 1861, at Baldwin County, Alabama, by Captain McCoy for the war. He was mortally wounded in the head at Battle of Shiloh on April 6, 1862, in the A. M. attack on the 1st Battery and captured at the hospital. He was admitted to USA Hospital No. 6 at Louisville, Kentucky, with gunshot wound on April 18, 1862, sent to prison hospital on June 24, 1862. He was received and placed in confinement at Camp Chase, Ohio, from Louisville on June 28, 1862. Age 19, six foot one and one half inches, blue eyes, light hair, born in Marengo County, Alabama. He was transferred from Camp Chase to Vicksburg, Mississippi, for exchange on August 25, 1862. He arrived near Vicksburg aboard the steamer *John H. Done* among 1020, prisoners. He appears present on a company muster roll for March 1, to June 30, 1863. Company muster roll for September/October 1863, reports him absent detached to fish by General Maury.

Whitbee, William, Pvt. Co. F

Enlisted on October 13, 1861, at Baldwin County, Alabama, by Captain McCoy for one year. He appears on a report for June 28, 1862, near Tupelo, Mississippi, wounded at Shiloh and furloughed on surgeons certificate on April 8. Sent from Corinth Hospital to interior hospital on May 28, 1862. He appears present on a company muster roll for bounty on September 24, 1862. He appears present on a company muster roll for March 1, to June 30, 1863, lost one canteen at 25 cents. Company muster roll for

September/October 1863, reports him absent detached to fish by General Maury on August 23, 1863. POW captured at Fort Gaines, Alabama, on August 8, 1864. He was received at Ship Island, Mississippi, from New Orleans on October 25, 1864, and exchanged at Ship Island on January 5, 1865. POW surrendered by Lt. General Richard Taylor at Citronelle, Alabama, on May 4, 1865, and paroled at Meridian, Mississippi, on May 13, 1865.

White, James S., Pvt. Co. A

POW captured at Fort Morgan, Alabama, on August 23, 1864. He was admitted to St. Louis USA General Hospital at New Orleans on August 26, 1864, with diarrhoea and returned to confinement on September 9, 1864. He was sent to New York from New Orleans on September 27, 1864, and received at Elmira, New York, on October 8, 1864. He was paroled at Elmira, New York, for exchange on March 2, 1864, and sent to James River. He was admitted to Receiving and Wayside Hospital No. 9 at Richmond, Virginia on March 8, 1864, and died of chronic diarrhoea and pneumonia on March 12, 1865.

White, Robert, Pvt. Co. A/K

Enlisted at Fort Gaines, Alabama, on January 13, 1862, by Lt. Cayce for the war. Wounded in his right leg at Shiloh on April 6, at 2:30 P. M. His name appears on a regimental return for June, 1862, wounded at Shiloh and furloughed on April 10, 1862. He appears absent detached at hospital in Mobile on a company muster roll for bounty on September 24, 1862. Muster roll for December 31, 1862, to April 30, 1863, reports him as Sgt. absent detailed November 10, 1864, at Ordinance Department at Choctaw Bluff. Muster roll for May/June 1964, report him as Sgt. present detailed on November 10, 1864, at Fort Stonewall (*near Choctaw Bluff*) by order of General Slaughter. Muster roll for September/October, 1863, reports him absent and reduced from 3rd Sgt. to ranks on September 1, 1863, attached July 30, 1863, with Ordinance Department at Fort Stonewall. He appears on a voucher for pay for January 1864, at Forts Stonewall and Sidney Johnston in Ordnance Service. Muster roll for September/October 1864, reports him absent as Battery Sgt Fort Tracy at August? 15, 1864. POW surrendered with Co. K, commanded by William L. Brainard at Citronelle, Alabama, by Lt. General Richard Taylor on May 4, 1865, and paroled at Meridian, Mississippi, on May 10, 1865. There is paper work in his file.*

White, Thomas, Pvt. Co. F

Enlisted on August 29, 1862, at Jefferson County, Alabama, by W. T. Poole for three years or the war. He appears present on company muster rolls for March 1, to June 30, 1863 and September/October 1863. From a hospital muster roll for March/April 1864, employed as a nurse at Post Hospital at Fort Morgan in November 1863, returned to his company on January 25, 1864, (here he is show as enlisting on August 28, 1862, at Blount County, Alabama). He was admitted to Ross Hospital at Mobile on January 16, 1864, with debility and returned to duty on January 20, 1864. POW captured at Fort Gaines, Alabama, on August 8, 1864. He was received at Ship Island, Mississippi, from New Orleans on October 25, 1864, and exchanged at Ship Island on January 5, 1865. He was admitted to Ross Hospital at Mobile, on April 2, 1865, with hypertrophia cardio (enlarged heart) and returned to duty on April 7, 1865. POW he was surrendered with

Co. F commanded by Captain Gwin at Citronelle, Alabama, by Lt. General Richard Taylor on May 4, 1865, and paroled at Meridian, Mississippi, on May 13, 1865. His residence as shown as Jefferson County, Alabama, on his parole.

Whitfield, Gains, Pvt./Sgt. Co. C

Enlisted on January 2, 1862, at Fort Gaines, Alabama, by Captain Rembert for three years or the war. He appears present on a company muster roll for December 31, 1862, to April 30, 1863. Muster roll for May/June 1863, reports him present, lost cartridge box at $2.50, waist belt at 75 cents, cap pouch at $1, plate, ? cartridges, 12 caps at $1 and bayonet, scabbard at $1. Muster roll for September/October 1863, reports him absent detached ACS Department August 22, 1863, by order of General Maury. He appears July 29, 1864, on a list of employees of Major H. R. Whitfiled, at Meridian Mississippi, as a clerk assigned on September 23, 1863. He had a surgeon's certificate of disability that is in his file. POW he was surrendered with detached units commanded by Major Girard at Citronelle, Alabama, by Lt. General Richard Taylor on May 4, 1865, and paroled at Meridian, Mississippi, May 10, 1865. His residence was shown as Marengo County, Alabama, on his parole. There is paper work in his file.*

Whiting, Nathan, 1st Lt. 2nd Lt. Co. A

Mustered into state service on April 1, 1861, and enlisted in Confederate Service on October 13, 1861, and elected 2nd Lt. on April 26, 1861. He resigned on March 20, 1862. He appears present on a return from Fort Gaines, Alabama, for November 1861. He was paid $160 for service for January and February 1862.

Whiting, S. (Samuel) C., Pvt./2nd Corp. Co. I

Enlisted on October 13, 1861, at Halls Mill, Alabama, by Major Hessee for the war. His name appears on a report for November 1862, "went with leave to Mobile for four days from November 4". He appears present on a company muster roll for bounty on September 24, 1862. Company muster rolls for July/August 1863 and September/October 1863, report him present. POW captured at Fort Gaines, Alabama, on August 8, 1864. He was received at Ship Island, Mississippi, from New Orleans on October 25, 1864, and exchanged at Ship Island on January 5, 1865.

Whitley, J. B., Pvt. Co. C

POW he was surrendered with a detachment of CSA Army at Citronelle, Alabama, by Lt. General Richard Taylor in May 1865, and paroled on June 9, 1865, at Demopolis, Alabama. His residence is shown as Marengo County, Alabama.

Whitly, J. M., Pvt. Co. C

His name appears on a regimental return for June 1862, June 12, Tupelo, transferred to Captain Myers Sharpshooters.

Whitly, W. B., Pvt. Co. F see **Witbee, William**

Wiena, Ant., Pvt. Co. G

His name appears on a regimental return for June 1862, sent to interior hospital June 28.

Wier, Robert G., Pvt. Co. G

Enlisted on October 13, 1861, at Mobile, Alabama, by Major Hessee for twelve months. His name appears on a regimental return for June 1862, as a clerk at Regimental A. C. S. He appears absent on a company muster roll for bounty on September 24, 1862, detached as hospital steward on August 5, 1862, on order of General Forney. Muster rolls for December 31, 862, to April 30, 1863, May/June 1863 and September/October 1863, all report him absent with the same notation. There are a number of Hospital Muster rolls from General Hospital Mobile and General Hospital Ross at Mobile from July 1862, until February 1864, that have his name listed on the roll. There is paper work in his file.*

Wignier, George, Pvt. Co. G

He was paid for service in May, and June, 1862, and he appears on two other receipt rolls for payment for commutation of rations. There is paperwork in his file.*

Wilder, Edward B.

Payment of claim for deceased soldier was made to Caleb Wilder his father on March 28, 1863.

Wilkinson, H. W., Pvt. Co. K

Enlisted on October 14, 1863, at Fort Morgan, Alabama, by Captain Dorgan for the war. Company muster roll for September/October 1863, reports him present and never been paid. POW captured at Fort Gaines, Alabama, on August 8, 1864. He was sent to New Orleans as a prisoner and signed an Oath of Allegiance to the USA on December 27, 1764. He is shown on a register of POW's at New Orleans confined on August 12, 1864, "deserter from the 21st Alabama". There is correspondence in his file about his Aunt who lived in New Orleans as that was his home as well. There are several communications in his file.*

Willard, Joseph, Pvt. Co. I

Enlisted on August 12, 1863, at Fort Morgan, Alabama, by Lt. Donovan for the war. He appears present on company muster rolls for July/August 1863 and September/October 1863. He was admitted to Post Hospital at Fort Morgan on September 5, 1863, with neuralgia and returned to duty on September 7, 1863. Company muster roll for September/October 1864, reports him absent sent to Hospital Moore on October 23, 1864.

Williams, ?, Pvt. Co. H

Enlisted on October 13, 1861, at Mobile, Alabama, by Major Hessee to serve twelve months. POW captured on April 8, 1862, at Pittsburg Landing. Discharged due to disability, age 34, five foot five inches, dark complexion, dark eyes, brown hair, a laborer by occupation.

Williams, Caleb, J., 1st Sgt. Co. C
Discharged.

Williams, C. C., Pvt. Co. C
Enlisted on February 11, 1863, at Choctaw Bluff, Alabama, by Captain Smith for three years or the war. He appears present on a company muster roll for December 31, 1862, to April 30, 1864. He was admitted to Post Hospital at Fort Morgan on January 24, 1864, with int. fev. and sent to general hospital on January 29, 1864. Muster roll for May/June 1864, reports him present sick in quarters. Muster roll for September/October 1863, reports him absent on furlough from October 28, 1863. POW captured at Fort Gaines, Alabama, on August 8, 1864. He was received at Ship Island, Mississippi, from New Orleans on October 25, 1864, and exchanged at Ship Island on January 5, 1865. POW surrendered with Company C commanded by Captain F. N. Smith at Citronelle, Alabama, by Lt. General Richard Taylor on May 4, 1865, and paroled at Meridian, Mississippi, on May 13, 1865. His residence is shown as Sumter County, Alabama.

Williams, C. H., Pvt./Sgt. Co. D see **Williams, Charles**

Williams, Charles (H.), Pvt./Sgt. Co. D
Enlisted on October 13, 1861, at Mobile, Alabama, by Captain Butt for the war. His name appears on a report for June 1861, sent to interior hospital at the evacuation of Corinth. He appears present on a company muster roll for bounty on September 24, 1862. Muster roll for November/December 1862, reports him present and promoted from Private to 4th Corporal on December 1, 1862. Company muster rolls for July/August 1863, September/October 1863 and November/December 1863, all report him present.

Williams, Charles, B., Pvt. Co. D
Killed at Shiloh on April 6, 1861, in the P. M. at the Old Field. Shot through the head. This is filed with Charles Williams above.

Williams, Charles M., Pvt. Co. A
He appears present on a company muster roll for bounty on September 24, 1862, refused to take bounty. He appears absent on company muster roll for September/October 1863, sent to General Hospital at Mobile on October 25, 1863. POW captured at Fort Morgan, Alabama, on August 23, 1864. He was admitted to St. Louis USA General Hospital at New Orleans on August 30, 1864, with intermittent fever and returned to confinement on September 27, 1864. He was received at Elmira, New York, from New Orleans on October 8, 1864. He signed the Oath of Allegiance to the USA on June 21, 1865, and was released at Elmira. Residence Mobile, Alabama, blue eyes, fair complexion, dark hair, and five foot ten and one half inches.

Williams, Daniel J., Corp., Co. G
Enlisted on August 25, 1862, at Henry County, Alabama, by Lt. Henry for the war. He appears absent on a company muster roll for September/October 1864, absent on fifteen-day furlough, promoted from the ranks on September 1, 1864. POW surrendered at Citronelle, Alabama, by Lt. General Richard Taylor on May 4, 1865, and paroled at

Meridian, Mississippi, on May 13, 1865. Residence shown as Abbeville, Henry County, Alabama.

Williams, E., Pvt./Sgt. Co. C

Enlisted on November 28, 1861, at Fort Gaines, Alabama, by Captain Rembert for twelve months. His name appears on a regimental return for June 1862, absent on sick furlough. He appears present on a company muster roll for bounty on September 24, 1862. He appears on a report near Tupelo, Mississippi, June 28, 1862, sent to interior hospital from Corinth. Company muster roll for December 31, 1862, to April 30, 1863, reports him present. Muster roll for May/June 1863, reports him present and promoted to 3rd Sergeant from the ranks on June 6, 1863. Muster roll for September/October 1863, reports him present. POW captured at Fort Gaines, Alabama, on August 8, 1864. He was received at Ship Island, Mississippi, from New Orleans on October 25, 1864, and exchanged at Ship Island on January 5, 1865.

Williams, F. D., Pvt. Co. D see **Williams, Fred**

Williams, Fred, Pvt. Co. D

Enlisted on October 13, 1861, at Mobile, Alabama, by Captain Butt for one year. He appears present on a company muster roll for bounty on September 24, 1862. His name appears on a regimental return for June 1862, sent to interior hospital at the evacuation of Corinth. Company muster rolls for November/December 1862, July/August 1863 and September/October 1864, all report him present. Company muster rolls for November/December 1863 and November/December 1864, report him present on daily duty as company cook. He was admitted to Post Hospital at Fort Morgan, Alabama, on April 27, 1863, with ulcer and returned to duty on May 4, 1863.

Williams, James M., 2nd Lt./Lt. Colonel

Mustered in to Confederate service on October 13, 1861. He was elected Captain on March 21, 1862, and promoted on May 8, 1862. His name appears on a regimental return for June 1862, present at Tupelo, Mississippi, elected Captain at organization. He was elected Major on August 30, 1862, He appears on a field return from Fort Morgan shown as a loss as he was transferred to Choctaw Bluff, Alabama, on October 6, 1862. Field and Staff muster roll for July/August 1863, reports him absent promoted to Lt. Colonel on May 1, 1863. F & S muster rolls for September/October 1863 and March/April 1864, report him present. He appears on several rolls of Non-com Staff of 1st Battalion Alabama Artillery, July/August 1863, September/October 1863, and April 30, 1864, certification as Inspection and Investigating Officer. He was paid $130 per month as Captain of Co. A and $170 per month as Lt. Colonel. *There is considerable paper work in his file that has reproduced poorly and not readable.* See **From that Terrible Field – Civil War Letters of James M. Williams**, published by The University Press, edited by John Kent Folmar.*

Williams, John, Drummer Co. D

Enlisted on October 13, 1861, at Mobile, Alabama, by Captain Butt for one year. His name appears on a regimental return for June 1862, sent to interior hospital at evacuation (of Corinth) Company muster rolls for November/December 1862, July/August 1863, September/October 1863, November/December 1863 and September/October 1864, all show him present. He was admitted to Ross Hospital at Mobile, Alabama, with febris intermittens tert. on October 10, 1864, and returned to duty on October 28, 1864. POW surrendered at Citronelle, Alabama, by Lt. General Richard Taylor on May 4, 1865, and paroled at Meridian, Mississippi, on May 13, 1865. Residence shown as Autauga County, Alabama.

Williams Jr., John B., 3rd Sgt. Co. E/Field and Staff
Enlisted on October 13, 1861, at Mobile, Alabama, by Captain Chamberlain for twelve months. A regimental return for June 1862, shows him 3rd Sgt. Co. E, May 19, Corinth, Mississippi, Ordnance Sergeant. Field and Staff muster roll for July/August 1863, reports him absent, on sick leave for 15 days. Field & Staff muster rolls for September/October 1863 and March/April 1864, reports him present. POW captured at Fort Gaines, Alabama, on August 8, 1864. He was admitted to St. Louis USA General Hospital in New Orleans on September 29, 1864, with fever remit. and returned to confinement on October 8, 1864. He was received at Ship Island, Mississippi, from New Orleans on October 25, 1864, and exchanged at Ship Island on January 5, 1865. There are several pay vouchers and his parole in his file.*

Williams, John G., Pvt. Co. C see **Williams, John S.**

Williams, John S., Pvt. Co. C
Enlisted on October 13, 1861, at Mobile, Alabama, by Captain Rembert for twelve months. He appears on a regimental return for June 1862, as regimental teamster. He appears present on a company muster roll for bounty on September 24, 1862. Muster roll for December 31, 1862, to April 30, 1864, reports him present. May/June 1863, muster roll reports him present, lost one canteen at 25 cents, one strap at 20 cents and one haversack at 20 cents. Muster roll for September/October 1863, reports him present and lost one haversack at $1. He was admitted to Ross Hospital in Mobile on January 28, 1864, with bronchitis and sent to General Hospital at Montgomery, Alabama, on February 17, 1864. POW captured at Fort Gaines, Alabama, on August 8, 1864. He was received at Ship Island, Mississippi, from New Orleans on October 25, 1864, and exchanged at Ship Island on January 5, 1865. POW surrendered at Citronelle, Alabama, by Lt. General Richard Taylor on May 4, 1865, and paroled at Meridian, Mississippi, on May 13, 1865. His residence was shown as Demopolis, Alabama.

Williams, J. T. F., Pvt. Co. B
Enlisted on October 13, 1861, at Mobile, Alabama, by Captain Butt for twelve months. He appears present on a company muster roll for bounty on September 24, 1862, refused to take bounty. Muster roll for November/December 1862, reports him present. POW captured at Blakeley, Alabama, on April 9, 1865. He was received at Ship Island, Mississippi, on April 15, 1865, and transferred to Vicksburg, Mississippi, for exchange on May 1, 1865. There are pay vouchers in his file.*

Williams, Junius, F., Pvt.? Corp. Co. A

Enlisted on October 13, 1861, at Mobile, Alabama, by Major Hessee for twelve months. He was captured on the ambulance squad at Shiloh Hospital on April 7, 1862, and exchanged. He appears present on a company muster roll for bounty on September 24, 1862. Muster rolls for December 31, 1862, to April 30, 1863 and May/June 1863, report him present. Muster roll for September/October 1863, reports him present and promoted to 3rd Corporal from the ranks. POW captured at Fort Morgan, Alabama, on August 23, 1864. He was sent to Elmira, New York, on October 8, 1864, from New Orleans. He signed and swore to the Oath of Allegiance to the USA at Elmira on June 14, 1865, and released. Residence shown as New Orleans, Louisiana, florid complexion, auburn hair, blue eyes, five foot nine inches. There is a pay voucher in his file.*

Williams, N. P., Pvt. Co. C

POW surrendered at Citronelle, Alabama, by Lt. General Richard Taylor in May 1865, paroled at Demopolis, Alabama, on June 9, 1865. Residence shown as Marengo County, Alabama.

Williams, William J., Corporal Co. G

POW captured at Fort Gaines, Alabama, on August 8, 1864. He was received at Ship Island, Mississippi, from New Orleans on October 25, 1864, where he applied to take the Oath of Allegiance to the USA. He was exchanged at Ship Island on January 4, 1865. POW surrendered with Co. G commanded by Edward Spalding at Citronelle, Alabama, by Lt. General Richard Taylor on May 4, 1865, and paroled at Meridian, Mississippi, on May 13, 1865. Residence shown as Curaton's Bridge, Henry County, Alabama.

Williams, W. P., Pvt. Co. D

Enlisted on March 15, 1861, at Selma, Alabama, by Captain Gee for three years. Company muster rolls for July/August 1863, September/October 1863 and November/December 1863, all report him present. He was admitted to Ross Hospital at Mobile, Alabama, on May 17, 1864, with anasarca (dropsy) and returned to duty on June 20, 1864. Muster roll for September/October 1864, reports him absent sent to General Hospital in Mobile on September 17, 1864. He was admitted to General Hospital (Soldiers Home Hospital) Shelby Springs, Alabama, from October 1, to October 13, 1864, with fever int. quotidian. He was admitted to 1st Mississippi USA Hospital at Jackson, Mississippi, on September 25, 1864, with typhoid dysenteria, and transferred on October 19, 1864. POW surrendered with Provost Guard, Clerks, and Couriers commanded by Lt. R. H. Douglas at Citronelle, Alabama, by Lt. General Richard Taylor on May 4, 1865, and paroled at Meridian, Mississippi, on May 13, 1865. His residence was shown as Selma, Alabama.

Williams, W., Pvt. Co. A

Captured at Fort Donaldson on February 16, 1862, and sent to Camp Morton, Indiana. Transferred from Camp Morton to Vicksburg, Mississippi, on August 24, 1862, for exchange. Received at Atkins Landing, near Vicksburg on November 10, 1862.

21ST ALABAMA INFANTRY VOLUNTEERS

Williamson, E. S., Pvt. Co. C

Enlisted February 17, 1863, at Marengo County, Alabama, by Lt. Northrup for three years or the war. Company muster roll for December 31, 1862, to April 30, 1863, reports him present. Muster roll for May/June 1863, reports him present sick in quarters. Muster roll for September/October 1863, reports him present. Claim for deceased soldier was filed on October 1, 1864, by Penelope M. Williamson his widow.

Williamson, William, Pvt. Co. B

Enlisted on October 13, 1861, at Mobile, Alabama, by Major Hessee for the war. His name appears on a report for June 28, 1862, near Tupelo, Mississippi, sent to Mobile from Blackland, by advice of Dr. Dubose. He appears present on a company muster roll for bounty on September 24, 1862. Company muster roll for May/June 1863, reports that he was discharged on May 24, 1863, on disability by order of General Maury. There are pay vouchers in his file.*

Willis, E., Pvt. Co. F

His name appears on a list of payments to discharged soldiers. Discharged on July 4, 1862.

Willis, J. S., Pvt. Co. F.

Enlisted on October 13, 1861, at Mobile, Alabama, by Captain McCoy for one year. He appears present on a company muster roll for bounty on September 24, 1862. Company muster roll for March 1, to June 30, 1863, reports him present. Muster roll for September/October 1863, reports him absent detached to fish by General Maury on August 23, 1863. He appears on a muster roll of Sossaman's Detachment for September/October, 1864, detailed at Battery Huger by Colonel Fuller. He was admitted to Ross Hospital at Mobile, Alabama, on October 21, 1864, with febris, intermitten quot. and acute dysentery then returned to duty on October 31, 1864.

Willis, J. W., Pvt. Co. D

Enlisted on October 13, 1861, at Halls Mill, Alabama, by Major Hessee for the war. Company muster roll for September/October 1864, reports him absent sent to General Hospital in Mobile on October 21, 1864. (Assigned to company by order)

Willoughby, A., Pvt. Co. K

Enlisted August 10, 1864, at Mobile, Alabama, by Major Stone for the war. Company muster roll for September/October 1864, reports that he deserted.

Wilmarth, A. M., Pvt. Co. K

Enlisted on October 13, 1861, at Mobile, Alabama, by Captain Stewart for the war. He appears absent detached in Commissary Department on the company muster roll for bounty on September 24, 1862. Muster roll for November/December 1862, reports him absent detached in A. C. S. Department since May 20, 1862. Muster rolls for July/August 1863 and September/October 1863, both show the same notation as preceding roll. Muster roll for September/October 1864, reports him absent detached with A. Q. M. Department. He appears on a report for December 1864, at Chief Clerk at

Marion, Alabama, for the Commissary District of Alabama, December 31, 1864. POW surrendered with Co. K commanded by W. L Bernard at Citronelle, Alabama, by Lt. General Richard Taylor on May 4, 1865, and paroled at Meridian, Mississippi, on May 13, 1865. Residence shown as Meridian Mississippi. There is paperwork in his file.

Wilmarth, A., Pvt. Co. K see **Walmarth, A. M.**

Wilson, Alton, R., Pvt. Co. E
    Enlisted on October 13, 1861, at Mobile, Alabama, by Lt. Chamberlain for the war. He appears present on a company muster roll for bounty on September 24, 1862. Company muster roll for November/December 1862, reports him present. Muster rolls for July/August 1863 and September/October 1863, report him absent detached with Signal Corps from January 5, 1863. POW captured at Fort Morgan, Alabama, on August 23, 1864. Received at Elmira, New York, on October 8, 1864, from New Orleans. He was paroled and transferred for exchange on March 14, 1865. There is paperwork in his file.**

Wilson, A. T., Pvt. Co. E.
    He was admitted to Way Hospital at Meridian, Mississippi, on January 13, 1865, with a wound and furloughed. *This note filed with Wilson, Alton R. above.*

Wilson, E., Pvt. Co. E.
    POW captured at Spanish Fort, Alabama, on April 8, 1865. He was received at Ship Island, Mississippi, on April 10, 1865, and transferred to Vicksburg, Mississippi, for exchange on May 1, 1865.

Wilson, James, Pvt. Co. F.
    Enlisted at Fort Morgan, Alabama, on August 12, 1862, by Captain Dade for the war. He appears present on a company muster roll for bounty on September 24, 1862. Company muster roll for March 1, to June 30, 1863, reports him present. He drew clothing on March 31, 1864.

Wilson, J. G., Pvt. Co. I
    Enlisted at Shelby County, Alabama, on September 17, 1862, by W. I. Davis for the war. Company muster roll for July/August 1863, reports him present. Muster roll for September/October 1863, reports him absent in arrest without leave for two days. POW captured at Fort Gaines, Alabama, on August 8, 1864. He was received at Ship Island, Mississippi, from New Orleans on October 25, 1864. He was to be exchanged at Ship Island, on January 4, 1865, but was left sick in hospital at Ship Island. POW surrendered and paroled among stragglers at Selma, Alabama, in June 1865.

Wilson, J. B., Ordnance Sgt.
    He was admitted to St. Louis USA General Hospital at New Orleans on August 24, 1864, with bronchitis and returned to confinement on October 22, 1864, age 26. *This filed with Wilson, J. G. above.*

Wilson, J. H., Pvt. Co. G/D

POW captured at Fort Gaines, Alabama, on August 8, 1864. He was received at Ship Island, Mississippi, from New Orleans on October 25, 1864. He was exchanged at Ship Island on January 4, 1865. He appears on a roll of soldiers on duty as mechanics or laborers at Mobile employed by Major Henry St. Paul or Major Stone as Engineer on the steamer *Reindeer*. Age 46.

Wilson, W. T., Pvt. Co. I

POW captured at Fort Gaines, Alabama, on August 8, 1864. He was confined at Steam Levee Press No. 4 at New Orleans and sent to St. Louis USA General Hospital at New Orleans on September 28, 1864, with rubeola. He was returned to confinement on October 5, 1864. He was received at Ship Island, Mississippi, from New Orleans on October 25, 1864. He was exchanged at Ship Island on January 4, 1865. He was admitted to Yandell Hospital at Meridian, Mississippi, on April 1, 1865. POW surrendered in hospital by Lt. General Richard Taylor at Citronelle, Alabama, on May 4, 1865, and paroled at Meridian, Mississippi, on May 12, 1865. Residence shown as Montevallo, Alabama.

Winders, J. T., Pvt. Co. C

His name appears on a register of effects of deceased soldiers. Left $42.50.

Wiseman, S. C., Pvt. Co. D

His name appears on a list of Confederate POW's captured and paroled at the Battle of Iuka September 19, 1862, filed at Corinth, Mississippi, on October 13, 1862.

Witherspoon, A. J., Chaplin, Field and Staff

Appointed on November 15, 1861, and resigned on April 23, 1864. He appears on a regimental return for December 1861, as present. POW captured at Pittsburg Landing, Tennessee, on April 7, 1862. He was received at Camp Chase, Ohio, on April 18, 1862, and transferred to Johnson's Island, Ohio, on April 26, 1862, born 1824 in South Carolina. He was released from Johnson's Island Prison by order of the Superintendent in August 1862. Field and Staff muster rolls for July/August 1863 and September/October 1863, report him present. Muster roll for March/April 1864, reports him absent sick on sick furlough extended thirty days from April 18, 1864. He was paid $60 per month. There are pay vouchers in his file.* *Company C The Marengo Rifles or Witherspoon guards from Clarke and Marengo Counties, Alabama is named for this man.*

Witherspoon, P. T., Co. E

POW captured at Fort Gaines, Alabama, on August 8, 1864. He was received at Ship Island, Mississippi, from New Orleans on October 25, 1864. He was exchanged at Ship Island on January 4, 1865. POW surrendered with Co. F commanded by Captain Middleton by Lt. General Richard Taylor at Citronelle, Alabama, on May 4, 1865, and paroled at Meridian, Mississippi, on May 13, 1865. Residence shown as Pontotoc Kemper County, Mississippi. *Records also show R. T, and P. F. Witherspoon.*

Wolf, W. T., Pvt. Co. K

Enlisted on September 10, 1863, at Fort Morgan, Alabama, by Captain Dorgan for the war. He appears present on company muster rolls for November/December 1862, July/August 1863, September/October 1863 and September/October 1864. POW he was surrendered with Co. K commanded by Lt. W. I. Brainard by Lt. General Richard Taylor at Citronelle, Alabama, on May 4, 1865, and paroled at Meridian, Mississippi, on May 13, 1865. His residence was shown as Mobile, Alabama.

Wood, Arthur F., Assistant Surgeon

His name appears on a register of Commissioned Officers of the CSA attached to the 21st Alabama Infantry.

Wood, C. S., Pvt. Co. C.

Enlisted on April 4, 1862, at Corinth, Mississippi, by Captain Rembert for the war. He appears present on a company muster roll for bounty on September 24, 1862. He appears on a regimental return for June 1862, sick on furlough. His name appears on a report June 28, 1862, near Tupelo, Mississippi, sent to interior hospital from Corinth.

Wright, Conoly, Pvt. Co. B

Enlisted September 8, 1862, at Mobile, Alabama, by Captain Johnson for the war. He appears present on a company muster roll for bounty on September 24, 1862. Company muster rolls for May/June 1863 and September/October 1864, report him present. He was admitted to Post Hospital at Fort Morgan, Alabama, on December 29, 1863, with pneumonia and sent to general hospital on January 11, 1865. He was admitted to Ross Hospital at Mobile on January 16, 1864, with debility and returned to duty on February 1, 1865. He signed an Oath of Allegiance to the USA at New Orleans on August 13, 1864, "deserter came into Federal line with the fleet before the capture of Fort Gaines." He took the Oath on August 13, 1864. *There are conflicting dates in this file.*

Wright, A. S., Pvt. Co. H

He was admitted to Ross Hospital, Mobile, Alabama, on August 8, 1864, with februs intermit tert.. and sent to General Hospital at Selma on August 8, 1864.

Wright, E. W., Pvt. Co. F

Company muster roll for March 1, to June 30, 1863, reports that him discharged for disability on May 2, 1863.

Wright, G. W., Pvt. Co. C

POW surrendered by Lt. General Richard Taylor at Citronelle, Alabama, in May 1865, and paroled at Meridian, Mississippi, on May 13, 1865. His residence was shown as Clarke County, Alabama.

Wright, John, Pvt. Co. A

His name appears among a roll of stragglers that were POW's surrendered and paroled at Selma, Alabama, in June 1865. Residence shown as Perry County, Alabama.

21ST ALABAMA INFANTRY VOLUNTEERS

Wright, P. W., Pvt. Co. C see **Wright, V. W.**

Wright, Robert, Pvt. Co. G
POW captured at Fort Gaines, Alabama, on August 8, 1864. He was received at Ship Island, Mississippi, from New Orleans on October 25, 1864 and exchanged at Ship Island on January 4, 1865.

Wright, R. W., Pvt. Co. B
He signed a Parole of Honor at Montgomery, Alabama, on May 30, 1865. His parole is in his file. Five foot three inches, dark hair, gray eyes, dark complexion.*

Wright, S., Pvt. Co. C
POW captured at Fort Gaines, Alabama, on August 8, 1864. He was admitted to St. Louis, USA General Hospital at New Orleans on October 9, 1864, with rubeola, and returned to confinement on October 15, 1864. He was received at Ship Island, Mississippi, from New Orleans on October 25, 1864. He was exchanged at Ship Island on January 4, 1865. POW surrendered by Lt. General Richard Taylor at Citronelle, Alabama, in May 1865, and paroled at Demopolis, Alabama, on June 14, 1865. His residence was shown as Clarke County, Alabama.

Wright, V. W., Pvt. Co. C
Enlisted on October 10, 1863, by Lt. Wragg for three years or the war. He appears present on a company muster roll for September/October 1864. POW captured at Fort Gaines, Alabama, on August 8, 1864. He was admitted to St. Louis USA General Hospital at New Orleans on August 26, 1864, with diarrhoea and returned to confinement on August 29, 1864. He was received at Ship Island, Mississippi, from New Orleans on October 25, 1864. He was exchanged at Ship Island on January 4, 1865.

Wright, Wade, Pvt. Co. G
POW captured at Fort Gaines, Alabama, on August 8, 1864. He was admitted to St. Louis, USA General Hospital at New Orleans on September 26, 1864, with diarrhoea and died on September 30, 1864. He was buried in Monument Cemetery grave No. 399.

Wright, ?, Pvt, Co. C
Enlisted on October 13, 1863, at Mobile, Alabama, by Captain Rembert for one year. His name appears on a report June 28, 1862, near Tupelo, Mississippi, sent to interior hospital. He appears present on a company muster roll for bounty on September 24, 1862. Muster roll for December 31, 1862, to April 30, 1863, reports him absent detached in Engineering Department at Choctaw Bluff. May/June 1863, muster roll reports him present detached in Engineering Department on May 25, sick in quarters.

Wunns, A., Pvt. Co. H
His name appears on a regimental return for June 1862.

Wynn, E., Pvt. Co. F

Enlisted on February 23, 1863, at Choctaw Bluff, Alabama, by Captain Dade for the war. He appears on a company muster roll for March 1, to June 30, 1863. Muster roll for September/October 1863, reports that he deserted from Point Clear, Alabama, on September? 11, 1863, carrying off gun, knapsack, haversack, canteen, and ? rounds of cartridges.

[*From Mobile Register and Advertiser Sunday April 2, 1865*] *Privates **Elam** and **Winn** of the 21st Alabama Regiment were shot to death with musketry at Blakeley at 6 o'clock P. M. on Friday – These men deserted to the enemy some time since but were subsequently apprehended, tired, condemned, as suffered the extreme penalty of the law, as above stated.*]

Y

Yancey, Fred, Corporal Co. F

His name appears on a regimental return for June 1862. Killed at Shiloh on April 6, 1862, at 8:30 A. M. at 1st Camp. Claim for deceased soldier filed by Amelia Young on October 13, 1864.

Yarborough, E. A., Pvt. Co. I

POW surrendered by Lt. General Richard Taylor at Citronelle, Alabama, in May 1865, and paroled at Meridian, Mississippi, on May 13, 1865. Residence shown as Marengo County, Alabama.

Yarrow, C. S. A., Pvt._

His name appears on a roll of POW's at Camp Douglas, Illinois, on August 1, 1862, captured at Fort Donaldson on February 16, 1862.

Yates, J. A., Pvt. Co. I

Admitted to Hospital in Richmond, Virginia.

Young, William, Pvt. Co. F

Enlisted at Baldwin County, Alabama, by Captain McCoy on October 13, 1861, for one year. He appears present on a company muster roll for bounty on September 24, 1862. Muster roll for March 1, to June 30, 1864, reports him present. Muster roll for September/October 1863, shows him absent detached on duty at Choctaw Bluff. POW captured at Fort Gaines, Alabama, on August 8, 1864. He was admitted to St. Louis, USA General Hospital at New Orleans on August 12, 1864, with gunshot wound, minnie ball fracture radius of left arm and returned to confinement on September 30, 1864. He was admitted again on October 10, 1864, and returned to confinement on October 22. Age 29. He was received at Ship Island, Mississippi, from New Orleans on October 25, 1864. He was exchanged at Ship Island on January 4, 1865.

Yuille, R. L., Pvt._

Enlisted on September 20, 1864, at Mobile, Alabama, by Major Stone for the war. He appears absent on company K muster roll for September/October 1864. Temporarily attached to the company

Z

Zeigler, J. J., Pvt. Co. D. see **Ziegler, J. J.**

Zeigler, W. H., Pvt. Co. D
    Enlisted on February 11, 1864, at Montgomery, Alabama, for the war. He appears absent on a company muster roll for September/October 1864, sent to General Hospital in Mobile. He was paroled at Montgomery in May 1865. His parole is in his file.* Five foot eight inches, dark hair, gray eyes, fair complexion.

Ziegler, J. J., Pvt. Co. D
    Enlisted July 22, 1863, at Montgomery, Alabama, by enrolling officer for the war. Company muster rolls for September/October 1863, and November/December 1863, report him present. Company muster roll for September/October 1863, reports him absent sent to General Hospital in Mobile, on September 26, 1864.

MOBILE CONFEDERATES

APPENDIX

The data supplied here unless otherwise noted is taken from the microfilm rolls of the Compiled Service Records of the 21st Alabama Infantry.

Field and Staff

Crawford, James	Colonel	Resigned April 30, 1862
Anderson, Charles D.	Colonel	
Ingersoll, Andrew J.	Lt. Col.	Resigned March 27, 1862
Cayce, Stewart W.	Lt. Co.	Resigned May 19, 1862
Stewart, Charles, S.	M – Lt. Col.	Killed April 30, 1863
Williams, James M.	M – Lt. Col.	
Stewart, Frederick K.	M	Resigned March 31, 1862
McCoy, F. J.	M	?
Johnson, Charles B.	M	Transferred to V. S. December 22, 1864
Anderson, William H.	Surg.	Transferred November 20, 1861
Beatty, William H.	Surg.	
Redwood, Robert H.	Surg.	Transferred to Price's Army
Payne, John F. Y.	Surg.	Transferred August 5, 1864
? on, B. M.	A. S.	
? , Arthur F.	A. S.	?
Dubose, M. W.	A. S.	
Hawthorn, A. B.	Chap.	Resigned Nov. 12, 1861
Witherspoon, Andrew J.	Chap.	Resigned April 23, 1864
Cluis, Frederick, V.	ACS	Transferred
Lyon, Thomas F. A.	ACS	Transferred March 19, 1862
Vass, Douglas	AQM	Retired August 26, 1864
Cayce, Stewart W.	Adj.	To Lt. Colonel
Vidmer, George	Adj.	
Collins, Charles LeB	Act. Adj.	Temporary
Parker, Gideon	Adj.	

Gibson, John, Major

Company Muster Rolls
Officers
Company A
Washington Light Infantry, No. 2, Mobile

Jewett, John	Captain	Not reelected
Cluie, F. V.	Lt.	To ACS
Whiting, Nathan	2nd Lt.	Not reelected
Williams, John W.	2nd Lt.	Not reelected
Williams, J. M.	2nd Lt. – Capt.	Promoted to Major
Cothran, Jno. F.	2nd Lt. – 1st Lt. – Capt.	
Dixon, Geo. E.	2nd Lt. – 1st Lt.	Died February 17, 1864
Badger, Wm. S.	2nd Lt	To 1st Lt. Co. H
Tell, C. L.	2nd Lt. – 1st Lt.	
Gaggam, H. M.	2nd Lt.	
Bure, Wm. H.	2nd Lt.	

Company B
Montgomery Guards

Johnson, Charles B.	Captain	Promoted to Major
Harmon, Patrick C.	1st Lt. – 2nd Lt.	Not reelected at 1st Lt., appointed 2nd Lt.
Bryne, M.	2nd Lt.	Ditto
Hatton, Thomas, J.	2nd Lt.	Ditto
O'Connor, Jno. F.	1st Lt. – Captain	
Toulmin, Jno. F.	2nd Lt. – 1st Lt.	
Burke, Michel	2nd Lt.	
McCullough, David S.	2nd Lt.	
Carlen, Thos. S.	2nd Lt.	Died August 17/23, 1863

Company A
Washington Light Infantry, No. 2, Mobile

Jewett, John	Captain	Not reelected
Cluie, F. V.	Lt.	To ACS
Whiting, Nathan	2nd Lt.	Not reelected
Williams, John W.	2nd Lt.	Not reelected
Williams, J. M.	2nd Lt. – Capt.	Promoted to Major
Cothran, Jno. F.	2nd Lt. – 1st Lt. – Capt.	
Dixon, Geo. E.	2nd Lt. – 1st Lt.	Died February 17, 1864
Badger, Wm. S.	2nd Lt	To 1st Lt. Co. H
Tell, C. L.	2nd Lt. – 1st Lt.	
Gaggam, H. M.	2nd Lt.	
Bure, Wm. H.	2nd Lt.	

Company B
Montgomery Guards

Johnson, Charles B.	Captain	Promoted to Major
Harmon, Patrick C.	1st Lt. – 2nd Lt.	Not reelected at 1st Lt., appointed 2nd Lt.
Bryne, M.	2nd Lt.	Ditto
Hatton, Thomas, J.	2nd Lt.	Ditto
O'Connor, Jno. F.	1st Lt. – Captain	
Toulmin, Jno. F.	2nd Lt. – 1st Lt.	
Burke, Michel	2nd Lt.	
McCullough, David S.	2nd Lt.	
Carlen, Thos. S.	2nd Lt.	Died August 17/23, 1863

Company C
Marengo Rifles or Witherspoon Guards

Rembert, J. M.	Captain	Died on April 8, 1862
Rogers, Thomas, W.	1st Lt.	Resigned July 6, 1862
Poellnitz, Bruno B.	2nd Lt.	Resigned July 6, 1862
Luther, J. G. M.	2nd Lt.	Dr. July 22, 1862
Smith, Frank N.	Captain	
Northrup, Albert	2nd Lt. – 1st Lt.	
Pollinitz, Edwin A.	2nd Lt.	
McLeod, A. D.	2nd Lt.	Died October 1863
Pollinitz, J. A.	2nd Lt.	

Company D
Battle Guards

Butt, Cary W.	Captain	Resigned August 13, 1862
Deas, Henry A.	1st Lt.	Not reelected
Savage, Thos. J.	2nd Lt. – 1st Lt.	
Butt, Melville C.	2nd Lt. – 1st Lt. – Capt.	
Cogburn, Jno. D.	2nd Lt.	
Demony, L. P.	2nd Lt.	
Minnia, James W.	2nd Lt.	To Co. H
Williams, Chas. H.	2nd Lt.	

Company E
Chamberlain Rifles – Woodruff Rifles or Mobile Rifles No. 2

Chamberlin, Jno. C.	Captain	Resigned May 2, 1862.
Barker, G. M.	1st Lt.	Not reelected

21ST ALABAMA INFANTRY VOLUNTEERS

Sossaman, Henry	2nd Lt.	Captain
Carrington, A. S.	2nd Lt. – 1st Lt.	To Captain Co. H
Rabby, Peter	2nd	Resigned April 25, 1863
Middleton, Robert	2nd Lt. – 1st Lt.	
Alliman, B. F.	2nd Lt.	
Baldwin, Ralph P.	2nd Lt.	

Company F
Baldwin Rifles No. 2

McCoy, F. J.	Captain	Not reelected
Dade, B. F.	1st Lt. – Captain	
Smith, Franklin N.	2nd Lt – 1st Lt.	To Captain Co. C
Gwin, Geo. B.	2nd Lt. – 1st Lt.	
Gabel, M. V.	2nd Lt.	Failed to pass
Macartney, M. Edwin	2nd Lt.	
Macartney, Thos N.	2nd Lt.	

Company G
Spanish Guards or Southern Star Guards

Festorazzi, A. S.	Captain	Discharged by order of Gen. Bragg
Felix, Sebastian	1st Lt.	Ditto
Horta, Peter	2nd Lt.	Ditto
Sequi, Joquin.	2nd Lt.	Ditto

Headquarters AW June 27, 1862. SO (Special Order) No. 48
The non-commissioned officers and privates of Captain Festorazzi's Co. G, 21st Alabama Regiment are transferred to the 1st Reg. La. Infantry.

Company G
Swanson Guards, No. 1

Spalding, Edward, R.	Captain	March 24, 1864
Donoho, O. C.	1st Lt.	Ditto
Demony, Wm.	2nd Lt.	Ditto
Andrews, W. H.	2nd Lt.	Ditto
Alexander, J. H.	Lt. Comdg.	

This company took the place of Captain Festorazzi's Company that was transferred to 1st La. Inf.

Company H
Swanson Guards, No. 2

Carrington, A. S.	Captain	March 24, 1864
Badger, William S.	1st Lt.	Ditto
Minnia, James M.	2nd Lt.	
Danzey, John M.	2nd Lt.	

This company took the place of Captain DeVaux's Company that was transferred to the 1st La. Infantry.

Company H
French Guards

DeVaux, Chas.	Captain	Dismissed GCM (G. Court Marshal) Oct. 12, 1863
Multra, J. Geo	1st Lt.	Detached by order General Bragg
Collins, Celestin	2nd Lt.	Resigned November 1, 1861
Augustine, Pierre	2nd Lt.	Detached by order of General Bragg

Headquarters AW Special Order No. 48
The non-commissioned officers and privates of Capt. DeVaux's Co. H, 21st Alabama, Infantry is hereby transferred to the 1st Reg. La. Inf.

Company I
United Rangers or Independent Rifles

Taylor, Smith S.	Captain	Died April 17, 1862
Talley, Horace	1st Lt.	Not reelected
Moon, Henry, G.	2nd	Not reelected
Gleason, Thos.	2nd Lt. – Capt.	Discharged
McInnia, M.	1st Lt.	
Crenshaw, M. V.	2nd Lt. – Capt.	
Donoho, O. C.	2nd Lt.	To 1st Lt. Co. G
Dantzler, G. B.	2nd Lt.	
Herbert, T. J.	2nd Lt.	
Thompson, Samuel	1st Lt.	Discharged
Bently, M.	2nd Lt.	Discharged

Company K
Mobile Cadets

Stewart, Chas. S.	Captain	To. Lt. Colonel
Shepherd, Thos. M.	1st Lt.	Killed April 6, 1862
Dorgan, A. P.	2nd Lt.- Capt.	R. August 3, 1864

Collins, Chas. L. B. 2nd Lt. – 1st Lt.
Brainard, Wm. J. 2nd Lt.
Hurtel, A. F. 2nd Lt.
Hopper, H. L. 2nd Lt. R. July 4, 1863

Field and Staff Muster Rolls

July and August 1863 Point Clear
September and October 1863 Fort Morgan
March and April 1864 Alabama Port

Captions, Records of Events and Reports of Casualties
21st Alabama Regiment

June 1862 Camp near Tupelo
November 1862 Fort Morgan (2nd Batt.)
December 1862 Fort Morgan (2nd Batt.)
September and October 1864
Capt. Sossaman's Detachment Mobile

Captions and Record of Events
21st Alabama Regiment

Company A

September 24, 1862 Fort Morgan for bounty
December 31, 1862, to April 30, 1863 Mobile, Ala.
April 26, 1863, Detached from the Battalion and ordered to report at Mobile. - May 5, 1863, ordered to report at Selma. - May 26, 1863, ordered from Selma to report to Gen. Slaughter at Mobile.
May and June, 1863 Fort Stonewall, Ala.
April 26, 1863, ordered from Choctaw Bluff to Mobile. – May 5, 1863, ordered from Mobile to Selma. – May 20, 1863, ordered from Selma to Mobile. – June 8, 1863, ordered from Mobile to Choctaw Bluff. – June 24, 1863, moved into camp three miles from Fort Stonewall Choctaw Bluff.
September and October 1863 Fort Morgan, Ala.
Ordered from Point Clear, Ala. to Spring Hill, Ala. October 24, 1863. - Arrived at Spring Hill October 26, 1863. - Ordered to Fort Morgan October 28, 1863. – Arrived at Fort Morgan October 29, 1863.

Company B

September 24, 1862 Fort Morgan, Ala.
March and April 1863 Oven Bluff
May and June 1863 Camp near Fort Stonewall Jackson – Removed from Fort Sidney Johnston (Oven Bluff) to Rosie Hill near Fort Stonewall Jackson (Choctaw Bluff) on the 25th day of June 1863.
September and October 1863 Fort Morgan

Company C

September 24, 1862	Fort Morgan for bounty
December 31, 1862 to April 30, 1863	Mobile, Ala.

April 26, 1863, detached from the Battalion and ordered to report at Mobile - May 5, 1863, Ordered to report at Selma. - May 20, 1863, Ordered to report to General Slaughter at Mobile.

May and June 1863	Fort Stonewall

Ordered to report to General C. D. Anderson at Choctaw Bluff on the 8th of June 1863, - Moved from Choctaw Bluff to Rosie Hill on the 24th of June 1863.

September and October 1863	Fort Morgan, Ala.

Company D

September 24, 1862	Fort Morgan for bounty
November and December 1862	Fort Morgan
July and August 1863	Fort Grant

Ordered from Fort Morgan to Fort Grant by Colonel Smith commanding the 3rd Brigade August 21, 1863.

September and October 1863	Fort Grant
November and December 1863	Fort Powell
September and October 1864	Battery Huger

Company E

September 24, 1862	Fort Morgan for bounty
November and December	Fort Morgan
July and August 1863	Fort Morgan
September and October 1863	Fort Morgan

Company F

September 24, 1862	Fort Morgan for bounty
March 1 to June 30, 1863	Fort Stonewall
September and October 1863	Fort Morgan

Ordered form Point Clear to Spring Hill near Mobile October 22, 1863. – Reached Spring Hill. October 23, 1863. – Ordered from Spring Hill to Fort Morgan on October 27, 1863. - Reached Fort Morgan on October 28, 1863.

Company I

September 24, 1862	Fort Morgan for bounty
July and August 1863	Fort Morgan
September and October 1863	Fort Morgan

Company K

November and December 1862	Fort Morgan
July and August 1863	Fort Morgan
September and October 1863	Fort Morgan
September and October 1864	Brown Warehouse – Mobile, Ala.

21ST ALABAMA INFANTRY VOLUNTEERS

The 21st regiment of Alabama Volunteers, 3rd Brigade, Dist. of Gulf; was organized in the months of April, May, June, July, August, and September 1861, and mustered into Confederate service on October 13, 1861, for 12 months. Also see Whiting, Nathan 1st Lt.

In the "*Mobile Evening News*," November 8, 1861, a report by the paper's camp correspondent, "Occasional," reports extensively on the 21st Alabama Regiment. The site is described as "Camp Gov. Moore." He states further that:

> "Our camp, as you are aware, is now situated about eleven miles from the city, in a high piney woods county, with considerable black-jack interspersed, and sufficiently removed from any house to prevent our disturbing the hen-roosts of our piney woods friends. Our camp, extending 1200 feet from front to rear, by 800 in width, presents to the eyes a level plane of ground for (crease in paper renders these word indecipherable) ... regimental parades as to satisfy the most fastidious military stickler for level parade grounds and fine front views.
>
> "This is not, however--I assure you, Mr. Editor--accomplished without much labor and many groans. Especially to those unaccustomed to swinging the axe and grubbing up stumps the work proved most fatiguing, and many anathema were launched against--well--against the tall, unconscious pine trees and the tough, sinewy white oak. But 'Labor *omnia vincit*'--the trees have been felled, the stumps removed, and the ground leveled, and evening finds us drawn up in regimental line for review by the staff."

"Occasional" goes on to specify the placing in the line of the particular companies (by name) of the 21st Alabama Infantry, with their respective captains (as of that date) as well as describing the field officers, staff, and NCOs of the regimental staff with the usual daily schedule starting with reveille.

Plate CX (110) of the Atlas to accompany the Official Records shows a location "Halls Mill" about 10 or 11 miles from the city, describing the surrounding country as "flat piney woods."

Camp Governor Moore and Camp Memminger were two names of Camps in the Halls Mill area, but there were at least nine Alabama infantry commands in the area. These were the 18th through 25th Alabama Regiments, plus the 2nd Alabama Battalion. It appears that the 21st Alabama was assigned to Col. W. L. Powell's command with the bay forts and would not have been at Hall's Mill very long.

The machinery at Hall's Mill was intended to manufacture turpentine, so we might expect the surrounding country to be a vast expanse of "flat piney woods".

Following an inspection, General Bragg describes these camps as 12 to 15 miles from Mobile, so we must be talking about at least three camps cut out of the woods as described here.

Letters from Pvt. Lewis B. Henley Co. F to his family in Clarke County, Alabama.

Fort Gaines, Ala June 30, 1864

Dear and Effectinated Mother

To you all I take the present opportunity of writhing a few lines to thee to inform thee that I am well and enjoying the best of health and I hope and trust to God that these few pend lines may find you enjoying the same good keeping of health.

Dear and Effectionated Mother I havent any news of interest to write you. Duty is hard on us and times is dull. It looks like there is no end to this war. It don't look like that we ever will conker the yanks without help from another nation. But still I hope we may and I hope we can conker them soon so what few men that are living can get home agane. Dear Mother I want to see you all very bad. They aint no chance to get a furlow now. But if I think they will commence giving furlows agane before long and if they do I will try to get one. But I expect it will be getting late in the fall before I get one. They is three or four that have been in the company longer that I have and they will get furlows fist so I will wait that subject.

I have just got back from school. I enjoyed myself finely while I was going to school. I got a letter from Father just before our school was disbanded and I never got time to answer it. I hope he will not think hard of me for it. I will write to him in a few days that is if I git the chance. I hardly ever have the chance to write. We are on duty ever day and at night we cant rest for the misquetoes. I think there is ten thousand to where there ever was one in Basis (Bashi) creek swamp.

Mother I want you to write to me and give my all the news that you have or can hear of. Tell Hannah and the rest of the girls to write. Give my love and best respects to the boys and to Mr. Lefore and expect the same for yourself. So I will close my short and

bad composed letter and excuse bad writhing and spelling. No more at present only I remain your true son until death.

L. B. Henley to
Malinda Henly

Lewis Henley was one of 14 children 6 were boys. His mother was Cherokee, Malinda Head-Spirit.

21ST ALABAMA INFANTRY VOLUNTEERS

To Mr. Joseph Henley from L. B. Henley

Fort Morgan December 15, 1864 [*Error in the date? Ft. Morgan surrendered August 23, 1864, could be December 1863?*]

Mr. Joseph Henley

Dear Father

  It is with the greatest of pleasure that I seat myself to write to you a few lines to inform you that I am well and hardy and truly hope that these lines may reach your far and distant land and find you and family enjoying the same blessing of health. Father I haven't any news to write you at present times is very hard here and I don't see any prospect of any better times. I would be very glad to see you all. It is out of the question to get a furlow unless I could get a recruit to come to this company. If I was at home and had to go into service I'd come to this place. It is an easy place to get along in. We have good quarters to stay in and good bunks to sleep on but w have a heap of duty to do but that's nothing after one gets use to it but we don't get much to eat. Something to eat is cornpone so I will quit that subject.

  I will close my short and bad composed and I will write a longer one when I get more time. Give my love to and best respects to Mother and all the rest of the family and accept the same for yourself. And I want you all to write me every chance you get. Give my love to Polly and her family and to Julia and her family and to Mr. Lefore. So no more at present I still remain your true and loving son until death.

          L. B. Henley

MOBILE CONFEDERATES

Notes on the preserved Flag of the 21st Alabama.

There exists a flag that provenance indicates was displayed by the 21st Alabama, probably at Blakeley. It is presently on display at the City of Mobile Museum and is marked appropriately. It was presented to City of Mobile Museum Department by Spring Hill College in 2000. The flag was found in 1941 in the personal effects of Father A. B. Fox, S. J. rector of the college chapel. The flag was presented to Father Fox in the 1930's by Mr. William E. Rodgers of Mobile who was a friend and who said his father, Robert E. Rodgers, had been color bearer and removed the flag after the surrender at Blakeley. The compiled service records of the 21st Alabama do not show a member by that name. He is not shown as a member of the 21st by either the National or State archives. Exactly how this person came into the possession of the flag is not known. This flag measures 35 inches on the leading edge and 48 inches on the fly. It is constructed in the pattern of a rectangular St. Andrews Cross with 12 five-pointed stars appliquéd to each side of the cross and has no border. There is about 10 percent of the material missing. The flag is reported to have been probably issued to the 21st Alabama Infantry by the Confederate Department of Alabama in 1864. It is further reported to likely been manufactured in Mobile by James Cameron.

Bibliography

The Mobile Cadets 1845 – 1945, edited by William S. Coker, Patagonia Press, Bagdad, FL 1993

From That Terrible Field Civil War letters of James M. Williams, Edited by John Kent Folmar, U of Alabama Press, University Alabama.

[OR] War of the Rebellion Official Records of the Union and Confederate Armies, Washington, Government Printing office 1880.

Confederate Military History Vol. VIII, Lt. General Joseph Wheeler CSA.

Confederate Mobile, Arthur W. Bergeron, Jr., University Press of Mississippi, Jackson and London.

Copyright Arthur E. Green

ABOUT THE AUTHOR

ART GREEN was born in Dallas County, Alabama in 1937. He is a direct descendant of Revolutionary War Patriot William Day of Edgefield District, South Carolina, who is buried in Dallas County. He is also the grandson of John C. Green who fought for Southern Independence in the War Between the States in the 38th Alabama Infantry Regiment Co. B.

He is retired from Alabama State Docks Department and has compiled several published regimental history books on South Alabama Confederate Regiments. Art is married to Karen Harvey Green who is a native Mobilian. They live in Mid-town Mobile. He has two children and two grandchildren. Art is a member of several historical, genealogical and heritage organizations including Mobile Genealogical Society. His books include:

Southerners at War: The 38th Alabama Infantry Volunteers

Gracie's Pride: The 43rd Alabama Infantry Volunteers

Too Little Too Late: The 63rd Alabama Infantry CSA

Southern Boots and Saddles: The 15th Confederate Cavalry

Misc. Alabama Commands in Confederate Service

*Mobile Confederates from Shiloh to Spanish Fort:
The Story of the 21st Alabama Infantry Volunteers*

www.ingramcontent.com/pod-product-compliance
Lightning Source LLC
Chambersburg PA
CBHW060506300426
44112CB00017B/2562